THE HOMILIES

The second Book of Homilies . . . doth contain a godly and wholesome Doctrine, and necessary for these times, as doth the former book of Homilies, which were set forth in the time of *Edward* the Sixth; and therefore we judge them to be read in Churches by the Ministers, diligently and distinctly, that they may be understanded of the people.

ARTICLE XXXV, *Of Homilies*

THE HOMILIES

APPOINTED TO BE READ IN CHURCHES

the edition of John Griffiths revised

Brynmill / Preservation Press

editing and typography copyright © 2006 The Brynmill Press Ltd

this edition first published 2006
by
The Brynmill Press Ltd
The Stonehouse Bishopstone Herefordshire HR4 7JE England
ISBNS 0 907839 82 7   978 0 907839 82 8

and in the United States of America
by
Preservation Press of the Prayer Book Society USA

ISBNS 1-879793-08-3   978-1-879793-08-8

typeset by the The Brynmill Press Ltd
printed in England by Antony Rowe Ltd
Bumper's Farm, Chippenham, Wiltshire SN14 6LH

British Library Cataloguing in Publication Data: a catalogue record of this
book is available from the British Library.

www.edgewaysbooks.com

Contents

abbreviated names of the Books of the Bible as used in marginal references

Bar. = Baruch
Chron. = Chronicles
Col. = Colossians
Cor. = Corinthians
Dan. = Daniel
Deut. = Deuteronomy
Eccles. = Ecclesiastes
Ecclus. = Ecclesiasticus
Eph. = Ephesians
Esth. = Esther
Exod. = Exodus
Ezek. = Ezekiel
Gal. = Galatians
Gen. = Genesis
Hab. = Habakkuk
Hag. = Haggai
Heb. = Hebrews
Hos. = Hosea
Isai. = Isaiah
Jer. = Jeremiah

Josh. = Joshua
Lev. = Leviticus
Mac. = Maccabees
Mal. = Malachi
Matt. = Matthew
Mic. = Micah
Neh. = Nehemiah
Num. = Numbers
Pet. = Peter
Phil. = Philippians
Prov. = Proverbs
Rev. = Revelation
Rom. = Romans
Sam. = Samuel
Thess. = Thessalonians
Tim. = Timothy
Tob. = Tobit
Wisd. = Wisdom of Solomon
Zech. = Zechariah

The names of other Books are given in full.

The Homilies
and this Edition

During the first century of her separation from Rome, three English books were of supreme importance to the Church of England. The first, in a sense embracing the other two, was the English Bible, which from 1539, still in the reign of Henry VIII, was given royal sanction, so that versions close to Tyndale's could be freely read (if only chained in churches) throughout the land. The second, the Book of Common Prayer, had to wait for the death of King Henry, who was far too reactionary a theologian to have countenanced it. These two books, in the form of the 1611 Bible, in direct descent from Tyndale, and the 1662 revision of the Prayer Book (with the Articles of Religion and the Ordinal usually bound in the one volume), are still in daily use.

The third member of the triad, the Homilies,* appeared in 1547, and went through two major expansions as well as many minor revisions in numerous editions, between then and 1623, after which there were many reprints.

Archbishop Thomas Cranmer had much to do with all three books. The need for the Homilies must have been urgently felt by Cranmer's generation, not excluding his anti-Reformation episcopal colleagues. The Prayer Book gave to the whole people (for Church attendance was at least in theory compulsory) in their own language, the liturgy of the Church, and forms of service to cover the major events of life, from baptism, by way of marriage, to burial. But a reliable and standard exposition of the Christian way, to be heard by all the people, was thought so urgently necessary that it preceded the first Prayer Book by two years.

The Homilies now republished differ from both earlier and later collections in their effort at complete coverage of essential Christian doctrine and life, and in their authority. In the near-century before the Civil War they were "appointed to be read in churches". By Royal Injunction of July 1547, one of the Homilies was to be read every

---

* They are usually known by this simple name, by which I shall call them, though many of the complicated title-pages of the early editions begin *Certain Homilies* . . .

Sunday.* Their authority is stated in Article XXXV as "a godly and wholesome doctrine, and necessary for these times". They are therefore "to be read in Churches by the Ministers, diligently and distinctly, that they may be understanded of the people". The 1801 edition of The Thirty-Nine Articles of the Episcopal Church of the United States of America reaffirmed the Article "so far as it declares the Books of Homilies to be an explication of Christian doctrine and instructive to piety and morals", though it discontinued the instruction that they be read in churches, and "all references to the constitution and laws of England are considered as inapplicable." In modern times it is unusual to hear one of the Homilies read in place of a sermon, but wherever the Anglican Way has gone and the Articles have been received as a Formulary in the new Province, the two Book of Homilies have naturally been included. So, for example, they are now part of the Standards of Faith of Anglican Churches in West and East Africa, from Nigeria to Uganda.

A move had been made in 1542, during the lifetime of King Henry VIII, to issue an authorised volume of homilies, but nothing came of it, perhaps because of the King's rooted hostility to the doctrines of the Reformation. Under the new king Edward VI, a great need was still felt for the Christian way to be expounded to the people. The parish priests could not always be relied upon to do so, and those who were capable were not all in line with the reformed doctrines.

Not all parish priests in the reigns of the protestant Tudors were licensed to preach. Usually a university degree, which in those days meant Oxford or Cambridge, was required. Where original preaching was not possible, the Homilies were to be used, according to the rubric still found in the Communion service of the Book of Common Prayer: *Then shall follow the Sermon, or one of the Homilies already set forth, or hereafter to be set forth, by authority.* The likelihood must be that Shakespeare heard a part of one the Homilies much more often than he heard a sermon.†

The first Book of Homilies was published only six months after the death of Henry VIII, in the summer of 1547, which must mean that plans if not texts had already been made before Henry's death. No

---

* This was still in the days of the Latin mass. The Book of Common Prayer makes provision for a sermon or homily only in Holy Communion, which was not as often celebrated as Archbishop Cranmer wished; but the more frequent Antecommunion would include sermon or homily.

† Richmond Noble, *Shakespeare's Biblical Knowledge and Use of the Book of Common Prayer*, 1935, gives a number of examples of direct quotations from the Homilies as well as more general indebtedness. Falstaff has Homily phrases on the tip of his tongue. Ulysses' speech on degree in *Troilus and Cressida* I.iii is (amongst other things) a reworking of the opening of the Exhortation to Obedience. Prospero's "prayer / Which pierces so, that it assaults / Mercy itself" (*The Tempest*, epilogue) reworks a passage of Ecclesiasticus quoted below, p. 263.

documentary evidence is known to survive of the details of compilation and editing, but it is probable that Archbishop Thomas Cranmer was the editor, as well as himself the author of three of the most theological Homilies (of Salvation, Faith and Good Works). The Homily on Charity is known to be by Bishop Bonner, one of the principal ecclesiastical opponents of Cranmer. The aim of the first Book of Homilies was surely to present, as far as practicable, agreed Christian doctrine, and if an author could be included from the anti-Reformation camp, it was thereby demonstrated that about something as important as the understanding of Christian love there was no difference between the evangelicals, as they were known, and their conservative opponents. Bishop Gardiner of Winchester, however, later a great thorn in the flesh to Cranmer, declined to contribute. In the other direction, Bishop Bonner was able to include the Sermon on the Misery of All Mankind (by John Harpsfield) in a collection set forth in 1555, during the time under Queen Mary I when our Homilies were proscribed.

The Homily against Adultery is proved to be the work of Thomas Becon, a chaplain of Cranmer's, by its inclusion in his collected Works. I think it is rather more than a guess that Cranmer edited it as well as all the other contributions, for the style of this Homily is not the same as Becon's elsewhere, and throughout the first collection a standard of effective expression is maintained which is of great importance in the history of English prose. The 1547 Homilies hardly ever lapse into the monstrous-length sentences which Bonner amongst others habitually wrote.

During the Roman reaction under Mary I all copies of the Homilies were ordered to be destroyed, but the survival of so many shows that the destruction was far from complete. The second Book, said to have been supervised by John Jewel, Bishop of Salisbury, first appeared in 1562, fulfilling a promise made at the end of the first Book to treat subjects it did not cover. The two volumes went on being printed separately for many years. In 1570, the year after the Northern Rising, the Homily against Disobedience and Wilful Rebellion appeared separately and in 1571 was added to the second Book. From 1582, so as to facilitate binding in one volume, the two Books were sometimes printed uniformly, and in 1623, the most recent edition to be issued on authority, they were at last published as one volume.

The urgency behind the Homilies is not hard to understand. It is certainly untrue that there was no preaching in the Middle Ages, but equally, a new emphasis on preaching came in with the Reformation. The Bible is the Word of God, but it is necessary to expound the Bible, to explain how it can save. The Book of Common Prayer is itself a kind of résumé of the Bible and in fact includes it, except for some of the

Apocrypha, by way of the lections. The Homilies make a fitting complement to the Book of Common Prayer in their expounding of Biblical doctrine, and in their range. They have a solid theological core, and explain salvation through grace by faith in language comprehensible to the ordinary worshipper but without oversimplification; there is subtlety as well as clarity in the reconciliation of Paul and James. And they inherit from the Middle Ages a determination to impart moral doctrine, moral in the widest sense of how to walk in the Christian way; and they go into practical detail.

The Homilies are "evangelical" in their theology but very characteristic of the Church of England of the sixteenth century in a catholic range of reference. The Bible is of course paramount, but for the English divines of the sixteenth century that included what we now call the Apocrypha. I have no statistics, but my impression (readers can check from marginal references) is that Ecclesiasticus is as frequently cited as Ecclesiastes, and the writers range the Apocrypha as freely as the Old Testament. They have another of Cranmer's great marks, the very frequent appeal to the Fathers. St John Chrysostom is not as frequently cited as St John the Evangelist, but is an authority often quoted. From pagan learning Plato is cited, and from the Schoolmen even at one point Duns Scotus, though not as having an authority equal to that of the Scriptures.

It is not, in my opinion, for an editor of a Formulary of the Church of England to air his views in a preface. (Anyone interested may find mine in an expanded version of these brief introductory remarks, on the publisher's website.) I will just say that with all their frequent strengths and occasional weaknesses, the Homilies provide a reliable guide to the Christian life; I regret that the Church of England has allowed them to fall into disuse; and I would not have given more time and effort to the present edition than I ever dreamt of when I began it, if I had thought them to be of only antiquarian interest. The Homilies are an important part of the English mind of the sixteenth century and necessary for several kinds of historical understanding. What interests me even more is that even today there are occasions when it could, imaginably, be more edifying than the sermon to hear a reading of one of the Homilies.

This Edition

The present text is not newly edited from original editions but revised from that of John Griffiths, Oxford, 1859. Though it is a long time since Griffiths did his work, his excellent edition is still unlikely to be superseded, and he established his text with such immense care that in the present edition only two typographical errors have been corrected. The present edition follows Griffiths in using modern spelling but reproducing proper names in their sixteenth-century forms. (A short list of unfamiliar versions of names will be found after the select Glossary.) Griffiths italicised Bible quotations which, as an aid to seeing how strongly Bible-based the Homilies are, I have also retained. This is wholly editorial. Italics were not used in the modern way in the original editions, and there are a few moments when a modern text cries out for emphasis, but I judged that it was worth foregoing this resource for the sake of reserving italics for the Bible. I have, however, italicised a few titles of books when they could not be mistaken for Biblical quotations.

Griffiths's edition is based for the first Book on the first Elizabethan edition, of 1559, the first edition of the second Book, and the second edition (the first to be divided into six parts) of the Homily against Disobedience and Wilful Rebellion. But as Griffiths knew well, there is no such thing as one best authentic text of the Homilies. In the sixteenth century, spelling was the preserve of the individual compositor and there could be a great number of different old-spelling texts. At first there were three publishers (the same three who published the first Prayer Book of 1549, Grafton and Whitchurch in London and Oswen in Worcester) and they had their different practices, as well as themselves varying from one edition to the next and even between copies of the same edition. It is quite possible that no two sixteenth-century copies of the Homilies are identical. Editions frequently differed in paragraphing and punctuation, as was normal in the sixteenth century. There was never any tendency to treat the text as unalterable, as the 1611 Bible has been since the eighteenth century, and any new edition between 1547 and 1623 would as a matter of course make minor alterations. In succeeding editions archaisms were replaced as they were noticed.

The 1547 collection was revised in 1549, to accompany the first Prayer Book, mainly by the division of homilies so as to make them of more acceptable length. One of the influential Martin Bucer's last acts was to oppose this, but the work was done with stylistic smoothness, so that the paragraphs introducing the newly divided sections do so on the whole without disrupting the flow of thought—though on one occasion half a quotation would be heard at one service and the rest at the next.

When in 1559 the first Book was reissued under Queen Elizabeth I the text was considerably altered, with the aim of making it more easily comprehensible to the ordinary congregation; and it is this edited text that Griffiths prints. Anglo-Saxonate words were substituted for Latinisms, or added in parentheses. In my opinion these alterations were often ill-judged and have not stood the test of time. In the twenty-first century we do not need to be told that the word *consequently* means *followingly* or *ascension*, *going up*; *transformed* need not be changed to *changed*, and we probably find the 1559 *cracking* harder to understand than the 1547 *ostentation*. The additions also sometimes clumsily damage the rhythm of this prose which, let us remember, was designed like that of the Prayer Book to be read aloud. I have frequently reinstated the 1547 text at these points. I have, however, allowed the Elizabethan substitution of *Queen* for the Edwardian *King* to stand at places where the English monarch is referred to.

The second collection was never revised so drastically, but time and again, especially in the 1623 edition, modern words were substituted for what had become archaic. If there is no compelling reason to use the older text I have frequently followed 1623 so as to make the text more reader-friendly four centuries later. I have not, however, taken the process of modernisation any further. There is room for the continuing replacement of archaic words, but the present edition does not attempt it.

So the present text of the first Book is closer to the Edwardian editions than Griffiths's in often rejecting the later glosses, but throughout is closer to 1623 in accepting replacements for archaisms.

The other principal departure from Griffiths's excellent text is in the punctuation. Griffiths uses modern punctuation (that is, of the age of Dickens) as well as modern spelling. By our standards Victorian punctuation can be fussy, using commas we would do without. Griffiths's punctuation, however, is by the standards of his own age very sparse, and at a number of places it seems to me the text demands additional punctuation by any modern standard. Griffiths's punctuation is nevertheless thoroughly modern in being *syntactic*. The first function of modern punctuation is to show relations within and between well-formed sentences, even where these relations are not expressed aloud by a pause or phrase-end. The examples that come to mind are the use of commas after the *that* of reported speech or after a conjunction, followed by a subordinate clause, which do not represent any pause in ordinary reading aloud. I have deleted most of these. The present edition nevertheless uses very many more commas than Griffiths, as do all the original editions—though not always in the same places as one another, for there was no more a standard Tudor punctuation than a standard spelling. In the sixteenth century, punctuation was still as much rhetorical as syntactic. Students of Shakespeare get used to commas or major punctuation where any punctuation would now be incorrect. The Homilies, especially the first collection, come at a critical moment for the emergence of modern prose, and though they are certainly written (unlike much medieval prose) in modern complex sentences, the writers equally certainly had the speaking voice consciously in mind; the editors and compositors punctuated accordingly. In texts designed for reading aloud the rhetorical commas are, I think, an aid we should use, and so I have retained many—not following any one edition precisely, but in the spirit of all the editions. An example of authentic original punctuation will be found in the last paragraph of page 85 and the first of page 86, for the latter of which there is only one edition as an authority. Particularly in the second Book, which has so many more very complex and long sentences than the first, I hope the hints given by old-style punctuation will be a help—once one gets used to it. For instance it is incorrect now to put a comma between subject and verb or verb and direct object, but such commas are found countless times in sixteenth-century texts, and in the present edition. READ ALOUD, phrase as indicated by the punctuation, and the modern reader will find the Homilies much easier to follow than in the *presto* silent reading we now habitually practise. Connoisseurs may nevertheless notice that the punctuation of the second Book is in this edition rather sparser than of the first; which represents my opinion that in the fifteen years between the two collections English prose had moved (not always to its advantage) in the direction of the long, complex, rather Latinate sentences habitually written by the Elizabethan learned.

Griffiths gives a very full textual apparatus, recording all significant verbal variants in all the editions, and extensively quoting sources in original languages. This is all on the page, not tucked away at the back, and the 1859 edition is a triumph of Victorian typography as well as Victorian scholarship, using different systems of reference for margin, footnote textual notes and footnote explanatory notes. Griffiths's edition is indispensable for scholarly use, but not the ideal one for the general reader or for reading aloud. The original editions gave marginal references to authorities quoted—principally the Scriptures but also numbers of the Fathers and lesser authorities. The present edition discards Griffiths's variant readings and scholarly apparatus but retains these original marginal notes. Griffiths identified a large number of Bible quotations and references not noted in the original editions, and since his use of italics for Bible quotations looks strange without a marginal reference most of Griffiths's additional references have been retained, though his references to passing glances not involving direct quotation have not. He was monumentally thorough. I may have supplied as many as three Biblical references he overlooked, but perhaps fewer. Griffiths also expanded the references of the original editions by including verse as well as chapter numbers, and I have followed him here, though a more modern system of referencing has been used. The abbreviated name of the Bible book is followed by chapter and then after a colon verse, all in arabic numerals. The original references to the Psalms are to their medieval numbering. Griffiths reports both these and modern Protestant numbering; in this edition the latter has been used. Samuel, Kings and Chronicles in the margins replace the Vulgate names and numbers, so there is occasionally what looks like a clash between text and margin. It is surprising how little the Homilists depended on the then new English translations of the Scriptures. The writers tended to use their own *ad hoc* translations often from the Latin Vulgate,* the version of the Bible that must have been second nature to the first-generation Reformers, and so their phrasing will not always ring a bell with the modern reader.

Griffiths's edition, complete with scholarly and textual apparatus, can be found at the following website:

http://www.footstoolpublications.com/Homilies/Homilies.htm

The present text is edited from Miss Irene Teas's transcription of Griffiths's text found there. It would have been slow and, because of the very extensive textual complications, tricky to scan Griffiths, and without Miss Teas's text, which has needed fewer corrections than I expected, I doubt whether the present edition would have been attempted.

I have done my best in the time at my disposal, but I claim no miracles, and it is hardly possible that no errors have remained or that no new ones have been introduced. The Publishers would be grateful to be informed of any remaining misprints, with a view to correction in any reprint.

The 1623 text is available at the University of Toronto English Library website, http://www.library.utoronto.ca/www/utel/index.html and an annotated old-spelling but modern-punctuation edition of the first Book, together with the Homily against Disobedience and Wilful Rebellion, was edited by Ronald B. Bond and published by University of Toronto Press in 1987.

Ian Robinson
Trinity 2006

---

* The original Latin is occasionally quoted, for instance below, pp. 166–7, 315. In the latter example the translated Vulgate text is a little easier to understand in a prophetic sense than the versions direct from the Hebrew.

Acknowledgements

The dedication of this edition, if it were in order to dedicate one of the formularies of the Church of England, would have been to John Griffiths. Any later editor of the Homilies must record gratitude to the excellent and thorough work of the Victorian editor. Miss Irene Teas, as just stated, has most kindly allowed us to use the text of her website copy of the Griffiths text, the making of which took more of her hours than I would like to guess. I am also most grateful to the Revd Dr Peter Toon who has encouraged the project throughout; and I am much obliged to Dr Robert Marchant, who devoted a period of enforced inactivity to proof-reading, and corrected a number of errors, and to Mrs Hannah Atherton, who read proofs with an eagle eye.

CERTAIN SERMONS

APPOINTED BY THE QUEEN'S MAJESTY
TO BE DECLARED AND READ
BY ALL PARSONS, VICARS AND CURATES
EVERY SUNDAY AND HOLY DAY
IN THEIR CHURCHES
AND BY HER GRACE'S ADVICE
PERUSED AND OVERSEEN
FOR THE BETTER UNDERSTANDING
OF THE SIMPLE PEOPLE

THE PREFACE

CONSIDERING HOW NECESSARY it is that the word of God, which is the only food of the soul, and that most excellent light that we must walk by in this our most dangerous pilgrimage, should at all convenient times be preached unto the people, that thereby they both learn their duty towards God, their Prince, and their neighbours, according to the mind of the Holy Ghost expressed in the Scriptures, and also to avoid the manifold enormities which heretofore by false doctrine have crept into the Church of God; and how that they which are appointed ministers have not the gift of preaching sufficiently to instruct the people which is committed unto them, whereof great inconveniences might rise, and ignorance still be maintained, if some honest remedy be not speedily found and provided; the Queen's Most Excellent Majesty, tendering the soul health of her loving subjects and the quieting of their consciences in the chief and principal points of Christian religion, and willing also by the true setting forth and pure declaring of God's word, which is the principal guide and leader unto all godliness and virtue, to expel and drive away as well all corrupt, vicious, and ungodly living, as also erroneous and poisoned doctrines tending to superstition and idolatry, hath by the advice of her most honourable counsellors, for her discharge in this behalf, caused a Book of Homilies, which heretofore was set forth by her most loving brother, a Prince of most worthy memory, Edward the Sixth, to be printed anew; wherein are contained certain wholesome and godly exhortations, to move the people to honour and worship Almighty God and diligently to serve him, every one according to their degree, state, and vocation. All which Homilies Her Majesty commandeth and straitly chargeth all Parsons, Vicars, Curates, and all other having spiritual cure, every Sunday and Holy Day in the year, at the ministering of the Holy Communion, or, if there be no Communion ministered that day, yet after the Gospel and Creed, in such order and place as is appointed in the Book of Common Prayers, to read and declare to their parishioners plainly and distinctly one of the said Homilies in such order as they stand in the Book; except there be a Sermon according as it is injoined in the book of her Highness'

Injunctions, and then for that cause only, and for none other, the reading of the said Homily to be deferred unto the next Sunday or Holy Day following. And, when the foresaid Book of Homilies is read over, Her Majesty's pleasure is, that the same be repeated and read again in suchlike sort as was before prescribed.

Furthermore Her Highness commandeth, that, notwithstanding this order, the said ecclesiastical persons shall read Her Majesty's Injunctions at such times and in such order as is in the book thereof appointed; and that the Lord's Prayer, the Articles of the Faith, and the Ten Commandments be openly read unto the people as in the said Injunctions is specified; that all her people, of what degree or condition soever they be, may learn how to invocate and call upon the Name of God, know what duty they owe both to God and man; so that they may pray, believe, and work according to knowledge while they shall live here, and after this life be with Him that with his blood hath bought us all. To whom, with the Father and the Holy Ghost, be all honour and glory for ever. Amen.

The Preface above is that which was set before the First Book of Homilies by Queen Elizabeth. King Edward's Preface was as follows:

THE KING'S MOST EXCELLENT MAJESTY, by the prudent advice of his most dear beloved uncle Edward Duke of Somerset, Governor of His Majesty's person and Protector of all His Highness' realms, dominions, and subjects, with the rest of his most honourable counsel, most graciously considering the manifold enormities which heretofore have crept into His Grace's realm through the false usurped power of the Bishop of Rome and the ungodly doctrine of his adherents, not only unto the great decay of Christian religion, but also (if God's mercy were not) unto the utter destruction of innumerable souls, which through hypocrisy and pernicious doctrine were seduced and brought from honouring of the alone true, living, and eternal God unto the worshipping of creatures, yea, of stocks and stones, from doing the commandments of God unto voluntary works and phantasies invented of men, from true religion unto popish superstition; considering also the earnest and fervent desire of his dearly beloved subjects to be delivered from all errors and superstitions and to be truly and faithfully instructed in the very word of God, that lively food of man's soul, whereby they may learn unfeignedly, and according to the mind of the Holy Ghost expressed in the Scriptures, to honour God and to serve their King with all humility and subjection, and godly and honestly to behave themselves toward all men; again, calling to remembrance that the next and most ready way to expel and avoid as well all corrupt, vicious, and ungodly living, as also erroneous doctrine tending to superstition and idolatry, and clearly to put away all contention which hath heretofore risen through diversity of preaching, is the true setting forth and pure declaring of God's word, which is the principal guide and leader unto all godliness and virtue; finally, that all Curates, of what learning soever they be, may have some godly and fruitful lessons in a readiness to read and declare unto their parishioners for their edifying, instruction, and comfort; hath caused a Book of Homilies to be made and set forth, wherein is contained certain wholesome and godly exhortations, to move the people to honour and worship Almighty God, and diligently to serve him, every one according to their degree, state, and vocation. The which Homilies His Majesty commandeth and straitly chargeth all Parsons, Vicars, Curates, and all other having spiritual cure, every Sunday in the year, at the Communion, when the people be most gathered, to read and declare to their parishioners plainly and distinctly in such order as they stand in the Book; except any Sermon be preached, and then for that cause only, and for none other, the reading of the said Homily to be deferred unto the next Sunday following. And, when the foresaid Book of Homilies is read over, the King's Majesty's pleasure is, that the same be repeated and read again, in suchlike sort as was before prescribed, unto such time as His Grace's pleasure shall further be known in this behalf.

Also His Majesty commandeth that the said ecclesiastical persons upon the first Holy Day falling in the week time of every quarter of the year, shall read his Injunctions openly and distinctly to the people in manner and form in the same expressed. And upon every other Holy and Festival Day through the year, likewise falling in the week time, they shall recite the Pater Noster, the Articles of our Faith, and the Ten Commandments in English openly before all the people, as in the said Injunctions is specified; that all degrees and all ages may learn to know God and to serve him according to his holy word. Amen.

A FRUITFUL EXHORTATION
TO THE READING
AND KNOWLEDGE
OF HOLY SCRIPTURE

The praise of
holy Scripture

The perfection
of holy Scripture

The knowledge
of holy Scripture
is necessary.

To whom the
knowledge of
holy Scripture is
sweet and
pleasant

Who be enemies
to holy Scripture

An apt
similitude,
declaring of
whom the
Scripture is
abhorred

An exhortation
unto the diligent
reading,
hearing, and
Matt. 4:4
searching of the
holy Scriptures

UNTO A CHRISTIAN MAN, there can be nothing either more necessary, or profitable, than the knowledge of holy Scripture; forasmuch as in it, is contained God's true word, setting forth his glory, and also man's duty. And there is no truth nor doctrine, necessary for our justification, and everlasting salvation, but that is, or may be, drawn out of that fountain, and well of truth. Therefore, as many as be desirous to enter into the right, and perfect way unto God, must apply their minds, to know holy Scripture; without the which, they can neither sufficiently know God, and his will, neither their office and duty. And as drink is pleasant to them that be dry, and meat to them that be hungry, so is the reading, hearing, searching, and studying of holy Scripture, to them that be desirous to know God, or themselves, and to do his will. And their stomachs only, do loathe and abhor the heavenly knowledge, and food of God's word, that be so drowned in worldly vanities, that they neither savour God, nor any godliness. For that is the cause, why they desire such vanities, rather than the true knowledge of God. As they that are sick of an ague, whatsoever they eat or drink, though it be never so pleasant, yet it is as bitter to them as wormwood, not for the bitterness of the meat, but for the corrupt and bitter humour, that is in their own tongue and mouth: even so is the sweetness of God's word, bitter, not of itself, but only unto them that have their minds corrupted, with long custom of sin, and love of this world.

Therefore, forsaking the corrupt judgement of fleshly men, which care not but for their carcase, let us reverently hear and read holy Scriptures, which is the food of the soul. Let us diligently search for the well of life, in the books of the New and Old Testament, and not run to the stinking puddles of men's traditions, devised by man's imagination,

4

for our justification and salvation. For in holy Scripture is fully contained, what we ought to do, and what to eschew, what to believe, what to love, and what to look for at God's hands at length. In those books, we shall find the Father, from whom, the Son, by whom, and the Holy Ghost, in whom, all things have their being and conservation; and these three Persons to be but one God, and one substance. In these books, we may learn to know ourselves, how vile and miserable we be; and also to know God, how good he is of himself; and how he communicateth his goodness unto us, and to all creatures. We may learn also in these books, to know God's will and pleasure, as much as for this present time is convenient for us to know. And, as the great clerk and godly preacher St John Chrysostom saith,

The holy Scripture is a sufficient doctrine for our salvation.

What things we may learn in the holy Scripture

Whatsoever is required to salvation of man, is fully contained in the Scripture of God. He that is ignorant may there learn, and have knowledge. He that is hardhearted, and an obstinate sinner, shall there find eternal torments, prepared of God's justice, to make him afraid, and to mollify him. He that is oppressed with misery in this world, shall there find relief, in the promises of eternal life, to his great consolation and comfort. He that is wounded by the devil unto death, shall find there medicine, whereby he may be restored again unto health.

What commodities and profits the knowledge of holy Scripture bringeth

"If it shall be requisite, to teach any truth, or reprove false doctrine, to rebuke any vice, to commend any virtue, to give good counsel, to comfort, or to exhort, or to do any other thing requisite for our salvation; all those things," saith St Chrysostom, "we may learn plentifully of the Scripture." "There is," saith Fulgentius, "abundantly enough, both for men to eat, and children to suck. There is whatsoever is convenient for all ages, and for all degrees and sorts of men."

These books therefore, ought to be much in our hands, in our eyes, in our ears, in our mouths, but most of all in our hearts. For the Scripture of God, is the heavenly meat of our souls: *the hearing and keeping of it maketh us blessed, sanctifieth* us, and maketh us holy: *it converteth our souls: it is a light lantern to our feet: it is a sure, a constant, and a perpetual* instrument of salvation: *it giveth wisdom to the humble and lowlyhearted: it comforteth, maketh glad, cheereth, and cherisheth our consciences: it is a more excellent jewel or treasure, than any gold or precious stone: it is more sweet than honey or honeycomb*: it is called *the best part*, which *Mary did choose*; for it hath in it, everlasting comfort. The words of holy Scripture be called, *words of everlasting life*; for they be God's instrument, ordained for the same purpose. They have power to convert, through God's promise, and they be effectual, through God's assistance; and being received in a faithful heart, they have ever, an heavenly spiritual working in them. They are *lively, quick, and mighty in operation, and sharper than any two-edged sword, and entereth through, even unto the dividing asunder of*

Holy Scripture ministereth sufficient doctrine for all Matt. 4:4 degrees and ages. Luke 11:28 John 17:17 Psalm 19:7–10

Luke 10:39, 42

John 6:68

Col. 1:5, 6, 25–8

Heb. 4:12

the soul and the spirit, of the joints and the marrow. Christ calleth him a wise builder, that buildeth upon his word, upon his sure and substantial foundation. By this word of God we shall be judged; for *the word that I speak*, saith Christ, *is it that shall judge, in the last day*. He that keepeth the word of Christ, is promised the love and favour of God, and that he shall be the mansion place, or temple, of the blessed Trinity. This word, whosoever is diligent to read, and in his heart to print that he readeth, the great affection to the transitory things of this world, shall be minished in him, and the great desire of heavenly things, that be therein promised of God, shall increase in him. And there is nothing, that so much establisheth our faith and trust in God, that so much conserveth innocency, and pureness of the heart, and also of outward godly life and conversation, as continual reading and meditation of God's word. For that thing, which by continual use of reading of holy Scripture, and diligent searching of the same, is deeply printed and graven in the heart, at length turneth almost into nature. And moreover the effect and virtue of God's word, is to illuminate the ignorant, and to give more light unto them that faithfully and diligently read it; to comfort their hearts, and to encourage them to perform, that which of God is commanded. It teacheth patience in all adversity, in prosperity humbleness; what honour is due unto God, what mercy and charity to our neighbour. It giveth good counsel in all doubtful things. It showeth of whom we shall look for aid, and help in all perils, and that God is the only Giver of victory, in all battles and temptations of our enemies, bodily and ghostly. And in reading of God's word, he most profiteth not always, that is most ready in turning of the book, or in saying of it without the book; but he that is most turned into it, that is most inspired with the Holy Ghost, most in his heart and life altered, and transformed into that thing which he readeth; he that is daily less and less proud, less wrathful, less covetous, and less desirous of worldly and vain pleasures; he that daily, forsaking his old vicious life, increaseth in virtue, more and more. And, to be short, there is nothing that more maintaineth godliness of the mind, and expelleth ungodliness, than doth the continual reading or hearing of God's word, if it be joined with a godly mind, and a good affection to know and follow God's will. For without a single eye, pure intent, and good mind, nothing is allowed for good before God. And on the other side, nothing more obscureth Christ, and the glory of God, nor induceth more blindness, and all kinds of vices, than doth the ignorance of God's word.

Matt. 7:24

John 12:48

John 14:23

1 Sam. 14:6–23
2 Chron. 20:1–30
1 Cor. 15:57
1 John 5:4

Who profit most
in reading God's
word

What
incommodities
the ignorance of
God's word
bringeth
Isai. 5: 13, 24;
Matt. 22:29
1 Cor. 14

THE SECOND PART
OF THE SERMON OF THE HOLY SCRIPTURE

IN THE FIRST PART of this Sermon, which exhorteth to the knowledge of holy Scripture, was declared, wherefore the knowledge of the same, is necessary and profitable to all men, and that by the true knowledge and understanding of Scripture, the most necessary points of our duty, towards God and our neighbours, are also known. Now as concerning the same matter, you shall hear what followeth.

If we profess Christ, why be we not ashamed to be ignorant in his doctrine, seeing that every man is ashamed to be ignorant, in that learning which he professeth? That man is ashamed to be called a philosopher, which readeth not the books of philosophy; and to be called a lawyer, an astronomer, or a physician, that is ignorant in the books of law, astronomy, and physic. How can any man then say, that he professeth Christ and his religion, if he will not apply himself, as far forth as he can or may conveniently, to read and hear, and so to know, the books of Christ's Gospel and doctrine? Although other sciences be good, and to be learned, yet no man can deny but this is the chief, and passeth all other incomparably. What excuse shall we therefore make, at the last day before Christ, that delight to read or hear men's phantasies and inventions, more than his most holy Gospel; and will find no time, to do that which chiefly, above all things, we should do; and will rather read other things, than that for the which we ought rather, to leave reading of all other things? Let us therefore apply ourselves, as far forth as we can have time and leisure, to know God's word, by diligent hearing and reading thereof, as many as profess God, and have faith and trust in him. *[God's word excelleth all sciences.]*

But they that have no good affection to God's word, to colour this their fault, allege commonly, two vain and feigned excuses. Some go about, to excuse them by their own frailness and fearfulness, saying that they dare not read holy Scripture, lest through their ignorance, they should fall into any error. Other pretend, that the difficulty to understand it, and the hardness thereof, is so great, that it is meet to be read only of clerks, and learned men. *[Vain excuses dissuading from the knowledge of God's word. The first. The second]*

As touching the first, ignorance of God's word is the cause of all error, as Christ himself affirmed to the Sadducees, saying, that *they erred, because they knew not the Scripture*. How should they then eschew error, that will be still ignorant? and how should they come out of ignorance, that will not read nor hear, that thing which should give them knowledge? He that now hath most knowledge, was at the first ignorant: yet he forbare not to read, for fear he should fall into error; but he diligently read, lest he should remain in ignorance, and through ignorance in error. And, if you will not know the truth of God (a thing *[Matt. 22:29]* most necessary for you), lest you fall into error, by the same reason you may then lie still, and never go, lest, if you go, you fall in the mire; nor eat any good meat, lest you take a surfeit; nor sow your corn, nor labour in your occupation, nor use your merchandise, for fear you lose your seed, your labour, your stock: and so, by that reason, it should be best for you to live idly, and never to take in hand, to do any manner of good thing, lest peradventure some evil thing may chance thereof. And, if you be afraid to fall into error, by reading of holy Scripture, I shall show you how you may read it, without danger of error. Read it humbly, with a meek and lowly heart, to the intent you may glorify God, and not yourself, with the knowledge of it; and read it not without daily praying to God, that he would direct your reading to good effect; and take upon you to expound it, no further than you can plainly understand it. For, as St Augustine saith, the knowledge of holy Scripture is a great, large, and a high palace, but the door is very low; so that the high and arrogant man cannot run in, but he must stoop low, and humble himself, that shall enter into it. Presumption and arrogancy is the mother of all error: and humility needeth to fear no error. For humility will only search to know the truth; it will search, and will bring together one place with another; and where it cannot find the sense, it will pray, it will inquire of other that know, and will not presumptuously and rashly, define any thing which it knoweth not. Therefore the humble man may search any truth, boldly in the Scripture, without any danger of error. And, if he be ignorant, he ought the more to read, and to search holy Scripture, to bring him out of ignorance. I say not nay, but a man may profit with only hearing; but he may much more profit, with both hearing and reading.

How most commodiously, and without all peril, the holy Scripture is to be read

This have I said, as touching the fear to read, through ignorance of the person. And concerning the difficulty of Scripture, he that is so weak, that he is not able to brook strong meat, yet he may suck the sweet and tender milk, and defer the rest until he wax stronger, and come to more knowledge. For God receiveth the learned and unlearned, and casteth away none, but is indifferent unto all. And the Scripture is full, as well of low valleys, plain ways, and easy for every man to use and to walk in, as also of high hills and mountains, which few men can ascend unto. And "whosoever giveth his mind to holy Scriptures with diligent study and fervent desire, it cannot be," saith St John Chrysostom,

Scripture in some places is easy, and in some places hard to be understood.

God leaveth no man untaught that hath a good will to know his word.

that he should be left without help. For either God Almighty will send him some godly doctor, to instruct him, as he did to instruct the Eunuch, a nobleman of Ethiope, and treasurer unto Queen Candace; who having a great affection to read the Scripture, although he understood it not, yet for the desire that he had, unto God's word, God sent his Apostle Philip, to declare unto him the true sense of the Scripture that he read; or else, if we lack a learned man to instruct and teach us, yet God himself from above, will give light unto our minds, and teach us those things, which are necessary for us, and wherein we be ignorant.

And in another place Chrysostom saith, that "man's human and worldly wisdom or science, is not needful to the understanding of Scripture, but the revelation of the Holy Ghost, who inspireth the true meaning, unto them that with humility and diligence do search therefore." *He that asketh shall have, and he that seeketh shall find, and he that knocketh shall have the door open.* If we read once, twice, or thrice, and understand not, let us not cease so, but still continue reading, praying, asking of other; and so, by still knocking, at the last the door shall be opened, as St Augustine saith. Although many things in the Scripture, be spoken in obscure mysteries, yet there is nothing, spoken under dark mysteries in one place, but the selfsame thing, in other places, is spoken more familiarly and plainly, to the capacity both of learned and unlearned. And those things in the Scripture, that be plain to understand, and necessary for salvation, every man's duty is to learn them, to print them in memory, and effectually to exercise them; and, as for the obscure mysteries, to be contented to be ignorant in them, until such time as it shall please God, to open those things unto him. In the mean season, if he lack either aptness or opportunity, God will not impute it to his folly: but yet it behoveth not, that such as be apt should set aside reading, because some other be unapt to read. Nevertheless, for the difficulty of such places, the reading of the whole ought not to be set apart. And briefly to conclude: as St Augustine saith, by the Scripture, all men be amended, weak men be strengthened, and strong men be comforted. So that surely none be enemies to the reading of God's word, but such as either be so ignorant, that they know not how wholesome a thing it is, or else be so sick, that they hate the most comfortable medicine that should heal them, or so ungodly, that they would wish the people still to continue in blindness, and ignorance of God.

Thus we have briefly touched some part, of the *benefits* commodities of God's holy word, which is one of God's chief and principal benefits, given and declared to mankind, here in earth. Let us thank God heartily, for this his great and special gift, beneficial favour, and fatherly providence. Let us be glad to *revive this* precious *gift*, of our heavenly Father. Let us hear, read, and know these holy rules, injunctions, and statutes of our Christian religion, and upon that we have made profession to God, at our baptism. Let us with fear and reverence, lay up in the chest of our hearts, these necessary and fruitful lessons. Let us *night and day* muse, and *have meditation* and contemplation *in them.* Let us ruminate, and as it were chew the cud, that we may have the sweet juice, spiritual effect,

How the knowledge of Scripture may be attained unto

Matt. 7:8

A good rule for the understanding of the Scripture

No man is excepted from the knowledge of God's will.

What persons would have ignorance to continue

The Holy Scripture is one of God's chief benefits.

2 Tim. 1:6
The right reading, use and fruitful studying in Holy Scripture

Psalm 1:2

marrow, honey, kernel, taste, comfort, and consolation of them. Let us stay, quiet, and certify our consciences, with the most infallible certainty, truth, and perpetual assurance of them. Let us pray to God, the only Author of these heavenly meditations, that we may speak, think, believe, live, and depart hence, according to the wholesome doctrine and verities of them. And by that means, in this world we shall have God's protection, favour, and grace, with the unspeakable solace of peace and quietness of conscience, and after this miserable life, we shall enjoy the endless bliss, and glory of heaven. Which he grant us all, that died for us all, Jesus Christ: to whom, with the Father, and Holy Ghost, be all honour and glory, both now and everlastingly. Amen.

A SERMON
OF THE MISERY OF ALL MANKIND
AND OF HIS CONDEMNATION
TO DEATH EVERLASTING
BY HIS OWN SIN

THE HOLY GHOST, in writing the holy Scripture, is in nothing more diligent, than to pull down man's vainglory and pride, which of all vices is most universally grafted in all mankind, even from the first infection of our first father Adam. And therefore we read in many places of Scripture, many notable lessons, against this old rooted vice, to teach us the most commendable virtue of humility, how to know ourselves, and to remember what we be of ourselves.

In the book of Genesis, Almighty God giveth us all a title and name in our great-grandfather Adam, which ought to admonish us all, to consider what we be, whereof we be, from whence we came, and whither we shall, saying thus: *In the sweat of thy face shalt thou eat thy bread, till thou be turned again into the ground; for out of it wast thou taken; inasmuch as thou art dust, and into dust shalt thou be turned again.* Here, as it were in a glass, we may learn to know ourselves to be but ground, earth, and ashes, and that to earth and ashes we shall return. Also the holy patriarch Abraham, did well remember this name and title, *dust,* earth, *and ashes,* appointed and assigned by God, to all mankind; and therefore he calleth himself by that name, when he maketh his earnest prayer for Sodom and Gomorre. And we read that Judith, Hester, Job, Jeremy, with other holy men and women, in the Old Testament, did use sackcloth, and to cast dust and ashes upon their heads, when they bewailed their sinful living. They called and cried to God, for help and mercy, with such a ceremony of sackcloth, dust, and ashes, that thereby they might declare to the whole world, what an humble and lowly estimation they had of themselves, and how well they remembered their name, and title aforesaid, their vile, corrupt, frail nature, dust, earth, and ashes.

Gen. 3:19

Judges 4:10 &
9:1;
Job 42:6;
Jer. 6:26 &
25:34

II

Wisd. 7:1–6

The book of Wisdom also, willing to pull down our proud stomachs, moveth us diligently to remember our mortal and earthly generation, which we have all, *of him that was first made*; and that *all men*, as well kings as subjects, *come into this world, and go out of the same in like sort*, that is, as of ourselves, full miserable, as we may daily see. And Almighty God

Isai. 40:6,7

commanded his Prophet Esay, to make a proclamation, and cry to the whole world: and Esay asking, *What shall I cry?* the Lord answered, *Cry that all flesh is grass, and that all the glory thereof, is but as the flower of the field: when the grass is withered, the flower falleth away, when the wind of the Lord bloweth upon it. The people surely is grass, the which drieth up, and the flower fadeth away.* And the holy Prophet Job, having in himself great experience, of the miserable and sinful estate of man, doth open the same to

Job 14:1–4

the world, in these words. *Man*, saith he, *that is born of a woman, living but a short time, is full of manifold miseries. He springeth up like a flower, and fadeth again, vanishing away as it were a shadow, and never continueth in one state. And dost thou judge it meet O Lord, to open thine eyes upon such a one, and to bring him to judgement with thee? Who can make him clean, that is conceived of an unclean seed?* And all men, of their evilness, and natural proneness, were so universally given to sin, that as the Scripture saith,

Gen. 6:6

God repented that ever he made man: and by sin, his indignation was so much provoked against the world, that he drowned all the world, with

Gen. 7

Noe's flood, except Noe himself, and his little household.

Jer. 22:29

It is not without great cause, that the Scripture of God doth, so many times, call all men here in this world, by this word Earth. *O thou earth, earth, earth*, saith Jeremy, *hear the word of the Lord.* This our right name, vocation, and title, *Earth, Earth, Earth*, pronounced by the Prophet, showeth what we be indeed, by whatsoever other style, title, or dignity men do call us. Thus he plainly nameth us, who knoweth best both what we be, and what we ought of right to be called. And thus he describeth

Rom. 3:9–18

us, speaking by his faithful Apostle St Paul: *All men, Jews and Gentiles, are under sin. There is none righteous, no not one; There is none that understandeth; there is none that seeketh after God. They are all gone out of the way; they are all unprofitable: there is none that doeth good, no not one. Their throat is an open sepulchre; with their tongues they have used craft and deceit; the poison of serpents is under their lips. Their mouth is full of cursing and bitterness; their feet are swift to shed blood. Destruction and wretchedness are in their ways, and the way of peace, have they not known: there is no fear of*

Rom. 11:32

God before their eyes. And in another place, St Paul writeth thus: *God hath wrapped all nations in unbelief, that he might have mercy on all. The*

Gal. 3:22

Scripture shutteth up all under sin, that the promise by the faith of Jesus Christ, should be given unto them that believe. St Paul in many places

Ephes. 2:3

painteth us out in our colours, calling us, *the children of the wrath of God when we be born*; saying also, that *we cannot think a good thought of ourselves*, much less we can say well, or do well of ourselves. And the Wise Man saith in the book of Proverbs, *The just man falleth, seven times a day.*

The most tried and approved man Job, *feared all his works.* St John the Baptist, being sanctified in his mother's womb, and praised before he was born, called *an angel*, and *great before the Lord, filled even from his birth with the Holy Ghost, the preparer of the way for* our Saviour *Christ*, and commended of our Saviour Christ, to be *more than a prophet* and *the greatest that ever was born of a woman*, yet he plainly granteth, that he *had need to be washed of Christ*; he worthily extolleth and glorifieth, his Lord and Master Christ, and humbleth himself, as *unworthy to unbuckle his shoes*, and giveth all honour and glory to God. So doth St Paul both oft and evidently, confess himself what he was of himself, ever giving, as a most faithful servant, all praise to his Master and Saviour. So doth blessed St John the Evangelist, in the name of himself, and of all other holy men, be they never so just, make this open confession: *If we say we have no sin, we deceive ourselves, and the truth is not in us. If we acknowledge our sins, God is faithful and just, to forgive us our sins, and to cleanse us from all unrighteousness. If we say we have not sinned, we make him a liar, and his word is not in us.* Wherefore the Wise Man, in the book called Ecclesiastes, maketh this true and general confession: *There is not one just man upon the earth, that doeth good and sinneth not.* And St David is ashamed of his sin, but not to confess his sin. How oft, how earnestly and lamentably, doth he desire God's great mercy, for his great offences, and that God should *not enter into judgement with him*! And again, how well weigheth this holy man his sins, when he confesseth, that they be so many in number, and so hid and hard to understand, that it is in a manner unpossible to know, utter, or number them! Wherefore, he having a true, earnest, and deep contemplation and consideration of his sins, and yet not coming to the bottom of them, he maketh supplication to God, *to forgive him his privy, secret, hid sins*, to the knowledge of the which he cannot attain. He weigheth rightly his sins, from the original root and spring-head, perceiving inclinations, provocations, stirrings, stingings, buds, branches, dregs, infections, tastes, feelings, and scents of them, to continue in him still. Wherefore he saith, *Mark and behold, I was conceived in sins.* He saith not sin, but in the plural number sins; forasmuch as out of one, as a fountain, springeth all the rest.

And our Saviour Christ saith, *There is none good but God*, and that *we can do nothing* that is good *without him*, nor *no man can come to the Father, but by him.* He commandeth us all, to say that *we be unprofitable servants, when we have done all that we can do.* He preferreth the penitent Publican, before the proud, holy, and glorious Pharisee. He calleth himself a *Physician, but not to them that be whole, but to them that be sick*, and have need of his salve for their sore. He teacheth us in our prayers,

Prov. 24:16

Job 9:28

Luke 1:15, 76

Luke 7:26, 28

Matt. 3:11, 14

Mark 1:7, 8

1 John 1: 8–10

Eccles. 7:20

Psalm 51

Psalm 143:2

Psalm 19:12

Psalm 51:5

Mark 10:18
Luke 18:9
John 15:5

Luke 17:10
Luke 18:14

Matt. 9:12

to acknowledge ourselves sinners, and to ask forgiveness and deliverance from all evils, at our heavenly Father's hand. He declareth that the sins of our own hearts, do defile our own selves. He teacheth that an evil word or thought, deserveth condemnation, affirming that *we shall give an account for every idle word.* He saith *he came not to save but the sheep that were utterly lost,* and cast away. Therefore, few of the proud, just, learned, wise, perfect, and holy Pharisees, were saved by him; because they justified themselves, by their counterfeit holiness before men. Wherefore good people, let us beware of such hypocrisy, vainglory, and justifying of ourselves. Let us look upon our feet; and then down peacock's feathers! down proud heart! down vile clay!—frail and brittle vessels.

Matt. 12:36

Matt. 15:24

THE SECOND PART OF THE SERMON OF THE MISERY OF MAN

FORASMUCH AS THE TRUE KNOWLEDGE of ourselves, is very necessary to come to the right knowledge of God, ye have heard in the last reading, how humbly, all godly men always have thought of themselves, and so to think and judge of themselves, are taught of God their Creator, by his holy word. For of ourselves, we be crabtrees, that can bring forth no apples. We be of ourselves, of such earth as can bring forth but weeds, nettles, brambles, briars, cockle, and darnel. Our fruits be declared, in the fifth chapter to the Galatians. We have neither faith, charity, hope, patience, chastity, nor any thing else that good is, but of God; and therefore these virtues be called there, *the fruits of the Holy Ghost,* and not the fruits of man.

Gal. 5:19–23

Let us therefore acknowledge ourselves before God, as we be indeed, miserable and wretched sinners. And let us earnestly repent, and humble ourselves heartily, and cry to God for mercy. Let us all confess with mouth and heart, that we be full of imperfections. Let us know our own works, of what imperfection they be; and then we shall not stand foolishly and arrogantly, in our own conceits, nor challenge any part of justification by our merits, or works. For truly, there be imperfections in our best works: we do not love God so much, as we are bound to do, with all our heart, mind, and power; we do not fear God so much, as we ought to do; we do not pray to God, but with great and many imperfections; we give, forgive, believe, love, and hope unperfectly; we speak, think, and do unperfectly; we fight against the devil, the world, and the flesh unperfectly. Let us therefore not be ashamed, to confess plainly our state of imperfection; yea, let us not be ashamed to confess imperfection, even in all our own best works. Let none of us be ashamed to say, with holy St

Peter, *I am a sinful man.* Let us all say, with the holy Prophet David, *We*   Luke 5:8
have sinned with our fathers; we have done amiss, and dealt wickedly. Let us   Psalm 106:6
all make open confession, with the prodigal son, to our Father, and say   Luke 15:18, 19
with him, *We have sinned against heaven, and before thee, O Father; we are*
not worthy to be called thy sons. Let us all say with holy Baruch, *O Lord our*   Bar. 2:6, 12
God, to us is worthily ascribed shame and confusion, and to thee righteousness:
we have sinned, we have done wickedly, we have behaved ourselves ungodly, in
all thy righteousness. Let us all say with the holy Prophet Daniel, *O Lord,*   Dan. 9: 7, 5
righteousness belongeth to thee; unto us belongeth confusion. We have sinned,
we have been naughty, we have offended, we have fled from thee, we have gone
back from all thy precepts and judgements. So we learn, of all good men in
holy Scripture, to humble ourselves, and to exalt, extol, praise, magnify,
and glorify God.

   Thus we have heard, how evil we be of ourselves; how of ourselves and
by ourselves, we have no goodness, help nor salvation, but contrariwise
sin, damnation, and death everlasting: which if we deeply weigh and consider, we shall the better understand the great mercy of God, and how
our salvation cometh only by Christ. For in ourselves, as of ourselves,   2 Cor. 3:5
we find nothing, whereby we may be delivered from this miserable
captivity, into the which we were cast, through the envy of the devil, by
transgressing of God's commandment in our first parent Adam. We are   Psalm 51:1–10
all become unclean: but we all are not able to cleanse ourselves, nor to
make one another of us clean. We are *by nature, the children of God's*   Ephes. 2:25
wrath: but we are not able to make ourselves, the children and inheritors
of God's glory. We are *sheep that run astray*: but we cannot of our own   1 Pet. 2
power, come again to the sheepfold; so great is our imperfection and
weakness. In ourselves therefore may not we glory, which of ourselves,
are nothing but sinful. Neither we may rejoice in any works that we do;
which all be so unperfect and unpure, that they are not able to stand,
before the righteous judgement seat of God, as the holy Prophet David
saith: *Enter not into judgement with thy servant, O Lord; for no man that*   Psalm 143:2
liveth, shall be found righteous in thy sight.

   To God therefore must we flee; or else shall we never find peace, rest,
and quietness of conscience in our hearts. For he is *the Father of mercies,*   2 Cor. 1:3
and God of all consolation. He is the Lord with whom *is plenteous*   Psalm 130:7
redemption. He is the God which, *of his own mercy saveth us*; and setteth   Titus 3:5
out his charity, and exceeding love toward us, in that of his own
voluntary goodness, when we were perished, he saved us, and provided
an everlasting kingdom for us. And all these heavenly treasures are given
us, not for our own deserts, merits, or good deeds, which of ourselves we
have none, but of his mere mercy freely. And for whose sake? Truly for
Jesus Christ's sake, that *pure and undefiled Lamb* of God. He is that   1 Peter 1:19
dearly beloved Son, for whose sake God is fully pacified, satisfied, and

John 1:29

Mark 7:37

1 Peter 2:22

John 14:30

John 8:46
Heb. 7:24–7

Heb. 10:14

1 Tim. 2:5–6

Rev. 5:9; 1:5
1 John 1:7
Psalm 103:3
Matt. 1:21

John 1:16

Col. 2:3

Hos. 13:9

set at one with man. He is *the Lamb of God, which taketh away the sins of the world*: of whom only, it may be truly spoken, that he did *all things well*, and *in his mouth was found no craft* nor subtilty. None but he alone may say, *The Prince of the World came, and in me he hath nothing*. And he alone may say also, *Which of you shall reprove me of any fault?* He is *that high and everlasting Priest, which hath offered himself, once for all* upon the altar of the cross, and *with that one oblation, hath made perfect for evermore them that are sanctified*. He is the *alone Mediator, between God and man*; which *paid our ransom to God, with his own blood*; and *with that hath he cleansed us all from sin*. He is the Physician *which healeth all our diseases*. He is that Saviour, which *saveth his people, from all their sins*. To be short, he is that flowing and most plenteous fountain, *of whose fulness all we have received*. For *in him alone, are all the treasures, of the wisdom and knowledge of God hidden*; and in him and by him, have we from God the Father, all good things pertaining either to the body or to the soul.

Oh how much are we bound to this our heavenly Father, for his great mercies, which he hath so plenteously declared unto us, in Christ Jesu our Lord and Saviour! What thanks worthy and sufficient, can we give to him? Let us all with one accord, burst out with joyful voices, ever praising and magnifying this Lord of mercy, for his tender kindness, showed to us in his dearly beloved Son, Jesus Christ our Lord.

Hitherto have we heard, what we are of ourselves; verily sinful, wretched, and damnable. Again we have heard, how that, of ourselves and by ourselves, we are not able either to think a good thought, or work a good deed: so that we can find in ourselves, no hope of salvation, but rather whatsoever maketh unto our destruction. Again we have heard, the tender kindness, and great mercy of God the Father toward us, and how beneficial he is to us, for Christ's sake, without our merits or deserts, even of his own mere mercy, and tender goodness. Now, how these exceeding great mercies of God, set abroad in Christ Jesu for us, be obtained, and how we be delivered, from the captivity of sin, death, and hell, it shall more at large, with God's help, be declared in the next Sermon. In the mean season, yea, and at all times, let us learn to know ourselves, our frailty and weakness, without any ostentation, or boasting of our own good deeds and merits. Let us also knowledge the exceeding mercy of God toward us, and confess, that as of ourselves cometh all evil, and damnation, so likewise of him, cometh all goodness and salvation; as God himself saith by the Prophet Osee: *O Israel, thy destruction cometh of thyself, but in me only is thy help* and comfort. If we thus humbly submit ourselves, in the sight of God, we may be sure that in the time of his visitation, he will lift us up, unto the kingdom of his dearly beloved Son Christ Jesu our Lord. To whom with the Father, and the Holy Ghost, be all honour and glory for ever. Amen.

A SERMON
OF THE SALVATION OF MANKIND
BY ONLY CHRIST OUR SAVIOUR
FROM SIN
AND DEATH EVERLASTING

BECAUSE ALL MEN BE SINNERS, and offenders against God, and breakers of his law and commandments, therefore can no man by his own acts, works, and deeds, seem they never so good, be justified and made righteous before God; but every man of necessity, is constrained to seek for another righteousness or justification, to be received at God's own hands, that is to say, the remission, pardon and forgiveness of his sins and trespasses, in such things as he hath offended. And this justification or righteousness, which we so receive by God's mercy and Christ's merits, embraced by faith, is taken, accepted and allowed of God, for our perfect and full justification.

For the more full understanding hereof, it is our parts and duty, ever to remember the great mercy of God; how that, all the world being wrapped in sin, by breaking of the law, God sent his only Son, our Saviour Christ, into this world, to fulfil the law for us, and by shedding of his most precious blood, to make a sacrifice and satisfaction, or (as it may be called), amends to his Father for our sins, to assuage his wrath and indignation, conceived against us for the same. Insomuch that infants, being baptised and dying in their infancy, are by this sacrifice washed from their sins, brought to God's favour, and made his children, and inheritors of his kingdom of heaven. And they which in act or deed, do sin after their baptism, when they convert, and turn again to God unfeignedly, they are likewise washed, by this sacrifice, from their sins, in such sort that there remaineth not any spot of sin, that shall be imputed to their damnation. This is that justification, or righteousness, which St Paul speaketh of, when he saith, *No man is justified by the works of the law,*

The efficacy of Christ's passion and oblation

Rom. 3:20, 22, 24

17

Gal. 2:16

but freely, by faith in Jesus Christ. And again he saith, *We believe in Christ Jesu, that we be justified freely, by the faith of Christ, and not by the works of the law; because that no man shall be justified by the works of the law.*

And, although this justification be free unto us, yet it cometh not so freely unto us, that there is no ransom paid therefore at all.

An objection

But here may man's reason be astonied, reasoning after this fashion. If a ransom be paid for our redemption, then it is not given us freely: for a prisoner that payeth his ransom, is not let go freely; for if he go freely, then he goeth without ransom; for what is it else to go freely, than to be set at liberty without payment of ransom?

An answer

This reason is satisfied by the great wisdom of God, in this mystery of our redemption; who hath so tempered his justice and mercy together, that he would neither by his justice condemn us, unto the perpetual captivity of the devil, and his prison of hell, remediless for ever without mercy, nor by his mercy deliver us clearly, without justice or payment of a just ransom; but with his endless mercy, he joined his most upright and equal justice. His great mercy he showed unto us, in delivering us from our former captivity, without requiring of any ransom to be paid, or amends to be made upon our parts; which thing by us had been impossible to be done. And whereas it lay not in us that to do, he provided a ransom for us, that was, the most precious body, and blood, of his own most dear and best beloved Son Jesu Christ; who besides his ransom,

Psalm 85:10

fulfilled the law for us perfectly. And so the justice of God, and his mercy, did embrace together, and fulfilled the mystery of our redemption. And of this justice and mercy of God, knit together, speaketh St Paul in the

Rom. 3:23–5

third chapter to the Romans: *All have offended, and have need of the glory of God, but are justified freely by his grace, by redemption which is in Jesu Christ; whom God hath set forth to us, for a reconciler and peacemaker, through faith*

Rom. 10:4

in his blood, to show his righteousness. And in the tenth chapter: *Christ is the end of the Law, unto righteousness to every man that believeth.* And in the

Rom. 8:3, 4

eighth chapter: *That which was impossible by the Law, inasmuch as it was weak by the flesh, God sending his own Son, in the similitude of sinful flesh, by sin damned sin in the flesh, that the righteousness of the Law might be fulfilled in us, which walk not after the flesh, but after the Spirit.*

Three things must go together in our justification.

In these foresaid places, the Apostle toucheth specially three things, which must concur and go together, in our justification: upon God's part, his great mercy and grace; upon Christ's part, justice, that is, the satisfaction of God's justice, or the price of our redemption, by the offering of his body, and shedding of his blood, with fulfilling of the law, perfectly and throughly; and upon our part, true and lively faith in the merits of Jesu Christ; which yet is not ours, but by God's working in us. So that in our justification, is not only God's mercy and grace, but also

Rom. 8:3, 4

his justice, which the Apostle calleth *the justice of God*; and it consisteth in paying our ransom, and fulfilling of the law. And so the grace of God, doth not exclude the justice of God in our justification, but only excludeth the justice of man, that is to say, the justice of our works, as to be merits of deserving our justification. And therefore St Paul declareth here nothing upon the behalf of man, concerning his justification, but only a true and lively faith; which nevertheless is *the gift of God,* and not man's only work without God. And yet that faith doth not exclude repentance, hope, love, dread, and the fear of God, to be joined with faith, in every man that is justified; but it excludeth them, from the office of justifying. So that although they be all present together, in him that is justified, yet they justify not all together. Nor that faith also, doth not shut out the justice of our good works, necessarily to be done afterward, of duty towards God (for we are most bounden to serve God, in doing good deeds, commanded by him in his holy Scripture, all the days of our life); but it excludeth them, so that we may not do them to this intent, to be made good by doing of them. For all the good works that we can do, be unperfect, and therefore not able to deserve our justification: but our justification doth come freely, by the mere mercy of God; and of so great and free mercy, that whereas all the world was not able of their selves, to pay any part towards their ransom, it pleased our heavenly Father, of his infinite mercy, without any our desert or deserving, to prepare for us the most precious jewels, of Christ's body and blood, whereby our ransom might be fully paid, the law fulfilled, and his justice fully satisfied. So that Christ is now the righteousness, of all them that truly do believe in him. He for them paid their ransom by his death. He for them fulfilled the law in his life. So that now in him, and by him, every true Christian man may be called a fulfiller of the law; forasmuch as that which their infirmity lacketh, Christ's justice hath supplied.

Eph. 2:8

How it is to be understood, that faith justifieth without works

THE SECOND PART
OF THE SERMON OF SALVATION

YE HAVE HEARD, of whom all men ought to seek their justification and righteousness, and how also, this righteousness cometh unto men, by Christ's death and merits. Ye heard also, how that three things are required, to the obtaining of our righteousness; that is, God's mercy, Christ's justice, and a true and a lively faith, out of the which faith springeth good works. Also before was declared at large, that no man can be justified by his own good works, because that no man fulfilleth the law, according to the strict rigour of the law. And St Paul in his Epistle to the Galathians, proveth the same, saying thus: *If there had been any law*

Gal. 3:21

Gal. 2:21

Gal. 5:4

Ephes. 2:8, 9

Rom. 11:6

Acts 10:43

Faith only
justifieth, is the
doctrine of old
doctors.

Phil. 3:9

Faith alone, how
it is to be under-
stood

given, *which could have justified, verily righteousness should have been by the law.* And again he saith, *If righteousness be by the law, then Christ died in vain.* And again he saith, *You that are justified in the law, are fallen away from grace.* And furthermore, he writeth to the Ephesians on this wise: *By grace are ye saved through faith; and that not of yourselves, for it is the gift of God; and not of works, lest any man should glory.* And to be short, the sum of all Paul's disputation is this: that if justice come of works, then it cometh not of grace; and if it come of grace, then it cometh not of works. And to this end, tendeth all the Prophets, as St Peter saith in the tenth of the Acts. *Of Christ all the Prophets,* saith St Peter, *do witness, that through his Name, all they that believe in him shall receive the remission of sins.*

And after this wise to be justified, only by this true and lively faith in Christ, speaketh all the old and ancient authors, both Greeks and Latins. Of whom I will specially rehearse three, Hilary, Basil, and Ambrose. St Hilary saith these words plainly, in the ninth Canon upon Matthew: "Faith only justifieth." And St Basil, a Greek author, writeth thus: "This is a perfect and a whole rejoicing in God, when a man avaunteth not himself, for his own righteousness, but knowledgeth himself, to lack true justice and righteousness, and to be justified by the only faith in Christ. And Paul," saith he, "doth glory, in the contempt of his own righteousness, and that he looketh for *the righteousness of God, by faith.*" These be the very words of St Basil. And St Ambrose, a Latin author, saith these words: "This is the ordinance of God, that he which believeth in Christ, should be saved without works, by faith only, freely receiving remission of his sins." Consider diligently these words. Without works, by faith only, freely we receive remission of our sins. What can be spoken more plainly, than to say that freely, without works, by faith only, we obtain remission of our sins?

These and other like sentences, that we be justified by faith only, freely and without works, we do read ofttimes, in the most best and ancient writers. As, beside Hilary, Basil, and St Ambrose before rehearsed, we read the same in Origen, St Chrysostom, St Cyprian, St Augustine, Prosper, Oecumenius, Photius, Bernardus, Anselm, and many other authors, Greek and Latin. Nevertheless, the sentence, that we be justified by faith only, is not so meant of them, that the said justifying faith is alone in man, without true repentance, hope, charity, dread, and fear of God, at any time or season. Nor when they say that we be justified freely, they mean not that we should, or might afterward be idle, and that nothing should be required of our parts afterward; neither mean they, that we are so to be justified, without our good works, that we should do no good works at all, like as shall be more expressed at large hereafter. But this proposition, that we be justified by faith only, freely, and without works, is spoken for to take away clearly, all merit of our works, as being insufficient, to deserve our justification at God's hands; and thereby most plainly, to express the weakness of man, and the goodness of God, the great infirmity of ourselves, and the might and power of God, the imperfectness of our own works, and the most abundant grace of our Saviour Christ; and thereby wholly to ascribe the merit, and deserving of our justification, unto Christ only, and his most precious bloodshedding.

This faith the holy Scripture teacheth: this is the strong rock and foundation, of Christian religion: this doctrine, all old and ancient authors of Christ's Church do approve: this doctrine advanceth, and setteth forth, the true glory of Christ, and suppresseth the vain glory of man: this whosoever denieth, is not to be reported for a true Christian man, nor for a setter forth of Christ's glory, but for an adversary of Christ, and his Gospel, and for a setter forth of men's vainglory.

> The profit of the doctrine of, "Faith only justifieth"

> What they be that impugn the doctrine of, "Faith only justifieth"

And although this doctrine be never so true, as it is most true indeed, that we be justified freely, without all merit of our own good works (as St Paul doth express it), and freely, by this lively and perfect faith in Christ only (as the ancient authors use to speak it), yet this true doctrine must be also truly understood, and most plainly declared, lest carnal men should take unjustly, occasion thereby to live carnally, after the appetite and will of the world, the flesh, and the devil. And because no man should err, by mistaking of this doctrine, I shall plainly and shortly, so declare the right understanding of the same, that no man shall justly think, that he may thereby take any occasion of carnal liberty, to follow the desires of the flesh, or that thereby any kind of sin shall be committed, or any ungodly living the more used.

First, you shall understand, that in our justification by Christ, it is not all one thing, the office of God unto man, and the office of man unto God. Justification is not the office of man, but of God. For man cannot justify himself, by his own works, neither in part, nor in the whole; for that were the greatest arrogancy and presumption of man, that Antichrist could set up against God, to affirm that a man might by his own works, take away and purge his own sins, and so justify himself. But justification is the office of God only, and is not a thing which we render unto him, but which we receive of him; not which we give to him, but which we take of him, by his free mercy, and by the only merits of his most dearly beloved Son, our only Redeemer, Saviour, and Justifier, Jesus Christ. So that the true understanding of this doctrine, We be justified freely, by faith without works, or that we be justified by faith in Christ only, is not that this our own act, to believe in Christ, or this our faith in Christ, which is within us, doth justify us, and merit our justification unto us; for that were to count ourselves to be justified by

> A declaration of this doctrine, Faith without works justifieth

> Justification is the office of God only.

some act, or virtue that is within ourselves. But the true understanding and meaning thereof is, that although we hear God's word, and believe it, although we have faith, hope, charity, repentance, dread, and fear of God within us, and do never so many good works thereunto, yet we must renounce the merit, of all our said virtues of faith, hope, charity, and all our other virtues and good deeds, which we either have done, shall do, or can do, as things that be far too weak, and insufficient and unperfect, to deserve remission of our sins, and our justification; and therefore we must trust, only in God's mercy, and in that sacrifice, which our High Priest and Saviour, Christ Jesus, the Son of God, once offered for us upon the cross, to obtain thereby God's grace, and remission, as well of our original sin, in baptism, as of all actual sin committed by us after our baptism, if we truly repent, and convert unfeignedly to him again. So that, as St John Baptist, although he were never so virtuous and godly a man, yet in this matter of forgiving of sin, he did put the people from him, and appointed them unto Christ, saying thus unto them, *Behold, yonder is the Lamb of God, which taketh away the sins of the world*; even so, as great and as godly a virtue as the lively faith is, yet it putteth us from itself, and remitteth or appointeth us unto Christ, for to have only by him, remission of our sins, or justification. So that our faith in Christ, as it were, saith unto us thus: It is not I that take away your sins, but it is Christ only; and to him only I send you for that purpose, renouncing therein all your good virtues, words, thoughts, and works, and only putting your trust in Christ.

John 1:29

THE THIRD PART OF
THE SERMON OF SALVATION

IT HATH BEEN MANIFESTLY DECLARED unto you, that no man can fulfil the law of God, and therefore by the law all men are condemned: whereupon it followeth necessarily, that some other thing should be required for our salvation than the law; and that is a true and a lively faith in Christ, bringing forth good works, and a life according to God's commandments. And also, you heard the ancient authors' minds of this proposition, "Faith in Christ only justifieth man," so plainly declared, that you see, that the very, true sense of this proposition, "We be justified by faith in Christ only," according to the meaning of the old ancient authors, is this: We put our faith in Christ, that we be justified by him only, that we be justified by God's free mercy, and the merits of our Saviour Christ only, and by no virtue, or good work of our own, that is in us, or that we can be able to have or to do, for to deserve the same, Christ himself only, being the cause meritorious thereof.

Here you perceive many words to be used, to avoid contention in words, with them that delight to brawl about words, and also to show the true meaning, to avoid evil taking and misunderstanding: and yet peradventure, all will not serve with them that be contentious; but contenders will ever forge matter of contention, even when they have none occasion thereto. Notwithstanding, such be the less to be passed upon, so that the rest may profit, which will be more desirous to know the truth than, when it is plain enough, to contend about it, and with contentious and captious cavillations, to obscure and darken it. Truth it is that our own works do not justify us, to speak properly of our justification; that is to say, our works do not merit, or deserve, remission of our sins, and make us, of unjust, just before God; but God of his mere mercy, through the only merits, and deservings of his Son, Jesus Christ, doth justify us. Nevertheless, because faith doth directly send us to Christ, for remission of our sins, and that by faith given us of God, we embrace the promise of God's mercy, and of remission of our sins, which thing none other of our virtues or works properly doeth, therefore Scripture useth to say, that faith without works doth justify. And, forasmuch that it is all one sentence in effect to say, Faith without works, and, Only faith, doth justify us, therefore the old ancient fathers of the Church, from time to time have uttered our justification, with this speech, "Only faith justifieth us"; meaning none other thing than St Paul meant, when he said, "Faith without works justifieth us." And, because all this is brought to pass, through the only merits and deservings of our Saviour Christ, and not through our merits, or through the merit of any virtue that we have within us, or of any work that cometh from us, therefore in that respect of merit and deserving, we renounce as it were altogether again faith, works, and all other virtues. For our own imperfection, is so great, through the corruption of original sin, that all is imperfect that is within us, faith, charity, hope, dread, thoughts, words, and works, and therefore not apt to merit and deserve, any part of our justification for us. And this form of speaking we use, in the humbling of ourselves to God, and to give all the glory to our Saviour Christ, which is best worthy to have it.

Here you have heard, the office of God in our justification, and how we receive it of him freely, by his mercy, without our deserts, through true and lively faith. Now you shall hear, the office and duty of a Christian man unto God, what we ought on our part, to render unto God again, for his great mercy and goodness. Our office is not to pass the time of this present life, unfruitfully and idly, after that we are baptised or justified, not caring how few good works we do, to the glory of God and profit of our neighbours: much less it is our office, after that we be once made Christ's members, to live contrary to the same, making ourselves

They that preach, Faith only justifieth, do not teach carnal liberty, or that we should do no good works.

members of the devil, walking after his enticements, and after the suggestions of the world and the flesh; whereby we know, that we do serve the world and the devil, and not God. For that faith which bringeth forth, without repentance, either evil works, or no good works is not a right, pure, and lively faith, but a dead, devilish, counterfeit, and feigned faith, as St Paul and St James call it. For even the devils know and believe, that Christ was born of a virgin, that he fasted forty days and forty nights, without meat and drink, that he wrought all kind of miracles, declaring himself very God. They believe also that Christ, for our sakes, suffered most painful death, to redeem us from eternal death, and that he rose again from death, the third day: they believe that he ascended into heaven, and that he sitteth on the right hand of the Father, and at the last end of this world, shall come again and judge both the quick and the dead. These articles of our faith the devils believe; and so they believe all things that be written in the New and Old Testament to be true: and yet for all this faith, they be but devils, remaining still in their damnable estate, lacking the very true Christian faith. For the right and true Christian faith, is not only to believe that holy Scripture, and all the foresaid articles of our faith are true, but also to have a sure trust and confidence, in God's merciful promises, to be saved from everlasting damnation, by Christ; whereof doth follow a loving heart, to obey his commandments. And this true Christian faith neither any devil hath, nor yet any man which, in the outward profession of his mouth, and in his outward receiving of the Sacraments, in coming to the church, and in all other outward appearances, seemeth to be a Christian man, and yet in his living and deeds, showeth the contrary. For how can a man have this true faith, this sure trust and confidence in God, that by the merits of Christ his sins be remitted, and he reconciled to the favour of God, and to be partaker of the kingdom of heaven by Christ, when he liveth ungodly, and denieth Christ in his deeds? Surely no such ungodly man can have this faith and trust in God. For as they know Christ to be the only Saviour of the world, so they know also, that wicked men shall not possess the kingdom of God. They know that God *hateth unrighteousness,* that *he will destroy all those that speak untruly;* that *those that have done good works,* which cannot be done without a lively faith in Christ, *shall come forth into the resurrection of life, and those that have done evil, shall come unto the resurrection of judgement.* And very well they know also, that *to them that be contentious, and to them that will not be obedient unto the truth, but will obey unrighteousness, shall come indignation, wrath, and affliction, &c.*

Therefore to conclude, considering the infinite benefits of God, showed and exhibited unto us mercifully, without our deserts; who hath not only created us of nothing, and from a piece of vile clay, of his infinite goodness, hath exalted us, as touching our soul, unto his own

Marginal notes:

The devils have faith, but not the true faith.

What is the true and justifying faith

They that continue in evil living have not true faith.

Psalm 5:5, 6

John 5:29

Rom. 2:8, 9

similitude and likeness; but also, whereas we were condemned to hell and death eternal, hath given his own natural Son (being God eternal, immortal, and equal unto himself in power and glory), to be incarnated, and to take our mortal nature upon him, with the infirmities of the same, and in the same nature, to suffer most shameful and painful death, for our offences, to the intent to justify us, and to restore us to life everlasting; so making us also his dear beloved children, brethren unto his only Son, our Saviour Christ, and inheritors for ever, with him, of his eternal kingdom of heaven: these great and merciful benefits of God, if they be well considered, do neither minister unto us occasion to be idle, and to live without doing any good works, neither yet stirreth us, by any means, to do evil things; but contrariwise, if we be not desperate persons, and our hearts harder than stones, they move us to render ourselves unto God, wholly with all our will, hearts, might, and power; to serve him in all good deeds, obeying his commandments during our lives; to seek in all things his glory and honour, not our sensual pleasures and vainglory; evermore dreading, willingly to offend such a merciful God, and loving Redeemer, in word, thought, or deed. And the said benefits of God deeply considered, do move us for his sake, also to be ever ready to give ourselves to our neighbours, and as much as lieth in us, to study with all our endeavour, to do good to every man. These be the fruits of the true faith: to do good, as much as lieth in us, to every man; and above all things, and in all things, to advance the glory of God, of whom only we have our sanctification, justification, salvation, and redemption. To whom be ever glory, praise, and honour, world without end. Amen.

A SHORT DECLARATION
OF THE TRUE, LIVELY,
AND CHRISTIAN FAITH

Faith

THE FIRST COMING UNTO GOD, good Christian people, is through faith; whereby as it is declared in the last Sermon, we be justified before God. And lest any man should be deceived, for lack of right understanding hereof, it is diligently to be noted, that faith is taken in the Scripture two manner of ways.

A dead faith

James 2:17, 19

There is one faith which in Scripture is called a *dead* faith; which bringeth forth no good works, but is idle, barren and unfruitful. And this faith, by the holy Apostle St James, is compared to the faith of *devils*; which *believe* God to be true and just, *and tremble* for fear, yet they do nothing well, but all evil. And such a manner of faith, have the wicked and

Titus 1:16

naughty Christian people; which *confess God*, as St Paul saith, *in their mouth, but deny him in their deeds, being abominable, and without the right faith, and to all good works reproveable*. And this faith is a persuasion and belief, in man's heart, whereby he knoweth that there is a God, and agreeth unto all truth of God's most holy word, contained in holy Scripture, so that it consisteth only, in believing of the word of God, that it is true. And this is not properly called faith: but as he that readeth Cesar's Commentaries, believing the same to be true, hath thereby a knowledge of Cesar's life and notable acts, because he believeth the history of Cesar, yet it is not properly said, that he believeth in Cesar, of whom he looketh for no help nor benefit; even so he that believeth, that all that is spoken of God in the Bible is true, and yet liveth so ungodly, that he cannot look to enjoy the promises and benefits of God, although it may be said, that such a man hath a faith and belief, to the words of God, yet it is not properly said, that he believeth in God, or hath such a faith and trust in God, whereby he may surely look for grace, mercy, and everlasting life at God's hand, but rather for indignation and punishment, according to the merits of his wicked life. For as it is written in a book intituled to be of Didymus Alexandrinus, "Forasmuch as faith without works is dead, it is not now faith; as a dead man is not a man."

This dead faith therefore, is not that sure and substantial faith, which saveth sinners.

Another faith there is in Scripture, which is not as the foresaid faith, idle, unfruitful, and dead, but *worketh by charity*, as St Paul declareth Gal. 5: which, as the other vain faith is called a dead faith, so may this be called a quick or lively faith. And this is not only the common belief, of the articles of our faith, but it is also a sure trust and confidence, of the mercy of God, through our Lord Jesus Christ, and a stedfast hope, of all good things to be received at God's hand; and that although we through infirmity, or temptation of our ghostly enemy, do fall from him by sin, yet if we return again unto him, by true repentance, that he will forgive and forget our offences, for his Son's sake, our Saviour Jesus Christ; and will make us inheritors with him, of his everlasting kingdom; and that in the mean time, until that kingdom come, he will be our protector and defender, in all perils and dangers, whatsoever do chance; and that though sometime he doth send us sharp adversity, yet that evermore he will be a loving Father unto us, correcting us for our sin, but not withdrawing his mercy finally from us, if we trust in him, and commit ourselves wholly unto him, hang only upon him, and call upon him, ready to obey and serve him. This is the true, lively, and unfeigned Christian faith, and is not in the mouth, and outward profession only, but it liveth and stirreth, inwardly in the heart. And this faith is not without hope and trust in God, nor without the love of God, and of our neighbours, nor without the fear of God, nor without the desire to hear God's word, and to follow the same in eschewing evil, and doing gladly all good works. This faith, as St Paul describeth it, is the sure ground and foundation of the benefits, which we ought to look for, and trust to receive of God, a certificate and sure looking for them, although they yet sensibly appear not unto us. And after he saith, *He that cometh to God, must believe both that he is, and that he is a merciful rewarder of well doers.* And nothing commendeth good men unto God so much, as this assured faith and trust in him.

Of this faith, three things are specially to be noted: first, that this faith doth not lie dead in the heart, but is lively and fruitful, in bringing forth good works; second, that without it can no good works be done, that shall be acceptable and pleasant to God; third, what manner of good works they be, that this faith doth bring forth.

For the first. As the light cannot be hid, but will show forth itself at one place or other; so a true faith cannot be kept secret, but when occasion is offered, it will break out, and show itself by good works. And as the living body of a man, ever exerciseth such things, as belongeth to a natural and living body, for nourishment and preservation of the same as it hath need, opportunity, and occasion; even so the soul that hath a

A lively faith
Gal. 5:6

Heb. 11:1

Ibid.:6

Three things are to be noted of faith.

Faith is full of good works.

lively faith in it, will be doing alway some good work, which shall declare
that it is living, and will not be unoccupied.

Therefore, when men hear in the Scriptures, so high commendations
of faith, that it maketh us to please God, to live with God, and to be the
children of God; if then they phantasy, that they be set at liberty from
doing all good works, and may live as they list, they trifle with God, and
deceive themselves. And it is a manifest token, that they be far from
having the true and lively faith, and also far from knowledge, what true
faith meaneth. For the very sure and lively Christian faith, is not only to
believe all things of God, which are contained in holy Scripture, but also
is an earnest trust and confidence in God, that he doth regard us, and
that he is careful over us, as the father is over the child whom he doth
love, and that he will be merciful unto us, for his only Son's sake; and
that we have our Saviour Christ, our perpetual Advocate and Priest; in
whose only merits, oblation, and suffering we do trust, that our offences
be continually washed and purged, whensoever we repenting truly, do
return to him with our whole heart, stedfastly determining with
ourselves, through his grace, to obey and serve him, in keeping his
commandments, and never to turn back again to sin. Such is the true
faith, that the Scripture doth so much commend: the which, when it
seeth and considereth what God hath done for us, is also moved,
through continual assistance of the Spirit of God, to serve and please
him, to keep his favour, to fear his displeasure, to continue his obedient
children, showing thankfulness again by observing (or keeping) his
commandments; and that freely, for true love chiefly, and not for dread
of punishment, or love of temporal reward, considering how clearly,
without our deservings, we have received his mercy and pardon freely.

This true faith will show forth itself, and cannot long be idle. For, as
it is written, *The just man doth live by faith,* he neither sleepeth nor is idle,
when he should wake and be well occupied. And God by his Prophet
Jeremy saith, that *he is a happy and blessed man, which hath faith and
confidence in God: for he is like a tree set by the water side, that spreadeth his
roots abroad toward the moisture, and feareth not heat when it cometh; his leaf
will be green, and will not cease to bring forth his fruit.* Even so faithful men,
putting away all fear of adversity, will show forth the fruit of their good
works, as occasion is offered to do them.

Hab. 2:4

Jer. 17:7, 8

*God is good to us first.
He wants us to be like he is.
Doing for each other as he does
for us.
That's what it means to be godly.*

THE SECOND PART
OF THE SERMON OF FAITH

YE HAVE HEARD in the first part of this Sermon, that there be two kinds of faith, a dead and an unfruitful faith, and a faith lively, *that worketh by charity*; the first to be unprofitable, the second necessary for the obtaining of our salvation; the which faith hath charity always joined unto it, and is fruitful, bringing forth all good works. Now as concerning the same matter, you shall hear what followeth.

Gal. 5:6

The Wise Man saith, *He that believeth in God, will hearken unto his commandments*. For if we do not show ourselves faithful in our conversation, the faith which we pretend to have, is but a feigned faith; because the true Christian faith, is manifestly showed by good living, and not by words only, as St Augustine saith, "Good living cannot be separated, from true *faith, which worketh by love*." And St Chrysostom saith, "Faith of itself is full of good works: as soon as a man doth believe, he shall be garnished with them."

Ecclus. 32:24

Lib. de Fide et Operibus c. 2

Sermo de Lege et Fide

How plentiful this faith is of good works, and how it maketh the work of one man, more acceptable to God than of another, St Paul teacheth at large, in the eleventh chapter to the Hebrews, saying that faith made the oblation of Abel, better than the oblation of Cain. This made Noe to build the ark. This made Abraham to forsake his country and all his friends, and to go unto a far country, there to dwell among strangers. So did also Isaac and Jacob, depending only, of the help and trust that they had in God. And when they came to the country, which God promised them, they would build no cities, towns, nor houses; but lived like strangers in tents, that might every day be removed. Their trust was so much in God, that they set but little by any worldly thing; for that God had prepared for them, better dwellingplaces in heaven, of his own foundation and building. This faith made Abraham ready at God's commandment, to offer his own son and heir Isaac, whom he loved so well, and by whom he was promised, to have innumerable issue, among the which one should be born, in whom all nations should be blessed; trusting so much in God, that though he were slain, yet that God was able by his omnipotent power, to raise him from death, and perform his promise. He mistrusted not the promise of God, although unto his reason, every thing seemed contrary. He believed verily that God would not forsake him, in dearth and famine, that was in the country. And in all other dangers, that he was brought unto, he trusted ever, that God would be his God, and his protector and defender, whatsoever he saw to the contrary. This faith wrought so in the heart of Moses, that he *refused to be taken, for King Pharao his daughter's son*, and to have great

Heb. 11

Gen. 4:4, 5;
Gen. 6:22;
Ecclus. 44:17
Gen. 11:31

Gen. 22:1–18
Ecclus. 44:20

Exod. 2:11

Heb. 11:24–7

inheritance in Egypt; *thinking it better, with the people of God to have affliction* and sorrow, *than* with naughty men, *in sin to live pleasantly for a time. By faith he cared not, for the threatening of King Pharao*: for his trust was so in God, that he passed not of the felicity of this world, but looked

Exod. 14:22;
Heb. 11:29

for the reward, to come in heaven; setting his heart upon *the invisible*

Josh. 6:20;
Heb. 11:30

God, as if he had seen him, ever present before his eyes. *By faith the children of Israel passed through the Red Sea. By faith the walls of Hierico fell down,* without stroke; and many other wonderful miracles have been wrought. In all good men that heretofore have been, faith hath brought forth their good work; and obtained the promises of God. Faith hath *stopped the*

Dan. 6:16–23;
Heb. 11:33
Dan. 3:13–28;
Heb. 11:34

lions' mouths: faith hath *quenched the force of fire*: faith hath *escaped the sword's edges*: faith hath given weak men strength, victory in battle;

Ibid.:36

overthrown the armies of infidels; raised the dead to life. Faith hath made good men, to take adversity in good part: *some have been mocked and whipped, bound and cast in prison*; some have lost all their goods, and

Ibid.:38

lived in great poverty; *some have wandered in mountains, hills and wilderness*; some have been racked, some slain, *some stoned, some sawn*, some

Ibid.:37

rent in pieces, some beheaded, some burnt without mercy, and would not be delivered, because they looked to rise again, to a better state.

All these fathers, martyrs, and other holy men, whom St Paul spake of, had their faith surely fixed in God, when all the world was against them. They did not only know God to be the Lord, Maker, and Governor, of all men in the world; but also they had a special confidence and trust, that he was and would be, their God, their comforter, aider, helper, maintainer, and defender. This is the Christian faith; which these holy men had, and we also ought to have. And, although they were not named Christian men, yet was it a Christian faith that they had; for they looked for all benefits of God the Father, through the merits of his Son Jesu Christ, as we now do. This difference is between them and us; for they looked when Christ should come, and we be in the time when

In Johan. Tract
45

he is come. Therefore saith St Augustine, "The time is altered and changed, but not the faith. For we have both one faith, in one Christ."

2 Cor. 4:13

The same Holy Ghost also that we have, had they, saith St Paul. For as the Holy Ghost doth teach us, to trust in God, and to call upon him as

Isai. 63:16

our Father, so did he teach them to say, as it is written, *Thou, Lord, art our Father and Redeemer, and thy Name is without beginning, and everlasting.* God gave them then grace to be his children, as he doth us now. But now, by the coming of our Saviour Christ, we have received more abundantly, the Spirit of God in our hearts, whereby we may conceive a greater faith, and a surer trust, than many of them had. But in effect they and we be all one: we have the same faith, that they had in God, and they the same that we have. And St Paul so much extolleth their faith, because we should no less, but rather more, give ourselves wholly unto

Christ, both in profession and living, now when Christ is come, than the old fathers did before his coming. And by all the declaration of St Paul, it is evident that the true, lively, and Christian faith is no dead, vain, or unfruitful thing; but a thing of perfect virtue, of wonderful operation and strength, bringing forth all good motions, and good works.

All holy Scripture agreeably beareth witness, that a true lively faith in Christ, doth bring forth good works: and therefore every man must examine, and try himself diligently, to know whether he have the same true, lively faith in his heart, unfeignedly or not; which he shall know by the fruits thereof. Many that professed the faith of Christ, were in this error, that they thought they knew God, and believed in him, when in their life they declared the contrary. Which error St John in his first Epistle confuting, writeth in this wise: *Hereby we are certified that we know* 1 John 2:3, 4 *God, if we observe his commandments. He that saith he knoweth God, and observeth not his commandments, is a liar, and the truth is not in him.* And again he saith, *Whosoever sinneth doth not see God, nor know him. Let no* 1 John 3:6, 7 *man deceive you, well beloved children.* And moreover he saith, *Hereby we* *Ibid.*:19–22 *know, that we be of the truth, and so we shall persuade our hearts before him. For if our own hearts reprove, God is above our hearts, and knoweth all things. Well beloved, if our hearts reprove not, then have we confidence in God, and shall have of him, whatsoever we ask, because we keep his commandments, and do those things that please him.* And yet further he saith, *Every man* 1 John 5:1, 18 *that believeth that Jesus is Christ, is born of God*: and, *We know that whosoever is born of God, doth not sin; but the generation of God purgeth him, and the devil doth not touch him.* And finally he concludeth, and showing the cause why he wrote this Epistle saith, *For this cause have I thus written* *Ibid.*:13 *unto you, that you may know, that you have everlasting life, which do believe in the Son of God.* And in his third Epistle, he confirmeth the whole matter of faith and works, in few words, saying, *He that doeth well, is of* 3 John:11 *God, and he that doeth evil, knoweth not God.* And as St John saith that the lively knowledge, and faith of God, bringeth forth good works, so saith he likewise of hope and charity, that they cannot stand with evil living. Of hope he writeth thus: *We know that when God shall appear, we shall be* 1 John 3:2, 3 *like unto him, for we shall see him, even as he is. And whosoever hath this hope in him, doth purify himself, like as God is pure.* And of charity he saith these words: *He that doth keep God's word* or commandment, *in him is truly the* 1 John 2:5 *perfect love of God.* And again he saith, *This is the love of God, that we should* 1 John 5:3 *keep his commandments.*

And St John wrote not this as a subtile saying, devised of his own phantasy, but as a most certain and necessary truth, taught unto him by Christ himself, the eternal and infallible Verity; who in many places doth most clearly affirm, that faith, hope, and charity cannot consist (or stand) without good and godly works. Of faith he saith, *He that believeth* John 3:36

in the Son, hath everlasting life; but he that believeth not in the Son, shall not see that life, but the wrath of God remaineth upon him. And the same he confirmeth, with a double oath, saying, *Forsooth and forsooth I say unto you, He that believeth in me, hath everlasting life.* Now forasmuch as *he that believeth in Christ, hath everlasting life*, it must needs consequently follow, that he that hath this faith, must have also good works, and be studious to observe God's commandments obediently. For to them that have evil works, and lead their life in disobedience and transgression (or breaking) of God's commandments, without repentance, pertaineth not everlasting life, but everlasting death, as Christ himself saith: *They that do well, shall go into life eternal, but they that do evil, shall go into the everlasting fire.* And again he saith, *I am the first letter and the last, the beginning and the ending. To him that is athirst, I will give of the well of the water of life freely. He that hath the victory, shall have all things, and I will be his God, and he shall be my Son: but they that be fearful, mistrusting God, and lacking faith, they that be cursed people, and murderers, and fornicators, and sorcerers, and idolaters, and all liars, shall have their portion, in the lake that burneth with fire and brimstone, which is the second death.* And, as Christ undoubtedly affirmeth, that true faith bringeth forth good works, so doth he say likewise of charity: *Whosoever hath my commandments and keepeth them, that is he that loveth me.* And after he saith, *He that loveth me, will keep my word*: and, *He that loveth me not, keepeth not my words.*

And as the love of God is tried by good works, so is the fear of God also; as the Wise Man saith: *The dread of God putteth away sin.* And also he saith, *He that feareth God, will do good works.*

Margin notes:
John 6:47

Matt.25:46

Rev. 21:6–8

Charity bringeth forth good works.
John 14:21, 23, 24

Ecclus. 1:21

Ecclus. 15:1

THE THIRD PART
OF THE SERMON OF FAITH

YOU HAVE HEARD, in the second part of this Sermon, that no man should think that he hath that lively faith, which Scripture commandeth, when he liveth not obediently to God's laws; for all good works spring out of that faith. And also it hath been declared unto you by examples, that faith maketh men stedfast, quiet, and patient in all afflictions. Now as concerning the same matter, you shall hear what followeth.

A man may soon deceive himself, and think in his own phantasy, that he by faith knoweth God, loveth him, feareth him, and belongeth to him, when in very deed, he doeth nothing less. For the trial of all these things, is a very godly and Christian life. He that feeleth his heart act to seek God's honour, and studieth to know the will and commandments of God, and to frame himself thereunto, and leadeth not his life after the desire of his own flesh, to serve the devil by sin, but setteth his mind, to serve God for God's own sake, and for his sake also, to love all his neighbours, whether they be friends or adversaries, doing good to every man, as opportunity serveth, and willingly hurting no man; such a man may well rejoice in God, perceiving by the trade of his life, that he unfeignedly hath the right knowledge of God, a lively faith, a stedfast hope, a true and unfeigned love and fear of God. But he that casteth away the yoke of God's commandments from his neck, and giveth himself to live without true repentance, after his own sensual mind and pleasure, not regarding to know God's word, and much less to live according thereunto; such a man clearly deceiveth himself, and seeth not his own heart, if he thinketh that he either knoweth God, loveth him, feareth him, or trusteth in him.

Some peradventure phantasy in themselves, that they belong to God, although they live in sin; and so they come to the church, and show themselves as God's dear children. But St John saith plainly, *If we say*   1 John 1:6
that we have any company with God, and walk in darkness, we do lie. Other do vainly think, that they know and love God, although they pass not of his commandments. But St John saith clearly, *He that saith, I know God,*   *Ibid.* 2:4
and keepeth not his commandments, he is a liar. Some falsely persuade themselves that they love God, when they hate their neighbours. But St John saith manifestly, *If any man say, I love God, and yet hateth his*   *Ibid.* 4:20;
brother, he is a liar. He that saith that he is in the light, and hateth his brother,   *Ibid.* 2:9–11
he is still in darkness. He that loveth his brother, dwelleth in the light: but he that hateth his brother is in darkness, and walketh in darkness, and knoweth not whither he goeth, for darkness hath blinded his eyes. And moreover he saith, *Hereby we manifestly know the children of God, from the children of the*   *Ibid.* 3:10
devil: he that doeth not righteously, is not the child of God, nor he that hateth his brother.

Deceive not yourselves therefore, thinking that you have faith in God, or that you love God, or do trust in him, or do fear him, when you live in sin; for then your ungodly and sinful life, declareth the contrary, whatsoever ye say or think. It pertaineth to a Christian man, to have this true Christian faith, and to try himself, whether he hath it or no, and to know what belongeth to it, and how it doth work in him. It is not the world that we can trust to: the world, and all that is therein, is but vanity. It is God that must be our defence, and protection against all temptation of wickedness and sin, errors, superstition, idolatry, and all evil. If all the world were on our side, and God against us, what could the world avail us? Therefore let us set our whole faith and trust in God, and neither the world, the devil, nor all the power of them, shall prevail against us.

Let us therefore, good Christian people, try and examine our faith, what it is: let us not flatter ourselves, but look upon our works, and so judge of our faith, what it is. Christ himself speaketh of this matter, and

Matt. 12:33

saith, *The tree is known by the fruit.* Therefore let us do good works, and thereby declare our faith, to be the lively Christian faith. Let us, by such virtues as ought to spring out of faith, show our election to be sure and stable; as St Peter teacheth: *Endeavour yourselves to make your calling and choosing certain, by good works.* And also he saith, *Minister* or declare *in your faith virtue, in virtue knowledge, in knowledge temperance, in temperance patience, again in patience godliness, in godliness brotherly charity, in brotherly charity love.* So shall we show indeed, that we have the very lively Christian faith; and may so both certify our conscience the better, that we be in the right faith, and also by these means, confirm other men. If these fruits do not follow, we do but mock with God, deceive ourselves, and also other men. Well may we bear the name of Christian men, but we do lack the true faith, that doth belong thereunto. For true faith doth ever bring forth good works; as St James saith, *Show me thy faith by thy deeds.* Thy deeds and works must be an open testimonial of thy faith; otherwise thy faith, being without good works, is but the devils' faith, the faith of the wicked, a phantasy of faith, and not a true Christian faith. And like as the devils and evil people, be nothing the better for their counterfeit faith, but it is unto them the more cause of damnation, so they that be christened, and have received knowledge of God, and of Christ's merits, and yet of a set purpose do live idly, without good works, thinking the name of a naked faith, to be either sufficient for them, or else setting their minds upon vain pleasures of this world, do live in sin without repentance, not uttering the fruits, that do belong to such an high profession; upon such presumptuous persons and wilful sinners, must needs remain the great vengeance of God, and eternal punishment in hell, prepared for the devil and wicked livers.

2 Peter 1:10

Ibid.:5–7

James 2:18

Therefore as you profess the name of Christ, good Christian people, let no such phantasy, and imagination of faith, at any time beguile you: but be sure of your faith; try it by your living; look upon the fruit that cometh of it; mark the increase of love and charity by it, toward God and your neighbour; and so shall you perceive it, to be a true lively faith. If you feel and perceive such a faith in you, rejoice in it, and be diligent to maintain it, and keep it still in you: let it be daily increasing, and more and more by well working: and so shall ye be sure, that you shall please God by this faith; and at the length, as other faithful men have done before, so shall you when his will is, come to him, and receive *the end* and final reward *of your faith,* as St Peter nameth it, *the salvation of your souls.* The which God grant us, that hath promised the same unto his faithful. To whom be all honour and glory, world without end. Amen.

1 Peter 1:9

A SERMON
OF GOOD WORKS
ANNEXED UNTO FAITH

IN THE LAST SERMON was declared unto you, what the lively and true faith of a Christian man is, that it causeth not a man to be idle, but to be occupied in bringing forth good works, as occasion serveth. Now by God's grace, shall be declared the second thing, that before was noted of faith, that without it, can no good work be done, acceptable and pleasant unto God. For, *as a branch cannot bear fruit of itself*, saith our Saviour Christ, *except it abide in the vine, so cannot you, except you abide in me. I am the vine, and you be the branches. He that abideth in me, and I in him, he bringeth forth much fruit: for without me, you can do nothing.* And St Paul proveth that Enoch had faith, *because he pleased God: for without faith*, saith he, *it is not possible to please God.* And again to the Romans he saith, *Whatsoever work is done without faith, it is sin.*

> No good work can be done without faith.
>
> John 15:4, 5
>
> Heb. 11:5, 6
>
> Rom. 14:23

Faith giveth life to the soul; and they be as much dead to God that lack faith, as they be to the world, whose bodies lack souls. Without faith, all that is done of us, is but dead before God, although the work seem never so gay and glorious, before man. Even as the picture graven or painted, is but a dead representation of the thing itself, and is without life, or any manner of moving, so be the works of all unfaithful persons, before God. They do appear to be lively works, and indeed they be but dead, not availing to the everlasting life. They be but shadows and shows, of lively and good things, and not good and lively things indeed. For true faith doth give life to the works; and out of such faith come good works, that be very good works indeed; and without it, no work is good before God.

As saith St Augustine: "We must set no good works before faith, nor think that before faith, a man may do any good work. For such works, although they seem unto men, to be praiseworthy, yet indeed they be but vain," and not allowed before God. "They be as the course of a horse, that runneth out of the way, which taketh great labour, but to no

> In Præfat. Psalm 31

35

purpose. Let no man therefore," saith he, "reckon upon his good works, before his faith: where as faith was not, good works were not. The intent," saith he, "maketh the good works; but faith must guide and order the intent of man." And Christ saith, *If thine eye be naught, thy whole body is full of darkness.* "The eye doth signify the intent," saith St Augustine, "wherewith a man doeth a thing." So that he which doeth not his good works with a godly intent, and a true *faith that worketh by love*, the whole body beside (that is to say, all the whole number of his works), is dark, and there is no light in it. For good deeds be not measured by the facts themselves, and so dissevered from vices, but by the ends and intents, for the which they be done. If a heathen man clothe the naked, feed the hungry, and do such other like works; yet, because he doeth them not in faith, for the honour and love of God, they be but dead, vain, and fruitless works to him. Faith is it, that doth commend the work to God: "For," as St Augustine saith, "whether thou wilt or no, that work that cometh not of faith, is naught." Where the faith of Christ is not the foundation, there is no good work, what building soever we make. There is one work, in the which be all good works, that is, *faith which worketh by charity.* If thou have it, thou hast the ground of all good works; for the virtues of strength, wisdom, temperance, and justice be all referred unto this same faith. Without this faith, we have not them, but only the names and shadows of them; as St Augustine saith: "All the life of them that lack the true faith, is sin; and nothing is good without him, that is the Author of goodness: where he is not, there is but feigned virtue, although it be in the best works." And St Augustine, declaring this verse of the Psalm, *The turtle hath found a nest, where she may keep her young birds,* saith that Jews, heretics, and pagans do good works; they clothe the naked, feed the poor, and do other works of mercy; but, because they be not done in the true faith, therefore the birds be lost. But if they remain in faith, then "faith is the nest" and safeguard "of their birds," that is to say, safeguard of their good works, that the reward of them be not utterly lost.

And this matter, which St Augustine at large in many books disputeth, St Ambrose concludeth in a few words saying, "He that by nature would withstand vice, either by natural will or reason, he doth in vain garnish the time of this life, and attaineth not the very true virtues: for without the worshipping of the true God, that which seemeth to be virtue is vice."

And yet most plainly to this purpose, writeth St John Chrysostom in this wise. "You shall find many, which have not the true faith, and be not of the flock of Christ, and yet as it appeareth, they flourish in good works of mercy; you shall find them full of pity, compassion, and given to justice; and yet for all that, they have no fruit of their works, because the chief work lacketh." "For when the Jews asked of Christ, what they

Marginalia:

Matt. 6:23

In Præfat. Psalm 31
Gal. 5:6

Psalm 84:3

de Vocatione Gentium Lib. I, cap. 3

In sermone de fide, lege, et Spiritu Sancto

should do to work good works, he answered, *This is the work of God, to* John 6:29
believe in him whom he sent: so that he called faith, *the work of God*. And as
soon as a man hath faith, anon he shall flourish in good works: for faith
of itself is full of good works, and nothing is good, without faith." And
for a similitude, he saith that "They which glister and shine in good
works, without faith in God, be like dead men, which have goodly and
precious tombs, and yet it availeth them nothing."

Faith may not be naked without good works; for then it is no true
faith: and when it is adjoined to works, yet it is above the works. For
as men that be very men indeed, first have life, and after be nourished;
so must our faith in Christ go before, and after be nourished with
good works. And life may be without nourishment, but nourishment
cannot be without life.

A man must needs be nourished, by good works, but first he must
have faith. He that doeth good deeds, yet without faith, he hath not
life. I can show a man that by faith without works, lived and came to
heaven: but without faith, never man had life. The thief that was
hanged when Christ suffered, did believe only, and the most merciful
God did justify him. And because no man shall say again, that he
lacked time to do good works, for else he would have done them,
truth it is, and I will not contend therein: but this I will surely affirm,
that faith only saved him. If he had lived, and not regarded faith and
the works thereof, he should have lost his salvation again. But this is
the effect that I say, that faith by itself saved him, but works by
themselves never justified any man.

Here ye have heard the mind of St Chrysostom; whereby you may
perceive, that neither faith is without works, having opportunity thereto,
nor works can avail to everlasting life, without faith.

THE SECOND PART
OF THE SERMON OF GOOD WORKS

OF THE THREE THINGS, which were in the former Sermon specially noted
of lively faith, two be declared unto you. The first was, that faith is never
idle, without good works, when occasion serveth; the second, that good
works acceptable to God, cannot be done without faith. Now to go forth What works they are that spring of faith
to the third part, that is, what manner of works they be, which spring out
of true faith, and lead faithful men, unto everlasting life.

This cannot be known so well, as by our Saviour Christ himself, who
was asked of a certain great man the same question. *What works shall I* Matt. 19:16–19
do, said a prince, *to come to everlasting life?* To whom Jesus answered, *If
thou wilt come to the everlasting life, keep the commandments.* But the

prince, not satisfied herewith, asked further, *Which commandments?* The Scribes and Pharisees had made so many of their own laws, and traditions to bring men to heaven, beside God's commandments, that this man was in doubt, whether he should come to heaven by those laws and traditions, or by the laws of God; and therefore he asked Christ, which commandments he meant. Whereunto Christ made him a plain answer, rehearsing the commandments of God, saying, *Thou shalt not kill, Thou shalt not commit adultery, Thou shalt not steal, Thou shalt not bear false witness, Honour thy father and mother,* and *Love thy neighbour as thyself.* By which words Christ declared, that the laws of God be the very way, that doth lead to everlasting life, and not the traditions and laws of men. So that this is to be taken for a most true lesson, taught by Christ's own mouth, that the works of the moral commandments of God, be the very true works of faith, which lead to the blessed life to come.

> The works that lead to heaven be the works of God's commandments.

> Man, from his first falling from God's commandments, hath ever been ready to do the like, and to devise works of his own phantasy to please God withal.

But the blindness and malice of man, even from the beginning, hath ever been ready to fall, from God's commandments. As Adam the first man, having but one commandment, that he should not eat of the fruit forbidden, notwithstanding God's commandment, he gave credit unto the woman seduced by the subtle persuasion of the serpent, and so followed his own will, and left God's commandment. And ever since that time, all that came of him hath been so blinded, through original sin, that they have been ever ready, to fall from God and his law, and to invent a new way unto salvation, by works of their own device; so much that almost all the world, forsaking the true honour of the only eternal living God, wandered about in their own phantasies, worshipping some the sun, the moon, the stars, some Jupiter, Juno, Diana, Saturnus, Apollo, Neptunus, Ceres, Bacchus, and other dead men and women. Some, therewith not satisfied, worshipped divers kinds of beasts, birds, fish, fowl, and serpents; every country, town, and house in a manner being divided, and setting up images, of such things as they liked, and worshipping the same. Such was the rudeness of the people, after they fell to their own phantasies, and left the eternal living God and his commandments, that they devised innumerable images and gods. In which error and blindness they did remain, until such time as Almighty God, pitying the blindness of man, sent his true Prophet Moses into the world, to reprove and rebuke this extreme madness, and to teach the people to know the only living God, and his true honour and worship.

> The devices and idolatry of the Gentiles

But the corrupt inclination of man, was so much given to follow his own phantasies, and (as you would say), to favour his own bird that he brought up himself, that all the admonitions, exhortations, benefits, and threatenings of God, could not keep him, from such his inventions. For, notwithstanding all the benefits of God, showed unto the people of Israel, yet when Moses went up into the mountain, to speak with

Almighty God, he had tarried there but a few days, when the people began to invent new gods; and as it came into their heads, they made a calf of gold, and kneeled down and worshipped it. And after that they followed the Moabites, and worshipped Beelphegor, the Moabites' god. Read the book of Judges, the books of the Kings, and the Prophets; and there you shall find, how unstedfast the people were, how full of inventions, and more ready to run after their own phantasies, than God's most holy commandments. There shall you read of Baal, Moloch, Chamos, Melchom, Baalpeor, Astaroth, Bel, the Dragon, Priapus, the Brazen Serpent, the Twelve Signs, and many other; unto whose images the people with great devotion, invented pilgrimages, preciously decking and censing them, kneeling down and offering to them, thinking that an high merit before God, and to be esteemed, above the precepts and commandments of God. And where at that time, God commanded no sacrifice to be made but in Jerusalem only, they did clean contrary; making altars and sacrifices everywhere, in hills, in woods, and in houses; not regarding God's commandments, but esteeming their own phantasies and devotion, to be better than them. And the error hereof was so spread abroad, that not only the unlearned people, but also the priests and teachers of the people, partly by glory and covetousness were corrupted, and partly by ignorance blindly deceived, with the same abominations; so much that, King Achab having but only Helias, a true teacher and minister of God, there were eight hundred and fifty priests, that persuaded him to honour Baal, and to do sacrifice in the woods or groves. And so continued that horrible error, until the three noble kings, as Josaphat, Ezechias, and Josias, God's chosen ministers, destroyed the same clearly, and brought again the people from such their feigned inventions, unto the very commandments of God: for the which thing, their immortal reward and glory doth and shall remain with God for ever.

And beside the foresaid inventions, the inclination of man to have his own holy devotions, devised new sects and religions, called Pharisees, Sadducees, and Scribes; with many holy and godly traditions and ordinances, as it seemed by the outward appearance, and goodly glistering of the works, but in very deed, all tending to idolatry, superstition, and hypocrisy; their hearts within being full of malice, pride, covetousness, and all wickedness. Against which sects, and their pretended holiness, Christ cried out, more vehemently than he did against any other persons, saying and often rehearsing these words: *Woe be to you, Scribes and Pharisees, ye hypocrites! for you make clean the vessel without, but within you be full of ravine and filthiness. Thou blind Pharisee and hypocrite, first make the inward part clean.* For, notwithstanding all the goodly traditions, and outward show of good works, devised of their own

The devices and idolatry of the Israelites
Exod. 32:1–6

1 Kings 18:19, 22

Religions and sects among the Jews

Matt. 23:25, 26

imagination, whereby they appeared to the world, most religious and holy of all men, yet Christ, who saw their hearts, knew that they were inwardly in the sight of God, most unholy, most abominable, and furthest from God of all men. Therefore said he unto them, *Hypocrites, the Prophet Esay spake full truly of you, when he said, This people honour me with their lips, but their heart is far from me: they worship me in vain, that teach doctrines and commandments of men. For you leave the commandments of God, to keep your own traditions.*

And though Christ said *they worship God in vain, that teach doctrines and commandments of men,* yet he meant not thereby, to overthrow all men's commandments; for he himself was ever obedient to the princes and their laws, made for good order, and governance of the people: but he reproved the laws and traditions, made by the Scribes and Pharisees, which were not made only for good order of the people (as the civil laws were), but they were set up so high, that they were made to be a right and pure worshipping of God, as they had been equal with God's laws, or above them; for many of God's laws could not be kept, but were fain to give place unto them. This arrogancy God detested, that man should so advance his laws, to make them equal with God's laws, wherein the true honouring and right worshipping of God standeth, and to make his laws for them to be left off. God hath appointed his laws, whereby his pleasure is to be honoured. His pleasure is also that all man's laws, being not contrary to his laws, shall be obeyed and kept, as good and necessary for every commonweal, but not as things wherein principally his honour resteth. And all civil and man's laws either be, or should be made, to bring in men the better to keep God's laws; that consequently, God should be the better honoured by them. Howbeit, the Scribes and Pharisees were not content, that their laws should be no higher esteemed than other positive and civil laws, nor would not have them called by the name of other temporal laws; but called them, holy and godly traditions, and would have them esteemed, not only for a right and true worshipping of God (as God's laws be indeed), but also to be the most high honouring of God, to the which the commandments of God, should give place. And for this cause, did Christ so vehemently speak against them, saying, *Your traditions, which men esteem so high, be abomination before God.*

For commonly, of such traditions followeth the transgression of God's commandments, and a more devotion in the keeping of such things, and a greater conscience in breaking of them, than of the commandments of God. As the Scribes and Pharisees so superstitiously and scrupulously kept the Sabbath, that they were offended with Christ, because he healed sick men, and with his Apostles, because they being sore hungry, gathered the ears of corn to eat, upon that day. And

Matt. 15:7–9

Isai. 29:13, 14

Man's laws must be observed and kept, but not as God's laws.

Holy traditions were esteemed as God's laws.

Luke 16:15

Holiness of man's device is commonly occasion that God is offended.

Matt. 12:1–14

because his disciples washed not their hands, so often as the traditions required, the Scribes and Pharisees quarrelled with Christ, saying *Why do thy disciples break the traditions of the seniors?* But Christ laid to their charge, that they, for to keep their own traditions, did teach men to break the very commandments of God. For they taught the people such a devotion, that they offered their goods, into the treasure house of the Temple, under the pretence of God's honour, leaving their fathers and mothers (to whom they were chiefly bound) unholpen; and so *they brake the commandments of God, to keep their own traditions.* They esteemed more an oath made by the gold or oblation in the Temple, than an oath made in the name of God himself or of the Temple. They were more studious, to pay their tithes of small things, than to do the greater things commanded of God, as works of mercy, or to do justice, or to deal sincerely, uprightly, and faithfully, with God and man. *These,* saith Christ, *ought to be done, and the other not left undone.* And, to be short, they were of so blind judgement, that they stumbled at a straw, and leaped over a block: they would, as it were nicely, take a fly out of their cup, and drink down a whole camel. And therefore Christ called them *blind guides,* warning his disciples from time to time, to eschew their doctrine. For although they seemed to the world, to be most perfect men, both in living and teaching, yet was their life but hypocrisy, and their doctrine but sour leaven, mingled with superstition, idolatry, and overthwart judgement, setting up the traditions and ordinances of man, in the stead of God's commandments.

Matt. 15:1–6

Mark 7:9

Matt. 23:16–22

Ibid.:23

Ibid.

THE THIRD PART OF
THE SERMON OF GOOD WORKS

THAT ALL MEN might rightly judge of good works, it hath been declared in the second part of this Sermon, what kind of good works they be, that God would have his people to walk in, namely, such as he hath commended in his holy Scripture, and not such works, as men have studied out of their own brain, of a blind zeal and devotion, without the word of God. And by mistaking the nature of good works, man hath most highly displeased God, and hath gone from his will and commandment. So that thus you have heard how much the world, from the beginning until Christ's time, was ever ready to fall from the commandments of God, and to seek other means to honour and serve him, after a devotion found out of their own heads, and how they did set up their own traditions, as high or above God's commandments. Which hath happened also in our times (the more it is to be lamented), no less than it did among the Jews; and that by the corruption, or at the least by the negligence, of them that chiefly, ought to have preferred God's commandments, and to have preserved the pure and heavenly doctrine, left by Christ.

What man having any judgement or learning, joined with a true zeal unto God, doth not see and lament to have entered into Christ's religion, such false doctrine, superstition, idolatry, hypocrisy, and other enormities and abuses; so as by little and little, through the sour leaven thereof, the sweet bread of God's holy word, hath been much hindered and laid apart? Never had the Jews in their most blindness, so many pilgrimages unto images, nor used so much kneeling, kissing, and censing of them, as hath been used in our time. Sects and feigned religions, were neither the forty part so many, among the Jews, nor more superstitiously and ungodly abused, than of the late days they have been among us. Which sects and religions, had so many hypocritical and feigned works in their state of religion (as they arrogantly named it), that their lamps, as they said, ran always over, able to satisfy, not only for their own sins, but also for all other their benefactors, brothers and sisters of their religion, as most ungodly and craftily, they had persuaded the multitude of ignorant people; keeping in divers places, as it were marts or markets of merits, being full of their holy reliques, images, shrines, and works of over-flowing abundance, ready to be sold. And all things which they had were called holy, holy cowls, holy girdles, holy pardoned beads, holy shoes, holy rules, and all full of holiness. And what thing can be more foolish, more superstitious, or ungodly, than that men, women, and children should wear a friar's coat to deliver them from agues or pestilence, or when they die, or when they be buried, cause it to be cast upon them, in hope thereby to be saved? Which superstition, although thanks be to God, it hath been little used in this realm, yet in divers other realms it hath been, and yet is used among many, both learned and unlearned.

But to pass over the innumerable superstitiousness, that hath been in strange apparel, in silence, in dormitory, in cloister, in chapter, in choice of meats and drinks, and in suchlike things, let us consider what enormities and abuses have been, in the three chief principal points, which they called the three essentials of religion, that is to say, obedience, chastity, and wilful poverty. First, under pretence of obedience to their father in religion (which obedience they made themselves), they were made free by their rules and canons, from the obedience of their natural father and mother, and from the obedience of emperor and king, and all temporal power, whom of very duty, by God's laws, they were bound to obey. And so the profession of their obedience not due, was a forsaking of their due obedience. And how their profession of chastity was kept, it is more honesty to pass over in silence, and let the world judge of that which is well known, than with unchaste words, by expressing of their

Sects and religions amongst Christian men

The three chief vows of religion

unchaste life, to offend chaste and godly ears. And as for their wilful poverty, it was such that, when in possessions, jewels, plate, and riches they were equal or above merchants, gentlemen, barons, earls, and dukes, yet by this subtile sophistical term, Proprium in communi, that is to say, Proper in common, they mocked the world, persuading that notwithstanding all their possessions and riches, yet they kept their vow and were in wilful poverty. But for all their riches, they might neither help father nor mother, nor other that were indeed very needy and poor, without the licence of their father abbot, prior, or warden. And yet they might take of every man, but they might not give aught to any man, no, not to them, whom the laws of God bound them to help. And so through their traditions and rules, the laws of God could bear no rule with them; and therefore of them might be most truly said, that which Christ spake unto the Pharisees: *You break the commandments of God, by your traditions. You honour God with your lips, but your hearts be far from him.* And the longer prayers they used, by day and by night, under pretence of such holiness, to get the favour of widows, and other simple folks, that they might sing trentals and service, for their husbands and friends, and admit them into their prayers, the more truly is verified of them, in the saying of Christ: *Woe be to you, Scribes and Pharisees, hypocrites! for you devour widows' houses, under colour of long prayers: therefore your damnation shall be the greater. Woe be to you, Scribes and Pharisees, hypocrites! for you go about by sea and by land, to make mo novices and new brethren, and when they be let in, or received of your sect, you make them the children of hell, worse than yourselves be.*

Matt. 15:3, 8

Matt. 23:14, 15

Honour be to God, who did put light in the heart of his faithful and true minister, of most famous memory, King Henry the Eighth, and gave him the knowledge of his word, and an earnest affection to seek his glory, and to put away all such superstitious and pharisaical sects, by Antichrist invented, and set up against the true word of God and glory of his most blessed Name; as he gave the like spirit, unto the most noble and famous princes Josaphat, Josias, and Ezechias. God grant all us, the Queen's Highness' faithful and true subjects, to feed of the sweet and savoury bread, of God's own word, and as Christ commanded, to eschew all our pharisaical and papistical leaven, of man's feigned religion. Which although it were before God, most abominable, and contrary to God's commandments, and Christ's pure religion, yet it was praised to be a most godly life, and highest state of perfection; as though a man might be more godly and more perfect, by keeping the rules, traditions, and professions of men, than by keeping the holy commandments of God.

And, briefly to pass over the ungodly and counterfeit religions, let us rehearse some other kinds of papistical superstitions and abuses, as of Beads, of Lady Psalters and Rosaries, of Fifteen Os, of St Bernard's

Other devices and superstitions

Verses, of St Agathe's Letters, of Purgatory, of Masses Satisfactory, of Stations and Jubilees, of feigned Reliques, of hallowed Beads, Bells, Bread, Water, Palms, Candles, Fire, and such other, of superstitious Fastings, of Fraternities, of Pardons, with suchlike merchandise; which were so esteemed and abused, to the great prejudice of God's glory and commandments, that they were made most high and most holy things, whereby to attain to the everlasting life, or remission of sin. Yea also vain inventions, unfruitful ceremonies, and ungodly laws, decrees, and Councils of Rome, were in such wise advanced, that nothing was thought comparable in authority, wisdom, learning, and godliness unto them: so that the laws of Rome, as they said, were to be received of all men as the four Evangelists; to the which all laws of princes, must give place; and the laws of God also partly were left off, and less esteemed, that the said laws, decrees, and Councils, with their traditions and ceremonies, might be more duly kept, and had in greater reverence. Thus was the people through ignorance, so blinded with the goodly show, and appearance of those things, that they thought the keeping of them to be a more holiness, a more perfect service and honouring of God, and more pleasing to God, than the keeping of God's commandments. Such hath been the corrupt inclination of man, ever superstitiously given to make new honouring of God, of his own head, and then to have more affection and devotion, to keep that, than to search out God's holy commandments, and to keep them; and furthermore, to take God's commandments for men's commandments, and men's commandments for God's commandments, yea, and for the highest and most perfect and holy, of all God's commandments. And so was all confused, that scant well learned men, and but a small number of them, knew (or at the least would know), and durst affirm the truth, to separate God's command-ments, from the commandments of men: whereupon did grow much error, superstition, idolatry, vain religion, overthwart judgement, great contention, with all ungodly living.

Wherefore, as you have any zeal, to the right and pure honouring of God, as you have any regard to your own souls, and to the life that is to come, which is both without pain and without end, apply yourselves chiefly above all things, to read and to hear God's word: mark diligently therein what his will is you shall do, and with all your endeavour apply yourselves to follow the same. First you must have an assured faith in God, and give yourselves wholly unto him, love him in prosperity and adversity, and dread to offend him evermore. Then, for his sake, love all men, friends and foes; because they be his creation and image, and redeemed by Christ, as ye are. Cast in your minds how you may do good unto all men, unto your powers, and hurt no man. Obey all your superiors and governors, serve your masters faithfully and diligently, as

Marginal notes:

Decrees and decretals

An exhortation to the keeping of God's command-ments

A brief rehearsal of God's commandments

well in their absence as in their presence, not for dread of punishment only, but for conscience sake, knowing that you are bound so to do, by God's commandments. Disobey not your fathers and mothers, but honour them, help them, and please them to your power. Oppress not, kill not, beat not, neither slander nor hate any man; but love all men, speak well of all men, help and succour every man as you may, yea, even your enemies that hate you, that speak evil of you, and that do hurt you. Take no man's goods, nor covet your neighbour's goods wrongfully, but content yourselves, with that which ye get truly, and also bestow your own goods charitably, as need and case requireth. Flee all idolatry, witchcraft, and perjury. Commit no manner of adultery, fornication, nor other unchasteness, in will nor in deed, with any other man's wife, widow, maid, or otherwise. And travailing continually during your life, thus in keeping the commandments of God, wherein standeth the pure, principal, and right honour of God, and which wrought in faith, God hath ordained to be the right trade, and pathway unto heaven, you shall not fail, as Christ hath promised, to come to that blessed and everlasting life, where you shall live in glory and joy, with God for ever. To whom be praise, honour, and empery, *authority* for ever and ever. Amen.

A SERMON
OF CHRISTIAN LOVE AND CHARITY

OF ALL THINGS THAT BE GOOD to be taught unto Christian people, there is nothing more necessary to be spoken of, and daily called upon, than charity; as well for that all manner of works of righteousness, be contained in it, as also that the decay thereof, is the ruin of the world, the banishment of virtue, and the cause of all vice. And forsomuch as almost every man maketh, and frameth to himself charity, after his own appetite, and how detestable soever his life be, both unto God and man, yet he persuadeth himself still, that he hath charity; therefore you shall hear now, a true and plain description of charity, not of men's imagination, but of the very words and example, of our Saviour Jesus Christ. In which description every man, as it were in a glass, may consider himself, and see plainly without error, whether he be in the true charity, or not.

What charity is
The love of God

Charity is to love God, with all our heart, all our life, and all our powers and strength. With all our heart: that is to say, that our heart, mind and study be set, to believe his word, to trust in him, and to love him, above all other things that we love best, in heaven or in earth. With all our life: that is to say, that our chief joy and delight be set, upon him and his honour, and our whole life given, unto the service of him, above all things, with him to live and die, and to forsake all other things, rather

Matt. 10:37

than him; for, *he that loveth his father or mother, son or daughter*, house or land, *more than me*, saith Christ, *is not worthy to have me*. With all our powers: that is to say, that with our hands and feet, with our eyes and ears, our mouths and tongues, and with all other parts and powers, both of body and soul, we should be given, to the keeping and fulfilling of his commandments. This is the first and principal part of charity, but it is

The love of thy
neighbour

not the whole: for charity is also, to love every man, good and evil, friend and foe; and whatsoever cause be given to the contrary, yet nevertheless to bear good will and heart, unto every man, to use ourselves well unto them, as well in words and countenance, as in all our outward acts and deeds. For so Christ himself taught, and so also he performed in deed.

46

Of the love of God he taught in this wise, unto a doctor of the law, that asked him, which was the great and chief commandment in the law. *Love thy Lord God*, said Christ, *with all thy heart, with all thy life, and with all thy mind.* And of the love that we ought to have, among ourselves each to the other, he teacheth us thus: *You have heard it taught in times past, Thou shalt love thy friend, and hate thy foe: but I tell you, Love your enemies, speak well of them that defame you, and speak evil of you, do well to them that hate you, pray for them that vex and persecute you; that you may be the children of your Father, that is in heaven; for he maketh his sun to rise, both upon the evil and good, and sendeth rain, to just and unjust. For if you love them that love you, what reward shall you have? do not the publicans likewise? And if you speak well only, of them that be your brethren and dear beloved friends, what great matter is that? do not the heathen the same also?* These be the very words of our Saviour, Christ himself, touching the love of our neighbour. And forasmuch as the Pharisees, with their most pestilent traditions, false interpretations and gloses, had corrupted, and almost clearly stopped up, this pure well of God's lively word, teaching that this love and charity, pertained only to a man's friends, and that it was sufficient for a man, to love them which do love him, and to hate his foes; therefore Christ opened this well again, purged it, and scoured it, by giving unto his godly law of charity, a true and clear interpretation, which is this, that we ought to love every man, both friend and foe; adding thereto, what commodity we shall have thereby, and what incommodity by doing the contrary. What thing can we wish so good for us, as the eternal heavenly Father, to reckon and take us for his children? And this shall we be sure of, saith Christ, if we love every man, without exception. And if we do otherwise, saith he, we be no better than the Pharisees, publicans, and heathen, and shall have our reward with them, that is, to be shut out, from the number of God's chosen children, and from his everlasting inheritance in heaven.

Thus of true charity Christ taught, that every man is bound to love God, above all things, and to love every man, friend and foe. And thus likewise he did use himself, exhorting his adversaries, rebuking the faults of his adversaries, and when he could not amend them, yet he prayed for them. First he loved God his Father, above all things, so much, that he sought not his own glory and will, but the glory and will of his Father. *I seek not*, said he, *mine own will, but the will of him that sent me.* Nor he refused not to die, to satisfy his Father's will, saying, *If it may be, let this cup of death, go from me; if not, thy will be done, and not mine.* He loved also not only his friends, but also his enemies; which in their hearts, bare exceeding great hatred against him, and in their tongues, spake all evil of him, and in their acts and deeds, pursued him with all their might and power, even unto death. Yet all this notwithstanding, he

Matt. 22:37

Matt. 5:43–7

John 5:30

Matt. 26:39, 42

withdrew not his favour from them; but still loved them, preached unto them, of love rebuked their false doctrine, their wicked living, and did good unto them, patiently taking, whatsoever they spake or did against him. When they gave him evil words, he gave none evil again; when they did strike him, he did not smite again; and when he suffered death, he did not slay them, nor threaten them, but prayed for them, and did put all things to his Father's will. And as a sheep that is led unto the shambles, to be slain, and as a lamb that is shorn of his fleece, make no noise nor resistance, even so went he unto his death, without any repugnance, or opening of his mouth to say any evil.

Isai. 53:7
Acts 8:32

Thus have I set forth unto you, what charity is, as well by the doctrine, as by the example, of Christ himself. Whereby also every man may, without error, know himself, what state and condition he standeth in, whether he be in charity, and so the child of the Father in heaven, or not. For although almost every man, persuadeth himself to be in charity, yet let him examine none other man, but his own heart, his life and conversation, and he shall not be deceived, but truly discern and judge, whether he be in perfect charity or not. For he that followeth not his own appetite and will, but giveth himself earnestly to God, to do all his will and commandments, he may be sure, that he loveth God, above all things: and else, surely he loveth him not, whatsoever he pretend. As Christ said, *If ye love me, keep my commandments*. For, *He that knoweth my commandments, and keepeth them, he it is*, saith Christ, *that loveth me*. And again he saith, *He that loveth me, will keep my word; and my Father will love him, and we will both come to him, and dwell with him*. And, *He that loveth me not, will not keep my words*. And likewise he that beareth good heart and mind, and useth well his tongue and deeds, unto every man, friend and foe, he may know thereby, that he hath charity. And then he is sure also, that Almighty God taketh him, for his dear beloved son; as St John saith, *Hereby manifestly are known the children of God, from the children of the devil: for whosoever doth not love his brother, belongeth not unto God.*

John 14: 15, 21, 23, 24

1 John 3:10

THE SECOND PART OF
THE SERMON OF CHARITY

YOU HAVE HEARD a plain and a fruitful setting forth of charity, and how profitable and necessary a thing charity is; how charity stretcheth itself, both to God and man, friend and foe, and that, by the doctrine and example of Christ; and also who may certify himself, whether he be in perfect charity or not. Now as concerning the same matter it followeth.

The perverse nature of man, corrupt with sin, and destitute of God's word and grace, thinketh it against all reason, that a man should love his enemy, and hath many persuasions, which bring him to the contrary. Against all which reasons, we ought as well to set the teaching as the living, of our Saviour Christ, who loving us, when we were his enemies, doth teach us to love our enemies. He did patiently, take for us many reproaches, suffered beating and most cruel death. Therefore we be no members of him, if we will not follow him. *Christ*, saith St Peter, *suffered for us, leaving an example, that we should follow him*. Furthermore we must consider, that to love our friends, is no more but that which thieves, adulterers, homicides, and all wicked persons do; insomuch that Jews, Turks, infidels, and all brute beasts, do love them that be their friends, of whom they have their living, or any other benefits: but to love enemies is the proper condition only, of them that be the children of God, the disciples and followers of Christ. Notwithstanding, man's froward and corrupt nature, weigheth over deeply many times, the offence and displeasure done unto him by enemies, and thinketh it a burden intolerable, to be bound to love them that hate him. But the burden should be easy enough, if on the other side, every man would consider, what displeasure he hath done to his enemy again, and what pleasure he hath received of his enemy. And if we find no equal recompence, neither in receiving pleasures of our enemy, nor in requiting displeasures unto him again, then let us ponder the displeasures, which we have done against Almighty God, how often and how grievously, we have offended him; whereof if we will have of God forgiveness, there is none other remedy, but to forgive the offences done unto us, which be very small, in comparison of our offences done against God. And, if we consider, that he which hath offended us, deserveth not to be forgiven of us, let us consider again, that we much less deserve, to be forgiven of God. And although our enemy deserve not, to be forgiven for his own sake, yet we ought to forgive him, for God's love; considering how great and many benefits, we have received of him, without our deserts, and that Christ hath deserved of us, that for his sake, we should forgive them their trespasses, committed against us.

But here may rise a necessary question, to be dissolved. If charity require to think, speak, and do well unto every man, both good and evil, how can magistrates execute justice upon malefactors, with charity? How can they cast evil men in prison, take away their goods, and sometime their lives, according to laws, if charity will not suffer them so to do?

Hereunto is a plain and a brief answer: that plagues and punishments be not evil of themselves, if they be well taken of the harmless; and to an evil man, they are both good and necessary, and may be executed according to charity, and with charity should be executed.

Margin notes:

Against carnal men, that will not forgive their enemies

1 Pet. 2:21

A question

An answer

Charity hath two
offices.

For declaration whereof you shall understand, that charity hath two offices, the one contrary to the other, and yet both necessary to be used, upon men of contrary sort and disposition. The one office of charity, is to cherish good and harmless men; not to oppress them with false accusations, but to encourage them with rewards, to do well and to continue in well doing, defending them with the sword, from their adversaries. And the office of bishops and pastors, is to praise good men for well doing, that they may continue therein, and to rebuke and correct, by the word of God, the offences and crimes of all evil-disposed persons. The other office of charity, is to rebuke, correct, and punish vice, without regard of persons; and this is to be used against them only, that be evil men and malefactors. And that it is as well the office of charity, to rebuke, punish, and correct them that be evil, as it is to cherish, and reward, them that be good and harmless, St Paul declareth

Rom. 13:1–4

(writing to the Romans), saying that *the high powers are ordained of God*, not to be dreadful to them that do well, but unto malefactors, to draw

1 Tim. 5:20

the sword, *to take vengeance of him that committeth the sin*. And St Paul biddeth Timothy, stoutly and earnestly to rebuke sin, by the word of God. So that both offices, should be diligently executed, to fight against the kingdom of the devil, the preacher with the word, and the governor with the sword: else they love neither God, nor them whom they govern, if for lack of correction, they wilfully suffer God to be offended, and them whom they govern, to perish. For, as every loving father correcteth his natural son, when he doeth amiss, or else he loveth him not, so all governors of realms, countries, towns, and houses, should lovingly correct them which be offenders, under their governance, and cherish them which live innocently, if they have any respect, either unto God and their office, or love unto them of whom they have governance. And such rebukes, and punishments of them that offend, must be done in due time, lest by delay, the offenders fall headlong, into all manner of mischief, and not only be evil themselves, but also do hurt unto many men, drawing other by their evil example, to sin and outrage after them: as one thief may both rob many men, and also make many thieves; and one seditious person may allure many, and annoy a whole town or country. And such evil persons, that be so great offenders of God and the commonweal, charity requireth to be cut off, from the body of the commonweal, lest they corrupt other good and honest persons; like as a good surgeon cutteth away, a rotten and festered member, for love he hath to the whole body, lest it infect other members adjoining to it.

Thus it is declared unto you, what true charity or Christian love is, so plainly, that no man need to be deceived. Which love whosoever keepeth, not only toward God, whom he is bound to love above all things, but also toward his neighbour, as well friend as foe, it shall surely keep him from all offence of God, and just offence of man. Therefore bear well away, this one short lesson, that by true Christian charity, God ought to be loved, above all things, and all men ought to be loved, good and evil, friend and foe; and to all such we ought, as we may, to do good; those that be good, of love to encourage and cherish, because they be good; and those that be evil, of love to procure and seek their correction, and due punishment, that they may thereby, either be brought to goodness, or at the least, that God and the commonwealth, may be the less hurt and offended. And if we thus direct our life, by Christian love and charity, then Christ doth promise and assure us, that he loveth us, that we be the children of our heavenly Father, reconciled to his favour, very members of Christ, and that after this short time, of this present and mortal life, we shall have with him, everlasting life, in his everlasting kingdom of heaven. Therefore to him, with the Father, and the Holy Ghost, be all honour and glory, now and ever. Amen.

AGAINST SWEARING AND PERJURY

ALMIGHTY GOD, to the intent his most holy Name should be had in honour, and evermore be magnified of the people, commandeth that no man should take his Name vainly in his mouth, threatening punishment unto him that unreverently abuseth it, by swearing, forswearing, and blasphemy. To the intent therefore that this commandment may be the better known and kept, it shall be declared unto you, both how it is lawful, for Christian people to swear, and also what peril and danger it is, vainly to swear or to be forsworn.

How and in what causes it is lawful to swear

First, when judges require oaths of the people, for declaration (or opening) of the truth, or for execution of justice, this manner of swearing is lawful. Also, when men make faithful promises, with calling to witness of the Name of God, to keep covenants, honest promises, statutes, laws, and good customs; as Christian princes do, in their conclusions of peace, for conservation of commonwealths; and private persons promise their fidelity, in matrimony, or one to another in honest and true friendship; and all men, when they do swear to keep common laws, or local statutes and good customs, for due order to be had, and continued among men; when subjects do swear, to be true and faithful, to their king and sovereign lord, and when judges, magistrates, and officers swear, truly to execute their offices; and when a man would affirm the truth, to the setting forth of God's glory, for the salvation of the people, in open preaching of the Gospel, or in giving of good counsel privately, for their souls' health: all these manner of swearings, for causes necessary and honest, be lawful. But when men do swear of custom, in reasoning, buying and selling, or other daily communication, as many be common and great swearers, such kind of swearing, is ungodly, unlawful, and forbidden by the commandment of God: for such swearing is nothing else, but taking of God's holy Name in vain.

And here is to be noted, that lawful swearing is not forbidden, but commanded, of Almighty God. For we have examples of Christ, and godly men in holy Scripture, that did swear themselves, and required oaths of other likewise. And God's commandment is, *Thou shalt dread thy Lord God, and shalt swear by his Name.* And Almighty

Deut. 6:13

52

God by his Prophet David saith, *All men shall be praised that swear by him.*

Psalm 63:11

Thus did our Saviour Christ swear, divers times, saying, *Verily, Verily.* And St Paul sweareth thus, *I call God to witness.* And Abraham waxing old, required an oath of his servant, that he should procure a wife for his son Isaac, which should come of his own kinred: and the servant did swear, that he would perform his master's will. Abraham also, being required, did swear, unto Abimelech the King of Geraris, that he should not hurt him, nor his posterity: and so likewise did Abimelech swear, unto Abraham. And David did swear, to be and continue a faithful friend to Jonathas: and Jonathas did swear, to become a faithful friend unto David.

John 3:3, 5, 11

2 Cor. 1:23

Gen. 24:1–9

Gen. 21:22–31

1 Sam. 18:3;
20:12–17, 42

Also God once commanded, that if a thing were laid to pledge to any man, or left with him to keep, if the same thing were stolen or lost, that the keeper thereof should be sworn, before judges, that he did not convey it away, nor used any deceit, in causing the same to be conveyed away, by his consent or knowledge. And St Paul saith, that in all matters of controversy, between two persons, where as one saith yea, and other nay, so as no due proof can be had of the truth, the end of every such controversy, must be an oath, ministered by a judge.

Exod. 22:10, 11

Heb. 6:16

And moreover God, by the Prophet Jeremy saith, *Thou shalt swear, The Lord liveth, in truth, in judgement, in righteousness.* So that whosoever sweareth, when he is required of a judge, let him be sure in his conscience, that his oath have these three conditions, and he shall never need to be afraid of perjury. First, he that sweareth must swear *truly*; that is, he must, setting apart all favour, and affection to the parties, have the truth only before his eyes, and for love thereof, say and speak, that which he knoweth to be truth, and no further. The second is, he that taketh an oath, must do it *with judgement*; not rashly and unadvisedly, but soberly, considering what an oath is. The third is, he that sweareth, must swear *in righteousness*; that is, for the very zeal and love, which he beareth to the defence of innocency, to the maintenance of the truth, and to the righteousness of the matter or cause, all profit, disprofit, all love and favour unto the person, for friendship or kinred, laid apart. Thus an oath, if it have with it these three conditions, is a part of God's glory, which we are bound by his commandment, to give unto him: for he willeth that we shall swear, only by his Name. Not that he hath pleasure in our oaths: but like as he commanded the Jews, to offer sacrifices unto him, not for any delight that he had in them, but to keep the Jews from committing of idolatry, so he commanding us to swear, by his holy Name, doth not teach us that he delighteth in swearing, but he thereby forbiddeth all men to give his glory, to any creature, in heaven, earth, or water.

Jer. 4:2

What conditions
an oath ought to
have
The first

The second

The third

Why we be
willed in
Scripture to
swear by the
name of God

Isai. 42:8,
Psalm 150:6

Hitherto you see that oaths lawful, are commanded of God, used of Patriarchs and Prophets, of Christ himself, and of his Apostle Paul.

Therefore Christian people must think lawful oaths, both godly and necessary. For by lawful promises and covenants, confirmed by oaths, princes and their countries are confirmed, in common tranquillity and peace. By holy promises, with calling the Name of God to witness, we be made lively members of Christ, when we profess his religion, receiving the Sacrament of Baptism. By like holy promise, the sacrament of matrimony knitteth man and wife, in perpetual love, that they desire not to be separated, for any displeasure or adversity, that shall after happen. By lawful oaths which kings, princes, judges, and magistrates do swear, common laws are kept inviolate, justice is indifferently ministered, harmless persons, fatherless children, widows, and poor men are defended, from murderers, oppressors, and thieves, that they suffer no wrong, nor take any harm. By lawful oaths, mutual society, amity, and good order is kept continually, in all commonalities, as boroughs, cities, towns, and villages. And by lawful oaths, malefactors are searched out, wrong doers are punished, and they which sustain wrong, are restored to their right. Therefore lawful swearing cannot be evil, which bringeth unto us so many godly, good, and necessary commodities.

Wherefore, when Christ so earnestly forbade swearing, it may not be so understood, as though he did forbid all manner of oaths: but he forbiddeth all vain swearing, and forswearing, both by God, and by his creatures, as the common use of swearing, in buying, selling, and in our daily communication; to the intent, every Christian man's word should be as well regarded in such matters, as if he should confirm his communication with an oath. For "every Christian man's word," saith St Jerome, "should be so true, that it should be regarded as an oath." And Chrysostom witnessing the same, saith, "It is not convenient to swear: for what needeth us to swear, when it is not lawful, for one of us to make a lie unto another?"

Peradventure some will say, I am compelled to swear, for else men that do commune with me, or do buy and sell with me, will not believe me. To this answereth St Chrysostom, that he that thus saith, showeth himself to be an unjust, and a deceitful person: for if he were a trusty man, and his deeds taken to agree with his words, he should not need to swear at all. For he that useth truth and plainness, in his bargaining and communication, he shall have no need, by such vain swearing, to bring himself in credence with his neighbours, nor his neighbours will not mistrust his sayings. And if his credence be so much lost indeed, that he thinketh no man will believe him, without he swear, then he may well think his credence is clean gone. For truth it is, as Theophylactus writeth, that "no man is less trusted, than he that useth much to swear." And Almighty God, by the Wise Man saith, *That man which sweareth much, shall be full of sin, and the scourge of God, shall not depart from his house.*

Margin notes:

Commodities had by lawful oaths made and observed

Vain swearing is forbidden.

An objection

An answer

Ecclus. 23:11

But here some men will say, for excusing of their many oaths in their daily talk, "Why should I not swear, when I swear truly?" To such men it may be said, that though they swear truly, yet in swearing often, unadvisedly, for trifles, without necessity, and when they should not swear, they be not without fault, but do take God's most holy Name in vain. Much more ungodly and unwise men, are they that abuse God's most holy Name, not only in buying and selling of small things, daily in all places, but also in eating, drinking, playing, communing, and reasoning; as if none of these things might be done, except in doing of them, the most holy Name, of God, be commonly used and abused, vainly and unreverently talked of, sworn by and forsworn, to the breaking of God's commandment, and procurement of his indignation.

Another objection

An answer

THE SECOND PART OF
THE SERMON OF SWEARING

YOU HAVE BEEN TAUGHT, in the first part of this Sermon, against swearing and perjury, what great danger it is, to use the Name of God in vain; and that all kind of swearing is not unlawful, neither against God's commandment; and that there be three things required, in a lawful oath; first, that it be made for the maintenance of the truth; second, that it be made with judgement, not rashly and unadvisedly; thirdly, for the zeal and love of justice. Ye heard also, what commodities cometh, of lawful oaths, and what danger cometh, of rash and unlawful oaths. Now as concerning the rest of the same matter, ye shall understand, that as well they use the Name of God in vain, that by an oath make lawful promises, of good and honest things, and perform them not, as they which do promise evil and unlawful things, and do perform the same.

Of such men, that regard not their godly promises, bound by an oath, but wittingly and wilfully breaketh them, we do read in holy Scripture, two notable punishments. First, Josue and the people of Israel, made a league and faithful promise, of perpetual amity and friendship, with the Gabaonites: notwithstanding, afterward, in the days of wicked Saul, many of the Gabaonites were murdered, contrary to the said faithful promise made. Wherewith Almighty God was so sore displeased, that he sent an universal famine, upon the whole country, which continued by the space of three years; and God would not withdraw his punishment, until the said offence was revenged, by the death of seven sons or next kinsmen, of King Saul. Also, whereas Sedechias King of Jerusalem, had promised fidelity to the King of Chaldea, afterward, when Sedechias, contrary to his oath and allegiance, did rebel against King Nabucho-

Lawful oaths and promises would be better regarded.
Josh. 9

2 Sam. 21:1–14

2 Kings 24:17–25:7

donozor, this heathen king, by God's permission and sufferance invading the land of Jewry, and besieging the city of Jerusalem, compelled the said King Sedechias, to flee, and in fleeing took him prisoner, slew his sons before his face, and put out both his eyes, and binding him with chains, led him prisoner miserably into Babylon. Thus doth God show plainly, how much he abhorreth breakers of honest promises, bound by an oath made in his name.

Unlawful oaths and promises are not to be kept.

Matt. 14:6–11

And of them that make wicked promises, by an oath, and will perform the same, we have example in the Scripture, chiefly of Herod, of the wicked Jews, and of Jephthah. Herod *promised by an oath*, unto the damsel which danced before him, *to give unto her, whatsoever she would ask*, when she was *instructed before, of her* wicked *mother* to ask the head of St John Baptist. Herod, as he took a wicked oath, so he more wickedly, performed the same, and cruelly slew the most holy Prophet.

Acts 23:12

Judges 11:30–9

Likewise *did* the malicious Jews *make an oath, cursing themselves, if they did either eat or drink, until they had slain St Paul*. And Jephthah, when God had given to him victory, of the children of Ammon, promised, of a foolish devotion unto God, to offer for a sacrifice unto him, that person which of his own house, should first meet with him, after his return home. By force of which fond and unadvised oath, he did slay his own and only daughter, which came out of his house, with mirth and joy, to welcome him home. Thus the promise, which he made most foolishly to God, against God's everlasting will, and the law of nature, most cruelly he performed, so committing against God, double offence. Therefore, whosoever maketh any promise, binding himself thereunto by an oath, let him foresee, that the thing which he promiseth, be good, honest, and not against the commandment of God, and that it be in his own power, to perform it justly: and such good promises, must all men keep evermore assuredly. But if a man at any time, shall either of ignorance or of malice, promise and swear, to do anything which is either against the law of Almighty God, or not in his power to perform, let him take it for an unlawful, and ungodly oath.

Against perjury

An oath before a judge

Now something to speak of perjury. To the intent you should know how great and grievous an offence, against God, this wilful perjury is, I will show you what it is, to take an oath before a judge, upon a book. First, when they, laying their hands upon the Gospel book, do swear truly to inquire, and to make a true presentment, of things wherewith they be charged, and not to let from saying the truth, and doing truly, for favour, love, dread, or malice of any person, as God may help them, and the holy contents of that book, they must consider, that in that book is contained, God's everlasting truth, his most holy and eternal word, whereby we have forgiveness of our sins, and be made inheritors of heaven, to live for ever, with God's angels and his saints, in joy and gladness. In the Gospel book is contained also, God's terrible threats to obstinate sinners, that will not amend their lives, nor believe the truth of God, his holy word, and the everlasting pain, prepared in hell for idolaters, hypocrites, for false and vain swearers, for perjured men, for false witness bearers, for false condemners of innocent and guiltless men, and for them which for favour, hide the crimes of evildoers, that they should not be punished. So that whosoever wilfully forsweareth themselves, upon Christ's holy Evangely, they utterly forsake God's mercy, goodness, and truth, the merits of our Saviour Christ's nativity, life, passion, death, resurrection, and ascension; they refuse the forgiveness of sins, promised to all penitent sinners, the joys of heaven, the company with angels and saints for ever; all which benefits and comforts, are promised unto true Christian persons, in the Gospel. And they, so being forsworn upon the Gospel, do betake themselves to the devil's service, the master of all lies, falsehood, deceit, and perjury, provoking the great indignation, and curse, of God against them, in this life, and the terrible wrath, and judgement, of our Saviour Christ, at the great day of the last judgement, when he shall justly judge, both the quick and the dead, according to their works. For whosoever forsaketh the truth, for love or displeasure of any man, or for lucre and profit to himself, doth forsake Christ, and with Judas, betrayeth him. And, although such perjured men's falsehood, be now kept secret, yet it shall be opened at the last day, when the secrets of all men's hearts, shall be manifest to all the world; and then the truth shall appear, and accuse them; and their own conscience, with all the blessed company of heaven, shall bear witness truly against them; and Christ, the righteous Judge, shall then justly condemn them, to everlasting shame, and death.

Though perjury do escape here unspied and unpunished, it shall not ever do so.

This sin of perjury Almighty God, by the Prophet Malachy, doth threaten to punish sore, saying unto the Jews, *I will come to you in judgement, and I will be a swift witness,* and a sharp judge, *upon sorcerers, adulterers, and perjured persons.* Which thing to that Prophet Zachary, God declareth in a vision, wherein the Prophet saw a book flying, which was twenty cubits long and ten cubits broad, God saying then unto him, *This is the curse that shall go forth, upon the face of the earth, for falsehood, false swearing, and perjury; and this curse shall enter in, to the house of the perjured man, and it shall remain, in the midst of his house, and consume him, the timber and stones of his house.* Thus you see how much, God doth hate perjury, and what punishment God hath prepared, for false swearers and perjured persons.

Mal. 3:5

Zech. 5:1–4

Thus you have heard how, and in what causes, it is lawful for a Christian man to swear; ye have heard, what properties and conditions, a lawful oath must have, and also how such lawful oaths, are both godly and necessary to be observed; ye have heard, that it is not lawful to swear vainly, that is, other ways than in such causes, and after such sort, as is declared; and finally ye have heard, how damnable a thing it is, either to forswear ourselves, or to keep an unlawful and unadvised oath. Wherefore let us earnestly call for grace, that all vain swearing and perjury set apart, we may only use such oaths, as be lawful and godly, and that we may truly, without all fraud, keep the same, according to God's will and pleasure. To whom, with the Son, and Holy Ghost, be all honour and glory. Amen.

A SERMON
HOW DANGEROUS A THING IT IS
TO FALL FROM GOD

OF OUR GOING FROM GOD, the Wise Man saith, that pride was the first Ecclus. 10:12, 13
beginning: for by it man's heart was turned, from God his Maker. *For
pride*, saith he, *is the fountain of all sin: he that hath it, shall be full of cursings,
and at the end, it shall overthrow him.* And as by pride and sin, we go from
God, so shall God, and all goodness with him, go from us. And the
Prophet Osee doth plainly affirm, that they which go away still from
God, by vicious living, and yet would go about, to pacify him otherwise
by sacrifice, and entertain him thereby, they labour in vain: for,
notwithstanding all their sacrifice, yet he goeth still away from them.
Forsomuch, saith the Prophet, as *they do not apply their minds, to return to* Hos. 5:4, 6
*God, although they go about, with whole flocks and herds to seek the Lord, yet
they shall not find him; for he is gone away from them.*

But as touching our turning to God, or from God, you shall
understand, that it may be done divers ways. Sometimes directly by
idolatry, as Israel and Juda then did. Sometimes men go from God, by
lack of faith, and mistrusting of God, whereof Esay speaketh in this
wise: *Woe to them that go down into Egypt, to seek for help, trusting in horses,* Isai. 31:1, 3
and having confidence in the number of chariots, and puissance (or power) *of
horsemen: they have no confidence, in the holy God of Israel, nor seek for the
Lord.* But what followeth? *The Lord shall let his hand full upon them, and
down shall come both the helper, and he that is holpen: they shall be destroyed,
all together.*

Sometime men go from God, by the neglecting of his commandments
concerning their neighbours, which commandeth them, to express
hearty love towards every man: as Zachary said unto the people, in
God's behalf, *Give true judgement, show mercy and compassion, every one* Zech. 7:9–14
*to his brother, imagine no deceit towards widows, or children fatherless and
motherless, towards strangers, or the poor; let no man forge evil in his heart,
against his brother. But these things they passed not of; they turned their backs,*

and went their way; they stopped their ears, that they might not hear; they hardened their hearts, as an adamant stone, that they might not listen to the law, and the words that the Lord had sent, through his Holy Spirit, by his ancient Prophets. Wherefore the Lord showed his great indignation upon them. It came to pass, saith the Prophet, even as I told them: as they would not hear, so when they cried, they were not heard, but were scattered, into all kingdoms which they never knew, and their land was made desolate.

Jer. 7:24

Origen. *super Exod.* Hom. XII

And to be short, all they that may not abide the word of God, but following the persuasions and stubbornness, of their own hearts, *go backward and not forward* (as it is said in Jeremy), they go and turn away from God. Insomuch that Origen saith, "He that with mind, with study, with deeds, with thought and care, applieth and giveth himself, to God's word, and thinketh upon his laws, day and night, giveth himself wholly to God, and in his precepts and commandments is exercised, this is he that is turned to God." And on the other part he saith,

> Whosoever is occupied with fables and tales, when the word of God is rehearsed, he is turned from God. Whosoever in time of reading God's word, is careful in his mind of worldly business, of money or of lucre, he is turned from God. Whosoever is entangled with the cares of possessions, filled with covetousness of riches, whosoever studieth for the glory and honour of this world, he is turned from God.

So that, after his mind, whosoever hath not a special mind, to that thing that is commanded, or taught of God; he that doth not listen unto it, embrace, and print it in his heart, to the intent that he may duly, fashion his life thereafter; he is plainly turned from God, although he do other things, of his own devotion and mind, which to him seem better, and more to God's honour.

1 Sam. 15:1–24

Which thing to be true, we be taught and admonished in the holy Scripture, by the example of King Saul; who being commanded of God by Samuel, that he should kill all the Amalechites, and destroy them clearly, with their goods and cattle, yet he being moved partly with pity, and partly (as he thought), with devotion unto God, saved Agag their king, and all the chief of their cattle, therewith to make sacrifice unto God. Wherewithal God being displeased highly, said unto the Prophet Samuel, *I repent, that ever I made Saul a king; for he hath forsaken me, and not followed my words;* and so he commanded Samuel to show him. And when Samuel asked, wherefore contrary to God's word, he had saved the cattle, he excused the matter, partly by fear, saying he durst do none other, for that the people would have it so; partly, for that they were goodly beasts, he thought God would be content, seeing it was done of a good intent and devotion, to honour God with the sacrifice of them.

But Samuel, reproving all such intents and devotions (seem they never so much to God's honour), if they stand not with his word, whereby we may be assured of his pleasure, said in this wise: *Would God have sacrifices and offerings, or rather that his word, should be obeyed? To obey him, is better than offerings, and to listen to him, is better than to offer the fat of rams. Yea, to repugn against his voice, is as evil as the sin of soothsaying, and not to agree to it, is like abominable idolatry. And now, forasmuch as thou hast cast away the word of the Lord, he hath cast away thee, that thou shouldest not be king.*

By all these examples of holy Scripture, we may know that as we forsake God, so shall he ever forsake us. And what miserable state doth consequently, and necessarily, follow thereupon, a man may easily consider, by the terrible threatenings of God. And, although he consider not all the said misery to the uttermost, being so great that it passeth any man's capacity, in this life, sufficiently to consider the same, yet he shall soon perceive so much thereof that, if his heart be not more than stony, or harder than the adamant, he shall fear, tremble, and quake, to call the same to his remembrance.

The turning of God from man

First, the displeasure of God toward us, is commonly expressed in the Scripture, by these two things, by showing his fearful countenance upon us, and by turning his face, or hiding it from us. By showing his dreadful countenance, is signified his great wrath; but by turning his face, or hiding thereof, is many times more signified, that is to say, that he clearly forsaketh us, and giveth us over. The which significations be taken of the properties of men's manners. For men towards them whom they favour, commonly bear a good, a cheerful, and loving countenance; so that by the face, or countenance of a man, it doth commonly appear what will or mind, he beareth towards other. So, when God doth show his dreadful countenance towards us, that is to say, doth send dreadful plagues, of sword, famine, or pestilence upon us, it appeareth, that he is greatly wroth with us. But when he withdraweth from us his word, the right doctrine of Christ, his gracious assistance and aid, which is ever joined to his word, and leaveth us to our own wit, our own will and strength, he declareth then, that he beginneth to forsake us. For, whereas God hath showed, to all them that truly believe his Gospel, his face of mercy, in Jesus Christ, which doth so lighten their hearts, that they, if they behold it as they ought to do, be transformed to his image, be made partakers of the heavenly light, and of his Holy Spirit, and be fashioned to him, in all goodness requisite to the children of God; so if they after do neglect the same, if they be unthankful unto him, if they order not their lives, according to his example and doctrine, and to the setting forth of his glory, he will take away from them his kingdom, his holy word, whereby he should reign in them, because they bring not forth the fruit thereof, that he looketh for.

2 Cor. 3:18; 4:4, 6

Nevertheless, he is so merciful, and of so long sufferance, that he doth not show upon us that great wrath suddenly. But when we begin to shrink from his word, not believing it, or not expressing it in our livings, first he doth send his messengers, the true preachers of his word, to admonish and warn us of our duty; that as he for his part, for the great love he bare unto us, delivered his own Son, to suffer death, that we by his death, might be delivered from death, and be restored to the life everlasting, evermore to dwell with him, and to be partakers, and inheritors with him, of his everlasting glory, and kingdom of heaven, so again that we for our parts, should walk in a godly life, as becometh his children to do. And if this will not serve, but still we remain disobedient, to his word and will, not knowing him, not loving him, not fearing him, not putting our whole trust and confidence in him; and, on the other side, to our neighbours, behaving ourselves uncharitably by disdain, envy, malice, or by committing murder, robbery, adultery, gluttony, deceit, lying, swearing, or other like detestable works, and ungodly behaviour; then he threateneth us, by terrible comminations, swearing in great anger, that *whosoever doeth these works, shall never enter into his rest*, which is, the kingdom of heaven.

Heb. 4:1–13
Psalm 95:11

THE SECOND PART OF
THE SERMON OF FALLING FROM GOD

IN THE FORMER PART of this Sermon, ye have learned, how many manner of ways, men fall from God; some by idolatry, some for lack of faith, some by the neglecting of their neighbours, some by not hearing God's word, some by the pleasure they take, in the vanities of worldly things. Ye have also learned, in what misery that man is, which is gone from God; and how that God yet, of his infinite goodness, to call again man from that his misery, useth first gentle admonitions, by his preachers; after, he layeth on terrible threatenings.

Now, if this gentle monition, and threatening together, do not serve, then God will show his terrible countenance upon us; he will pour intolerable plagues upon our heads; and after he will take away from us, all his aid and assistance, wherewith before he did defend us, from all such manner of calamity. As the evangelical Prophet Esay, agreeing with Christ's parable, doth teach us, saying that God had made a goodly vineyard, for his beloved children; *he hedged it*, he walled it round about, *he planted it with chosen vines, and made a turret, in the midst thereof, and therein also a wine-press; and when he looked, that it should bring him forth good grapes, it brought forth wild grapes*. And after it followeth: *Now shall I show you*, saith God, *what I will do, with my vineyard. I will pluck down the*

Isai. 5:1–6
Matt. 21:33–41

hedges, that it may perish; I will break down the walls, that it may be trodden under foot: I will let it lie waste; it shall not be cut, it shall not be digged, but briars and thorns shall overgrow it; and I shall command the clouds, that they shall no more rain upon it.

By these threatenings, we are monished and warned, that if we, which are the chosen vineyard of God, bring not forth good grapes, that is to say, good works, that may be delectable and pleasant in his sight, when he looketh for them, when he sendeth his messengers, to call upon us for them, but rather bring forth wild grapes, that is to say, sour works, unsweet, unsavoury, and unfruitful, then will he pluck away all defence, and suffer grievous plagues, of famine and battle, dearth and death, to light upon us: finally, if these do not yet serve, he will let us lie waste; he will give us over; he will turn away from us; he will dig and delve no more about us; he will let us alone, and suffer us to bring forth, even such fruit as we will, to bring forth brambles, briers, and thorns, all naughtiness, all vice, and that so abundantly, that they shall clean overgrow us, choke, strangle, and utterly destroy us.

But they that in this world, live not after God, but after their own carnal liberty, perceive not this great wrath of God towards them, that he will not dig nor delve, any more about them, that he doth let them alone, even to themselves: but they take this, for a great benefit of God, to have all at their own liberty; and so they live, as if carnal liberty were the true liberty, of the Gospel. But God forbid, good people, that ever we should desire such liberty. For although God suffer sometimes, the wicked to have their pleasure, in this world, yet the end of ungodly living, is at length, endless destruction. The murmuring Israelites had that they longed for: they had quails enough, yea, till they were weary of them. But what was the end thereof? Their sweet meat had sour sauce: even *whiles the meat was in their mouths*, the plague of God, lighted upon them, and suddenly they died. So, if we live ungodly, and God suffereth us, to follow our own wills, to have our own delights and pleasures, and correcteth us not, with some plague, it is no doubt, but he is almost utterly displeased with us.

Num. 11:4–6, 31-3

Psalm 78:30, 31

And although it be long or he strike, yet many times, when he striketh such persons, he striketh them at once, for ever. So that when he doth not strike us, when he ceaseth to afflict us, to punish or beat us, and suffereth us to run headlong, into all ungodliness, and pleasures of this world that we delight in, without punishment and adversity, it is a dreadful token, that he loveth us no longer, that he careth no longer for us, but hath given us over, to our own selves. As long as a man doth prune his vines, doth dig at the roots, and doth lay fresh earth to them, he hath a mind to them, he perceiveth some token of fruitfulness, that may be recovered in them: but when he will bestow no more, such cost and labour about them, then it is a sign, that he thinketh they will never be good. And the father, as long as he loveth his child, he looketh angerly, he correcteth him, when he doeth amiss: but, when that serveth not, and upon that he ceaseth, from correction of him, and suffereth him to do what he list himself, it is a sign, that he intendeth to disinherit him, and to cast him away, for ever.

So surely nothing should pierce our heart so sore, and put us in such horrible fear, as when we know in our conscience, that we have grievously offended God, and do so continue, and that yet he striketh not, but quietly suffereth us, in the naughtiness that we have delight in.

Psalm 51:11

Psalm 27:9

Psalm 143:7

Then specially it is time to cry, and to cry again, as David did, *Cast me not away from thy face, and take not away thy Holy Spirit from me. Lord, turn not away thy face from me; cast not thy servant away, in displeasure. Hide not thy face from me, lest I be like to them, that go down into hell.* The which lamentable prayers of him, as they do certify us, what horrible danger they be in, from whom God turneth his face, for that time and as long as he so doth, so should they move and stir us, to cry upon God, with all our heart, that we may not be brought into that state; which doubtless is so sorrowful, so miserable, and so dreadful, as no tongue can sufficiently express, or any heart can think. For what deadly grief may a man suppose it is, to be under the wrath of God; to be forsaken of him; to have his Holy Spirit, the Author of all goodness, to be taken from him; to be brought to so vile a condition, that he shall be left meet for no better purpose, than to be for ever condemned to hell! For not only such places of David, do show that upon the turning of God's face from any persons, they shall be left bare from all goodness, and far from hope of remedy, but also the place rehearsed last before, of Esay, doth mean the same; which showeth, that God at length doth so forsake his unfruitful vineyard, that he will not only, suffer it to bring forth weeds, *briers, and thorns,* but also, further to punish the unfruitfulness of it, he saith he will not cut it, he will not deliver it, and he *will command the clouds, that they shall not rain upon it*; whereby is signified, the teaching of his holy word (which St Paul after a like manner, expresseth by planting

1 Cor. 3:6–8

and watering), meaning that he will take that away from them. So that they shall be no longer, of his kingdom; they shall be no longer, governed by his Holy Spirit; they shall be put from the grace, and benefits that they had, and ever might have enjoyed, through Christ; they shall be deprived, of the heavenly light and life, which they had in Christ, whiles they abode in him; they shall be (as they were once), as men *without God in this world,* or rather in worse taking; and to be short, they shall be given into the power of the devil, which beareth the rule, in all them that

1 Sam. 15:23–55

Ephes. 2:2

be cast away from God, as he did in Saul, and Judas, and generally in all such, as work after their own wills, *the children of mistrust and unbelief.*

Let us beware therefore, good Christian people, lest that we rejecting God's word, by the which we obtain and retain, true faith in God, be not at length cast off so far, that we become, as the children of unbelief. Which be of two sorts, far diverse, yea, almost clean contrary, and yet both, be very far from returning to God. The one sort, only weighing their sinful and detestable living, with the right judgement and straightness of God's righteousness, be so without counsel, and be so comfortless (as all they must needs be, from whom *the Spirit of counsel* and comfort is gone), that they will not be persuaded in their hearts, but that either God cannot, or else that he will not, take them again to his favour and mercy. The other, hearing the loving and large promises, of God's mercy, and so not conceiving a right faith thereof, make those promises larger, than ever God did; trusting that, although they continue, in their sinful and detestable living, never so long, yet that God at the end of their life, will show his mercy upon them, and that then they will return. And both these two sorts of men, be in a damnable state: and yet nevertheless God, who *willeth not the death of the wicked*, hath showed means, whereby both the same, if they take heed in season, may escape.

Isai. 11:2

Ezek. 18:23, 32; 33:11

The first, as they do dread God's rightful justice, in punishing sinners (whereby they should be dismayed, and should despair indeed, as touching any hope that may be in themselves), so if they would constantly believe, that God's mercy is the remedy, appointed against such despair and distrust, not only for them, but generally for all that be sorry and truly repentant, and will therewithal stick to God's mercy, they may be sure, they shall obtain mercy, and enter into the port, or haven of safeguard; into the which whosoever doth come, be they beforetime never so wicked, they shall be out of danger, of everlasting damnation. As God by Ezechiel saith: *What time soever, the wicked doth return*, and take earnest and true repentance, I will forget all his wickedness.

Against desperation

Ezek. 33:12, 14–16, 19

The other, as they be ready to believe God's promises, so they should be as ready, to believe the threatenings of God. As well they should believe the Law, as the Gospel; as well that there is an hell and everlasting fire, as that there is an heaven and everlasting joy. As well they should believe damnation, to be threatened to the wicked and evildoers, as salvation, to be promised to the faithful in word and works. As well they should believe God to be true, in the one as in the other. And the sinners that continue in their wicked living, ought to think that the promises of God's mercy, and the Gospel, pertain not unto them, being in that state, but only the Law, and those Scriptures which contain the wrath and indignation of God, and his threatenings: which should certify them, that as they do overboldly, presume of God's mercy, and live dissolutely, so doth God, still more and more, withdraw his mercy from them; and he is so provoked thereby, to wrath at length, that he

Against presumption

destroyeth such presumers, many times suddenly. For of such St Paul said thus: *When they shall say, It is peace, There is no danger, then shall sudden destruction come upon them.* Let us beware therefore, of such naughty boldness to sin. For God, which hath promised his mercy, to them that be truly repentant, although it be at the latter end, hath not promised to the presumptuous sinner, either that he shall have long life, or that he shall have true repentance, at his last end. But for that purpose, hath he made every man's death uncertain, that he should not put his hope in the end, and in the mean season, to God's high displeasure, live ungodly.

Wherefore let us all follow the counsel of the Wise Man: let us *make no tarrying, to turn unto the Lord*; let us *not put off from day to day: for suddenly, shall his wrath come, and in time of vengeance, he shall destroy* the wicked. Let us therefore turn betimes: and when we turn, let us pray to God, as Osee teacheth, saying *Forgive us all our sins, receive us graciously.* And if we turn to him, with an humble and a very penitent heart, he will receive us, to his favour and grace, for his holy Name's sake, for his promise sake, for his truth and mercy's sake, promised to all faithful believers in Jesus Christ, his only natural Son. To whom, the only Saviour of the world, with the Father, and the Holy Ghost, be all honour, glory, and power, world without end. Amen.

1 Thess. 5:3

Ecclus. 5:7

Hos. 14:2

AN EXHORTATION
AGAINST THE FEAR OF DEATH

IT IS NOT TO BE MARVELLED, that worldly men do fear to die. For death depriveth them, of all worldly honours, riches, and possessions: in the fruition whereof, the worldly man counteth himself happy, so long as he may enjoy them at his own pleasure; and otherwise, if he be dispossessed of the same, without hope of recovery, then he can none other think of himself, but that he is unhappy, because he hath lost his worldly joy and pleasure. "Alas!" thinketh this carnal man, "shall I now depart for ever, from all my honours, all my treasures, from my country, friends, riches, possessions, and worldly pleasures, which are my joy, and heart's delight? Alas! that ever that day shall come, when all these I must bid farewell at once, and never to enjoy any of them after!" Wherefore it is not without great cause spoken, of the Wise Man, *O death, how bitter and sour, is the remembrance of thee, to a man that liveth in peace and prosperity, in his substance, to a man living at ease, leading his life after his own mind, without trouble, and is therewithal well pampered and fed!* Ecclus. 41:1

There be other men, whom this world doth not so greatly laugh upon, but rather vex and oppress with poverty, sickness, or some other adversity; yet they do fear death, partly because the flesh abhorreth naturally, his own sorrowful dissolution, which death doth threaten unto them, and partly by reason of sicknesses, and painful diseases, which be most strong pangs, and agonies in the flesh, and use commonly, to come to sick men before death, or at the least accompany death, whensoever it cometh.

Although these two causes seem great and weighty, to a worldly man, whereupon he is moved to fear death, yet there is another cause, much greater than any of these afore rehearsed, for which indeed, he hath just cause to fear death; and that is the state and condition, whereunto at the last end, death bringeth all them that have their hearts, fixed upon this world, without repentance and amendment. This state and condition is called, *the second death*; which unto all such shall ensue, after this bodily death. And this is that death, which indeed ought to be dread and Rev. 21:8

feared: for it is the everlasting loss, without remedy, of the grace and favour of God, and of everlasting joy, pleasure, and felicity. And it is not only the loss for ever, of all these eternal pleasures, but also it is the condemnation, both of body and soul, without either appellation, or hope of redemption, unto everlasting pains, in hell. Unto this state, death sent the unmerciful and ungodly rich man, that Luke speaketh of in his Gospel; who living in all wealth, and pleasure in this world, and cherishing himself daily, with dainty fare and gorgeous apparel, despised poor Lazarus, that lay pitifully at his gate, miserably plagued, and *full of sores*, and also grievously pined with hunger. Both these two were arrested of death; which sent Lazarus, the poor miserable man, by angels anon unto Abraham's bosom, a place of rest, pleasure, and consolation. But the unmerciful rich man, descended down, into hell; and *being in torments*, he cried for comfort, complaining of the intolerable pain that he suffered, in that flame of fire: but it was too late. So unto this place, bodily death sendeth all them, that in this world have their joy and felicity, all them that in this world, be unfaithful unto God, and uncharitable unto their neighbours, so dying without repentance, and hope of God's mercy. Wherefore it is no marvel, that the worldly man feareth death: for he hath much more cause so to do, than he himself doth consider.

Thus we see three causes, why worldly men fear death; one, because they shall lose thereby, their worldly honours, riches, possessions, and all their heart's desires; another, because of the painful diseases, and bitter pangs, which commonly men suffer, either before or at the time of death; but the chief cause, above all other, is the dread, of the miserable state of eternal damnation, both of body and soul, which they fear shall follow after their departing, out of the worldly pleasures of this present life. For these causes, be all mortal men which be given to the love of this world, both in fear and state of death through sin, as the holy Apostle saith, so long as they live here in this world.

But, everlasting thanks be to Almighty God for ever! there is never one of all these causes, no, nor yet they all together, that can make a true Christian man afraid to die, which is the very member of Christ, the temple of the Holy Ghost, the son of God, and the very inheritor, of the everlasting kingdom of heaven; but, plainly contrary, he conceiveth great and many causes, undoubtedly grounded, upon the infallible and everlasting truth, of the word of God, which move him, not only to put away the fear of bodily death, but also, for the manifold benefits, and singular commodities which ensue, unto every faithful person, by reason of the same, to wish, desire, and long heartily for it. For death shall be to him, no death at all, but a very deliverance from death, from all pains, cares, and sorrows, miseries, and wretchedness of this world, and the

Marginal notes:

Luke 16:19–31

The first

The second

The third

Heb. 2:15

1 Cor. 3:16

very entry into rest, and a beginning of everlasting joy, a tasting of heavenly pleasures, so great that neither tongue is able to express, neither eye to see, nor ear to hear them, no, nor for any earthly man's heart to conceive them. So exceeding great benefits they be, which God our heavenly Father, by his mere mercy, and for the love of his Son, Jesus Christ, hath laid up in store, and prepared for them that humbly submit themselves to God's will, and evermore unfeignedly love him, from the bottom of their hearts.

1 Cor. 2:9

And we ought to believe, that death being slain by Christ, cannot keep any man that stedfastly trusteth in Christ, under his perpetual tyranny and subjection, but that he shall rise from death again, unto glory at the last day, appointed by Almighty God, like as Christ our Head did rise again, according to God's appointment, the third day. For St Augustine saith, the Head going before, the members trust to follow, and come after. And St Paul saith, if Christ be risen from the dead, we shall rise also from the same. And, to comfort all Christian persons herein, holy Scripture calleth this bodily death *a sleep*; wherein man's senses be, as it were, taken from him for a season, and yet, when he awaketh, he is more fresh than he was when he went to bed. So although we have our souls separated from our bodies, for a season, yet at the general resurrection, we shall be more fresh, beautiful, and perfect, than we be now. For now we be mortal, then we shall be immortal; now infected with divers infirmities, then clearly void of all mortal infirmities; now we be subject to all carnal desires, then we shall be all spiritual, desiring nothing but God's glory, and things eternal.

1 Cor. 15:20–3

John 11:11,13;
Acts 7:60;
1 Thess. 4:13–18

Thus is this bodily death a door, or entering unto life; and therefore not so much dreadful, if it be rightly considered, as it is comfortable; not a mischief, but a remedy of all mischief; no enemy, but a friend; not a cruel tyrant, but a gentle guide; leading us, not to mortality, but to immortality, not to sorrow and pain, but to joy and pleasure, and that to endure for ever; if it be thankfully taken, and accepted as God's messenger, and patiently borne of us, for Christ's love, that suffered most painful death for our love, to redeem us, from death eternal. According hereunto St Paul saith, *our life is hid with Christ in God, but when our Life shall appear, then shall we also appear with him, in glory.*

Col. 3:3–4

Why then shall we fear to die, considering the manifold and comfortable promises of the Gospel, and of holy Scriptures? *God the Father hath given us everlasting life,* saith St John, *and this life is in his Son. He that hath the Son, hath life; and he that hath not the Son, hath not life.* And, *This I wrote,* saith St John, *to you that believe in the Name, of the Son of God, that you may know, that you have everlasting life, and that you do believe upon the Name, of the Son of God.* And our Saviour Christ saith, *He that believeth in me hath life everlasting, and I will raise him from death to life, at the last day.*

1 John 5:11–13

John 6:40, 47

1 Cor. 1:30, 31

St Paul also saith, that *Christ is ordained, and made of God our righteous-ness, our holiness and redemption, to the intent that he which will glory, should*

Phil. 3:7–11

glory in the Lord. St Paul did contemn and set little by, *all other things, esteeming them as dung, which before, he had in very great price, that he might be found in Christ,* to have everlasting life, true holiness, righteousness,

Rom. 8:32

and redemption. Finally, St Paul maketh a plain argument, in this wise: *If our heavenly Father, would not spare his own natural Son, but did give him to death for us, how can it be, that with him, he should not give us all things?* Therefore, if we have Christ, then have we with him, and by him, all good things, whatsoever we can in our hearts wish, or desire; as, victory over death, sin, and hell; we have the favour of God, peace with him, holiness, wisdom, justice, power, life, and redemption; we have by him perpetual health, wealth, joy, and bliss everlasting.

THE SECOND PART
OF THE SERMON
OF THE FEAR OF DEATH

IT HATH BEEN HERETOFORE SHOWED YOU, that there be three causes, wherefore men do commonly fear death; first, the sorrowful departing from worldly goods and pleasures; the second, the fear of the pangs and pains, that come with death; last and principal cause, is the horrible fear, of extreme misery, and perpetual damnation, in time to come. And yet none of these three causes, troubleth good men; because they stay themselves by true faith, perfect charity, and sure hope of the endless joy, and bliss everlasting.

All those therefore, have great cause to be full of joy, that be joined to Christ with true faith, stedfast hope, and perfect charity, and not to fear death, nor everlasting damnation. For death cannot deprive them of Jesu Christ, nor any sin can condemn them, that are grafted surely in him, which is their only joy, treasure, and life. Let us repent our sins, amend our lives, trust in his mercy and satisfaction, and death can

Rom. 14:8, 9

neither take him from us, nor us from him. For then, as St Paul saith, *whether we live or die, we be the Lord's own.* And again he saith, *Christ did die, and rose again, because he should be Lord, both of the dead and quick.* Then if we be the Lord's own, when we be dead, it must needs follow that such temporal death, not only cannot harm us, but also that it shall much be to our profit, and join us unto God, more perfectly. And thereof the Christian heart may surely be certified, by the infallible truth of holy

2 Cor. 5:5–8

Scripture. *It is God,* saith St Paul, *which hath prepared us, unto immortality, and the same is he, which hath given us an earnest, of the Spirit. Therefore let us be always of good comfort: for we know, that so long as we be in the body, we be as it were far from God*, in a strange country, subject to many perils, *walking without* perfect *sight* and knowledge, of Almighty God, *only* seeing him, *by faith* in holy Scriptures; *but we have a courage, and desire rather to be at home, with God and our Saviour, Christ, far from the body*, where *we may behold his Godhead, as he is, face to face*, to our everlasting comfort. These be St Paul's words in effect: whereby we may perceive, that the life in this world, is resembled and likened to a pilgrimage, in a strange country far from God; and that death, delivering us from our bodies, doth send us straight home, into our own country, and maketh us to dwell presently, with God for ever, in everlasting rest and quietness. So that to die is no loss, but profit and winning, to all true Christian people.

What lost the thief, that hanged on the cross with Christ, by his bodily death? Yea, how much did he gain by it! Did not our Saviour say unto him, *This day thou shalt be with me, in Paradise*? And Lazarus, that pitiful person, that lay before the rich man's gate, pained with sores and pined with hunger, did not death highly profit and promote him, which by the ministry of angels, sent him unto Abraham's bosom, a place of rest, joy, and heavenly consolation? Let us think none other, good Christian people, but Christ hath prepared, and made ready before, the same joy and felicity for us, that he prepared for Lazarus and the thief. Wherefore let us stick unto his salvation, and gracious redemption, and believe his word, serve him from our hearts, love and obey him; and, whatsoever we have done heretofore, contrary to his most holy will, now let us repent in time, and hereafter study to correct our life, and doubt not, but we shall find him as merciful unto us, as he was either to Lazarus, or to the thief: whose examples are written in holy Scripture, for the comfort of them that be sinners, and subject to sorrows, miseries, and calamities in this world; that they should not despair in God's mercy, but ever trust, thereby to have forgiveness of their sins, and life everlasting, as Lazarus and the thief had.

Thus I trust every Christian man perceiveth, by the infallible word of God, that bodily death cannot harm nor hinder, them that truly believe in Christ, but contrary, shall profit and promote the Christian souls, which being truly penitent for their offences, depart hence in perfect charity, and in sure trust that God is merciful to them, forgiving their sins, for the merits of Jesus Christ, his only natural Son.

The second cause why some do fear death, is sore sickness and grievous pains, which partly come before death, and partly accompany death, whensoever it cometh. This fear, is the fear of the frail flesh, and a natural passion, belonging unto the nature of a mortal man. But true faith in God's promises, and regard of the pains and pangs, which Christ upon the cross suffered, for us miserable sinners, with consideration of

Luke 23:43
Luke 16:20-2

The second cause why some do fear death

the joy and everlasting life to come, in heaven, will mitigate those pains, and moderate this fear, that it shall never be able, to overthrow the hearty desire and gladness, that the Christian soul hath, to be separated from this corrupt body, that it may come to the gracious presence, of our Saviour, Jesus Christ. If we believe stedfastly the word of God, we shall perceive, that such bodily sickness, pangs of death, or whatsoever dolorous pains we suffer, either before or with death, be nothing else in Christian men, but the rod of our heavenly and loving Father; wherewith he mercifully correcteth us, either to try and declare the faith of his patient children, that they may be found laudable, glorious, and honourable in his sight, when Jesus Christ shall be openly showed, to be the Judge of all the world, or else to chasten and amend in them, whatsoever offendeth his fatherly and gracious goodness, lest they should perish everlastingly. And this his correcting rod, is common to all them that be truly his.

Heb. 12:1–11   Therefore *let us cast away the burden of sin, that lieth so heavy* in our necks, and return unto God, by true penance, and amendment of our lives. *Let us with patience run this course that is appointed*; suffering for his sake that died, for our salvation, all sorrows and pangs of death, and death itself joyfully, when God sendeth it to us; *having our eyes fixed*, and set fast ever, *upon the Head and Captain of our faith, Jesus Christ; who, considering the joy, that he should come unto*, cared neither for the shame, nor pain of death, but willingly conforming his will, to his Father's will, *most patiently suffered, the* most shameful and painful *death, of the cross*, being innocent; and how therefore he is exalted in heaven, *and* everlastingly *sitteth on the right hand, of the throne of God* the Father. Let
Phil. 2:9   us call to our remembrance therefore, the life and joys of heaven, that are kept for all them that patiently, do suffer here with Christ; and *consider that Christ suffered* all his painful passion, *by sinners*, and for sinners; and then we shall with patience, and the more easily, suffer such sorrows and pains, when they come. *Let us not set at light, the chastising of the Lord*; nor grudge at him, *nor fall from him, when of him we be corrected: for the Lord loveth, them whom he doth correct, and beateth every one whom he taketh to be his child. What child is that*, saith St Paul, *whom the father loveth, and doth not chastise? If ye be without God's correction, which all his well beloved and true children have, then be you but bastards*, smally regarded of God, *and not his true children. Therefore, seeing that when we have in earth, our carnal fathers to be our correctors, we do fear them, and reverently take their correction, shall we not much more, be in subjection to God our spiritual Father, by whom we shall have eternal life? And our carnal fathers sometime correct us, even as pleaseth them*, without cause: *but this Father* justly correcteth us, either for our sin, to the intent we should amend, or *for our commodity and wealth, to make us thereby, partakers of his holiness.* Furthermore, all

correction which God sendeth us, *in this present time seemeth to have no joy* and comfort, *but sorrow* and pain; yet it bringeth with it, a taste of God's mercy and goodness, towards them that be so corrected, and a sure hope, of God's everlasting consolation, in heaven.

If then these sorrows, diseases, and sicknesses, and also death itself, be nothing else but our heavenly Father's rod, whereby he certifieth us, of his love and gracious favour, whereby he trieth and purifieth us, whereby he giveth unto us holiness, and certifieth us, that we be his children, and he our merciful Father; shall not we then with all humility, *as obedient* and loving *children*, joyfully kiss our heavenly Father's rod, and ever say in our heart, with our Saviour Jesus Christ, *Father, if this* anguish and sorrow which I feel, and death, which I see approach, *may not pass*, but that thy will is, that I must suffer them, *thy will be done?*

1 Pet. 1:14

Matt. 26:42

THE THIRD PART
OF THE SERMON
OF THE FEAR OF DEATH

IN THIS SERMON against the Fear of Death, two causes were declared, which commonly move worldly men, to be in much fear to die; and yet the same do nothing trouble the faithful, and good livers, when death cometh, but rather giveth them occasion, greatly to rejoice, considering that they shall be delivered, from the sorrow and misery of this world, and be brought to the great joy and felicity, of the life to come.

Now the third and special cause, why death indeed is to be feared, is the miserable state of the worldly and ungodly people, after their death. But this is no cause at all, why the godly and faithful people, should fear death; but rather contrariwise, their godly conversation in this life, and belief in Christ, cleaving continually to his merits, should make them, to long sore after that life, that remaineth for them undoubtedly after this bodily death. Of this immortal state, after this transitory life, where we shall live evermore, in the presence of God, in joy and rest, after victory over all sickness, sorrows, sin, and death, there be many plain places of holy Scripture, which confirm the weak conscience, against the fear of all such dolours, sicknesses, sin, and bodily death, to assuage such trembling, and ungodly fear, and to encourage us, with comfort and hope of a blessed state, after this life. St Paul wisheth unto the Ephesians *that God the Father of glory, would give unto them the spirit of wisdom and revelation, that the eyes of their hearts, might have light to know him,* and to perceive how great things, he had called them unto, and how rich inheritance, he hath prepared after this life, for them that pertain unto him. And St Paul himself declareth, *the desire* of his heart, which was *to*

The third cause why death is to be feared

Ephes. 1:17, 18

Phil. 1:23–4

be dissolved, and loosed from his body, *and to be with Christ*, which as he said, was *much better for him, although to them it was more necessary, that he should live*, which he refused not for their sakes. Even like as St Martin said, "Good Lord, if I be necessary for thy people, to do good unto them, I will refuse no labour: but else, for mine own self, I beseech thee to take my soul."

Now the holy fathers of the old Law, and all faithful and righteous men, which departed before our Saviour Christ's ascension into heaven, did by death, depart from troubles unto rest, from the hands of their enemies, into the hands of God, from sorrows and sicknesses, unto joyful refreshing, into Abraham's bosom, a place of all comfort and consolation; as Scriptures do plainly, by manifest words testify. The

Wisd. 3:1–3

Book of Wisdom saith, *that the righteous men's souls, be in the hand of God, and no torment shall touch them. They seemed to the eyes of foolish men, to die; and their death was counted miserable, and their departing out of this world*

Ibid. 5:15–16

wretched: but they be in rest. And another place saith *that the righteous shall live for ever, and their reward is with the Lord, and their minds be with God, who is above all: therefore they shall receive a glorious kingdom, and a beautiful*

Ibid. 4:7

crown, at the Lord's hand. And in another place the same Book saith, *The righteous, though he be prevented with sudden death, nevertheless he shall be*

Luke 16:22–5

there, where he shall be refreshed. Of Abraham's bosom Christ's words be so plain, that a Christian man needeth no more proof of it.

Now then, if this were the state of the holy fathers, and righteous men before the coming of our Saviour, and before he was glorified, how much more then, ought all we to have a stedfast faith, and a sure hope, of this blessed state and condition, after our death; seeing that our Saviour, now hath performed the whole work of our redemption, and is

John 17:24

gloriously, ascended into heaven, *to prepare our dwelling places* with him, and said unto his Father, *Father, I will that where I am, my servants shall be with me*. And we know, that whatsoever Christ will, his Father will the same: wherefore it cannot be but, if we be his faithful servants, our souls shall be with him, after our departing, out of this present life.

St Stephen, when he was stoned to death, even in the midst of his

Acts 7:55–9

torments, what was his mind most upon? *When he was full of the Holy Ghost*, saith holy Scripture, *having his eyes lifted up into heaven, he saw the glory of God, and Jesus, standing on the right hand of God*. The which truth after he had confessed boldly, before the enemies of Christ, *they drew him out of the city, and there they stoned him; who cried unto God, saying, Lord Jesu Christ, take my spirit*. And doth not our Saviour say plainly, in

John 5:24

St John's Gospel, *Verily, verily, I say unto you, He that heareth my word, and believeth on him that sent me, hath everlasting life, and cometh not into judgement, but shall pass from death to life*? Shall we not then think that death to be precious, by the which we pass into life? Therefore it is a true saying of the Prophet, *The death of the holy and righteous men, is precious in the Lord's sight.* Holy Simeon, after that he had his heart's desire, in seeing our Saviour, that he ever longed for all his life, *he embraced him in his arms, and said, Now, Lord, let me depart in peace, for mine eyes have beholden that Saviour, which thou hast prepared for all nations.* It is truth therefore, that the death of the righteous is called *peace,* and *the benefit of the Lord;* as the Church saith, in the name of the righteous departed out of this world, *My soul, turn thee to thy rest, for the Lord hath been good to thee, and rewarded thee.* And we see by holy Scripture, and other ancient histories of Martyrs, that the holy, faithful, and righteous, ever since Christ's ascension, in their death did not doubt, but that they went to be with Christ in spirit, which is our life, health, wealth, and salvation.

Psalm 116:15

Luke 2:28–31

Psalm 96:7

John in his holy Revelation, saw a hundred forty and four thousand virgins and innocents, of whom he said, *These follow the Lamb,* Jesu Christ, *wheresoever he goeth.* And shortly after, in the same place he saith, *I heard a voice from heaven, saying unto me, Write, Happy and blessed, are the dead which die in the Lord: from henceforth surely, saith the Spirit, they shall rest from their pains and labours: for their works do follow them.* So that then they shall reap with joy and comfort, that which they sowed with labours and pains. *They that sow in the spirit, of the spirit shall reap, everlasting life. Let us therefore never be weary of well doing: for when the time* of reaping or reward *cometh, we shall reap, without any weariness,* everlasting joy. *Therefore, while we have time,* as St Paul exhorteth us, *let us do good to all men;* and *not lay up our treasures in earth, where rust and moths corrupt it;* which *rust,* as St James saith, *shall bear witness against us,* at the great day, condemn us, *and shall like* most burning *fire, torment our flesh.*

Rev. 14:1–5, 13

Gal. 6:8–10

Matt. 6:19
James 5:3

Let us beware therefore, as we tender our own wealth, that we be not in the number of those miserable, covetous, and wretched men, which St James biddeth mourn and lament, for their greedy gathering and ungodly keeping of goods. Let us be wise in time, and learn to follow the wise example of the wicked Steward. Let us so wisely order our goods and possessions, committed unto us here by God, for a season, that we may truly hear and obey, this commandment of our Saviour Christ: *I say unto you,* saith he, *Make you friends of the wicked mammon, that they may receive you, into everlasting tabernacles* (or dwellings). Riches he calleth *wicked,* because the world abuseth them, unto all wickedness; which are otherwise the good gift of God, and instruments, whereby God's servants do truly serve him, in using of the same. He commanded them not to make them rich friends, to get high dignities, and worldly promotions, to give great gifts to rich men, that have no need thereof; but to make them friends of poor and miserable men, unto whom whatsoever they give, Christ taketh it as given to himself. And to these friends, Christ in the Gospel giveth so great honour, and pre-eminence,

Ibid. 5:1–4

Luke 16:1–9

that he saith, *they shall receive* them that do good unto them, *into everlasting houses*: not that men shall be our rewarders, for our well doing, but that Christ will reward us, and take it to be done unto himself, whatsoever is done to such friends. Thus making poor wretches our friends, we make our Saviour Christ our friend, whose members they are: whose misery, as he taketh for his own misery, so their relief, succour, and help, he taketh for his succour, relief, and help; and will as much thank us, and reward us for our goodness showed to them, as if he himself, had received like benefit at our hands; as he witnesseth in the

Matt. 25:40   Gospel, saying, *Whatsoever ye have done to any of these simple persons, which do believe in me, that have ye done to myself.*

     Therefore let us diligently foresee, that our faith and hope, which we have conceived in Almighty God, and in our Saviour Christ, wax not faint, nor that the love, which we bear in hand to bear to him, wax not cold; but let us study daily and diligently, to show ourselves to be the true honourers and lovers of God, by keeping of his commandments, by doing of good deeds unto our needy neighbours, relieving by all means that we can their poverty, with our abundance and plenty, their ignorance with our wisdom and learning, and comfort their weakness with our strength and authority, calling all men back from evil doing, by godly counsel and good example, persevering still in well doing, so long as we live. So shall we not need to fear death, for any of those three causes aforementioned, nor yet for any other cause, that can be imagined. But contrary, considering the manifold sicknesses, troubles, and sorrows, of this present life, the dangers of this perilous pilgrimage, and the great encumbrance, which our spirit hath by this sinful flesh, and frail body, subject to death; considering also the manifold sorrows, and dangerous deceits of this world, on every side, the intolerable pride, covetousness, and lechery in time of prosperity, the impatient murmuring of them that be worldly, in time of adversity, which cease not to withdraw and pluck us from God, our Saviour Christ, from our life, wealth, or eternal joy, and salvation; considering also the innumerable assaults of our ghostly enemy the devil, with all his fiery darts of ambition, pride, lechery, vainglory, envy, malice, detraction (or backbiting), with other his innumerable deceits, engines, and snares, whereby he goeth busily about, to catch all men under his

1 Pet. 5:8   dominion, ever *like a roaring lion*, by all means *searching, whom he may devour*: the faithful Christian man which considereth all these miseries, perils, and incommodities, whereunto he is subject, so long as he here liveth upon earth, and on the other part, considereth that blessed and comfortable state, of the heavenly life to come, and the sweet condition, of them that depart in the Lord, how they are delivered, from the continual encumbrances of their mortal and sinful body, from all the

malice, crafts, and deceits of this world, from all the assaults of their ghostly enemy the devil, to live in peace, rest, and endless quietness, to live in the fellowship of innumerable Angels, and with the congregation of perfect just men, as Patriarchs, Prophets, Martyrs, and Confessors, and finally unto the presence of Almighty God, and our Saviour Jesus Christ: he that doth consider all these things, and believeth them assuredly, as they are to be believed, even from the bottom of his heart, being stablished in God in this true faith, having a quiet conscience in Christ, a firm hope, and assured trust in God's mercy, through the merits of Jesu Christ, to obtain this quietness, rest, and everlasting joy, shall not only be without fear of bodily death, when it cometh, but certainly, as St Paul did, so shall he gladly, according to God's will, and when it please God to call him out of this life, greatly desire it in his Phil. 1:23 heart, that he may be rid, from all these occasions of evil, and live ever to God's pleasure, in perfect obedience of his will, with our Saviour Jesus Christ: to whose gracious presence, the Lord, of his infinite mercy and grace, bring us, to reign with him in life everlasting. To whom, with our heavenly Father, and the Holy Ghost, be glory, in worlds without end. Amen.

AN EXHORTATION CONCERNING GOOD ORDER AND OBEDIENCE TO RULERS AND MAGISTRATES

ALMIGHTY GOD hath created and appointed all things, in heaven, earth, and waters, in a most excellent, and perfect order. In heaven, he hath appointed distinct orders and states, of archangels and angels. In earth, he hath assigned and appointed kings and princes, with other governors under them, all in good and necessary order. The water above is kept, and raineth down, in due time and season. The sun, moon, stars, rainbow, thunder, lightning, clouds, and all birds of the air, do keep their order. The earth, trees, seeds, plants, herbs, corn, grass, and all manner of beasts, keep themselves in their order. All the parts of the whole year, as winter, summer, months, nights, and days, continue in their order. All kinds of fishes in the sea, rivers and waters, with all fountains and springs, yea, the seas themselves, keep their comely course and order. And man himself also, hath all his parts, both within and without, as soul, heart, mind, memory, understanding, reason, speech, with all and singular corporal members of his body, in a profitable, necessary, and pleasant order. Every degree of people, in their vocation, calling, and office, hath appointed to them their duty and order. Some are in high degree, some in low; some kings and princes, some inferiors and subjects; priests and laymen, masters and servants, fathers and children, husbands and wives, rich and poor; and every one have need of other. So that in all things, is to be lauded and praised, the goodly order of God: without the which no house, no city, no commonwealth, can continue and endure; for where there is no right order, there reigneth all abuse, carnal liberty, enormity, sin, and Babylonical confusion. Take away kings, princes, rulers, magistrates, judges, and such estates of God's order, no man shall ride or go by the highway, unrobbed; no man shall sleep in his own house or bed, unkilled; no man shall keep his wife, children, and possessions, in quietness; all things shall be common; and there must needs follow all mischief, and utter destruction, both of souls, bodies, goods, and commonwealths.

But blessed be God! that we in this realm of England, feel not the horrible calamities, miseries, and wretchedness, which all they undoubtedly feel and suffer, that lack this godly order. And praised be God! that we know the great excellent benefit of God, showed toward us in his behalf. God hath sent us his high gift, our most dear sovereign Lady Queen Elizabeth, with a godly, wise, and honourable council, with other superiors and inferiors, in a beautiful order, and goodly. Wherefore let us subjects do our bounden duties, giving hearty thanks to God, and praying for the preservation of this godly order. Let us all obey, even from the bottom of our hearts, all their godly proceedings, laws, statutes, proclamations, and injunctions, with all other their godly order. Let us consider the Scriptures of the Holy Ghost, which persuade and command us all, obediently to be subject, first and chiefly to the Queen's Majesty, Supreme Governor over all, and next to her honourable council, and to all other noblemen, magistrates, and officers, which by God's goodness, be placed and ordered.

For Almighty God, is the only author and provider, of this forenamed state and order; as it is written of God, in the Book of Proverbs: *Through me kings do reign; through me counsellors make just laws: through me do princes bear rule, and all judges of the earth execute judgement: I am loving to them that love me.* Here let us mark well and remember, that the high power and authority of kings, with their making of laws, judgements, and officers, are the ordinances, not of man, but of God; and therefore is this word, *Through me,* so many times repeated. Here is also well to be considered, and remembered, that this good order is appointed of God's wisdom, favour, and love, specially for them that love God; and therefore he saith, *I love them that love me.* Prov. 8:15–17

Also in the Book of Wisdom, we may evidently learn that a king's power, authority, and strength, is a great benefit of God, given of his great mercy, to the comfort of our great misery. For thus we read there spoken to kings: *Hear, O ye kings, and understand; learn, ye that be judges of the ends of the earth; give ear, ye that rule the multitudes: for the power is given you, of the Lord, and the strength from the Highest.* Let us learn also here, by the infallible word of God, that kings, and other their officers, are ordained of God, who is Most Highest; and therefore they are here diligently taught, to apply and give themselves, to knowledge and wisdom, necessary for the ordering of God's people, to their governance committed. And they be here also taught, by Almighty God, that they should acknowledge themselves, to have all their power and strength, not from Rome, but immediately of God Most Highest. Wisd. 6:1–3

We read in the Book of Deuteronomy, that all punishment pertaineth to God, by this sentence: *Vengeance is mine, and I will reward*. But this sentence, we must understand to pertain also to the magistrates, which do exercise God's room, in judgement and punishing, by good and godly laws here in earth. And the places of Scripture which seem, to remove from among all Christian men, judgement, punishment, or killing ought to be understood, that no man of his own private authority, may be judge over other, may punish, or may kill, but we must refer all judgement to God, to kings and rulers, and judges under them, which be God's officers to execute justice, and by plain words of Scripture, have their authority, and use of the sword, granted from God; as we are taught by St Paul, the dear and chosen Apostle, of our Saviour Christ, whom we ought diligently to obey, even as we would obey our Saviour Christ, if he were present. Thus St Paul writeth to the Romans: *Let every soul submit himself, unto the authority of the higher powers. For there is no power, but of God: the powers that be, be ordained of God. Whosoever therefore withstandeth the power, withstandeth the ordinance of God: but they that resist, shall receive to themselves damnation. For rulers are not fearful to them that do good, but to them that do evil. Wilt thou be without fear of that power? do well then, and so shalt thou be praised of the same: for he is the minister of God, for thy wealth. But and if thou do that which is evil, then fear: for he beareth not the sword for naught; for he is the minister of God, to take vengeance, on him that doeth evil. Wherefore ye must needs obey, not only for fear of vengeance, but also because of conscience. And even for this cause, pay ye tribute: for they are God's ministers, serving for the same purpose.*

Here let us all learn of St Paul, the *chosen vessel* of God, that all persons having souls (he excepteth none, nor exempteth none, neither priest, apostle, nor prophet, saith St Chrysostom), do owe, of bounden duty, and even in conscience, obedience, submission, and subjection to the high powers, which be set in authority by God; forasmuch as they be God's lieutenants, God's presidents, God's officers, God's commissioners, God's judges, ordained of God himself, of whom only, they have all their power, and all their authority. And the same St Paul, threateneth no less pain, than everlasting damnation, to all disobedient persons, to all resisters, against this general and common authority; forasmuch as they resist not man, but God; not man's device and invention, but God's wisdom, God's order, power, and authority.

Deut. 32:35

Rom. 13:1–6

Acts 9:15

THE SECOND PART OF
THE SERMON OF OBEDIENCE

FORASMUCH AS GOD hath created, and disposed all things, in a comely order, we have been taught in the first part of this Sermon, concerning good Order and Obedience, that we also ought, in all commonwealths, to observe and keep a due order, and to be obedient to the powers, their ordinances and laws; and that all rulers are appointed of God, for a godly order, to be kept in the world; and also how the magistrates, ought to learn how to rule and govern, according to God's laws; and that all subjects, are bounden to obey them as God's ministers, yet although they be evil, not only for fear, but also for conscience' sake.

And here, good people, let us all mark diligently, that it is not lawful, for inferiors and subjects in any case, to resist the superior powers: for St Paul's words be plain, that *whosoever withstandeth, shall get to themselves* | Rom. 13:2
damnation; for *whosoever withstandeth, withstandeth the ordinance of God.* Our Saviour Christ himself, and his Apostles, received many and divers injuries, of the unfaithful and wicked men in authority: yet we never read, that they, or any or them, caused any sedition or rebellion, against authority. We read oft, that they patiently suffered all troubles, vexations, slanders, pangs, and pains, and death itself, obediently, without tumult or resistance. They *committed their cause, to him that judgeth righteously*, | 1 Pet. 2:23
and prayed for their enemies, heartily and earnestly. They knew, that the authority of the powers, was God's ordinance; and therefore, both in their words and deeds, they taught ever, obedience to it, and never taught nor did the contrary. The wicked judge Pilate said to Christ, *Knowest thou not, that I have power to crucify thee, and have power also to* | John 19:10, 11
loose thee? Jesus answered, Thou couldest have no power at all against me, except it were given thee, from above. Whereby Christ taught us plainly, that even the wicked rulers, have their power and authority from God. And therefore it is not lawful for their subjects, by force to withstand them, although they abuse their power; much less then it is lawful for subjects, to withstand their godly and Christian princes, which do not abuse their authority, but use the same to God's glory, and to the profit and commodity of God's people.

The holy Apostle St Peter, commandeth servants to be obedient to their masters, *not only if they be good and gentle, but also if they be evil and* | 1 Pet. 2:18–21
froward, affirming that the vocation and calling, of God's people, is to be patient, and of the suffering side. And there he bringeth in, the patience of our Saviour Christ, to persuade obedience to governors, yea, although they be wicked, and wrong doers. But let us now hear St Peter himself speak, for his own words certify best our conscience. Thus he

uttereth them, in his first Epistle: *Servants, obey your masters with fear, not only if they are good and gentle, but also if they be froward. For it is thankworthy, if a man for conscience toward God, endureth grief, and suffereth wrong undeserved. For what praise is it, when ye be beaten for your faults, if ye take it patiently? But when ye do well, if you then suffer wrong, and take it patiently, then is there cause, to have thank of God. For hereunto verily were ye called: for so did Christ suffer for us, leaving us an example, that we should follow his steps.* All these be the very words of St Peter.

I Sam. 18, 19, 20

St David also teacheth us a good lesson in this behalf: who was many times, most cruelly and wrongfully persecuted, of King Saul, and many times also, put in jeopardy, and danger of his life, by King Saul and his people; yet he never withstood, neither used any force, or violence against King Saul, his mortal enemy, but did ever to his liege lord and master, King Saul, most true, most diligent, and most faithful service. Insomuch that, when the Lord God had given King Saul, into David's I Sam. 24 hands, in his own cave, he would not hurt him, when he might without all bodily peril, easily have slain him; no, he would not suffer any of his servants, once to lay their hands upon King Saul, but prayed to God, in this wise: *Lord, keep me from doing that thing unto my master, the Lord's anointed; keep me that I lay not my hand upon him, seeing he is the anointed, of the Lord. For, as truly as the Lord liveth, except the Lord smite him, or except his day come, or that he go down to war, and in battle perish, the Lord be merciful unto me, that I lay not my hand upon the Lord's anointed.* And that David might have killed his enemy King Saul, it is evidently proved, in the first Book of the Kings, both by the cutting off the lap of Saul's garment, and also by the plain confession of King Saul. Also another Ibid. 26:7–12 time, as it is mentioned in the same Book, when the most unmerciful, and most unkind King Saul, did persecute poor David, God did again, give King Saul into David's hands, by casting of King Saul and his whole army, into a dead sleep; so that David, and one Abisai with him, came in the night into Saul's host, where *Saul lay sleeping, and his spear stack in the ground, at his head. Then said Abisai unto David, "God hath delivered thine enemy, into thy hands at this time: now therefore let me smite him once, with my spear to the earth, and I will not smite him again, the second time"*; meaning thereby to have killed him, with one stroke, and to have made him sure for ever. *And David* answered, and *said to Abisai, "Destroy him not: for who can lay his hands, on the Lord's anointed, and be guiltless?" And David said furthermore, "As sure as the Lord liveth, the Lord shall smite him, or his day shall come to die, or he shall descend into battle, and there perish. The Lord keep me, from laying my hands upon the Lord's anointed: but take thou now, the spear that is at his head, and the cruse of water, and let us go"*: and so he did. Here is evidently proved, that we may not withstand, nor in any ways hurt an anointed king; which is

God's lieutenant, vicegerent, and highest minister, in that country where he is king.

But peradventure some here would say, that David in his own defence, might have killed King Saul lawfully, and with a safe conscience. But holy David did know, that he might in no wise withstand, hurt, or kill his sovereign lord and king: he did know, that he was but King Saul's subject, though he were in great favour with God, and his enemy King Saul, out of God's favour. Therefore, though he were never so much provoked, yet he refused utterly, to hurt the Lord's anointed. He durst not, for offending God and his own conscience (although he had occasion and opportunity), once lay his hands, upon God's high officer the King, whom he did know to be a person reserved, and kept for his office' sake, only to God's punishment and judgement. Therefore he prayeth, so oft and so earnestly, that he lay not his hands, upon the Lord's anointed. And by these two examples, St David, being named in Scripture *a man after God's own heart*, giveth a general rule and lesson, to all subjects in the world, not to withstand, their liege lord and king, not to take a sword, by their private authority, against their king, God's anointed; who only, beareth the sword by God's authority, for the maintenance of the good, and for the punishment of the evil; who only, by God's law, hath the use of the sword, at his commandment, and also hath all power, jurisdiction, regiment, coercion, and punishment, as supreme governor, of all his realms and dominions, and that, even by the authority of God, and by God's ordinances.

Yet another notable story and doctrine, is in the second Book of the Kings, that maketh also for this purpose. When an Amalechite, by King Saul's own consent and commandment, had killed King Saul, he went to David, supposing to have had great thank, for his message that he had killed David's deadly enemy; and therefore he made great haste, to tell to David the chance, bringing with him, King Saul's crown that was upon his head, and his bracelet, that was upon his arm, to persuade his tidings to be true. But godly David, was so far from rejoicing at this news, that immediately and forthwith, he rent his clothes, off his back, he mourned and wept, and said to the messenger, *How is it, that thou wast not afraid, to lay thy hand on the Lord's anointed, to destroy him?* And by and by, David made one of his servants, to kill the messenger, saying, *Thy blood be on thine own head; for thy own mouth, hath testified against thee, granting that thou hast slain, the Lord's anointed.*

These examples being so manifest and evident, it is an intolerable ignorance, madness, and wickedness, for subjects to make any murmuring, rebellion, resistance, commotion, or insurrection, against their most dear, and most dread, sovereign lord and king, ordained and appointed of God's goodness, for their commodity, peace, and quietness.

Marginal notes:

Objection
Answer

Psalm 89:3, 20–6

2 Sam. 1:1–16

Yet let us believe undoubtedly, good Christian people, that we may not obey, kings, magistrates, or any other, though they be our own fathers, if they would command us, to do any thing contrary to God's commandments. In such a case, we ought to say with the Apostles, *We must rather obey God, than man.* But nevertheless, in that case, we may not in any wise, withstand violently, or rebel against rulers, or make any insurrection, sedition, or tumults, either by force of arms, or other ways, against the anointed of the Lord, or any of his appointed officers; but we must in such case, patiently suffer all wrongs and injuries, referring the judgement of our cause, only to God. Let us fear, the terrible punishment of Almighty God, against traitors or rebellious persons, by the example of Core, Dathan, and Abiron, which repugned and grudged against God's magistrates and officers, and therefore the earth opened, and swallowed them up alive. Other for their wicked murmuring and rebellion, were by a sudden fire, sent of God, utterly consumed. Other for their froward behaviour, to their rulers and governors, God's ministers, were suddenly, stricken with a foul leprosy. Other were stinged to death, with wonderful strange, fiery serpents. Other were sore plagued, so that there was killed in one day, the number of fourteen thousand and seven hundred, for rebellion against them, whom God had appointed, to be in authority. Absalon also rebelling, against his father King David, was punished with a strange and notable death.

Acts 5:29

Num. 16:1–33

Ibid. 11:1

Ibid. 12:1–10

Ibid. 21:5, 6

Ibid. 16:41–9

2 Sam. 18:9, 10

THE THIRD PART OF
THE SERMON OF OBEDIENCE

YE HAVE HEARD BEFORE, in this Sermon of Good Order and Obedience, manifestly proved, both by Scriptures and examples, that all subjects are bounden, to obey their magistrates, and for no cause to resist, rebel, or make any sedition against them, yea, although they be wicked men. And let no man think, that he can escape unpunished, that committeth treason, conspiracy, or rebellion, against his sovereign lord the King, though he commit the same, never so secretly, either in thought, word, or deed, never so privily, in his privy chamber by himself, or openly communicating, and consulting with others. For treason will not be hid; treason will out at length. God will have that most detestable vice, both opened and punished; for that it is so directly against his ordinance, and against his high principal judge, and anointed, in earth. The violence and injury, that is committed against authority, is committed against God, the common weal, and the whole realm; which God will have known, and condignly punished, one way or other. For it is notably

written of the Wise Man, in Scripture, in the book called Ecclesiastes,   Eccles. 10:20
Wish the King no evil in thy thought, nor speak no hurt of him in thy privy
chamber; for a bird of the air, shall betray thy voice, and with her feathers,
shall she bewray thy words.

These lessons and examples, are written for our learning. Let us all
therefore fear, the most detestable vice of rebellion, ever knowing and
remembering, that he that resisteth common authority, resisteth God
and his ordinance, as it may be proved, by many other mo places, of holy
Scripture.

And here let us take heed, that we understand not these, or such other
like places, which so straitly command obedience to superiors, and so
straitly punished rebellion and disobedience to the same, to be meant,
in any condition, of the pretensed power, of the Bishop of Rome. For
truly, the Scripture of God, alloweth no such usurped power, full of
enormities, abusions, and blasphemies: but the true meaning of these,
and such places, be to extol and set forth, God's true ordinance, and the
authority of God's anointed kings, and of their officers appointed under
them.

And concerning the usurped power of the Bishop of Rome, which he
most wrongfully challengeth, as the successor of Christ, and Peter: we
may easily perceive how false, feigned, and forged it is, not only in that,
it hath no sufficient ground in holy Scripture, but also, by the fruits and
doctrine thereof. For our Saviour Christ and St Peter, teach most
earnestly and agreeably obedience to kings, as to the chief and supreme
rulers in this world, next under God. But the Bishop of Rome teacheth
immunities, privileges, exemptions, and disobedience, most clearly
against Christ's doctrine, and St Peter's. He ought therefore rather to be
called Antichrist, and the successor of the Scribes and Pharisees, than
Christ's vicar, or St Peter's successor, seeing that, not only in this point,
but also in other weighty matters of Christian religion, in matters of
remission of sins, and of salvation, he teacheth so directly against, both
St Peter, and against our Saviour Christ. Who not only taught obedience
to kings, but also practised obedience, in their conversation and living.
For we read that they both paid tribute to the King. And also we read,   Matt. 17:24–7
that the holy Virgin Mary, mother to our Saviour Christ, and Joseph,
who was taken for his father, at the Emperor's commandment, went to
the city of David, named Bethleem, to be taxed among other, and to
declare their obedience, to the Magistrates, for God's ordinances' sake.
And here let us not forget the blessed Virgin Mary's obedience: for   Luke 2:4–7
although, she was highly in God's favour, and Christ's natural mother,
and was also great with child that same time, and so nigh her travail, that
she was delivered in her journey: yet, she gladly without any excuse or
grudging (for conscience sake) did take that cold and foul winter

journey, being in the mean season so poor, that she lay in the stable, and there she was delivered of Christ.

Luke 12:14
John 6:15

Luke 22:25–6

Our Saviour Christ refused the office of a worldly judge, and so he did the office of a worldly king: commanding his disciples, and all that believe in him, that they should not contend for superiority, neither for worldly dominion in this world. For ambition and pride is detestable in all Christian persons of every degree. And the Apostles in that place, do not represent the persons of bishops, and priests only, but also (as ancient authors do write) they represent the persons of kings and princes: whose worldly rule and governance, they then ambitiously desired. So that in that place Christ teacheth also Christian emperors, kings and princes, that they should not rule their subjects by will, and to their own commodity, and pleasure only: but that they should govern their subjects, by good and godly laws. They should not make themselves so to be lords over the people, to do with them and their goods what they list, and to make what laws they list, without dread of God and of his laws, without consideration of their honour and office, whereunto God hath called them, (as heathen kings and princes do) but to think themselves to be God's officers, ordained by God to be his ministers unto the people, for their salvation, common quietness and wealth: to punish malefactors, to defend innocents, and to cherish welldoers.*

1 Pet. 2:13–15

And according to the same: lo, how St Peter agreeth, writing by express words, in his first Epistle: *Submit yourselves*, saith he, *unto kings, as unto the chief heads, or unto rulers, as unto them that are sent of him, for the punishment of evil doers, and for the praise of them that do well: for so is the will of God.* I need not expound these words, they be so plain of themselves. St Peter doth not say, Submit yourselves unto me, as supreme head of the Church; neither he saith, Submit yourselves from time to time, to my successors in Rome: but he saith, *Submit yourselves unto your king, your supreme head*, and unto those that he appointeth, in authority under him; *for* that ye shall so show your obedience, *it is the will of God*; God will, that you be in subjection to your head and king. This is God's ordinance, God's commandment, and God's holy will, that the whole body of every realm, and all the members and parts of the same,

1 Pet. 2:13

Rom. 13:7

shall be subject to their head, their king; and that, as St Peter writeth, *for the Lord's sake*, and, as St Paul writeth, *for conscience sake*, and not for fear only.

Matt. 22:21
Rom. 13:7

Thus we learn, by the word of God, to yield to our king, that is due to our king, that is, honour, obedience, payments of due taxes, customs, tributes, subsidies, love, and fear.

---

* This paragraph is found only in one issue of the first Grafton edition of 1547. The punctuation (but not capitalisation) of this and the preceding paragraph is original, as in the Bodleian Library copy.

Thus we know partly our bounden duties to common authority: now let us learn, to accomplish the same. And let us most instantly and heartily, pray to God, the only author of all authority, for all them that be in authority; according as St Paul willeth, writing thus to Timothy in his first Epistle. *I exhort therefore that, above all things, prayers, supplic-*   1 Tim. 2:1–3
ations, intercessions, and giving of thanks, be done for all men, for kings, and for all that be in authority, that we may live a quiet, and a peaceable life, with all godliness and honesty: for that is good, and accepted in the sight of God, our Saviour. Here St Paul maketh an earnest and an especial exhortation, concerning giving of thanks, and prayer for kings and rulers, saying, *Above all things*, as he might say, In any wise principally and chiefly, *let prayer be made for kings.* Let us heartily thank God, for his great and excellent benefit and providence, concerning the state of kings. Let us pray for them, that they may have God's favour, and God's protection. Let us pray, that they may ever in all things, have God before their eyes. Let us pray that they may have wisdom, strength, justice, clemency, zeal to God's glory, to God's verity, to Christian souls, and to the common wealth. Let us pray that they may rightly, use their sword and authority, for the maintenance and defence of the catholic faith, contained in holy Scripture, and of their good and honest subjects, and for the fear and punishment, of the evil and vicious people. Let us pray that they may faithfully, follow the most faithful kings and captains in the Bible, David, Ezechias, Josias, Moses, with such other. And let us pray for ourselves, that we may live godly in holy and Christian conversation: so we shall have God on our side; and then let us not fear, what man can do   Judith 5:17, 21
against us: so we shall live in true obedience, both to our most merciful King in heaven, and to our most Christian Queen in earth: so shall we please God, and have the exceeding benefit, peace of conscience, rest, and quietness, here in this world; and after this life we shall enjoy a better life, rest, peace, and the everlasting bliss of heaven. Which he grant us all, that was *obedient* for us all, *even to the death of the cross,* Jesus   Phil. 2:8
Christ: to whom, with the Father, and the Holy Ghost, be all honour and glory both now and ever. Amen.

A SERMON
AGAINST WHOREDOM
AND UNCLEANNESS

ALTHOUGH THERE WANT NOT, good Christian people, great swarms of vices, worthy to be rebuked, unto such decay is true godliness, and virtuous living now come, yet above all other vices, the outrageous seas of adultery (or breaking of wedlock), whoredom, fornication, and uncleanness have not only burst in, but also overflowed, almost the whole world, unto the great dishonour of God, the exceeding infamy of the name of Christ, the notable decay of true religion, and the utter destruction of the public wealth; and that so abundantly, that through the customable use thereof, this vice is grown, into such an height, that in a manner, among many it is counted no sin at all, but rather a pastime, a dalliance, and but a touch of youth; not rebuked, but winked at; not punished, but laughed at. Wherefore it is necessary at this present, to intreat of the sin, of whoredom and fornication, declaring unto you, the greatness of this sin, and how odious, hateful, and abominable it is, and hath alway been reputed, before God and all good men, and how grievously it hath been punished, both by the law of God, and the laws of divers princes; again, to show you certain remedies, whereby ye may through the grace of God, eschew this most detestable sin, of whoredom and fornication, and lead your lives, in all honesty and cleanness.

And that ye may perceive, that fornication and whoredom, are in the sight of God, most abominable sins, ye shall call to remembrance, this commandment of God, *Thou shalt not commit adultery*. By the which word *adultery*, although it be properly understood of the unlawful commixtion (or joining together), of a married man with any woman beside his wife, or of a wife, with any man beside her husband: yet thereby is signified also, all unlawful use of those parts which be ordained for generation. And this one commandment forbidding adultery, doth sufficiently paint and set out before our eyes, the greatness of this sin of whoredom, and manifestly declareth how greatly, it ought to be abhorred,

Exod. 20:14

of all honest and faithful persons. And, that none of us all shall think himself excepted, from this commandment, whether we be old or young, married or unmarried, man or woman, hear what God the Father saith, by his most excellent Prophet Moses: *There shall be no whore, among the daughters of Israel, nor no whoremonger, among the sons of Israel.* Deut. 23:17

Here is whoredom, fornication, and all uncleanness, forbidden to all kinds of people, all degrees, and all ages, without exception. And that we shall not doubt, but that this precept pertaineth to us indeed, hear what Christ, the perfect Teacher of all truth, saith in the New Testament. *Ye have heard*, saith Christ, *that it was said to them of the old time, Thou shalt not commit adultery: but I say unto you, Whosoever seeth a woman, to have his lust of her, hath committed adultery with her, already in his heart.* Here our Saviour Christ, doth not only confirm and stablish, the law against adultery, given in the Old Testament of God the Father, by his servant Moses, and maketh it of full strength, continually to remain, among the professors of his Name in the new law; but he also— condemning the gross interpretation, of the Scribes and Pharisees, which taught that the aforesaid commandment, only required to abstain from the outward adultery, and not from the filthy desires and unpure lusts—teacheth us an exact and full perfection of purity, and cleanness of life, both to keep our bodies undefiled, and our hearts pure and free from all evil thoughts, carnal desires, and fleshly consents. How can we then be free from this commandment, where so great charge is laid upon us? May a servant do what he will in any thing, having a commandment of his master, to the contrary? Is not Christ our Master? are not we his servants? How then may we neglect our Master's will and pleasure, and follow our own will and phantasy? *Ye are my friends*, saith Christ, *if you keep those things that I command you.* Now hath Christ our Master commanded us, that we should forsake all uncleanness and lechery, both in body and spirit: this therefore must we do, if we look to please God. Matt. 5:27–8 John 15:14

In the Gospel of St Matthew we read, that the Scribes and Pharisees were grievously offended with Christ, because his disciples did not keep the traditions of the forefathers, for they washed not their hands, when they went to dinner or supper; and among other things Christ answered and said, *Hear and understand. Not that thing which entereth into the mouth, defileth the man, but that which cometh out of the mouth, defileth the man. For those things which proceed out of the mouth, come forth from the heart, and they defile the man. For out of the heart, proceed evil thoughts, murders, breaking of wedlock, whoredom, thefts, false witness, blasphemies. These are the things which defile a man.* Here may we see, that not only murder, theft, false witness, and blasphemy, defile men, but also evil thoughts, breaking of wedlock, fornication, and whoredom. Matt. 15:1–20

Who is now of so little wit, that he will esteem whoredom, and fornication, to be things of small importance, and of no weight before God? Christ, which is *the Truth*, and *cannot lie*, saith that evil thoughts, breaking of wedlock, whoredom, and fornication, defile a man, that is to say, corrupt both the body and the soul of man, and make them, of the temples of the Holy Ghost, the filthy dunghill or dungeon, of all unclean spirits; of the mansion of God, the dwelling place of Satan.

Again, in the Gospel of St John, when the woman taken in adultery, was brought unto Christ, said not he unto her, *Go thy way, and sin no more?* Doth not he here call whoredom, sin? And what is *the reward of sin*, but everlasting *death?* If whoredom be sin, then is it not lawful for us to commit it. For St John saith, *He that committeth sin, is of the devil*. And our Saviour saith, *Every one that committeth sin, is the servant of sin*. If whoredom had not been sin, surely St John Baptist, would never have rebuked King Herod, for taking his brother's wife: but he told him plainly, that it was not lawful for him, to take his brother's wife. He winked not at that whoredom of Herod, although he were a king of great power, but boldly reproved him, for his wicked and abominable living, although for the same he lost his head. But he would rather suffer death than see God so dishonoured, by the breaking of his holy precept; than to suffer whoredom to be unrebuked, even in a king. If whoredom had been but a pastime, a dalliance, and a thing not to be passed of, as many count it nowadays, truly John had been more than twice mad, if he would have had the displeasure of a king, if he would have been cast into prison, and lost his head for a trifle. But John knew right well, how filthy, stinking, and abominable, the sin of whoredom is, in the sight of God: therefore would not he leave it unrebuked, no not in a king. If whoredom be not lawful in a king, neither is it lawful in a subject. If whoredom be not lawful in a public officer, neither is it lawful in a private person. If it be not lawful, neither in king nor subject, neither in common officer nor private person, truly, then is it lawful in no man, nor woman, of whatsoever degree or age they be.

Furthermore, in the Acts of the Apostles we read, that when the Apostles and elders, with the whole congregation, were gathered together, to pacify the hearts of the faithful, dwelling at Antioch, which were disquieted, through the false doctrine of certain Jewish preachers, they sent word to the brethren, that it seemed good to the Holy Ghost, and to them, to charge them, with no more than with necessary things; among other, they willed them, to abstain from idolatry and fornication; *from which*, said they, *if ye keep yourselves, ye shall do well*. Note here, how these holy and blessed fathers of Christ's Church, would charge the congregation, with no mo things than were necessary. Mark also how, among those things, from the which they commanded the brethren of

Marginal references:
John 14:6;
Titus 1:2

John 8:11

Rom. 6:23

1 John 3:8

John 8:34;
Rom. 6:16

Matt. 14:3–10

Acts 15:22–9

Antioch to abstain, fornication and whoredom, is numbered. It is therefore necessary, by the determination and consent of the Holy Ghost, and the Apostles and elders, with the whole congregation, that as from idolatry and superstition, so likewise we must abstain, from fornication and whoredom. Is it necessary unto salvation, to abstain from idolatry? So is it, to abstain from whoredom. Is there any nigher way to lead unto damnation, than to be an idolater? No. Even so, neither is there a nearer way to damnation, than to be a fornicator, and an whoremonger. Now where are those people, which so lightly esteem breaking of wedlock, whoredom, fornication, and adultery? It is necessary, saith the Holy Ghost, and blessed Apostles, the elders, with the whole congregation of Christ; it is necessary to salvation, say they, to abstain from whoredom. If it be necessary unto salvation, then woe be to them, which neglecting their salvation, give their minds to so filthy and stinking sin, to so wicked vice, to such detestable abomination.

THE SECOND PART OF
THE SERMON AGAINST ADULTERY

YOU HAVE BEEN TAUGHT, in the first part of this Sermon against Adultery, how that vice, at this day reigneth most, above all other vices, and what is meant by this word Adultery, and how holy Scripture dissuadeth, from doing that filthy sin, and finally what corruption cometh to man's soul, through the sin of adultery.

Now to proceed further, let us hear, what the blessed Apostle St Paul saith to this matter. Writing to the Romans he hath these words: *Let us*   Rom. 13:12–14
cast away the works of darkness, and put on the armour of light. Let us walk honestly, as it were in the daytime, not in eating and drinking, neither in chamberings and wantonness, neither in strife and envying: but put ye on the Lord Jesus Christ, and make not provision for the flesh, to fulfil the lusts of it. Here the holy Apostle exhorteth us, to cast away the works of darkness; which among other, he calleth gluttonous eating, drinking, chambering, and wantonness; which all are ministers unto that vice, and preparations to induce and bring in, the filthy sin of the flesh. He calleth them, the deeds and works of darkness, not only because they are customably done in darkness, or in the night time (*for everyone that doeth evil, hateth*   John 3:20
the light, neither cometh he to the light, lest his works should be reproved), but that they lead the right way, unto that *utter darkness, where weeping and*   Matt. 13:42, 50
gnashing of teeth shall be. And he saith in another place, of the same Epistle, *They that are in the flesh, cannot please God. We are debtors not to the*   Rom. 8:8, 12, 13
flesh, that we should live after the flesh: for, if ye live after the flesh, ye shall die.

1 Cor. 6:18–20

Again he saith, *Fly from whoredom. For every sin that a man committeth, is without his body; but whosoever committeth whoredom, sinneth against his own body. Do ye not know, that your members are the temple of the Holy Ghost, which is in you, whom also ye have of God, and ye are not your own? for ye are dearly bought. Glorify God in your body,* &c. And a little before he saith,

Ibid.:15–17

Do ye not know, that your bodies are the members of Christ? Shall I then take the members of Christ, and make them the members of an whore? God forbid. Do ye not know, that he which cleaveth to an whore, is made one body with her? There shall be two in one flesh, saith he. *But he that cleaveth to the Lord, is one spirit.* What godly reasons doth the blessed Apostle St Paul bring

1 Cor. 3:17

forth here, to dissuade us from whoredom, and all uncleanness! *Your members,* saith he, *are the temple of the Holy Ghost: which whosoever doth defile, God will destroy him,* as saith St Paul. If we be the temple of the Holy Ghost, how unfitting then is it, to drive that Holy Spirit from us, through whoredom, and in his place, to set the wicked spirits of uncleanness and fornication, and to be joined and do service to them! *Ye are dearly bought,* saith he: *therefore glorify God in your bodies.* Christ, that innocent Lamb of God, hath bought us from the servitude of the

1 Pet. 1:18, 19

devil, *not with corruptible gold and silver, but with his most precious* and dear heart *blood.* To what intent? That we should fall again, unto our old uncleanness and abominable living? Nay verily: but that we should *serve*

Luke 1:74, 75,

him all the days of our life, in holiness and righteousness, that we should

Isai. 38:20

glorify him in our bodies, by purity and cleanness of life. He declareth also, that *our bodies are the members of Christ.* How unseemly a thing is it then, to cease to be incorporate, and one with Christ, and through whoredom, to be joined and made all one with an whore! What greater dishonour or injury, can we do to Christ, than to take away from him, the members of his body, and to join them to whores, devils, and wicked spirits? And what more dishonour can we do to ourselves, than through uncleanness, to lose so excellent a dignity and freedom, and to become bondslaves, and miserable captives to the spirits of darkness? Let us therefore consider first, the glory of Christ, and then our estate, our dignity, and freedom, wherein God hath set us, by giving us his Holy Spirit; and let us valiantly defend the same, against Satan and all his crafty assaults, that Christ may be honoured, and that we lose not our liberty, but still remain in one spirit with him.

Eph. 5:3–5

Moreover, in his Epistle to the Ephesians, the blessed Apostle willeth us to be so pure, and free from adultery, *fornication, and all uncleanness, that we not once name them among us, as it becometh saints; nor filthiness, nor foolish talking, nor jesting, which are not comely; but rather giving of thanks. For this ye know,* saith he, *that no whoremonger, either unclean person, or*

Gal. 5:19–21

covetous person, which is an idolater, hath any inheritance, in the kingdom of Christ and God. And that we should remember to be holy, pure, and free

from all uncleanness, the holy Apostle calleth us *saints*, because we are
sanctified, and made holy in the blood of Christ, through the Holy
Ghost. Now if we be saints, what have we to do with the manners of the
heathen? St Peter saith, *As he which called you is holy, even so be ye holy
also, in all your conversation; because it is written, Be ye holy, for I am holy.*

1 Cor. 6:11

1 Pet. 1:15,
Lev. 11:44, 19:2

Hitherto have we heard, how grievous a sin, fornication and
whoredom is, and how greatly God doth abhor it, throughout the whole
Scripture. How can it any otherwise be, than a sin of most abomination,
seeing it once may not be named, among the Christians, much less it
may in any point be committed? And surely, if we would weigh the
greatness of this sin, and consider it in the right kind, we should find the
sin of whoredom, to be that most filthy lake, foul puddle, and stinking
sink, whereinto all kinds of sins and evils flow, where also they have their
resting place, and abiding. For hath not the adulterer a pride in his
whoredom? As the Wise Man saith: *They are glad when they have done
evil, and rejoice in things that are stark naught.* Is not the adulterer also
idle, and delighteth in no godly exercise, but only in that his most filthy
and beastly pleasure? Is not his mind plucked, and utterly drawn away,
from all virtuous studies, and fruitful labours, and only given to carnal,
and fleshly imaginations? Doth not the whoremonger, give his mind to
gluttony, that he may be the more apt, to serve his lusts and carnal
pleasures? Doth not the adulterer, give his mind to covetousness, and to
polling and pilling of other, that he may be the more able, to maintain
his harlots and whores, and to continue, in his filthy and unlawful love?
Swelleth he not also, with envy against other, fearing that his prey
should be allured, and taken away from him? Again, is he not ireful, and
replenished with wrath and displeasure, even against his best beloved, if
at any time, his beastly and devilish request be letted? What sin or kind
of sin is it, that is not joined with fornication and whoredom? It is a
monster of many heads. It receiveth all kinds of vices, and refuseth all
kinds of virtues. If one several sin bringeth damnation, what is to be
thought of that sin, which is accompanied with all evils, and hath
waiting on it, whatsoever is hateful to God, damnable to man, and
pleasant to Satan?

Prov. 2:14

Great is the damnation, that hangeth over the heads of fornicators
and adulterers. What shall I speak of other incommodities, which issue
and flow out of this stinking puddle, of whoredom? Is not that treasure,
which before all other, is most regarded of honest persons, the good
fame and name, of man and woman, lost, through whoredom? What
patrimony, what substance, what goods, what riches, doth whoredom
shortly consume, and bring to naught! What valiantness and strength, is
many times made weak, and destroyed with whoredom! What wit is so
fine, that it is not doted and defaced, through whoredom? What beauty,

although it were never so excellent, is not disfigured, through whoredom? Is not whoredom, an enemy to the pleasant flower of youth? and bringeth it not grey hairs, and old age before the time? What gift of nature, although it were never so precious, is not corrupted with whoredom? Come not the French pocks, with other diverse diseases, of whoredom? From whence come so many bastards, and misbegotten children, to the high displeasure of God, and dishonour of holy wedlock, but of whoredom? How many consume all their substance and goods, and at the last fall into such extreme poverty, that afterward they steal, and so are hanged, through whoredom! What contention and manslaughter cometh of whoredom! How many maidens be deflowered, how many wives corrupted, how many widows defiled, through whoredom! How much is the public and common weal impoverished, and troubled through whoredom! How much is God's word contemned, and depraved, by whoredom and whoremongers!

Of this vice, cometh a great part of the divorces, which nowadays be so commonly accustomed, and used by men's private authority, to the great displeasure of God, and the breach of the most holy knot and bond, of matrimony. For when this most detestable sin, is once crept into the breast of the adulterer, so that he is entangled, with unlawful and unchaste love, straightways his true and lawful wife, is despised; her presence is abhorred; her company stinketh, and is loathsome; whatsoever she doeth is dispraised; there is no quietness in the house, so long as she is in sight: therefore to make short tale, must she away, for her husband can brook her no longer. Thus through whoredom, is the honest and harmless wife put away, and an harlot received in her stead: and in like sort, it happeneth many times in the wife, towards her husband. Oh abomination! Christ our Saviour, very God and man, coming to restore the law of his heavenly Father, unto the right sense, understanding, and meaning, among other things, reformed the abuse of this law of God. For whereas the Jews used, of a long sufferance, by custom to put away their wives, at their pleasure for every cause, Christ correcting that evil custom, did teach, that if any man put away his wife, and marrieth another, for any cause, except only for adultery (which then was death by the law), he was an adulterer; and forced also his wife, so divorced, to commit adultery, if she were joined to any other man; and the man also so joined with her, to commit adultery. In what case then are those adulterers, which for the love of an whore, put away their true and lawful wife, against all law, right, reason, and conscience? Oh damnable is the state, wherein they stand! Swift destruction shall fall on them, if they repent not, and amend not. For God will not ever suffer, holy wedlock thus to be dishonoured, hated, and despised. He will once punish, this fleshly and licentious manner of living, and cause that his

Matt. 19:8, 9

holy ordinance, shall be had in reverence and honour. For surely *wedlock*, as the Apostle saith, *is honourable among all men, and the bed* Heb. 13:4 *undefiled; but whoremongers and fornicators, God will judge*, that is to say, punish and condemn.

But to what purpose is this labour taken, to describe and set forth the greatness of the sin of whoredom, and the incommodities that issue and flow out of it, seeing that breath and tongue shall sooner fail any man, than he shall or may be able, to set it out according to the abomination, and heinousness thereof? Notwithstanding, this is spoken to the intent, that all men should flee whoredom, and live in the fear of God. God grant, that it may not be spoken in vain!

THE THIRD PART OF
THE SERMON AGAINST ADULTERY

IN THE SECOND PART of this Sermon against Adultery, that was last read, you have learned how earnestly, the Scripture warneth us to avoid the sin of adultery, and to embrace cleanness of life; and that through adultery, we fall into all kinds of sins, and are made bondslaves to the devil; through cleanness of life, we are made members of Christ; and finally how far adultery bringeth a man, from all goodness, and driveth him headlong, into all vices, mischief, and misery. Now will I declare unto you in order, with what grievous punishments, God in times past plagued adultery, and how certain worldly princes also, did punish it, that ye may perceive, that whoredom and fornication be sins no less detestable, in the sight of God, and all good men, than I have hitherto uttered.

In the first book of Moyses we read, that when mankind began to be Gen. 6 multiplied upon the earth, the men and women gave their minds so greatly, to fleshly delight and filthy pleasure, that they lived without all fear of God. God, seeing this their beastly and abominable living, and perceiving that they amended not, but rather increased daily more and more, in their sinful and unclean manners, repented that he ever had made man: and, to show how greatly he abhorred adultery, whoredom, fornication, and all uncleanness, he made all the fountains of the deep earth, to burst out, and the sluices of heaven to be opened, so that the rain came down upon the earth, by the space of forty days and forty nights; and by this means, destroyed the whole world, and all mankind, eight persons only excepted, that is to say, Noe, the *preacher of righteous-* 2 Pet. 2:5 *ness* (as St Peter calleth him), and his wife, his three sons and their wives. Oh what a grievous plague did God cast here, upon all living creatures, for the sin of whoredom! For the which God took vengeance, not only of man, but also of beasts, fowls, and all living creatures. Manslaughter Gen. 4

was committed before; yet was not the world destroyed for that: but for whoredom, all the world, few only except, was overflowed with waters, and so perished. An example worthy to be remembered! that ye may learn to fear God.

We read again, that for the filthy sin of uncleanness, Sodom and Gomorre, and the other cities nigh unto them, were destroyed with fire and brimstone, from heaven, so that there was neither man, woman, child, nor beast, nor any thing that grew upon the earth, there left undestroyed. Whose heart trembleth not, at the hearing of this history? Who is so drowned in whoredom and uncleanness, that will not now for ever after, leave this abominable living? seeing that God so grievously punisheth uncleanness, to rain fire and brimstone from heaven, to destroy whole cities, to kill man, woman, and child, and all other living creatures there abiding, to consume with fire, all that ever grew. What can be more manifest tokens of God's wrath, and vengeance against uncleanness, and impurity of life? Mark this history, good people, and fear the vengeance of God!

Do we not read also, that *God did smite Pharao and his house, with great plagues*, because that he ungodly desired Sara, the wife of Abraham? Likewise read we of Abimelech King of Gerar, although he touched her not by carnal knowledge.

These plagues and punishments, did God cast upon filthy and unclean persons, before the Law was given, the law of nature only, reigning in the hearts of men, to declare how great love he had, to matrimony, and again how much he abhorred adultery, fornication, and all uncleanness. And when the law that forbade whoredom, was given by Moses to the Jews, did not God command, that the breakers thereof should be put to death? The words of the law be these: *Whoso committeth adultery, with any man's wife, shall die the death, both the man and the woman, because he hath broken wedlock, with his neighbour's wife.* In the Law also it was commanded, that a damsel and a man taken together in whoredom, should be both stoned to death. In another place we also read, that God commanded Moses, to take all the head rulers and princes of the people, and to hang them upon gibbets openly, that every man might see them, because they either committed, or did not punish, whoredom. Again, did not God send such a plague among the people, for fornication and uncleanness, that they died in one day, three and twenty thousand?

I pass over for lack of time, many other histories of the holy Bible, which declare the grievous vengeance, and heavy displeasure of God, against whoremongers and adulterers. Certes this extreme punishment appointed of God, showeth evidently, how greatly God hateth whoredom.

Gen. 19:1–29

Gen. 12:14–19

Gen. 20

Lev. 20:10

Deut. 22:23, 24

Num. 25:4

Ibid.:9

And let us not doubt, but that God at this present, abhorreth all manner of uncleanness, no less than he did in the old Law, and will undoubtedly punish it, both in this world, and in the world to come. For he is a God that can abide no wickedness: therefore ought it to be eschewed, of all that tender the glory of God, and the salvation of their own souls. St Paul saith, *all these things are written for our example*, and to teach us the fear of God, and the obedience to his holy law. For, *if God spared not the natural branches*, neither will he spare us, that be but grafts, if we commit like offence. If God destroyed many thousands of people, many cities, yea, the whole world, for whoredom, let us not flatter ourselves, and think we shall escape free and without punishment. For he hath promised in his holy law, to send most grievous plagues, upon them that transgress his holy commandments.

Psalm 5:4

1 Cor. 10:6, 11

Rom. 11:21, 22

Thus have we heard, how God punisheth the sin of adultery. Let us now hear certain laws, which the civil magistrates devised in divers countries, for the punishment thereof, that we may learn how uncleanness hath ever been detested, in all well-ordered cities and commonwealths, and among all honest persons. The law among the Lepreians was this, that when any were taken in adultery, they were bound, and carried three days through the city, and afterward as long as they lived, were they despised, and with shame and confusion, counted as persons void of all honesty. Among the Locrensians, the adulterers had both their eyes thrust out. The Romans in times past, punished whoredom, sometime by fire, sometime by sword. If a man among the Egyptians, had been taken in adultery, the law was that he should openly, in the presence of all the people, be scourged naked with whips, unto the number of a thousand stripes: the woman that was taken with him, had her nose cut off, whereby she was known ever after, to be a whore, and therefore to be abhorred, of all men. Among the Arabians, they that were taken in adultery, had their heads stricken from their bodies. The Athenians punished whoredom, by death in like manner. So likewise did the barbarous Tartarians. Among the Turks even at this day, they that be taken in adultery, both man and woman, are stoned straightways to death, without mercy. Thus see we what godly acts, were devised in times past, of the high powers, for the putting away of whoredom, and for the maintaining of holy matrimony, and pure conversation. And the authors of these acts, were not Christians, but heathen: yet were they so inflamed with the love of honesty, and pureness of life, that for the maintenance and conservation of that, they made godly statutes, suffering neither fornication nor adultery, to reign in their realms unpunished.

Laws devised for the punishment of whoredom

Christ said to the people, *The Ninivites shall rise at the judgement, with this nation*, meaning the unfaithful Jews, *and shall condemn them: for they repented, at the preaching of Jonas; but behold,* saith he, *a greater than Jonas*

Matt. 12:41

is here, meaning himself, and yet they repent not. Shall not, think you, likewise the Locrensians, Arabians, Athenians, with such other, rise up at the judgement, and condemn us? forasmuch as they ceased from whoredom, at the commandment of man, and we have the law, and manifest precepts and commandments, of God, and yet forsake we not our filthy conversation. Truly, truly, it shall be easier at the day of judgement, to those heathen, than to us, except we repent and amend. For although death of body seemeth to us, a grievous punishment in this world for whoredom, yet is that pain nothing, in comparison of the grievous torments, which adulterers, fornicators, and all unclean persons shall suffer, after this life. For all such shall be excluded, and shut out of the kingdom of heaven, as St Paul saith: *Be not deceived; for neither whoremongers, nor worshippers of images, nor adulterers, nor softlings, nor sodomites, nor thieves, nor covetous persons, nor drunkards, nor cursed speakers, nor pillers, shall inherit the kingdom of God.* And St John in his Revelation saith, that *whoremongers shall have their part* with murderers, sorcerers, enchanters, liars, idolaters, and such other, *in the lake which burneth with fire and brimstone, which is the second death.* The punishment of the body, although it be death, hath an end; but the punishment of the soul, which St John calleth *the second death*, is everlasting: there shall be *fire and brimstone*; there *shall be weeping and gnashing of teeth; the worm* that shall there gnaw the conscience of the damned, *shall never die.* Oh whose heart distilleth not, even drops of blood, to hear and consider these things? If we tremble and shake, at the hearing and naming of these pains, oh what shall they do, that shall feel them, that shall suffer them, yea, and ever shall suffer, worlds without end? God have mercy upon us! Who is now so drowned in sin, and past all ungodliness, that he will set more, by a filthy and stinking pleasure, which soon passeth away, than by the loss of everlasting glory? Again, who will so give himself, to the lusts of the flesh, that he feareth nothing at all, the pains of hell fire?

But let us hear, how we may eschew the sin of whoredom and adultery, that we may walk in the fear of God, and be free from those most grievous and intolerable torments, which abide all unclean persons. To avoid fornication, adultery, and all uncleanness, let us provide that above all things, we may keep our hearts pure and clean, from all evil thoughts, and carnal lusts; for if that be once infected and corrupt, we fall headlong, into all kind of ungodliness. This shall we easily do, if when we feel inwardly, that Satan our old enemy tempteth us unto whoredom, we by no means consent to his crafty suggestions, but valiantly resist, and withstand him by strong faith, in the word of God, alleging against him always in our heart, this commandment of God: Scriptum est, *Non moechaberis*; It is written, *Thou shalt not commit whoredom.* It shall be good also for us, ever to live in the fear of God, and

1 Cor. 6:9, 10;
Gal. 5:19–21;
Eph. 5:5

Rev. 21:8

Matt. 13:42;
Luke 3:17

Remedies,
whereby to avoid
fornication and
adultery

Exod. 20:14,

to set before our eyes, the grievous threatenings of God, against all ungodly sinners; and to consider in our mind, how filthy, beastly, and short that pleasure is, whereunto Satan moveth us, and again, how the pain appointed for that sin, is intolerable and everlasting. Moreover, to use a temperance and sobriety, in eating and drinking, to eschew unclean communication, to avoid all filthy company, to flee idleness, to delight in reading of holy Scripture, to watch in godly prayers and virtuous meditations, and at all times, to exercise some godly travails, shall help greatly, unto the eschewing of whoredom.

And here are all degrees to be monished, whether they be married or unmarried, to love chastity and cleanness of life. For the married are bound by the law of God, so purely to love one another, that neither of them seek any strange love. The man must only cleave to his wife, and the wife again, only to her husband. They must so delight one in another's company, that none of them covet any other. And as they are bound thus to live together, in all godliness and honesty, so likewise it is their duty, virtuously to bring up their children, and to provide that they fall not into Satan's snare, nor into any uncleanness, but that they come pure and honest, unto holy wedlock, when time requireth. So likewise ought all masters and rulers to provide, that no whoredom, nor any point of uncleanness, be used among the servants. And again, they that are single, and feel in themselves, that they cannot live without the company of a woman, let them get wives of their own, and so live godly together. *For it is better to marry than to burn*: and, *to avoid fornication*, saith the Apostle, *let every man have his own wife, and every woman her own husband.* Finally, all such as feel in themselves, a sufficiency and ability, through the working of God's Spirit, to lead a sole and continent life, let them praise God for his gift, and seek all means possible, to maintain the same; as by reading of holy Scriptures, by godly meditations, by continual prayers, and such other virtuous exercises. 1 Cor. 6:2, 9

If we all on this wise will endeavour ourselves, to eschew fornication, adultery, and all uncleanness, and lead our lives in all godliness, and honesty, serving God, with a pure and clean heart, and glorifying him in our bodies, by leading an innocent and harmless life, we may be sure, to be in the number of those, of whom our Saviour Christ speaketh in the Gospel, on this manner: *Blessed are the pure in heart, for they shall see God.* Matt. 5:8 To whom alone be glory, honour, rule, and power, worlds without end. Amen.

A SERMON
AGAINST CONTENTION
AND BRAWLING

THIS DAY good Christian people, shall be declared unto you, the unprofitableness, and shameful unhonesty, of contention, strife, and debate; to the intent that when you shall see, as it were in a table painted before your eyes, the evil-favouredness and deformity, of this most detestable vice, your stomachs may be moved, to rise against it, and to detest and abhor that sin, which is so much to be hated, and so pernicious and hurtful to all men.

But among all kinds of contention, none is more hurtful, than is contention in matters of religion. *Eschew*, saith St Paul, *foolish and unlearned questions, knowing that they breed strife. It becometh not the servant of God, to fight* or strive, *but to be meek, toward all men.* This contention and strife, was in St Paul's time among the Corinthians, and is at this time among us Englishmen. For too many there be, which upon the ale benches, or other places, delight to set forth certain questions, not so much pertaining to edification, as to vain glory, and showing forth of their cunning; and so unsoberly to reason and dispute, that, when neither party will give place to other, they fall to chiding and contention, and sometime from hot words, to further inconvenience. St Paul could not abide to hear among the Corinthians, these words of discord or dissension: *I hold of Paul, I of Cephas, and I of Apollo.* What would he then say, if he heard these words of contention, which be now almost in every man's mouth: He is a Pharisee, He is a Gospeller, He is of the new sort, He is of the old faith, He is a new-broached brother, He is a good catholic father, He is a papist, He is an heretic? Oh how the Church is divided! Oh how the cities be cut and mangled! Oh how the coat of Christ, that was without seam, is all to-rent and torn! Oh body mystical of Christ, where is that holy and happy unity, out of the which whosoever is, he is not in Christ? If one member be pulled from another, where is the body? If the body be drawn from the head, where is the life

1 Tim. 1:4
2 Tim. 2:23, 24

1 Cor. 3:4

of the body? We cannot be jointed to Christ our Head, except we be glued with concord and charity, one to another. For he that is not in this unity, is not of the Church of Christ; which is a congregation, or unity together, and not a division.

St Paul saith, that *as long as emulation* (or envying), *contention, and factions be among us, we be carnal, and walk according to the fleshly man.* And St James saith, *If you have bitter emulation* (or envying), *and contention in your hearts, glory not of it. For, where as contention is, there is unstedfastness, and all evil deeds.* And why do we not hear St Paul, which prayeth us, whereas he might command us, saying, *I beseech you in the name of our Lord Jesus Christ, that you will speak all one thing, and that there be no dissension among you, but that you will be one whole body, of one mind, and of one opinion* in the truth. If his desire be reasonable and honest, why do we not grant it? If his request be for our profit, why do we refuse it? And if we list not to hear his petition or prayer, yet let us hear his exhortation, where he saith, *I exhort you, that you walk as it becometh the vocation in the which you be called, with all submission and meekness, with lenity and softness of mind, bearing one another by charity, studying to keep the unity of the Spirit, by the bond of peace: for there is one body, one Spirit, one faith, one baptism.* There is, he saith, but *one body*: of the which he can be no lively member, that is at variance with the other members. There is *one Spirit*, which joineth and knitteth all things in one: and how can this one Spirit reign in us, when we among ourselves, be divided? There is but *one faith*: and how can we then say, He is of the old faith, and, He is of the new faith? There is but *one baptism*: and then shall not all they which be baptised, be one? Contention causeth division: wherefore it ought not to be among Christians, whom one faith and baptism joineth in an unity. But if we contemn St Paul's request and exhortation, yet at the least, let us regard his earnest entreating; in the which he doth very earnestly charge us, and as I may so speak, conjure us, in this form and manner: *If there be any consolation in Christ, if there be any comfort of love, if you have any fellowship of the Spirit, if you have any bowels of pity and compassion, fulfil my joy, being all like affected, having one charity, being of one mind, of one opinion, that nothing be done by contention or vain glory.* Who is he that hath any bowels of pity, that will not be moved with these words so pithy? Whose heart is so stony, that the sword of these words, which be *more sharp than any two-edged sword,* may not cut and break asunder? Wherefore let us endeavour ourselves, to fulfil St Paul's joy, here in this place, which shall be at length, to our great joy in another place.

Let us so read the Scripture, that by reading thereof we may be made the better livers, rather than the more contentious disputers. If any thing is necessary to be taught, reasoned, or disputed, let us do it with all

1 Cor. 3:3

James 3:14, 16

1 Cor. 1:10

Ephes. 4:1–5

Phil. 2:1–3

Heb. 4:12

How we should read the Scripture

meekness, softness, and lenity. If any thing shall chance to be spoken uncomely, let one bear another's frailty. He that is faulty, let him rather amend, than defend that which he hath spoken amiss, lest he fall by contention, from a foolish error, into an obstinate heresy. For it is better to give place meekly, than to win the victory with the breach of charity; which chanceth, where every man will defend his opinion obstinately. If we be Christian men, why do we not follow Christ? which saith, *Learn of me, for I am meek, and lowly in heart.* A disciple must learn the lesson of his schoolmaster, and a servant must obey the commandment of his master. *He that is wise and learned,* saith St James, *let him show his goodness by his good conversation, and soberness of his wisdom. For where there is envy and contention, that wisdom cometh not from God, but is worldly wisdom, man's wisdom, and devilish wisdom. For the wisdom that cometh from above,* from the Spirit of God, *is chaste* and pure, corrupted with no evil affections; *it is* quiet, meek, and *peaceable,* abhorring all desire of contention; *it is tractable,* obedient, not grudging to learn, and to give place, to them that teach better for their reformation. For there shall never be an end of striving and contention, if we contend, who in contention shall be master, and have the overhand: we shall heap error upon error, if we continue to defend that obstinately, which was spoken unadvisedly. For truth is, that stiffness in maintaining an opinion, breedeth contention, brawling, and chiding; which is a vice, among all other, most pernicious and pestilent to common peace, and quietness.

And as it standeth betwixt two persons and parties (for no man commonly doth chide with himself), so it comprehendeth two most detestable vices: the one is picking of quarrels, with sharp and contentious words; the other standeth in froward answering, and multiplying evil words again. The first is so abominable, that St Paul saith, *If any that is called a brother, be a worshipper of idols, a brawler or picker of quarrels, a thief or an extortioner, with him that is such a man, see that ye eat not.* Now here consider that St Paul numbereth a scolder, a brawler, or a picker of quarrels, among thieves and idolaters. And many times cometh less hurt of a thief, than of a railing tongue: for the one taketh away a man's good name, the other taketh but his riches, which is of much less value and estimation, than is his good name. And a thief hurteth but him from whom he stealeth; but he that hath an evil tongue, troubleth all the town where he dwelleth, and sometime the whole country. And a railing tongue is a pestilence, so full of contagiousness, that St Paul willeth Christian men, to forbear the company of such, and neither to eat nor drink with them. And, whereas he will not, that a Christian woman should forsake her husband, although he be an infidel, nor that a Christian servant should depart from his master, which is an infidel and heathen, and so suffereth a Christian man to keep company

Matt. 11:29

James 3:13–17

Against quarrel picking
1 Cor. 5:11

1 Cor. 7:13;

1 Tim. 6:1

with an infidel, yet he forbiddeth us, to eat or drink with a scolder or a quarrel picker. And also in the sixth chapter to the Corinthians he saith thus: *Be not deceived; for neither fornicators, neither worshippers of idols,* *neither thieves nor drunkards, neither cursed speakers, shall dwell in the* *kingdom of heaven.* It must needs be a great fault, that doth move and cause the father, to disherit his natural son: and how can it otherwise be, but that this cursed speaking, must needs be a most damnable sin, the which doth cause God, our most merciful and loving Father, to deprive us of his most blessed kingdom of heaven?

1 Cor. 6:9–10

Against the other sin, that standeth in requiting taunt for taunt, speaketh Christ himself. *I say unto you*, saith our Saviour Christ, *Resist* *not evil; but love your enemies, and say well by them that say evil by you, do* *well unto them that do evil to you, and pray for them that do hurt and* *persecute you; that you may be the children of your Father, which is in heaven,* *who suffereth his sun, to rise both upon good and evil, and sendeth his rain,* *both to the just and unjust.* To this doctrine of Christ, agreeth very well the teaching of St Paul, that *chosen vessel* of God, who ceaseth not to exhort and call upon us, saying, *Bless them that curse you; bless, I say, and curse* *not. Recompense to no man evil for evil. If it be possible, as much as lieth in* *you, live peaceably with all men.*

Against froward
answering
Matt. 5:39, 44,
45

Acts 9:15

Rom. 12:14, 17,
18

THE SECOND PART OF
THE SERMON AGAINST CONTENTION

IT HATH BEEN DECLARED unto you, in this Sermon against strife and brawling, what great inconvenience cometh thereby, and specially of such contention, as groweth in matters of religion; and how, when as no man will give place to another, there is none end of contention and discord, and that unity which God requireth of Christians, is utterly thereby neglected and broken; and that this contention, standeth chiefly in two points, as in picking of quarrels, and making froward answers.

Now you shall hear St Paul's words, saying, *Dearly beloved, avenge not* *yourselves, but rather give place unto wrath: for it is written, Vengeance is mine,* *I will revenge, saith the Lord. Therefore, if thine enemy hunger, feed him; if he* *thirst, give him drink. Be not overcome with evil, but overcome evil with* *goodness.* All these be the words of St Paul.

Rom. 12:19–21

Deut. 32:35

But they that be so full of stomach, and set so much by themselves, that they may not abide so much as one evil word to be spoken of them, peradventure will say, If I be evil reviled, shall I stand still, like a goose or a fool, with my finger in my mouth? Shall I be such an idiot and dizzard, to suffer every man to speak upon me what they list, to rail what they list, to spew out all their venom against me, at their pleasures? Is it not

An objection

An answer

convenient, that he that speaketh evil, should be answered accordingly? If I shall use this lenity and softness, I shall both increase mine enemy's frowardness, and provoke other to do like. Such reasons make they that can suffer nothing, for the defence of their impatience. And yet, if by froward answering to a froward person, there were hope to remedy his frowardness, he should less offend, that should so answer, doing the same not of ire or malice, but only of that intent, that he that is so froward or malicious, may be reformed: but he that cannot amend another man's fault, or cannot amend it without his own fault, better it were, that one should perish than two. Then, if he cannot quiet him with gentle words, at the least let him not follow him, in wicked and uncharitable words. If he can pacify him with suffering, let him suffer; and if not, it is better to suffer evil than to do evil, to say well than to say evil: for to speak well against evil, cometh of the Spirit of God; but to render evil for evil, cometh of the contrary spirit. And he that cannot temper nor rule his own anger, is but weak and feeble, and rather more like a woman or a child, than a strong man: for the true strength and manliness, is to overcome wrath, and to despise injury, and other men's foolishness. And besides this, he that shall despise the wrong done unto him by his enemy, every man shall perceive that it was spoken or done without cause; whereas contrarily, he that doth fume and chafe at it, shall help the cause of his adversary, giving suspicion, that the thing is true. And so, in going about to revenge evil, we show ourselves to be evil; and while we will punish and revenge another man's folly, we double and augment our own folly.

But many pretences find they that be wilful, to colour their impatience. Mine enemy, say they, is not worthy to have gentle words or deeds, being so full of malice or frowardness. The less he is worthy, the more art thou allowed of God, the more art thou commended of Christ, for whose sake thou shouldest render good for evil, because he hath commanded thee, and also deserved that thou shouldest so do. Thy neighbour hath peradventure, with a word offended thee: call thou to thy remembrance, with how many words and deeds, how grievously, thou hast offended thy Lord God. What was man, when Christ died for him? Was he not his enemy, and unworthy to have his favour and mercy? Even so, with what gentleness and patience doth he forbear and tolerate thee, although he is daily offended by thee! Forgive therefore a light tresspass to thy neighbour, that Christ may forgive thee many thousands of trespasses, which art every day an offender. For if thou forgive thy brother, being to thee a trespasser, then hast thou a sure sign and token, that God will forgive thee, to whom all men be debtors, or trespassers. How wouldest thou have God merciful to thee, if thou wilt be cruel unto thy brother? Canst thou not find in thine heart, to do that toward another, that is thy fellow, which God hath done to thee, that art but his servant? Ought not one sinner to forgive another, seeing that Christ, which was no sinner, did pray to his Father, for them that without mercy and despitefully, put him to death? *Who when he was reviled, did not use reviling words again; and, when he suffered wrongfully, he did not threaten; but gave all vengeance, to the judgement of his Father, which judgeth rightfully.* And what crackest thou of thy Head, if thou labour not to be in the body? Thou canst be no member of Christ, if thou follow not the steps of Christ: who as the Prophet saith, was *led to death like a lamb*, not opening his mouth to reviling, but opening his mouth to praying, for them that crucified him, saying, *Father, forgive them, for they cannot tell what they do.* The which example, anon after Christ, St Stephen did follow, and after, St Paul. *We be evil spoken of*, saith he, *and we speak well; we suffer persecution, and take it patiently; men curse us, and we gently entreat.* Thus St Paul taught that he did, and he did that he taught. *Bless you*, saith he, *them that persecute you; bless you, and curse not.* Is it a great thing, to speak well to thine adversary, to whom Christ doth command thee to do well? David, when Semei did call him all to naught, did not chide again, but said patiently, *Suffer him to speak evil, if perchance the Lord will have mercy on me.*

1 Pet. 2:23

Isai. 53:7

Luke 23:34

Acts 7:60

1 Cor. 4:12, 13

Rom. 12:14

2 Sam. 16:11, 12

Histories be full of examples of heathen men, that took very meekly, both opprobrious and reproachful words, and injurious or wrongful deeds. And shall those heathen men excel in patience us, that profess Christ, the teacher and example of all patience? Lysander, when one did rage against him, in reviling of him, he was nothing moved, but said, "Go to, go to, speak against me, as much and as oft as thou wilt, and leave out nothing; if perchance by this means, thou mayest discharge thee of those naughty things, with the which it seemeth that thou art full laden." Many men speak evil of all men, because they can speak well of no man. After this sort, this wise man avoided from him the reproachful words spoken unto him, imputing and laying them, to the natural sickness of his adversary. Pericles, when a certain scolder, or a railing fellow, did revile him, he answered not a word again, but went into a gallery; and after, toward night, when he went home, this scolder followed him, raging still more and more, because he saw the other to set nothing by him; and after that he came to his gate, being dark night, Pericles commanded one of his servants to light a torch, and to bring the scolder home, to his own house. He did not only with quietness, suffer this brawler patiently, but also recompensed an evil turn, with a good turn, and that to his enemy. Is it not a shame for us, that profess Christ, to be worse than heathen people, in a thing chiefly pertaining to Christ's religion? Shall philosophy persuade them, more than God's word shall persuade us? Shall natural reason prevail more with them, than religion shall do with us? Shall man's wisdom lead them, to that thing whereunto the heavenly doctrine cannot lead us? What blindness, wilfulness, or rather madness is this! Pericles, being provoked to anger, with many villainous words, answered not a word. But we, stirred but with one little word, what foul work do we make! how do we fume, rage, stamp, and stare like mad men! Many men, of every trifle will make a great matter, and of the spark of a little word, will kindle a great fire, taking all things in the worst part. But how much better is it, and more like to the example and doctrine of Christ, to make rather of a great fault in our neighbour, a small fault, reasoning with ourselves after this sort: He spake these words, but it was in a sudden heat; or the drink spake them, and not he; or he spake them at the motion of some other; or he spake them being ignorant of the truth; he spake them not against me, but against him whom he thought me to be.

Reasons to move men from quarrel picking

But as touching evil speaking, he that is ready to speak evil against other men, first let him examine himself, whether he be faultless, and clear of the fault which he findeth in another. For it is a shame, when he that blameth another for any fault, is guilty himself, either in the same fault, or in a greater. It is a shame for him that is blind, to call another man blind: and it is more shame for him that is whole blind, to call him blinkard that is but purblind; for this is to see a straw in another man's eye, when a man hath a block in his own eye. Then let him consider, that he that useth to speak evil, shall commonly be evil spoken of again, and he that speaketh what he will, for his pleasure, shall be compelled to hear that he would not, to his displeasure. Moreover, let him remember

Matt. 12:36

that saying, that we *shall give an account for every idle word*. How much more then, shall we make a reckoning for our sharp, bitter, brawling, and chiding words, which provoke our brother to be angry, and so to the breach of his charity!

Reasons to move men from froward answering

And as touching evil answering, although we be never so much provoked, by other men's evil speaking, yet we shall not follow their frowardness, by evil answering, if we consider that anger is a kind of madness, and that he which is angry, is as it were for the time, in a frenzy. Wherefore let him beware, lest in his fury he speak any thing, whereof afterward, he may have just cause to be sorry. And he that will defend that anger is no fury, but that he hath reason even when he is most angry, then let him reason thus with himself, when he is angry: Now I am so moved and chafed, that within a little while after, I shall be otherways minded: wherefore then should I now speak any thing, in mine anger, which hereafter, when I should fainest, cannot be changed? Wherefore shall I do any thing now, being (as it were) out of my wit, for the which, when I shall come to myself again, I shall be very sad? Why doth not reason, why doth not godliness, yea, why doth not Christ, obtain that thing now of me, which hereafter time shall obtain of me? If a man be called an adulterer, usurer, drunkard, or by any other shameful name, let him consider earnestly, whether he be so called truly, or falsely. If truly, let him amend his fault, that his adversary may not after, worthily charge him with such offences. If these things be laid against him falsely, yet let him consider, whether he hath given any occasion, to be suspected of such things; and so he may both cut off that suspicion, whereof this slander did arise, and in other things shall live more warily. And thus using ourselves, we may take no hurt, but rather much good, by the rebukes and slanders of our enemy. For the reproach of an enemy, may be to many men, a quicker spur to the amendment of their life, than the gentle monition of a friend. Philippus the King of Macedony, when he was evil spoken of, by the chief rulers of the city of Athens, he did thank them heartily, because by them he was made better, both in his words and deeds: "For I study," said he, "both by my sayings and doings, to prove them liars."

THE THIRD PART OF THE SERMON AGAINST CONTENTION

YE HEARD IN THE LAST LESSON, of the Sermon against strife and brawling, how we may answer them, which maintain their froward sayings in contention, and that will revenge with words, such evil as other men do to them; and finally how we may, according to God's will, order ourselves, and what to consider towards them, when we are provoked to contention and strife, with railing words. Now to proceed in the same matter, you shall know the right way, how to disprove and overcome your adversary and enemy.

This is the best way to improve a man's adversary: so to live, that all which shall know his honesty, may bear witness, that he is slandered unworthily. If the fault whereof he is slandered, be such that for the defence of his honesty, he must needs make answer, yet let him answer quietly and softly, on this fashion, that those faults be laid against him falsely. For it is truth that the Wise Man saith: *A soft answer assuageth anger, and a hard and sharp answer, doth stir up rage and fury.* The sharp answer of Nabal, did provoke David to cruel vengeance; but the gentle words of Abigail, quenched the fire again, that was all in a flame. And a special remedy against malicious tongues, is to arm ourselves with patience, meekness, and silence; lest with multiplying words with the enemy, we be made as evil as he.

But they that cannot bear one evil word, peradventure for their own excuse, will allege that which is written: "He that despiseth his good name is cruel." Also we read, *Answer a fool according to his foolishness.* And

Prov. 15:1

1 Sam. 25:10–35

An objection
Augustine
Serm. 355
Prov. 26:5

John 19:9

Matt. 11:19;
13:55

John 8:48

Answer

Prov. 26:5

Ibid.: 4

Matt. 3:7; Gal.
3:1; Titus. 1:12

Phil. 3:2

Matt. 23:16–33

Matt. 16:25

Acts 13:10, 11

Acts 5:3

John 2:15

Exod. 32:15–19,
27, 28

Num. 25: 8, 14,
15
But these
examples are not
to be followed of
every body, but
as men be called
to office, and set
in authority.

our Lord Jesus did hold his peace at certain evil sayings, but to some he answered diligently. He heard men call him *a Samaritan, a carpenter's son, a wine drinker,* and he held his peace: but when he heard them say, *Thou hast a devil within thee,* he answered to that earnestly.

Truth it is indeed, that there is a time, when it is convenient to *answer a fool according to his foolishness, lest he should seem in his own conceit, to be wise.* And sometime it is not profitable, to *answer a fool according to his foolishness,* lest the wise man be made, like to the fool. When our infamy (or the reproach that is done unto us) is joined with the peril of many, then it is necessary in answering, to be quick and ready. For we read that many holy men of good zeals, have sharply and fiercely, both spoken and answered tyrants and evil men; which sharp words came not of anger, rancour, or malice, or desire of vengeance, but of a fervent desire, to bring them to the true knowledge of God, and from ungodly living, by an earnest and sharp rebuke and chiding. In this zeal, St John Baptist called the Pharisees *adders' brood*; and St Paul called the Galathians, *fools*; and the men of Crete, he called *liars, evil beasts,* and *sluggish bellies*; and the false apostles he called *dogs,* and *crafty workmen.* And this zeal is godly, and to be allowed, as it is plainly proved, by the example of Christ; who although he were the fountain and spring, of all meekness, gentleness, and softness, yet he calleth the obstinate Scribes and Pharisees, *blind guides, fools, painted graves, hypocrites, serpents, adders'. brood, a corrupt and wicked generation.* Also he rebuketh Peter eagerly, saying, *Go behind me, Satan.* Likewise St Paul reproveth Elymas, saying *O thou full of all craft and guile, enemy to all justice, thou ceasest not to destroy the right ways of God: and now, lo, the hand of the Lord is upon thee, and thou shalt be blind, and not see for a time.* Also St Peter reprehendeth Ananias very sharply, saying, *Ananias, how is it that Satan hath filled thy heart, that thou shouldest lie unto the Holy Ghost?*

This zeal hath been so fervent, in many good men, that it hath stirred them, not only to speak bitter and eager words, but also to do things, which might seem to some to be cruel; but indeed they be very just, charitable, and godly, because they were not done of ire, malice, or contentious mind; but of a fervent mind, to the glory of God, and the correction of sin, executed by men called to that office. For in this zeal, our Lord Jesus Christ, did drive with a whip the buyers and sellers, out of the Temple. In this zeal, Moses brake the two tables, which he had received at God's hand, when he saw the Israelites dancing about a calf, and caused to be killed, twenty and three thousand of his own people. In this zeal, Phinees the son of Eleazar, did thrust through with his sword Zambri and Cozbi, whom he found together joined, in the act of lechery.

Wherefore, now to return again to contentious words, and specially in matters of religion and God's word, which would be used with all

modesty, soberness, and charity, the words of St James ought to be well marked, and borne in memory, where he saith that of contention riseth all evil. And the wise King Solomon saith, *Honour is due to a man that*   Prov. 20:3
keepeth himself from contention, and all that mingle themselves therewith, be fools. And because this vice is so much hurtful, to the society of a commonwealth, in all well ordered cities, these common brawlers and scolders be punished, with a notable kind of pain, as to be set on the cucking stool, pillory, or suchlike. And they be unworthy to live in a commonwealth, the which do as much as lieth in them, with brawling and scolding, to disturb the quietness and peace of the same. And whereof cometh this contention, strife, and variance, but of pride and vainglory? Let us therefore *humble ourselves, under the mighty hand of*   1 Pet. 5:6
God, which hath promised to rest upon them that be humble and low in spirit. If we be good and quiet Christian men, let it appear in our speech   Luke 1:52
and tongues. If we have forsaken the devil, let us use no more devilish tongues. He that hath been a railing scolder, now let him be a sober counsellor. He that hath been a malicious slanderer, now let him be a loving comforter. He that hath been a vain railer, now let him be a ghostly teacher. He that hath abused his tongue in cursing, now let him use it in blessing. He that hath abused his tongue in evil speaking, now let him use it in speaking well. *All bitterness, anger, railing and blasphemy,*   Eph. 4:31
let it be avoided from you. If you may, and it be possible, in no wise be angry. But if you may not be clean void of this passion, then yet so temper and bridle it, that it stir you not to contention and brawling. If you be provoked with evil speaking, arm yourself with patience, lenity, and silence; either speaking nothing, or else being very soft, meek, and gentle in answering. Overcome thine adversaries with benefits, and gentleness. And above all things, keep peace and unity: be no peace breakers, but peace makers. And then there is no doubt, but that God, the Author of comfort and peace, will grant us peace of conscience, and such concord and agreement, *that with one mouth and mind, we may*   Rom. 15:6
glorify God, the Father of our Lord, Jesus Christ. To whom be all glory, now and ever. Amen.

HEREAFTER SHALL FOLLOW Sermons of Fasting, Praying, Alms deeds; of the Nativity, Passion, Resurrection, and Ascension of our Saviour Christ; of the due receiving of his blessed body and blood under the form of bread and wine; against Idleness, against Gluttony and Drunkenness, against Covetousness, against Envy, Ire, and Malice; with many other matters as well fruitful as necessary to the edifying of Christian people and the increase of godly living.

GOD SAVE THE QUEEN

THE SECOND TOME
OF HOMILIES

OF SUCH MATTERS AS WERE PROMISED
AND ENTITLED
IN THE FORMER PART OF HOMILIES

SET OUT BY THE AUTHORITY
OF THE QUEEN'S MAJESTY

AND TO BE READ IN EVERY PARISH CHURCH
AGREEABLY

AN ADMONITION
TO ALL MINISTERS ECCLESIASTICAL

Matt. 24:45 FOR THAT THE LORD doth require of his *servant, whom he hath set over his household,* to show both faithfulness and prudence in his office, it shall be necessary that ye, above all other, do behave yourself most faithfully and diligently, in your so high a function; that is, aptly, plainly, and distinctly to read the sacred Scriptures, diligently to instruct the youth in their Catechism, gravely and reverently to minister his most holy Sacraments, prudently also to choose out such Homilies as be most meet for the time, and for the more agreeable instruction of the people committed to your charge, with such discretion, that where the Homily may appear too long for one reading, to divide the same to be read part in the forenoon and part in the afternoon. And, where it may so chance some one or other chapter of the Old Testament to fall in order to be read upon the Sundays or Holy Days, which were better to be changed with some other of the New Testament of more edification, it shall be well done to spend your time, to consider well of such chapters beforehand, whereby your prudence and diligence in your office may appear; so that your people may have cause to glorify God for you, and be the readier to embrace your labours, to your better commendation, to the discharge of your consciences and their own.

AN HOMILY
OF THE RIGHT USE OF THE
CHURCH OR TEMPLE OF GOD
AND OF THE REVERENCE DUE
UNTO THE SAME

THE FIRST PART

WHERE THERE APPEARETH at these days great slackness and negligence, of a great sort of people, in resorting to the church, there to serve God their heavenly Father, according to their most bounden duty; as also much uncomely and unreverent behaviour of many persons in the same, when they be there assembled; and thereby may just fear arise, of the wrath of God, and his dreadful plagues hanging over our heads, for our grievous offence in this behalf, amongst other many and great sins, which we daily and hourly commit before the Lord: therefore, for the discharge of all our consciences, and the avoiding of the common peril and plague hanging over us, let us consider, what may be said out of God's holy book, concerning this matter; whereunto I pray you give good audience, for that it is of great weight, and concerneth you all.

Although the eternal and incomprehensible Majesty of God, the *Lord of heaven and earth*, whose *seat is heaven and the earth his footstool*, cannot be enclosed *in temples*, or houses *made with* man's *hand*, as in dwelling-places able to receive or contain his Majesty (according as is evidently declared of the Prophet Esay, and by the doctrine of St Stephen and St Paul, in the Acts of the Apostles, and where King Salomon, who builded unto the Lord the most glorious temple that ever was made, saith, *Who shall be able to build a meet or worthy house for him? if heaven, and the heaven above all heavens, cannot contain him, how much less can that which I have builded!* and further confesseth, *What am I, that I should be able to build thee an house, O Lord? but yet for this purpose only it is made, that thou*

Matt. 11:25

Isai. 66:1

Acts 7:48, 49
and 17:24
1 Kings 8:27;
2 Chron. 2:6
and 6:18, 19

mayest regard the prayer of thy servant, and his humble supplication; much less then, be our churches meet dwellingplaces to receive the incomprehensible Majesty of God): and indeed the chief and special temples of God, wherein he hath greatest pleasure, and most delighteth to dwell and continue in, are the bodies and minds of true Christians, and the chosen people of God (according to the doctrine of the holy Scripture, declared in the first Epistle to the Corinthians: *Know ye not*, saith St Paul, *that ye be the temple of God, and that the Spirit of God doth dwell in you? if any man defile the temple of God, him will God destroy; for the temple of God is holy, which ye are*: and again in the same Epistle: *Know ye not that your body is the temple of the Holy Ghost, dwelling in you, whom ye have given you of God, and that ye be not your own? for ye be dearly bought: glorify ye now therefore God, in your body and in your spirit, which are God's*): and therefore, as our Saviour Christ teacheth in the Gospel of St John, they that *worship God the Father, in spirit and truth*, in what place soever they do it, worship him aright; *for such worshippers doth God the Father look for*: for *God is a Spirit; and those which worship him, must worship him in Spirit and truth*, saith our Saviour Christ: yet, all this notwithstanding, the material church or temple is a place appointed, as well by the usage and continual examples expressed in the Old Testament as in the New, for the people of God to resort together unto, there to hear God's holy word, to call upon his holy Name, to give him thanks for his innumerable and unspeakable benefits bestowed upon us, and duly and truly to celebrate his holy Sacraments; in the unfeigned doing and accomplishing of the which, standeth that true and right worshipping of God aforementioned. And the same church or temple, is by the Scriptures, both of the Old Testament and the New, called the house and temple of the Lord, for the peculiar service there done, to his Majesty, by his people, and for the effectuous presence of his heavenly grace, wherewith he by his said holy word, endueth his people so there assembled. And to the said house or temple of God, at times by common order appointed, are all people that be godly indeed, bound with all diligence to resort, unless by sickness, or other most urgent causes, they be letted therefro. And all the same so resorting thither, ought with all quietness and reverence, there to behave themselves, in doing their bounden duty and service to Almighty God, in the congregation of his saints. All which things are evident to be proved by God's holy word, as hereafter shall plainly appear.

And first of all, I will declare by the Scriptures, that it is called, as it is indeed, *the house of God*, and *temple of the Lord. He that sweareth by the Temple*, saith our Saviour Christ, *sweareth by it, and him that dwelleth therein*, meaning God the Father: which he also expresseth plainly in the Gospel of St John, saying, *Do not make the house of my Father the house of*

1 Cor. 3:16–17

Ibid. 6:19–20

John 4:23, 24

Matt. 23:21

John 2:16

merchandise. And in the book of the Psalms, the Prophet David saith, *I will enter into thine house: I will worship in thy holy temple, in thy fear*. And it is in almost infinite places of the Scripture, specially in the Prophets and book of Psalms, called *the house of God*, or *the house of the Lord*. Sometime it is named *the tabernacle of the Lord*, and sometime *the sanctuary*, that is to say, the holy house or place, *of the Lord*.

> Psalm 5:7

> Psalm 132:5, 7
> Exod. 25:8;
> Lev. 19:30

And it is in like wise called *the house of prayer*. As Salomon, who builded the Temple of the Lord at Jerusalem, doth oft call it the house of the Lord; in the which the Lord's name should be called upon. And Esay in the fifty-sixth chapter: *My house shall be called the house of prayer, amongst all nations*: which text our Saviour Christ allegeth in the New Testament, as doth appear in three of the Evangelists. And in the parable of the Pharisee and the Publican which went to pray,* our Saviour Christ saith, they *went up into the Temple to pray*. And Anna, the holy widow and prophetess, *served the Lord, in fasting and prayer in the Temple, night and day*. And in the story of the Acts it is mentioned, how that *Peter and John went up into the Temple, at the hour of prayer*. And St Paul, praying in the Temple at Jerusalem, was rapt in spirit, and did see Jesus speaking unto him. And, as in all convenient places prayer may be used of the godly privately, so is it most certain, that the church or temple is the due and appointed place, for common and public prayer.

> 1 Kings 8, 29–49,
> 2 Chron. 2:4 and
> 6:10, 20–40
> Isaiah 56:7

> Matt. 21:13,
> Mark 11:17,
> Luke 19:46

> Luke 18:10

> Luke 2:37

> Acts 3:1

> Acts 22:17, 18

Now, that it is likewise the place of thanksgiving unto the Lord, for his innumerable and unspeakable benefits bestowed upon us, appeareth notably in the latter end of the Gospel of St Luke, and the beginning of the story of the Acts; where it is written, that the Apostles and disciples, after the ascension of the Lord, *continued with one accord daily in the Temple, always praising and blessing God*. And it is likewise declared in the first Epistle to the Corinthians, that the church is the due place appointed for the reverent use of the Sacraments.

> Luke 24:53,
> Acts 2:46

> 1 Cor. 11:20–34

It remaineth now to be declared, that the church or temple is the place where the lively word of God (and not man's inventions), ought to be read and taught, and that the people are bound thither with all diligence to resort; and this proof likewise to be made by the Scriptures, as hereafter shall appear.

In the story of the Acts of the Apostles we read, that Paul and Barnabas *preached the word of God in the temples of the Jews* at Salamin. And when *they came to Antiochia, they entered on the sabbath day into the synagogue* or church, *and sat down; and after the lesson*, or reading *of the Law and the Prophets, the ruler of the temple sent unto them, saying, "Ye men and brethren, if any of you have any exhortation to make unto the people, say it." And so Paul standing up, and making silence with his hand, said, "Ye men that be Israelites, and ye that fear God, give ear*," and so forth, preaching to

> Acts 13:5, 14–41

---

* Griffiths records all texts as reading "... went to pray; in which parable our Saviour ...."

them a sermon out of the Scriptures, as there at large appeareth. And in

Acts 17:1–3

the same story of the Acts, the seventeenth chapter, is testified how Paul preached Christ *out of the Scriptures* at Thessalonica. And in the fifteenth chapter James the Apostle, in that holy council and assembly of his

Acts 15:21

fellow Apostles, saith: *Moses of old time hath, in every city, certain that preach him in the synagogues* or temples, *where he is read every sabbath day*. By these places, ye may see the usage of reading of the Scriptures of the Old Testament among the Jews in their synagogues every sabbath day, and sermons usually made upon the same. How much more then is it convenient, that the Scriptures of God, and specially the Gospel of our Saviour Christ, should be read and expounded to us, that be Christians, in our churches; specially our Saviour Christ, and his Apostles, allowing this most godly and necessary usage, and by their examples confirming the same!

Matt. 4:23, 9:35,
Mark 1:14, 39,
Luke 4:15, 44,
Matt. 13:54,
Mark 6:2,
Luke 13:10

It is written in the stories of the Gospels, in divers places, that *Jesus went round about all Galilee, teaching in their synagogues, and preaching the Gospel of the kingdom*; in which places is his great diligence in continual preaching, and teaching of the people, most evidently set forth. In Luke

Luke 4:16–22

ye read how Jesus, *according to his accustomed use, came into the temple*, and how *the book of Esay the Prophet was delivered him*; how he read a text therein, and made a sermon upon the same. And in the nineteenth is

Luke 19:47

expressed, how he taught daily in the Temple. And it is thus written in

John 8:2

the eighth of John: *Jesus came again early in the morning into the Temple, and all the people came unto him, and he sat down and taught them*. And in

John 18:20

the eighteenth of John, our Saviour testifieth before Pilate, that he *spake openly unto the world*, and that he *always taught in the synagogue and in the Temple, whither all the Jews resorted, and* that *secretly* he *spake nothing*. And

Luke 21:37–8

in St Luke: *Jesus taught in the Temple, and all the people came early in the morning unto him, that they might hear him in the Temple*. Here ye see, as well the diligence of our Saviour, in teaching the word of God in the Temple daily, and specially on the sabbath days, as also the readiness of the people resorting all together, and that early in the morning, into the Temple to hear him.

The same example of diligence, in preaching the word of God in the Temple, shall ye find in the Apostles, and the people resorting unto

Acts 5:21, 28,
40, 42

them (Acts the fifth); how the Apostles, although they had been whipped and scourged the day before, and by the high priest commanded that they should preach no more in the name of Jesus, yet the day following, *they entered early in the morning into the Temple*, and *did not cease to teach,*

Acts 13, 15, 17

and declare Jesus Christ. And in sundry other places of the story of the Acts, ye shall find like diligence, both in the Apostles in teaching, and in the people in coming to the temple, to hear God's word.

Luke 1:9, 10

And it is testified in the first of Luke, that when Zachary, the holy priest, and father to John Baptist, did sacrifice within the Temple, *all the people stood without a long time, praying*: such was their zeal and fervency at that time. And in the second of Luke appeareth, what great journeys men, women, yea, and children took, to come to the Temple on the feast day, there to serve the Lord; and specially the example of Joseph, the blessed Virgin Mary, mother to our Saviour Christ, and of our Saviour Christ himself, being yet but a child; whose examples are worthy for us to follow. So that if we would compare our negligence, in resorting to the house of the Lord, there to serve him, to the diligence of the Jews in coming daily, very early, sometime great journeys, to their Temple, and, when the multitude could not be received within the Temple, the fervent zeal that they had, declared in standing long without and praying, we may justly, in this comparison, condemn our slothfulness and negligence, yea, plain contempt, in coming to the Lord's house (standing so near unto us) so seldom, and scarcely at noon time; so far is it from a great many of us, to come early in the morning, or give attendance without, who disdain to come into the temple. And yet we abhor the very name of the Jews, when we hear it, as of a most wicked and ungodly people. But it is to be feared, that in this point, we be far worse than the Jews, and that they shall rise at the day of judgement, to our condemnation, who in comparison to them, show such slackness and contempt in resorting to the house of the Lord, there to serve him, according as we are of duty most bound.

Luke 2:41–4

And besides this most horrible dread, of God's just judgement in the great day, we shall not in this life escape his heavy hand and vengeance, for this contempt of the house of the Lord, and his due service in the same, according as the Lord himself threateneth, in the first chapter of his Prophet Aggeus, after this sort: *Because you have left my house desert and without company, saith the Lord, and ye have made haste, every man to his own house; for this cause are the heavens stayed over you, that they should give no dew, and the earth is forbidden, that it shall bring forth his fruit; and I have called drought upon the earth, and upon the mountains, and upon corn, and upon wine, and upon oil, and upon all things that the earth bringeth forth, and upon men, and upon beasts, and upon all things that men's hands labour for.* Behold, if we be such worldlings, that we care not for the eternal judgements of God (which yet of all other, are most dreadful and horrible), we shall not escape the punishment of God in this world, by drought and famine, and the taking away of all worldly commodities, which we as worldlings seem only to regard and care for.

Hag. 1:9–11

Whereas on the contrary part, if we would amend this fault of negligence, slothfulness, and contempt of the house of the Lord, and his due service there, and with diligence resort thither together, to serve the Lord, with one accord and consent, in all holiness and righteousness before him, we have promises of benefits, both heavenly and worldly.

Matt. 18:20

Wheresoever two or three be gathered in my name, saith our Saviour Christ, *there am I in the midst of them*. And what can be more blessed, than to have our Saviour Christ amongst us? Or what again can be more unhappy or mischievous, than to drive our Saviour Christ from amongst us, and to leave a place for his and our most ancient and mortal enemy, the old dragon and serpent, Satan the devil, in the midst of us? In the second of Luke it is written, how that the mother of Christ, and Joseph, when they had long sought Christ, whom they had lost, and could find him no where, that at the last *they found him in the Temple, sitting in the midst of the doctors*. So if we lack Jesus Christ, that is to say, the Saviour of our souls and bodies, we shall not find him in the market place, or in the guild hall, much less in the alehouse or tavern, amongst good fellows (as they call them), so soon as we shall find him in the temple, the Lord's house, amongst the teachers and preachers of his word, where indeed he is to be found. And as concerning worldly commodities, we have a sure promise of our Saviour Christ: *Seek ye first the kingdom of God, and the righteousness thereof, and all these things shall withal be given unto you.*

Luke 2:46

Matt. 6:33

And thus we have, in the first part of this Homily, declared by God's word, that the temple or church is the house of the Lord, for that the service of the Lord (as teaching and hearing of his holy word, calling upon his holy Name, giving thanks to him for his great and innumerable benefits, and due ministering of his Sacraments) is there used. And it is likewise declared already, by the Scriptures, how all godly and Christian men and women ought, at times appointed, with diligence to resort unto the house of the Lord, there to serve him and to glorify him, as he is most worthy, and we most bound. To whom be all glory and honour, world without end. Amen.

THE SECOND PART OF THE HOMILY OF THE RIGHT USE OF THE CHURCH

IT WAS DECLARED in the first part of this Homily, by God's word, that the temple or church is the house of the Lord, for that the service of the Lord (as teaching and hearing of his holy word, calling upon his holy Name, giving thanks to him for his great and innumerable benefits, and due ministering of his Sacraments), is there used. And it is likewise already declared by the Scriptures, how all godly and Christian men and women ought, at all times appointed, with diligence to resort unto the house of the Lord, there to serve him, and to glorify him, as he is most worthy, and we most bounden. Now it remaineth, in this second part of the Homily concerning the right use of the temple of God, to be likewise declared by God's word, with what quietness, silence, and reverence, those that resort to the house of the Lord, ought there to use and behave themselves.

It may teach us sufficiently, how well it doth become us Christian men, reverently to use the church and holy house of our prayers, by considering in how great reverence and veneration, the Jews in the old law had their Temple; which appeareth by sundry places, whereof I will note unto you certain. In the twenty-sixth of Matthew it was laid to our Saviour Christ's charge, before a temporal judge, as a matter worthy death, by the two false witnesses, that he had said he could destroy the Temple of God, and in three days build it again; not doubting but, if they might make men to believe that he had said any thing against the honour and majesty of the Temple, he should seem to all men most worthy of death. And in the twenty-first of the Acts, when the Jews found Paul in the Temple, they *laid hands upon him, crying, Ye men Israelites, help: this is that man who teacheth all men everywhere, against the people and the law, and against this place; besides that he hath brought the Gentiles into the Temple, and hath profaned this holy place.* Behold how they took it for a like offence, to speak against the Temple of God, as to speak against the law of God; and how they judged it convenient, that none but godly persons, and the true worshippers of God, should enter into the temple of God. And the same fault is laid to Paul's charge by Tertullus, an eloquent man, and by the Jews, in the twenty-fourth of the Acts, before a temporal judge, as a matter worthy death, that he *went about to pollute the Temple* of God. And in the twenty-seventh of Matthew, when the chief priests had received again the pieces of silver at Judas' hand, they said, *It is not lawful to put them into Corban* (which was the treasure house of the Temple), *because it is the price of blood.* So that they could not abide that not only any unclean person, but also any other dead thing that was judged unclean, should once come into the Temple, or any place thereto belonging.

And to this end is St Paul's saying, in the second Epistle to the Corinthians, the sixth chapter, to be applied: *What fellowship is there, betwixt righteousness and unrighteousness? or what communion, between light and darkness? or what concord, between Christ and Belial? or what part can the faithful have with the unfaithful? or what agreement can there be, between the Temple of God and images?* Which sentence, although it be chiefly referred to the temple of the mind of the godly, yet seeing that the similitude and pith of the argument is taken from the material Temple, it enforceth that no ungodliness, specially of images or idols, may be suffered in the temple of God, which is the place of worshipping God, and therefore can no more be suffered to stand there, than light can agree with darkness, or Christ with Belial; for that the true worshipping of God, and the worshipping of images, are most contrary, and the

Matt. 26:61

Acts 21:27–8

Acts 24:6

Matt. 27:6

2 Cor. 6:14–16

setting of them up in the place of worshipping, may give great occasion to the worshipping of them.

But to return to the reverence that the Jews had to their Temple. You will say they honoured it superstitiously, and a great deal too much, crying out, *The Temple of the Lord, The Temple of the Lord*, being notwithstanding the most wicked in life, and be therefore most justly reproved in Jeremy, the Prophet of the Lord. Truth it is, that they were superstitiously given to the honouring of their Temple. But I would we were not as far too short from the due reverence of the Lord's house, as they overshot themselves therein. And if the Prophet justly reprehended them, hearken also what the Lord requireth at our hands, that we may know whether we be blameworthy or no.

It is written in Ecclesiastes, the fourth chapter: *When thou dost enter into the house of God*, saith he, *take heed to thy feet; draw near that thou mayest hear: for obedience is much more worth, than the sacrifice of fools, which know not what evil they do. Speak nothing rashly there, neither let thine heart be swift to utter words before God: for God is in heaven, and thou art upon the earth; therefore let thy words be few.* Note, well-beloved, what quietness in gesture and behaviour, what silence in talk and words, is required in *the house of God*, for so he calleth it. See whether they *take heed to their feet* (as they be here warned) which never cease from uncomely walking, and jetting up and down, and overthwart the church, showing an evident signification of notable contempt, both of God and all good men there present: and what heed they take to their tongues and speech, which do not only *speak words swiftly and rashly before the Lord* (which they be here forbidden), but also oftentimes speak filthily, covetously, and ungodly, talking of matters scarce honest or fit for the alehouse or tavern, in the house of the Lord; little considering that they speak *before God*, who dwelleth *in heaven* (as is here declared), when they be but vermins, here creeping *upon the earth*, in comparison to his eternal Majesty; and less regarding that they must *give an account at the great day of every idle word*, wheresoever it be spoken, much more of filthy, unclean or wicked words, spoken in the Lord's house to the great dishonour of his Majesty, and offence of all that hear them.

And indeed, concerning the people and multitude, the temple is prepared for them to be hearers, rather than speakers; considering that as well the word of God is there read or taught (whereunto they are bound to give diligent ear, with all reverence and silence), as also that common prayer and thanksgiving are rehearsed and said, by the public minister, in the name of the people, and the whole multitude present: whereunto they giving their ready audience should assent, and should say *Amen*, as St Paul teacheth in the first Epistle to the Corinthians; and in another place, *Glorifying God with one spirit and mouth*, which cannot

Jer. 7:1–15

Eccles. 5:1–2 [English numbering; 4:17; Vulgate 5:1]

Matt. 12:36

1 Cor. 14:16

Rom. 15:6

be when every man and woman, in several pretence of devotion, prayeth privately, one asking, another giving thanks, another reading doctrine, and not regarding to hear the common prayer of the minister. And peculiarly, what due reverence is to be used in the ministering of the Sacraments in the temple, the same St Paul teacheth in his Epistle to the Corinthians, rebuking such as did unreverently use themselves in that behalf. *Have ye not houses to eat and drink in?* saith he. *Do ye despise the Church* or congregation *of God? What shall I say to you? Shall I praise you? In this I praise you not.*

1 Cor. 11:22

And God requireth not only this outward reverence of behaviour and silence in his house, but all inward reverence, in cleansing of the thoughts of our hearts; threatening by his Prophet Ose, in the ninth chapter, that *for the malice of the inventions* and devices of the people, he *will cast them out of his house;* whereby is also signified, the eternal casting of them out of his heavenly house and kingdom, which is most horrible. And therefore in the nineteenth of Leviticus God saith, *Fear you with reverence my sanctuary, for I am the Lord.* And according to the same, the Prophet David saith, *I will enter into thine house, I will worship in thy holy temple in thy fear;* showing what inward reverence, and humbleness of mind, the godly men ought to have in the house of the Lord.

Hos. 9:15

Lev. 19:30

Psalm 5:7

And to allege somewhat concerning this matter out of the New Testament, in what honour God would have his house or temple kept, and that by the example of our Saviour Christ, whose authority ought of good reason, with all true Christians to be of most weight and estimation. It is written of all the four Evangelists, as a notable act, and worthy to be testified by many holy witnesses, how that our Saviour Jesus Christ, that merciful and mild Lord, compared for his meekness to a sheep suffering with silence his fleece to be shorn from him, and to a lamb led without resistance to the slaughter, which *gave his body to them that did smite him,* answered not him that reviled, *nor turned away his face from them that did reproach him, and spit upon him,* and according to his own example, gave precepts of mildness and sufferance to his disciples, yet when he seeth the Temple, and holy house of his heavenly Father, misordered, polluted, and profaned, useth great severity and sharpness, overturneth the tables of the exchangers, subverteth the seats of them that sold doves, maketh a whip of cords, and scourgeth out those wicked abusers and profaners of the Temple of God, saying, *My house shall be called a house of prayer, but ye have made it a den of thieves;* and in the second of John, *Do not ye make the house of my Father, the house of merchandise.* For as it is the house of God, when God's service is duly done in it, so when we wickedly abuse it, with wicked talk or covetous bargaining, we make it a den of thieves, or house of merchandise. Yea, and such reverence would Christ should be showed therein, that *he*

Matt. 21:12, 13,
Mark 11:15, 17,
Luke 19:45, 46,
John 2:15

Isai. 53:7
Acts 8:32
Isai. 50:6
1 Pet. 2:23

Matt. 5:38–48

John 2:16

Mark 11:16

would not suffer any vessel to be carried through the Temple. And, whereas our Saviour Christ (as is before mentioned out of St Luke) could be found nowhere, when he was sought, but only in the Temple, amongst the doctors, and now again exerciseth his authority and jurisdiction, not in castles and princely palaces, amongst soldiers, but in the Temple: ye may hereby understand in what place his spiritual kingdom, which he denieth to be *of this world*, is soonest to be found, and best to be known, of all places in this world.

John 18:36

And according to this example of our Saviour Christ, in the primitive Church (which was most holy and godly, and in the which due discipline, with severity, was used against the wicked) open offenders were not suffered once to enter into the house of the Lord, nor admitted to common prayer and the use of the holy Sacraments, with other true Christians, until they had done open penance, before the whole church. And this was practised not only upon mean persons, but also upon the rich, noble, and mighty persons, yea,* upon Theodosius, that puissant and mighty Emperor, whom, for committing a grievous and wilful murder, St Ambrose, Bishop of Millain, reproved sharply, and did also excommunicate† the said Emperor, and brought him to open penance.

Chrysostom

And they that were so justly exempted, and banished (as it were) from the house of the Lord, were taken (as they be indeed) for men divided and separated from Christ's Church, and in most dangerous estate, yea,

1 Cor. 5:5

as St Paul saith, even *given unto Satan* the devil for a time; and their company was shunned and avoided, of all godly men and women, until such time as they by repentance and public penance were reconciled. Such was the honour of the Lord's house in men's hearts, and outward reverence also at that time; and so horrible a thing was it, to be shut out of the church and house of the Lord in those days, when religion was most pure, and nothing so corrupt as it hath been of late days. And yet we willingly, either by absenting ourselves from the house of the Lord, do, as it were, excommunicate ourselves from the Church and fellowship of the saints of God; or else, coming thither, by uncomely and unreverent behaviour there, by hasty, rash, yea, unclean and wicked thoughts and words, before the Lord our God, horribly dishonour his holy house, the Church of God, and his holy Name and Majesty, to the great danger of our souls, yea, and certain damnation also, if we do not speedily and earnestly repent us of this wickedness.

Thus ye have heard, dearly beloved, out of God's word, what reverence is due to the holy house of the Lord, how all godly persons ought with diligence, at times appointed, thither to repair, how they

---

* The people's fault was most grievous; the sentence executed otherwise and more cruel than it should. [*margin* 1623]

† He was only dehorted from receiving the sacrament until by Repentance he might be better prepared. [*margin* 1623]

ought to behave themselves there with reverence and dread before the Lord, what plagues and punishments, as well temporal as eternal, the Lord in his holy word threateneth, as well to such as neglect to come to his holy house, as also to such who, coming thither, do unreverently, by gesture or talk, there behave themselves. Wherefore, if we desire to have seasonable weather, and thereby to enjoy the good fruits of the earth; if we will avoid drought and barrenness, thirst and hunger, which are plagues threatened unto such as make haste to go to their own houses, to alehouses, and to taverns, and leave the house of the Lord empty and desolate; if we abhor to be scourged, not with whips made of cords out of the material temple only (as our Saviour Christ served the defilers of the house of God in Jerusalem), but also to be beaten and driven out of the eternal temple and house of the Lord (which is his heavenly kingdom), with the iron rod of everlasting damnation, and *cast into outward darkness, where is weeping and gnashing of teeth*: if we fear, dread, and abhor this, I say, as we have most just cause so to do, then let us amend this our negligence and contempt in coming to the house of the Lord, this our unreverent behaviour in the house of the Lord; and, resorting thither diligently together, let us there—with reverent hearing of the Lord's holy word, calling on the Lord's holy Name, giving of hearty thanks unto the Lord, for his manifold and inestimable benefits, daily and hourly bestowed upon us, celebrating also reverently of the Lord's holy Sacraments—serve the Lord in his holy house, as becometh the servants of the Lord, *in holiness and righteousness before him, all the days of our life*: and then we shall be assured after this life, to *rest in his holy hill*, and to *dwell in his tabernacle*, there to *praise* and magnify *his* holy *Name in the congregation of his saints*, in the holy house of his eternal kingdom of heaven, which he hath purchased by the death and shedding of the precious blood of his Son, our Saviour Jesus Christ. To whom with the Father, and the Holy Ghost, one immortal Majesty of God, be all honour, glory, praise, and thanksgiving world without end. Amen.

Hag. 1:9–11

Matt. 8:12, 22:13, 25:30

Luke 1:75

Psalm 15:1

Psalm 149:1, 3

Eph. 2:21, 3:21

AN HOMILY
AGAINST PERIL OF IDOLATRY
AND SUPERFLUOUS
DECKING OF CHURCHES

THE FIRST PART

IN WHAT POINTS the true ornaments of the church or temple of God do consist and stand, hath been declared in the two last Homilies, intreating of the right use of the temple or house of God, and of the due reverence that all true Christian people are bound to give unto the same. The sum whereof is, that the church or house of God is a place appointed by the holy Scriptures, where the lively word of God ought to be read, taught, and heard, the Lord's holy Name called upon by public prayer, hearty thanks given to his Majesty, for his infinite and unspeakable benefits bestowed upon us, his holy Sacraments duly and reverently ministered; and that therefore all that be godly indeed, ought both with diligence, at times appointed, to repair together to the said church, and there with all reverence to use and behave themselves before the Lord; and that the said church, thus godly used by the servants of the Lord in the Lord's true service, for the effectual presence of God's grace (wherewith he doth by his holy word and promises endue his people there present and assembled, to the attainment as well of commodities worldly, necessary for us, as also for all heavenly gifts and life everlasting), is called by the word of God (as it is indeed) *the temple of the Lord,* and *the house of God*; and that therefore the due reverence thereof is stirred up in the hearts of the godly, by the consideration of these true ornaments of the said house of God, and not by any outward ceremonies, or costly and glorious decking of the said house or temple of the Lord. Contrary to the which most manifest doctrine of the Scriptures, and contrary to the usage of the primitive Church, which was most pure and uncorrupt, and contrary to the sentences and judgements of the most ancient, learned, and godly doctors of the Church (as hereafter shall appear), the corruption of these latter days hath brought into the church infinite multitudes of images; and the same, with other parts of the temple also, have decked with gold and silver, painted with colours, set them with stone and pearl, clothed them with silks and precious vestures, phantasing untruly that to be the chief decking and adorning of the temple or house of God, and that all people should be the more moved to the due reverence of the same, if all corners thereof were glorious and glistering with gold and precious stones: whereas indeed they by the said images, and such glorious decking of the temple, have nothing at all profited such as were wise and of understanding; but have thereby greatly hurt the simple and unwise, occasioning them thereby to commit most horrible idolatry, and the covetous persons, by the same occasion, seeming to worship, and peradventure worshipping indeed, not only the images, but also the matter of them, gold and silver, as that vice is of all others in the Scriptures peculiarly called *idolatry*, or worshipping of images.

Eph. 5:5, Col. 3:5

Against the which foul abuses and great enormities, shall be alleged unto you, first, the authority of God's holy word, as well out of the Old Testament as of the New; and secondly, the testimonies of the holy and ancient learned fathers and doctors, out of their own works, and ancient histories ecclesiastical; both that you may at once know their judgements, and withal understand what manner of ornaments were in the temples in the primitive Church, in those times which were most pure and sincere: thirdly, the reasons and arguments made for the defence of images or idols, and the outrageous decking of temples and churches with gold, silver, pearl, and precious stone, shall be confuted, and so this whole matter concluded.

But lest any should take occasion by the way of doubting, by words or names, it is thought good here to note, first of all, that although in common speech we use to call the likeness or similitudes of men or other things images, and not idols, yet the Scriptures use the said two words, *idols* and *images*, indifferently for one thing alway. They be words of diverse tongues and sounds, but one in sense and signification in the Scriptures. The one is taken of the Greek word εἴδωλον, an idol, and the other of the Latin word Imago, an image; and so both used as English terms in the translating of Scriptures indifferently, according as the Septuaginta have in their translation in Greek, εἴδωλα, and St Jerome in his translation of the same places in Latin hath Simulacra, in English *images*. And in the New Testament, that which St John calleth εἴδωλον, St Jerome likewise translateth Simulacrum, as in all other like places of Scripture, usually he doth so translate. And Tertullian, a most ancient doctor, and well learned in both the tongues, Greek and Latin,

1 John 5:21

Lib. *de Corona*
Militis

interpreting this place of St John, *Beware of idols*, "that is to say," saith
Tertullian, "of the images themselves," the Latin words which he useth
be Effigies and Imago, to say, an image. And therefore it forceth not,
whether in this process we use the one term or the other, or both
together, seeing they both (though not in common English speech, yet
in Scripture) signify one thing. And though some, to blind men's eyes,
have heretofore craftily gone about, to make them to be taken for words
of diverse signification in matters of religion, and have therefore usually
named the likeness or similitude of a thing, set up amongst the heathen
in their temples or other places to be worshipped, an Idol, but the like
similitude with us set up in the church, the place of worshipping, they
call an Image; as though these two words, *idol* and *image*, in Scripture
did differ in propriety and sense, which (as is aforesaid) differ only in
sound and language, and in meaning be indeed all one, specially in the
Scriptures and matters of religion; and our images also have been, and
be, and, if they be publicly suffered in churches and temples, ever will be
also worshipped, and so idolatry committed to them, as in the last part
of this Homily shall at large be declared and proved: wherefore our
images in temples and churches be indeed none other but idols, as unto
the which idolatry hath been, is, and ever will be committed.

And first of all, the Scriptures of the Old Testament, condemning and
abhorring as well all idolatry or worshipping of images, as also the very
idols or images themselves, specially in temples, are so many and
plentiful, that it were almost an infinite work, and to be contained in no
small volume, to record all the places concerning the same. For, when
God had chosen to himself a peculiar and special people, from
amongst all other nations that knew not God, but worshipped idols
and false gods, he gave unto them certain ordinances and laws, to be
kept and observed of his said people: but concerning none other
matter did he give either mo, or more earnest and express, laws to his
said people, than those that concerned the true worshipping of him, and
the avoiding and fleeing of idols and images and idolatry; for that, that
both the said idolatry is most repugnant to the right worshipping of him
and his true glory, above all other vices, and that he knew the proneness
and inclination of man's corrupt kind and nature, to that most odious
and abominable vice. Of the which ordinances and laws, so given by the
Lord to his people concerning that matter, I will rehearse and allege
some that be most special for this purpose, that you by them may judge
of the rest.

Deut. 4:1–2

In the fourth chapter in the book named Deuteronomy is a notable
place, and most worthy with all diligence to be marked, which
beginneth thus: *And now Israel, hear the commandments and judgements
which I teach thee*, saith the Lord, *that thou doing them mayest live, and*

enter and possess the land, which the Lord God of your fathers will give you. Ye shall put nothing to the word which I speak to you, neither shall ye take any thing from it. Keep ye the commandments of the Lord your God, which I command you. And by and by after, he repeateth the same sentence three or four times, before he come to the matter that he would specially warn them of, as it were for a preface, to make them take the better heed unto it. *Take heed to thyself,* saith he, *and to thy soul with all carefulness, lest thou*   *Ibid.:9* *forgettest the things which thine eyes have seen, and that they go not out of thy heart, all the days of thy life: thou shalt teach them to thy children and nephews* or posterity. And shortly after: *The Lord spake unto you, out of the middle of*   *Ibid.:12* *fire: you heard the voice* or sound *of his words, but you did see no form* or shape *at all.* And by and by followeth: *Take heed therefore diligently unto*   *Ibid.:15–19* *your souls: you saw no manner of image, in the day in the which the Lord spake unto you in Horeb, out of the midst of the fire: lest peradventure you being deceived, should make to yourselves any graven image, or likeness of man or woman, or the likeness of any beast which is upon the earth, or of the birds that fly under heaven, or of any creeping thing that is moved on the earth, or of the fishes that do continue in the waters; lest peradventure thou, lifting up thine eyes to heaven, do see the sun and the moon and the stars of heaven, and so thou, being deceived by error, shouldest honour and worship them, which the Lord thy God hath created to serve all nations that be under heaven.* And again: *Beware that thou forget not the covenant of the Lord thy*   *Ibid.:25–8* *God, which he made with thee, and so make to thyself any carved image of them, which the Lord hath forbidden to be made: for the Lord thy God is a consuming fire, and a jealous God. If thou have children and nephews, and do tarry in the land, and being deceived, do make to yourselves any similitude, doing evil before the Lord your God, and provoke him to anger, I do this day call upon heaven and earth to witness, that ye shall quickly perish out of the land which you shall possess: you shall not dwell in it any long time; but the Lord will destroy you, and will scatter you amongst all nations; and ye shall remain but a very few, amongst the nations whither the Lord will lead you away; and then shall you serve gods which are made with man's hands, of wood and stone, which see not, nor hear not, neither eat nor smell*: and so forth. This is a notable chapter, and intreateth almost altogether of this matter; but because it is too long to write out the whole, I have noted you certain principal points out of it: first, how earnestly and oft he calleth upon them to mark and to take heed, and that upon the peril of their souls, to the charge which he giveth them; then, how he forbiddeth, by a solemn and long rehearsal of all things in heaven, in earth, and in the water, any image or likeness of any thing at all to be made; thirdly, what penalty and horrible destruction he solemnly, with invocation of heaven and earth for record, denounceth and threateneth to them, their children and posterity, if they, contrary to this commandment, do make or worship any image or similitude, which he so straitly hath forbidden. And when they, this notwithstanding, partly by inclination of man's corrupt nature, most prone to idolatry, and partly occasioned by the Gentiles and heathen people dwelling about them, who were idolaters, did fall to the making and worshipping of images, God, according to his word, brought upon them all those plagues, which he threatened them with; as appeareth in the Books of the Kings and the Chronicles, in sundry places at large.

And agreeable hereunto are many other notable places in the Old Testament. Deuteronomy 27: *Cursed be he that maketh a carved image, or a cast* or molten *image, which is abomination before the Lord, the work of the artificer's hand, and setteth it up in a secret corner: and all the people shall say, Amen.*

Deut. 27:15

Read the thirteenth and fourteenth chapters of the Book of Wisdom, concerning idols or images, how they be made, set up, called upon, and offered unto; and how he praiseth the tree whereof the gibbet is made, as happy in comparison to the tree that an image or idol is made of, even by these very words : *Happy is the tree wherethrough righteousness cometh,* meaning the gibbet; *but cursed is the idol that is made with hands, yea, both it, and he that made it*: and so forth. And by and by, he showeth how that the things which were the good *creatures of God* before, as trees or stones, when they be once altered, and fashioned into images to be worshipped, *become abomination, a temptation unto the souls of men, and a snare for the feet of the unwise.* And why? *The seeking out of images is the beginning of whoredom,* saith he; *and the bringing up of them is the destruction of life. For they were not from the beginning, neither shall they continue for ever. The wealthy idleness of men hath found them out upon earth: therefore shall they come shortly to an end.* And so forth to the end of the chapter, containing these points: how idols or images were first invented and offered unto; how *by an ungracious custom* they were established; how tyrants compel men to worship them; how the ignorant and the common people are deceived, by the cunning of the workman and the beauty of the image, to do honour unto it, and so to err from the knowledge of God; and of other great and many mischiefs, that come by images. And for a conclusion, he saith that *the honouring of abominable images is the cause, the beginning, and end of all evil,* and that the worshippers of them be *either mad,* or most wicked. See and view the whole chapter with diligence, for it is worthy to be well considered, specially that is written of the deceiving of the simple and unwise common people, by idols and images, and repeated twice or thrice, lest it should be forgotten. And in the chapter following be these words: *The painting of the picture and carved image with divers colours, enticeth the ignorant, so that he honoureth and loveth the picture of a dead image, that hath no soul. Nevertheless, they*

Wisd. 14:7, 8

Ibid.:11–14

Ibid.:16

Ibid.:27, 28

Ibid. 15:4–6

that love such evil things, they that trust in them, they that make them, they that favour them, and they that honour them, are all worthy of death: and so forth.

In the book of Psalms, the Prophet curseth the image-honourers, in divers places. *Confounded be all they that worship carven images, and that delight or glory in them. Like be they unto the images that make them, and all they that put their trust in them.*

Psalm 97:7, 115:8, 135:18

And in the Prophet Esay saith the Lord: *Even I am the Lord, and this is my name; and my glory will I give to none other, neither my honour to graven images.* And by and by: *Let them be confounded with shame, that trust in idols or images, or say to them, You are our gods.* And in the fortieth chapter, after he hath set forth the incomprehensible Majesty of God, he asketh, *To whom then will ye make God like? or what similitude will ye set up unto him? Shall the carver make him a carved image? And shall the gold-smith cover him with gold, and cast him into a form of silver plates? And for the poor man, shall the image-maker frame an image of timber, that he may have somewhat to set up also?* And after this he crieth out, O wretches, *heard ye never of this? Hath it not been preached unto you since the beginning?* and so forth, how by the creation of the world, and the greatness of the work, they might understand the Majesty of God, the Creator and Maker of all, to be greater than that it could be expressed, or set forth, in any image or bodily similitude.

Isai. 42:8

Ibid.:17

Isai. 40:18–21

And besides this preaching, even in the law of God, *written with his own finger* (as the Scripture speaketh), and that in the first table, and the beginning thereof, is this doctrine aforesaid against images, not briefly touched, but at large set forth and preached, and that with denunciation of destruction to the contemners and breakers of this law, and their posterity after them. And lest it should yet not be marked, or not remembered, the same is written and reported, not in one, but in sundry places of the word of God, that by oft reading and hearing of it, we might once learn and remember it. As you also hear daily read in the church: *God spake these words and said, I am the Lord thy God. Thou shalt have none other gods but me. Thou shalt not make to thyself any graven image, nor the likeness of any thing that is in heaven above, or in the earth beneath, nor in the water under the earth: thou shalt not bow down to them, nor worship them: for I the Lord thy God am a jealous God, and visit the sin of the fathers upon the children, unto the third and fourth generation of them that hate me, and show mercy unto thousands in them that love me, and keep my commandments.* All this notwithstanding, neither could the notableness of the place, being the very beginning of the living Lord's law, make us to mark it; nor the plain declaration, by recounting of all kind of similitudes, cause us to understand it; nor the oft repeating and reporting of it, in divers and sundry places, the oft reading and hearing of it, could cause us to remember it; nor the dread

Exod. 21:18

Exod. 20:4, 5

Exod. 20:23, Lev. 19:4, Deut. 5:8, 9

of the horrible penalty to ourselves and our children, and posterity after us, fear us from transgressing of it; nor the greatness of the reward to us, and our children after us, move us any thing to obedience, and the observing of this the Lord's great law: but as though it had been written in some corner, and not at large expressed, but briefly and obscurely touched; as though no penalty to the transgressors, nor reward to the obedient, had been adjoined unto it; like blind men, without all knowledge and understanding, like unreasonable beasts, without dread of punishment or respect of reward, we* have diminished and dishonoured the high Majesty of the living God, by the baseness and vileness of sundry and divers images, of dead stocks, stones, and metals.

And as the Majesty of God, whom we have left, forsaken, and dishonoured, and therefore the greatness of our sin and offence against his Majesty, cannot be expressed, so is the weakness, vileness, and foolishness in device, of the images whereby we have dishonoured him, expressed at large in the Scriptures; namely, the Psalms, the Book of Wisdom, the Prophet Esay, Ezechiel, and Baruch; specially in these places and chapters of them, Psalm 115 and 135, Esay 40 and 44, Ezechiel 6, Wisdom 13, 14, 15, Baruch 6. The which places, as I exhort you often and diligently to read, so are they too long, at this present to be rehearsed in an homily. Notwithstanding, I will make you certain brief or short notes out of them, what they say of these idols or images. First, that they be made but of small pieces of wood, stone, or metal; and therefore they cannot be any similitudes of the great Majesty of God, whose *seat is heaven, and the earth his footstool.* Secondarily, that they be dead, *have eyes and see not, hands and feel not, feet and cannot go,* &c.; and therefore they cannot be fit similitudes of the living God. Thirdly, that they have no power to do good nor harm to others; though some of them have an axe, some a sword, some a spear in their hands, yet do thieves come into their temples and rob them, and they cannot once stir, to defend themselves from the thieves; nay, if the temple or church be set afire, that their priests can run away and save themselves, but they cannot once move, but tarry still, like blocks as they are, and be burned; and therefore they can be no meet figures of the puissant and mighty God, who alone is able, both to save his servants, and to destroy his enemies everlastingly. They be trimly decked in gold, silver, and stone, as well the images of men as of women, like wanton wenches (saith the Prophet Baruch) that love paramours; and therefore can they not teach us, nor our wives and daughters, any soberness, modesty, and chastity. And therefore, although it is now commonly said that they be the layman's books, yet we see they teach no good lesson, neither of God nor godliness, but all error and wickedness.

* "we" is an editorial addition.

Places of the
Scripture against
idols or images

Isai. 66:1

Psalm 115:5, 7

Bar. 6:9, 11

Therefore God, by his word, as he forbiddeth any idols or images to be made or set up, so doth he command such as we find made and set up, to be pulled down, broken, and destroyed. And it is written in the book of Numbers, the twenty-third chapter, that there was *no idol in Jacob*, nor there was *no image seen in Israel*, and that *the Lord God was with that people.* Where note, that the true Israelites, that is, the people of God, have no images among them; but that God was with them, and that therefore their enemies cannot hurt them, as appeareth in the process of that chapter. And as concerning images already set up, thus saith the Lord in Deuteronomy: *Overturn their altars, and break them to pieces, cut down their groves, burn their images: for thou art an holy people unto the Lord.* And the same is repeated more vehemently again, in the twelfth chapter of the same book. Here note, what the people of God ought to do to images, where they find them. But lest any private persons, upon colour of destroying of images, should make any stir or disturbance in the commonwealth, it must always be remembered, that the redress of such public enormities, appertaineth to the magistrates and such as be in authority only, and not to private persons. And therefore the good Kings of Juda, Asa, Ezechias, Josaphat, and Josias, are highly commended for the breaking down and destroying of the altars, idols, and images; and the Scriptures declare, that they specially in that point *did that which was right before the Lord.* And contrariwise Hieroboam, Achab, Joas, and other princes, which either set up or suffered such altars or images undestroyed, are by the word of God, reported to have *done evil before the Lord.* And if any, contrary to the commandment of the Lord, will needs set up such altars or images, or suffer them undestroyed amongst them, the Lord himself threateneth, in the first chapter of the book of Numbers, and by his holy Prophets Ezechiel, Micheas, and Abacuc, that he will come himself, and pull them down. And how he will handle, punish, and destroy the people that so set up or suffer such altars, images, or idols undestroyed, he denounceth by his Prophet Ezechiel, on this manner: *I myself, saith the Lord, will bring a sword over you, to destroy your high places; I will cast down your altars, and break down your images; your slain men will I lay before your gods, and the dead carcases of the children of Israel will I cast before their idols; your bones will I strow round about your altars and dwellingplaces; your cities shall be desolate, the hill chapels laid waste, your altars destroyed and broken, your gods cast down and taken away, your temples laid even with the ground, your own works clean rooted out; your slain men shall lie amongst you: that ye may learn to know, how that I am the Lord:* and so forth to the chapter's end, worthy with diligence to be read, that *they that be near shall perish with the sword, they that be far off with the pestilence,* they that flee into holds or wilderness with hunger, and if any be yet left, that they shall be carried

Num. 23:21

Deut. 7:5, 6

Deut. 12:2, 3

1 Kings 15:11–14, 2 Chron. 14:2–5, 15:8, 16, 31:1, 20, 17:3–6, 34:2–7

1 Kings 14:9, 16:30–3, 2 Chron. 24:17–24, 2 Kings 13:11

Num. 1, Mic. 1:3–7, Hab. 2:18, 19

Ezek. 6:3–7

Ibid.:9, 12

away prisoners, to servitude and bondage. So that, if either the multitude or plainness of the places might make us to understand, or the earnest charge that God giveth in the said places move us to regard, or the horrible plagues, punishments, and dreadful destruction threatened to such worshippers of images or idols, setters up or maintainers of them, might ingender any fear in our hearts, we would once leave and forsake this wickedness, being in the Lord's sight so great an offence and abomination. Infinite places almost, might be brought out of the Scriptures of the Old Testament concerning this matter, but these few at this time shall serve for all.

You will say peradventure, these things pertain to the Jews, what have we to do with them? Indeed they pertain no less to us Christians than to them. For if we be the people of God, how can the word and law of God not appertain to us? St Paul, alleging one text out of the Old Testament, concludeth generally for other Scriptures of the Old Testament, as well

Rom. 15:4

as that, saying, *Whatsoever is written before*, meaning in the Old Testament, *is written for our instruction*: which sentence is more specially true of such writings of the Old Testament, as contain the immutable law and ordinances of God, in no age or time to be altered, nor of any persons, of any nations or age, to be disobeyed, such as the above rehearsed places be. Notwithstanding, for your further satisfying herein, according to my promise, I will, out of the Scriptures of the New Testament, or Gospel of our Saviour Christ, likewise make a confirmation of the said doctrine against idols or images, and of our duty concerning the same.

First, the Scriptures of the New Testament do, in sundry places, make mention with rejoicing, as for a most excellent benefit and gift of God, that they which received the faith of Christ, were *turned from their dumb*

Rom. 1:25
Acts 14:15, 17:30
Rom. 11:30
1 Cor. 12:2, 3,
Gal. 4:8,9,
1 Thess. 1:4–9

and dead *images, unto the true and living God, who is* to be *blessed for ever;* namely, in these places: the fourteenth and seventeenth of the Acts of the Apostles; the eleventh to the Romans; the first Epistle to the Corinthians, the twelfth chapter; to the Galathians, the fourth; and the first to the Thessalonians, the first chapter.

And in like wise the said idols or images, and worshipping of them, are, in the Scriptures of the New Testament, by the Spirit of God much abhorred and detested, and earnestly forbidden: as appeareth both in

Acts 7:41, 42;
15:20, 29
Rom. 1:23–32

the forenamed places, and also many others besides; as in the seventh and fifteenth of the Acts of the Apostles; the first to the Romans: where is set forth the horrible plague of idolaters, given over by God *into a reprobate sense*, to work all wickedness, and abominations not to be spoken, as usually spiritual and carnal fornication go together. In the

1 Cor. 5:11

first Epistle to the Corinthians, the fifth chapter, we are forbidden once *to keep company*, or *to eat* and drink, *with such as be called brethren* or

Gal. 5:20

Christians *that do worship images*. In the fifth to the Galathians, the worshipping of images is numbered amongst *the works of the flesh*: and in the first to the Corinthians, the tenth, it is called the service of devils, and that such as use it shall be destroyed. And in the sixth chapter of the said Epistle, and the fifth to the Galathians, is denounced, that such *image worshippers shall never come into the inheritance of the kingdom of heaven*. And in sundry other places is threatened, that the *wrath of God shall come upon all such*. And therefore St John in his Epistle exhorteth us, as his *dear children*, to *beware of images*. And St Paul warneth us, to *flee from the worshipping of them, if we be wise*, that is to say, if we care for health, and fear destruction, if we regard the kingdom of God, and life everlasting, and dread the wrath of God, and everlasting damnation: for it is not possible that we should be worshippers of images and the true servants of God also; as St Paul teacheth, the second to the Corinthians, the sixth chapter, affirming expressly that *there can be no more consent or agreement, between the temple of God*, which all true Christians be, *and images, than between righteousness and unrighteousness, between light and darkness, between the faithful and the unfaithful, or between Christ and the devil*. Which place enforceth, both that we should not worship images, and that we should not have images in the temple, for fear and occasion of worshipping them, though they be of themselves things indifferent; for the Christian is the holy temple, and lively image of God, as the place well declareth, to such as will read and weigh it.

And whereas all godly men did ever abhor that any kneeling and worshipping, or offering, should be used to themselves when they were alive, for that it was the honour due to God only, as appeareth in the Acts of the Apostles by St Peter forbidding it to Cornelius, and by St Paul and Barnabas forbidding the same to the citizens in Lystra, yet we like mad men, fall down before the dead idols or images of Peter and Paul, and give that honour to stocks and stones, which they thought abominable to be given to themselves being alive. And the good angel of God, as appeareth in the book of St John's Revelation, refused to be kneeled unto, when that honour was offered him of John. *Beware*, saith the angel, *that thou do it not; for I am thy fellow-servant*. But the evil angel, Satan, desireth nothing so much as to be kneeled unto, and thereby at once both to rob God of his due honour, and work the damnation of such as make him so low courtesy, as in the story of the Gospel appeareth in sundry places. Yea, and he offered our Saviour Christ all earthly goods, on the condition that he would kneel down and worship him. But our Saviour repelleth Satan, by the Scriptures, saying, *It is written, Thou shalt worship thy Lord God, and him alone shalt thou serve*. But we, by not worshipping and serving God alone, as the Scriptures teach us, and by worshipping of images contrary to the Scriptures, pluck Satan to us, and are ready without reward to follow his desire; yea, rather than fail, we

1 Cor. 10:20–2

1 Cor. 6:9, 10

Gal. 5:20, 21

1 John 5:21;
1 Cor. 10:14, 15, 21

2 Cor. 6:14–16

Acts 10:25, 26;
14: 14–18

Rev. 19:10

Matt. 4:10,
Luke 4:8

will offer him gifts and oblations, to receive our service. But let us brethren, rather follow the counsel of the good angel of God, than the suggestion of subtile Satan, that wicked angel and old serpent; who according to the pride whereby he first fell, attempteth alway, by such sacrilege, to deprive God (whom he envieth) of his due honour, and because his own face is horrible and ugly, to convey it to himself, by the mediation of gilt stocks and stones, and withal to make us the enemies of God, and his own suppliants and slaves, and in the end to procure us, for a reward, everlasting destruction and damnation. Therefore above all things, if we take ourselves to be Christians indeed, as we be named, let us credit the word, obey the law, and follow the doctrine and example, of our Saviour and Master Christ, repelling Satan's suggestion to idolatry and worshipping of images, according to the truth alleged and taught out of the Testament and Gospel of our said heavenly Doctor and

Rom. 9:5

Schoolmaster, Jesus Christ, *who is God*, to be *blessed for ever*. Amen.

THE SECOND PART
OF THE HOMILY
AGAINST PERIL OF IDOLATRY

YOU HAVE HEARD, well beloved, in the first part of this Homily, the doctrine of the word of God against idols and images, against idolatry and worshipping of images, taken out of the Scriptures of the Old Testament and the New, and confirmed by the examples as well of the Apostles as of our Saviour Christ himself. Now, although our Saviour

John 5:34

Christ *taketh not* or needeth not *any testimony of men*, and that which is once confirmed by the certainty of his eternal truth, hath no more need of the confirmation of man's doctrine and writings, than the bright sun at noon tide hath need of the light of a little candle to put away darkness and to encrease his light; yet, for your further contentation, it shall in this second part be declared (as in the beginning of the first part was promised) that this truth and doctrine, concerning the forbidding of images and worshipping of them, taken out of the holy Scriptures as well of the Old Testament as the New, was believed and taught of the old holy fathers, and most ancient learned doctors, and received in the old primitive Church, which was most uncorrupt and pure. And this declaration shall be made out of the said holy doctors' own writings, and out of the ancient histories ecclesiastical to the same belonging.

Lib. *Contra Coronandi Morem*

Tertullian, a most ancient writer and doctor of the Church, who lived about one hundred and threescore years after the death of our Saviour Christ, both in sundry other places of his works, and specially in his book written against the manner of Crowning, and in another little treatise entitled, *Of the Soldier's Crown or Garland*, doth most sharply and vehemently write and inveigh against images and idols; and upon St John's words, the first Epistle and fifth chapter, saith thus. "St John," saith he,

1 John 5:21

> deeply considering the matter, saith, *My little children, keep yourselves from* images or *idols*. He saith not now, Keep yourselves from idolatry, as it were from the service and worshipping of them; but from the images or idols themselves, that is, from the very shape and likeness of them. For it were an unworthy thing, that the image of the living God should become the image of a dead idol.

Do not, think you, those persons which place images or idols in churches and temples, yea, shrine them even over the Lord's table, even as it were of purpose to the worshipping and honouring of them, take good heed to either St John's counsel or Tertullian's? For so to place images and idols, is it to keep themselves from them, or else to receive and embrace them?

Clemens in his book to James, brother of the Lord, saith:

Lib. v ad Jacob. Domini

> What can be so wicked or so unthankful, as to receive a benefit of God, and to give thanks therefore unto stocks and stones? Wherefore away ye, and understand your health. For God hath need of no man, nor requireth any thing, nor can be hurt in any thing: but we be they which are either holpen or hurt, in that we be thankful to God or unthankful.

Origines in his book against Celsus, saith thus: "Christian men and Jews, when they hear these words of the Law, *Thou shalt fear the Lord thy God*, and *shalt not make any image*, do not only abhor the temples, altars, and images of the gods, but if need be, will rather die, than they should defile themselves with any impiety." And shortly after, he saith: "In the commonwealth of the Jews, the carver of idols and image maker was cast far off and forbidden, lest they should have any occasion to make images, which might pluck certain foolish persons from God, and turn the eyes of their souls, to the contemplation of earthly things." And in another place of the same book: "It is not only," saith he, "a mad and frantic part to worship images, but also once to dissemble or wink at it." And, "A man may know God and his only Son, and those which have had such honour given them by God that they be called *gods*; but it is not possible that any should by worshipping of images, get any knowledge of God."

Deut. 6:13

Exod. 20:4

Exod. 22:28, Psalm 82:1, 6, John 10:34, 35

Athanasius in his book against the Gentiles hath these words:

> Let them tell, I pray you, how God may be known by an image. If it be by the matter of the image, then there needeth no shape or form, seeing that God hath appeared in all material creatures, which do testify his glory. Now if they say he is known by the form or fashion,

is he not better to be known by the living things themselves, whose fashions the images express? For of surety, the glory of God should be more evidently known, if it were declared by reasonable and living creatures, rather than by dead and unmoveable images. Therefore, when ye do carve or paint images, to the end to know God thereby, surely ye do an unworthy and unfit thing.

And in another place of the same book he saith: "The invention of images came of no good, but of evil; and whatsoever hath an evil beginning, can never in any thing be judged good, seeing it is altogether naught." Thus far Athanasius, a very ancient, holy, and learned bishop and doctor, who judgeth both the first beginning, and the end, and all together of images or idols, to be naught.

Lactantius likewise, an old and learned writer, in his book *Of the Origin of Error* hath these words:

> God is above man, and is not placed beneath, but is to be sought in the highest region. Wherefore there is no doubt, but that no religion is in that place wheresoever any image is. For, if religion stand in godly things, and there is no godliness but in heavenly things, then be images without religion.

Lib. 2, cap. 16

These be Lactantius' words, who was above thirteen hundred years ago, and within three hundred years after our Saviour Christ.

Cyrillus, an old and holy doctor, upon the Gospel of St John hath these words: "Many have left the Creator, and have worshipped the creature; neither have they been abashed to say unto a stock, Thou art my father; and unto a stone, Thou begottest me. For many, yea, almost all, alas for sorrow! are fallen unto such folly, that they have given the glory of deity" (or godhead) "to things without sense or feeling".

Epiphanius, Bishop of Salamine in Cyprus, a very holy and learned man, who lived in Theodosius the Emperor's time, about three hundred and ninety years after our Saviour Christ's ascension, writeth thus to John, Patriarch of Jerusalem. "I entered," saith Epiphanius,

> into a certain church to pray: I found there a linen cloth hanging in the church door, painted, and having in it the image of Christ, as it were, or for some other Saint (for I remember not well whose image it was): therefore when I did see the image of a man, hanging in the church of Christ contrary to the authority of the Scriptures, I did tear it, and gave counsel to the keepers of that church, that they should wind a poor man that was dead in the said cloth, and so bury him.

And afterwards the same Epiphanius, sending another unpainted cloth, for that painted one which he had torn, to the said Patriarch, writeth thus:

> I pray you, will the elders of that place to receive this cloth, which I have sent by this bearer, and command them that from henceforth, no

such painted cloths, contrary to our religion, be hanged in the church of Christ. For it becometh your goodness rather to have this care, that you take away such scrupulosity; which is unfitting for the church of Christ, and offensive to the people committed to your charge.

And this epistle, as worthy to be read of many, did St Jerome himself translate into the Latin tongue. And that ye may know that St Jerome had this holy and learned Bishop Epiphanius in most high estimation, and therefore did translate this epistle as a writing of authority, hear what a testimony the said St Jerome giveth him in another place, in his treaty against the errors of John, Bishop of Jerusalem, where he hath these words: "Thou hast," saith St Jerome, "Pope Epiphanius, which doth openly in his letters call thee an heretic. Surely thou art not to be preferred before him, neither for age, nor learning, nor godliness of life, nor by the testimony of the whole world." And shortly after, in the same treaty, saith St Jerome: "Bishop Epiphanius was ever of so great veneration and estimation, that Valens the Emperor," who was a great persecutor, "did not once touch him. For heretics, being princes, thought it their shame, if they should persecute such a notable man." And in the *Tripartite Ecclesiastical History*, the ninth book and forty-eighth chapter, is testified, that Epiphanius, being yet alive, did work miracles; and that after his death, devils being expelled at his grave or tomb did roar. Thus you see what authority St Jerome, and that most ancient History, give unto the holy and learned Bishop Epiphanius: whose judgement of images in churches and temples, then beginning by stealth to creep in, is worthy to be noted.

All notable bishops were then called popes.

Lib. 9, cap. 48

First, he judged it contrary to Christian religion, and the authority of the Scriptures, to have any images in Christ's church. Secondly, he rejected not only carved, graven, and molten images, but also painted images, out of Christ's church. Thirdly, that he regarded not whether it were the image of Christ or of any other Saint, but being an image, would not suffer it in the church. Fourthly, that he did not only remove it out of the church, but with a vehement zeal tare it asunder, and exhorted that a corse should be wrapped and buried in it, judging it meet for nothing but to rot in the earth; following herein the example of the good King Ezechias, who brake the brazen serpent into pieces, and burned it to ashes, for that idolatry was committed to it. Last of all, that Epiphanius thinketh it the duty of vigilant bishops, to be careful that no images be permitted in the church, for that they be occasion of scruple and offence, to the people committed to their charge.

2 Kings 18:4

Now, whereas neither St Jerome, who did translate the said epistle, nor the authors of that most ancient *History Ecclesiastical Tripartite*, who do most highly commend Epiphanius (as is aforesaid), nor no other godly or learned bishop at that time or shortly after, have written any thing against Epiphanius' judgement concerning images, it is an evident proof

that in those days, which were about four hundred years after our
Saviour Christ, there were no images publicly used and received in the
church of Christ, which was then much less corrupt, and more pure, than
now it is. And whereas images began at that time, secretly and by stealth,
to creep out of private men's houses into the churches, and that first in
painted cloths and walls: such bishops as were godly and vigilant, when
they espied them, removed them away, as unlawful and contrary to Christian religion, as did here Epiphanius: to whose judgement you have not
only St Jerome, the translator of his epistle, and the writer of the Holy
Tripartite, but also all the learned and godly bishops and clerks, yea, and
the whole Church of that age, and so upward to our Saviour Christ's time,
by the space of about four hundred years, consenting and agreeing.

This is written the more largely of Epiphanius, for that our image
maintainers nowadays, seeing themselves so pressed with this most
plain and earnest act and writing of Epiphanius, a bishop and doctor of
such antiquity, holiness, and authority, labour by all means (but in vain
against the truth), either to prove that this epistle was neither of Epiphanius' writing, nor St Jerome's translation, either if it be, say they, it is of
no great force; for this Epiphanius, say they, was a Jew, and being converted
to the Christian faith, and made a bishop, retained the hatred which
Jews have to images, still in his mind, and so did and wrote against them
as a Jew, rather than as a Christian. Oh Jewish impudency and malice of
such devisers! It would be proved, and not said only, that Epiphanius
was a Jew. Furthermore, concerning the reason they make, I would
admit it gladly. For if Epiphanius' judgement against images is not to be
admitted, for that he was of a Jew (an enemy to images, which be God's
enemies) converted to Christ's religion, then likewise followeth it, that no
sentence in the old doctors and fathers, sounding for images, ought to
be of any authority, for that in the primitive Church, the most part of
learned writers, as Tertullian, Cyprian, Ambrose, Austin, and infinite
others, were of Gentiles (which be favourers and worshippers of images)
converted to the Christian faith, and so let somewhat slip out of their pens
sounding for images, rather as Gentiles than Christians; as Eusebius in
his History Ecclesiastical, and St Jerome saith plainly, that images came
first from the Gentiles to us Christians. And much more doth it follow,
that the opinion of all the rabblement of the popish church, maintaining
images, ought to be esteemed of small or no authority; for that it is no
marvel that they, which have from their childhood been brought up
amongst images and idols, and have drunk in idolatry almost with their
mother's milk, hold with images and idols, and speak and write for
them. But indeed it would not be so much marked, whether he were of
a Jew or a Gentile converted to Christ's religion that writeth, as how
agreeably or contrarily to God's word he doth write, and so to credit or

discredit him. Now, what God's word saith of idols and images, and the worshipping of them, you heard at large, in the first part of this Homily.

St Ambrose, in his treaty of the death of Theodosius the Emperor, saith: "Helene found the cross and the title on it: she worshipped the King, and not the wood surely, for that is an heathenish error and the vanity of the wicked, but she worshipped him that hanged on the cross, and whose name was written in the title" and so forth. See both the godly Empress' fact, and St Ambrose' judgement at once. They thought it had been an heathenish error, and vanity of the wicked, to have worshipped the cross itself, which was embrued with our Saviour Christ's own precious blood: and we fall down before every cross piece of timber, which is but an image of that cross.

St Augustine, the best learned of all ancient doctors, in his forty-fourth Epistle to Maximus, saith: "Know thou, that none of the dead, nor any thing that is made of God, is worshipped as God of the catholic Christians, of whom is a Church also in your town." Note that by St Augustine such as worshipped the dead or creatures be no catholic Christians. The same St Augustine teacheth, in the twenty-second book of *The City of God*, the tenth chapter, that neither temples or churches ought to be builded or made for Martyrs or Saints, but to God alone; and that there ought no priests to be appointed for Martyr or Saint, but to God only. The same St Augustine, in his book of *The Manners of the Catholic Church*, hath these words: "I know that many be worshippers of tombs and pictures; I know that there be many that banquet most riotously, over the graves of the dead, and giving meat to dead carcases, do bury themselves upon the buried, and attribute their gluttony and drunkenness to religion." See, he esteemeth worshipping of Saints' tombs and pictures, as good religion as gluttony and drunkenness, and no better at all. St Augustine greatly alloweth Marcus Varro, affirming that religion is most pure without images. And saith himself: "Images be of more force to crooken an unhappy soul, than to teach and instruct it." And saith further: "Every child, yea, every beast knoweth, that it is not God that they see. Wherefore then doth the Holy Ghost so often monish us, of that which all men know?" Whereunto St Augustine himself answereth thus: "For," saith he, "when images are placed in temples, and set in honourable sublimity, and begin once to be worshipped, forthwith breedeth the most vile affection of error." This is St Augustine's judgement of images in churches, that by and by they breed error and idolatry.

It would be too tedious to rehearse all other places, which might be brought out of the ancient doctors, against images and idolatry: wherefore we shall hold ourself contented with these few at this present.

Now as concerning Histories Ecclesiastical touching this matter, that you may know why, and when, and by whom, images were first used

Lib. IV *de Civ. Dei*, cap. 31
In Psalm 36 et 113

privately, and afterwards not only received into the Christians' churches and temples, but in conclusion worshipped also, and how the same was gainsaid, resisted, and forbidden, as well by godly bishops and learned doctors, as also by sundry Christian princes: I will briefly collect into a compendious history, that which is at large, and in sundry places, written by divers ancient writers and historiographers, concerning this matter.

As the Jews, having most plain and express commandment of God, that they should neither make nor worship any image (as it is at large before declared), did notwithstanding, by the example of the Gentiles or heathen people that dwelt about them, fall to the making of images and worshipping of them, and so to the committing of most abominable idolatry; for the which God, by his holy Prophets, doth most sharply reprove and threaten them, and afterward did accomplish his said threatenings, by extreme punishing of them (as is also above specified): even so some of the Christians in old time, which were converted from worshipping of idols and false gods, unto the true living God, and to our Saviour Jesus Christ, did of a certain blind zeal, and as men long accustomed to images, paint or carve images of our Saviour Christ, his mother Mary, and of the Apostles, thinking that this was a point of gratitude and kindness, towards those by whom they had received the true knowledge of God, and the doctrine of the Gospel. But these pictures or images came not yet into churches, nor were not worshipped of a long time after.

And, lest you should think that I do say this of mine own head only, without authority, I allege for me Eusebius, Bishop of Cesarea, and the most ancient author of the *Ecclesiastical History* (who lived about the three hundred and thirtieth year of our Lord, in Constantinus Magnus' days, and his son Constantius, Emperors), in the seventh book of his *History Ecclesiastical*, the fourteenth chapter, and St Jerome upon the tenth chapter of the Prophet Jeremy; who both expressly say, that the "error" of images (for so St Jerome calleth it), "hath" come in and "passed" to the Christians from the Gentiles "by an heathenish use" and custom. The cause and means Eusebius showeth, saying,

> It is no marvel, if they which being Gentiles before, and did believe, seemed to offer this as a gift unto our Saviour, for the benefits which they had received of him. Yea, and we do see now, that images of Peter and Paul, and our Saviour himself, be made, and tables to be painted: which me think to have been observed, and kept indifferently by an heathenish custom; for the heathen are wont so to honour them whom they judged honour worthy. For that some tokens of old men should be kept for the remembrance of posterity, is a token of their honour that were before, and the love of those that come after.

Thus far I have rehearsed Eusebius' words. Where note ye, that both St Jerome and he agree herein, that these images came in amongst

Christian men by such as were Gentiles, and accustomed to idols, and being converted to the faith of Christ, retained yet some remnants of Gentility not throughly purged; for St Jerome calleth it an "error" manifestly. And the like example we see, in the Acts of the Apostles, of the Jews: who, when they were converted to Christ, would have brought in their circumcision (whereunto they were so long accustomed) with them into Christ's religion; with whom the Apostles, namely St Paul, had much ado for the staying of that matter. But of circumcision was less marvel, for that it came first in by God's ordinance and command-ment. A man may most justly wonder of images, so directly against God's holy word and strait commandment, how they should enter in. But images were not yet worshipped in Eusebius' time, nor publicly set up in churches and temples; and they who privately had them, did err of a certain zeal, and not by malice: but afterwards they crept out of private houses, into churches, and so bred first superstition, and last of all idolatry, amongst Christians, as hereafter shall appear. Acts 15

In the time of Theodosius and Martian, Emperors, who reigned about the year of our Lord 460, and eleven hundred years ago, when the people of the city of Nola, once a year did celebrate the birthday of St Felix, in the temple, and used to banquet there sumptuously, Pontius Paulinus, Bishop of Nola, caused the walls of the temple to be painted with stories taken out of the Old Testament, that the people beholding and considering those pictures, might the better abstain from too much surfeiting and riot. And about the same time Aurelius Prudentius, a very learned and Christian poet, declareth how he did see painted in a church, the history of the passion of St Cassian, a schoolmaster and martyr, whom his own scholars, at the commandment of the tyrant, tormented with the pricking, or stabbing in of their pointels or brazen pens, into his body, and so by a thousand wounds and mo (as saith Prudentius), most cruelly slew him. And these were the first paintings in churches that were notable of anti-quity. And so by this example came in painting, and afterward, images of timber and stone and other matter, into the churches of Christians.

Now, and ye will consider this beginning, men are not so ready to worship a picture on a wall, or in a window, as an embossed and gilt image, set with pearl and stone. And a process of a story, painted with the gestures and actions of many persons, and commonly the sum of the story written withal, hath another use in it, than one dumb idol or image standing by itself. But from learning by painted stories, it came by little and little to idolatry. Which when godly men, as well emperors and learned bishops as others, perceived, they commanded that such pictures, images or idols, should be used no more. And I will, for a declaration thereof, begin with the decree of the ancient Christian Emperors Valens and Theodosius the Second, who reigned about four hundred years after our Saviour Christ's ascension, who forbad that any images should be made or painted privately; for certain it is, that there was none in temples publicly in their time. These Emperors did write unto the Captain of the Army, attending on the Emperors, after this sort:

> Valens and Theodosius, Emperors, unto the Captain of the Army. Whereas we have a diligent care to maintain the religion of God above all things, we will grant to no man to set forth, grave, carve, or paint the image of our Saviour Christ, in colours, stone, or any other matter; but, in what place soever it shall be found, we command that it be taken away, and that all such as shall attempt anything contrary to our decrees or commandment herein, shall be most sharply punished.

This decree is written in the books named *Libri Augustales*, the *Imperial Books*, gathered by Tribonianus, Basilides, Theophilus, Dioscorus, and Satira, men of great authority and learning, at the commandment of the emperor Justinian, and is alleged by Petrus Crinitus, a notable learned man, in the ninth book and ninth chapter of his work entitled *de Honesta Disciplina*, that is to say, *Of Honest Learning*. Here you see what Christian princes, of most ancient times, decreed against images, which then began to creep in amongst the Christians. For it is certain, that by the space of three hundred years and more, after the death of our Saviour Christ, and before these godly Emperors' reign, there were no images publicly in churches or temples. How would the idolaters glory, if they had so much antiquity and authority for them, as is here against them!

Now shortly after these days, the Goths, Vandals, Huns, and other barbarous and wicked nations, burst into Italy and all parts of the West countries of Europe, with huge and mighty armies, spoiled all places, destroyed cities, and burned libraries; so that learning and true religion went to wrack, and decayed incredibly. And so the bishops of those latter days being of less learning, and in the middle of wars taking less heed also than did the bishops afore, by ignorance of God's word and negligence of bishops, and specially barbarous princes, not rightly instructed in true religion, bearing the rule, images came into the Church of Christ in the said West parts, where these barbarous people ruled, not now in painted cloths only, but embossed in stone, timber, metal, and other like matter; and were not only set up, but began to be worshipped also. And therefore Serenus, Bishop of Massile, the head town of Gallia Narbonensis (now called the Province), a godly and learned man, who was about six hundred years after our Saviour Christ, seeing the people, by occasion of images, fall to most abominable idolatry, brake to pieces all the images of Christ and Saints which were in that city; and was therefore complained upon to Gregory, the first of that name Bishop of Rome, who was the first learned bishop that did allow the open having of images in churches, that can be known by any writing or history of antiquity.

And upon this Gregory do all image worshippers at this day ground their defence. But, as all things that be amiss have, from a tolerable beginning, grown worse and worse, till they at the last became untolerable, so did this matter of images. First, men used privately, stories painted in tables, cloths, and walls; afterwards, gross and embossed images, privately in their own houses. Then afterwards pictures first, and after them embossed images, began to creep into churches, learned and godly men ever speaking against them. Then by use, it was openly maintained that they might be in churches, but yet forbidden that they should be worshipped. Of which opinion was Gregory, as by the said Gregory's Epistle to the forenamed Serenus, Bishop of Massile, plainly appeareth; which Epistle is to be found in the book of the Epistles of Gregory, or Register, in the tenth part of the fourth Epistle, where he hath these words: "That thou didst forbid images to be worshipped, we praise altogether; but that thou didst break them, we blame. For it is one thing to worship the picture, and another by the picture of the story to learn what is to be worshipped. For that which Scripture is to them that read, the same doth picture perform unto idiots" (or the unlearned) "beholding": and so forth. And after a few words: "Therefore it should not have been broken, which was set up, not to be worshipped in churches, but only to instruct the minds of the ignorant." And a little after:

> Thus thou shouldest have said, If you will have images in the church, for that instruction wherefore they were made in old time, I do permit that they may be made, and that you may have them. And show them that not the sight of the story which is opened by the picture, but that worshipping which was inconveniently given to the pictures, did mislike you. And if any would make images, not to forbid them, but avoid by all means to worship any image.

By these sentences, taken here and there out of Gregory's Epistle to Serenus (for it were too long to rehearse the whole), ye may understand whereunto the matter was now come, six hundred years after Christ; that the having of images or pictures in the churches, were then maintained in the West part of the world (for they were not so froward yet in the East Church), but the worshipping of them, was utterly forbidden. And you may withal note, that seeing there is no ground for worshipping of images in Gregory's writing, but a plain condemnation thereof, that such as do worship images, do unjustly allege Gregory for them. And further, if images in the Church do not teach men, according to Gregory's mind, but rather blind them, it followeth that images should not be in the church, by his sentence, who only would they should be placed there, to the end that they might teach the ignorant.

Wherefore, if it be declared that images have been and be worshipped, and also that they teach nothing but errors and lies (which shall by God's grace hereafter be done), I trust that then by Gregory's own determination, all images and image-worshippers shall be overthrown.

But in the mean season, Gregory's authority was so great in all the West Church, that by his encouragement, men set up images in all places: but their judgement was not so good to consider why he would have them set up, but they fell all on heaps to manifest idolatry, by worshipping of them, which Bishop Serenus (not without just cause) feared would come to pass. Now if Serenus his judgement, thinking it meet that images whereunto idolatry was committed should be destroyed, had taken place, idolatry had been overthrown; for to that which is not, no man committeth idolatry. But of Gregory's opinion, thinking that images might be suffered in churches, so it were taught that they should not be worshipped, what ruin of religion, and what mischief ensued afterward to all Christendom, experience hath to our great hurt and sorrow proved: first, by the schism rising between the East and the West church about the said images; next, by the division of the Empire into two parts, by the same occasion of images, to the great weakening of all Christendom; whereby, last of all, hath followed the utter overthrow of the Christian religion, and noble Empire, in Greece and all the East parts of the world, and the encrease of Mahomet's false religion, and the cruel dominion and tyranny of the Saracens and Turks; who do now hang over our necks also, that dwell in the West parts of the world, ready at all occasions to overrun us. And all this do we owe unto our idols and images, and our idolatry in worshipping of them.

Eutrop. Lib: *de Rebus Rom. 23*

But now give you ear a little to the process of the history. Wherein I do much follow the Histories of Paulus Diaconus and others, joined with Eutropius, an old writer: for though some of the authors were favourers of images, yet do they most plainly and at large prosecute the histories of those times: whom Baptist Platina also, in his *History of Popes*, as in the *Lives of Constantine and Gregory the Second*, Bishops of Rome, and other places where he entreateth of this matter, doth chiefly follow. After

Platina *in Vitis Constantini et Greg. II*

Gregory's time, Constantine, Bishop of Rome, assembled a Council of bishops in the West Church, and did condemn Philippicus, then Emperor, and John, Bishop of Constantinople, of the heresy of the Monothelites, not without a cause indeed, but very justly. When he had so done, by the consent of the learned about him, the said Constantine, Bishop of Rome, caused the images of the ancient fathers, which had been at those six Councils which were allowed and received of all men, to be painted in the entry of St Peter's church at Rome. When the Greeks had knowledge hereof, they began to dispute and reason the matter of images with the Latins, and held this opinion, that images could have no place in Christ's Church; and the Latins held the contrary, and took part with the images. So the East and West Churches, which agreed evil before, upon this contention about images, fell to utter enmity, which was never well reconciled yet. But in the mean season Philippicus and Arthemius or Anastasius, Emperors, commanded images and pictures to be pulled down and rased out, in every place of their dominion. After them came Theodosius the Third: he commanded the defaced images to be painted again in their places. But this Theodosius reigned but one year. Leo, the third of that name, succeeded him; who was a Syrian born, a very wise, godly, merciful, and valiant prince. This Leo, by proclamation, commanded that all images set up in churches to be worshipped, should be plucked down and defaced, and required specially the Bishop of Rome, that he should do the same; and himself in the mean season, caused all images that were in the imperial city Constantinople, to be gathered on an heap into the middle of the city, and there publicly burned them to ashes, and whited over and rased out all pictures painted upon the walls of the temples, and punished sharply divers maintainers of images. And when some did therefore report him to be a tyrant, he answered, that such of all other were most justly punished, which neither worshipped God aright, nor regarded the imperial majesty and authority, but maliciously rebelled against wholesome and profitable laws. When Gregorius, the third of that name Bishop of Rome, heard of the Emperor's doings in Greece concerning images, he assembled a Council of Italian bishops against him; and there made decrees for images, and that more reverence and honour should yet be given to them than was before; and stirred up the Italians against the Emperor, first at Ravenna, and moved them to rebellion. And as Auspurgensis, and Anthonius Bishop of Florence, testify in their Chronicles, he caused Rome and all Italy at the last to refuse their obedience, and the payment of any more tribute to the Emperor, and so by treason and rebellion maintained their idolatry. Which example other bishops of Rome have continually followed, and gone through withal most stoutly.

Treason and rebellion for the defence of images

After this Leo, which reigned twenty-four years, succeeded his son Constantine the Fifth; who after his father's example, kept images out of the temples. And being moved, with the Council which Gregory had assembled in Italy for images, against his father, he also assembled a Council of all the learned men and bishops of Asia and Greece; although some writers place this Council in Leo Isauricus his father's latter days. In this great assembly they sat in Council, from the fourth of the Idus of February, to the sixth of the Idus of August, and made concerning the use of images this decree: "It is not lawful, for them that believe in God through Jesus Christ, to have any images, neither of the Creator nor of any creatures, set up in temples to be worshipped; but rather that all images, by the law of God and for the avoiding of offence, ought to be

A Council against images

taken out of churches." And this decree was executed in all places where any images were found, in Asia or Greece. And the Emperor sent the determination of this Council, holden at Constantinople, to Paul, then Bishop of Rome, and commanded him to cast all images out of the churches: which he, trusting in the friendship of Pipine, a mighty prince, refused to do. And both he and his successor Stephanus the Third, who assembled another Council in Italy for images, condemned the Emperor and the Council of Constantinople of heresy; and made a decree, that "the holy images" (for so they called them), of Christ, the blessed Virgin, and other Saints, were indeed worthy honour and worshipping. When Constantine was dead, Leo the Fourth his son reigned after him; who married a woman of the city of Athens, named Theodora, who also

Or Eirene was called Hirene, by whom he had a son, named Constantine the Sixth; and dying whilst his son was yet young, left the regiment of the empire, and governance of his young son, to his wife Hirene. These things were done in the Church about the year of our Lord 760.[*]

Note here, I pray you, in this process of the story, that in the churches of Asia and Greece there were no images publicly, by the space of almost seven hundred years. And there is no doubt but the primitive Church next the Apostles' times was most pure. Note also, that when the contention began about images, how of six Christian Emperors, who were the chief magistrates by God's law to be obeyed, only one, which was Theodosius (who reigned but one year), held with images. All the other Emperors, and all the learned men and bishops of the east Church, and that in assembled Councils, condemned them; besides the two Emperors before mentioned, Valens and Theodosius the Second, who were long before these times, who straitly forbad that any images should be made. And universally after this time all the Emperors of Greece, only Theodosius excepted, destroyed continually all images. Now on the contrary part note ye, that the Bishops of Rome, being no ordinary magistrates appointed of God out of their diocese, but usurpers of princes' authority contrary to God's word, were the maintainers of images against God's word, and stirrers up of sedition and rebellion, and workers of continual treason against their sovereign lords, contrary to God's law and the ordinances of all human laws, being not only enemies to God, but also rebels and traitors against their princes. These be the first bringers in of images openly into churches; these be the maintainers of them in the churches; and these be the means whereby they have maintained them, to wit, conspiracy, treason, and rebellion against God and their princes.

Now to proceed in the history most worthy to be known. In the nonage of Constantine the Sixth, the Empress Hirene his mother, in whose

---

[*] Correcting the Homilist, who follows a mistake in Bullinger, Griffiths observes that Theodora and Eirene are not the same person, and gives accurate dates: Leo IV reigned 775–80.

hands the regiment of the empire remained, was governed much by the advice of Theodore, Bishop, and Tharasius, Patriarch of Constantinople, who practised and held with the Bishop of Rome, in maintaining of images most earnestly. By whose counsel and entreaty, the Empress first most wickedly digged up the body of her father in law, Constantine the Fifth, and commanded it to be openly burned, and the ashes to be thrown into the sea. Which example (as the constant report goeth) had like to have been put in practice with princes' corses in our days, had the authority of the holy father continued but a little longer. The cause why the Empress Hirene thus used her father-in-law was, for that he when he was alive, had destroyed images, and had taken away the sumptuous ornaments of churches, saying that Christ, whose temples they were, allowed poverty, and not pearls and precious stones. Afterward the said Hirene, at the persuasion of Adrian, Bishop of Rome, and Paul the Patriarch of Constantinople, and his successor Tharasius, assembled a Council of the bishops of Asia and Greece, at the city Nicea; where, the Bishop of Rome's legates being presidents of the Council, and ordering all things as they listed, the Council which was assembled before, under the Emperor Constantine the Fifth, and had decreed that all images should be destroyed, was condemned as an heretical Council and assembly, and a decree was made, that images should be set up in all the churches of Greece, and that honour and worship also should be given unto the said images. And so the Empress, sparing no diligence in setting up of images, nor cost in decking them in all churches, made Constantinople within a short time altogether like Rome itself. And now you may see that come to pass, which Bishop Serenus feared, and Gregory the First forbad in vain, to wit, that images should in no wise be worshipped. For now not only the simple and unwise, unto whom images (as the Scriptures teach) be specially a snare, but the bishops and learned men also, fall to idolatry by occasion of images, yea, and make decrees and laws also, for the maintenance of the same. So hard is it, and indeed impossible, any long time to have images publicly in churches and temples, without idolatry; as by the space of a little more than one hundred years, betwixt Gregory the First forbidding most straitly the worshipping of images, and Gregory the Third, Paul, and Leo the Third, Bishops of Rome, with this Council, commanding and decreeing that images should be worshipped, most evidently appeareth.

A decree that images should be worshipped

Now, when Constantine the young Emperor came to the age of twenty years, he was daily in less and less estimation. For such as were about his mother persuaded her, that it was God's determination that she should reign alone, and not her son with her. The ambitious woman believing the same, deprived her son of all imperial dignity, and compelled all the men of war, with their captains, to swear to her, that they would not suffer her son Constantine to reign during her life. With which indignity the young prince being moved, recovered the regiment of the empire unto himself, by force; and being brought up in true religion in his father's time, seeing the superstition of his mother Hirene, and the idolatry committed by images, cast down, brake, and burned all the idols and images that his mother had set up. But within a few years after, Hirene the Empress, taken again into her son's favour, after she had persuaded him to put out Nicephorus his uncle's eyes, and to cut out the tongues of his four other uncles, and to forsake his wife, and by such means to bring him in hatred with all his subjects, now further to declare that she was no changeling, but the same woman that had before, digged up and burned her father-in-law's body, and that she would be as natural a mother, as she had been kind daughter, seeing the images which she loved so well, and had with so great cost set up, daily destroyed by her son the Emperor, by the help of certain good companions, deprived her son of the empire; and first, like a kind and loving mother, put out both his eyes, and laid him in prison; where, after long and many torments, she at the last most cruelly slew him. In this History joined to Eutropius it is written, that the sun was darkened, by the space of seventeen days, most strangely and dreadfully, and that all men said, that for the horribleness of that cruel and unnatural fact of Hirene, and the putting out of the Emperor's eyes, the sun had lost his light. But indeed God would signify, by the darknesss of the sun, into what darkness and blindness, of ignorance and idolatry, all Christendom should fall, by the occasion of images, the bright sun of his eternal truth, and light of his holy word, by the mists and black clouds of men's traditions being blemished and darkened: as by sundry most terrible earthquakes, happening about the same time God signified, that the quiet state of true religion should by such idolatry, be most horribly tossed and turmoiled.

And here may you see, what a gracious and virtuous lady this Hirene was, how loving a niece to her husband's uncles, how kind a mother-in-law to her son's wife, how loving a daughter to her father-in-law, how natural a mother to her own son, and what a stout and valiant captain the bishops of Rome had of her, for the setting up and maintenance of their idols or images. Surely they could not have found a meeter patron, for the maintenance of such a matter, than this Hirene, whose ambition and desire of rule was insatiable, whose treason, continually studied and wrought, was most abominable, whose wicked and unnatural cruelty passed Medea and Progne; whose detestable parricides have ministered matter to poets to write their horrible tragedies. And yet certain historiographers, who do put in writing all these her horrible wickedness, for love they had to images, which she maintained, do praise her as a godly

Empress, and as sent from God. Such is the blindness of false superstition, if it once take possession in a man's mind, that it will both declare the vices of wicked princes, and also commend them. But not long after, the said Hirene, being suspected to the princes and lords of Greece of treason, in alienating the empire to Charles King of the Francons, and for practising a secret marriage between herself and the said king, and being convicted of the same, was by the said lords deposed, and deprived again of the empire, and carried into exile into the island Lesbos, where she ended her lewd life.

While these tragedies about images were thus in working in Greece, the same question, of the use of images in churches, began to be moved in Spain also. And at Elibery, a noble city now Granate, was a Council of Spanish bishops and other learned men assembled; and there, after long deliberation and debating of the matter, it was concluded at length, of the whole Council, after this sort, in the thirty-sixth article: "We think that pictures ought not to be in churches, lest that which is honoured or worshipped be painted on walls." And in the forty-first canon of that Council it is thus written: "We thought good to admonish the faithful, that as much as in them lieth, they suffer no images to be in their houses: but if they fear any violence of their servants, at the least let them keep themselves clean and pure from images; if they do not so, let them be accounted as none of the Church." Note here, I pray you, how a whole and great country, in the West and South parts of Europe, nearer to Rome a great deal than to Greece in situation of place, do agree with the Greeks against images, and do not only forbid them in churches, but also in private houses, and do excommunicate them that do the contrary. And another Council of the learned men of all Spain also, called Concilium Toletanum Duodecimum, decreed and determined likewise, against images and image-worshippers. But when these decrees of the Spanish Council, at Elibery, came to the knowledge of the Bishop of Rome and his adherents, they, fearing lest all Germany also would decree against images, and forsake them, thought to prevent the matter, and by the consent and help of the Prince of Francons (whose power was then most great in the West parts of the world), assembled a Council of Germans, at Frankford, and there procured the Spanish Council against images aforementioned, to be condemned, by the name of the Felician heresy (for that Felix, Bishop of Aquitania, was chief in that Council), and obtained that the acts of the second Nicene Council, assembled by Hirene (the holy empress whom ye heard of before), and the sentence of the Bishop of Rome for images, might be received. For much after this sort do the papists report the history of the Council of Frankford. Notwithstanding, the book of Carolus Magnus his own writing (as the title showeth), which is now put in print, and commonly

Another Council against images

Decrees of the Council against images

Yet another Council against images

in men's hands, showeth the judgement of that prince, and of the whole Council of Frankford also, to be against images, and against the second Council of Nice, assembled by Hirene for images; and calleth it an arrogant, foolish, and ungodly Council; and declareth the assembly of the Council of Frankford, to have been directly made and gathered, against that Nicene Council, and the errors of the same. So that it must needs follow, that either there were in one prince's time two Councils assembled at Frankford, one contrary to another, which by no history doth appear, or else that, after their custom, the popes and papists have most shamefully corrupted that Council, as their manner is to handle, not only Councils, but also all Histories and writings of the old doctors, falsifying and corrupting them for the maintenance of their wicked and ungodly purposes, as hath in times of late come to light, and doth in our days more and more continually appear most evidently. Let the forged gift of Constantine, and the notable attempt to falsify the first Nicene Council for the pope's supremacy, practised by popes in St Augustine's time, be a witness hereof; which practice indeed had then taken effect, had not the diligence and wisdom of St Augustine, and other learned and godly bishops in Afrike, by their great labour and charges, also resisted and stopped the same.

The forged gift of Constantine, &c. Nicene Council like to be falsified

Now to come towards an end of this history, and to show you the principal point that came to pass by the maintenance of images. Whereas, from Constantinus Magnus' time until that day, all authority imperial and princely dominion, of the Empire of Rome, remained continually in the right and possession of the Emperors, who had their continuance and seat imperial at Constantinople, the city royal, Leo the Third, then Bishop of Rome, seeing the Greek Emperors so bent against his *gods of gold and silver, timber and stone*, and having the King of the Francons or Frenchmen, named Charles, whose power was exceeding great in the West countries, very appliable to his mind, for causes hereafter appearing, under the pretence that they of Constantinople were for that matter of images, under the Pope's ban and curse, and therefore unworthy to be Emperors, or to bear rule, and for that the Emperors of Greece, being far off, were not ready at a beck, to defend the Pope against the Lombards his enemies, and others with whom he had variance: this Leo the Third, I say, attempted a thing exceeding strange, and unheard of before, and of incredible boldness and presumption; for he, by his papal authority, doth translate the government of the Empire, and the crown and name imperial, from the Greeks, and giveth it unto Charles the Great, King of the Francons; not without the consent of the forenamed Hirene, Empress of Greece, who also sought to be joined in marriage with the said Charles. For the which cause, the said Hirene was by the lords of Greece deposed and banished, as one

Dan. 5:4, 23

that had betrayed the Empire, as ye before have heard. And the same princes of Greece did, after the deprivation of the said Hirene, by common consent elect and create (as they always had done) an Emperor, named Nicephorus: whom the Bishop of Rome, and they of the West, would not acknowledge for their Emperor, for they had already created them another. And so there became two Emperors: and the Empire, which was before one, was divided into two parts, upon occasion of idols and images, and the worshipping of them; even as the kingdom of the Israelites was in old time, for the like cause of idolatry, divided in King Roboam his time. And so the Bishop of Rome, having the favour of Charles the Great by this means assured to him, was wondrously enhanced in power and authority, and did in all the West Church, specially in Italy, what he lust; where images were set up, garnished, and worshipped of all sorts of men. But images were not so fast set up and so much honoured in Italy and the West, but Nicephorus Emperor of Constantinople, and his successors Scauratius, the two Michaels, Leo, Theophilus, and other Emperors their successors in the Empire of Greece, continually pulled them down, brake them, burned them, and destroyed them as fast. And when Theodorus Emperor would, at the Council of Lyons, have agreed with the Bishop of Rome, and have set up images, he was by the nobles of the Empire of Greece deprived, and another chosen in his place. And so rose a jealousy, suspicion, grudge, hatred, and enmity between the Christians and Empires of the East countries and West, which could never be quenched nor pacified. So that, when the Saracens first, and afterward the Turks, invaded the Christians, the one part of Christendom would not help the other. By reason whereof, at the last, the noble Empire of Greece, and the city imperial Constantinople, was lost, and is come into the hands of the infidels, who now have overrun almost all Christendom, and possessing past the middle of Hungary, which is part of the West Empire, do hang over all our heads, to the utter danger of all Christendom.

Thus we see, what a sea of mischiefs, the maintenance of images hath brought with it; what an horrible schism, between the East and the West Church; what an hatred, between one Christian and another; Councils against Councils, Church against Church, Christians against Christians, princes against princes; rebellions, treasons, unnatural and most cruel murders; the daughter digging up and burning her father the emperor his body; the mother, for love of idols, most abominably murdering her own son, being an emperor; at the last, the tearing in sunder of Christendom and the Empire, into two pieces, till the Infidels, Saracens, and Turks, common enemies to both parts, have most cruelly vanquished, destroyed, and subdued the one part, the whole Empire of Greece, Asia the Less, Thracia, Macedonia, Epirus, and many other great and goodly

These things were done about the 803 year of our Lord.

Or, Stauratius

countries and provinces, and have won a great piece of the other Empire, and put the whole in dreadful fear, and most horrible danger. For it is (not without a just and great cause) to be dread, lest, as the Empire of Rome was, even for the like cause of images and the worshipping of them, torn in pieces and divided, as was for idolatry the kingdom of Israel in old time divided, so like punishment, as for the like offence fell upon the Jews, will also light upon us; that is, lest the cruel tyrant, and enemy of our commonwealth and religion, the Turk, by God's just vengeance, in like wise partly murder, and partly lead away into captivity us Christians, as did the Assyrian and Babylonian kings murder, and lead away the Israelites; and lest the Empire of Rome, and Christian religion, be so utterly brought under foot, as was then the kingdom of Israel, and true religion of God. Whereunto the matter already, as I have declared, shrewdly inclineth on our part; the greater part of Christendom, within less than three hundred years' space, being brought in captivity, and most miserable thraldom, under the Turks, and the noble Empire of Greece clean everted: whereas, if the Christians, divided by these image matters, had holden together, no infidels and miscreants could thus have prevailed against Christendom. And all this mischief and misery which we have hitherto fallen into, do we owe to

Dan. 5:4, 23 our mighty *gods of gold and silver, stock and stone*; in whose help and defence, where they cannot help themselves, we have trusted so long, until our enemies the infidels, have overcome and overrun us almost altogether: a just reward, for those that have left the mighty living God, the Lord of hosts! and have stooped, and given the honour due to him,

Psalm 115:5–8, 97:7; Deut. 27:15; Isai. 42:17; 14:16; Wisd. 14:8 to dead blocks and stocks, who *have eyes and see not, ears and hear not, feet and cannot go*, and so forth, and are *cursed* of God, *and all they that make them, and that put their trust in them.*

Thus you understand, well beloved in our Saviour Christ, by the judgement of the old learned and godly doctors of the Church, and by ancient Histories Ecclesiastical, agreeing to the verity of God's word, alleged out of the Old Testament and the New, that images and image worshipping were in the primitive Church, which was most pure and uncorrupt, abhorred and detested, as abominable and contrary to true Christian religion; and that, when images began to creep into the Church, they were not only spoken and written against, by godly and learned bishops, doctors, and clerks, but also condemned by whole councils, of bishops and learned men assembled together; yea, the said images by many Christian emperors and bishops were defaced, broken, and destroyed, and that above seven hundred and eight hundred years ago; and that therefore it is not of late days, as some would bear you in hand, that images and image worshipping have been spoken and written against. Finally, you have heard what mischief and misery hath, by the occasion of the said images, fallen upon whole Christendom, besides the loss of infinite souls, which is most horrible of all. Wherefore let us beseech God, that we, being warned by his holy word forbidding all idolatry, and by the writings of old godly doctors, and Ecclesiastical Histories, written and preserved, by God's ordinance, for our admonition and warning, may flee from all idolatry, and so escape the horrible punishment and plagues, as well worldly as everlasting, threatened for the same. Which God our heavenly Father grant us, for our only Saviour and Mediator Jesus Christ's sake. Amen.

THE THIRD PART OF THE HOMILY AGAINST IMAGES AND THE WORSHIPPING OF THEM

CONTAINING
THE CONFUTATION OF THE PRINCIPAL ARGUMENTS
WHICH ARE USED TO BE MADE
FOR THE MAINTENANCE OF IMAGES
WHICH PART MAY SERVE
TO INSTRUCT THE CURATES THEMSELVES
OR MEN OF GOOD UNDERSTANDING

NOW YE HAVE HEARD how plainly, how vehemently, and that in many places, the word of God speaketh against not only idolatry and worshipping of images, but also against idols and images themselves (I mean always thus herein, in that we be stirred and provoked by them to worship them, and not as though they were simply forbidden by the New Testament without such occasion and danger). And ye have heard likewise, out of Histories Ecclesiastical, the beginning, proceeding, and success of idolatry by images, and the great contention in the Church of Christ about them, to the great trouble and decay of Christendom. And withal ye have heard the sentences of old ancient fathers, and godly learned doctors and bishops, against images and idolatry, taken out of their own writings. It remaineth, that such reasons as be made for the maintenance of images, and excessive painting, gilding, and decking, as well of them as of temples or churches, also be answered and confuted, partly by application of some places before alleged to their reasons, and partly by otherwise answering the same. Which part hath the last place in this treatise, for that it cannot well be understood of the meaner sort, nor the arguments of image maintainers can without prolixity too much tedious be answered, without the knowledge of the treatise going before. And although divers things before mentioned, be here rehearsed again, yet this repetition is not superfluous, but in a manner necessary, for that the simple sort cannot else understand, how the foresaid places are to be applied to the arguments of such as do maintain images, wherewith otherwise they might be abused.

First, it is alleged by them that maintain images, that all laws, prohibitions, and curses, noted by us out of the holy Scripture, and sentences of the doctors also by us alleged, against images, and the worshipping of them, appertain to the idols of the Gentiles or Pagans, as the idol of Jupiter, Mars, Mercury, &c., and not to our images of God, of Christ, and his Saints. But it shall be declared, both by God's word and the sentences of the ancient doctors, and judgement of the primitive Church, that all images, as well ours as the idols of the Gentiles, be forbidden and unlawful, namely in churches and temples.

And first this is to be replied out of God's word, that the images of God the Father, the Son, and the Holy Ghost, either severally, or the images of the Trinity, which we had in every church, be by the Scriptures expressly and directly forbidden and condemned, as appeareth by these

Deut. 4:12, 16

places: *The Lord spake unto you out of the middle of fire: you heard the voice* or sound *of his words, but you did see no form* or shape *at all. Lest peradventure you, being deceived, should make to yourself any graven image or likeness*: and so forth, as is at large rehearsed in the first part of this treatise against images. And therefore in the old Law, the middle of the propitiatory, which represented God's seat, was empty, lest any should take occasion to make any similitude or likeness of him. Esay, after he

Isai. 40:18–21

hath set forth the incomprehensible Majesty of God, he asketh, *To whom then will ye make God like? or what similitude will ye set up unto him? Shall the carver make him a carven image? And shall the goldsmith cover him with gold, or cast him into a form of silver plates? And for the poor man, shall the image maker frame an image of timber, that he may have somewhat to set up also?* And after this he crieth out, O wretches, *heard ye never of this? Hath it not been preached to you since the beginning*, how by the creation of the world, and the greatness of the work, they might understand the Majesty of God, the Maker and Creator of all, to be greater than that it could be expressed or set forth, in any image or bodily similitude? Thus far the Prophet Esay; who from the forty-fourth chapter to the forty-

Acts 17:29

ninth, intreateth in a manner of no other thing. And St Paul, in the Acts of the Apostles, evidently teacheth the same, that no similitude can be made unto God in *gold, silver, stone,* or any other matter. By these, and many other places of Scripture, it is evident that no image either ought,

John 1:18; 4:24

or can, be made unto God. For how can *God, a* most pure *Spirit*, whom *man never saw*, be expressed by a gross, bodily, and visible similitude? How can the infinite Majesty and greatness of God, incomprehensible to man's mind, much more not able to be compassed with the sense, be expressed in a finite and little image? How can a dead and *dumb image* express *the living God?* What can an image, which when it is fallen cannot rise up again, which can neither help his friends nor hurt his enemies, express of the most puissant and mighty God, who alone is able to reward his friends, and to destroy his enemies everlastingly? A man might justly cry with the Prophet Habacuc, *Shall such images* instruct or *teach* any thing right of God? or shall they become doctors? Wherefore men that have made an image of God, whereby to honour him, have thereby dishonoured him most highly, diminished his Majesty, blemished his glory, and falsified his truth. And therefore St Paul saith, that such as have framed any similitude or image of God, like a mortal man or any other likeness, in timber, stone, or other matter, *have changed his truth into a lie.* For both they thought it to be no longer that which it was, a stock or a stone, and took it to be that which it was not, as God, or an image of God. Wherefore an image of God is not only a lie, but a double lie also. But *the devil is a liar, and the father of lies*: wherefore the lying images which be made of God, to his great dishonour and horrible danger of his people, came from the devil. Wherefore they be convict of foolishness and wickedness, in making of images of God or the Trinity: for that no image of God ought or can be made, as by the Scriptures and good reason evidently appeareth; yea, and once to desire an image of God, cometh of infidelity, thinking not God to be present, except they might see some sign or image of him, as appeareth by the Hebrews in the wilderness willing Aaron to make them gods, whom they might see go before them.

Where they object, that seeing in Esaias and Daniel be certain descriptions of God, as sitting on a high seat, &c., why may not a painter likewise set him forth in colours to be seen, as it were a judge, sitting in a throne, as well as he is described in writing of the Prophets, seeing that scripture or writing, and picture, differ but a little? First it is to be answered, that things forbidden by God's word, as painting of images of God, and things permitted of God, as such descriptions used of the Prophets, be not all one; neither ought nor can man's reason (although it show never so goodly), prevail any thing against God's express word and plain statute law, as I may well term it. Furthermore the Scripture, although it have certain descriptions of God, yet, if you read on forth, it expoundeth itself, declaring that *God is a pure Spirit*, infinite, who *replenisheth heaven and earth*: which the picture doth not, nor expoundeth not itself, but rather, when it hath set God forth, in a bodily similitude, leaveth a man there, and will easily bring one into the heresy of the Anthropomorphites, thinking God to have hands and feet, and to sit as a man doth; which they that do, saith St Augustine in his book *De Fide et Symbolo,* cap. vii, fall "into that sacrilege, which the Apostle detesteth in

2 Kings 19:4;
Acts 14:15

Hab. 2:19

Rom. 1:25

John 8:44

Exod. 32:1

Isai. 6:1;
Dan. 7:9, 10

John 4:24;
1 Kings 8:27
Acts 17:24, 25
Jer. 23:24

Rom. 1:23

those who *have changed the glory of the incorruptible God, into the similitude of a corruptible man*. For it is wickedness for a Christian to erect such an image to God in a temple; and much more wickedness, to erect such a one in his heart" by believing of it.

But to this they reply, that this reason notwithstanding, images of Christ may be made, for that he took upon him flesh, and became man. It were well that they would first grant, that they have hitherto done most wickedly, in making and maintaining of images of God, and of the Trinity, in every place, whereof they are by force of God's word and good reason convicted: and then to descend to the trial for other images.

Now concerning their objection, that an image of Christ may be made, the answer is easy: for in God's word and religion, it is not only inquired whether a thing may be done or no, but also whether it be lawful, and agreeable to God's word, to be done or no. For all wickedness may be, and is, daily done, which yet ought not to be done. And the words of the reasons, above alleged out of the Scriptures, are that images neither ought, nor can be, made unto God. Wherefore to reply, that images of Christ may be made, except withal it be proved that it is lawful for them to be made, is rather than to hold one's peace, to say somewhat, but nothing to the purpose.

Jer. 10:14, 51:17;
Rom. 1:25

And yet it appeareth, that no image can be made of Christ but a lying image, as the Scripture peculiarly calleth images *lies*. For Christ is God and man: seeing therefore that of the Godhead, which is the most excellent part, no image can be made, it is falsely called the image of Christ: wherefore images of Christ be not only defects, but also lies. Which reason serveth also for the images of Saints, whose souls, the more excellent parts of them, can by no images be represented and expressed: wherefore they be no images of Saints, whose souls reign in joy with God, but of the bodies of Saints, which as yet lie putrified in the graves. Furthermore, no true image can be made of Christ's body, for it is unknown now of what form and countenance he was. And there be in Greece and at Rome, and in other places, divers images of Christ, and none of them like to another, and yet every of them affirmeth, that theirs is the true and lively image of Christ, which cannot possibly be. Wherefore, as soon as an image of Christ is made, by and by is a lie made of him, which by God's word is forbidden. Which also is true of the images of any Saints of antiquity, for that it is unknown of what form and countenance they were. Wherefore, seeing that religion ought to be grounded upon truth, images, which cannot be without lies, ought not to be made, or put to any use of religion, or to be placed in churches and temples, places peculiarly appointed to true religion, and service of God. And thus much, that no true image of God, our Saviour Christ, or his Saints, can be made: wherewithal is also confuted that their allegation, that images be the laymen's books. For it is evident, by that which is before rehearsed, that they teach no things of God, of our Saviour Christ, and of his Saints, but lies and errors. Wherefore either they be no books, or if they be, they be false and lying books, the teachers of all error.

And now, if it should be admitted and granted, that an image of Christ could truly be made, yet is it unlawful that it should be made, yea, or that the image of any Saint should be made, specially to be set up in temples, to the great and unavoidable danger of idolatry, as hereafter shall be proved.

And first, concerning the image of Christ, that though it might be had truly, yet it were unlawful to have it in churches publicly, is a notable place in Ireneus; who reproved the heretics called Gnostici, for that they carried about the image of Christ, made truly after his own proportion in Pilate's time, as they said, and therefore more to be esteemed, than those lying images of him which we now have. The which Gnostici also used to set garlands upon the head of the said image, to show their affection to it.

Lib. i, cap. 24

But to go to God's word. Be not, I pray you, the words of the Scripture plain? *Beware lest thou, being deceived, make to thyself* to say, to any use of religion, *any graven image, or any similitude of any thing*, &c. And, *Cursed be the man that maketh a graven or molten image, abomination before the Lord*, &c. Be not our images such? Be not our images of Christ and his Saints either carved, or molten and cast, or similitudes of men and women? It is happy that we have not followed the Gentiles in making of images of beasts, fishes, and vermins also. Notwithstanding, the image of an horse, as also the image of the ass that Christ rode on, have in divers places been brought into the church and temple of God. And is not that which is written, in the beginning of the Lord's most holy law, and daily read unto you, most evident also? *Thou shalt not make any likeness of any thing in heaven above, in earth beneath, or in the water under the earth*, &c. Could any more be forbidden and said than this, either of the kinds of images, which be either *carved, molten*, or otherwise *similitudes*, or of things whereof images are forbidden to be made? Are not all things either *in heaven, earth, or water under the earth*? And be not our images of Christ and his Saints, *likenesses of things in heaven, earth, or in the water*?

Lev. 26:1;
Deut. 5:8

Sculptile, Fusile,
Similitudo
Deut. 27:15

Exod. 20:4–5

If they continue in their former answer, that these prohibitions concern the idols of the Gentiles, and not our images, first, that answer is already confuted, concerning the images of God and the Trinity at large, and concerning the images of Christ also, by Ireneus. And that the law of God is likewise to be understood against all our images, as well of Christ as his Saints, in temples and churches, appeareth further, by the judgement of the old doctors, and the primitive Church. Epiphanius rending a painted cloth, wherein was the picture of Christ, or of some

Saint, affirming it to be against our religion, that any such image should be had in the temple or church (as is before at large declared), judged that not only idols of the Gentiles, but that all images of Christ, and his Saints also, were forbidden by God's word, and our religion. Lactantius, affirming it to be certain that no true religion can be, where an image or picture is (as is before declared), judged, that as well all images and pictures, as the idols of the Gentiles, were forbidden; else would he not so generally have spoken and pronounced of them. And St Augustine (as is before alleged), greatly alloweth M. Varro, affirming that religion is most pure without images; and saith himself, "Images be of more force to crook an unhappy soul, than to teach and instruct it." And he saith further: "Every child, yea, every beast knoweth, that it is not God that they see. Wherefore then doth the Holy Ghost so often monish us, of that which all men know?" Whereunto St Augustine answereth thus: "For," saith he, "when images are placed in temples, and set in honourable sublimity, and begin once to be worshipped, forthwith breedeth the most vile affection of error." This is St Augustine's judgement of images in churches, that by and by they breed error and idolatry. The Christian emperors, the learned bishops, all the learned men of Asia, Greece, and Spain, assembled in Councils at Constantinople and in Spain, seven and eight hundred years ago and more, condemning and destroying all images, as well of Christ as of the Saints, set up by the Christians (as is before at large declared), testify that they understood God's word so, that it forbad our images as well as the idols of the Gentiles. And as it is written (Sap. xiv), that *images were not from the beginning, neither shall they continue to the end*, so were they not in the beginning in the primitive Church: God grant they may in the end be destroyed! For all Christians in the primitive Church, as Origen against Celsus, Cyprian also, and Arnobius do testify, were sore charged and complained on, that they had no altars nor images. Wherefore did they not, I pray you, conform themselves to the Gentiles, in making of images, but for lack of them sustained their heavy displeasure, if they had taken it to be lawful, by God's word, to have images? It is evident therefore, that they took all images to be unlawful, in the church or temple of God, and therefore had none, though the Gentiles therefore were most highly displeased, following this rule, *We must obey God rather than men*. And Zephyrus in his notes upon the *Apology* of Tertullian gathereth, that all his vehement persuasion "should be but cold, except we know this once for all, that Christian men in his time did most hate images, with their ornaments." And Ireneus (as is above declared), reproveth the heretics called Gnostici, for that they carried about the image of Christ. And therefore the primitive Church, which is specially to be followed, as most incorrupt and pure, had publicly in churches neither idols of the

Gentiles, nor any other images, as things directly forbidden by God's word.

And thus it is declared by God's word, the sentences of the doctors, and the judgement of the primitive Church, which was most pure and sincere, that all images, as well ours as the idols of the Gentiles, be by God's word forbidden, and therefore unlawful, specially in temples and churches.

Now if they, as their custom is, flee to this answer, that God's word forbiddeth not absolutely all images to be made, but that they should not be made to be worshipped; and that therefore we may have images, so we worship them not, for that they be things indifferent, which may be abused, or well used (which seemeth also to be the judgement of Damascene, and Gregory the First as is above declared; and this is one of their chief allegations for the maintenance of images, which hath been alleged since Gregory the First's time): well, then we be come to their second allegation, which in part, we would not stick to grant them. For we are not so superstitious or scrupulous, that we do abhor either flowers wrought in carpets, hangings, and other arras, either the images of princes printed or stamped in their coins, which when Christ did see in a Roman coin, we read not that he reprehended it; neither do we condemn the arts of painting and image making, as wicked of themselves. But we would admit and grant them, that images used for no religion, or superstition rather, we mean images of none worshipped, nor in danger to be worshipped of any, may be suffered. But images placed publicly in temples, cannot possibly be without danger of worshipping, and idolatry: wherefore they are not publicly to be had or suffered, in temples and churches.

The Jews, to whom this law was first given (and yet, being a moral commandment, and not ceremonial, as all doctors interpret it, bindeth us as well as them); the Jews, I say, who should have the true sense and meaning of God's law, so peculiarly given unto them, neither had in the beginning any images publicly in their Temple (as Origenes and Josephus at large declareth), neither after the restitution of the Temple would by any means consent to Herod, Pilate, or Petronius, that images should be placed only in the Temple at Jerusalem, although no worshipping of images was required at their hands, but rather offered themselves to the death, than to assent that images should once be placed in the Temple of God. Neither would they suffer any image-maker among them: and Origen addeth this cause: lest their minds should be plucked from God, to the contemplation of earthly things. And they are much commended for this earnest zeal, in maintaining of God's honour and true religion. And truth it is, that the Jews and Turks, who abhor images and idols, as directly forbidden by God's word, will

Damasc. Lib. 4 de Fide Orth. cap. 17. Gregor. in Epist. ad Seren. Massil.

Orig. Contr. Cels. Lib. 4. Joseph. Ant. Lib. 17, cap. 8; Lib. 18, cap. 5; Lib. 18, cap. 15

never come to the truth of our religion, whiles these stumbling-blocks of images remain amongst us, and lie in their way. If they object yet the brazen serpent, which Moses did set up, or the images of the cherubins, or any other images which the Jews had in their Temple, the answer is easy. We must in religion obey God's general law, which bindeth all men, and not follow examples of particular dispensation, which be no warrants for us; else we may, by the same reason, resume circumcision, and sacrificing of beasts, and other rites permitted to the Jews. Neither can those images of cherubin, set in secret, where no man might come nor behold, be any example for our public setting up of images, in churches and temples.

But to let the Jews go. Where they say that images, so they be not worshipped, as things indifferent may be tolerated in temples and churches; we infer and say for the adversative, that all our images of God, our Saviour Christ, and his Saints, publicly set up in churches and temples, places peculiarly appointed to the true worshipping of God, be not things indifferent, nor tolerable, but against God's law and commandment, taking their own interpretation and exposition of it. First, for that all images so set up publicly, have been worshipped of the unlearned and simple sort, shortly after they have been publicly so set up, and, in conclusion, of the wise and learned also. Secondly, for that they are worshipped in sundry places, now in our time also. And thirdly, for that it is impossible that images of God, Christ, or his Saints, can be suffered, specially in temples and churches, any while or space, without worshiping of them; and that idolatry, which is most abominable before God, cannot possibly be escaped and avoided, without the abolishing and destruction of images and pictures, in temples and churches; for that idolatry is to images, specially in temples and churches, an inseparable accident (as they term it); so that images in churches, and idolatry, go always both together, and that therefore the one cannot be avoided, except the other, specially in all public places, be destroyed. Wherefore, to make images, and publicly to set them up in temples and churches, places appointed peculiarly to the service of God, is to make images to the use of religion, and not only against this precept, *Thou shalt make no manner of image*, but against this also, *Thou shalt not bow down to them, nor worship them*: for they being so set up, have been, be, and ever will be worshipped.

Exod. 20:4, 5

And the full proof, of that which in the beginning of the first part of this treaty was touched, is here to be made and performed, to wit, that our images, and idols of the Gentiles, be all one, as well in the things themselves, as also in that our images have been before, be now, and ever will be, worshipped, in like form and manner as the idols of the Gentiles were worshipped, so long as they be suffered in churches and temples. Whereupon it followeth, that our images in churches have been, be, and ever will be, none other but abominable idols, and be therefore no things indifferent. And every of these parts shall be proved in order, as hereafter followeth.

And first, that our images, and the idols of the Gentiles, be all one concerning themselves, is most evident, the matter of them being *gold, silver,* or other metal, stone, wood, clay, or plaster, as were *the idols of the Gentiles*; and so, being either *molten* or cast, either *carved, graven,* hewed, or otherwise formed and fashioned, after the similitude and *likeness of man or woman,* be dead and dumb *works of man's hands,* having *mouths and speak not, eyes and see not, hands and feel not, feet and go not*; and so as well in form as matter, be altogether like the idols of the Gentiles: insomuch that all the titles, which be given to the idols in the Scriptures, may be verified in our images. Wherefore no doubt, but the like curses which are mentioned in the Scriptures, will light upon the makers and worshippers of them both.

Simulacra gentium, argentum et aurum. Fusile. Sculptile. Similitudo. Simulacrum. Opera manuum hominum. Psalm 115:4, 5, 7; Deut. 4:16, 27:15

Secondly, that they have been and be worshipped in our time, in like form and manner as were the idols of the Gentiles, is now to be proved. And for that idolatry standeth chiefly in the mind, it shall in this part first be proved, that our image-maintainers have had, and have, the same opinions and judgement of Saints, whose images they have made and worshipped, as the Gentiles idolaters had of their gods. And afterward shall be declared, that our image maintainers and worshippers have used, and use, the same outward rites, and manner of honouring and worshipping their images, as the Gentiles did use before their idols, and that therefore they commit idolatry, as well inwardly and outwardly, as did the wicked Gentiles idolaters.

And concerning the first part, of the idolatrous opinions of our image maintainers. What, I pray you, be such Saints with us, to whom we attribute the defence of certain countries, spoiling God of his due honour herein, but Dii Tutelares of the Gentiles idolaters? such as were Belus to the Babylonians and Assyrians, Osiris and Isis to the Egyptians, Vulcan to the Lemnians, and such other. What be such Saints, to whom the safeguard of certain cities are appointed, but Dii Praesides with the Gentiles idolaters; such as were at Delphos Apollo, at Athens Minerva, at Carthage Juno, at Rome Quirinus, &c.? What be such Saints to whom, contrary to the use of the primitive Church, temples and churches be builded, and altars erected, but Dii Patroni of the Gentiles idolaters? such as were in the Capitol Jupiter, in Paphus Temple Venus, in Ephesus Temple Diana, and suchlike. Alas! we seem in this thinking and doing, to have learned our religion, not out of God's word, but out of the pagan poets; who say,

Dii Tutelares

Dii Praesides

Dii Patroni

> Excessere omnes adytis arisque relictis
> Di, quibus imperium hoc steterat, &c.

Virgil, *Aeneid* II.351

that is to say, "All the gods, by whose defence this empire stood, are gone out of the temples, and have forsaken their altars."

And where one saint hath images in divers places, the same saint hath divers names thereof, most like to the Gentiles. When you hear of our Lady of Walsingham, our Lady of Ipswich, our Lady of Wilsdon, and such other, what is it, but an imitation of the Gentiles idolaters' Diana Agrotera, Diana Coryphea, Diana Ephesia, &c., Venus Cypria, Venus Paphia, Venus Gnidia? Whereby is evidently meant, that the saint for the image sake should in those places, yea, in the images themselves, have a dwelling: which is the ground of their idolatry; for where no images be, they have no such means. Terentius Varro showeth that there were three hundred Jupiters in his time: there were no fewer Veneres and Dianae: we had no fewer Christophers, Ladies, and Mary Magdalenes, and other saints. Oenomaus and Hesiodus show, that in their time there were thirty thousand gods: I think we had no fewer Saints, to whom we gave the honour due to God.

And they have not only spoiled the true living God of his due honour, in temples, cities, countries, and lands, by such devices and inventions, as the Gentiles idolaters have done before them, but the sea and waters have as well special saints with them, as they had gods with the Gentiles, Neptune, Triton, Nereus, Castor and Pollux, Venus, and such other; in whose places be come St Christopher, St Clement, and divers other, and specially our Lady, to whom shipmen sing, Ave, maris stella. Neither hath the fire scaped their idolatrous inventions: for instead of Vulcan and Vesta, the Gentiles' gods of the fire, our men have placed St Agatha, and make letters on her day, for to quench fire with. Every artificer and profession hath his special saint, as a peculiar god: as for example, scholars have St Nicholas and St Gregory, painters St Luke; neither lack soldiers their Mars, nor lovers their Venus amongst Christians. All diseases have their special saints, as gods, the curers of them; the pocks St Roch, the falling evil St Cornelis, the toothache St Appoline, &c. Neither do beasts and cattle lack their gods with us: for St Loy is the horseleach, and St Anthony the swineherd, &c.

Psalm 89:11, 50:12, 144:10, 21:12, 74:12, 127:1, 36:6

Where is God's providence and due honour in the mean season? who saith, *The heavens be mine, and the earth is mine, the whole world and all that in it is: I do give victory, and I put to flight: Of me be all counsels and help, &c.: Except I keep the city, in vain doth he watch that keepeth it: Thou, Lord, shalt save both men and beasts.* But we have left him neither heaven, nor earth, nor water, nor country, nor city, peace, nor war, to rule and govern, neither men, nor beasts, nor their diseases to cure; that a godly man might justly for zealous indignation cry out, O heaven, O earth and seas, what madness, and wickedness against God, are men fallen into! what dishonour do the creatures to their Creator and Maker! And, if we remember God sometime, yet, because we doubt of his ability or will to help, we join to him another helper, as he were a noun adjective, using these sayings: such as learn, God and St Nicholas be my speed; such as sneeze, God help and St John; to the horse, God and St Loy save thee. Thus are we become *like horses and mules, which have no understanding.* For is there not one God only, who by his power and wisdom made all things, and by his providence governeth the same, and by his goodness maintaineth and saveth them? Be not *all things of him,* by him, *and through him?* Why dost thou turn from the Creator to the creatures? This is the manner of the Gentiles idolaters: but thou art a Christian, and therefore *by Christ* alone hast *access to* God *the Father,* and help of him only.

Psalm 32:9

Rom. 11:36

Eph. 2:18;
1 Tim. 2:5

These things are not written to any reproach of the Saints themselves, who were the true servants of God, and did give all honour to him, taking none unto themselves, and are blessed souls with God; but against our foolishness and wickedness, making of the true servants of God false gods, by attributing to them the power and honour which is God's, and due to him only. And, for that we have such opinions of the power, and ready help of Saints, all our Legends, Hymns, Sequences, and Masses did contain stories, lauds, and praises of them, and prayers to them, yea, and sermons also altogether of them, and to their praises, God's word being clean laid aside. And this we do altogether agreeable to the Saints, as did the Gentiles idolaters to their false gods. For these opinions, which men have had of mortal persons, were they never so holy, the old most godly and learned Christians have written against the feigned gods of the Gentiles; and Christian princes have destroyed their images: who, if they were now living, would doubtless likewise both write against our false opinions of Saints, and also destroy their images. For it is evident, that our image maintainers have the same opinion of Saints, which the Gentiles had of their false gods, and thereby are moved to make them images, as the Gentiles did.

If answer be made, that they make Saints but intercessors to God, and means for such things as they would obtain of God; that is even, after the Gentiles' idolatrous usage, to make them, of Saints, gods called Dii Medioximi, to be mean intercessors, and helpers to God, as though he did not hear, or should be weary if he did all alone. So did the Gentiles teach that there was one chief power, working by other as means; and so they made all gods subject to fate or destiny: as Lucian in his Dialogues feigneth, that Neptune made suit to Mercury, that he might speak with Jupiter. And therefore in this also, it is most evident, that our image maintainers be all one in opinion with the Gentiles idolaters.

Medioximi Dii

Now remaineth the third part, that their rites and ceremonies, in honouring or worshipping of the images or Saints, be all one with the rites which the Gentiles idolaters used, in honouring their idols.

First, what meaneth it, that Christians, after the example of the Gentiles idolaters, go on pilgrimage to visit images, where they have the like at home, but that they have a more opinion of holiness and virtue in some images than other some, like as the Gentiles idolaters had? Which is the readiest way to bring them to idolatry, by worshipping of them, and directly against God's word, who saith, *Seek me, and ye shall live; and do not seek Bethel, neither enter not into Gilgal, neither go to Bersaba.* And against such as had any superstition in the holiness of the place, as though they should be heard for the place sake, saying, *Our fathers worshipped in this mountain, and ye say that at Jerusalem is the place where men should worship*, our Saviour Christ pronounceth: *Believe me, the hour cometh, when you shall worship the Father, neither in this mountain nor at Jerusalem, but true worshippers shall worship the Father, in spirit and truth.* But it is too well known, that by such pilgrimage-going Lady Venus, and her son Cupid, were rather worshipped wantonly in the flesh, than God the Father, and our Saviour Christ his Son, truly worshipped in the spirit. And it was very agreeable (as St Paul teacheth), that they which fell to idolatry, which is spiritual fornication, should also fall into carnal fornication, and all uncleanliness, by the just judgements of God delivering them over to abominable concupiscences.

What meaneth it, that Christian men, after the use of the Gentiles idolaters, cap and kneel before images? Which, if they had any sense and gratitude, would kneel before men: carpenters, masons, plasterers, founders, and goldsmiths, their makers and framers, by whose means they have attained this honour, which else should have been evil favoured and rude lumps of clay or plaster, pieces of timber, stone, or metal, without shape or fashion, and so without all estimation and honour; as that idol in the pagan poet confesseth, saying, "I was once a vile block, but now I am become a god," &c. What a fond thing is it for man, who hath life and reason, to bow himself to a dead and unsensible image, the work of his own hand! Is not this stooping and kneeling before them *adoration* of them, which is forbidden so earnestly by God's word? Let such as so fall down before images of Saints know and confess, that they exhibit that honour to dead stocks and stones, which the Saints themselves, Peter, Paul, and Barnabas, would not to be given them being alive, which the angel of God forbiddeth to be given to him.

And if they say they exhibit such honour, not to the image, but to the Saint whom it representeth, they are convicted of folly, to believe that they please Saints with that honour which they abhor as a spoil of God's honour: for they be no changelings, but now both, having greater understanding and more fervent love of God, do more abhor to deprive him of his due honour, and being now like unto the angels of God, do

Amos 5:4

John 4:20–3

Rom. 1:23–9

Horatius

Adorare

Gen. 23:7, 12 and 33:3
1 Kings 1:16, 23
Acts 10:25, 26 and 14:13–18

Rev. 19:10

with angels flee to take unto them, by sacrilege, the honour due to God. And herewithal is confuted their lewd distinction of Latria and Dulia: where it is evident, that the Saints of God cannot abide, that as much as any outward worshipping be done or exhibited to them. But Satan, God's enemy, desiring to rob God of his honour, desireth exceedingly that such honour might be given to him. Wherefore those which give the honour due to the Creator, to any creature, do service acceptable to no Saints, who be the friends of God, but unto Satan, God's and man's mortal and sworn enemy. And to attribute such desire of divine honour to Saints, is to blot them with a most odious and devilish ignominy and villainy, and indeed of Saints, to make them Satans, and very devils, whose property is to challenge to themselves, the honour which is due to God only.

Matt. 4:9

And furthermore, in that they say that they do not worship the images, as the Gentiles did their idols, but God and the Saints, whom the images do represent, and therefore that their doings before images be not like the idolatry of the Gentiles before their idols, St Augustine, Lactantius, and Clemens do prove evidently, that by this their answer they be all one with the Gentiles idolaters. "The Gentiles," saith St Augustine, "which seem to be of the purer religion, say, 'We worship not the images, but by the corporal image, we do behold the signs of the things which we ought to worship.'" And Lactantius saith: "The Gentiles say, 'We fear not the images, but them after whose likeness the images be made, and to whose names they be consecrated.'" Thus far Lactantius. And Clemens saith: "That serpent the devil uttereth these words by the mouth of certain men, 'We to the honour of the invisible God worship visible images': which surely is most false." See how, in using the same excuses which the Gentiles idolaters pretended, they show themselves to be all one with them in idolatry. For notwithstanding this excuse, St Augustine, Clemens, and Lactantius prove them idolaters. And Clemens saith that the serpent, the devil, putteth such excuses in the mouth of idolaters. And the Scriptures saith they worshipped the stocks and stones, notwithstanding this excuse, even as our image maintainers do. And Ezechiel therefore calleth the gods of the Assyrians *stocks and stones*, although they were but images of their gods. So are our images, of God and the Saints, named by the names of God and his Saints, after the use of the Gentiles. And the same Clemens saith thus in the same book: "They dare not give the name of the Emperor to any other, for he punisheth his offender and traitor by and by; but they dare give the name of God to other, because he for repentance suffereth his offenders." And even so do our image worshippers give both names of God and the Saints, and also the honour due to God, to their images, even as did the Gentiles idolaters to their idols.

Augustine
Psalm 113

Lactantius
Lib. 2 *Instit.*

Lib. 5 *ad Jacobum
Domini Fratrem*

Deut. 4:28
Ezek. 20:32
2 Kings 19:18

What should it mean, that they, according as did the Gentiles idolaters, light candles at noon time or at midnight before them, but therewith to honour them? For other use is there none in so doing. For in the day it needeth not, but was ever a proverb of foolishness, to light a candle at noon time; and in the night it availeth not to light a candle before the blind; and God hath neither use nor honour thereof. And concerning this candle lighting, it is notable that Lactantius, above a thousand years ago, hath written after this manner:

Lib. 6 *Instit.*
cap. 2

> If they would behold the heavenly light of the sun, then should they perceive that God hath no need of their candles, who for the use of man hath made so goodly a light. And whereas in so little a circle of the sun, which for the great distance seemeth to be no greater than a man's head, there is so great brightness, that the sight of man's eye is not able to behold it, but if one stedfastly look upon it a while, his eyes will be dulled and blinded with darkness; how great light, how great clearness, may we think to be with God, with whom is no night nor darkness?

and so forth. And by and by he saith: "Seemeth he therefore to be in his right mind, which offereth up to the Giver of all light, the light of a wax candle for a gift? He requireth another light of us, which is not smoky, but bright and clear, even the light of the mind and understanding." And shortly after he saith:

> But their gods, because they be earthly, have need of light, lest they remain in darkness. Whose worshippers, because they understand no heavenly thing, do draw the religion which they use, down to the earth; in the which, being dark of nature, is need of light. Wherefore they give to their gods no heavenly, but the earthly understanding of mortal men. And therefore they believe those things to be necessary and pleasant unto them, which are so to us; who have need either of meat when we be hungry, or drink when we be thirsty, or clothing when we be acold, or when the sun is set, candle light, that we may see.

Thus far Lactantius, and much more, too long here to write, of candle lighting in temples, before images and idols, for religion: whereby appeareth, both the foolishness thereof, and also that in opinion and act, we do agree altogether in our candle religion, with the Gentiles idolaters.

What meaneth it, that they, after the example of the Gentiles idolaters, burn incense, offer up gold to images, hang up crutches, chains, and ships, legs, arms, and whole men and women of wax, before images, as though by them or Saints (as they say) they were delivered from lameness, sickness, captivity, or shipwreck? Is not this *Colere* *imagines, to worship images,* so earnestly forbidden in God's word? If they deny it, let them read the eleventh chapter of Daniel the Prophet; who saith of Antichrist, *He shall worship god whom his fathers knew not, with*

Colere

Dan. 11:38

gold, silver, and with precious stone, and other things of pleasure: in which place the Latin word is *Colet*. And in the second of Paralipomenon, the twenty-ninth chapter, all the outward rites and ceremonies, as burning of incense and such other, wherewith God in the Temple was honoured, is called *Cultus*, to say *worshipping*; which is forbidden straitly, by God's word, to be given to images. Do not all stories ecclesiastical declare, that our holy Martyrs, rather than they would bow and kneel, or offer up one crumb of incense, before an image or idol, have suffered a thousand kinds of most horrible and dreadful death? And what excuse soever they make, yet, that all this running on pilgrimage, burning of incense and candles, hanging up of crutches, chains, ships, arms, legs, and whole men and women of wax, kneeling, and holding up of hands, is done to the images, appeareth by this: that where no images be, or where they have been and be taken away, they do no such things at all; but the places frequented when the images were there, now they be taken away, be forsaken and left desert; nay, now they hate and abhor the place deadly: which is an evident proof, that that which they did before, was done in respect of the images.

Wherefore, when we see men and women, on heaps, to go on pilgrimage to images, kneel before them, hold up their hands before them, set up candles, burn incense before them, offer up gold and silver unto them, hang up ships, crutches, chains, men and women of wax before them, attributing health and safeguard, the gifts of God, to them or the Saints whom they represent (as they rather would have it); who, I say, who can doubt, but that our image maintainers, agreeing in all idolatrous opinions, outward rites and ceremonies, with the Gentiles idolaters, agree also with them in committing most abominable idolatry?

And to increase this madness, wicked men, which have the keeping of such images, for their more lucre and advantage, after the example of the Gentiles idolaters, have reported and spread abroad, as well by lying tales as written fables, divers miracles of images: as that such an image miraculously was sent from heaven, even like Palladium or *Magna Diana Ephesiorum*; such another was as miraculously found in the earth, as the man's head was in Capitol, or the horse head in Capua. Such an image was brought by angels; such an one came itself far from the East to the West, as dame Fortune flit to Rome. Such an image of our Lady was painted by St Luke, whom of a physician they have made a painter for that purpose. Such an one a hundred yokes of oxen could not move; like Bona Dea, whom the ship could not carry; or Jupiter Olympius, which laughed the artificers to scorn, that went about to remove him to Rome. Some images, though they were hard and stony, yet for tender heart and pity, wept. Some, like Castor and Pollux, helping their friends in battle, sweat, as marble pillars do in dankish weather. Some spake more mon-

2 Chron. 29:11, 35

Cultus

Acts 19:28, 34, 35

strously than ever did Balaam's ass, who had life and breath in him. Such a cripple came and saluted this Saint of oak, and by and by he was made whole; and lo, here hangeth his crutch! Such an one in a tempest vowed to St Christopher, and scaped; and behold, here is his ship of wax! Such an one by St Leonard's help brake out of prison; and see where his fetters hang! And infinite thousands mo miracles, by like or more shameless lies, were reported. Thus do our image maintainers, in earnest, apply to their images, all such miracles as the Gentiles have feigned of their idols. And if it were to be admitted, that some miraculous acts were, by illusion of the devil, done where images be (for it is evident that the most part were feigned lies, and crafty jugglings of men), yet followeth it not therefore, that such images are either to be honoured, or suffered to remain; no more than Ezechias left the brazen serpent undestroyed, when it was worshipped, although it were both set up by God's commandment, and also approved by a great and true miracle, for as many as beheld it were by and by healed: neither ought miracles to persuade us to do contrary to God's word. For the Scriptures have, for a warning hereof, foreshowed that the kingdom of Antichrist shall be mighty in miracles and wonders, to the strong illusion of all the reprobate.

2 Kings 18:4, Num. 21:8, 9

Matt. 24:24, 2 Thess. 2:9–12, Rev. 13:13, 14

But in this they pass the folly and wickedness of the Gentiles: that they honour and worship the reliques and bones of our Saints, which prove that they be mortal men, and dead, and therefore no gods to be worshipped; which the Gentiles would never confess of their gods, for very shame. But the reliques we must kiss and offer unto, specially on Relique Sunday. And while we offer, that we should not be weary or repent us of our cost, the music and minstrelsy goeth merrily, all the offertory time, with praising and calling upon those Saints whose reliques be then in presence. Yea, and the water also, wherein those reliques have been dipped, must with great reverence be reserved, as very holy and effectuous. Is this agreeable to St Chrysostom, who writeth thus of reliques? "Do not regard the ashes of the Saint's bodies, nor the reliques of their flesh and bones, consumed with time; but open the eyes of thy faith, and behold them clothed with heavenly virtue, and the grace of the Holy Ghost, and shining with the brightness of the heavenly light." But our idolaters found too much vantage of reliques, and relique water, to follow St Chrysostom's counsel. And because reliques were so gainful, few places were there, but they had reliques provided for them. And for more plenty of reliques, some one Saint had many heads, one in one place, and another in another place. Some had six arms and twenty-six fingers. And where our Lord bare his cross alone, if all the pieces of the reliques thereof were gathered together, the greatest ship in England would scarcely bear them: and yet the greatest part of it, they say, doth yet remain in the hands of the infidels; for the which they pray in their

Homilia de Septem Macchabeis

beads' bidding, that they may get it also into their hands, for such godly use and purpose. And not only the bones of the Saints, but every thing appertaining to them, was an holy relique. In some place they offer a sword, in some the scabbard, in some a shoe, in some a saddle that had been set upon some holy horse, in some the coals wherewith St Laurence was roasted, in some place the tail of the ass which our Lord Jesus Christ sat on, to be kissed and offered to for a relique. For, rather than they would lack a relique, they would offer you a horse bone instead of a virgin's arm, or the tail of the ass, to be kissed and offered unto for reliques. Oh wicked, impudent, and most shameless men, the devisers of these things! Oh seely, foolish, and dastardly daws, and more beastly than the ass whose tail they kissed, that believe such things! Now God be merciful to such miserable and seely Christians, who by the fraud and falsehood, of those which should have taught them the way of truth and life, have been made, not only more wicked than the Gentiles idolaters, but also no wiser than asses, *horses, and mules, which have no understanding!*   Psalm 32:9

Of these things already rehearsed, it is evident, that our image maintainers have not only made images, and set them up in temples, as did the Gentiles idolaters their idols, but also that they have had the same idolatrous opinions of the Saints, to whom they have made images, which the Gentiles idolaters had of their false gods; and have not only worshipped their images with the same rites, ceremonies, superstition, and all circumstances, as did the Gentiles idolaters their idols, but in many points also have far exceeded them in all wickedness, foolishness, and madness. And if this be not sufficient to prove them image worshippers, that is to say idolaters, lo, you shall hear their own open confession. I mean not only the decrees of the second Nicene Council under Hirene, [and] the Roman Council under Gregory the Third; in which, as they teach that images are to be honoured and worshipped (as is before declared), so yet do they it warily and fearfully: in comparison to the blasphemous, bold blazing of manifest idolatry to be done to images, set forth of late, even in these our days, the light of God's truth so shining that, above other their abominable doings and writings, a man would marvel most at their impudent, shameless, and most shameful blustering boldness, who would not at the least have chosen them a time of more darkness, as meeter to utter their horrible blasphemies in, but have now taken an harlot's face, not purposed to blush, in the setting abroad the furniture of their spiritual whoredom. And here the plain blasphemy of the reverend father in God, James Naclantus, Bishop of Clugium, written in his exposition of St Paul's Epistle to the Romans, and the first chapter, and put in print now of late at Venice, may stand in stead of all: whose words of image-worshipping be these in Latin, as he did write them, not one syllable altered.

Ergo non solum fatendum est, fideles in Ecclesia adorare coram imagine, ut nonnulli ad cautelam forte loquuntur, sed et adorare imaginem, sine quo volueris scrupulo: quin et eo illam venerantur cultu, quo et prototypon ejus. Propter quod, si illud habet adorari latria, et illa latria: si dulia vel hyperdulia, et illa pariter ejusmodi cultu adoranda est.

The sense whereof in English is this: "Therefore it is not only to be confessed, that the faithful in the Church do worship before an image (as some peradventure do warily speak), but also do worship the image itself, without any scruple of doubt at all: yea, and they worship the image with the same kind of worship, wherewith they worship the copy of the image" (or the thing whereafter the image is made). "Wherefore, if the copy itself is to be worshipped with divine honour" (as is God the Father, Christ, and the Holy Ghost), "the image of them is also to be worshipped with divine honour; if the copy ought to be worshipped with inferior honour, or higher worship, the image also is to be worshipped with the same honour or worship."

Thus far hath Naclantus: whose blasphemies let Pope Gregorius the First confute, and by his authority damn them to hell, as his successors have horribly thundered. For although Gregory permitteth images to be had, yet he forbiddeth them by any means to be worshipped, and praiseth much Bishop Serenus, for the forbidding the worship of them, and willeth him to teach the people, to avoid by all means to worship any image. But Naclantus bloweth forth his blasphemous idolatry, willing images to be worshipped, with the highest kind of adoration and worship. And lest such wholesome doctrine should lack authority, he groundeth it upon Aristotle, in his book *de Somno et Vigilia*, that is, *Of Sleeping and Waking*, as by his printed book, noted so in the margin, is to be seen. Whose impudent wickedness, and idolatrous judgement, I have therefore more largely set forth, that ye may (as Virgil speaketh of Sinon), "of one know all" these image worshippers and idolaters, and understand to what point in conclusion, the public having of images in temples and churches hath brought us, comparing the times and writings of Gregory the First with our days, and the blasphemies of such idolaters as this beast of Belial, named Naclantus, is.

Wherefore now it is—by the testimony of the old godly fathers and doctors, by the open confession of bishops assembled in Councils, by most evident signs and arguments, opinions, idolatrous acts, deeds, and worshipping done to our images, and by their own open confession and doctrine, set forth in their books—declared and showed, that our images have been, and be, commonly worshipped, yea, and that they ought so to be; I will, out of God's word, make this general argument against all such makers, setters up, and maintainers of images in public places. And

Gregor. Epist. ad Seren. Massil

Of image worshipping

first of all, I will begin with the words of our Saviour Christ: *Woe be to*   Matt.18:6, 7
that man by whom an offence is given.Woe be to him that offendeth one of these
little ones, or weak ones. *Better were it for him, that a millstone were hanged*
about his neck, and he cast into the middle of the sea, and drowned, than he
should offend one of these little ones, or weak ones. And in Deuteronomy,   Deut. 27:18
God himself denounceth him *accursed, that maketh the blind to wander in*
his way. And in Leviticus: *Thou shalt not lay a stumbling-block*, or stone,   Lev. 19:14
before the blind. But images in churches and temples have been, and be,
and (as afterward shall be proved), ever will be, offences or stumbling-
blocks, specially to the weak, simple, and common people, deceiving
their hearts, by the cunning of the artificer, as the Scripture expressly, in
sundry places, doth testify, and so bringing them to idolatry. Therefore   Wisd. 13:10,
woe be to the erecter, setter up, and maintainer of images in churches   14:18–21
and temples! for a greater penalty remaineth for him, than the death of
the body.

If answer be yet made, that this offence may be taken away, by diligent
and sincere doctrine and preaching of God's word, as by other means;
and that images in churches and temples therefore, be not things
absolutely evil to all men, although dangerous to some; and therefore
that it were to be holden, that the public having of them in churches and
temples, is not expedient: as a thing perilous, rather than unlawful as a
thing utterly wicked—then followeth the third article to be proved,
which is this, that it is not possible, if images be suffered in churches and
temples, either by preaching of God's word, or by any other means, to
keep the people from worshipping of them, and so to avoid idolatry.

And first concerning preaching. If it should be admitted that,
although images were suffered in churches, yet might idolatry, by
diligent and sincere preaching of God's word, be avoided; it should
follow of necessity, that sincere doctrine might always be had and
continue, as well as images, and so, that wheresoever, to offence, were
erected an image, there also, of reason, a godly and sincere preacher
should, and might, be continually maintained. For it is reason, that the
warning be as common as the stumbling-block, the remedy as large as is
the offence, the medicine as general as the poison. But that is not
possible, as both reason and experience teacheth. Wherefore preaching
cannot stay idolatry, images being publicly suffered.

For an image, which will last for many hundred years, may for a little
be bought; but a good preacher cannot without much be continually
maintained.

Item, if the Prince will suffer it, there will be by and by many, yea,
infinite images; but sincere preachers were, and ever shall be, but a few,
in respect of the multitude to be taught. For our Saviour Christ saith,
The harvest is plentiful, but the workmen be but a few: which hath been   Matt.9:37

hitherto continually true, and will be to the world's end; and in our time, and here in our country, so true, that every shire should scarcely have one good preacher, if they were divided.

Now images will continually to the beholders preach their doctrine, that is, the worshipping of images and idolatry; to the which preaching mankind is exceeding prone, and enclined to give ear and credit, as experience of all nations and ages doth too much prove. But a true preacher, to stay this mischief, is in very many places, scarcely heard once in an whole year, and somewheres not once in seven years, as is evident to be proved. And that evil opinion which hath been long rooted in men's hearts, cannot suddenly, by one sermon, be rooted out clean. And as few are inclined to credit sound doctrine, as many, and almost all, be prone to superstition and idolatry. So that herein appeareth not only a difficulty, but also an impossibility, of the remedy.

Further, it appeareth not, by any story of credit, that true and sincere preaching hath endured in any one place, above one hundred years; but it is evident that images, superstition, and worshipping of images, and idolatry, have continued many hundred years. For all writings and experience do testify, that good things do, by little and little, ever decay, until they be clean banished; and contrariwise evil things do more and more encrease, till they come to be a full perfection of wickedness. Neither need we to seek examples far off, for a proof hereof: our present matter is an example. For preaching of God's word, most sincere in the beginning, by process of time waxed less and less pure, and after corrupt, and last of all, altogether laid down and left off, and other inventions of men crept in place of it. And on the other part, images among Christian men were first painted, and that in whole stories together, which had some signification in them; afterwards they were embossed, and made of timber, stone, plaster, and metal. And first they were only kept privately in private men's houses; and then after they crept into churches and temples: but first by painting, and after by embossing; and yet were they nowhere at the first worshipped. But shortly after, they began to be worshipped of the ignorant sort of men, as appeareth by the Epistle that Gregory, the first of that name Bishop of Rome, did write to Serenus, Bishop of Marcelles. Of the which two bishops, Serenus, for idolatry committed to images, brake them and burned them; Gregory, although he thought it tolerable to let them stand, yet he judged it abominable that they should be worshipped, and thought, as is now alleged, that the worshipping of them might be stayed by teaching of God's word, according as he exhorteth Serenus to teach the people, as in the same Epistle appeareth. But whether Gregory's opinion, or Serenus' judgement, were better herein, consider ye, I pray you; for experience by and by confuteth Gregory's opinion. For notwithstanding Gregory's writing, and the preaching of others, images being once publicly set up in temples and churches, simple men and women, shortly after, fell on heaps to worshipping of them; and at the last, the learned also were carried away with the public error, as with a violent stream or flood; and at the second Council Nicene the bishops and clergy decreed, that images should be worshipped: and so, by occasion of these stumbling-blocks, not only the unlearned and simple, but the learned and wise, not the people only, but the bishops, not the sheep, but also the shepherds themselves (who should have been guides in the right way, and light to shine in darkness), being blinded by the bewitching of images, as blind guides of the blind, fell both into the pit of damnable idolatry. In the which all the world, as it were drowned, continued until our age, by the space of about eight hundred years, unspoken against in a manner. And this success had Gregory's order: which mischief had never come to pass, had Bishop Serenus' way been taken, and all idols and images been utterly destroyed and abolished; for no man worshippeth that that is not. And thus you see how, from having of images privately, it came to public setting of them up in churches and temples, although without harm at the first, as was then of some wise and learned men judged; and from simple having them there, it came at last to worshipping of them; first by the rude people, who specially (as the Scriptures teachen), are in danger of superstition and idolatry, and afterwards by the bishops, the learned, and by the whole clergy. So that laity and clergy, learned and unlearned, all ages, sects, and degrees of men, women, and children of whole Christendom (an horrible and most dreadful thing to think), have been at once drowned in abominable idolatry, of all other vices most detested of God, and most damnable to man, and that by the space of eight hundred years and more. And to this end is come that beginning, of setting up of images in churches: then judged harmless, in experience proved not only harmful, but exitious and pestilent, and to the destruction and subversion of all good religion universally. So that I conclude, as it may be possible in some one city, or little country, to have images set up in temples and churches, and yet idolatry, by earnest and continual preaching of God's true word, and the sincere Gospel of our Saviour Christ, may be kept away for a short time; so is it impossible that, images once set up and suffered in temples and churches, any great countries, much less the whole world, can any long time be kept from idolatry. And the godly will respect not only their own city, country, and time, and the health of men of their age, but be careful for all places and times, and the salvation of men of all ages: at the least they will not lay such stumbling-blocks and snares, for the feet of other countrymen and ages, which experience hath already proved to have been the ruin of the world.

Wisd. 13 and 14

Wherefore I make a general conclusion, of all that I have hitherto said. If the stumbling-blocks and poisons of men's souls, by setting up of images will be many, yea infinite, if they be suffered, and the warnings of the said stumbling-blocks, and remedies for the said poisons, by preaching, but few, as is already declared; if the stumbling-blocks be easy to be laid, the poisons soon provided, and the warnings and remedies hard to know or come by; if the stumbling-blocks lie continually in the way, and poison be ready at hand everywhere, and warnings and remedies but seldom given; and if all men be more ready of themselves to stumble and be offended, than to be warned, all men more ready to drink of the poison, than to taste of the remedy (as is before partly, and shall hereafter more fully be declared); and so, in fine, the poison continually, and deeply, drunk of many, the remedy seldom, and faintly, tasted of a few; how can it be, but infinite of the weak and infirm shall be offended, infinite by ruin shall break their necks, infinite by deadly venom be poisoned in their souls? And how is the charity of God, or love of our neighbour in our hearts then, if when we may remove such dangerous stumbling-blocks, such pestilent poisons, we will not remove them? What shall I say of them, which will lay stumbling-blocks where before was none, and set snares for the feet, nay, for the souls of weak and simple ones, and work the danger of the eternal ruin, for whom our Saviour Christ shed his precious blood? Where better it were that the arts of painting, plastering, carving, graving, and founding, had never been found nor used, than one of them whose souls in the sight of God are so precious, should by occasion of image or picture, perish and be lost.

And thus is it declared, that preaching cannot possibly stay idolatry, if images be set up publicly in temples and churches. And as true is it, that no other remedy, as writing against idolatry, councils assembled, decrees made against it, severe laws likewise, and proclamations of princes and emperors, neither extreme punishments and penalties, nor any other remedy, could, or can be, possibly devised for the avoiding of idolatry, if images be publicly set up and suffered.

For concerning writing against images, and idolatry to them committed, there hath been alleged unto you, in the second part of this treatise, a great many places out of Tertullian, Origen, Lactantius, St Augustine, Epiphanius, St Ambrose, Clemens, and divers other learned and holy bishops, and doctors of the Church. And besides these, all Histories Ecclesiastical, and books of other godly and learned bishops and doctors, are full of notable examples and sentences, against images and the worshipping of them. And as they have most earnestly written, so did they sincerely and most diligently, in their time, teach and preach according to their writings and examples. For they were then preaching bishops, and more often seen in pulpits, than in princes' palaces; more

often occupied in his legacy who said, *Go ye into the whole world, and* Matt. 16:15
preach the gospel to all men, than in embassages, and affairs of princes of
this world. And as they were most zealous and diligent, so were they of
excellent learning, and godliness of life, and by both, of great authority
and credit with the people, and so of more force and likelihood to
persuade the people, and the people more like to believe, and follow
their doctrine. But if their preachings could not help, much less could
their writings; which do but come to the knowledge of a few that be
learned, in comparison to continual preaching, whereof the whole
multitude is partaker.

Neither did the old fathers, bishops, and doctors severally, only by
preaching and writing, but also together, great numbers of them
assembled in synods and councils, make decrees and ecclesiastical laws,
against images and the worshipping of them; neither did they so once or
twice, but divers times and in divers ages and countries, assemble
synods and councils, and made severe decrees against images and
worshipping of them; as hath been at large in the second part of this
Homily before declared. But all their writing, preaching, assembling in
councils, decreeing, and making of laws ecclesiastical, could nothing
help, either to pull down images to whom idolatry was committed, or
against idolatry, whilst images stood. For those blind books and dumb
schoolmasters, I mean images and idols (for they call them laymen's
books and schoolmasters), by their carved and painted writings, teaching and preaching idolatry, prevailed against all their written books, and
preaching with lively voice, as they call it.

Well, if preaching and writing could not keep men from worshipping
of images and idolatry, if pens and words could not do it, you would
think that penalty and swords might do it, I mean that princes, by severe
laws and punishments, might stay this unbridled affection of all men to
idolatry, though images were set up and suffered. But experience
proveth, that this can no more help against idolatry, than writing and
preaching. For Christian Emperors, whose authority ought of reason,
and by God's law, to be greatest, above eight in number, and six of them
successively reigning one after another (as is in the histories before
rehearsed), making most severe laws and proclamations against idols
and idolatry, images and the worshipping of images, and executing most
grievous punishments, yea, the penalty of death, upon the maintainers
of images, and upon idolaters and image worshippers, could not bring
to pass, that either images, once set up, might throughly be destroyed, or
that men should refrain from the worshipping of them, being set up.
And what think you then will come to pass, if men of learning should
teach the people to make them, and should maintain the setting up of
them, as things necessary in religion?

To conclude: it appeareth evidently, by all stories and writing and experience of times past, that neither preaching, neither writing, neither the consent of the learned, nor authority of the godly, nor the decrees of councils, neither the laws of princes, nor extreme punishments of the offenders in that behalf, nor no other remedy or means, can help against idolatry, if images be suffered publicly. And it is truly said, that times past are schoolmasters of wisdom, to us that follow and live after. Therefore, if in times past the most virtuous, most and best learned, the most diligent also, and in number almost infinite, ancient fathers, bishops, and doctors, with their writing, preaching, industry, earnestness, authority, assemblies, and councils, could do nothing against images, and idolatry to images once set up; what can we, neither in learning, nor holiness of life, neither in diligence, neither authority, to be compared with them, but men in contempt, and of no estimation (as the world goeth now), a few also in number, in so great a multitude and malice of men—what can we do, I say, or bring to pass, to the stay of idolatry or worshipping of images, if they be allowed to stand publicly in temples and churches? And if so many, so mighty emperors, by so severe laws and proclamations, so rigorous and extreme punishments and executions, could not stay the people from setting up and worshipping of images, what will ensue, think you, when men shall commend them, as necessary books of the laymen? Let us therefore, of these latter days, learn this lesson of the experience of the ancient antiquity, that idolatry cannot possibly be separated from images any long time; but that as an unseparable accident, or as a shadow followeth the body when the sun shineth, so idolatry followeth, and cleaveth to, the public having of images in temples and churches; and finally, as idolatry is to be abhorred and avoided, so are images, which cannot be long without idolatry, to be put away and destroyed.

Besides the which experiments, and proofs of times before, the very nature and origin of images themselves, draweth to idolatry most violently, and man's nature and inclination also, is bent to idolatry so vehemently, that it is not possible to sever or part images, nor to keep men, from idolatry, if images be suffered publicly.

That I speak of the nature and origin of images is this. Even as the first invention of them is naught, and no good can come of that which had an evil beginning—for they be altogether naught, as Athanasius, in his book against the Gentiles declareth; and St Jerome also upon the Prophet Jeremy, the sixth chapter, and Eusebius, the seventh book of his *Ecclesiastical History*, the eighteenth chapter, testify, that they first came from the Gentiles, which were idolaters and worshippers of images, unto us—and as *the invention of them was the beginning of spiritual fornication*, as the word of God testifieth, Sap. 14; so will they, naturally

Wisd. 14:12

as it were, and of necessity, turn to their origin from whence they came, and draw us with them most violently to idolatry, abominable to God and all godly men. For if the origin of images, and worshipping of them, as it is recorded in the eighth chapter of the Book of Wisdom, began of a blind love of a fond father, framing for his comfort an image of his son being dead, and so at the last men fell to the worshipping of the image, of him whom they did know to be dead; how much more will men and women fall to the worshipping of the images of God, our Saviour Christ, and his Saints, if they be suffered to stand in churches and temples publicly! For, the greater the opinion is, of the majesty and holiness of the person, to whom an image is made, the sooner will the people fall to the worshipping of the said images. Wherefore the images of God, our Saviour Christ, the blessed Virgin Mary, the Apostles, Martyrs, and other of notable holiness, are of all other images most dangerous for the peril of idolatry; and therefore greatest heed [is] to be taken, that none of them be suffered to stand publicly, in churches and temples. For there is no great dread, lest any should fall to the worshipping of the images of Annas, Cayphas, Pilate, or Judas the traitor, if they were set up. But to the other, it is already at full proved, that idolatry hath been, is, and is most like continually to be, committed.

Now, as was before touched, and is here more largely to be declared, the nature of man is none otherwise bent to worshipping of images, if he may have them and see them, than it is bent to whoredom and adultery, in the company of harlots. And, as unto a man given to the lust of the flesh, seeing a wanton harlot, sitting by her, and embracing her, it profiteth little for one to say, *Beware of fornication; God will condemn fornicators and adulterers*—for neither will he, being overcome with greater enticements of the strumpet, give ear or take heed to such godly admonitions; and when he is left afterwards alone with the harlot, nothing can follow but wickedness—even so, suffer images to be in sight in churches and temples, ye shall in vain bid them *beware of images* (as St John doth), and *flee idolatry* (as all the Scriptures warn us); ye shall in vain preach and teach them against idolatry. For a number will notwithstanding fall headlong unto it, what by the nature of images, and by the inclination of their own corrupt nature. Wherefore, as a man given to lust, to sit down by a strumpet is to tempt God, so is it likewise, to erect an idol in this proneness of man's nature to idolatry, nothing but a tempting. Now if any will say that this similitude proveth nothing, yet I pray them, let the word of God, out of the which the similitude is taken, prove something. Doth not the word of God call idolatry spiritual *fornication*? Doth it not call a gilt or painted idol or image, a strumpet with a painted face? Be not the spiritual wickedness of an idol's enticing, like the flatteries of a wanton harlot? Be not men and women as prone to

Wisd. 14 [*sic*]:15

1 Cor. 6:18,
1 Thess. 4:3
Heb. 13:4

1 John 5:21

Lev. 17:7, 20:5,
Num. 25:1, 2
Deut. 31:16
Bar. 6:9–11

spiritual fornication, I mean idolatry, as to carnal fornication? If this be denied, let all nations upon the earth which have been idolaters (as by all stories appeareth), prove it true. Let the Jews and the people of God, which were so often and so earnestly warned, so dreadfully threatened, concerning images and idolatry, and so extremely punished therefore, and yet fell unto it, prove it to be true; as in almost all the books of the Old Testament, namely, the Kings and the Chronicles and the Prophets, it appeareth most evidently. Let all ages and times, and men of all ages and times, of all degrees and conditions, wise men, learned men, princes, idiots, unlearned, and commonalty, prove it to be true. If you require examples: for wise men, ye have the Egyptians and the Indian Gymnosophists, the wisest men of the world; you have Salomon, the wisest of all other; for learned men, the Greeks, and namely the Athenians, exceeding all other nations in superstition and idolatry, as in the history of the Acts of the Apostles St Paul chargeth them; for princes and governors, you have the Romans, the rulers of the roast (as they say); you have the same forenamed King Salomon, and all the kings of Israel and Juda after him, saving David, Ezechias, and Josias, and one or two more. All these, I say, and infinite others, wise, learned, princes and governors, being all idolaters, have you for examples, and a proof of men's inclination to idolatry. That I may pass over with silence, in the mean time, infinite multitudes and millions of idiots and unlearned, the ignorant and gross people, *like unto horses and mules, in whom is no understanding*, whose peril and danger to fall on heaps to idolatry, by occasion of images, the Scriptures specially foreshow and give warning of. And indeed, how should the unlearned, simple, and foolish, scape the nets and snares of idols and images, in the which the wisest and best learned have been so entangled, trapped, and wrapped? Wherefore the argument holdeth this ground sure, that men be as inclined, of their corrupt nature, to spiritual fornication as to carnal: which the wisdom of God foreseeing, to the general prohibition, that *none should make to themselves any image or similitude*, addeth a cause depending of man's corrupt nature: *Lest*, saith God, *thou being deceived with error, honour and worship them.*

And of this ground of man's corrupt inclination, as well to spiritual fornication as to carnal, it must needs follow, that as it is the duty of the godly magistrate, loving honesty and hating whoredom, to remove all strumpets and harlots, specially out of places notoriously suspected, or resorted unto of naughty-packs, for the avoiding of carnal fornication; so is it the duty of the same godly magistrate, after the examples of the godly kings Ezechias and Josias, to drive away all spiritual harlots, I mean idols and images, specially out of suspected places, churches and temples, dangerous for idolatry to be committed to images placed there,

Acts 17:16, 22
Rom. 1:23

Psalm 32:9

Wisd. 13, 14 &c.

Deut. 4:15–19

as it were in the appointed place, and height of honour and worship (as St Augustine saith), where the living God only, and not dead stones nor stocks, is to be worshipped: it is, I say, the office of godly magistrates, likewise to avoid images and idols out of churches and temples, as spiritual harlots out of suspected places, for the avoiding of idolatry, which is spiritual fornication. August. in Psal. 36 et 113; et Lib. 4, cap. 3, *de Civ. Dei*

And as he were the enemy of all honesty, that would bring strumpets and harlots out of their secret corners, into the public market place, there freely to dwell, and occupy their filthy merchandise, so is he the enemy of the true worshipping of God, that bringeth idols and images, into the temple and church, the house of God, there openly to be worshipped, and to spoil the *zealous God* of his honour, who *will not give it to any other, nor his glory to carven images*; who is as much forsaken, and the bond of love between man and him as much broken, by idolatry, which is spiritual fornication, as is the knot and bond of marriage broken, by carnal fornication. Let all this be taken as a lie, if the word of God enforce it not to be true. *Cursed be the man*, saith God in Deuteronomy, *that maketh a carven or molten image, and placeth it in a secret corner: and all the people shall say, Amen.* Thus saith God: for at that time no man durst have or worship images openly, but in corners only; and the whole world, being the great temple of God, he that in any corner thereof, robbeth God of his glory, and giveth it to stocks and stones, is pronounced by God's word accursed. Now he that will bring these spiritual harlots out of their lurking corners, into public churches and temples, that spiritual fornication may there openly, of all men and women, without shame, be committed with them: no doubt that person is cursed of God, and twice cursed, and all good and godly men and women will say, *Amen*, and their *Amen* will take effect also. Isai. 42:8

Deut. 27:15

Yea, and furthermore, the madness of all men professing the religion of Christ, now by the space of a sort of hundred years, and yet even in our time, in so great light of the Gospel, very many running on heaps by sea and land, to the great loss of their time, expense and waste of their goods, destitution of their wives, children, and families, and danger of their own bodies and lives, to Compostella, Rome, Jerusalem, and other far countries, to visit dumb and dead stocks and stones, doth sufficiently prove the proneness of man's corrupt nature, to the seeking of idols once set up, and the worshipping of them.

And thus, as well by the origin and nature of idols and images themselves, as by the proneness and inclination of man's corrupt nature to idolatry, it is evident, that neither images, if they be publicly set up, can be separated, nor men, if they see images in temples and churches, can be stayed and kept, from idolatry.

Now, whereas they yet allege, that howsoever the people, princes, learned, and wise of old time have fallen into idolatry, by occasion of images, that yet in our time the most part, specially the learned, wise, and of any authority, take no hurt nor offence by idols and images, neither do run into far countries to them and worship them; and that they know well what an idol or image is, and how to be used: and that therefore it followeth, images in churches and temples to be an indifferent thing, as the which of some is not abused; and that therefore they may justly hold (as was in the beginning of this part by them alleged), that it is not unlawful or wicked absolutely, to have images in churches and temples, though it may, for the danger of the simpler sort, seem to be not altogether expedient: whereunto may be well replied, that Salomon also, the wisest of all men, did well know what an idol or image was, and neither took any harm thereof a great while himself, and

Wisd. 13, 14

also, with his godly writings, armed others against the danger of them; but yet afterward the same Salomon, suffering his wanton paramours to bring their idols into his court and palace, was by carnal harlots persuaded and brought at the last, to the committing of spiritual fornication with idols, and of the wisest and godliest prince, became the most foolishest and wickedest also. Wherefore it is better even for the

Ecclus. 3:26 and 13:1
1 Cor. 10:12

wisest to regard this warning, *He that loveth danger shall perish therein*, and, *Let him that standeth beware he fall not*, rather than wittingly and willingly, to lay such a stumbling-block for his own feet and others, that may perhaps bring at last to breakneck.

The good King Ezechias did know well enough, that the brazen serpent was but a dead image, and therefore he took no hurt himself thereby through idolatry to it. Did he therefore let it stand, because himself took no hurt thereof? No, not so; but being a good king, and therefore regarding the health of his seely subjects deceived by that image, and committing idolatry thereto, he did not only take it down,

2 Kings 18:4
Num. 21:8, 9
John 3:14, 15

but also brake it to pieces. And this he did to that image that was set up by the commandment of God, in the presence whereof great miracles were wrought, as that which was a figure of our Saviour Christ to come, who should deliver us from the mortal sting of the old serpent Satan. Neither did he spare it in respect of the ancientness or antiquity of it, which had continued about seven hundred years; nor for that it had been suffered and preserved by so many godly kings, before his time. How, think you, would that godly prince, if he were now living, handle our idols, set up against God's commandment directly, and being figures of nothing but folly, and for fools to gaze on, till they become as wise as the blocks themselves which they stare on, and so fall down as dared larks in that gaze, and being themselves alive, worship a dead stock or stone, gold or silver, and so become idolaters, abominable and cursed before the living God, giving the honour due unto him which made them when they were nothing, and to our Saviour Christ, who redeemed them being lost, to the dead and dumb idol, *the work of man's hand*, which never did nor can do any thing for them, no, is not able to stir, nor once to move, and therefore worse than a vile worm, which can move and creep? The excellent king Josias also did take himself no hurt of images and idols, for he did know well what they were. Did he therefore, because of his own knowledge, let idols and images stand? Much less did he set any up. Or rather did he not, by his knowledge and authority also, succour the ignorance of such as did not know what they were, by utter taking away of all such stumbling-blocks as might be occasion of ruin to his people and subjects?

Deut. 4:28; Isai. 46:7

Will they, because a few took no hurt by images or idols, break the general law of God, *Thou shalt make to thee no similitude*, &c? They might as well, because Moyses was not seduced by Jethro's daughter, nor Boos by Ruth, being strangers, reason that all the Jews might break the general law of God, forbidding his people to join their children in marriage with strangers, lest they seduce their children that they should not follow God. Wherefore they which thus reason, "Though it be not expedient, yet is it lawful, to have images publicly," and do prove that lawfulness by a few picked and chosen men; if they object that indifferently to all men, which a very few can have without hurt and offence, they seem to take the multitude for "vile souls" (as he saith in Virgil), of whose loss or safeguard no reputation is to be had—for whom yet Christ paid as dearly as for the mightiest princes, or the wisest and best learned in the earth. And they that will have it generally to be taken for indifferent, for that a very few take no hurt of it, though infinite multitudes besides perish thereby, show that they put little difference between the multitude of Christians, and brute beasts, whose danger they do so little esteem.

Exod. 20:4

Exod. 24:16; Deut. 7:3–4

Besides this, if they be bishops or parsons, or otherwise having charge of men's consciences, that thus reason, "It is lawful to have images publicly, though it be not expedient," what manner of pastors show they themselves to be to their flock, which thrust unto them that which they themselves confess not to be expedient for them, but to the utter ruin of the souls committed to their charge, for whom they shall give a strait account before *the Prince of pastors*, at the last day? For indeed to object to the weak, and ready to fall of themselves, such stumbling-blocks, is a thing not only not expedient, but unlawful, yea, and most wicked also. Wherefore it is to be wondered, how they can call images set up in churches and temples—to no profit or benefit of any, and to so great peril and danger, yea, hurt and destruction of many or rather infinite—things indifferent. Is not the public setting up of them rather a snare for

1 Pet. 5:4

all men, and the tempting of God? I beseech these reasoners to call to mind their own accustomed ordinance and decree, whereby they determined that the Scripture, though by God himself commanded to be known of all men, women, and children, should not be read of the simple, nor had in the vulgar tongue, for that (as they said) it was dangerous, by bringing the simple people into errors. And will they not forbid images to be set up in churches and temples, which are not commanded but forbidden most straitly by God, but let them still be there, yea, and maintain them also, seeing the people are brought not in danger only, but indeed into most abominable error and detestable idolatry thereby? Shall God's word, by God commanded to be read unto all, and known of all, for danger of heresy (as they say) be shut up? and idols and images, notwithstanding they be forbidden by God, and notwithstanding the danger of idolatry by them, shall they yet be set up, suffered, and maintained in churches and temples? O worldly and fleshly wisdom! ever bent to maintain the inventions and traditions of men by carnal reason, and by the same to disannul or deface the holy ordinances, laws, and honour of the eternal God, who is to be honoured and praised for ever. Amen

Now IT REMAINETH, for the conclusion of this treatise, to declare as well the abuse of churches and temples, by too costly and sumptuous decking and adorning of them, as also the lewd painting, gilding, and clothing of idols and images, and so to conclude the whole treatise.

In Tertullian's time, an hundred and threescore years after Christ, Christians had none other temples but common houses, whither they for the most part secretly resorted. And so far off was it that they had before his time any goodly or gorgeous-decked temples, that laws were made, in Antoninus Verus and Commodus the Emperors' times, that no Christians should dwell in houses, come in public baths, or be seen in streets or any where abroad; and that if they were once accused to be Christians, they should by no means be suffered to escape. As was practised in Apollonius, a noble senator of Rome, who being accused of his own bondman and slave, that he was a Christian, could neither by his defence and apology, learnedly and eloquently written and read publicly in the senate, nor in respect that he was a citizen, nor for the dignity of his order, nor for the vileness and unlawfulness of his accuser (being his own slave, by likelihood of malice moved to forge lies against his lord), nor for no other respect or help,* be delivered from death. So that Christians were then driven to dwell in caves and dens, so far off was it that they had any public temples adorned and decked as they now be. Which is here rehearsed to the confutation of those impudent

Deut. 31:10–13

Tertull. *Apol.* cap. 39

Euseb. Lib. 5 *Eccles. Hist.*

Hieronymus

* All texts repeat "could" here.

shameless liars, which report such glorious glosed fables of the goodly and gorgeous temples, that St Peter, Linus, Cletus, and those thirty bishops their successors had at Rome, until the time of the Emperor Constantine, and which St Polycarp should have in Asia, or Ireneus in France; by such lies, contrary to all true histories, to maintain the superfluous gilding and decking of temples nowadays, wherein they put almost the whole sum and pith of our religion. But in those times the world was won to Christendom, not by gorgeous, gilded, and painted temples of Christians, which had scarcely houses to dwell in, but by the godly, and as it were golden minds, and firm faith, of such as in all adversity and persecution professed the truth of our religion.

And after these times, in Maximian and Constantius the Emperors' proclamation, the places where Christians resorted to public prayer were called "Conventicles". And in Galerius Maximinus the Emperor's Epistle, they are called Oratories and Dominica, to say, places dedicate to the service of the Lord. (And here by the way it is to be noted, that at that time there were no churches or temples erected unto any Saint, but to God only; as St Augustine also recordeth, saying, "We build no temples unto our Martyrs.") And Eusebius himself calleth churches "houses of prayer", and showeth that in Constantine the Emperor's time, all men rejoiced, seeing, "instead of low conventicles," which tyrants had destroyed, "high temples to be builded." Lo, until the time of Constantine, by the space of above three hundred years after our Saviour Christ, when Christian religion was most pure and indeed golden, Christians had but low and poor conventicles, and simple oratories, yea, caves under the ground, called Cryptae, where they, for fear of persecution, assembled secretly together; a figure whereof remaineth, in the vaults which yet are builded under great churches, to put us in remembrance of the old state of the primitive Church before Constantine: whereas in Constantine's time, and after him, were builded great and goodly temples for Christians, called Basilicae, either for that the Greeks used to call all great and goodly places Basilicas, or for that the high everlasting King, God and our Saviour Christ, was served in them. But although Constantine and other princes, of good zeal to our religion, did sumptuously deck and adorn Christians' temples, yet did they dedicate, at that time, all churches or temples to God, or our Saviour Christ, and to no Saint; for that abuse began long after, in Justinian's time.

And that gorgeousness then used, as it was borne with, as rising of a good zeal, so was it signified of the godly learned, even at that time, that such cost might otherwise have been better bestowed. Let St Jerome, although otherwise too great a liker and allower of external and outward things, be a proof hereof, who hath these words in his Epistle to Demetriades. "Let other," saith St Jerome,

Marginal notes:

Euseb. Lib. 8, cap. 19; et Lib. 9, cap. 9

De Civitate Lib. 8, cap. 1

Cryptae

Basilicae

Nov. Const. 3 et 67

build churches, cover walls with tables of marble, carry together huge pillars, and gild their tops or heads, which do not feel or understand their precious decking and adorning; let them deck the doors with ivory and silver, and set the golden altars with precious stones. I blame it not. Let every man abound in his own sense: and better is it so to do, than carefully to keep their riches laid up in store. But thou hast another way appointed thee, to clothe Christ in the poor, to visit him in the sick, feed him in the hungry, lodge him in those who do lack harbour, and *specially such as be of the household of faith.*

Matt. 25:40

Gal. 6:10

And the same St Jerome toucheth the same matter somewhat more freely, in his *Treatise of the Life of Clerks to Nepotian*, saying thus:

Many build walls, and erect pillars of churches; the smooth marbles do glister, the roof shineth with gold, the altar is set with precious stones; but of the ministers of Christ, there is no election or choice. Neither let any man object, and allege against me the rich Temple that was in Jewry, the table, candlesticks, incense-ships, platters, cups, mortars, and other things all of gold. Then were these things allowed of the Lord, when the priests offered sacrifices, and the blood of beasts was accounted the redemption of sins. Howbeit *all these things* went before *in figure, and they were written for us, upon whom the end of the world is come.* And now, when that our Lord, being poor, hath dedicate the poverty of his house, let us remember his cross, and we shall esteem riches as mire or dung. What do we marvel at that which Christ calleth *wicked mammon*? Whereto do we so highly esteem and love, that which St Peter doth for a glory testify that he had not?

1 Cor. 10:11

Luke 16:11

Acts 3:6

Hitherto St Jerome. Thus ye see how St Jerome teacheth the sumptuousness amongst the Jews to be a figure, to signify, and not an example to follow, and that those outward things were suffered for a time, until Christ our Lord came, who turned all those outward things into spirit, faith, and truth. And the same St Jerome upon the seventh chapter of Jeremy saith:

God commanded both the Jews at that time, and now us who are placed in the Church, that we have no trust in the goodliness of building, and gilt roofs, and in walls covered with tables of marble, and say, *The Temple of the Lord, the Temple of the Lord, the Temple of the Lord.* For that is the temple of the Lord, wherein dwelleth true faith, godly conversation, and the company of all virtues.

And upon the Prophet Agge he describeth the true and right decking or ornaments of the temple after this sort. "I," saith St Jerome

Psalm 41:6

do think the silver, wherewith the house of God is decked, to be the doctrine of the Scriptures, of the which it is spoken, *The doctrine of the Lord is a pure doctrine, silver tried in fire, purged from dross, purified seven times.* And I do take gold to be that which remaineth in the hid sense of the saints, and the secret of the heart, and shineth with the true light of God. Which is evident that the Apostle also meant, of the saints that *build upon the foundation of Christ,* some *silver,* some *gold,* some *precious stones*; that by the gold the hid sense, by silver godly utterance, by precious stones works which please God, might be signified. With these metals, the Church of our Saviour is made more goodly and gorgeous, than was the Synagogue in old time: with these lively stones is the Church and house of Christ builded, and peace is given to it for ever.

1 Cor. 3:12

All these be St Jerome's sayings.

No more did the old godly bishops, and doctors of the Church, allow the outrageous furniture of temples and churches, with plate, vessels of gold, silver, and precious vestures. St Chrysostom saith, in the ministry of the holy Sacraments there is no need of golden vessels, but of golden minds. And St Ambrose saith: "Christ sent his Apostles without gold, and gathered his Church without gold. The Church hath gold, not to keep it, but to bestow it on the necessities of the poor." "The Sacraments look for no gold, neither do they please God for the commendation of gold, which are not bought for gold. The adorning and decking of the Sacraments is the redemption of captives." Thus much St Ambrose. St Jerome commendeth Exuperius, Bishop of Tolose, that he carried the Sacrament of the Lord's Body in a wicker basket, and the Sacrament of his Blood in a glass, and so cast covetousness out of the church. And Bonifacius, Bishop and Martyr, as it is recorded in the Decrees, testifieth that in old time, the ministers used wooden, and not golden vessels. And Zephyrinus, the sixteenth Bishop of Rome, made a decree that they should use vessels of glass. Likewise were the vestures used in the Church in old time, very plain and single, and nothing costly. And Rabanus at large declareth, that this costly and manifold furniture of vestments, of late used in the Church, was fetched from the Jewish usage, and agreeth with Aaron's apparelling almost altogether. For the maintenance of the which, Innocentius the Pope pronounceth boldly, that all the customs of the old Law be not abolished, that we might in such apparel, of Christians, the more willingly become Jewish.

2 *Offic.* cap. 28

Tit. *de Consecr.* Can. *Triburien.*

Lib.1 *Instit.* cap. 14

This is noted, not against churches and temples, which are most necessary, and ought to have their due use and honour (as is in another Homily for that purpose declared), nor against the convenient cleanliness and ornaments thereof, but against the sumptuousness and abuses of temples and churches. For it is a church or temple also, that glistereth with no marble, shineth with no gold nor silver, glittereth with no pearls nor precious stones, but with plainness and frugality, signifieth no proud doctrine nor people, but humble, frugal, and nothing

Psalm 45:13

esteeming earthly and outward things, but gloriously decked with inward ornaments, according as the Prophet declareth, saying, *The King's daughter is altogether glorious inwardly.*

Now concerning outrageous decking of images and idols, with painting, gilding, adorning with precious vestures, pearl, and stone: what is it else, but for the further provocation and enticement to spiritual fornication, to deck spiritual harlots most costly and wantonly? Which the idolatrous Church understandeth well enough. For she, being indeed not only an harlot (as the Scriptures calleth her), but also a foul, filthy, old, withered harlot (for she is indeed of ancient years), and understanding her lack of natural and true beauty, and great loathsomeness which of herself she hath, doth (after the custom of such harlots) paint herself, and deck and tire herself, with gold, pearl, stone, and all kind of precious jewels; that she, shining with the outward beauty and glory of them, may please the foolish fantasy of fond lovers, and so entice them to spiritual fornication with her—who if they saw her, I will not say naked, but in simple apparel, would abhor her as the foulest and filthiest harlot that ever was seen; according as appeareth by the description of the garnishing of *the great strumpet* of all strumpets, *the mother of whoredom*, set forth by St John in his Revelation, who by her glory provoked the princes of the earth to commit whoredom with her. Whereas on the contrary part, the true Church of God, as a chaste matron, *espoused* (as the Scripture teacheth) *to one husband, our Saviour Jesus Christ*, whom alone she is content only to please and serve, and looketh not to delight the eyes or phantasies of any other strange lovers or wooers, is content with her natural ornaments, not doubting, by such sincere simplicity best to please him, which can well skill of the difference between a painted visage and true natural beauty.

Rev. 17, 18

2 Cor. 11:2

And concerning such glorious gilding and decking of images, both God's word written in the tenth chapter of the Prophet Jeremy, and St Jerome's commentaries upon the same, are most worthy to be noted. First, the words of the Scriptures be these: *The workman with his axe hewed the timber out of the wood, with the work of his hands: he decked it with gold and silver: he joined it with nails and pins, and the stroke of an hammer, that it might hold together. They be made smooth as the palm, and they cannot speak: if they be borne, they remove, for they cannot go. Fear ye them not, for they can neither do evil nor good.* Thus saith the Prophet. Upon which text St Jerome hath these words:

Jer. 10:3–5

This is the description of idols, which the Gentiles worship. Their matter is vile and corruptible. And whereas the artificer is mortal, the things he maketh must needs be corruptible. *He decketh it with silver and gold*, that with the glittering or shining of both metals, he may deceive the simple. Which error indeed hath passed over from the Gentiles, that we should judge religion to stand in riches.

And by and by after he saith: "They have the beauty of metals, and be beautified by the art of painting, but good or profit is there none in them." And shortly after again:

> They make great promises, and devise an image of vain worshipping, of their own phantasies: they make great brags to deceive every simple body: they dull and amaze the understanding of the unlearned, as it were with golden sentences, and eloquence shining with the brightness of silver. And of their own devisers and makers are these images advanced and magnified: in the which is no utility nor profit at all, and the worshipping of the which properly pertaineth to the Gentiles and heathen, and such as know not God.

Thus far of St Jerome's words. Whereupon you may note as well his judgement of images themselves, as also of the painting, gilding, and decking of them: that it is an error which came from the Gentiles; that it persuadeth religion to remain in riches; that it amazeth and deceiveth the simple and unlearned, with golden sentences and silver-shining eloquence; and that it appertaineth properly to the Gentiles and heathens, and such as know not God. Wherefore the having, painting, gilding, and decking of images, by St Jerome's judgement, is erroneous, seducing and bringing into error (specially the simple and unlearned), heathenish, and void of the knowledge of God. Surely the Prophet Daniel, in the eleventh chapter, declareth such sumptuous decking of images with gold, silver, and precious stones to be a token of Antichrist's kingdom, who, as the Prophet foreshoweth, shall worship God with such gorgeous things. _{Dan. 11:38}

Now usually, such outrageous adorning and decking of images, hath risen and been maintained, either of offerings provoked by superstition and given in idolatry, or of spoils, robberies, usury, or goods otherwise unjustly gotten, whereof wicked men have given part to the images or Saints (as they call them), that they might be pardoned of the whole; as of divers writings and old monuments, concerning the cause and end of certain great gifts, may well appear. And indeed such money, so wickedly gotten, is most meet to be put to so wicked an use. And that which they take to be amends for the whole before God, is more abominable in his sight, than both the wicked getting, and the more wicked spending, of all the rest. For how the Lord alloweth such gifts, he declareth evidently in the Prophet Esay, saying, *I (saith the Lord) do love* *judgement, and I hate spoil and raveny offered in sacrifice.* Which the very Gentiles understood: for Plato showeth that such men as suppose that God doth pardon wicked men, if they give part of their spoils and ravine

Isai. 61:8

Dialogo de Legibus 10

to him, take him to be like a dog, that would be entreated and hired with part of the prey, to suffer the wolves to worry the sheep.

And in case the goods wherewith images be decked were justly gotten, yet is it extreme madness, so foolishly and wickedly to bestow goods purchased by wisdom and truth. Of such lewdness Lactantius writeth thus:

Lib. 2 *Instit.* cap. 4

> Men do in vain deck images of the gods with gold, ivory, and precious stone, as though they could take any pleasure of these things. For what use have they of precious gifts, which understand nor feel nothing? Even the same that dead men have. For with like reason, do they bury dead bodies farced with spices and odours, and clothed with precious vestures, and deck images, which neither felt or knew when they were made, nor understand when they be honoured, for they get no sense and understanding by their consecration.

Thus far Lactantius, and much more, too long here to rehearse, declaring, that as little girls play with little puppets, so be these decked images great puppets, for old fools to play with. And that we may know what not only men of our religion, but ethnics also, judge of such decking of dead images, it is not unprofitable to hear what Seneca, a wise and excellent learned senator of Rome, and philosopher, saith concerning the foolishness of ancient and grave men, used in his time, in worshipping and decking of images. "'We,' saith Seneca,* 'be not twice children, as the common saying is, but always children: but this is the difference, that we being elder, play the children.' And in these plays they bring in before great and well decked puppets," for so he calleth images, "ointments, incense, and odours. To these puppets they offer up sacrifice, which have a mouth, but not the use of teeth. Upon these they put attiring and precious apparel, which have no use of clothes. To these they give gold and silver, which they who receive it," meaning the images, "lack as well as they that have given it from them." And Seneca much commendeth Dionysius, King of Sicily, for his merry robbing of such decked and jewelled puppets.

But you will ask, "What doth this appertain to our images, which is written against the idols of the Gentiles?" Altogether surely. For what use or pleasure have our images of their decking and precious ornaments? Did our images understand when they were made? or know when they be so trimmed and decked? Be not these things bestowed upon them as much in vain as upon dead men which have no sense? Wherefore it followeth, that there is like foolishness and lewdness in decking of our images, as great puppets for old fools, like children, to play the wicked play of idolatry before, as was amongst the ethnics and Gentiles. Our churches stand full of such great puppets, wondrously decked and

---

* The Homilist is quoting Seneca from Lactantius. See Griffiths's note.

adorned; garlands and coronets be set on their heads, precious pearls hanging about their necks; their fingers shine with rings set with precious stone; their dead and stiff bodies are clothed with garments stiff with gold. You would believe that the images of our men Saints were some princes of Persy land, with their proud apparel, and the idols of our women Saints were nice and well trimmed harlots, tempting their paramours to wantonness: whereby the Saints of God are not honoured, but most dishonoured, and their godliness, soberness, chastity, contempt of riches and of the vanity of the world, defaced and brought in doubt by such monstrous decking, most differing from their sober and godly lives. And, because the whole must thoroughly be played, it is not enough thus to deck idols, but at the last come in the priests themselves, likewise decked with gold and pearl, that they may be meet servants for such lords and ladies, and fit worshippers of such gods and goddesses. And with a solemn pace, they pass forth before these golden puppets, and down to the ground on their marrowbones, before these honourable idols, and then, rising up again, offer up odours and incense unto them, to give the people an example of double idolatry, by worshipping not only the idol, but the gold also and riches, wherewith it is garnished. Which things the most part of our old Martyrs rather than they would do, or once kneel or offer up one crumb of incense before an image, suffered most cruel and terrible deaths, as the histories of them at large to declare.

And here again, their allegation out of Gregory the First and Damascene, that images be the laymen's books, and that picture is the scripture of idiots, and simple persons, is worthy to be considered. For as it hath been touched in divers places before, how they be books teaching nothing but lies, as by St Paul, in the first chapter to the Romans, evidently appeareth of the images of God, so, what manner of books and scripture these painted and gilt images of Saints be unto the common people, note well, I pray you. For after that our preachers shall have instructed and exhorted the people, to the following of the virtues of the Saints, as, contempt of this world, poverty, soberness, chastity, and suchlike virtues, which undoubtedly were in the Saints, think you, as soon as they turn their faces from the preacher, and look upon the graven books, and painted scripture, of the glorious gilt images and idols, all shining and glittering with metal and stone, and covered with precious vestures, or else, with Chaerea in Terence, behold "a painted table", wherein is set forth by the art of the painter, an image with a nice and wanton apparel and countenance, more like to Venus or Flora than Mary Magdalene—or, if like to Mary Magdalene, it is when she played the harlot rather than when she wept for her sins—when, I say, they turn about from the preacher, to these books and schoolmasters and painted scriptures, shall they not find them lying books, teaching other manner

Gregor. *Epist. ad Seren. Massil.* Damasc. *de Fide Orthod.* Lib. 4, cap. 17

of lessons, of esteeming of riches, of pride and vanity and apparel, of niceness and wantonness, and peradventure of whoredom? as Chaerea of like pictures was taught, and in Lucian one learned of Venus Gnidia a lesson too abominable here to be remembered. Be not these, think you, pretty books and scriptures, for simple people, and specially for wives and maidens, to look in, read on, and learn such lessons of? What will they think either of the preacher, who taught them contrary lessons of the Saints, and therefore by these carven doctors are charged with a lie, or of the Saints themselves, if they believe these graven books and painted scriptures of them, who make the Saints now reigning in heaven with God, to their great dishonour, schoolmasters of such vanity, which they in their lifetime most abhorred? For what lessons of contempt of riches, and vanity of this world, can such books, so besmeared with gold, set with stone, covered with silks, teach? What lessons of soberness and chastity, can our women learn of these pictured scriptures, with their nice apparel and wanton looks?

But away, for shame, with these coloured cloaks of idolatry, of the books and scriptures of images and pictures to teach idiots, nay, to make idiots and stark fools and beasts of Christians. Do men, I pray you, when they have the same books at home with them, run on pilgrimage to seek like books at Rome, Compostella, or Jerusalem, to be taught by them, when they have the like to learn of at home? Do men reverence some books, and despise and set light by other of the same sort? Do men kneel before their books, light candles at noon time, burn incense, offer up gold and silver and other gifts, to their books? Do men either feign or believe miracles to be wrought by their books? I am sure that the New Testament of our Saviour Jesus Christ, containing the word of life, is a more lively, express, and true image of our Saviour, than all carved, graved, molten, and painted images in the world be; and yet none of all these things be done to that book, or scripture of the Gospel of our Saviour, which be done to images and pictures, the books and scriptures of laymen and idiots, as they call them. Wherefore, call them what they list, it is most evident by their deeds, that they make of them none other books nor scriptures, than such as teach most filthy and horrible idolatry, as the users of such books daily prove, by continual practising of the same. O books and scriptures, in the which the devilish schoolmaster Satan hath penned the lewd lessons of wicked idolatry, for his dastardly disciples and scholars to behold, read, and learn, to God's most high dishonour, and their most horrible damnation! Have not we been much bound, think you, to those which should have taught us the truth out of God's book, and his holy Scripture, that they have shut up that book and Scripture from us (and none of us so bold as once to open it or read on it), and instead thereof, to spread us abroad these goodly carven and gilted books, and painted scriptures, to teach us such good and godly lessons? Have not they done well, after they ceased to stand in pulpits themselves, and to teach the people committed to their instruction, keeping silence of God's word, and become *dumb dogs* (as the Prophet calleth them), to set up in their stead, on every pillar and corner of the church, such goodly doctors, as dumb, but more wicked than themselves be? We need not to complain of the lack of one dumb parson, having so many dumb devilish vicars, I mean these idols and painted puppets, to teach in their stead!

Isai. 56:10

Now in the mean season, whilst the dumb and dead idols stand thus decked and clothed, contrary to God's law and commandment, the poor Christian people, the lively images of God, commended to us so tenderly by our Saviour Christ, as most dear to him, stand naked, shivering for cold, and their teeth chattering in their heads, and no man covereth them; are pined with hunger and thirst, and no man giveth them a penny to refresh them; whereas pounds be ready at all times, contrary to God's word and will, to deck and trim dead stocks and stones, which neither feel cold, hunger, nor thirst. Clemens hath a notable sentence concerning this matter, saying thus:

Lib. 5 *ad Jacobum Domini*

That serpent the devil, doth by the mouth of certain men utter these words, "We for the honour of the invisible God, do worship visible images": which doubtless is most false. For if you will truly honour the image of God, you should, by doing well to man, honour the true image of God in him. For the image of God, is in every man: but the likeness of God, is not in every one, but in those only which have a godly heart and pure mind. If you will therefore truly honour the image of God, we do declare to you the truth, that ye do well to man, who is *made after the image of God*, that you give honour and reverence to him, and refresh the hungry with meat, the thirsty with drink, the naked with clothes, the sick with attendance, the stranger harbourless with lodging, the prisoners with necessaries: and this shall be accounted as truly bestowed upon God. And these things are so directly appertaining to God's honour, that whosoever doeth not this, shall seem to have reproached and done villainy to the image of God. For what honour of God is this, to run to images of stock and stone, and to honour vain and dead figures as God, and to despise man, in whom is the true image of God?

James 3:9

And by and by after he saith: "Understand ye therefore, that this is the suggestion of the serpent Satan lurking within you, which persuadeth you, that you are godly, when you honour insensible and dead images, and that you be not ungodly, when you hurt, or leave unsuccoured, the lively and reasonable creatures." All these be the words of Clemens. Note, I pray you, how this most ancient and learned doctor, within one hundred years of our Saviour Christ's time, most plainly teacheth, that no service of God, or religion acceptable to him, can be in honouring of dead images, but in succouring of the poor, the lively images of God; according to St James, who saith *This is the pure and true religion, before God the Father, to succour fatherless and motherless children, and widows in their affliction, and to keep himself undefiled from this world.*

James 1:27

    True religion then, and pleasing of God, standeth not in making, setting up, painting, gilding, clothing, and decking of dumb and dead images, which be but great puppets and mammets, for old fools in dotage and wicked idolatry, to dally and play with; nor in kissing of them, capping, kneeling, offering to them, in censing of them, setting up of candles, hanging up of legs, arms, or whole bodies of wax before them, or praying and asking of them, or of Saints, things belonging only to God to give: but all these things be vain and abominable, and most damnable before God. Wherefore all such do not only bestow their money and labour in vain, but with their pains and cost, purchase to themselves God's wrath, in utter indignation and everlasting damnation, both of body and soul. For ye have heard it evidently proved, in these Homilies against Idolatry—by God's word, the doctors of the Church, Ecclesiastical Histories, reason, and experience—that images have been and be worshipped, and so idolatry committed to them, by infinite multitudes, to the great offence of God's Majesty, and danger of infinite souls; and that idolatry cannot possibly be separated from images set up in churches and temples, gilded and decked gorgeously; and that therefore, our images be indeed, very idols, and so all the prohibitions, laws, curses, threatenings of horrible plagues, as well temporal as eternal, contained in the holy Scripture, concerning idols and the makers, maintainers, and worshippers of them, appertain also to our images, set up in churches and temples, to the makers, maintainers, and worshippers of them. And all those names of abomination, which God's word in the holy Scripture, giveth to the idols of the Gentiles, appertain to our images, being idols like to them, and having like idolatry committed unto them: and God's own mouth in the holy Scriptures, calleth them *vanities, lies, deceits, uncleanliness,* filthiness, dung, mischief, and *abomination before the Lord.* Wherefore, God's horrible wrath, and our most dreadful danger, cannot be avoided, without the destruction, and utter abolishing, of all such images and idols, out of the church and temple of God: which to accomplish, God put in the minds of all Christian princes!

Deut. 32:21; Jer. 16:19; Amos 2:4; 2 Chron. 29:5; Deut. 27:15

    And in the mean time, let us take heed and be wise, O ye beloved of the Lord, and let us have no strange gods, but one only God, who made us when we were nothing, the Father of our Lord Jesus Christ, who redeemed us when we were lost, and with his Holy Spirit who doth sanctify us. For *this is life everlasting, to know him to be the only true God,*

John 17:3

and Jesus Christ, whom he hath sent. Let us honour and worship for religion's sake, none but him: and him let us worship and honour as he will himself, and hath declared by his word that he will be honoured and worshipped; not in, nor by, images or idols, which he hath most straitly forbidden, neither in kneeling, lighting of candles, burning of incense, offering up of gifts unto images and idols, to believe that we shall please him; for all these be abomination before God; but let us honour and worship God, *in spirit and truth*, fearing and loving him above all things, John 4:23, 24 trusting in him only, calling upon him, and praying to him only, praising and lauding of him only, and all other, in him and for him. For *such worshippers* doth our heavenly Father love, who is the most purest Spirit, and therefore will be worshipped *in spirit and truth*. And such worshippers were Abraham, Moses, David, Helias, Peter, Paul, John, and all other the holy Patriarchs, Prophets, Apostles, Martyrs, and all true Saints of God; who all, as the true friends of God, were enemies and destroyers of images and idols, as the enemies of God, and his true religion.

Wherefore take heed and be wise, O ye beloved of the Lord; and that which others, contrary to God's word, bestow wickedly, and to their damnation, upon dead stocks and stones (no images, but enemies, of God and his Saints), that bestow ye, as the faithful servants of God, according to God's word, mercifully upon poor men and women, fatherless children, widows, sick persons, strangers, prisoners, and such others that be in any necessity; that ye may, at that great day of the Lord, hear that most blessed and comfortable saying, of our Saviour Christ: *Come, ye blessed, into the kingdom of my Father, prepared for you before the* Matt. 25:34–40 *beginning of the world. For I was hungry, and ye gave me meat; thirsty, and ye gave me drink; naked, and ye clothed me; harbourless, and ye lodged me; in prison, and ye visited me; sick, and ye comforted me. For whatsoever ye have done for the poor and needy, in my name and for my sake, that have ye done for me.* To the which his heavenly kingdom God *the Father of mercies* 2 Cor. 1:3 bring us, for Jesus Christ's sake, our only Saviour, Mediator, and Advocate: to whom with the Holy Ghost, one immortal, invisible, and most glorious God, be all honour, and thanksgiving, and glory, world without end. Amen.

AN HOMILY
FOR REPAIRING
AND KEEPING CLEAN
AND COMELY ADORNING
OF CHURCHES

IT IS A COMMON CUSTOM used of all men, when they intend to have their friends or neighbours, to come to their houses, to eat or drink with them, or to have any solemn assembly, to treat and talk of any matter, they will have their houses, which they keep in continual reparations, to be clean and fine, lest they should be counted sluttish, or little to regard their friends and neighbours. How much more then ought the house of God, which we commonly call the church, to be sufficiently repaired in all places, and to be honourably adorned and garnished, and to be kept clean and sweet, to the comfort of the people that shall resort thereto!

It appeareth in the holy Scripture, how God's house, which was called his holy Temple, and was the mother church of all Jewry, fell sometimes into decay, and was oftentimes profaned and defiled, through the negligence and ungodliness of such as had charge thereof. But when godly kings and governors were in place, then commandment was given forthwith, that the church and Temple of God should be repaired, and the devotion of the people to be gathered, for the reparation of the same. We read in the fourth Book of the Kings, how that King Joas, being a godly prince, gave commandment to the priests, to convert certain offerings of the people, towards the reparation and amendment of God's Temple. Like commandment gave that most godly King Josias, concerning the reparation and re-edification of God's Temple, which in his time he found in sore decay. It hath pleased Almighty God, that these histories touching the re-edifying and repairing of his holy Temple, should be written at large, to the end we should be taught thereby first, that God is well pleased that his people should have a convenient place to resort unto, and to

2 Kings 12:4–5

Ibid. 22:3–6

194

come together to praise and magnify God's holy Name. And secondly, he is highly pleased, with all those which diligently and zealously, go about to amend and restore such places as are appointed for the congregation of God's people to resort unto, and wherein they humbly and jointly render thanks to God, for his benefits, and with one heart and voice, praise his holy Name. Thirdly, God was sore displeased with his people, because they builded, decked, and trimmed up their own houses, and suffered God's house to be in ruin and decay, to lie uncomely and fulsomely. Wherefore God was sore grieved with them, and plagued them, as appeareth in the Prophet Haggeus: *Thus saith the Lord: Is it time* Hag. 1:2, 4, 6 *for you to dwell in your ceiled houses, and the Lord's house not regarded? Ye have sowed much, and gathered in but little; your meat and your clothes have neither filled you, nor made you warm; and he that had his wages put it in a bottomless purse.* By these plagues, which God laid upon his people for neglecting of his Temple, it may evidently appear, that God will have his temple, his church, the place where his congregation shall resort to magnify him, well edified, well repaired, and well maintained.

Some, neither regarding godliness nor the place of godly exercise, will say the Temple, in the old law, was commanded to be built and repaired, by God himself, because it had great promises annexed unto it, and because it was a figure, a sacrament, or a signification of Christ, and also of his Church. To this may be easily answered, first that our churches are not destitute of promises, forasmuch as our Saviour Christ saith, *Where two or three are gathered in my name, there am I in the midst* Matt. 18:20 *among them.* A great number therefore coming to church together, in the name of Christ, have there, that is to say in the church, their God and Saviour Christ Jesus, present among the congregation of his faithful people by his grace, by his favour and godly assistance, according to his most assured and comfortable promises. Why then ought not Christian people to build them temples and churches, having as great promises of the presence of God, as ever had Salomon for the material Temple which he did build? As touching the other point, that Salomon's Temple was a figure of Christ, we know that now, in the time of the clear light of Christ Jesus the Son of God, all shadows, figures, and significations are utterly gone, all vain and unprofitable ceremonies, both Jewish and heathenish, fully abolished; and therefore our churches are not set up for figures and significations of Messias and Christ to come, but for other godly and necessary purposes: that is to say, that like as every man hath his own house to abide in, to refresh himself in, to rest in, with suchlike commodities, so Almighty God will have his house and palace, whither the whole parish and congregation shall resort. Which is called the church and temple of God, for that the Church, which is the company of God's people, doth there assemble, and come together to

2 Chron. 2:6

serve him; not meaning hereby that the Lord, *whom the heaven of heavens is not able to hold* or comprise, doth dwell in the church of lime and stone, made with man's hands, as wholly and only contained therewithin and nowhere else; for so he never dwelt in Salomon's Temple. Moreover, the church or temple is counted and called holy, yet not of itself, but because God's people resorting thereunto are holy, and exercise themselves in holy and heavenly things.

And to the intent ye may understand further, why churches were built among Christian people, this was the greatest consideration: that God might have his place, and that God might have his time, duly to be honoured and served, of the whole multitude in the parish; first, there to hear and learn the blessed word and will, of the everlasting God; secondly, that there the blessed Sacraments, which our Lord and Saviour Christ Jesus hath ordained and appointed, should be duly, reverently, and honourably ministered; thirdly, that there the whole multitude of God's people in the parish, should with one voice and heart, call upon the Name of God, magnify and praise the Name of God, render earnest and hearty thanks to our heavenly Father, for his heap of benefits, daily and plentifully poured upon us, not forgetting to bestow our alms upon God's poor, to the intent God may bless us the more richly.

Thus ye may well perceive and understand, wherefore churches were built and set up amongst Christian people, and dedicated and appointed to these godly uses, and utterly exempted, from all filthy, profane, and worldly uses. Wherefore, all they that have little mind or devotion, to repair and build God's temple, are to be counted people of much ungodliness, spurning against good order in Christ's Church, despising the true honour of God, with evil example offending and hindering their neighbours, otherwise well and godly disposed. The world thinketh it but a trifle, to see their church in ruin and decay; but whoso doth not lay to their helping hands, they sin against God, and his holy congregation. For, if it had not been sin, to neglect and slightly regard the re-edifying, and building up again of his temple, God would not have been so much grieved, and so soon have plagued his people, because they builded and decked their own houses so gorgeously, and despised the house of God their Lord.

It is sin and shame, to see so many churches so ruinous, and so foully decayed, almost in every corner. If a man's private house, wherein he dwelleth, be decayed, he will never cease, till it be restored up again. Yea, if his barn, where he keepeth his corn, be out of reparations, what diligence useth he, to make it in perfect state again! If his stable for his horse, yea the sty for his swine, be not able to hold out water and wind, how careful is he, to do cost thereon! And shall we be so mindful of our common base houses, deputed to so low occupying, and be forgetful toward that house of God, wherein be ministered the words of our eternal salvation, wherein be ministered the Sacraments and mysteries of our redemption? The fountain of our regeneration is there presented to us; the partaking of the Body and Blood of our Saviour Christ, is there offered unto us; and shall we not esteem the place, where so heavenly things be handled? Wherefore, if ye have any reverence to the service of God, if ye have any common honesty, if ye have any conscience, in keeping of necessary and godly ordinances, keep your churches in good repair! whereby ye shall not only please God, and deserve his manifold blessings, but also deserve the good report of all godly people.

The second point which appertaineth to the maintenance of God's house, is to have it well adorned and comely, and clean kept: which things may be the more easily performed, when the church is well repaired. For like as men are well refreshed and comforted, when they find their houses having all things in good order, and all corners clean and sweet, so when God's house, the church, is well adorned with places convenient to sit in, with the pulpit for the preacher, with the Lord's table for the ministration of his Holy Supper, with the font to Christen in, and also is kept clean, comely, and sweetly, the people is the more desirous and the more comforted to resort thither, and to tarry there the whole time appointed them.

With what earnestness, with what vehement zeal, did our Saviour Christ drive the buyers and sellers out of the Temple of God! and hurled down the tables of the changers of money, and the seats of the dove-sellers, and could not abide that any man should carry a vessel through the Temple. He told them that they had made his Father's house *a den of thieves*, partly through their superstition, hypocrisy, false worship, false doctrine, and insatiable covetousness, and partly through contempt, abusing that place with walking and talking, with worldly matters, without all fear of God and due reverence to that place. What dens of thieves the churches of England have been made, by the blasphemous buying and selling the most precious Body and Blood of Christ, in the mass, as the world was made to believe, at diriges, at month's minds, in trentals, in abbeys and chantries, beside other horrible abuses, God's holy name be blessed for ever! we now see and understand. All these abominations they that supply the room of Christ have cleansed, and purged the churches of England of, taking away all such fulsomeness and filthiness as, through blind devotion and ignorance, hath crept into the Church this many hundred years.

Wherefore, O ye good Christian people, ye dearly beloved in Christ Jesu, ye that glory not in worldly and vain religion, in fantastical adorning and decking, but rejoice in heart, to see the glory of God truly

Matt. 21:12, 13

Mark 11:16

set forth, and the churches restored to their ancient and godly use, render your most hearty thanks to the goodness of Almighty God, who hath in our days, stirred up the hearts, not only of his godly preachers and ministers, but also of his faithful and most Christian magistrates and governors, to bring such godly things to pass. And forasmuch as your churches are scoured and swept, from the sinful and superstitious filthiness wherewith they were defiled and disfigured, do ye your parts, good people, to keep your churches comely and clean: suffer them not to be defiled with rain and weather, with dung of doves and owls, stares and choughs, and other filthiness, as it is foul and lamentable to behold in many places of this country. It is the house of prayer, not the house of talking, of walking, of brawling, of minstrelsy, of hawks, of dogs. Provoke not the displeasure and plagues of God, for despising and abusing his holy house, as the wicked Jews did. But have God in your heart: be obedient to his blessed will: bind yourselves, every man and woman to their power, toward the reparations and clean keeping of your church; to the intent ye may be partakers of God's manifold blessings, and that ye may the better be encouraged to resort to your parish church, there to learn your duties toward God and your neighbour, there to be present and partakers of Christ's holy Sacraments, there to render thanks to your heavenly Father, for the manifold benefits which he daily poureth upon you, there to pray together, and to call upon God's holy Name. Which be blessed, world without end. Amen.

AN HOMILY
OF GOOD WORKS
AND FIRST OF FASTING

THE LIFE WHICH WE LIVE IN THIS WORLD, good Christian people, is of the free benefit of God lent us, yet not to use it at our pleasure, after our own fleshly will, but to trade over the same, in those works which are beseeming them that are become new creatures in Christ. These works the Apostle calleth *good works*, saying, *We are God's workmanship, created in Christ Jesu to good works, which God hath ordained, that we should walk in them*. And yet his meaning is not by these words to induce us to have any affiance, or to put any confidence, in works, as by the merit and deserving of them to purchase to ourselves and others, remission of sin, and so consequently, everlasting life. For that were mere blasphemy against God's mercy, and great derogation to the bloodshedding of our Saviour Jesus Christ. For it is of the free grace and mercy of God, by the mediation of the blood of his Son Jesus Christ, without merit or deserving on our part, that our sins are forgiven us, that we are reconciled and brought again into his favour, and are made heirs of his heavenly kingdom. "Grace," saith St Augustine, "belongeth to God, who doth call us: and then hath he good works, whosoever received grace. Good works then bring not forth grace, but are brought forth by grace. The wheel," saith he, "turneth round, not to the end that it may be made round, but, because it is first made round, therefore it turneth round. So no man doeth good works, to receive grace by his good works; but because he hath first received grace, therefore consequently he doeth good works." And in another place he saith: "Good works go not before in him which shall afterward be justified; but good works do follow after, when a man is first justified." St Paul therefore teacheth that we must do good works, for divers respects: first, to show ourselves obedient children, unto our heavenly Father, who *hath ordained them, that we should walk in them*; secondly, for that they are good declarations and testimonies, of our justification; thirdly, that others *seeing our good*

Eph. 2:10

August. *de Diver. Quaest. ad Simplic.* Lib. I, Qu. 28

August. *de Fide et Operibus* cap. 4

Matt. 5:16

199

works, may the rather by them be stirred up and excited, to *glorify our Father, which is in heaven.* Let us not therefore be slack to do good works, seeing it is the will of God that we should walk in them, assuring ourselves that at the last day, every man shall receive of God, for his labour done in true faith, a greater reward than his works have deserved. And because somewhat shall now be spoken of one particular good work, whose commendation is both in the Law and in the Gospel, thus much is said in the beginning, generally of all good works; first, to remove out of the way of the simple and unlearned, this dangerous stumbling-block, that any man should go about, to purchase or buy heaven with his works; secondly, to take away (so nigh as may be) from envious minds, and slanderous tongues, all just occasion of slanderous speaking, as though good works were rejected.

This good work which shall now be entreated of is fasting: which is found in the Scriptures to be of two sorts; the one outward, pertaining to the body; the other inward, in the heart and mind. This outward fast is an abstinence from meat, drink, and all natural food, yea from all delicious pleasures and delectations worldly. When this outward fast pertaineth to one particular man, or to a few, and not to the whole number of the people, for causes which hereafter shall be declared, then it is called "a private fast". But when the whole multitude, of men, women, and children, in a township or city, yea through a whole country, do fast, it is called "a public fast". Such was that fast, which the whole multitude of the children of Israel, were commanded to keep, the tenth day of the seventh month, because Almighty God appointed that day, to be a cleansing day, a day of atonement, a time of reconciliation, a day wherein the people were cleansed from their sins. The order and manner how it was done, is written in the sixteenth and twenty-third chapter of Leviticus. That day the people did lament, mourn, weep, and bewail their former sins. And whosoever upon that day did not humble his soul, bewailing his sins, as is said, abstaining from all bodily food until the evening, *that soul,* saith Almighty God, *should be destroyed from among his people.* We do not read that Moses ordained by order of law any days of public fast throughout the whole year, more than that one day. The Jews, notwithstanding, had more times of common fasting, which the Prophet Zachary reciteth to be: *the fast of the fourth, the fast of the fifth, the fast of the seventh, and the fast of the tenth month.* But for that it appeareth not in the Levitical law when they were instituted, it is to be judged that those other times of fasting, more than the fast of the seventh month, were ordained among the Jews by the appointment of their governors, rather of devotion, than by any open commandment given from God.

Upon the ordinance of this general fast, good men took occasion to appoint to themselves private fasts, at such times as they did either

Lev. 16:29–34, 23:27–32

Lev. 23:29

Zech. 8:19

earnestly lament and bewail their sinful lives, or did addict themselves to more fervent prayer, that it might please God, to turn his wrath from them, when either they were admonished, and brought to the consideration thereof, by the preaching of the Prophets, or otherwise when they saw present danger to hang over their heads. This sorrowfulness of heart, joined with fasting, they uttered sometime by their outward behaviour, and gesture of body, putting on sackcloth, sprinkling themselves with ashes and dust, and sitting or lying upon the earth. For when good men feel in themselves the heavy burden of sin, see damnation to be the reward of it, and behold with the eye of their mind the horror of hell, they tremble, they quake, and are inwardly touched with sorrowfulness of heart, for their offences, and cannot but accuse themselves, and open this their grief unto Almighty God, and call unto him for mercy. This being done seriously, their mind is so occupied, partly with sorrow and heaviness, partly with an earnest desire to be delivered from this danger, of hell and damnation, that all lust of meat and drink is laid apart, and loathsomeness of all worldly things and pleasures cometh in place; so that nothing then liketh them more, than to weep, to lament, to mourn, and both with words and behaviour of body, to show themselves weary of this life. Thus did David fast, when he made intercession to Almighty God, for the child's life, begotten in adultery of Bethsabe, Ury's wife. King Achab fasted after this sort, when it repented him of murdering of Naboth, and bewailed his own sinful doings. Such was the Ninivites' fast, brought to repentance by Jonas' preaching. When forty thousand of the Israelites were slain in battle against the Benjamites, the Scripture saith, *all the children of Israel, and the whole multitude of people, went out to Bethel, and sat there weeping before the Lord, and fasted all that day until night.* So did Daniel, Hester, Nehemias, and many others in the Old Testament fast.

2 Sam. 12:16–23

1 Kings 21:27–9

Jonah 3:5–10

Judges 20:21–6

Dan. 9:3, 10:2–3
Esth. 4:16,
Neh. 1:4

But if any man will say, "It is true, so they fasted indeed; but we are not now under that yoke of the Law, we are set at liberty by the freedom of the Gospel; therefore those rites and customs of the old Law bind not us, except it can be showed by the Scriptures of the New Testament, or by examples out of the same, that fasting now under the Gospel is a restraint of meat, drink, and all bodily food and pleasures from the body," as before: first, that we ought to fast, is a truth more manifest, than that it should here need to be proved; the Scriptures which teach the same are evident. The doubt therefore that is, is whether when we fast, we ought to withhold from our bodies, all meat and drink during the time of our fast, or no. That we ought so to do, may be well gathered upon a question moved by the Pharisees to Christ, and by his answer again to the same. "*Why,* say they, *do John's disciples fast often, and pray,*

Luke 5:33–5

and we likewise, but thy disciples eat and drink, and fast not at all?" In this smooth question they, couch up subtilly this argument or reason. "Whoso fasteth not, that man is not of God. For fasting and prayer are works both commended and commanded of God, in his Scriptures; and all good men, from Moses till this time, as well the Prophets as others, have exercised themselves in these works. John also, and his disciples at this day, do fast oft, and pray much; and so do we the Pharisees, in like manner. But thy disciples fast not at all: which if thou wilt deny, we can easily prove it. For whosoever eateth and drinketh, fasteth not: thy disciples eat and drink: therefore they fast not. Of this we conclude," say they, "necessarily, that neither art thou, nor yet thy disciples, of God." Christ maketh answer, saying, *"Can ye make that the children of the wedding shall fast, while the bridegroom is with them? The days shall come, when the bridegroom shall be taken from them: in those days shall they fast."* Our Saviour Christ, like a good Master, defendeth the innocency of his disciples, against the malice of the arrogant Pharisees, and proveth, that his disciples are not guilty of transgressing any jot of God's law, although as then they fasted not; and in his answer reproveth the Pharisees, of superstition and ignorance. Superstition, because they put a religion in their doings, and ascribed holiness to the outward work wrought, not regarding to what end fasting is ordained. Of ignorance, for that they could not discern between time and time:

Eccles. 3:4   they knew not, that there is a time of rejoicing and mirth, and a time again of lamentation and mourning; which both he teacheth in his answer (as shall be touched more largely hereafter, when we shall show what time is most fit to fast in). But here, beloved, let us note, that our Saviour Christ, in making his answer to their question, denied not, but confessed, that his disciples fasted not, and therefore agreeth to the Pharisees in this, as unto a manifest truth, that whoso eateth and drinketh fasteth not. Fasting then, even by Christ's assent, is a withholding of meat, drink, and all natural food from the body, for the determined time of fasting.

And that it was used in the primitive Church, appeareth most evidently by the Chalcedon Council, one of the four first general Councils. The fathers assembled there, to the number of six hundred and thirty, considering with themselves how acceptable a thing fasting is to God, when it is used according to his word; again, having before their eyes also, the great abuses of the same crept into the Church at those days, through the negligence of them which should have taught the people the right use thereof, and by vain gloses devised of men; to reform the said abuses, and to restore this so good and godly a work, to the true use thereof, decreed in that Council, that every person, as well in his private as public fast, should continue all the day without meat and drink, till after the Evening Prayer, and whosoever did eat or drink, before the Evening Prayer was ended, should be accounted, and reputed, not to consider the purity of his fast. This canon teacheth so evidently how fasting was used in the primitive Church, as by words it cannot be more plainly expressed. Fasting then, by the decree of those six hundred and thirty fathers—grounding their determination in this matter upon the sacred Scriptures, and long continued usage or practice both of the Prophets, and other godly persons before the coming of Christ, and also of the Apostles, and other devout men in the New Testament—is a withholding of meat, drink, and all natural food, from the body, for the determined time of fasting.

Thus much is spoken hitherto, to make plain unto you, what fasting is. Now hereafter, shall be showed the true and right use of fasting.

Good works are not all of one sort. For some are of themselves, and of their own proper nature, always good; as: to love God above all things, to love my neighbour as myself, to honour father and mother, to honour the higher powers, to give to every man that which is his due, and suchlike. Other works there be, which considered in themselves without further respect, are of their own nature mere indifferent, that is, neither good nor evil, but take their denomination, of the use or end whereunto they serve. Which works, having a good end, are called good works, and are so indeed; but yet that cometh not of themselves, but of the good end whereunto they are referred. On the other side, if the end that they serve unto be evil, it cannot then otherwise be, but that they must needs be evil also. Of this sort of works is fasting, which of itself is a thing merely indifferent, but is made better or worse, by the end that it serveth unto. For when it respecteth a good end, it is a good work; but the end being evil, the work itself is also evil.

To fast then with this persuasion of mind, that our fasting and other good works can make us good, perfect, and just men, and finally bring us to heaven, this is a devilish persuasion, and that fast so far off from pleasing God, that it refuseth his mercy, and is altogether derogatory to the merits of Christ's death, and his precious bloodshedding. This doth the parable of the Pharisee and the Publican teach. *"Two men,"* saith Christ, *"went up together to the Temple to pray, the one a Pharisee, the other a publican. The Pharisee stood and prayed thus within himself: 'I thank thee, O God, that I am not as other men are, extortioners, unjust, adulterers, and as this publican is: I fast twice in the week, I give tithes of all that I possess.' The publican stood afar off, and would not lift up his eyes to heaven; but smote his breast, and said, 'God, be merciful to me a sinner.'"* In the person of this Pharisee, our Saviour Christ setteth out, to the eye and to the judgement of the world, a perfect, just, and righteous man, such one as is not spotted with those vices that men commonly are infected with: extortion, Luke 18:10–13 bribery, polling and pilling their neighbours, robbers and spoilers of commonweals, crafty and subtile in chopping and changing, using false weights and detestable perjury, in their buying and selling, fornicators, adulterers, and vicious livers. This Pharisee was no such man, neither faulty in any suchlike notorious crime; but, where other transgressed by leaving things undone, which yet the law required, this man did more than was requisite by law, for he fasted twice in the week, and gave tithes of all that he had. What could the world then justly blame in this man? yea, what outward thing more, could be desired to be in him, to make him a more perfect and a more just man? Truly, nothing by man's judgement: and yet our Saviour Christ, preferreth the poor Publican without fasting, before him with his fast. The cause why he doth so is manifest. For the Publican, having no good works at all to trust unto, yielded up himself unto God, confessing his sins, and hoped certainly to be saved by God's free mercy only. The Pharisee gloried and trusted so much to his works, that he thought himself sure enough, without mercy, and that he should come to heaven by his fasting, and other deeds. To this end serveth that parable; for it is spoken to them *that trusted in themselves that they were righteous, and despised other.* Now, because the Pharisee directed his works to an evil end, seeking by them justification, which indeed is the proper work of God, without our merits, his fasting twice in the week, and all his other works, though they were never so many, and seemed to the world never so good and holy, yet, in very deed, before God, they are altogether evil and abominable.

Luke 18:9

The mark also that the hypocrites shoot at with their fast, is to appear holy in the eye of the world, and so to win commendation and praise, of men. But our Saviour Christ saith of them, *"They have their reward,"* that is, they have praise and commendation of men, but of God they have none at all. For whatsoever tendeth to an evil end is itself, by that evil end, made evil also.

Matt. 6:16

Again, so long as we keep ungodliness in our hearts, and suffer wicked thought to tarry there, though we fast as oft as did either St Paul, or John Baptist, and keep it as straitly as did the Ninivites, yet shall it be not only unprofitable to us, but also a thing that greatly displeaseth Almighty God. For he saith that *his soul abhorreth and hateth such fastings, yea they are a burden unto him, and he is weary of bearing them.* And therefore he inveigheth most sharply against them, saying by the mouth of the Prophet Esay, *Behold, when ye fast, your lust remaineth still, for ye do no less violence to your debtors. Lo, ye fast to strife and debate, and to smite with the fist of wickedness. Now ye shall not fast thus, that you may make your voice to be heard above. Think ye this fast pleaseth me, that a man should chasten himself for a day? Should that be called a fasting, or a day that pleaseth the Lord?*

Isai. 1:13, 14

Isai. 58:3, 4, 5

Now, dearly beloved, seeing that Almighty God alloweth not our fast for the work sake, but chiefly respecteth our heart, how it is affected, and then esteemeth our fast either good or evil, by the end that it serveth for, it is our part to *rend our hearts, and not our garments*, as we are advertised by the Prophet Joel; that is, our sorrow and mourning must be inward, in the heart, and not in outward show only; yea, it is requisite that first, before all things, we cleanse our hearts from sin, and then to direct our fast to such an end as God will allow to be good.

Joel 2:13

There be three ends, whereunto if our fast be directed, it is then a work profitable to us and accepted of God. The first is, to chastise the flesh, that it be not too wanton, but tamed, and brought in subjection to the spirit. This respect had St Paul in his fast, when he said, "*I chastise my body, and bring it into subjection, lest by any means it cometh to pass, that when I have preached to other, I myself be found a castaway.*" The second, that the spirit may be more fervent and earnest in prayer. To this end fasted the prophets and teachers that were at Antioch, before they sent forth Paul and Barnabas, to preach the Gospel. The same two Apostles fasted, for the like purpose, when they commended to God, by their earnest prayers, the congregations that were at Antioch, Pisidia, Iconium, and Lystra; as we read in the Acts of the Apostles. The third, that our fast be a testimony and witness with us, before God, of our humble submission to his high Majesty, when we confess and acknowledge our sins unto him, and are inwardly touched with sorrowfulness of heart, bewailing the same, in the affliction of our bodies. These are the three ends or right uses of fasting. The first belongeth most properly to private fast; the other two are common as well to public fast as to private. And thus much for the use of fasting.

1 Cor. 9:27

Acts 13:1–3
Acts 14:23

Lord, have mercy upon us, and give us grace, that while we live in this miserable world, we may through thy help, bring forth this and such other fruits of the Spirit, commended and commanded in thy holy word, to the glory of thy Name, and to our comforts, that after the race of this wretched life, we may live everlastingly with thee, in thy heavenly kingdom; not for the merits and worthiness of our works, but for thy mercies' sake, and the merits of thy dear Son Jesus Christ: to whom with thee, and the Holy Ghost, be all laud, honour, and glory, for ever and ever. Amen.

THE SECOND PART OF THE HOMILY
OF FASTING

IN THE FORMER HOMILY, beloved, was showed, that among the people of
the Jews, fasting, as it was commanded them from God by Moyses, was
to abstain the whole day, from morrow till night, from meat, drink, and
all manner of food that nourisheth the body; and that whoso tasted
aught, before the evening on the day appointed to fasting, was
accounted among them a breaker of his fast. Which order, though it
seemeth strange to some in these our days, because it hath not been so
used generally in this realm, of many years past, yet that it was so among
God's people (I mean the Jews, whom, before the coming of our Saviour
Christ, God did vouchsafe to choose unto himself, a peculiar people
above all other nations of the earth), and that our Saviour Christ so
understood it, and the Apostles after Christ's ascension did so use it,
was there sufficiently proved, by the testimonies and examples of the
holy Scriptures, as well of the New Testament as of the Old. The true use
of fasting was there also showed. In this second part of this Homily,
shall be showed, that no constitution or law made by man, for things
which of their own proper nature be mere indifferent, can bind the
conscience of Christian men, to a perpetual observation and keeping
thereof; but that the higher powers have full liberty to alter and change
every such law and ordinance, either ecclesiastical or political, when
time and place shall require.

But first an answer shall be made, to a question that some may make,
demanding what judgement we ought to have, of such abstinences as
are appointed by public order, and laws made by princes and by the
authority of the magistrates, upon policy, not respecting any religion at
all in the same; as when in any realm are appointed fasts,* in consideration of the maintaining of fisher towns bordering upon the seas, and for
the encrease of fishermen, of whom do spring mariners, to go upon the
sea, to the furnishing of the navy of the realm, whereby not only the
commodities of other countries may be transported, but also may be a
necessary defence, to resist the invasion of the adversary.

For the better understanding of this question, it is necessary that we
make a difference between the policies of princes, made for the ordering
of their commonweals, in provision of things serving to the more sure
defence of their subjects and countries, and between ecclesiastical
policies in prescribing such works, by which, as by secondary means,
God's wrath may be pacified, and his mercy purchased. Positive laws
made by princes, for conservation of their policy not repugnant unto
God's law, ought of all Christian subjects with reverence of the

---

* The words "are appointed fasts" are an editorial addition.

magistrate to be obeyed, not only for fear of punishment, *but also*, as the Apostle saith, *for conscience sake*; conscience, I say, not of the thing, which of its own nature is indifferent, but of our obedience, which by the law of God we owe unto the magistrate, as unto *God's minister*. By which positive laws though we subjects, for certain times and days appointed, be restrained from some kinds of meats and drink, which God, by his holy word, hath left free to be taken and used of all men, *with thanksgiving* in all places and at all times; yet, for that such laws of princes and other magistrates, are not made to put holiness in one kind of meat and drink more than another, to make one day more holy than another, but are grounded merely upon policy, all subjects are bound in conscience to keep them, by God's commandment: who by the Apostle willeth all, without exception, to submit themselves unto the authority of *the higher powers*.

Rom. 13:4, 51

Tim. 4:3–4

Rom. 13:1

And in this point, concerning our duties which be here dwelling in England, environed with the sea as we be, we have great occasion in reason, to take the commodities of the water which Almighty God by his divine providence hath laid so nigh unto us, whereby the encrease of victuals upon the land may the better be spared and cherished, to the sooner reducing of victuals to a more moderate price, to the better sustenance of the poor. And doubtless he seemeth to be too dainty an Englishman, who considering the great commodities which may ensue, will not forbear some piece of his licentious appetite, upon the ordinance of his Prince, with the consent of the wise of the realm. What good English heart would not wish that the old ancient glory should return to the realm, wherein it hath with great commendations excelled before our days, in the furniture of the navy of the same? What will more daunt the hearts of the adversary, than to see us as well fenced and armed on the sea, as we be reported to be on the land? If the Prince requested our obedience, to forbear one day from flesh more than we do, and to be contented with one meal in the same day, should not our own commodity thereby persuade us to subjection? But now that two meals be permitted on that day to be used, which sometime our elders, in very great numbers in the realm, did use with one only spare meal, and that in fish only, shall we think it so great a burden that is prescribed? Furthermore, consider the decay of the towns nigh the seas, which should be most ready, by the number of the people there, to repulse the enemy; and we which dwell further off upon the land, having them as our buckler to defend us, should be the more in surety. If they be our neighbours, why should we not wish them to prosper? If they be our defence, as nighest at hand to repel the enemy, to keep out the rage of the seas, which else would break upon our fair pastures, why should we not cherish them?

Neither do we urge, that in the ecclesiastical policy prescribing a form of fasting, to humble ourselves in the sight of Almighty God, that that order which was used among the Jews, and practised by Christ's Apostles after his ascension, is of such force and necessity, that that only ought to be used among Christians, and none other: for that were to bind God's people unto the yoke and burden of Moyses' policy; yea, it were the very way to bring us, which are set at liberty by the freedom of Christ's Gospel, into the bondage of the Law again, which God forbid that any man should attempt or purpose! But to this end it serveth, to show how far the order of fasting, now used in the Church at this day, differeth from that which then was used. God's Church ought not neither may it be so tied, to that or any other order now made, or hereafter to be made and devised by the authority of man, but that it may lawfully, for just causes, alter, change, or mitigate those ecclesiastical decrees and orders, yea, recede wholly from them, and break them, when they tend either to superstition or to impiety, when they draw the people from God, rather than work any edification in them.

This authority Christ himself used, and left it unto his Church. He used it, I say, for the order or decree made by the elders for washing ofttimes; which was diligently observed of the Jews, yet tending to superstition, our Saviour Christ altered and changed the same, in his Church, into a profitable Sacrament, the Sacrament of our regeneration or new birth.

This authority, to mitigate laws and decrees ecclesiastical, the Apostles practised, when they writing from Jerusalem, unto the congregation that was at Antioch, signified unto them, that they would *not lay any further burden upon them, but these necessaries,* that is, *that they should abstain from things offered unto idols, from blood, from that which is strangled, and from fornication,* notwithstanding that Moyses' law required many other observances.

Acts 15:28–9

This authority, to change the orders, decrees, and constitutions of the Church, was after the Apostles' time, used of the fathers about the manner of fasting, as it appeareth in the *Tripartite History,* where it is thus written. "Touching fasting, we find that it was diversely used in divers places by divers men. For they at Rome fast three weeks together before Easter, saving upon the Saturdays and Sundays, which fast they call Lent." And after a few lines in the same place it followeth:

Tripart. Hist.
Lib. 9, cap. 38

> They have not all one uniform order in fasting. For some do fast and abstain both from fish and flesh. Some when they fast, eat nothing but fish. Others there are, which when they fast, eat of all water fowls as well as of fish, grounding themselves upon Moyses, that such fowls have their substance of the water, as the fishes have. Some others, when they fast, will neither eat herbs nor eggs. Some fasters

there are, that eat nothing but dry bread. Others when they fast, eat nothing at all, no not so much as dry bread. Some fast from all manner of food till night, and then eat without making any choice or difference of meats. And a thousand suchlike divers kinds of fasting may be found in divers places of the world, of divers men diversely used.

Euseb. Lib. 5, cap. 24

And for all this great diversity in fasting, yet charity, the very, true bond of Christian peace, was not broken, neither did the diversity of fasting, break at any time, their agreement and concord in faith. "To abstain sometime from certain meats, not because the meats are evil, but because they are not necessary, this abstinence," saith St Augustine, "is not evil. And to restrain the use of meats, when necessity and time shall require: this," saith he, "doth properly pertain to Christian men."

Dogm. Ecclesiast. cap. 66

Thus ye have heard, good people, first, that Christian subjects are bound, even in conscience, to obey princes' laws which are not repugnant to the laws of God. Ye have also heard that Christ's Church is not so bound to observe any order, law, or decree made by man, to prescribe a form in religion, but that the Church hath full power and authority from God, to change and alter the same, when need shall require; which hath been showed you, by the example of our Saviour Christ, by the practice of the Apostles, and of the fathers since that time.

Now shall be showed briefly, what time is meet for fasting: for all times serve not for all things; but, as the Wise Man saith, "*All things have their times. There is a time to weep, and a time again to laugh; a time to mourn, and a time to rejoice,* &c." Our Saviour Christ excused his disciples, and reproved the Pharisees, because they neither regarded the use of fasting, nor considered what time was meet for the same. Which both he teacheth in his answer, saying, "*The children of the marriage cannot mourn while the bridegroom is with them.*" Their question was of fasting, his answer is of mourning: signifying unto them plainly, that the outward fast of the body is no fast before God, except it be accompanied with the inward fast, which is a mourning, and a lamentation in the heart, as is before declared. Concerning the time of fasting, he saith, "*The days will come, when the bridegroom shall be taken from them: in those days they shall fast.*" By this it is manifest, that it is no time of fasting while the marriage lasteth, and the bridegroom is there present, but when the marriage is ended, and the bridegroom gone, then is it a meet time to fast.

Eccles. 3:1, 4

Matt. 9:15

Matt. 9:15; Luke 5:35

Now: to make plain unto you, what is the sense and meaning of these words, "We are at the marriage," and again, "The bridegroom is taken from us." Ye shall note, that so long as God revealeth his mercy unto us, and giveth us of his benefits, either spiritual or corporal, we are said to be with the bridegroom at the marriage. So was that good old father Jacob at the marriage, when he understood that his son Joseph was alive

Gen. 45:26–8

1 Sam. 17:49–58 and ruled Egypt under King Pharao. So was David in the marriage with the bridegroom, when he had gotten the victory of great Goliah, and had smitten off his head. Judith, and all the people of Bethulia, were the children of the wedding, and had the bridegroom with them, when God had by the hand of a woman slain Holofernes, the grand captain of the Judith 13–16 Assyrians' host, and discomfited all their enemies. Thus were the Apostles the children of the marriage, while Christ was corporally present with them, and defended them from all dangers, both spiritual and corporal. But the marriage is said then to be ended, and the bridegroom to be gone, when Almighty God smiteth us with affliction, and seemeth to leave us in the midst of a number of adversities. So God sometime striketh private men privately with sundry adversities, as trouble of mind, loss of friends, loss of goods, long and dangerous sicknesses, &c. Then is it a fit time for that man to humble himself to Almighty God, by fasting, and to mourn and bewail his sins with a sorrowful heart, and to pray unfeignedly, saying with the Prophet David, Psalm 51:9 *Turn away thy face, O Lord, from my sins, and blot out of thy remembrance all mine offences.* Again, when God shall afflict a whole region or country with wars, with famine, with pestilence, with strange diseases, and unknown sicknesses, and other suchlike calamities, then is it time for all states and sorts of people, high and low, men, women, and children, to humble themselves by fasting, and bewail their sinful living before God, and pray with one common voice, saying thus, or some other suchlike prayer: "Be favourable, O Lord, be favourable unto thy people, which turneth unto thee in weeping, fasting, and praying: spare thy people, whom thou has redeemed with thy precious blood, and suffer not thine inheritance to be destroyed, and brought to confusion."

Fasting thus used with prayer is of great efficacy, and weigheth much Tob. 12:8 with God. So the angel Raphael told Tobias. It also appeareth, by that which our Saviour Christ answered to his disciples, demanding of him why they could not cast forth the evil spirit, out of him that was brought Matt. 17:21 unto them. *"This kind,"* saith he, *"is not cast out but by fasting and prayer."* How available fast is, how much it weigheth with God, and what it is able to obtain at his hand, cannot better be set forth, than by opening unto you, and laying before you, some of those notable things that have been brought to pass by it.

Fasting was one of the means, whereby Almighty God was occasioned to alter the thing which he had purposed, concerning Ahab for 1 Kings 21:17–29 murdering the innocent man Naboth, to possess his vineyard. *God spake unto Elia, saying, "Go thy way, and say unto Ahab, 'Hast thou killed, and also gotten possession? Thus saith the Lord: In the place where dogs licked the blood of Naboth, shall dogs even lick thy blood also. Behold, I will bring evil upon thee, and will take away thy posterity: yea, the dogs shall eat him of Ahab's stock, that dieth in the city, and him that dieth in the fields, shall the fowls of the air eat.'*" This punishment had Almighty God determined for Ahab in this world, and to destroy all the male kind that was begotten of Ahab's body, besides that punishment which should have happened unto him in the world to come. *When Ahab heard this, he rent his clothes, and put sackcloth upon him, and fasted, and lay in sackcloth, and went barefooted. Then the word of the Lord came to Elia, saying, "Seest thou how Ahab is humbled before me? Because he submitteth himself before me, I will not bring that evil in his days; but in his son's days will I bring it upon his house."* Although Ahab, through the wicked counsel of Jezabel his wife, had committed shameful murder, and against all right disherited, and dispossessed for ever Naboth's stock of that vineyard; yet, upon his humble submission in heart unto God, which he declared outwardly by putting on sackcloth and fasting, God changed his sentence, so that the punishment which he had determined, fell not upon Ahab's house in his time, but was deferred unto the days of Joram his son. Here we may see of what force our outward fast is, when it is accompanied with the inward fast of the mind, which is (as is said), a sorrowfulness of heart, detesting and bewailing our sinful doings.

The like is to be seen in the Ninivites. For when God had determined to destroy the whole city of Ninive, and the time which he had appointed was even now at hand, he sent the Prophet Jonas to say unto them, *"Yet forty days, and Ninive shall be overthrown." The people by and by* Jonah 3:4–10 *believed God, and gave themselves to fasting: yea the King, by the advice of his Council, caused to be proclaimed, saying, "Let neither man nor beast, bullock nor sheep, taste any thing, neither feed nor drink water; but let man and beast put on sackcloth, and cry mightily unto God; yea, let every man turn from his evil way, and from the wickedness that is in their hands. Who can tell if God will turn and repent, and turn away from his fierce wrath, that we perish not?"* And upon this their hearty repentance, thus declared outwardly with fasting, rending of their clothes, putting on sackcloth, and sprinkling themselves with dust and ashes, the Scripture saith, *God saw their works, that they turned from their evil ways, and God repented of the evil that he had said that he would do unto them, and he did it not.*

Now beloved, ye have heard, first what fasting is, as well that which is outward in the body, as that which is inward in the heart. Ye have heard also, that there are three ends or purposes, whereunto if our outward fast be directed, it is a good work, that God is pleased with. Thirdly hath been declared, what time is most meet for to fast, either privately or publicly. Last of all, what things fasting hath obtained of God, by the examples of Ahab and the Ninivites. Let us therefore, dearly beloved, seeing there are many more causes of fasting and mourning in these our days, than hath been of many years heretofore in any one age, endeavour ourselves, both inwardly in our hearts and also outwardly with our bodies, diligently to exercise this godly exercise of fasting, in such sort and manner as the holy Prophets, the Apostles, and divers other devout persons for their time used the same. God is now the same God that was then; *God that loveth righteousness, and* that *hateth iniquity*; God which *willeth not the death of a sinner, but rather that he turn from his wickedness, and live*; God that hath promised to turn to us, if we refuse not to turn unto him. Yea, if we *turn our evil works from before his eyes, cease to do evil, learn to do well, seek to do right, relieve the oppressed, be a right judge to the fatherless, defend the widow, break our bread to the hungry, bring the poor that wander, into our house, clothe the naked, and despise not our brother which is our own flesh; then shalt thou call,* saith the Prophet, *and the Lord shall answer; thou shalt cry, and he shall say,* "Here I am." Yea, God which heard Ahab and the Ninivites, and spared them, will also hear our prayers, and spare us, so that we after their example, will unfeignedly turn unto him: yea, he will bless us with his heavenly benedictions, the time that we have to tarry in this world, and after the race of this mortal life, he will bring us to his heavenly kingdom, where we shall reign in everlasting blessedness, with our Saviour Christ. To whom, with the Father, and the Holy Ghost, be all honour and glory, for ever and ever. Amen.

Psalm 14:7

Ezek. 33:11

Zech. 1:3;
Mal. 3:7
Isai. 1:16–17;
58:7, 9

AN HOMILY AGAINST GLUTTONY AND DRUNKENNESS

YE HAVE HEARD in the former Sermon, well beloved, the description and the virtue of fasting, with the true use of the same. Now ye shall hear how foul a thing gluttony and drunkenness is before God, the rather to move you to use fasting the more diligently. Understand ye therefore, that Almighty God, to the end that we might *keep ourselves undefiled*, and *serve him in holiness and righteousness*, according to his word, hath charged in his Scriptures so many as *look for the glorious appearing of our Saviour Christ, to lead their lives in all sobriety, modesty, and temperance.* Whereby we may learn how necessary it is, for every Christian that will not be found unready at the coming of our Saviour Christ, to *live soberminded in this present world*: forasmuch as otherwise, being unready, he cannot enter with Christ into glory; and being unarmed in this behalf, he must needs be in continual danger of that cruel *adversary, the roaring lion*, against whom the Apostle Peter warneth us to prepare ourselves in continual sobriety, that we may *resist, being stedfast in faith.* To the extent therefore that this soberness may be used in all our behaviour, it shall be expedient for us to declare unto you, how much all kind of excess offendeth the Majesty of Almighty God, and how grievously he punisheth the immoderate abuse of those his creatures, which he ordained to the maintenance of this our needy life—as meats, drinks, and apparel—and again to show the noisome diseases, and great mischiefs, that commonly do follow them that inordinately give up themselves to be carried headlong, with such pleasures as are joined either with dainty and overlarge fare, or else with costly and sumptuous apparel.

And first, that ye may perceive how detestable and hateful, all excess in eating and drinking is, before the face of Almighty God, ye shall call to mind what is written by St Paul to the Galathians, where he numbereth gluttony and drunkenness among those horrible crimes with the which (as he saith) *no man shall inherit the kingdom of heaven.* He reckoneth them among *the deeds of the flesh,* and coupleth them with idolatry, whoredom, and murder, which are the greatest offences that can be

James 1:27;
Luke 1:74–5

Titus 2:12–13

1 Pet. 5:8, 9

Gal. 5:19–21

named among men. For the first spoileth God of his honour; the second defileth his holy temple, that is to wit, our own bodies; the third maketh us companions of Cain, in the slaughter of our brethren; and whoso committeth them, as St Paul saith, *cannot inherit the kingdom of God*. Certainly, that sin is very odious, and loathsome before the face of God, which causeth him to turn his favourable countenance so far from us, that he should clean bar us out of the doors, and disherit us of his heavenly kingdom. But he so much abhorreth all beastly banqueting, that by his Son our Saviour Christ in the Gospel, he declareth this terrible indignation against all belly gods, in that he pronounceth them accursed, saying, *Woe be to you that are full, for ye shall hunger*. And by the Prophet Esay he crieth out, *Woe be to you that rise up early, to give yourselves to drunkenness, and set all your minds so on drinking, that ye sit sweating thereat until it be night. The harp, the lute, the shalm, and plenty of wine are at your feasts: but the words of the Lord ye do not behold, neither consider the works of his hands. Woe be unto you that are strong to drink wine, and are mighty to advance drunkenness*. Here the Prophet plainly teacheth, that feasting and banqueting maketh men forgetful of their duty towards God, when they give themselves to all kinds of pleasure, not considering nor regarding *the works of the Lord*, who *hath created meats* and drinks, as St Paul saith, *to be received thankfully of them that believe and know the truth*. So that the very beholding of these creatures, being the handywork of Almighty God, might teach us to use them thankfully, as God hath ordained. Therefore they are without excuse before God, which either filthily feed themselves, not respecting the sanctification which is *by the word of God and prayer*, or else unthankfully abuse the good creatures of God, by surfeiting and drunkenness: forasmuch as God's ordinance in his creatures plainly forbiddeth it.

They that give themselves therefore to bibbing and banqueting, being altogether without consideration of God's judgements, are suddenly oppressed in the day of vengeance. And thereof our Saviour Christ warneth his disciples saying, *Take heed to yourselves, lest at any time your hearts be overcome with surfeiting and drunkenness, and cares of this world, and so that day come on you unwares*. Whosoever then will take warning at Christ, let him take heed to himself lest, his heart being overwhelmed by surfeiting and drowned in drunkenness, he be taken unwares, with that unthrifty *servant*, which thinking not on his master's coming, began to smite his fellow servants, *and to eat and drink, and to be drunken*, and being suddenly taken, hath his just reward, *with unbelieving* hypocrites. They that use to drink deeply, and to feed at full, wallowing themselves in all kind of wickedness, are brought asleep, in that slumbering forgetfulness of God's holy will and commandments. Therefore Almighty God crieth by the Prophet Joel, *Awake, ye drunkards; weep and howl, all ye*

Luke 6:25
Isai. 5:11, 12, 22

1 Tim. 4:3

Ibid.:5

Luke 21:34

Luke 12:45, 46

Joel 1:5

drinkers of wine, because the new wine shall be pulled from your mouth. Here the Lord terribly threateneth, to withdraw his benefits from such as abuse them, and to pull the cup from the mouth of drunkards. Here we may learn, not to sleep in drunkenness and surfeiting, lest God deprive us of the use of his creatures, when we unkindly abuse them. For certainly the Lord our God will not only take away his benefits when they are unthankfully abused, but also, in his wrath and heavy displeasure, take vengeance on such as immoderately abuse them.

If our first parents, Adam and Eve, had not obeyed their greedy appetite in eating the forbidden fruit, neither had they lost the fruition of God's benefits, which they then enjoyed in Paradise, neither had they brought so many mischiefs, both to themselves and to all their posterity. But when they passed the bonds that God had appointed them, as unworthy of God's benefits they are expelled, and driven out of Paradise; they may no longer eat the fruits of that garden, which by excess they had so much abused; as transgressors of God's commandment, they, and their posterity, are brought to a perpetual shame and confusion; and as accursed of God, they must now sweat for their living, which before had abundance at their pleasure. Even so, if we in eating and drinking exceed, when God of his large liberality sendeth plenty, he will soon change plenty into scarceness; and whereas we gloried in fullness, he will make us empty, and confound us with penury; yea, we shall be compelled to labour and travail with pains, in seeking for that which we sometime enjoyed at ease. Thus the Lord will not leave them unpunished, which not regarding his works, follow the lust and appetite of their own hearts. `Gen. 3`

The patriarch Noah, whom the Apostle calleth the *preacher of righteousness*, a man exceedingly in God's favour, is in holy Scripture made an example, whereby we may learn to avoid drunkenness. For when he had poured in wine more than was convenient, in filthy manner he lay naked in his tent, his privities discovered. And whereas sometime he was much esteemed, he is now become a laughing-stock to his wicked son Cham, no small grief to Sem and Japheth, his other two sons, which were ashamed of their father's beastly behaviour. Here we may note that drunkenness bringeth with it shame and derision, so that it never escapeth unpunished. `Noah, 2 Pet. 2:5` `Gen. 9:20–3`

Lot, in like manner, being overcome with wine, committed abominable incest with his own daughters. So will Almighty God give over drunkards, to shameful lusts of their lewd hearts. Here is Lot by drinking, fallen so far beside himself, that he knoweth not his own daughters. Who would have thought that an old man, in that heavy case, having lost his wife and all that he had, which had seen even now God's vengeance, in fearful manner declared on the five cities, for their vicious living, should `Lot, Gen. 19:30–8`

Epist. 84

be so far past the remembrance of his duty? But men overcome with drink are altogether mad, as Seneca saith. He was deceived by his daughters: but now many deceive themselves, never thinking that God, by his horrible punishments, will be avenged on them that offend by excess. It is no small plague that Lot purchased by his drunkenness. For he had copulation most filthily with his own daughters, which conceived thereby; so that the matter is brought to light, it can no longer be hid. Two incestuous children are born, Ammon and Moab; of whom came two nations, the Ammonites and Moabites, abhorred of God, and cruel adversaries to his people the Israelites. Lo, Lot hath gotten to himself, by drinking, sorrow and care, with perpetual infamy and reproach, unto the world's end. If God spared not his servant Lot, being otherwise a godly man, nephew unto Abraham, one that entertained the angels of God, what will he do to these beastly belly-slaves, which void of all godliness or virtuous behaviour, not once, but continually, day and night, give themselves wholly to bibbing and banqueting?

Gen. 19:1–3

But let us yet further behold the terrible examples of God's indignation against such as greedily follow their unsatiable lusts. Amnon the son of David, feasting himself with his brother Absalon, is cruelly murdered of his own brother. Holofernes, a valiant and mighty captain, being overwhelmed with wine, had his head stricken from his shoulders by that seely woman Judith. Simon the high priest, and his two sons Mattathias and Judas, being entertained by Ptolemy the son of Abobus, who had before married Simon's daughter, after much eating and drinking were traitorously murdered of their own kinsman. If the Israelites had not given themselves to belly cheer, they had never so often fallen to idolatry. Neither would we at this day be so addict to superstition, were it not that we so much esteemed the filling of our bellies. The Israelites, when they served idols, *sat down to eat and drink, and rose again to play,* as the Scripture reporteth: therefore, seeking to serve their bellies, they forsook the service of the Lord their God. So are we drawn to consent unto wickedness, when our hearts are over-whelmed by drunkenness and feasting. So Herod, setting his mind on banqueting, was content to grant that the holy man of God, John the Baptist, should be beheaded, at the request of his whore's daughter. Had not the rich glutton been so greedily given to the pampering of his belly, he would never have been so unmerciful to the poor Lazarus, neither had he felt the torments of unquenchable fire. What was the cause that God so horribly punished Sodom and Gomorra? was it not their *proud banqueting and continual idleness,* which caused them to be so lewd of life, and so unmerciful towards the poor? What shall we now think of the horrible excess, whereby so many have perished and been brought to destruction?

Amnon
2 Sam. 13:23–9
Judith 13:2–8

1 Mac. 16:11–16

Exod. 32:6,
1 Cor. 10:7

Matt. 14:6–11

Luke 16:19–25

Ezek. 16:49, 50

The great Alexander, after that he had conquered the whole world, Alexander was himself overcome by drunkenness; insomuch that being drunken, he slew his faithful friend Clitus; whereof when he was sober, he was so much ashamed, that for anguish of heart he wished death. Yet, notwithstanding, after this he left not his banqueting, but in one night swilled in so much wine, that he fell into a fever; and when as by no means he would abstain from wine, within few days after, in miserable sort he ended his life. The conqueror of the whole world is made a slave by excess, and becometh so mad, that he murdereth his dear friend: he is plagued with sorrow, shame, and grief of heart, for his intemperancy, yet can he not leave it; he is kept in captivity; and he which sometime had subdued many, is become a subject to the vile belly. So are drunkards and gluttons, altogether without power of themselves, and the more they drink, the drier they wax; one banquet provoketh another; they study to fill their greedy stomachs. Therefore it is commonly said, "A drunken man is always dry," and, "A glutton's gut is never filled."

Unsatiable truly are the affections and lusts of man's heart; and therefore we must learn to bridle them, with the fear of God, so that we yield not to our own lusts, lest we kindle God's indignation against ourselves, when we seek to satisfy our beastly appetite. St Paul teacheth us, *whether we eat or drink, or whatsoever we do, to do all to the glory of God.* 1 Cor. 10:31 Where he appointeth, as it were by a measure, how much a man may eat and drink: that is to wit, so much that the mind be not made sluggish, by cramming in meat and pouring in drink, so that it cannot lift up itself to the praise and glory of God. Whatsoever he be then, that by eating and drinking makes himself unlusty to serve God, let him not think to escape unpunished.

Ye have heard how much Almighty God detesteth the abuse of his creatures, as he himself declareth, as well by his holy word, as also by the fearful examples of his just judgements. Now, if neither the word of God can restrain our raging lusts, and greedy appetites, neither the manifest examples of God's vengeance fear us from riotous and excessive eating and drinking, let us yet consider the manifold mischiefs that proceed thereof; so shall we know the tree by the fruits. It hurteth the body; it infecteth the mind; it wasteth the substance; and is noisome to the neighbours. But who is able to express the manifold dangers and inconveniences, that follow of intemperate diet?

Oft cometh sudden death by banqueting: sometime the members are dissolved, and so the whole body is brought into a miserable state. He that eateth and drinketh unmeasurably, kindleth ofttimes such an unnatural heat in his body, that his appetite is provoked thereby, to desire more than it should; or else it overcometh his stomach, and filleth all the body full of sluggishness; makes it unlusty, and unfit to serve either God or man, not nourishing the body, but hurting it; and last of all bringeth many kinds of incurable diseases, whereof ensueth sometimes desperate death. But what should I need to say any more in this behalf? For except God bless our meats, and give them strength to feed us; again, except God give strength to nature to digest, so that we may take profit by them; either shall we filthily vomit them up again, or else shall they lie stinking in our bodies, as in a loathsome sink or canal, and so diversely infect the whole body. And surely the blessing of God, is so far from such as use riotous banqueting, that in their faces be sometimes seen, the express tokens of this intemperancy, as Salomon noteth in his Proverbs. *To whom is woe?* saith he; *to whom is sorrow? to whom is brawling? to whom are wounds without cause? and for whom is the redness of eyes? Even to them that tarry long at the wine.* Mark, I beseech you, the terrible tokens of God's indignation. *Woe* and *sorrow, strife* and *brawling, wounds without cause,* disfigured face, and *redness of eyes* are to be looked for, when men set themselves to excess and gourmandise, devising all means to encrease their greedy appetites, by tempering the wine, and saucing it in such sort, that it may be more delectable and pleasant unto them. It were expedient, that such delicate persons should be ruled by Salomon, who in consideration of the foresaid inconveniences, forbiddeth the very sight of wine. *Look not upon the wine,* saith he, *when it is red, and when it showeth his colour in the cup, or goeth down pleasantly. For in the end thereof, it will bite like a serpent, and hurt like a cockatrice. Thine eyes shall look upon strange women, and thine heart shall speak lewd things. And thou shalt be as one that sleepeth in the midst of the sea, and as he that sleepeth in the top of the mast.* "They have stricken me," shalt thou say, "but I was not sick; they have beaten me, but I felt it not; therefore will I seek it yet still." Certainly that must needs be very hurtful, which biteth and infecteth like a poisoned serpent, whereby men are brought to filthy fornication, which causeth the heart to devise mischief. He doubtless is in great danger, that sleepeth in the midst of the sea, for soon is he overwhelmed with waves. He is like to fall suddenly, that sleepeth in the top of the mast. And surely he hath lost his senses, that cannot feel when he is stricken, that knoweth not when he is beaten. So, surfeiting and drunkenness bites by the belly, and causeth continual gnawing in the stomach, brings men to whoredom and lewdness of heart, with dangers unspeakable, so that men are bereaved and robbed of their senses, and are altogether without power of themselves. Who seeth not now the miserable estate, whereinto men are brought by these foul filthy monsters, gluttony and drunkenness? The body is so much disquieted by them, that as Jesus the son of Sirach affirmeth, the unsatiable feeder never sleepeth quietly, such an unmeasurable heat is kindled, whereof ensueth continual ache and pain, to the whole body.

Prov. 23:29–35

Ecclus. 31:20

And no less, truly, is the mind also annoyed, by surfeiting banquets. For sometimes men are stricken with frenzy of mind, and are brought in manner to mere madness; some wax so brutish and blockish, that they become altogether void of understanding. It is an horrible thing, that any man should maim himself, in any member; but for a man of his own accord, to bereave himself of his wits, is a mischief intolerable. The Prophet Osee, in the fourth chapter, saith that *wine and drunkenness* Hos. 4:11 *taketh away the heart.* Alas then, that any man should yield unto that whereby he might bereave himself of the possession of his own heart! *Wine and women lead wise men out of the way, and bring men of understanding* Ecclus. 19:2 *to reproof and shame*, saith Jesus the son of Sirach. Yea, he asketh, *What is* *Ibid.* 31:27, 29 *the life of man that is overcome with drunkenness? Wine drunken with excess maketh bitterness of mind, and causeth brawling and strife.* In magistrates it causeth cruelty instead of justice, as that wise philosopher Plato perceived right well, when he affirmed, that "a drunken man hath a tyrannous heart," and therefore will rule all at his pleasure, contrary to right and reason. And certainly, drunkenness maketh men forget both law and equity: which caused King Salomon so straitly to charge, that no wine should be given unto rulers, *lest peradventure, by drinking they* Prov. 31:4, 5 *forget what the law appointeth them, and so change the judgement of all the children of the poor.* Therefore among all sorts of men, excessive drinking is more intolerable in a magistrate, or man of authority, as Plato saith. For *de Republ.* Lib. 3 a drunkard knoweth not where he is himself: if then a man of authority should be a drunkard, alas! how might he be a guide unto other men, standing in need of a governor himself? Besides this, a drunken man can keep nothing secret; many fond, foolish, and filthy words are spoken, when men are at their banquets. "Drunkenness," as Seneca affirmeth,

> discovereth all wickedness, and bringeth it to light; it removeth all shamefastness, and encreaseth all mischief. The proud man, being drunken, uttereth his pride, the cruel man his cruelty, and the envious man his envy, so that no vice can lie hid in a drunkard. Moreover, in that he knoweth not himself, fumbleth and stammereth in his speech, staggereth to and fro in his going, beholdeth nothing stedfastly with his staring eyes, believeth that the house runneth round about him.

It is evident that the mind is brought clean out of frame by excessive drinking: so that *whosoever is deceived by wine or strong drink* becometh, Prov. 20:1 as Salomon saith, *a mocker or a mad man, so that he can never be wise.* If any man think that he may drink much wine, and yet be well in his wits, he may as well suppose, as Seneca saith, "that when he hath drunken poison, he shall not die." For, wheresoever excessive drinking is, there must needs follow, perturbation of mind; and where the belly is stuffed with dainty fare, there the mind is oppressed with slothful sluggishness.

Ad Sororem
Serm. 24
"A full belly maketh a gross understanding," saith St Bernard, and much meat maketh a weary mind.

But alas! nowadays men pass little either for body or mind: so they have worldly wealth, and riches abundant to satisfy their unmeasurable lusts, they care not what they do. They are not ashamed to show their drunken faces, and to play the mad man openly. They think themselves in good case, and that all is well with them, if they be not pinched by lack and poverty. Lest any of us therefore might take occasion to flatter himself, in this beastly kind of excess, by the abundance of riches, let us call to mind what Salomon writeth, in the twenty-first of his Proverbs.
Prov. 21:17
He that loveth wine and fat fare, shall never be rich, saith he. And in the twenty-third chapter he maketh a vehement exhortation, on this wise:
Prov. 23:20, 21
Keep not company with drunkards and gluttons, for the glutton and drunkard shall come to poverty. He that draweth his patrimony through his throat, and eateth and drinketh more in one hour or in one day, than he is able to earn in a whole week, must needs be an unthrift, and come to beggary.

But some will say, "What need any to find fault with this? he hurteth no man but himself, he is no man's foe but his own." Indeed I know this is commonly spoken, in defence of these beastly belly gods: but it is easy to see how hurtful they are, not only to themselves, but also to the commonwealth, by their example. Every one that meeteth them, is troubled with brawling and contentious language; and ofttimes, raging
Jer. 5:8
in beastly lusts, *like fed horses, they neigh on their neighbours' wives,* as Jeremy saith, and defile their children and daughters. Their example is evil to them among whom they dwell; they are an occasion of offence to many; and whiles they waste their substance in banqueting, their own household is not provided of things necessary, their wives and their children are evil entreated, they have not wherewith to relieve their poor neighbours in time of necessity, as they might have if they lived soberly. They are unprofitable to the commonwealth; for a drunkard is neither fit to rule, nor to be ruled. They are a slander to the Church or con-
1 Cor. 5:11
gregation of Christ; and therefore St Paul doth excommunicate them, among whoremongers, idolaters, covetous persons, and extortioners, forbidding Christians to eat with any such.

Let us therefore good people, eschew, every one of us, all intemperancy; let us love sobriety, and moderate diet, oft give ourselves to abstinence and fasting, whereby the mind of man is more lift up to God, more ready to all godly exercises, as prayer, hearing and reading of God's word, to his spiritual comfort. Finally, whosoever regardeth the health and safety of his own body, or wisheth always to be well in his wits, or desireth quietness of mind, and abhorreth fury and madness; he that would be rich and escape poverty; he that is willing to live without the hurt of his neighbour, a profitable member of the commonwealth, a Christian without slander of Christ and his Church: let him avoid all riotous and excessive banqueting; let him learn to keep such measure, as behoveth him that professeth true godliness; let him follow St Paul's rule, and so *eat and drink to the glory* and praise *of God*, who *hath created all good things, to be* soberly *used with thanksgiving.* To whom be all honour and glory, for ever. Amen.

1 Cor. 10:31; 1 Tim. 4:3, 4

AN HOMILY
AGAINST EXCESS OF APPAREL

WHERE YE HAVE HERETOFORE been excited and stirred to use temperance of meats and drinks, and to avoid the excess thereof, many ways hurtful to the state of the commonwealth, and also odious before Almighty God, being the Author and Giver of such creatures, to comfort and stablish our frail nature with thanks unto him, and not by abusing of them, to provoke his liberality to severe punishing of that disorder: in like manner it is convenient, that ye be admonished of another foul and chargeable excess, I mean of apparel, at these days so outrageous, that neither Almighty God by his word can stay our proud curiosity in the same, neither yet godly and necessary laws, made of our princes and oft repeated with the penalties, can bridle this detestable abuse; whereby both God is openly contemned, and the Prince's laws manifestly disobeyed, to the great peril of the realm. Wherefore, that sobriety also in this excess may be espied among us, I shall declare unto you, both the moderate use of apparel, approved by God in his holy word, and also the abuses thereof, which he forbiddeth and disalloweth, as it may appear by the inconveniences which daily encrease, by the just judgement of God, where that measure is not kept, which he himself hath appointed.

If we consider the end and purpose, whereunto Almighty God hath ordained his creatures, we shall easily perceive that he alloweth us apparel, not only for necessity's sake, but also for an honest comeliness. Even as in herbs, trees, and sundry fruits, we have not only divers necessary uses, but also the pleasant sight and sweet smell to delight us withal; wherein we may behold the singular love of God towards mankind, in that he hath provided, both to relieve our necessities, and also to refresh our senses with an honest and moderate recreation. Therefore David in the hundred and fourth Psalm, confessing God's careful providence, showeth that God not only provideth things necessary for men, as herbs and other meats, but also such things as may rejoice and comfort, as *wine to make glad the heart, oils and ointments to make the face to shine.* So that they are altogether past the limits of humanity which,

Psalm 104: 14, 15

yielding only to necessity, forbid the lawful fruition of God's benefits. With whose traditions we may not be led, if we give ear to St Paul, who writing to the Colossians, willeth them not to hearken unto such men as shall say, *Touch not, Taste not, Handle not,* superstitiously bereaving them of the fruition of God's creatures.

Col. 2:21

And no less truly ought we to beware, lest under pretence of Christian liberty, we take licence to do what we list, advancing ourselves in sumptuous apparel, and despising other, preparing ourselves in fine bravery, to wanton, lewd, and unchaste behaviour. To the avoiding whereof, it behoveth us to be mindful of four lessons, taught in holy Scripture, whereby we shall learn to temper ourselves, and to restrain our immoderate affections, to that measure which God hath appointed. The first is, that *we make not provision for the flesh, to accomplish the lusts thereof,* with costly apparel; as that harlot did of whom Salomon speaketh, Proverbs the seventh, which *perfumed her bed, and decked it with costly ornaments of Egypt,* to the fulfilling of her lewd lust: but rather ought we by moderate temperance, to cut off all occasions whereby the flesh might get the victory. The second is written by St Paul in the seventh chapter of his first Epistle to the Corinthes, where he teacheth us to *use this world as though we used it not*: whereby he cutteth away, not only all ambition, pride, and vain pomp in apparel, but also all inordinate care and affection, which withdraweth us from the contemplation of heavenly things, and consideration of our duty towards God. They that are much occupied in caring for things pertaining to the body, are most commonly negligent and careless in matters concerning the soul. Therefore our Saviour Christ willeth us, *not to take thought what we shall eat, or what we shall drink, or wherewith we shall be clothed, but rather to seek the kingdom of God, and the righteousness thereof.* Whereby we may learn to beware, lest we use those things to our hindrance, which God hath ordained for our comfort, and furtherance towards his kingdom. The third is, that we take in good part our estate and condition, and content ourselves with that which God sendeth, whether it be much or little. He that is ashamed of base and simple attire, will be proud of gorgeous apparel, if he may get it. We must learn therefore of the Apostle St Paul, both *to use plenty and also to suffer penury,* remembering that we must yield accounts of those things which we have received, unto him who abhorreth all excess, pride, ostentation, and vanity; who also utterly condemneth and disalloweth, whatsoever draweth us from our duty towards God, or diminisheth our charity towards our neighbours and brethren, whom we ought to love as ourselves. The fourth and last rule is, that every man behold and consider his own vocation, inasmuch as God hath appointed every man his degree and office, within the limits whereof, it behoveth him to keep himself. Therefore all may not look to

Four lessons

1
Rom. 13:14

Prov. 7:16, 17

2

1 Cor. 7:31

Matt. 6:31, 33

3

Phil. 4:12

4

wear like apparel, but every one according to his degree, as God hath placed him. Which if it were observed, many one doubtless should be compelled to wear a russet coat, which now ruffleth in silks and velvets, spending more by the year in sumptuous apparel, than their fathers received for the whole revenue of their lands. But alas! nowadays how many may we behold, occupied wholly in pampering the flesh, taking no care at all but only how to deck themselves, setting their affection altogether on worldly bravery, abusing God's goodness, when he sendeth plenty, to satisfy their wanton lusts, having no regard to the degree wherein God hath placed them.

The Israelites were contented with such apparel as God gave them, although it were base and simple; and God so blessed them, that their

Deut. 29:5

shoes and clothes lasted forty years: yea, and those clothes which their fathers had worn, the children were content to use afterward. But we are never contented, and therefore we prosper not; so that most commonly he that ruffleth in his sables, in his fine furred gown, corked slippers, trim buskins, and warm mittons, is more ready to chill for the cold, than the poor labouring man, which can abide in the field all the day long, when the north wind blows, with a few beggarly clouts about him. We are loth to wear such as our fathers have left us; we think not that sufficient or good enough for us. We must have one gown for the day, another for the night; one long, another short; one for winter, another for summer; one through furred, another but faced; one for the working day, another for the holy day; one of this colour, another of that colour; one afore dinner, another after; one of the Spanish fashion, another Turkey: and to be brief, never content with sufficient. Our Saviour Christ bad his disciples

Matt. 10:10

they should not have two coats: but the most men, far unlike to his scholars, have their presses so full of apparel, that many know not how many sorts they have. Which thing caused St James to pronounce this

James 5:1, 2, 5

terrible curse, against such wealthy worldlings: *Go to, ye rich men, weep and howl on your wretchedness that shall come upon you: your riches are corrupt, and your garments are motheaten: ye have lived in pleasure on the earth, and in wantonness; ye have nourished your hearts as in the day of slaughter.* Mark, I beseech you: St James calleth them miserable, notwithstanding their riches and plenty of apparel, forasmuch as they pamper their

Luke 16:19–25

bodies to their own destruction. What was the rich glutton the better for his fine fare and costly apparel? Did not he nourish himself to be

1 Tim. 6:8, 9

tormented in hell fire? Let us learn therefore, to *content ourselves, having food and raiment,* as St Paul teacheth; lest, *desiring to be enriched* with abundance, we *fall into temptations, snares, and many noisome lusts, which drown men in perdition and destruction.*

Certainly, such as delight in gorgeous apparel, are commonly puffed

Isai. 3:16–23

up with pride, and filled with divers vanities. So were *the daughters of Sion* and people of Jerusalem, whom Esay the Prophet threateneth, because they *walked with stretched-out necks, and wandering eyes, mincing as they went, and nicely treading with their feet,* that Almighty *God should make their heads bald, and discover their shame. In that day,* saith he, *shall the Lord take away the ornament of the slippers, and the cauls, and the round attires, and the sweet balls, and the bracelets, and the attires of the head, and the slops, and the headbands, and the tablets, and the ear-rings, the rings, and the mufflers, the costly apparel, and the veils, and wimples, and the crisping pin, and the glasses, and the fine linen, and the hoods, and the lawns.* So that Almighty God would not suffer his benefits to be vainly and wantonly abused, no, not of that people whom he most tenderly loved, and had chosen to himself before all other.

No less truly is the vanity that is used amongst us in these days. For the proud and haughty stomachs of the daughters of England, are so maintained, with divers disguised sorts of costly apparel, that (as Tertullian, an ancient father, saith), "There is left no difference in apparel, between an honest matron and a common strumpet." Yea, many men are become so effeminate, that they care not what they spend in disguising themselves, ever desiring new toys, and inventing new fashions. Therefore a certain man that would picture every countryman in his accustomed apparel, when he had painted other nations, he pictured the Englishman all naked, and gave him cloth under his arm, and bad him make it himself as he thought best, for he changed his fashion so often, that he knew not how to make it. Thus with our phantastical devices, we make laughing-stocks to other nations; while one spendeth his patrimony upon pounces and cuts, and another bestoweth more on a dancing shirt, than might suffice to buy him honest and comely apparel for his whole body. Some hang their revenues about their necks, ruffling in their ruffs; and many a one jeopardeth his best joint, to maintain himself in sumptuous raiment. And every man, nothing considering his estate and condition, seeketh to excel other in costly attire. Whereby it cometh to pass that, in abundance and plenty of all things, we yet complain of want and penury, while one man spendeth that which might serve a multitude, and no man distributeth of the abundance which he hath received, and all men excessively waste that which should serve to supply the necessities of other.

There hath been very good provision made against such abuses, by divers good and wholesome laws; which if they were practised as they ought to be, of all true subjects, they might in some part serve, to diminish this raging and riotous excess in apparel. But alas! there appeareth amongst us little fear and obedience, either of God or man. Therefore must we needs look for God's fearful vengeance from heaven, to overthrow our presumption and pride, as he overthrew Herod, who

Apol. con. Gentes cap. 6

The cause of dearth

Acts 12:21-3

in his royal apparel, forgetting God, was smitten of an angel, and eaten up of worms. By which terrible example, God hath taught us, that we are but worms' meat, although we pamper ourselves never so much, in gorgeous apparel. Here we may learn that which Jesus the son of Sirach teacheth, *not to be proud of clothing and raiment, neither to exalt ourselves in the day of honour, because the works of the Lord are wonderful and glorious, secret and unknown,* teaching us with humbleness of mind, every one to be mindful of the vocation, whereunto God hath called him.

Ecclus. 11:4

Let Christians therefore endeavour themselves, to quench the care of pleasing the flesh. Let us use the benefits of God in this world, in such wise that we be not too much occupied in providing for the body. Let us content ourselves quietly, with that which God sendeth, be it never so little. And if it please him to send plenty, let us not wax proud thereof, but let us use it moderately, as well to our own comfort, as to the relief of such as stand in necessity. He that in abundance and plenty of apparel, hideth his face from him that is naked, *despiseth his own flesh,* as Esay the Prophet saith. Let us learn to know ourselves, and not to despise other. Let us remember, that we stand all, before the Majesty of Almighty God, who shall judge us by his holy word, wherein he forbiddeth excess, not only to men, but also to women: so that none can excuse themselves, of what estate or condition soever they be. Let us therefore present ourselves before his throne, as Tertullian exhorteth, with the ornaments which the Apostle speaketh of, Ephesians the sixth chapter, *having our loins girt about with the verity, having the breastplate of righteousness, and shod with shoes prepared by the Gospel of peace.* Let us take unto us simplicity, chastity, and comeliness, submitting our necks to the sweet yoke of Christ. Let women be subject to their husbands, and they are sufficiently attired, saith Tertullian. The wife of one Philo, an heathen philosopher, being demanded why she ware no gold, she answered, that she thought her husband's virtues sufficient ornaments. How much more ought Christian women, instructed by the word of God, content themselves in their husbands! Yea, how much more ought every Christian to content himself, in our Saviour Christ, thinking himself sufficiently garnished with his heavenly virtues!

Isai. 58:7

Eph. 6:14–15

Matt. 11:30

But it will be here objected and said, of some nice and vain women, that all which we do in painting our faces, in dyeing our hair, in embalming our bodies, in decking us with gay apparel, is to please our husbands, to delight his eyes, and to retain his love toward us. Oh vain excuse, and most shameful answer, to the reproach of thy husband! What couldest thou more say to set out his foolishness, than to charge him to be pleased and delighted with the devil's tire? Who can paint her face, and curl her hair, and change it into an unnatural colour, but therein doth work reproof to her Maker, who made her, as though she could make herself more comely than God hath appointed the measure of her beauty? What do these women but go about to reform that which God hath made, not knowing that all things natural are the work of God, and things disguised and unnatural be the works of the devil? and as though a wise and a Christian husband should delight, to see his wife in such painted and flourished visages, which common harlots mostly do use, to train therewith their lovers to naughtiness; or as though an honest woman could delight, to be like an harlot for pleasing of her husband.

Nay, nay, these be but the vain excuses, of such as go about to please rather others than their husbands. And such attires be but to provoke her to show herself abroad to entice others: a worthy matter! She must keep debate with her husband to maintain such apparel, whereby she is the worse housewife, the seldomer at home to see to her charge, and so to neglect his thrift, by giving great provocation to her household to waste and wantonness, while she must wander abroad, to show her own vanity and her husband's foolishness. By which her pride she stirreth up much envy of others, which be so vainly delighted as she is. She doth but deserve mocks and scorns, to set out all her commendation in Jewish and ethnic apparel, and yet brag of her Christianity. She doth but waste superfluously her husband's stock by such sumptuousness, and sometime is the cause of much bribery, extortion, and deceit in her husband's dealings, that she may be the more gorgeously set out, to the sight of the vain world, to please the devil's eyes, and not God's, who giveth to every creature, sufficient and moderate comeliness; wherewith we should be contented, if we were of God. What other thing doest thou by those means, but provokest others to tempt thee, to deceive thy soul, by the bait of thy pomp and pride? What else doest thou, but settest out thy pride, and makest of thy undecent apparel of thy body the devil's net, to catch the souls of them which behold thee? O thou woman, not a Christian, but worse than a paynim, thou minister of the devil, why pamperest thou that carrion flesh so high, which sometime doth stink and rot on the earth as thou goest? Howsoever thou perfumest thyself, yet cannot thy beastliness be hidden or overcome, with thy smells and savours, which do rather deform and misshape thee, than beautify thee. What meant Salomon to say of such trimming of vain women, when he said, *A fair woman, with-* Prov. 11:22 *out good manners and conditions, is like a sow which hath a ring of gold upon her snout,* but that the more thou garnish thyself with these outward blazings, the less thou carest for the inward garnishing of thy mind, and so dost but defoul thyself by such array, and not beautify thyself?

Hear, hear, what Christ's holy Apostles do write. *Let not the outward* 1 Pet. 3:3–5 *apparel of women,* saith St Peter, *be decked with the braiding of hair, with wrapping on of gold, or goodly clothing: but let the mind and the conscience, which is not seen with the eyes, be pure and clean: that is,* saith he, *an*

1 Tim. 2:9, 10

acceptable and an excellent thing before God. For so the old ancient holy women attired themselves, and were obedient to their husbands. And St Paul saith, that *women should apparel themselves with shamefastness, and soberness, and not with braids of their hair, or gold, or pearl, or precious clothes, but as women should do, which will express godliness by their good outward works.* If we will not keep the Apostles' precepts, at the least let us hear what pagans, which were ignorant of Christ, have said in this matter. Democrates saith, "The ornament of a woman standeth in scarcity of speech and apparel." Sophocles saith of such apparel thus: "It is not an ornament, O thou fool, but a shame, and a manifest show of thy folly." Socrates* saith that "that is a garnishing to a woman, which declareth out her honesty." The Grecians use it in a proverb, "It is not gold or pearl which is a beauty to a woman, but good conditions." And Aristotle biddeth that "a woman should use less apparel than the law doth suffer; for it is not the goodliness of apparel, nor the excellency of beauty, nor the abundance of gold, that maketh a woman to be esteemed, but modesty, and diligence to live honestly in all things." This outrageous vanity is now grown so far, that there is no shame taken of it. We read in histories, that when King Dionysius sent to the women of Lacedemon rich robes, they answered and said that "they shall do us more shame than honour," and therefore refused them. The women in Rome in old time, abhorred that gay apparel which King Pyrrhus sent to them, and none were so greedy and vain to accept them. And a law was openly made of the senate, and a long time observed, "that no woman should wear over half an ounce of gold, nor should wear clothes of divers colours."

But perchance, some dainty dame will say and answer me, that they must do something to show their birth and blood, to show their husband's riches: as though nobility were chiefly seen by these things, which be common to those which be most vile! as though thy husband's riches were not better bestowed than in such superfluities! as though, when thou wast christened, thou didst not renounce the pride of the world, and the pomp of the flesh! I speak not against convenient apparel, for every state agreeable, but against the superfluity, against the vain delight to covet such vanities, to devise new fashions to feed thy pride with, to spend so much upon thy carcase, that thou and thy husband are compelled to rob the poor, to maintain thy costliness. Hear how that noble holy woman, Queen Hester, setteth out these goodly ornaments (as they be called), when in respect of saving God's people, she was compelled to put on such glorious apparel, knowing that it was a fit stale, to blind the eyes of carnal fools. Thus she prayed: *Thou knowest, O Lord, the necessity which I am driven to, to put on this apparel, and that I abhor this sign of pride, and of this glory which I bear on my head, and that I defy it as*

Esth. 14:16

---

* Griffiths points out, citing Plutarch, that this should be Crates.

a filthy cloth, and that I wear it not when I am alone. Again, by what means was Holofernes deceived, but by the glittering show of apparel? which that holy woman Judith did put on her, not as delighting in them, nor seeking vain voluptuous pleasure by them; but she ware it of pure necessity, by God's dispensation using this vanity, to overcome the vain eyes of God's enemy. Such desire was in those holy noble women, being very loth and unwilling otherwise, to wear such sumptuous apparel, by the which others should be caused to forget themselves. These be commended in Scripture for abhorring such vanities, which by constraint and great necessity, against their hearts' desire, were compelled to wear them for a time. And shall such women be worthy commendations, which neither be comparable with these women aforesaid in nobility, nor comparable to them in their good zeals to God and his people, whose daily delight and seeking, is to flourish in such gay shifts and changes, never satisfied, nor regarding who smarteth for their apparel, so they may come by it? Oh vain men, which be subjects to their wives, in these inordinate affections! Oh vain women! to procure so much hurt to themselves, by the which they come the sooner to misery in this world, and in the mean time be abhorred of God, hated and scorned of wise men, and in the end like to be joined with such who in hell, too late repenting themselves, shall openly complain with these words: *What hath our pride profited us? or what profit hath the pomp of riches brought us? All those things are passed away like a shadow. As for virtue, we did never show any sign thereof; and thus are we consumed in our wickedness.*

Judith 10:3, 4, 23; 12:15; 16:8, 9

Wisd. 5: 8, 9, 13

If thou sayest that the custom is to be followed, and the use of the world doth compel thee to such curiosity; then I ask of thee, whose custom should be followed? wise folks' manners, or fools'? If thou sayest, the wise; then I say, follow them, for fools' customs who should follow but fools? Consider that the consent of wise men ought to be alleged for a custom. Now, if any lewd custom be used, be thou the first to break it; labour to diminish it and lay it down; and more laud afore God, and more commendation shalt thou win by it, than by all the glory of such superfluity.

Thus ye have heard declared unto you, what God requireth by his word, concerning the moderate use of his creatures. Let us learn to use them moderately, as he hath appointed. Almighty God hath taught us, to what end and purpose we should use our apparel. Let us therefore learn so to behave ourselves in the use thereof, as it becometh Christians, always showing ourselves thankful to our heavenly Father, for his great and merciful benefits; who giveth unto us *our daily bread,* that is to say, all things necessary for this our needy life; unto whom we shall render accounts for all his benefits at *the glorious appearing of our Saviour Christ.* To whom, with the Father, and the Holy Ghost, be all honour, praise, and glory, for ever and ever. Amen.

Matt. 6:11

Titus 2:13

AN HOMILY OR SERMON
CONCERNING PRAYER

THERE IS NOTHING in all man's life, well beloved in our Saviour Christ, so needful to be spoken of, and daily to be called upon, as hearty, zealous, and devout prayer; and the necessity whereof is so great, that without it nothing may be well obtained at God's hand. For as the Apostle James saith, *every good and perfect gift cometh from above, and proceedeth from the Father of lights*: who is also said to be *rich and liberal towards all them that call upon him*, not because he either will not or cannot give without asking, but because he hath appointed prayer, as an ordinary means between him and us.

There is no doubt but he always *knoweth what we have need of*, and is always most ready to give abundance of those things that we lack. Yet, to the intent we might acknowledge him to be the Giver of all good things, and behave ourselves thankfully towards him in that behalf, loving, fearing, and worshipping him, sincerely and truly, as we ought to do, he hath profitably and wisely ordained, that in time of necessity, we should humble ourselves in his sight, pour out the secrets of our heart before him, and crave help at his hands, with continual, earnest, and devout prayer. By the mouth of his holy Prophet David he saith on this wise: *Call upon me in the days of thy trouble, and I will deliver thee*. Likewise in the Gospel, by the mouth of his well beloved Son Christ, he saith, *Ask, and it shall be given you; knock, and it shall be opened: for whosoever asketh receiveth; whosoever seeketh findeth; and to him that knocketh it shall be opened*. St Paul also, most agreeably consenting hereunto, *willeth men to pray everywhere, and to continue therein, with thanksgiving*. Neither doth the blessed Apostle St James in this point any thing dissent, but earnestly exhorting all men to diligent prayer, saith, *If any man lack wisdom, let him ask it of God, which giveth liberally to all men, and reproacheth no man*. Also in another place: *Pray one for another*, saith he, *that ye may be healed; for the righteous man's prayer availeth much, if it be fervent*. What other thing are we taught by these and such other places, but only this, that Almighty God, notwithstanding his heavenly wisdom

Margin notes:
James 1:17
Rom. 10:12

Matt. 6:8

Psalm 50:15

Matt. 7:7, 8

1 Tim. 2:8,
Phil. 4:6,
Col. 4:2

James 1:5

James 5:16

and foreknowledge, will be prayed unto, that he will be called upon, that he will have us no less willing on our part to ask, than he on his part is willing to give?

Therefore, most fond and foolish is the opinion and reason of those men, which therefore think all prayer to be superfluous and vain, because God *searcheth the heart and the reins*, and knoweth the meaning of the spirit before we ask. For if this fleshly and carnal reason were sufficient to disannul prayer, then why did our Saviour Christ so often cry to his disciples, *Watch and pray*? why did he prescribe them a form of prayer, saying, *When ye pray, pray after this sort, Our Father, which art in heaven*, &c? why did he pray so often and so earnestly himself, before his passion? finally, why did the Apostles, immediately after his ascension, gather themselves together into one several place, and there continue a long time in prayer? Either they must condemn Christ and his Apostles of extreme folly, or else they must needs grant, that prayer is a thing most necessary, for all men, at all times, and in all places. *Psalm 7:9; Rom. 8:27* *Matt. 26:41* *Matt. 6:9, Luke 11:2 Luke 22:41–4* *Acts 1:13, 14*

Sure it is, that there is nothing more expedient or needful for mankind, in all the world, than prayer. *Pray always*, saith St Paul, *with all manner of prayer and supplication, and watch thereto with all diligence*. Also in another place, he willeth us to *pray* continually, *without any intermission* or ceasing, meaning thereby, that we ought never to slack nor faint in prayer, but to continue therein to our lives' end. A number of other such places might here be alleged, of like effect, I mean, to declare the great necessity and use of prayer: but what need many proofs in a plain matter, seeing there is no man so ignorant but he knoweth, no man so blind but he seeth, that prayer is a thing most needful, in all estates and degrees of men? For only by the help hereof, we attain to those heavenly and everlasting treasures, which God our heavenly Father hath reserved and laid up for us his children, in his dear and well beloved Son, Jesus Christ, with this covenant and promise, most assuredly confirmed and sealed unto us: that if we ask, we shall receive. *Eph. 6:18* *1 Thess. 5:17* *John 16:23–7*

Now, the great necessity of prayer being sufficiently known, that our minds and hearts may be the more provoked and stirred thereunto, let us briefly consider, what wonderful strength and power it hath, to bring strange and mighty things to pass. We read in the Book of Exodus that Josua, fighting against the Amalekites, did conquer and overcome them, not so much by virtue of his own strength, as by the earnest and continual prayer of Moyses; who as long as he held up his hands to God, so long did Israel prevail; but when he fainted, and let his hands down, then did Amalek and his people prevail; insomuch that Aaron and Hur, being in the mount with him, were fain to stay up his hands, until the going down of the sun, otherwise had the people of God that day been utterly discomfited, and put to flight. Also we read in another place of Josua *Exod. 17:10–13* *Josh. 10:12, 13* himself, how he at the besieging of Gibeon, making his humble petition to Almighty God, caused the sun and the moon to stay their course, and to stand still in the midst of heaven, for the space of a whole day, until such time the people were sufficiently avenged upon their enemies. And

2 Chron. 20:1–24

was not Jehosaphat's prayer of great force and strength, when God at his request, caused his enemies to fall out among themselves, and wilfully to destroy one another? Who can marvel enough at the effect and virtue of Elia's prayer?

James 5:17, 18; 1 Kings 17:1; 18:42–5; Luke 4:25

He, being a man subject to affections as we are, prayed to the Lord that it might not rain, and there fell no rain upon the earth, for the space of three years and six months. Again he prayed that it might rain, and there fell great plenty, so that the earth brought forth her encrease most abundantly. It

Judith 9; 12:8; 13:4–9; Esth. 4:16; 14; Susanna 42–4

were too long to tell of Judith, Esther, Susanna, and of divers other godly men and women, how greatly they prevailed in all their doings, by giving their minds earnestly and devoutly to prayer. Let it be sufficient at this time, to conclude with the sayings of Augustine and Chrysostom,

Aug. Serm. 226 *de Tempore*; Chrys. *sup. Matt.* 22

whereof the one calleth prayer "the key of heaven", the other plainly affirmeth that "there is nothing in all the world more strong, than a man that giveth himself to fervent prayer."

Now then, dearly beloved, seeing prayer is so needful a thing, and of so great strength before God, let us, according as we are taught by the example of Christ and his Apostles, be earnest and diligent in calling on the Name of the Lord. Let us never faint, never slack, never give over; but let us daily and hourly, early and late, in season and out of season, be occupied in godly meditations and prayers. What if we obtain not our petition at the first? yet let us not be discouraged, but let us continually cry and call upon God: he will surely hear us at length, if for no other cause, yet for very importunity's sake. Remember the parable of the unrighteous judge and the poor widow, how she by her importunate

Luke 18:1–7

means, caused him to do her justice against her adversary, although otherwise he feared neither God nor man. *Shall not God much more avenge his elect,* saith our Saviour Christ, *which cry unto him day and night?* Thus he taught his disciples, and in them all other true Christian men, *to pray always, and never to faint* or shrink. Remember also the example of the woman of Chanaan, how she was rejected of Christ, and

Matt. 15:22–8

called dog, as one most unworthy of any benefit at his hands; yet she gave not over, but followed him still, crying and calling upon him, to be good and merciful unto her daughter; and at length, by very importunity, she obtained her request. Oh let us learn by these examples, to be earnest and fervent in prayer! assuring ourselves, that *whatsoever we ask*

John 16:23

of God the Father, in the name of his son Christ, and *according to his will,* he will undoubtedly grant it. He is truth itself; and as truly as he hath promised it, so truly will he perform it. God, for his great mercy's sake, so work in our hearts by his Holy Spirit, that we may always make our humble prayers unto him, as we ought to do, and always obtain the thing which we ask, through Jesus Christ our Lord! To whom with the Father, and the Holy Ghost, be all honour and glory, world without end. Amen.

THE SECOND PART OF THE HOMILY CONCERNING PRAYER

IN THE FIRST PART OF THIS SERMON, ye heard the great necessity, and also the great force, of devout and earnest prayer, declared and proved unto you, both by divers weighty testimonies, and also by sundry good examples of holy Scripture. Now shall you learn, whom you ought to call upon, and to whom ye ought always to direct your prayers.

We are evidently taught in God's holy Testament, that Almighty God is the only fountain and wellspring of all goodness, and that whatsoever we have in this world, we receive it only at his hands. To this effect serveth the place of St James: *Every good and perfect gift*, saith he, *cometh from above, and proceedeth from the Father of lights*. To this effect also serveth the testimony of Paul, in divers places of his Epistles, witnessing that *the spirit of wisdom*, the spirit of knowledge *and revelation*, yea, every good and heavenly gift, as faith, hope, charity, *grace, and peace*, cometh only and solely of God. In consideration whereof he bursteth out into a sudden passion, and saith, *O man, what thing hast thou, which thou hast not received?* Therefore, whensoever we need or lack anything, pertaining either to the body or the soul, it behoveth us to run only unto God, who is the only giver of all good things. Our Saviour Christ in the Gospel, teaching his disciples how they should pray, sendeth them to the Father in his name, saying, *Verily, verily, I say unto you, Whatsoever ye ask the Father in my name, he will give it unto you*. And in another place: *When ye pray, pray after this sort, Our Father, which art in heaven*, &c. And doth not God himself, by the mouth of his Prophet David, will and command us to call upon him? The Apostle wisheth *grace and peace to all them that call on the Name* of the Lord, and *of his Son Jesus Christ*: as doth also the Prophet Joel, saying, *And it shall come to pass, that whosoever shall call on the Name of the Lord, shall be saved.*

Thus then it is plain, by the infallible word of truth and life, that in all our necessities we must flee unto God, direct our prayers unto him, call upon his holy Name, desire help at his hands, and at no other's. Whereof if ye will yet have a further reason, mark that which followeth. There are certain conditions most requisite to be found, in every such a one that must be called upon, which if they be not found in him unto whom we pray, then doth our prayer avail us nothing, but is altogether in vain. The

James 1:17

Rom. 1:7, 1 Cor. 12:8, Eph. 1:17, 2:8, 1 Thess. 3:12

1 Cor. 4:7

John 16:25

Matt. 6:9, Luke 11:2

Psalm 1:15

1 Cor. 1:2, 3

Joel 2:32, Acts 2:21

first is this, that he to whom we make our prayers be able to help us. The second is, that he will help us. The third is, that he understand better than we ourselves, what we lack, and how far we have need of help. If these things be to be found in any other, saving only God, then may we lawfully call upon some other besides God. But what man is so gross, but he well understandeth, that these things are only proper to him which is omnipotent, and *knoweth all things*, even *the very secrets of the* *heart*, that is to say, only and to God alone? Whereof it followeth, that we must call neither upon angel, nor yet upon saint, but only and solely upon God. As St Paul doth write: *How shall men call upon him in whom* *they have not believed?* So that invocation or prayer may not be made, without faith in him on whom we call, but that we must believe in him, before we can make our prayers unto him: whereupon we must only and solely pray unto God. For to say that we should believe either in angel, or saint, or in any other living creature, were most horrible blasphemy against God, and his holy word; neither ought this fancy enter into the heart of any Christian man, because we are expressly taught, in the word of the Lord, only to repose our faith in the blessed Trinity, in whose only Name we are also baptised, according to the express commandment of our Saviour Jesus Christ, in the last of Matthew.

But, that the truth hereof may the better appear, even to them that be most simple and unlearned, let us consider what prayer is. St Augustine calleth it "a lifting up of the mind to God, that is to say, a humble and lowly pouring out of the heart to God". Isidorus saith that "it is an affection of the heart, and not a labour of the lips." So that, by these places, true prayer doth consist, not so much in the outward sound and voice of words, as in the inward groaning, and crying of the heart to God. Now then, is there any angel, any virgin, any patriarch or prophet among the dead, that can understand or know the meaning of the heart? The Scripture saith *it is God that searcheth the heart and reins*, and that *he* *only knoweth the hearts of the children of men*. As for the Saints, they have so little knowledge of the secrets of the heart, that many of the ancient fathers greatly doubt, whether they know anything at all, that is commonly done on earth. And albeit some think they do, yet St Augustine, a doctor of great authority and also antiquity, hath this opinion of them, that they know no more what we do on earth, than we know what they do in heaven. For proof whereof he allegeth the words of Esay the Prophet, where it is said, *Abraham is ignorant of us, and Israel* *knoweth us not*. His mind therefore is this, not that we should put any religion in worshipping them, or praying unto them, but that we should honour them by following their virtuous and godly life. For as he witnesseth in another place, the Martyrs and holy men in times past, were wont after their death to be remembered, and named of the priest

1 John 3:20,
Psalm 44:21

Rom. 10:14

Matt. 28:19

de Spir. et Lit.
cap. 50
de Summo Bono
cap. 8, Lib. 3

Psalm 8, Rev. 2,
Jer. 17,
2 Chron. 6

Lib. de Cura pro
Mort. agenda cap.
13;
Isai. 53:16
de vera Relig. cap.
55

Lib. 22 de Civ.
Dei, cap. 10

at Divine Service, but never to be invocated or called upon. And why so? "Because the priest," saith he, "is God's priest, and not theirs:" whereby he is bound to call upon God, and not upon them.

Thus you see, that the authority both of Scripture, and also of Augustine, doth not permit that we should pray unto them. Oh that all men would studiously read and *search the Scriptures*! then should they not be drowned in ignorance, but should easily perceive the truth, as well of this point of doctrine, as of all the rest. For there doth the Holy Ghost plainly teach us, that Christ is our only mediator and intercessor with God, and that we must seek and run to no other. *If any man sinneth*, saith St John, *we have an advocate with the Father, Jesus Christ the righteous; and he is the propitiation for our sins.* St Paul also saith, *There is one God, and one mediator between God and man, even the man Jesus Christ.* Whereunto agreeth the testimony of our Saviour himself, witnessing that *no man cometh to the Father, but only by him*, who is *the way, the truth, the life,* yea, and *the* only *door* whereby we must enter into the kingdom of heaven, because God is pleased in no other but him. For which cause also, he crieth and calleth unto us, that we should come unto him, saying, *Come unto me, all ye that labour and be heavy laden, and I shall refresh you.* Would Christ have us so necessarily come unto him? and shall we most unthankfully leave him, and run unto other? This is even that which God so greatly complaineth of, by his Prophet Jeremy, saying, *My people have committed two great offences; they have forsaken me, the fountain of the waters of life, and have digged to themselves broken pits, that can hold no water.* Is not that man, think you, unwise that will run for water to a little brook, when he may as well go to the head spring? Even so may his wisdom be justly suspected, that will flee unto Saints in time of necessity, when he may boldly, and without fear, declare his grief, and direct his prayer, unto the Lord himself.

If God were strange, or dangerous to be talked withal, then might we justly draw back, and seek to some other. But *the Lord is nigh unto them that call upon him, in faith* and *truth*: and *the prayer of the humble and meek hath always pleased him.* What if we be sinners? shall we not therefore pray unto God? or shall we despair to obtain any thing at his hands? Why did Christ then teach us to ask forgiveness of our sins, saying, *And forgive us our trespasses, as we forgive them that trespass against us*? Shall we think that the Saints are more merciful, in hearing sinners, than God? David saith, that *the Lord is full of compassion and mercy, slow to anger, and of great kindness.* St Paul saith, that *he is rich in mercy towards all them that call upon him.* And he himself, by the mouth of his Prophet Esay, saith, *For a little while have I forsaken thee, but with great compassion will I gather thee: for a moment in mine anger, I have hid my face from thee, but with everlasting mercy have I had compassion upon thee.* Therefore the sins of

John 5:39

1 John 2:1, 2

1 Tim. 2:5

John 14:6
John 10:9
Matt. 17:5

Matt. 11:28

Jer. 2:13

Psalm 145:18
Judith 9

Matt. 6:12

Psalm 103:8
Ephes. 2:4
Isai. 54:7, 8

any man ought not to withhold him, from praying unto the Lord his God; but if he be truly penitent, and stedfast in faith, let him assure himself, that the Lord will be merciful unto him, and hear his prayers.

"Oh but I dare not" (will some man say) "trouble God at all times with my prayers: we see that in kings' houses, and courts of princes, men cannot be admitted, unless they first use the help and means of some special noblemen, to come unto the speech of the king, and to obtain the thing that they would have." To this reason doth St Ambrose answer very well, writing upon the first chapter to the Romans. "Therefore," saith he, "we use to go unto the king by officers and noblemen, because the king is a mortal man, and knoweth not to whom he may commit the government of the commonwealth. But to have God our friend, from whom nothing is hid, we need not any helper, that should further us with his good word, but only a devout and godly mind." And if it be so, that we need one to entreat for us, why may we not content ourselves with that *one Mediator, which is at the right hand of God* the Father, and there *liveth for ever to make intercession for us*? As the blood of Christ did redeem us on the cross, and cleanse us from our sins, even so it is now *able to save all them that come unto God* by it. For Christ, sitting in heaven, *hath an everlasting priesthood*, and always prayeth to his Father, for them that be penitent, obtaining by virtue of his wounds, which are evermore in the sight of God, not only perfect remission of our sins, but also all other necessaries that we lack in this world: so that his only mediation is sufficient in heaven, and needeth no other's to help him.

Why then do we pray one for another in this life? some man perchance will here demand. Forsooth, we are willed so to do, by the express commandment both of Christ and his disciples, to declare therein, as well the faith that we have in Christ towards God, as also the mutual charity that we bear one towards another, in that we pity our brother's case, and make our humble petition to God for him. But that we should pray unto Saints, neither have we any commandment in all the Scripture, nor yet example which we may safely follow. So that, being done without authority of God's word, it lacketh the ground of faith, and therefore cannot be acceptable before God. *For whatsoever is not of faith is sin*: and the Apostle saith, that *faith cometh by hearing, and hearing by the word of God.*

Yet thou wilt object further, that the Saints in heaven do pray for us, and that their prayer proceedeth of an earnest charity, that they have towards their brethren on earth. Whereto it may be well answered, first, that no man knoweth, whether they do pray for us or no. And if any will go about to prove it, by the nature of charity, concluding that, because they did pray for men on earth, therefore they do much more the same now in heaven; then may it be said by the same reason, that as oft as we do weep on earth, they do also weep in heaven, because while they lived

Ambros. super cap. 1 Rom.

Heb. 7:25

Heb. 7:24; 9:12, 24; 10:12

Matt. 5:44, 6:9– 13, James 5:16, Col. 3:3, 1 Tim. 2:1–2

Heb. 11:6

Rom. 14:23

Rom. 10:17

in this world, it is most certain and sure they did so. As for that place which is written in the Apocalypse, namely, that the angel did offer up the prayers of the saints, upon the golden altar: it is properly meant, and ought properly to be understood, of those saints that are yet living on earth, and not of them that are dead; otherwise what need were it, that the angel should offer up their prayers, being now in heaven before the face of Almighty God? But, admit the Saints do pray for us, yet do we not know how, whether specially for them which call upon them, or else generally for all men, wishing well to every man alike. If they pray specially for them which call upon them, then it is like they hear our prayers, and also know our hearts' desire. Which thing to be false, it is already proved, both by the Scriptures, and also by the authority of Augustine. *Rev. 8:3, 4*

Let us not therefore put our trust or confidence in the Saints, or Martyrs that be dead. Let us not call upon them, nor desire help at their hands: but let us always lift up our hearts to God in the name of his dear Son Christ; for whose sake as God hath promised to hear our prayers, so he will truly perform it. Invocation is a thing proper unto God: which if we attribute unto the Saints, it soundeth to their reproach, neither can they well bear it at our hands. When Paul had healed a certain lame man, which was impotent in his feet, at Lystra, the people would have done sacrifice to him and Barnabas; who, rending their clothes, refused it, and exhorted them to worship the true God. Likewise in the Revelation, when St John fell before the angel's feet, to worship him, the angel would not permit him to do it, but commanded him that he should *worship God.* Which examples declare unto us, that the saints, and angels in heaven, will not have us do any honour unto them that is due and proper unto God. He only is our Father; he only is omnipotent; he only knoweth and understandeth all things; he only can help us at all times and in all places; *he suffereth the sun to shine upon the good and the bad; he feedeth the young ravens that cry unto him; he saveth both man and beast; he will not that any one hair of our head shall perish*, but is always ready to help and preserve, all them that put their trust in him, according as he hath promised, saying, *Before they call, I will answer; and whiles they speak, I will hear.* Let us not therefore any thing mistrust his goodness; let us not fear to come before the throne of his mercy; let us not seek the aid and help of Saints; but *let us come boldly* ourselves, nothing doubting, but God for Christ's sake, *in whom he is well pleased*, will hear us without a spokesman, and accomplish our desire, in all such things as shall be agreeable to his most holy will. So saith Chrysostom, an ancient doctor of the Church; and so must we stedfastly believe, not because he saith it, but much more, because it is the doctrine of our Saviour Christ himself, who hath promised, that if we pray to the Father in his name, we shall

Acts 14:8–18

Rev. 19:10, 22:8–9

Matt. 5:45; Psalm 147:9, 36:6; Luke 12:7, 21:18

Isai. 65:24

Heb. 4:16; 10:19–23 Matt. 17:5

Chrysost. 6 Hom. de Profect. Evang.

John 14:13–14, 15:16, 16:23–7

certainly be heard, both to the relief of our necessities, and also to the
salvation of our souls, which he hath purchased unto us, *not with gold or
silver, but with his precious blood*, shed once for all upon the cross.

To him therefore, with the Father and the Holy Ghost, three
Persons and one God, be all honour, praise, and glory, for ever and ever.
Amen.

1 Pet. 1:18–19

THE THIRD PART OF THE HOMILY
OF PRAYER

YE WERE TAUGHT in the other part of this Sermon, unto whom ye ought
to direct your prayers in time of need and necessity, that is to wit, not
unto angels or saints, but unto the eternal and everliving God: who
because he is merciful, is always ready to hear us, when we call upon him
in true and perfect faith; and because he is omnipotent, he can easily
perform, and bring to pass the thing that we request to have at his hands.
To doubt of his power, it were a plain point of infidelity, and clean against
the doctrine of the Holy Ghost, which teacheth that he is all in all. And as
touching his goodwill in this behalf, we have express testimonies in the
Scripture, how that he will help us, and also *deliver* us, if we *call upon him
in time of trouble*. So that in both these respects, we ought rather to call
upon him, than upon any other. Neither ought any man therefore to
doubt to come boldly unto God, because he is a sinner. For *the Lord*, as
the Prophet David saith, *is gracious and merciful*; yea, *his mercy and goodness
endureth for ever*. He that sent his own Son into the world *to save sinners*,
will he not also hear sinners, if with a true penitent heart, and a stedfast
faith, they pray unto him? Yes, *if we acknowledge our sins, God is faithful
and just to forgive us our sins, and to cleanse us from all unrighteousness*; as
we are plainly taught by the examples of David, Peter, Mary Magdalene,
the Publican, and divers other. And, whereas we must needs use the help
of some mediator and intercessor, let us content ourselves with him that
is the true and only *Mediator of the New Testament*, namely, the Lord and
Saviour, Jesus Christ. For as St John saith, *if any man sin, we have an
advocate with the Father, Jesus Christ the righteous, who is the propitiation for
our sins*. And St Paul, in his first Epistle to Timothy, saith, *There is one
God, and one mediator between God and man, even the man Jesus Christ; who
gave himself a ransom for all men, to be a testimony in due time*.

Now, after this doctrine established, you shall be instructed for what
kind of things, and what kind of persons, ye ought to make your prayers
unto God. It greatly behoveth all men when they pray, to consider well
and diligently with themselves, what they ask and require at God's hands,
lest, if they desire the thing which they ought not, their petitions be

Psalm 50:15

Psalm 107:1

1 Tim. 1:16

1 John 1:9

2 Sam. 12:13;
Mark 16:7, 9
Luke 18:14;
John 21:15–19

Heb. 12:24

1 John 2:1–2

1 Tim. 2:5, 6

made void, and of none effect. There came on a time unto Agesilaus the King, a certain importunate suitor, who requested him in a matter earnestly, saying, "Sir, and it please your grace, you did once promise me." "Truth," quoth the King, "if it be just that thou requirest, then I promised thee; otherwise I did only speak it, and not promise it." The man would not so be answered at the King's hand, but still urging him more and more, said, "It becometh a king, to perform the least word he hath spoken, yea, if he should only beck with his head." "No more," saith the King, "than it behoveth one that cometh to a king, to speak and ask those things which are rightful and honest." Thus the King cast off this unreasonable and importunate suitor. Now, if so great consideration be to be had, when we kneel before an earthly king, how much more ought to be had, when we kneel before the heavenly King, who is only delighted with justice and equity, neither will admit any vain, foolish, or unjust petition! Therefore it shall be good and profitable, throughly to consider and determine with ourselves, what things we may lawfully ask of God, without fear of repulse, and also what kind of persons we are bound to commend unto God in our daily prayers.

Two things are chiefly to be respected, in every good and godly man's prayer: his own necessity, and the glory of Almighty God. Necessity belongeth either outwardly to the body, or else inwardly to the soul. Which part of man, because it is much more precious and excellent than the other, therefore we ought first of all to crave such things as properly belong to the salvation thereof; as, the gift of repentance, the gift of faith, the gift of charity and good works, remission and forgiveness of sins, patience in adversity, lowliness in prosperity, and such other like *fruits of the Spirit*, as *hope, love, joy, peace, long-suffering, gentleness, goodness, meekness, and temperancy*; which things God requireth of all them that profess themselves to be his children, saying unto them on this wise, *Let your light so shine before men, that they may see your good works, and glorify your Father which is in heaven.* And in another place he also saith, *Seek first the kingdom of God and his righteousness, and then all other things shall be given unto you.* Wherein he putteth us in mind, that our chief and greatest care ought to be, for those things which pertain to the health and safeguard of the soul, because *we have here*, as the Apostle saith, *no continuing city, but do seek after another, in the world to come.* Gal. 5:22, 23 Matt. 5:16 Matt. 6:33 Heb. 13:14

Now, when we have sufficiently prayed for things belonging to the soul, then may we lawfully, and with safe conscience, pray also for our bodily necessities, as meat, drink, clothing, health of body, deliverance out of prison, good luck in our daily affairs, and so forth, according as we shall have need. Whereof what better example can we desire to have than of Christ himself? who taught his disciples, and all other Christian men, first to pray for heavenly things, and afterward for earthly things, as is to

Matt. 6:33,
Luke 11:2–4

1 Kings 3:5–13

be seen in that prayer which he left unto his Church, commonly called the Lord's Prayer. In the third Book of Kings and third chapter it is written, that *God appeared by night in a dream, unto Salomon the King, saying, "Ask of me whatsoever thou wilt, and I will give it thee."* Salomon made his humble prayer, and asked a wise and prudent heart, that might judge and understand what were good and what were ill, what were godly and what were ungodly, what were righteous and what were unrighteous in the sight of the Lord. *It pleased God wondrously, that he had asked this thing. And God said unto him, "Because thou hast requested this word, and hast not desired many days, and long years upon the earth, neither abundance of riches and goods, nor yet the life of thine enemies which hate thee, but hast desired wisdom to sit in judgement, behold, I have done unto thee according to thy words: I have given thee a wise heart, full of knowledge and understanding, so that there was never none like thee beforetime, neither shall be in time to come. Moreover, I have besides this, given thee that which thou hast not required, namely worldly wealth and riches, princely honour and glory, so that thou shalt therein also, pass all kings that ever were."* Note in this example how Salomon, being put to his choice to ask of God whatsoever he would, requested not vain and transitory things, but the high and heavenly treasures of wisdom; and that in so doing he obtaineth, as it were in recompense, both riches and honour. Wherein is given us to understand, that in our daily prayers, we should chiefly and principally, ask those things which concern the kingdom of God, and the salvation of our own souls, nothing doubting but all other things shall, according to the promise of Christ, be given unto us.

But here we must take heed, that we forget not that other end, whereof mention was made before: namely, the glory of God. Which unless we mind, and set before our eyes in making our prayers, we may not look to be heard, or to receive any thing of the Lord. In the twentieth chapter of

Matt. 20:20–3

Matthew *the mother of the two sons of Zebedee came unto Jesus, worshipping him, and saying, "Grant that my two sons may sit in thy kingdom, the one at thy right hand, and the other at thy left hand."* In this petition she did not respect the glory of God, but plainly declared the ambition and vainglory of her own mind; for which cause, she was also most worthily repelled, and rebuked at the Lord's hand. In like manner, we read in the Acts of one

Acts 8:18–20

Simon Magus, a sorcerer, how that *he, perceiving that through laying on of the apostles' hands, the Holy Ghost was given, offered them money, saying, "Give me also this power, that on whomsoever I lay my hands, he may receive the Holy Ghost."* In making this request, he sought not the honour and glory of God, but his own private gain and lucre, thinking to get great store of money by this feat; and therefore it was justly said unto him, *Thy money perish with thee, because thou thinkest that the gift of God may be obtained with money.* By these and such other examples we are taught, whensoever we make our prayers unto God, chiefly to respect the honour and glory of his Name. Whereof we have this general precept in the Apostle Paul: *Whether ye eat or drink, or whatsoever you do, look that you do it to the glory of God.* Which thing we shall best of all do, if we follow the example of our Saviour Christ, who praying, that the bitter cup of death might pass from him, would not therein have his own will fulfilled, but referred the whole matter to the good will and pleasure of his Father.

> 1 Cor. 10:31, Col. 3:17
>
> Matt. 26:39

And hitherto concerning those things that we may lawfully and boldly ask of God.

Now it followeth, that we declare what kind of persons we are bound in conscience to pray for. St Paul, writing to Timothy, exhorteth him to make *prayers and supplications for all men,* exempting none, of what degree or state soever they be. In which place he maketh mention by name of *kings and rulers, which are in authority,* putting us thereby to knowledge, how greatly it concerneth the profit of the commonwealth, to pray diligently for the higher powers. Neither is it without good cause, that he doth so often, in all his Epistles crave the prayers of God's people for himself. For in so doing, he declareth to the world, how expedient and needful it is, daily to call upon God, for the ministers of his holy word and sacraments, that they *may have the door of utterance opened* unto them, that they may truly understand the Scriptures, that they may effectually preach the same unto the people, and bring forth the true fruits thereof, to the example of all other. After this sort did the congregation continually pray for Peter at Jerusalem, and for Paul among the Gentiles, to the great encrease and furtherance of Christ's Gospel. And if we, following their good example herein, will study to do the like, doubtless it cannot be expressed, how greatly we shall both help ourselves, and also please God.

> 1 Tim. 2:1, 2
>
> Col. 4:3–4, Rom. 15:30–2, 2 Thess. 3:1, 2, Eph. 6:19, 20
>
> Col. 4:3
>
> Acts 12:5; 2 Cor. 1:11; Phil. 1:19; Philemon 22

To discourse and run through all degrees of persons, it were too long: therefore ye shall briefly take this one conclusion for all. Whomsoever we are bound by express commandment to love, for those also we are bound in conscience to pray: but we are bound by express commandment, to love all men as ourselves: therefore we are also bound to pray for all men, even as well as if it were for ourselves, notwithstanding we know them to be our extreme and deadly enemies; for so doth our Saviour Christ plainly teach us in his holy Gospel, saying, *Love your enemies, bless them that curse you, do good to them that hate you, pray for them that persecute you, that ye may be the children of your Father, which is in heaven.* And as he taught his disciples, so did he practise himself, in his lifetime, praying for his enemies upon the cross, and desiring his Father to forgive them, because they knew not what they did: as did also that holy and blessed Martyr Stephen, when he was cruelly stoned to death, of the stubborn and stiffnecked Jews, to the example of all them that will truly and unfeignedly follow their Lord and Master Christ, in this miserable and mortal life.

> Matt. 5:44, 45
>
> Luke 23:34
>
> Acts 7:60

Now to entreat of that question, whether we ought to pray for them that are departed out of this world, or no. Wherein if we will cleave only unto the word of God, then must we needs grant, that we have no commandment so to do. For the Scripture doth acknowledge but two places after this life, the one proper to the elect and blessed of God, the other to the reprobate and damned souls; as may be well gathered by the parable of Lazarus and the rich man. Which place St Augustine expounding, saith on this wise:

Luke 16:19–26

Lib. 2 *Evang.*
Quaest. cap. 38

> That which Abraham speaketh unto the rich man, in Luke's Gospel, namely that the just cannot go into those places where the wicked are tormented, what other things doth it signify, but only this, that the just, by reason of God's judgement, which may not be revoked, can show no deed of mercy in helping them, which after this life are cast into prison *until they pay the uttermost farthing?*

These words, as they confound the opinion of helping the dead by prayer, so they do clean confute, and take away, the vain error of purgatory, which is grounded upon this saying of the Gospel: *Thou shalt not depart thence, until thou hast paid the uttermost farthing.* Now doth St Augustine say, that those men which are cast into prison after this life, on that condition may in no wise be holpen, though we would help them never so much. And why? Because the sentence of God is unchangeable, and cannot be revoked again. Therefore let us not deceive ourselves, thinking that either we may help other, or other may help us by their good and charitable prayers, in time to come. For, as the Preacher saith, *When the tree falleth, whether it be toward the south, or toward the north, in what place soever the tree falleth, there it lieth*; meaning thereby, that every mortal man dieth either in the state of salvation, or damnation, according as the words of the Evangelist John do also plainly import, saying, *He that believeth on the Son of God, hath eternal life; but he that believeth not on the Son, shall never see life, but the wrath of God abideth upon him.* Where is then the third place, which they call purgatory? or where shall our prayers help and profit the dead? St Augustine doth only acknowledge two places after this life: heaven and hell. As for the third place, he doth plainly deny, that there is any such to be found in all Scripture.

Matt. 5:26

Eccles. 11:3

John 3:36

Lib. 5.
Hypognost.

Chrysost. *in
Heb.* 2, Homil. 4
Cyprian. *contra
Demetrianum*

Chrysostom likewise is of this mind, that unless we wash away our sins in this present world, we shall find no comfort afterward. And St Cyprian saith, that after death "repentance and sorrow of pain shall be without fruit; weeping also shall be in vain, and prayer shall be to no purpose." Therefore he counselleth all men, to make provision for themselves while they may, because, "When they are once departed out of this life, there is no place for repentance, nor yet for satisfaction." Let these and such other places be sufficient, to take away the gross error of purgatory out of our heads; neither let us dream any more, that the souls of the dead, are anything at all holpen by our prayers: but as the Scripture teacheth us, let us think that the soul of man, passing out of the body, goeth straightways either to heaven or else to hell, whereof the one needeth no prayer, and the other is without redemption.

The only purgatory wherein, we must trust to be saved, is the death and blood of Christ; which if we apprehend with a true and stedfast faith, it purgeth and cleanseth us from all our sins, even as well as if he were now hanging upon the cross. *The blood of Christ*, saith St John, *hath cleansed us from all sin. The blood of Christ*, saith St Paul, *hath purged our consciences from dead works, to serve the living God.* Also in another place he saith, *We be sanctified* and made holy, *by the offering up of the body of Jesus Christ*, done *once for all.* Yea, he addeth more, saying, *With* the *one oblation* of his blessed body, and precious blood, *he hath made perfect, for ever and ever, all them that are sanctified.* This then is that purgatory, wherein all Christian men must put their whole trust and confidence, nothing doubting, but if they truly repent them of their sins, and die in perfect faith, that then they shall forthwith, pass from death to life. If this kind of purgation will not serve them, let them never hope to be released by other men's prayers, though they should continue therein, unto the world's end. He that cannot be saved by faith in Christ's blood, how shall he look to be delivered by man's intercessions? Hath God more respect to man on earth, than he hath to Christ in heaven? *If any man sin*, saith St John, *we have an advocate with the Father, even Jesus Christ the righteous, and he is the propitiation for our sins.* But we must take heed that we call upon this Advocate, while we have space given us in this life, lest when we are once dead, there be no hope of salvation left unto us. For, as every man sleepeth with his own cause, so every man shall rise again with his own cause. And look in what state he dieth, in the same state he shall be also judged, whether it be to salvation, or damnation.

Let us not therefore dream either of purgatory, or of prayer for the souls of them that be dead; but let us earnestly and diligently, pray for them which are expressly commanded, in holy Scripture, namely for kings and rulers, for ministers of God's holy word and sacraments, for the saints of this world, otherwise called the faithful: to be short, for all men living, be they never so great enemies to God, and his people, as Jews, Turks, pagans, infidels, heretics, &c. Then shall we truly fulfil the commandment of God, in that behalf, and plainly declare ourselves, to be the true *children of our heavenly Father, which suffereth the sun to shine upon the good, and the bad, and the rain to fall upon the just, and the unjust.* For which, and all other benefits, most abundantly bestowed upon mankind from the beginning, let us give him hearty thanks, as we are most bound, and praise his Name, for ever and ever. Amen.

1 John 1:7

Heb. 9:14

Heb. 10:10

*Ibid.:*14

1 John 2:1–2

Matt. 5:45

AN HOMILY OF
THE PLACE AND TIME OF PRAYER

GOD, THROUGH HIS ALMIGHTY POWER, wisdom, and goodness, created in the beginning heaven and earth, the sun, the moon, the stars, the fowls of the air, the beasts of the earth, the fishes in the sea, and all other creatures, for the use and commodity of man; whom also he had created, to his own image and likeness, and given him the use and government over them all, to the end he should use them, in such sort as he had given him in charge and commandment, and also that he should declare himself thankful and kind, for all those benefits, so liberally and so graciously bestowed upon him, utterly without any deserving on his behalf. And although we ought at all times, and in all places, to have in remembrance, and to be thankful to, our gracious Lord—according as it is written, *I will magnify the Lord at all times*, and again, *Wheresoever the Lord beareth rule, O my soul, praise the Lord*—yet it appeareth to be God's good will and pleasure, that we should at special times, and in special places, gather ourselves together, to the intent his name might be renowned, and his glory set forth, in the congregation and the assembly of his saints.

Psalm 34:1, 103:22

As concerning the time, which Almighty God hath appointed his people to assemble together solemnly: it doth appear by the Fourth Commandment of God. *Remember*, saith God, *that thou keep holy the Sabbath day*. Upon the which day, as is plain in the Acts of the Apostles, the people accustomably resorted together, and heard diligently the Law and the Prophets read among them. And, albeit this Commandment of God doth not bind Christian people so straitly to observe, and keep the utter ceremonies of the Sabbath day, as it was given unto the Jews, as touching the forbearing of work and labour, in time of great necessity, and as touching the precise keeping of the seventh day, after the manner of the Jews (for we keep now the first day, which is our Sunday, and make that our Sabbath, that is, our day of rest, in the honour of our Saviour Christ, who as upon that day rose from death, conquering the same most triumphantly); yet notwithstanding, whatsoever is found in

Exod. 20:8
Acts 13:14, 15, 42

the Commandment appertaining to the law of nature, as a thing most godly, most just, and needful for the setting forth of God's glory, it ought to be retained, and kept of all good Christian people. And therefore, by this Commandment, we ought to have a time, as one day in a week, wherein we ought to rest, yea, from our lawful and needful works. For, like as it appeareth by this Commandment, that no man in the six days ought to be slothful or idle, but diligently to labour in that state wherein God hath set him, even so, God hath given express charge to all men, that upon the Sabbath day, which is now our Sunday, they should cease from all weekly and workday labour; to the intent that, like as God himself wrought six days, and rested the seventh, and blessed and sanctified it, and consecrated it to quietness and rest from labour, even so God's obedient people should use the Sunday holily, and rest from their common and daily business, and also give themselves wholly to heavenly exercises of God's true religion and service. So that, God doth not only command the observation of this holy day, but also, by his own example, doth stir and provoke us to diligent keeping of the same. Good natural children will not only become obedient to the commandment of their parents, but also have a diligent eye to their doings, and gladly follow the same. So, if we will be the children of our heavenly Father, we must be careful to keep the Christian Sabbath day, which is the Sunday; not only for that it is God's express commandment, but also to declare ourselves to be loving children, in following the example of our gracious Lord and Father. Thus it may plainly appear, that God's will and commandment was, to have a solemn time, and standing day in the week, wherein the people should come together, and have in remembrance his wonderful benefits, and to render him thanks for them, as appertaineth to loving, kind, and obedient people.

Exod. 20:8–11

This example and commandment of God, the godly Christian people began to follow, immediately after the ascension of our Lord Christ, and began to choose them a standing day in the week, to come together in; yet not the seventh day, which the Jews kept, but the Lord's day, the day of the Lord's resurrection, the day after the seventh day, which is the first of the week. Of the which day mention is made by St Paul, on this wise: *In the first day of the sabbath, let every man lay up what he thinketh good*, meaning for the poor. By *the first day of the sabbath* is meant our Sunday, which is the first day after the Jews' seventh day. And in the Apocalypse it is more plain, whereas St John saith: *I was in the Spirit upon the Sunday*. Sithence which time, God's people hath always, in all ages, without any gainsaying, used to come together upon the Sunday, to celebrate and honour the Lord's blessed Name, and carefully to keep that day in holy rest and quietness, both men, women, child, servant, and stranger. For the transgression and breach of which day, God hath

1 Cor. 16:2

Rev. 1:10

Num. 15:32–6

declared himself much to be grieved, as it may appear by him who for gathering of sticks on the Sabbath day, was stoned to death.

But alas! all these notwithstanding, it is lamentable to see the wicked boldness of those that will be counted God's people, who pass nothing at all of keeping and hallowing the Sunday. And these people are of two sorts. The one sort, if they have any business to do, though there be no extreme need, they must not spare for the Sunday; they must ride and journey on the Sunday; they must drive and carry on the Sunday; they must row and ferry on the Sunday; they must buy and sell on the Sunday; they must keep markets and fairs on the Sunday: finally, they use all days alike; workdays and holy days are all one. The other sort is worse. For although they will not travail nor labour on the Sunday, as they do on the week day, yet they will not rest in holiness, as God commandeth; but they rest in ungodliness and in filthiness, prancing in their pride, pranking and pricking, pointing and painting themselves, to be gorgeous and gay; they rest in excess and superfluity, in gluttony and drunkenness, like rats and swine; they rest in brawling and railing, in quarrelling and fighting; they rest in wantonness, in toyish talking, in filthy fleshliness; so that it doth too evidently appear, that God is more dishonoured, and the devil better served, on the Sunday, than upon all the days in the week beside. And, I assure you, the beasts, which are commanded to rest on the Sunday, honour God better than this kind of people; for they offend not God, they break not their holy day. Wherefore, O ye people of God, lay your hands upon your hearts; repent, and amend this grievous and dangerous wickedness; stand in awe of the commandment of God; gladly follow the example of God himself; be not disobedient to the godly order of Christ's Church, used and kept from the Apostles' time until this day; fear the displeasure, and just plagues of Almighty God, if ye be negligent, and forbear not labouring and travailing on the Sabbath day or Sunday, and do not resort together to celebrate and magnify God's blessed Name, in quiet holiness, and godly reverence.

Now, concerning the place where the people of God ought to resort together, and where especially they ought to celebrate and sanctify the Sabbath day, that is, the Sunday, the day of holy rest. That place is called God's temple or the church, because the company and congregation of God's people, which is properly called the Church, doth there assemble themselves, on the days appointed for such assemblies and meetings. And, forasmuch as Almighty God hath appointed a special time to be honoured in, it is very meet, godly, and also necessary, that there should be a place appointed, where these people should meet and resort, to serve their gracious God and merciful Father.

Truth it is, the holy Patriarchs, for a great number of years, had neither temple nor church to resort unto. The cause was, they were not stayed in any place, but were in a continual peregrination and wandering, that they could not conveniently build any church. But so soon as God had delivered his people from their enemies, and set them in some liberty in the wilderness, he set them up a costly and a curious tabernacle, which was as it were the parish church, a place to resort unto of the whole multitude, a place to have his sacrifices made in, and other observances and rites to be used in. Furthermore, after that God, according to the truth of his promise, had placed and quietly settled his people, in the land of Canaan, now called Jewry, he commanded a great and a magnificent Temple to be builded, by King Salomon, as seldom the like hath been seen; a Temple so decked and adorned, so gorgeously garnished, as was meet and expedient for people of that time, which would be allured and stirred with nothing so much, as with such outward goodly gay things. This was now the Temple of God, indued also with many gifts and sundry promises: this was the parish church, and the mother church of all Jewry: here was God honoured and served: hither was the whole realm of all the Israelites bound to come, at three solemn feasts in the year, to serve their Lord God here. But let us proceed further. In the time of Christ and his Apostles, there were yet no temples nor churches for Christian men; for why? they were always, for the most part, in persecution, vexation, and trouble; so that there could be no liberty nor license obtained for that purpose. Yet God delighted much, that they should often resort together in a place, and therefore, after his ascension, they remained together in an upper chamber. Sometimes they entered into the Temple, sometimes into the synagogues; sometimes they were in prisons, sometimes in their houses, sometimes in the fields, &c. And this continued so long, till the faith of Christ Jesu began to multiply, in a great part of the world. Now, when divers realms were established in God's true religion, and God had given them peace and quietness, then began kings, noblemen, and the people also, stirred up with a godly zeal and ferventness, to build up temples and churches, whither the people might resort, the better to do their duty towards God, and to keep holy their Sabbath day, the day of rest. And to these temples have the Christians customably used to resort, from time to time, as unto meet places, where they might, with common consent, praise and magnify God's Name, yielding him thanks, for the benefits that he daily poureth upon them, both mercifully and abundantly; where they might also hear his holy word read, expounded, and preached sincerely, and receive his holy sacraments, ministered unto them duly and purely.

True it is, that the chief and special temples of God, wherein he hath greatest pleasure, and most delighteth to dwell in, are the bodies and minds of true Christians, and the chosen people of God, according to the doctrine of holy Scriptures declared by St Paul. *Know ye not*, saith

Exod. 25–31, 35–40

1 Chron. 22

Exod. 23:14–17; Deut. 16:1–17; 2 Chron. 8:12–13

1 Cor. 3:16, 17

he, *that ye be the temple of God, and that the Spirit of God doth dwell in you? The temple of God is holy, which ye are.* And again in the same Epistle:

1 Cor. 6:19

Know ye not that your body is the temple of the Holy Ghost, dwelling in you, whom you have given you of God, and that ye be not your own? Yet, this notwithstanding, God doth allow the material temple, made of lime and stone (so oft as his people do come together into it, to praise his holy Name) to be his house, and the place where he hath promised to be present, and where he will hear the prayers of them that call upon him. The which thing both Christ and his Apostles, with all the rest of holy fathers, do sufficiently declare by this; that albeit they certainly knew that their prayers were heard, in what place soever they made them, though it were in caves, in woods, and in deserts, yet so oft as they could conveniently, they resorted to the material temples, there with the rest of the congregation to join in prayer, and true worship.

Wherefore, dearly beloved, you that profess yourselves to be Christians, and glory in that name, and disdain not to follow the example of your Master Christ, whose scholars (you say) ye be; show you to be like them whose schoolmates you take upon you to be, that is, the Apostles and disciples of Christ. Lift up *pure hands*, with clean hearts, in all places

1 Tim. 2:8,
Heb. 10:22

and at all times. But do the same in the temples and churches, upon the Sabbath days also. Our godly predecessors, and the ancient fathers of the primitive Church, spared not their goods to build churches; no, they spared not to venture their lives, in time of persecution, and to hazard their blood, that they might assemble themselves together in churches. And shall we spare a little labour to come unto churches? Shall neither their example, nor our duty, nor the commodities that thereby should come unto us, move us? If we will declare ourselves to have the fear of God, if we will show ourselves true Christians, if we will be the followers of Christ our Master, and of those godly fathers that have lived before us, and now have received the reward of true and faithful Christians, we must both willingly, earnestly, and reverently, come unto the material churches and temples to pray, as unto fit places appointed for that use; and that upon the Sabbath day, as at most convenient time for God's people to cease from bodily and worldly business, to give themselves to holy rest and godly contemplation, pertaining to the service of Almighty God: whereby we may reconcile ourselves to God, be partakers of his holy Sacraments, and be devout hearers of his holy word; so to be established in faith to Godward, in hope against all adversity, and in charity toward our neighbours; and thus running our course, as good Christian people, we may at the last attain the reward of everlasting glory, through the merits of our Saviour, Jesus Christ. To whom with the Father, and the Holy Ghost, be all honour and glory. Amen.

THE SECOND PART OF THE HOMILY OF THE PLACE AND TIME OF PRAYER

IT HATH BEEN DECLARED UNTO YOU, good Christian people, in the former Sermon read unto you, at what time, and into what place, ye shall come together to praise God. Now I intend to set before your eyes, first, how zealous and desirous ye ought to be, to come to your church, secondly, how sore God is grieved with them that do despise, or little regard, to come to the church, upon the holy restful day.

It may well appear by the Scriptures, that many of the godly Israelites, being now in captivity for their sins, among the Babylonians, full often wished and desired, to be again at Jerusalem. And at their return through God's goodness, though many of the people were negligent, yet the fathers were marvellous devout, to build up the Temple, that God's people might repair thither, to honour him. And King David, when he was a banished man out of his country, out of Jerusalem the holy city, from the sanctuary, from the holy place, and from the tabernacle of God, what desire, what ferventness was in him towards that holy place! what wishings and prayers made he to God, to be a dweller in the house of the Lord! *One thing*, saith he, *have I asked of the Lord, and this will I still crave, that I may resort and have my dwelling, in the house of the Lord, so long as I live.* Again, *Oh how I joyed when I heard these words, "We shall go into the Lord's house"!* And in other places of the Psalms, he declareth for what intent and purpose, he hath such a fervent desire, to enter into the temple and church of the Lord. *I will fall down*, saith he, *and worship in the holy temple of the Lord.* Again, *I have appeared in thy holy place, that I might behold thy might and power, that I might behold thy glory and magnificence.* Finally he saith, *I will show forth thy Name to my brethren, I will praise thee in the midst of the congregation.* Why then had David such an earnest desire to the house of God? First, because there he would worship and honour God. Secondly, there he would have a contemplation, and a sight of the power and glory of God. Thirdly, there he would praise the Name of God, with all the congregation and company of the people. These considerations of this blessed Prophet of God, ought to stir up and kindle in us, the like earnest desire, to resort to the church, especially upon the holy restful days; there to do our duties and to serve God; there to call to remembrance, how God, even of his mere mercy, and for the glory of his Name sake, worketh mightily to conserve us in health, and wealth, and godliness, and mightily preserveth us, from the assaults and rages of our fierce and cruel enemies; and there joyfully, in the number of his faithful people, to praise and magnify the Lord's holy Name. Set before your eyes also, that ancient father Simeon, of

Psalm 137, Dan. 9

Ezra 1, 3, 5, 6, Hag. 1

Psalm 27:4

Psalm 122:1

Psalm 138:2

Psalm 63:2

Psalm 22:22

Luke 2:25–38

whom the Scripture speaketh thus, to his great commendation, and an encouragement for us to do the like. *There was a man at Jerusalem, named Simeon, a just man, fearing God: he came by the Spirit of God into the Temple, and was told by the same Spirit, that he should not die, before he saw the Anointed of the Lord.* In the Temple his promise was fulfilled; in the Temple he saw Christ, and *took him in his arms*; in the Temple he brake out into the mighty praise of God his Lord. *Anna also, a prophetess, an old widow, departed not out of the Temple, giving herself to prayer and fasting, day and night: and she, coming about the same time,* was likewise inspired, and confessed, and spake of the Lord, to all them who looked for the redemption of Israel. This blessed man and this blessed woman were not disappointed of wonderful fruit, commodity, and comfort, which God sent them by their diligent resorting to God's holy Temple.

Anna

Now ye shall hear, how grievously God hath been offended with his people, for that they passed so little upon his holy Temple, and foully either despised or abused the same. Which thing may plainly appear by the notable plagues and punishments, which God hath laid upon his people, especially in this, that he stirred up their adversaries horribly to beat down, and utterly to destroy, his holy Temple, with a perpetual desolation. Alas! how many churches, countries, and kingdoms of Christian people, have of late years been plucked down, overrun, and left waste, with grievous and intolerable tyranny and cruelty, of the enemy of our Lord Christ, the great Turk; who hath so universally scourged the Christians, that never the like was heard or read of! Above thirty years past, the great Turk had overrun, conquered, and brought into his dominion and subjection, twenty Christian kingdoms, turning away the people from the faith of Christ, poisoning them with the devilish religion of wicked Mahomet, and either destroying their churches utterly, or filthily abusing them, with their wicked and detestable errors. And now this great Turk, this bitter and sharp scourge of God's vengeance, is even at hand in this part of Christendom, in Europe, at the borders of Italy, at the borders of Germany, greedily gaping to devour us, to overrun our country, to destroy our churches also, unless we repent our sinful life, and resort more diligently to the church, to honour God, to learn his blessed will, and to fulfil the same.

The Jews in their time, provoked justly the vengeance of God, for that partly they abused his holy Temple, with the detestable idolatry of the heathen, and superstitious vanities of their own inventions, contrary to God's commandment; partly they resorted unto it as hypocrites, spotted, imbrued, and foully defiled with all kind of wickedness, and sinful life; partly many of them passed little upon the holy Temple, and cared not whether they came thither or no. And have not the Christians of late days, and even in our days also, in like manner provoked the displeasure and indignation of Almighty God? partly because they have profaned and defiled their churches, with heathenish and Jewish abuses, with images and idols, with numbers of altars too too superstitiously and intolerably abused, with gross abusing and filthy corrupting of the Lord's holy Supper, the blessed Sacrament of his Body and Blood, with an infinite number of toys and trifles, of their own devices, to make goodly outward show, and to deface the homely, simple, and sincere religion of Christ Jesus. Partly, they resort to the church like hypocrites, full of all iniquity and sinful life, having a vain and a dangerous fancy and persuasion, that if they come to the church, besprinkle them with holy water, hear a mass, and be blessed with the chalice, though they understand not one word of the whole service, nor feel one motion of repentance in their hearts, all is well, all is sure. Fie upon such mocking and blaspheming of God's holy ordinance! Churches were made for another purpose, that is, to resort thither and to serve God truly, there to learn his blessed will, there to call upon his mighty Name, there to use the holy Sacraments, there to travail how to be in charity with thy neighbour, there to have thy poor and needy neighbour in remembrance, from thence to depart better and more godly, than thou camest thither. Finally, God's vengeance hath been, and is, daily provoked, because much wicked people pass nothing to resort to the church, either for that they are so sore blinded, that they understand nothing of God and godliness, and care not with devilish example to offend their neighbours; or else for that they see the church altogether scoured of such gay gazing sights, as their gross fantasy was greatly delighted with, because they see the false religion abandoned, and the true restored, which seemeth an unsavoury thing to their unsavoury taste; as may appear by this: that a woman said to her neighbour, "Alas! gossip, what shall we now do at church, since all the saints are taken away, since all the goodly sights we were wont to have are gone, since we cannot hear the like piping, singing, chanting, and playing upon the organs, that we could before?" But, dearly beloved, we ought greatly to rejoice, and give thanks that our churches are delivered of all those things, which displeased God so sore, and filthily defiled his holy house, and his place of prayer; for the which he hath justly destroyed many nations, according to the saying of St Paul, *If any man defile the temple of God, God will him* 1 Cor. 3:17 *destroy*. And this ought we greatly to praise God for, that such superstitious and idolatrous manners, as were utterly naught, and defaced God's glory, are utterly abolished, as they most justly deserved, and yet those things that either God was honoured with, or his people edified, are decently retained, and in our churches comely practised.

But now, forasmuch as ye perceive it is God's determinate pleasure ye should resort unto your churches, upon the day of holy rest; seeing ye hear what displeasure God conceiveth, what plagues he poureth upon his disobedient people; seeing ye understand what blessings of God are given, what heavenly commodities come, to such people as desirously and zealously, use to resort unto their churches; seeing also ye are now friendly bidden and jointly called, beware that ye slack not your duty; take heed that you suffer nothing to let you hereafter, to come to the church at such times as you are orderly appointed and commanded.

Luke 14:16–24   Our Saviour Christ telleth in a parable, that *a great supper* was prepared, guests were bidden, many excused themselves, and would not come: *I tell you*, saith Christ, *none of them that were called, shall taste of my supper.* This *great supper* is the true religion of Almighty God, wherewith he will be worshipped, in the due receiving of his Sacraments, and sincere preaching and hearing of his holy word, and practising the same by godly conversation. This feast is now prepared in God's banqueting house, the church; you are thereunto called and jointly bidden; if you refuse to come, and make your excuses, the same will be answered to you that was unto them.

Now come therefore dearly beloved, without delay, and cheerfully enter into God's feasting-house, and become partakers of the benefits provided and prepared for you. But see that ye come thither with your holyday garment, not like hypocrites, not of a custom and for manners' sake, not with loathsomeness, as though ye had rather not come than come, if ye were at your liberty. For God hateth and punisheth such

Matt. 22:12, 13   counterfeit hypocrites, as appeareth by Christ's former parable. *My friend*, saith God, *how camest thou in, without a wedding garment?* and therefore *commanded his servants to bind him hand and foot, and to cast him into the utter darkness, where shall be weeping, and wailing, and gnashing of teeth.* To the intent ye may avoid the like danger at God's hand, come to the church on the holyday, and come in your holyday garment; that is to say, come with a cheerful and a godly mind; come to seek God's glory, and to be thankful unto him; come to be at one with thy neighbour, and to enter in friendship and charity with him. Consider that all thy doings stink before the face of God, if thou be not in charity with thy neighbour. Come, with an heart sifted and cleansed from worldly and carnal affections and desires. Shake off all vain thoughts, which may hinder thee from God's true service. The bird, when she will fly, shaketh her wings: shake and prepare thyself, to fly higher than all the birds in the air; that after thy duty duly done, in this earthly temple and church, thou mayest fly up, and be received into the glorious temple of God, in heaven, through Christ Jesus our Lord. To whom, with the Father, and the Holy Ghost, be all glory and honour. Amen.

AN HOMILY WHEREIN IS DECLARED
THAT COMMON PRAYER
AND SACRAMENTS
OUGHT TO BE MINISTERED
IN A TONGUE THAT IS
UNDERSTOOD OF THE HEARERS

AMONG THE MANIFOLD EXERCISES of God's people, dear Christians, there is none more necessary for all estates, and at all times, than is Public Prayer, and the due use of Sacraments. For in the first, we beg at God's hand, all such things as otherwise we cannot obtain; and in the other, he embraceth us, and offereth himself to be embraced of us. Knowing therefore that these two exercises are so necessary for us, let us not think it unmeet to consider, first, what Prayer is, and what a Sacrament is; and then, how many sorts of Prayer there be, and how many Sacraments: so shall we the better understand how to use them aright.

To know what they be, St Augustine teacheth us. In his book entitled *Of the Spirit and the Soul*, he saith this of Prayer: "Prayer is," saith he, "the devotion of the mind, that is to say, the returning to God, through a godly and humble affection; which affection is a certain willing, and sweet inclining of the mind itself towards God." And in the second book *Against the Adversary of the Law and Prophets*, he calleth Sacraments "holy signs". And writing to Bonifacius of the baptism of infants he saith: "If Sacraments had not a certain similitude of those things whereof they be Sacraments, they should be no Sacraments at all. And of this similitude, they do for the most part receive the names of the self things they signify." By these words of St Augustine it appeareth, that he alloweth the common description of a Sacrament, which is, that it is a visible sign of an invisible grace, that is to say, that setteth out to the eyes and other outward senses, the inward working of God's free mercy, and doth, as it

Augustin. *de Spiritu et Anima*

Augustin. Lib. 2 *contr. Advers. Leg. et Proph.*
Augustin. *ad Bonifacium*

were, seal in our hearts the promises of God. And so was Circumcision a Sacrament, which preached unto the outward senses, the inward cutting away of the foreskin of the heart, and sealed and made sure, in the hearts of the circumcised, the promise of God touching the promised seed, that they looked for.

Now let us see how many sorts of Prayer, and how many Sacraments there be. In the Scriptures we read of three sorts of Prayer, whereof two are private, and the third is common. The first is that which St Paul

1 Tim. 2:8

speaketh of, in his Epistle to Timothy, saying, *I will that men pray in every place, lifting up pure hands, without wrath and striving*; and it is the devout lifting up of the mind to God, without the uttering of the heart's grief or desire, by open voice. Of this Prayer we have example in the first Book of the Kings, in Anna the mother of Samuel, when in the heaviness of her

1 Sam. 1:13

heart, she prayed in the Temple, desiring to be made fruitful. *She prayed in her heart*, saith the text, *but there was no voice heard*. After this sort must all Christians pray, not once in a week, or once in a day only, but as

1 Thess. 5:17
James 5:16

St Paul writeth to the Thessalonians, *without ceasing*: and as St James writeth, *the continual prayer of a just man is of much force*.

Matt. 6:6

The second sort of Prayer is spoken of in the Gospel of Matthew, where it is said, *When thou prayest, enter into thy secret closet, and, when thou hast shut the door to thee, pray unto thy Father in secret; and thy Father, which seeth in secret, shall reward thee*. Of this sort of Prayer there be sundry examples in the Scriptures; but it shall suffice to rehearse one,

Acts 10:1, 2, 30

which is written in the Acts of the Apostles. Cornelius, *a devout man, a captain of the Italian army*, saith to Peter, that *being in his house in prayer, at the ninth hour, there appeared unto him one in a white garment*, &c. This man prayed unto God in secret, and was rewarded openly. These be the two private sorts of Prayer; the one mental, that is to say, the devout lifting up of the mind to God; and the other vocal, that is to say, the secret uttering of the griefs and desires of the heart, with words, but yet in a secret closet or some solitary place.

The third sort of Prayer is Public or Common. Of this Prayer

Matt. 18:19, 20

speaketh our Saviour Christ, when he saith, *If two of you shall agree upon earth upon any thing, whatsoever ye shall ask, my Father which is in heaven shall do it for you: for, wheresoever two or three be gathered together, in my name, there am I in the midst of them*. Although God hath promised to hear us when we pray privately, so it be done faithfully and devoutly (for

Psalm 50:15;
James 5:17, 18

he saith, *Call upon me in the day of thy trouble, and I will hear thee*; and *Helias, being but a mortal man*, saith St James, *prayed, and heaven was shut three years and six months; and again he prayed, and the heaven gave rain*), yet by the histories of the Bible, it appeareth that Public and Common Prayer is most available before God; and therefore it is much to be lamented, that it is no better esteemed among us, which profess to be but one body in Christ. When the city of Ninive was threatened to be destroyed within forty days, the Prince and people joined themselves together in public prayer and fasting, and were preserved. In the prophet Joel, God commandeth a fasting to be proclaimed, and the people to be gathered together, young and old, man and woman, and are taught to say with one voice, *Spare us, O Lord, spare thy people, and let not thine inheritance be brought to confusion.* When the Jews should have been destroyed all in one day, through the malice of Haman, at the commandment of Hester they fasted and prayed, and were preserved. When Holofernes besieged Bethulia, by the advice of Judith they fasted and prayed, and were delivered. When Peter was in prison, the congregation joined themselves together in prayer, and Peter was wonderfully delivered. By these histories it appeareth, that Common or Public Prayer is of great force, to obtain mercy and deliverance at our heavenly Father's hand. *Therefore, brethren, I beseech you,* even *for the tender mercies of God,* let us no longer be negligent in this behalf; but as a people willing to receive at God's hand, such good things as in the Common Prayer of the Church are craved, let us join ourselves together, in the place of Common Prayer, and with one voice, and one heart, beg of our heavenly Father, all those things which he knoweth to be necessary for us. I forbid you not private prayer, but I exhort you to esteem Common Prayer as it is worthy. And before all things be sure, that in all these three sorts of Prayer, your minds be devoutly lifted up to God; else are your prayers to no purpose, and this saying shall be verified in you, *This people honoureth me with their lips, but their heart is far from me.*

Thus much for the three sorts of Prayer whereof we read in the Scriptures.

Now, with like or rather more brevity, you shall hear how many Sacraments there be, that were instituted by our Saviour Christ, and are to be continued and received of every Christian, in due time and order, and for such purpose as our Saviour Christ willed them to be received. And as for the number of them, if they should be considered according to the exact signification of a Sacrament, namely, for visible signs expressly commanded in the New Testament, whereunto is annexed the promise of free forgiveness of our sin, and of our holiness, and joining in Christ, there be but two: namely, Baptism, and the Supper of the Lord. For although Absolution hath the promise of forgiveness of sin, yet by the express word of the New Testament, it hath not this promise annexed and tied to the visible sign, which is imposition of hands. For this visible sign, I mean laying on of hands, is not expressly commanded in the New Testament to be used in Absolution, as the visible signs in Baptism and the Lord's Supper are; and therefore Absolution is no such Sacrament as Baptism and the Communion are. And though the

Marginal references:
Jonah 3:4–10
Joel 2:15–17
Esth. 4:16
Judith 8:17–27
Acts 12:5–12
Rom. 12:1
Isai. 29:13, Matt. 15:8

Ordering of Ministers hath his visible sign and promise, yet it lacks the promise of remission of sin, as all other Sacraments besides do. Therefore neither it, nor any other Sacrament else, be such Sacraments as Baptism and the Communion are. But in a general acception, the name of a Sacrament may be attributed, to any thing whereby an holy thing is signified. In which understanding of the word, the ancient writers have given this name, not only to the other five, commonly of late years taken and used for supplying the number of the seven Sacraments, but also to divers and sundry other ceremonies, as to oil, washing of feet, and suchlike; not meaning thereby to repute them as Sacraments in the same signification that the two forenamed Sacraments are. And therefore St Augustine, weighing the true signification and exact meaning of the word, writing to Januarius, and also in the third book of Christian Doctrine, affirmeth that the Sacraments of the Christians, as they are "most excellent in signification", so are they "most few in number"; and in both places maketh mention expressly of two, the Sacrament of Baptism, and the Supper of the Lord. And although there are retained, by the order of the Church of England, besides these two, certain other rites and ceremonies, about the Institution of Ministers in the Church, Matrimony, Confirmation of children (by examining them of their knowledge in the Articles of the Faith, and joining thereto the prayers of the Church for them), and likewise for Visitation of the Sick; yet no man ought to take these for Sacraments, in such signification and meaning as the Sacrament of Baptism and the Lord's Supper are, but either for godly states of life, necessary in Christ's Church, and therefore worthy to be set forth by public action and solemnity, by the ministry of the Church, or else judged to be such ordinances, as may make for the instruction, comfort, and edification of Christ's Church.

Now, understanding sufficiently what Prayer is, and what a Sacrament is also, and how many sorts of prayers there be, and how many Sacraments of our Saviour Christ's institution, let us see whether the Scriptures, and the example of the primitive Church, will allow any vocal prayer—that is, when the mouth uttereth the petitions with voice, or any manner of Sacrament, or other public and common rite, or action pertaining to the profit and edifying of the unlearned—to be ministered in a tongue unknown, or not understood of the minister or people; yea, and whether any person may privately use any vocal prayer in a language that he himself understandeth not. To this question we must answer, No.

And first of Common Prayer, and administration of Sacraments. Although reason, if it might rule, would soon persuade us, to have our Common Prayer, and administration of Sacraments, in a known tongue, both for that to pray commonly is, for a multitude to ask one and the self thing with one voice, and one consent of mind, and to administer a

Dionysius;
Bern. *de Coen.*
Dom. et Ablut.
Pedum

Sacrament is, by the outward word and element, to preach to the receiver the inward and invisible grace of God; and also for that both these exercises were first instituted, and are still continued, to the end that the congregation of Christ might, from time to time, be put in remembrance of their unity in Christ, and that, as members all of one body, they ought, both in prayers and otherwise, to seek and desire one another's commodity, and not their own without other's: yet we shall not need to fly to reason's proofs in this matter, sith we have both the plain and manifest words of the Scripture, and also the consent of the most learned and ancient writers, to commend the prayers of the congregation in a known tongue.

First, Paul to the Corinthians saith, *Let all things be done to edifying.* Which cannot be, unless common prayers, and administration of Sacraments, be in a tongue known to the people. For where the prayers spoken by the minister, and the words in the administration of the Sacraments, be not understood of them that be present, they cannot thereby be edified. For as, when the trumpet that is blown in the field giveth an uncertain sound, no man is thereby stirred up, to prepare himself to the fight; and as, when an instrument of music maketh no distinct sound, no man can tell what is piped; even so, when prayers or administration of Sacraments shall be in a tongue unknown to the hearers, which of them shall be thereby stirred up, to lift up his mind to God, and to beg with the minister at God's hand, those things which in the words of his prayers the minister asketh? or who shall in the ministration of the Sacraments, understand what invisible grace is to be craved of the hearer, to be wrought in the inward man? Truly no man at all. For, saith St Paul, *he that speaketh in a tongue unknown, shall be unto the hearer an alien*: which in a Christian congregation is a great absurdity. For we are *not strangers* one to another, *but* we are *the citizens of the saints, and of the household of God, yea, and members all of one body.* And therefore, whiles our minister is in rehearsing the prayer that is made in the name of us all, we must give diligent ear to the words spoken by him, and in heart beg at God's hand, those things that he beggeth in words. And to signify that we so do, we say, Amen, at the end of the prayer that he maketh in the name of us all. And this thing can we not do, for edification, unless we understand what is spoken. Therefore it is required of necessity, that the Common Prayer be had, in a tongue that the hearers do understand. If ever it had been tolerable to use strange tongues in the congregation, the same might have been, in the time of Paul and the other Apostles, when they were miraculously endued with the gift of tongues. For it might then have persuaded some to embrace the Gospel, when they had heard men that were Hebrews born, and unlearned, speak the Greek, the Latin, and other languages. But Paul thought it not tolerable then; and

1 Cor. 14:26

Ibid.:7, 8

Ibid.:2, 11

Eph. 2:19
1 Cor. 10:17 and 12: 12–27

shall we use it now, when no man cometh by the knowledge of tongues, otherwise than by diligent and earnest study? God forbid: for we should by that means bring all our Church exercises to frivolous superstition, and make them altogether unfruitful.

Luke writeth, that when Peter and John were discharged, by the princes and high priests of Jerusalem, *they came to their fellows, and told them all that the princes of the priests and elders had spoken unto them. Which when they heard, they lifted up their voice together to God, with one assent, and said, "Lord, thou art he that hast made heaven and earth, the sea, and all things that are in them,"* &c. Thus could they not have done, if they had prayed in a strange tongue, that they had not understood. And no doubt of it, they did not all speak with several voices, but some one of them spake in the name of them all, and the rest, giving diligent ear to his words, consented thereunto; and therefore it is said, that *they lifted up their voice together.* St Luke saith not, *their voices,* as many, but, *their voice,* as one. That one voice therefore, was in such language as they all understood, otherwise they could not have lifted it up, with the consent of their hearts; for no man can give consent, to the thing he knoweth not.

Acts 4:23, 24

As touching the times before the coming of Christ, there was never man yet that would affirm, that either the people of God, or other, had their prayers, or administrations of Sacraments, or sacrifices, in a tongue that they themselves understood not. As for the time since Christ, till that usurped power of Rome began to spread itself, and to enforce all the nations of Europe to have the Romish language in admiration, it appeareth, by the consent of the most ancient and learned writers, that there was no strange or unknown tongue used, in the congregations of Christians.

Justinus Martyr, who lived about one hundred and sixty years after Christ, saith this, of the administration of the Lord's Supper in his time:

Justin. *Apol.* 2

> Upon the Sunday assemblies are made, both of them that dwell in cities, and of them that dwell in the country also: amongst whom, as much as may be, the writings of the Apostles and Prophets are read. Afterwards, when the reader doth cease, the chief minister maketh an exhortation, exhorting them to follow so honest things. After this we rise all together, and offer prayers: which being ended, as we have said, bread and wine and water are brought forth; then the head minister offereth prayers and thanksgiving, with all his power, and the people answer, "Amen."

These words, with their circumstances being duly considered, do declare plainly, that not only the Scriptures were read in a known tongue, but also that prayer was made in the same, in the congregations of Justin's time.

Basilius Magnus, and Johannes Chrysostomus, did in their time prescribe public orders of public administration, which they call

Liturgies; and in them they appointed the people to answer to the prayers of the minister, sometime, "Amen," sometime, "Lord have mercy upon us," sometime, "And with thy spirit," and, "We have our hearts lifted up to the Lord," &c.; which answers, the people could not have made in due time, if the prayers had not been made in a tongue that they understood. The same Basil, writing to the clergy of Neocaesarea, saith thus of his usage in Common Prayer: "Appointing one to begin the song, the rest follow; and so, with divers songs and prayers passing over the night, at the dawning of the day, all together, even as it were with one mouth and one heart, they sing unto the Lord a song of confession, every man framing unto himself meet words of repentance." In another place he saith: "If the sea be fair, how is not the assembly of the congregation much more fair? in which a joined sound of men, women, and children, as it were of the waves beating on the shore, is sent forth in our prayers unto our God." Mark his words: "a joined sound," saith he, "of men, women, and children;" which cannot be, unless they all understand the tongue wherein the prayer is had. And Chrysostom, upon the words of Paul saith, so soon as the people hear these words, "World without end," they all do forthwith answer, "Amen." This could they not do, unless they understood the word spoken by the priest.

Epist. 63

Basil. Hom. 4

1 Cor. 14:16

Dionysius saith, that hymns were said of the whole multitude of people, in the administration of the communion.

Dionysius

Cyprian saith: "The priest doth prepare the minds of the brethren, with a preface before the prayer, saying, 'Lift up your hearts,' that, whiles the people doth answer, 'We have our hearts lifted up to the Lord,' they may be admonished, that they ought to think on none other thing than the Lord."

Cyprian. Serm. 6 de Orat. Dom.

St Ambrose, writing upon the words of St Paul, saith: "This is it that he saith, because he which speaketh in an unknown tongue, speaketh to God, for he knoweth all things; but men know not, and therefore there is no profit of this thing." And again upon these words: *If thou bless*, or give thanks, *with the spirit, how shall he that occupieth the room of the unlearned say, Amen, at thy giving thanks, seeing he understandeth not what thou sayest?*

1 Cor. 14:2

Ibid.:16

> That is, [saith Ambrose], if thou speak the praise of God in a tongue unknown to the hearers. For the unlearned, hearing that which he understandeth not, knoweth not the end of the prayer, and answereth not, Amen, which word is as much to say as, Truth, that the blessing or thanksgiving may be confirmed. For the confirmation of the prayer is fulfilled, by them that do answer, Amen, that all things spoken might be confirmed in the minds of the hearers, through the testimony of the truth.

And after many weighty words to the same end he saith: "The conclusion is this, that nothing should be done in the Church in vain; and that this thing ought chiefly to be laboured for, that the unlearned also might take profit, lest any part of the body should be dark, through ignorance." And lest any man should think all this to be meant of preaching, and not of prayer, he taketh occasion of these words of St Paul, *If there be not an interpreter, let him keep silence in the Church*, to say as followeth: "Let him pray secretly, or speak to God, who heareth all things that be dumb: for in the Church must he speak that may profit all persons."

Ibid.:28

St Jerome, writing upon these words of St Paul, *How shall he that supplieth the place of the unlearned* &c., saith: "It is the layman, whom Paul understandeth here to be in the place of the ignorant man, which hath no ecclesiastical office. How shall he answer, "Amen," to the prayer that he understandeth not?" And a little after, upon these words of St Paul, *For if I should pray in a tongue* &c., he saith thus: "This is Paul's meaning: if any man speak in strange and unknown tongues, his mind is made unfruitful, not to himself, but to the hearer; for, whatsoever is spoken, he knoweth it not."

Ibid.:16

Ibid.:14

St Augustine, writing upon the eighteenth Psalm, saith: "What this should be we ought to understand, that we may sing with reason of man, not with chattering of birds. For ousels and popinjays and ravens and pies, and other suchlike birds, are taught by men to prate they know not what; but to sing with understanding, is given by God's holy will, to the nature of man." Again, the same Augustine saith: "There needeth no speech when we pray, saving perhaps as the priests do, for to declare their meaning, not that God, but that men may hear them, and so being put in remembrance, by consenting with the priest, they may hang upon God."

Psalm 18

de Magist.

Thus are we taught, both by the Scriptures and ancient doctors, that in the administration of Common Prayer and Sacraments, no tongue unknown to the hearers ought to be used. So that for the satisfying of a Christian man's conscience, we need to spend no more time in this matter. But yet, to stop the mouths of the adversaries, which stay themselves much upon general decrees, it shall be good to add to these testimonies of Scriptures and doctors, one Constitution made by Justinian the Emperor, who lived five hundred and twenty and seven years after Christ, and was Emperor of Rome. The Constitution is this.

Nov. Const. 123

We command, that all bishops and priests do celebrate the holy oblation, and the prayers used in holy Baptism, not speaking low, but with a clear or loud voice, which may be heard of the people, that thereby the mind of the hearers may be stirred up, with great devotion, in uttering the praises of the Lord God. For so the holy Apostle teacheth, in his first Epistle to the Corinthians, saying, *Truly, if thou only bless*, or give thanks, *in spirit, how doth he which occupieth the place of the unlearned say, Amen, at thy giving of thanks unto God?*

1 Cor. 14:16, 17

for he understandeth not what thou sayest. Thou verily givest thanks well, but the other is not edified. And again, in the epistle to the Romans, he saith: *With the heart a man believeth unto righteousness, and with the mouth confession is made unto salvation.* Therefore for these causes it is convenient, that among other prayers, those things also which are spoken in the holy oblation, be uttered and spoken of the most religious bishops and priests, unto our Lord Jesus Christ, our God with the Father and the Holy Ghost, with a loud voice. And let the most religious priests know this, that if they neglect any of these things, that they shall give an account for them, in the dreadful judgement *of the great God and Saviour Jesus Christ*; neither will we, when we know it, rest and leave it unrevenged.

Rom. 10:10

Titus 2:13

This Emperor, as Sabellicus writeth, favoured the Bishop of Rome; and yet we see, how plain a decree he maketh, for the praying and administering of Sacraments in a known tongue, that the devotion of the hearers might be stirred up by knowledge, contrary to the judgement of them that would have ignorance to make devotion. He maketh it also a matter of damnation, to do these things in a tongue that the hearers understand not. Let us therefore conclude, with God and all good men's assent, that no Common Prayer, or Sacraments, ought to be ministered in a tongue that is not understood of the hearers.

Now a word or two of private prayer in an unknown tongue. We took in hand, where we began to speak of this matter, not only to prove that no Common Prayer, or administration of Sacraments, ought to be in a tongue unknown to the hearers, but also that no person ought to pray privately in that tongue, that he himself understandeth not. Which thing shall not be hard to prove, if we forget not what prayer is. For if prayer be that devotion of the mind, which enforceth the heart to lift up itself to God, how should it be said, that that person prayeth, that understandeth not the words that his tongue speaketh in prayer? Yea, how can it be said that he speaketh? For to speak, is by voice to utter the thought of the mind; and the voice that a man uttereth in speaking, is nothing else but the messenger of the mind, to bring abroad the knowledge, of that which otherwise lieth secret in the heart, and cannot be known, according to that which St Paul writeth: *What man*, saith he, *knoweth the things that appertain to man, saving only the spirit of man, which is in man?* He therefore that doth not understand the voices that his tongue doth utter, cannot properly be said to speak, but rather to counterfeit, as parrots and such other birds use to counterfeit men's voices. No man therefore, that feareth to provoke the wrath of God against himself, will be so bold to speak to God unadvisedly, without regard of reverent understanding, in his presence; but he will prepare his heart, before he presume to speak unto God. And therefore in our Common Prayer, the minister doth oftentimes say, "Let

1 Cor. 2:11

us pray," meaning thereby to admonish the people, that they should prepare their ears, to hear what he shall crave at God's hand, and their hearts to consent to the same, and their tongues to say, "Amen," at the end thereof. On this sort did the Prophet David prepare his heart, when he said, *My heart is ready, O God, my heart is ready, I will sing and declare a psalm.* The Jews also, when in the time of Judith they did with all their heart pray God, to visit his people of Israel, had so prepared their hearts before they began to pray. After this sort had Manasses prepared his heart, before he prayed and said, *And now, O Lord, do I bow the knees of mine heart, asking of thee, part of thy merciful kindness.* When the heart is thus prepared, the voice, uttered from the heart, is harmonious in the ears of God. Otherwise he regardeth it not, to accept it; but, forasmuch as the person that so babbleth his words without sense, in the presence of God, showeth himself not to regard the Majesty of him that he speaketh to, he taketh him as a contemner of his Almighty Majesty, and giveth him his reward among hypocrites, which make an outward show of holiness, but their hearts are full of abominable thoughts, even in the time of their prayers. For it is *the heart* that *the Lord looketh upon,* as it is written in the history of Kings. If we therefore will, that our prayers be not abominable before God, let us so prepare our hearts, before we pray, and so understand the things that we ask when we pray, that both our hearts and voices, may together sound in the ears of God's Majesty, and then we shall not fail to receive, at his hand, the things that we ask; as good men which have been before us did, and so have from time to time received, that which for their soul's health, they did at any time desire.

St Augustine seemeth to bear in this matter: for he saith thus of them which, being brought up in grammar and rhetoric, are converted to Christ, and so must be instructed in Christian religion:

de Catechizandis Rudibus

> Let them know also [saith he], that it is not the voice, but the affection of the mind, that cometh to the ears of God. And so shall it come to pass, that if haply they shall mark, that some bishops or ministers in the Church, do call upon God, either with barbarous words, or with words disordered, or that they understand not, or do disorderly divide the words that they pronounce, they shall not laugh them to scorn.

Hitherto he seemeth to bear with praying in an unknown tongue; but in the next sentence he openeth his mind thus:

> Not for that things ought not to be amended, that the people might say, Amen, to that which they do plainly understand. But yet these things must be godly borne withal, of these catechists, or instructors of the faith, that they may learn, that as in the common place where matters are pleaded, the goodness of an oration consisteth in sound, so in the Church it consisteth in devotion.

Margin notes:
Psalm 57:7
Judith 4:9–15
2 Paral. 36 [Prayer of Manasses]
1 Sam. 16:7

So that he alloweth not the praying in a tongue not understood of him that prayeth, but he instructeth the skilful orator, to bear with the rude tongue of the devout simple minister.

To conclude. If the lack of understanding the words that are spoken in the congregation, do make them unfruitful to the hearers, how should not the same make the words read unfruitful to the reader? The merciful goodness of God grant us his grace, to call upon him as we ought to do, to his glory and our endless felicity; which we shall do, if we humble ourselves in his sight, and in all our prayers, both common and private, have our minds fully fixed upon him. *For the prayer of them that humble* Ecclus. 35: 17, 18 *themselves shall pierce through the clouds; and till it draw nigh unto God, it will not be answered; and till the Most High do regard it, it will not depart. And the Lord will not be slack, but he will deliver the just, and execute judgement.* To him therefore be all honour and glory, for ever and ever. Amen.

AN INFORMATION
FOR THEM WHICH TAKE OFFENCE
AT CERTAIN PLACES OF
THE HOLY SCRIPTURE

THE FIRST PART

THE GREAT UTILITY AND PROFIT, that Christian men and women may take if they will, by hearing and reading the holy Scriptures, dearly beloved, no heart can sufficiently conceive, much less is any tongue able with words to express. Therefore Satan our old enemy, seeing the Scriptures to be the very mean and right way to bring the people to the true knowledge of God, and that Christian religion is greatly furthered, by diligent hearing and reading of them, he also perceiving what an hindrance and let they be to him and his kingdom, doeth what he can, to drive the reading of them out of God's Church. And for that end he hath always stirred up, in one place or other, cruel tyrants, sharp persecutors, and extreme enemies unto God and his infallible truth, to pull with violence the holy Bibles out of the people's hands, and hath most spitefully destroyed and consumed the same to ashes, in the fire, pretending most untruly, that the much hearing and reading of God's word, is an occasion of heresy, carnal liberty, and the overthrow of all good order, in all well ordered commonweals.

If to know God aright be an occasion of evil, then must we needs grant, that the hearing and reading of the holy Scriptures, is the cause of heresy, carnal liberty, and the subversion of all good orders. But the knowledge of God, and of ourselves, is so far off from being an occasion of evil, that it is the readiest, yea, the only mean to bridle carnal liberty, and to kill all our fleshly affections. And the ordinary way to attain this 2 Tim. 3:16   knowledge, is with diligence to hear and read the holy Scriptures. For *the whole Scriptures*, saith St Paul, *were given by the inspiration of God*: and shall we Christian men think to learn the knowledge of God, and of ourselves, in any earthly man's work or writing, sooner or better than in the holy Scriptures, written by the inspiration of the Holy Ghost? *The Scriptures were not brought unto us by the will of man; but holy men of God,* as witnesseth St Peter, *spake as they were moved by the holy Spirit of God.* The Holy Ghost is the Schoolmaster of truth, which leadeth his scholars, as our Saviour Christ saith of him, *into all truth.* And whoso is not led and taught by this Schoolmaster, cannot but fall into deep error, how goodly soever his pretence is, what knowledge and learning soever he hath of all other works and writings, or how fair soever a show or face of truth he hath, in the estimation and judgement of the world.

    2 Pet. 1:21

    John 16:13

If some man will say, I would have a true pattern and a perfect description, of an upright life approved in the sight of God, can we find, think ye, any better, or any such again, as Christ Jesus is, and his doctrine? whose virtuous conversation and godly life, the Scripture so lively painteth, and setteth forth before our eyes, that we beholding that pattern, might shape and frame our lives, as nigh as may be, agreeable to the perfection of the same. *Follow you me,* saith St Paul, *as I follow Christ.* And St John in his Epistle saith, *Whoso abideth in Christ, must walk even so as he walked before him.* And where shall we learn the order of Christ's life, but in the Scripture?

    1 Cor. 11:1
    1 John 2:6

Another would have a medicine, to heal all diseases and maladies of the mind. Can this be found or gotten otherwheres than out of God's own book, his sacred Scriptures? Christ taught so much, when he said to the obstinate Jews, *Search the Scriptures, for in them ye think to have eternal life.* If the Scriptures contain in them everlasting life, it must needs follow that they have also present remedy, against all that is an hindrance and let unto eternal life.

    John 5:39

If we desire the knowledge of heavenly wisdom, why had we rather learn the same of man, than of God himself, who as St James saith, is the Giver of wisdom? Yea, why will we not learn it at Christ's own mouth? who promising to be present with his Church till the world's end, doth perform his promise, in that he is not only with us by his grace and tender pity, but also in this, that he speaketh presently unto us, in the holy Scriptures, to the great and endless comfort of all them that have any feeling of God at all in them. Yea, he speaketh now in the Scriptures more profitably to us, than he did by word of mouth to the carnal Jews, when he lived with them here upon earth. For they, I mean the Jews, could neither hear nor see those things, which we may now both hear and see, if we will bring with us those ears and eyes that Christ is heard and seen with, that is, diligence to hear and read his holy Scriptures, and true faith to believe his most comfortable promises.

    James 1:5

    Matt. 28:20

If one could show but the print of Christ's foot, a great number, I think, would fall down and worship it: but to the holy Scriptures, where we may see daily, if we will, I will not say the print of his feet only, but the whole shape and lively image of him, alas! we give little reverence, or none at all. If any could let us see Christ's coat, a sort of us would make hard shift, except we might come nigh to gaze upon it, yea, and kiss it too: and yet all the clothes that ever he did wear, can nothing so truly nor so lively express him unto us, as do the Scriptures. Christ's image, made in wood, stone, or metal, some men, for the love they bear to Christ, do garnish and beautify the same, with pearl, gold, and precious stone: and should we not, good brethren, much rather embrace and reverence God's holy books, the sacred Bible, which do represent Christ unto us more truly than can any image? The image can but express the form or shape of his body, if it can do so much: but the Scripture doth in such sort set forth Christ, that we may see him both God and man; we may see him, I say, speaking unto us, healing our infirmities, dying for our sins, rising from death for our justification. And to be short, we may in the Scriptures so perfectly see whole Christ, with the eye of faith, as we lacking faith, could not with these bodily eyes see him, though he stood now present here before us.

Let every man, woman, and child therefore, with all their heart, thirst and desire God's holy Scriptures, love them, embrace them, have their delight and pleasure in hearing and reading them; so as at length we may be transformed, and changed into them. For the Holy Scriptures are God's treasure house, wherein are found all things needful for us to see, to hear, to learn, and to believe, necessary for the attaining of eternal life.

Thus much is spoken, only to give you a taste of some of the commodities which ye may take, by hearing and reading the holy Scriptures; for as I said in the beginning, no tongue is able to declare and utter all. And although it is more clear than the noon day, that to be ignorant of the Scriptures is the cause of error—as Christ saith to the Sadducees, *Ye err, not knowing the Scriptures*—and that error doth hold back and pluck men away from the knowledge of God; and as St Jerome saith, "Not to know the Scriptures is to be ignorant of Christ;" yet this notwithstanding, some there be that think it not meet, for all sorts of men to read the Scriptures, because they are, as they think, in sundry places stumbling-blocks to the unlearned; first, for that the phrase of the Scripture is sometime so homely, gross, and plain, that it offendeth the fine and delicate wits of some courtiers; furthermore, for that the Scripture also reporteth, even of them that have their commendation to be the children of God, that they did divers acts, whereof some are contrary to the law of nature, some repugnant to the law written, and other some seem to fight manifestly against public honesty; all which things, say they, are unto the simple an occasion of great offence, and cause many to think evil of the Scriptures, and to discredit their

Matt. 22:29

authority. Some are offended, at the hearing and reading of the diversity of the rites and ceremonies, of the sacrifices and oblations of the Law. And some worldly-witted men think it a great decay, to the quiet and prudent governing of their commonwealths, to give ear to the simple and plain rules and precepts, of our Saviour Christ in his Gospel; as being offended, that a man should be ready to turn his right ear to him that strake him on the left, and to him which would take away his coat, to offer him also his cloak, with such other sayings of perfection in Christ's meaning: for carnal reason, being alway an enemy to God, and not perceiving the things of God's Spirit, doth abhor such precepts; which yet rightly understood, infringeth no judicial policies, nor Christian men's governments. And some there be, which hearing the Scriptures to bid us to live without carefulness, without study or forecasting, do deride the simplicity of them. Therefore, to remove and put away occasions of offence, so much as may be, I will answer orderly to these objections. `Matt. 5:39, 40`

First, I shall rehearse some of those places that men are offended at, for the homeliness and grossness of speech, and will show the meaning of them.

In the book of Deuteronomy it is written, that Almighty God made a law, if a man died without issue, his brother or next kinsman should marry his widow, and the child that were first born between them, should be called his child that was dead, that the dead man's name might not be put out in Israel; and if the brother or next kinsman would not marry the widow, then she before the magistrates of the city, should pull off his shoe, and spit in his face, saying, *So be it done to that man, that will not build his brother's house.* Here, dearly beloved, the pulling off his shoe, and spitting in his face, were ceremonies, to signify unto all the people of that city, that the woman was not now in fault, that God's law in that point was broken, but the whole shame and blame thereof, did now redound to that man which openly, before the magistrates, refused to marry her: and it was not a reproach to him alone, but to all his posterity also; for they were called ever after, *The house of him whose shoe is pulled off.* `Deut. 25:5-10`

Another place, out of the Psalms: *I will break,* saith David, *the horns of the ungodly, and the horns of the righteous shall be exalted.* By *an horn* in the Scripture is understood power, might, strength, and sometime rule of government. The Prophet then, saying, *I will break the horns of the ungodly,* meaneth, that all the power, strength, and might of God's enemies, shall not only be weakened and made feeble, but shall at length also be clean broken and destroyed; though for a time, for the better trial of his people, God suffereth the enemies to prevail, and have the upper hand. In the hundred and thirty second Psalm it is said, *I will make David's horn to flourish.* Here *David's horn* signifieth his kingdom. `Psalm 75:10`

`Psalm 132:17`

Almighty God therefore, by this manner of speaking, promiseth to give David victory over all his enemies, and to stablish him in his kingdom, spite of all his enemies.

Psalm 60:8

And in the threescore Psalm it is written, *Moab is my washpot, and over Edom will I cast out my shoe,* &c. In that place, the Prophet showeth, how graciously God hath dealt with his people, the children of Israel, giving them great victories upon their enemies on every side. For, the Moabites and Idumeans, being two great nations, proud people, stout and mighty, God brought them under and made them servants to the Israelites; servants, I say, to stoop down to pull off their shoes, and wash their feet. Then, *Moab is my washpot, and over Edom will I cast out my shoe,* is as if he had said, "The Moabites and the Idumeans, for all their stoutness against us in the wilderness, are now made our subjects, our servants, yea, underlings to pull off our shoes, and wash our feet." Now, I pray you, what uncomely manner of speech is this, so used in common phrase among the Hebrews? It is a shame that Christian men should be so light headed, to toy as ruffians do of such manner speeches, uttered in good grave signification, by the Holy Ghost. More reasonable it were, for vain man to learn to reverence the form of God's words, than to gaud at them, to his damnation.

Some again are offended, to hear that the godly fathers had many wives and concubines, although after the phrase of the Scripture, a concubine is an honest name; for every concubine is a lawful wife, but every wife is not a concubine. And that ye may the better understand this to be true, ye shall note that it was permitted, to the fathers of the Old Testament, to have at one time mo wives than one: for what purpose ye shall afterward hear. Of which wives, some were free women born, some were bond women and servants. She that was free born had a prerogative, above those that were servants and bond women. The free born woman was by marriage, made the ruler of the house, under her husband, and is called the mother of the household, the mistress, or the dame of the house, after our manner of speaking, and had by her marriage an interest, a right, and an ownership in his goods, unto whom she was married. Other servants and bond women, were given by the owners of them, as the manner was then, I will not say always, but for the most part, unto their daughters, at the day of their marriage, to be handmaidens unto them. After such a sort did Pharao King of Egypt give unto Sara, Abraham's wife, Agar the Egyptian, to be her maid. So did

Gen. 29:24, 29

Laban give unto his daughter Lia, at the day of her marriage, Zilpha to be her handmaid; and to his other daughter Rahel he gave another bondmaid, named Bilha. And the wives, that were the owners of their handmaids, gave them in marriage to their husbands, upon divers

Gen. 16:3
Gen. 30:9

occasions. Sara gave her maid Agar in marriage to Abraham. Lia gave in like manner her maid Zilpha, to her husband Jacob. So did Rahel, his other wife, give him Bilha her maid, saying unto him, *Go in unto her, and she shall bear upon my knees*: which is as if she had said, "Take her to wife, and the children that she shall bear, will I take upon my lap, and make of them as if they were mine own." These handmaidens, or bond women, although by marriage they were made wives, yet they had not this prerogative, to rule in the house, but were still underlings, and in subjection to their mistress, and were never called mothers of the household, mistresses, or dames of the house, but are called sometimes wives, sometimes concubines. The plurality of wives was, by a special prerogative, suffered to the fathers of the Old Testament, not for satisfying their carnal and fleshly lusts, but to have many children; because every one of them hoped, and begged ofttimes of God in their prayers, that that blessed seed which God promised should come into the world, to break the serpent's head, might come and be born of his stock and kinred.

Now: of those which take occasion of carnality and evil life, by hearing and reading in God's book what God hath suffered, even in those men whose commendation is praised in the Scripture. As that Noe, whom St Peter calleth the eighth *preacher of righteousness*,was so drunk with wine, that in his sleep he uncovered his own privities. The just man Lot was, in like manner, drunken, and in his drunkenness, lay with his own daughters, contrary to the law of nature. Abraham, whose faith was so great, that for the same he deserved to be called, of God's own mouth, *a father of many nations, the father of all believers*, besides with Sara his wife, had also carnal company with Agar, Sara's handmaid. The Patriarch Jacob had to his wives, two sisters at one time. The Prophet David, and King Salomon his son, had many wives and concubines, &c. Which things we see plainly to be forbidden us, by the law of God, and are now repugnant to all public honesty. These and suchlike in God's book, good people, are not written that we should or may do the like, following their examples, or that we ought to think that God did allow every of these things in those men: but we ought rather to believe and to judge, that Noe in his drunkenness offended God highly, Lot lying with his daughters committed horrible incest. We ought then to learn by them this profitable lesson, that if so godly men as they were—which otherwise felt inwardly God's Holy Spirit, inflaming their hearts with the fear and love of God—could not, by their own strength, keep themselves from committing horrible sin, but did so grievously fall, that without God's great mercy they had perished everlastingly, how much more ought we then, miserable wretches, which have no feeling of God within us at all, continually to fear, not only that we may fall as they did, but also be overcome and drowned in sin, which they were not! and so, by considering their fall, take the better occasion to acknowledge our own infirmity,

2 Pet. 2:5; Gen. 9:21

Gen. 19:30–6

Gen. 17:4–5; Rom. 4:11–18

Gen. 16:4

Gen. 29:23–30

and weakness, and therefore more earnestly to call unto Almighty God, with hearty prayer incessantly, for his grace, to strengthen us, and to defend us from all evil. And though through infirmity we chance at any time to fall, yet we may, by hearty repentance and true faith, speedily rise again, and not sleep and continue in sin, as the wicked doth.

Thus, good people, should we understand such matters expressed in the divine Scriptures, that this holy *table* of God's word be not turned to us to be *a snare, a trap, and a stumbling-stone,* to take hurt by the abuse of our understanding: but let us esteem them in such a reverent humility, that we may find our necessary food therein, to strengthen us, to comfort us, to instruct us, as God of his great mercy hath appointed them, in all necessary works; so that we may be perfect before him, in the whole course of our life. Which he grant us who hath redeemed us, our Lord and Saviour Jesus Christ: to whom with the Father, and the Holy Ghost, be all honour and glory, for evermore. Amen.

Psalm 69:22

THE SECOND PART OF THE INFORMATION FOR THEM WHICH TAKE OFFENCE AT CERTAIN PLACES OF THE HOLY SCRIPTURE

YE HAVE HEARD, good people, in the Homily last read unto you, the great commodity of holy Scriptures: ye have heard how ignorant men, void of godly understanding, seek quarrels to discredit them: some of their reasons have ye heard answered. Now we will proceed, and speak of such politic wise men which be offended, for that Christ's precepts should seem to destroy all order in governance, as they do allege for example such as these be. *If any man strike thee on the right cheek, turn the other unto him also. If any will contend to take thy coat from thee, let him have cloak and all. Let not thy left hand know what thy right hand doeth. If thine eye, thine hand, thy foot offend thee, pull out thine eye, cut off thy hand, thy foot, and cast it from thee. If thine enemy,* saith St Paul, *be hungered, give him meat; if he thirst, give him drink: so doing, thou shalt heap hot burning coals upon his head.* These sentences, good people, unto a natural man seem mere absurdities, contrary to all reason. *For a natural man,* as St Paul saith, *understandeth not the things that belong to God, neither can he,* so long as old Adam dwelleth in him. Christ therefore meaneth, that he would have his faithful servants so far from vengeance, and resisting wrong, that he would rather have him ready to suffer another wrong, than by resisting, to break charity, and to be out of patience. He would have our good deeds so far from carnal respects, that he would not have our nighest friends know of our well doing, to win a vain glory. And, though our friends and kinsfolks be as dear as our right eyes, and our

Matt. 5:39, 40

Matt. 6:3
Matt. 18:8, 9

Rom. 12:20

1 Cor. 2:14

right hands, yet if they would pluck us from God, we ought to renounce them, and forsake them.

Thus, if ye will be profitable hearers and readers of the holy Scriptures, you must first deny yourselves, and keep under your carnal senses, taken by the outward words, and search the inward meaning; reason must give place to God's Holy Spirit; you must submit your worldly wisdom and judgement, unto his divine wisdom and judgement. Consider that the Scripture, in what strange form soever it be pronounced, is the word of the living God. Let that always come to your remembrance, which is so oft repeated of the Prophet Esay. *The mouth of the Lord*, saith he, *hath spoken it.* The almighty and everlasting *God, who* with his only word *created heaven and earth*, hath decreed it. *The Lord of hosts, whose ways are in the seas, whose paths are in the deep waters,* that Lord and God by whose word, all things in heaven and in earth are created, governed, and preserved, hath so provided it. *The God of gods and Lord of all lords,* yea, God that is *God alone*, incomprehensible, almighty, and everlasting, he hath spoken it: it is his word. It cannot therefore be but truth, which proceedeth from the God of all truth; it cannot be but wisely and prudently commanded, what Almighty God hath devised; how vainly soever, through want of grace, we miserable wretches do imagine and judge of his most holy word.

Isai. 1:20; 40:5; 58:14
Isai. 43:5; 44:24; 45:18
Psalm 77:19; Isai. 43:16; 51:15; 54:5; 2 Pet. 3:5,7

Deut. 10:17; Psalm 86:10

The Prophet David, describing an happy man, saith *Blessed is the man, that hath not walked after the counsel of the ungodly, nor stood in the way of sinners, nor sat in the seat of the scornful.** There are three sorts of people whose company the Prophet would have him to flee and avoid, which shall be an happy man, and partaker of God's blessing. First, he may not *walk after the counsel of the ungodly.* Secondly, he may not *stand in the way of sinners.* Thirdly, he must not *sit in the seat of the scornful.* By these three sorts of people, *ungodly men, sinners,* and *scorners,* all impiety is signified, and fully expressed. By *the ungodly,* he understandeth those which have no regard of Almighty God, being void of all faith, whose hearts and minds are so set upon the world, that they study only how to accomplish their worldly practices, their carnal imaginations, their filthy lust and desire, without any fear of God. The second sort he calleth *sinners*: not such as do fall through ignorance, or of frailness; for then who should be found free? what man ever lived upon earth, Christ only excepted, but he hath sinned? *The just man falleth seven times, and riseth again.* Though the godly do fall, yet they walk not on purposely in sin; they stand not still, to continue and tarry in sin; they sit not down like careless men, without all fear of God's just punishment for sin; but defying sin, through God's great grace and infinite mercy, they rise again, and fight against sin. The Prophet then calleth them *sinners,* whose hearts are clean turned from

Psalm 1:1

Prov. 24:16

* The original editions read ". . . stand nor sit . . . ."

God, and whose whole conversation of life is nothing but sin: they delight so much in the same, that they choose continually to abide and dwell in sin. The third sort he calleth *scorners*, that is, a sort of men, whose hearts are so stuffed with malice, that they are not contented to dwell in sin, and to lead their lives in all kind of wickedness, but also they do contemn and scorn in other, all godliness, true religion, all honesty and virtue.

Of the two first sorts of men, I will not say but they may take repentance, and be converted unto God. Of the third sort, I think I may, without danger of God's judgement, pronounce that never any yet converted unto God, by repentance, but continued on still in their abominable wickedness, heaping up to themselves damnation, against the day of God's inevitable judgement. Examples of such scorners we read of in the second book of Chronicles. When the good King Ezechias, in the beginning of his reign, had destroyed idolatry, purged the Temple, and reformed religion in his realm, he sent messengers into every city, to gather the people unto Jerusalem, to solemnise the feast of Easter, in such sort as God had appointed it. *The posts went from city to city, through the land of Ephraim and Manasses, even unto Zabulon.* And what did the people, think ye? Did they laud and praise the name of the Lord, which had given them so good a king, so zealous a prince to abolish idolatry, and to restore again God's true religion? No, no. The Scripture saith, the people *laughed them to scorn, and mocked the King's messengers.* And in the last chapter of the same book, it is written that Almighty *God, having compassion upon his people, sent his messengers the Prophets unto them,* to call them from their abominable idolatry, and wicked kind of living. *But they mocked his messengers, they despised his words, and misused his Prophets, until the wrath of the Lord arose against his people, and till there was no remedy*: for he gave them up into the hands of their enemies, even unto Nabuchodonozor, King of Babylon, who spoiled them of their goods, burnt their city, and led them, their wives, and their children, captives unto Babylon. The wicked people that were in the days of Noe, made but a mock at the word of God, when Noe told them that God would take vengeance upon them for their sins. The flood therefore came suddenly upon them, and drowned them, with the whole world. Lot preached to the Sodomites, that except they repented, both they and their city should be destroyed. They thought his sayings impossible to be true, they mocked and scorned his admonition, and reputed him as an old doating fool. But when God, by his holy angels, had taken Lot, his wife, and two daughters, from among them, he rained down fire and brimstone from heaven, and burnt up those scorners, and mockers of his holy word. And what estimation had Christ's doctrine among the Scribes and Pharisees? what reward had he among them? The Gospel reporteth thus: *The Pharisees, which were covetous, did scorn him in his doctrine.* Oh then ye see

2 Chron. 30: 1–10

2 Chron. 36: 15–20

Gen. 6, 7

Gen. 19

Luke 16:14

that worldly rich men scorn the doctrine of their salvation. The worldly wise men scorn the doctrine of Christ, as foolishness to their understanding. These scorners have ever been, and ever shall be, till the world's end. For St Peter prophesied that such scorners should be in the world, before the latter day. Take heed therefore, my brethren, take heed! Be not ye scorners of God's most holy word. Provoke him not to pour out his wrath now upon you, as he did then upon those gibers and mockers. Be not wilful murderers of your own souls. Turn unto God while there is yet time of mercy: ye shall else repent it, in the world to come, when it shall be too late; for there shall be *judgement without mercy*.

2 Pet. 3:3, 4

James 2:13

This might suffice to admonish us, and cause us henceforth to reverence God's holy Scriptures: but *all men have not faith*. This therefore shall not satisfy and content all men's minds; but as some are carnal, so they will still continue, and abuse the Scripture carnally, to their greater damnation. *The unlearned and unstable*, saith St Peter, *pervert the holy Scriptures, to their own destruction.* Jesus Christ, as St Paul saith, is *to the Jews an offence, to the Gentiles foolishness; but to God's children, as well of the Jews as of the Gentiles, he is the power and wisdom of God.* The holy man Simeon saith, *that he is set forth for the fall and rising again of many in Israel.* As Christ Jesus is a fall to the reprobate, which yet perish through their own default, so is his word, yea, the whole book of God, a cause of damnation unto them, through their incredulity. And as he is a rising up to none other than those which are God's children by adoption, so is his word, yea, the whole Scripture, *the power of God to salvation, to them* only *that do believe it.* Christ himself, the Prophets before him, the Apostles after him, all the true ministers of God's holy word, yea, every word in God's book, is unto the reprobate *the savour of death unto death.* Christ Jesus, the Prophets, the Apostles, and all the true ministers of his word, yea, every jot and tittle in the holy Scripture, have been, is, and shall be for evermore, *the savour of life unto* eternal *life*, unto all those whose hearts God hath purified, by true faith. Let us earnestly take heed, that we make no jesting-stock of the books of holy Scriptures. The more obscure and dark the sayings be to our understanding, the further let us think ourselves to be from God and his Holy Spirit, who was the Author of them. Let us with more reverence endeavour ourselves, to search out the wisdom hidden in the outward bark of the Scripture. If we cannot understand the sense and the reason of the saying, yet let us not be scorners, jesters, and deriders; for that is the uttermost token and show of a reprobate, of a plain enemy to God, and his wisdom. They be no idle fables to jest at, which God doth seriously pronounce; and for serious matters let us esteem them.

2 Thess. 3:2

2 Pet. 3:16

1 Cor. 1:23, 24

Luke 2:34

Rom. 1:16

2 Cor. 2:16

And though in sundry places of the Scriptures, be set out divers rites and ceremonies, oblations and sacrifices, let us not think strange of them, but refer them to the times and people for whom they served;

although yet to learned men they be not unprofitable to be considered, but to be expounded as figures, and shadows of things and persons afterward openly revealed, in the New Testament. Though the rehearsal of the genealogies, and pedigrees of the fathers, be not to much edification of the plain ignorant people, yet is there nothing so impertinently uttered, in all the whole book of the Bible, but may serve to spiritual purpose in some respect, to all such as will bestow their labours to search out the meanings. These may not be condemned, because they serve not to our understanding, nor make not to our edification. But let us turn our labour to understand, and to carry away, such sentences and stories as be more fit for our capacity and instruction.

And, whereas we read in divers Psalms, how David did wish to the adversaries of God sometimes shame, rebuke, and confusion, sometime the decay of their offspring and issue, sometime that they might perish and come suddenly to destruction (as he did wish to the captains of the Philistians, *Cast forth*, saith he, *thy lightning, and tear them; shoot out thine arrows, and consume them*), with such other manner of imprecations; yet ought we not to be offended at such prayers of David, being a Prophet as he was, singularly beloved of God, and rapt in spirit, with an ardent zeal to God's glory. He spake them not as of a private hatred, and in a stomach against their persons, but wished spiritually, the destruction of such corrupt errors and vices, which reigned in all devilish persons set against God. He was of like mind as St Paul was, when he did deliver Hymeneus and Alexander, with the notorious fornicator, to Satan, to their temporal confusion, *that their spirit might be saved, against the day of the Lord*. And when David did profess in some places, that he hated the wicked, yet in other places of his Psalms, he professeth that he hated them *with a perfect hate*, not with a malicious hate, to the hurt of the soul. Which perfection of spirit, because it cannot be performed in us, so corrupted in affections as we be, we ought not to use in our private causes, the like words in form, for that we cannot fulfil the like words in sense. Let us not therefore be offended; that we may the more reverently judge of such sayings, though strange to our carnal understandings, yet to them that be spiritually minded, judged to be zealously and godly pronounced.

God therefore, for his mercy's sake, vouchsafe to purify our minds, through faith in his Son Jesus Christ, and to instil the heavenly drops of his grace, into our hard stony hearts, to supple the same; that we be not contemners and deriders of his infallible word, but that with all humbleness of mind, and Christian reverence, we may endeavour ourselves to hear and to read his sacred Scriptures, and inwardly so to digest them, as shall be to the comfort of our souls, and sanctification of his holy Name. To whom, with the Son, and the Holy Ghost, three Persons and one living God, be all laud, honour, and praise, for ever and ever. Amen.

Psalm 144:6

1 Tim. 1:20;
1 Cor. 5:5

Psalm 26:5;
31:6; 129:21, 22

AN HOMILY OF ALMSDEEDS
AND MERCIFULNESS
TOWARD THE POOR AND NEEDY

AMONGST THE MANIFOLD DUTIES that Almighty God requireth of his faithful servants, the true Christians, by the which he would that both his Name should be glorified, and the certainty of their vocation declared, there is none that is either more acceptable unto him, or more profitable for them, than are the works of mercy and pity, showed upon the poor, which be afflicted with any kind of misery. And yet, this notwithstanding, such is the slothful sluggishness of our dull nature, to that which is good and godly, that we are almost in nothing more negligent, and less careful, than we are therein. It is therefore a very necessary thing, that God's people should awake their sleepy minds, and consider their duty on this behalf. And meet it is, that all true Christians should desirously seek and learn, what God by his holy word doth herein require of them; that first knowing their duty, whereof many by their slackness, seem to be very ignorant, they may afterwards diligently endeavour to perform the same. By the which, both the godly charitable persons may be encouraged, to go forwards and continue in their merciful deeds of giving alms to the poor, and also, such as hitherto have either neglected or contemned it, may yet now at length, when they shall hear how much it appertaineth to them, advisedly consider it, and virtuously apply themselves thereunto.

And, to the intent that every one of you may the better understand that which is taught, and also easilier bear away, and so take more fruit of, that shall be said, when several matters are severally handled, I mind particularly, and in this order, to speak and entreat of these points.

First, I will show how earnestly Almighty God, in his holy word, doth exact the doing of almsdeeds of us, and how acceptable they be unto him.

Secondly, how profitable it is for us to use them, and what commodity and fruit they will bring unto us.

Thirdly and last, I will show out of God's word, that whoso is liberal to the poor, and relieveth them plenteously, shall notwithstanding have sufficient for himself, and evermore be without danger of penury and scarcity.

Concerning the first, which is the acceptation, and dignity or price, of almsdeeds before God, know this: that to help and succour the poor, in their need and misery, pleaseth God so much, that as the holy Scripture in sundry places recordeth, nothing can be more thankfully taken, or accepted of God. For first we read, that Almighty God doth account that to be given and to be bestowed upon himself, that is bestowed upon the poor. For so doth the Holy Ghost testify unto us, by the Wise Man,

Prov. 19:17

saying, *He that hath pity upon the poor, lendeth unto the Lord* himself. And Christ in the Gospel avoucheth, and as a most certain truth bindeth it with an oath, that the alms bestowed upon the poor, was bestowed upon him, and so shall be reckoned at the last day. For thus he saith to the charitable almsgivers, when he sitteth as Judge, in the Doom, to give sentence of every man according to his deserts: *Verily I say unto you,*

Matt. 25:35–40

Whatsoever good and merciful deed *you did, upon any of the least of these my brethren, ye did the same unto me.* In relieving their hunger, *ye relieved mine*; in quenching their thirst, *ye quenched mine*; in clothing them, *ye clothed me*; and when ye harboured them, *ye lodged me* also; when ye visited them, *being sick or in prison, ye visited me.* For as he that receiveth a prince's ambassadors, and entertaineth them well, doth honour the prince from whom those ambassadors do come, so he that receiveth the poor and needy, and helpeth them in their affliction and distress, doth thereby receive and honour Christ their Master: who, as he was poor and needy himself, whilst he lived here amongst us, to work the mystery of our salvation, so at his departure hence, he promised in his stead to send unto us, those that were poor, by whose means his absence should be supplied; and therefore, that we would do unto him, we must do unto them. And for this cause doth Almighty God say unto Moyses, *The land*

Deut. 15:11

wherein you dwell, shall never be without poor men, because he would have continual trial of his people, whether they loved him or no; that in showing themselves obedient unto his will, they might certainly assure themselves, of his love and favour towards them, and nothing doubt, but that as his law and ordinances wherein he commanded them, that they should *open their hand unto their brethren, that were poor and needy in the land*, were accepted of them, and willingly performed, so he would on his part, lovingly accept them, and truly perform his promises, that he had made unto them.

The holy apostles and disciples of Christ, who by reason of his daily conversation, saw by his deeds, and heard in his doctrine, how much he tendered the poor; the godly fathers also, that were both before and since

Christ, indued without doubt with the Holy Ghost, and most certainly certified of God's holy will; they both do most earnestly exhort us, and in all their writings almost continually admonish us, that we would remember the poor, and bestow our charitable alms upon them. St Paul crieth unto us after this sort: *Comfort the feeble-minded, lift up the weak, and be charitable toward all men.* And again: *To do good to the poor, and to distribute alms gladly, see that thou do not forget; for with such sacrifices is God pleased.* Esay the Prophet teacheth on this wise: *Deal thy bread to the hungry, and bring the poor wandering home to thy house. When thou seest the naked, see thou clothe him, and hide not thy face from thy poor neighbour, neither despise thou thine own flesh.* And the holy father Toby giveth this counsel: *Give alms,* saith he, *of thine own goods, and turn never thy face from the poor. Eat thy bread with the hungry, and cover the naked with thy clothes.* And the learned and godly doctor Chrysostom giveth this admonition: "Let merciful alms be always with us as a garment;" that is, as mindful as we will be to put our garments upon us, to cover our nakedness, to defend us from the cold, and to show ourselves comely, so mindful let us be, at all times and seasons, that we give alms to the poor, and show ourselves merciful towards them. But what mean these often admonitions and earnest exhortations of the Prophets, Apostles, fathers, and holy doctors? Surely, as they were faithful to Godward, and therefore discharged their duty truly, in telling us what was God's will, so, of a singular love to usward, they laboured not only to inform us, but also to persuade with us, that to give alms, and to succour the poor and needy, was a very acceptable thing, and an high sacrifice to God, wherein he greatly delighted, and had a singular pleasure. For so doth the wise man the son of Sirach teach us, saying, *Whoso is merciful and giveth alms, he offereth the right thank offering.* And he addeth thereunto, *The right thank offering maketh the altar fat, and a sweet smell is it before the Highest; it is acceptable before God, and shall never be forgotten.*

And the truth of this doctrine is verified, by the examples of those holy and charitable fathers, of whom we read in the Scriptures, that they were given to merciful compassion towards the poor, and charitable relieving of their necessities. Such a one was Abraham, in whom God had so great pleasure, that he vouchsafed to come unto him in form of an angel, and to be entertained of him at his house. Such was his kinsman Lot, whom God so favoured, for receiving his messengers into his house, which otherwise should have lain in the street, that he saved him with his whole family, from the destruction of Sodom and Gomorra. Such were the holy fathers Job and Toby, with many others, who felt most sensible proofs of God's especial love towards them. And as all these, by their mercifulness and tender compassion, which they showed to the miserable afflicted members of Christ in the relieving, helping,

1 Thess. 5:14

Heb. 13:16

Isai. 58:7

Tob. 4:7, 16

Ad Pop. Antioch.
Hom. 35

Ecclus. 35:2, 6, 7

and succouring them, with their temporal goods in this life, obtained God's favour, and were dear, acceptable, and pleasant in his sight; so now they themselves take pleasure in the fruition of God, in the pleasant joys of heaven, and are also, in God's eternal word, set before us as perfect examples, ever before our eyes, both how we shall please God in this our mortal life, and also how we may come to live in joy with them, in everlasting pleasure and felicity. For most true is that saying which St Augustine hath, that the giving of alms, and relieving of the poor, is the right way to heaven. Via coeli pauper est; "The poor man," saith he, "is the way to heaven." They used in times past, to set in highways' sides the picture of Mercury, pointing with his finger, which was the right way to the town. And we use in cross-ways to set up a wooden or stone cross, to admonish the travelling man which way he must turn, when he cometh thither, to direct his journey aright. But God's word, as St Augustine saith, hath set in the way to heaven, the poor man and his house; so that whoso will go aright thither, and not turn out of the way, must go by the poor. The poor man is that Mercury, that shall set us the ready way; and, if we look well to this mark, we shall not wander much out of the right path.

The manner of wise worldly men among us, is that if they know a man of meaner estate than themselves, to be in favour with the prince or any other nobleman, whom they either fear or love, such a one they will be glad to benefit and pleasure, that when they have need, he may become their spokesman, either to help with his good word to obtain a commodity, or to escape a displeasure. Now surely, it ought to be a shame to us, that worldly men, for temporal things, that last but for a season, should be more wise and provident in procuring them, than we in heavenly. Our Saviour Christ testifieth of poor men, that they are dear unto him, and that he loveth them especially: for he calleth them his *little ones*, by a name of tender love; he saith they be his *brethren*. And St James saith, that God hath chosen them to be heirs of his kingdom. *Hath not God*, saith he, *chosen the poor of this world to himself, to make them hereafter the rich heirs of that kingdom, which he hath promised to them that love him?* And we know that the prayer which they make for us, shall be acceptable and regarded of God. Their complaint shall be heard also. Thereof doth Jesus the son of Sirach certainly assure us, saying, *If the poor complain of thee, in the bitterness of his soul, his prayer shall be heard; even he that made him shall hear him. Be courteous therefore unto the poor.* We know also, that he who acknowledgeth himself to be their Master and Patron, and refuseth not to take them for his servants, is both able to pleasure and displeasure us, and that we stand every hour in need of his help. Why should we then be either negligent or unwilling, to procure their friend-ship and favour, by the which also we may be assured to get his favour,

Matt. 10:42;
25:40

James 2:5

Ecclus. 4:6, 7

that is both able and willing to do us all pleasures that are for our commodity and wealth? Christ doth declare by this, how much he accepteth our charitable affection toward the poor, in that he promiseth a reward unto them that give but a cup of cold water, in his name, to them that have need thereof: and that reward is the kingdom of heaven. No doubt is it therefore, but that God regardeth highly, that which he rewardeth so liberally. For he that promiseth a princely recompence, for a beggarly benevolence, declareth, that he is more delighted with the giving, than with the gift, and that he as much esteemeth the doing of the thing, as the fruit and commodity that cometh of it. *Matt. 10:42, Mark 9:41*

Whoso therefore, hath hitherto neglected to give alms, let him know, that God now requireth it of him; and he that hath been liberal to the poor, let him know that his godly doings are accepted, and thankfully taken at God's hands, which he will requite with double and treble. For so saith the Wise Man: *He which showeth mercy to the poor, doth lay his money in bank to the Lord, for a large interest and gain*; the gain being chiefly the possession of the life everlasting, thorough the merits of our Saviour Jesus Christ. To whom, with the Father, and the Holy Ghost, be all honour and glory, for ever. Amen. *Prov. 19:17*

THE SECOND PART
OF THE SERMON OF ALMSDEEDS

YE HAVE HEARD before, dearly beloved, that to give alms unto the poor, and to help them in time of necessity, is so acceptable unto our Saviour Christ, that he counteth that to be done to himself, that we do for his sake unto them. Ye have heard also, how earnestly both the Apostles, Prophets, holy fathers, and doctors, do exhort us unto the same. And ye see how well-beloved and dear unto God they were, whom the Scriptures report unto us, to have been good almsmen. Wherefore, if either their good examples, or the wholesome counsel of godly fathers, or the love of Christ, whose especial favour we may be assured by this means to obtain, may move us, or do any thing at all with us, let us provide, that from henceforth, we show unto Godward this thankful service, to be mindful and ready, to help them that be poor and in misery.

Now will I, this second time that I entreat of almsdeeds, show unto you, how profitable it is, for us to exercise them, and what fruit thereby shall arise unto us, if we do them faithfully. Our Saviour Christ, in the Gospel, teacheth us, that it profiteth a man nothing, to have in possession all the riches of the whole world, and the wealth or glory thereof, if in the mean season he lose his soul, or do that thing whereby *Matt. 16:26* it should become captive unto death, sin, and hell fire. By the which saying, he not only instructeth us, how much the soul's health is to be preferred, before worldly commodities, but also, serveth to stir up our minds, and to prick us forwards, to seek diligently, and learn by what means we may preserve and keep our souls ever in safety; that is, how we may recover their health, if it be lost or impaired, and how it may be defended and maintained, if we once have it. Yea, he teacheth us also thereby, to esteem that as a precious medicine, and an inestimable jewel, that hath such strength and virtue in it, that can either procure or preserve so incomparable a treasure. For if we greatly regard that medicine or salve, that is able to heal sundry and grievous diseases of the body, much more will we esteem that which hath like power over the soul. And because we might be the better assured, both to know and have in readiness that so profitable a remedy, he, as a most faithful and loving teacher, showeth, himself, both what it is, and where we may find it, and how we may use and apply it. For, when both he and his disciples were grievously accused of the Pharisees, to have defiled their souls in breaking the constitutions of the elders, because they went to meat, and washed not their hands before, according to the custom of the Jews, Christ answering their superstitious complaint, teacheth them an especial remedy, how to keep clean their souls, notwithstanding the breach of such superstitious orders: *Give alms*, saith he, *and behold, all things are clean unto you*. He teacheth them, that to be merciful and charitable, in helping the poor, is the means to keep the soul pure and clean, in the sight of God. We are taught therefore by this, that merciful almsdealing is profitable, to purge the soul from the infection and filthy spots of sin. The same lesson doth the Holy Ghost also teach in sundry places of the Scripture, saying, *Mercifulness and almsgiving purgeth from all sins, and delivereth from death, and suffereth not the soul to come into darkness. A great confidence may they have, before the high God, that show mercy and compassion to them that are afflicted.* The wise Preacher the son of Sirach confirmeth the same, when he saith that, *as water quencheth burning fire, even so mercy and alms resisteth and reconcileth sins.* And sure it is, that mercifulness quaileth the heat of sin so much, that they shall not take hold upon man to hurt him; or if he have by any infirmity and weakness been touched and annoyed with them, straightways shall mercifulness wipe and wash them away, as salves and remedies to heal their sores and grievous diseases. And thereupon, that holy father Cyprian taketh good occasion to exhort earnestly, to the merciful work of giving alms, and helping the poor; and there he admonisheth to consider, how wholesome and profitable it is, to relieve the needy and help the afflicted, by the which we may purge our sins, and heal our wounded souls.

Luke 11:41

Tob. 4:10, 11;
Prov. 16:6

Ecclus. 3:30

But here some will say unto me, "If almsgiving, and our charitable works towards the poor, be able to wash away sins, to reconcile us to God, to deliver us from the peril of damnation, and make us the sons and heirs of God's kingdom, then is Christ's merit defaced, and his blood shed in vain; then are we justified by works, and by our deeds may we merit heaven; then do we in vain believe that *Christ died for to put away our sins, and that he rose for our justification,* as St Paul teacheth." But ye shall understand, dearly beloved, that neither those places of Scripture before alleged, neither the doctrine of the blessed Martyr Cyprian, neither any other godly and learned man, when they in extolling the dignity, profit, fruit, and effect of virtuous and liberal alms, do say that it washeth away sins, and bringeth us to the favour of God, do mean that our work, and charitable deed, is the original cause of our acceptation before God, or that, for the dignity or worthiness thereof, our sins be washed away, and we purged and cleansed of all the spots of our iniquity; for that were indeed to deface Christ, and to defraud him of his glory. But they mean this, and this is the understanding of those and suchlike sayings: that God, of his mercy, and especial favour towards them whom he hath appointed to everlasting salvation, hath so offered his grace effectually, and they have so received fruitfully, that although by reason of their sinful living, outwardly they seemed before to have been the children of wrath and perdition, yet now, the Spirit of God mightily working in them, unto obedience to God's will and commandments, they declare by their outward deeds and life, in showing of mercy and charity, which cannot come but of the Spirit of God and his especial grace, that they are the undoubted children of God, appointed to everlasting life: and so, as by their wickedness and ungodly living they showed themselves, according to the judgement of men (which follow *the outward appearance*), to be reprobates and castaways, so now by their obedience unto God's holy will, and by their mercifulness and tender pity (wherein they show themselves to be like unto God, who is the fountain and spring of all mercy), they declare openly and manifestly unto the sight of men, that they are the sons of God, and elect of him unto salvation.

For as the good fruit is not the cause that the tree is good, but the tree must first be good, before it can bring forth good fruit; so the good deeds of man are not the cause that maketh man good, but he is first made good by the Spirit and grace of God, that effectually worketh in him, and afterward he bringeth forth good fruits. And then, as the good fruit doth argue the goodness of the tree, so doth the good and merciful deed of the man argue, and certainly prove, the goodness of him that doeth it, according to Christ's saying, *Ye shall know them by their fruits.* And if any man will object, that evil and naughty men do sometimes, by their deeds,

Margin notes:
Titus 2:4; Rom. 4:25

1 Sam. 16:7

Matt. 7:16

appear to be very godly and virtuous, I will answer, that so doth the crab and choke-pear seem outwardly, to have sometime as fair a red, and as mellow a colour, as the fruit which is good indeed, but he that will bite, and take a taste, shall easily judge betwixt the sour bitterness of the one, and the sweet savouriness of the other. And as the true Christian man— in thankfulness of his heart, for the redemption of his soul, purchased by Christ's death—showeth kindly, by the fruit of his faith, his obedience to God, so the other, as a merchant with God, doeth all for his own gain, thinking to win heaven by the merit of his works, and so defaceth and obscureth the price of Christ's blood, who, only, wrought our purgation.

The meaning then, of these sayings in the Scriptures, and other holy writings, *Almsdeeds do wash away our sins*, and, "Mercy to the poor doth blot out our offences," is, that we doing these things according to God's will, and our duty, have our sins indeed washed away, and our offences blotted out, not for the worthiness of them, but by the grace of God *which worketh all in all*; and that for the promise that God hath made, to them that are obedient unto his commandment, that he which is the Truth might be justified, in performing the truth due to his true promise. Almsdeeds do wash away our sins, because God doth vouchsafe then, to repute us as clean and pure, when we do them for his sake, and not because they deserve or merit our purging, or for that they have any such strength and virtue in themselves.

I know that some men, too much addict to the advancing of their good works, will not be contented with this answer; and no marvel, for such men can no answer content nor suffice. Wherefore, leaving them to their own wilful sense, we will rather have regard of the reasonable and godly; who, as they most certainly know, and persuade themselves, that all goodness, all bounty, all mercy, all benefits, all forgiveness of sins, and whatsoever can be named good and profitable, either for the body or for the soul, do come only of God's mercy, and mere favour, and not of themselves, so, though they do never so many and so excellent good deeds, yet are they never puffed up, with the vain confidence of them. And though they hear and read in God's word, and otherwhere in godly men's works, that almsdeeds, mercy, and charitableness, doth wash away sin, and blot out iniquity, yet do they not arrogantly and proudly stick or trust unto them, or brag themselves of them, as the proud Pharisee did, lest with the Pharisee they should be condemned; but rather, with the humble and poor Publican, confess themselves sinful wretches, and unworthy to look up to heaven, calling and craving for mercy, that with the Publican they may be pronounced of Christ to be justified. The godly do learn, that when the Scriptures say that by good and merciful works, we are reconciled to God's favour, we are taught then to know what Christ, by his intercession and mediation, obtaineth

Tob. 12:9;
Prov. 16:6;
Dan. 4:27

1 Cor. 12:6

Luke 18:10–14

for us of his Father, when we be obedient to his will; yea, they learn in such manners of speaking, a comfortable argument, of God's singular favour and love, that attributeth that unto us, and to our doings, that he by his Spirit worketh in us, and through his grace procureth for us. And yet this notwithstanding, they cry out with St Paul, *Oh wretches that we are!* and acknowledge, as Christ teacheth, that *when they have all done, they are but unprofitable servants*; and with the blessed King David, in respect of the just judgements of God, they do tremble, and say, *Who shall be able to abide it, Lord, if thou wilt give sentence according to our deserts?* Thus they humble themselves, and are exalted of God; they count themselves vile, and of God are counted pure and clean; they condemn themselves, and are justified of God; they think themselves unworthy of the earth, and of God are thought worthy of heaven. Thus of God's word are they truly taught, how to think rightly of merciful dealing of alms, and of God's especial mercy and goodness, are made partakers of those fruits that his word hath promised.

Rom. 7:24

Luke 17:10

Psalm 130:3

Let us then follow their examples, and both show obediently in our life, those works of mercy that we are commanded, and have that right opinion and judgement of them that we are taught; and we shall, in like manner as they, be made partakers, and feel the fruits and rewards that follow such godly living. So shall we know by proof, what profit and commodity doth come of giving alms, and succouring of the poor.

THE THIRD PART
OF THE HOMILY OF ALMSDEEDS

Ye HAVE ALREADY HEARD two parts of this Treatise of Almsdeeds: the first, how pleasant and acceptable before God the doing of them is; the second, how much it behoveth us, and how profitable it is, to apply ourselves unto them. Now in this third part will I take away that let, that hindereth many from doing them. There be many, that when they hear how acceptable a thing, in the sight of God, the giving of alms is, and how much God extendeth his favour towards them that are merciful, and what fruits and commodities doth come to them by it, they wish very gladly with themselves, that they also might obtain these benefits, and be counted such of God, as whom he would love or do for. But yet these men are with greedy covetousness so pulled back, that they will not bestow one halfpenny, or one piece of bread, that they might be thought worthy of God's benefits, and so to come into his favour. For they are evermore fearful and doubting, lest by often giving, although it were but a little at a time, they should consume their goods, and so impoverish themselves, that even themselves at length should not be able to live, but should be driven to beg, and live of other men's alms. And thus they seek excuses, to withhold themselves from the favour of God, and choose with pinching covetousness, rather to lean unto the devil, than by charitable mercifulness, either to come unto Christ, or to suffer Christ to come unto them. Oh that we had some cunning and skilful physician, that were able to purge them of this so pestilent an humour, that so sore infecteth, not their bodies, but their minds, and so by corrupting their souls, bringeth their bodies and souls into danger of hell fire!

Now, lest there be any such among us, dearly beloved, let us diligently search for that physician, which is Jesus Christ, and earnestly labour, that of his mercy he will truly instruct us, and give us a present medicine against so perilous a disease.

Hearken then, whosoever thou art, that fearest lest by giving to the poor, thou shouldest bring thyself to beggary. That which thou takest from thyself, to bestow upon Christ, can never be consumed and wasted away. Wherein thou shalt not believe me; but if thou have faith, and be a true Christian, believe the Holy Ghost, give credit to the authority of God's word, that thus teacheth. For thus saith the Holy Ghost by Salomon: *He that giveth unto the poor, shall never want.* Men suppose that by hoarding, and laying up still, they shall at length be rich, and that by distributing and laying out, although it be for most necessary and godly uses, they shall be brought to poverty. But the Holy Ghost, which knoweth all truth, teacheth us another lesson, contrary to this. He teacheth us, that there is a kind of dispending, that shall never diminish the stock, and a kind of saving that shall bring a man to extreme poverty. For, where he saith that the good almsman shall never have scarcity, he addeth, *But he that turneth away his eyes, from such as be in necessity, shall suffer great poverty himself.* How far different then is the judgement of man, from the judgement of the Holy Ghost!

The holy Apostle Paul, a man full of the Holy Ghost, and made privy even of the secret will of God, teacheth that the liberal almsgiver shall not thereby be impoverished. *He that ministereth*, saith he, *seed unto the sower, will minister also bread unto you for food; yea, he will multiply your seed, and increase the fruits of your righteousness.* He is not content here to advertise them that they shall not lack, but he showeth them also, after what sort God will provide for them. Even as he provideth seed for the sower, in multiplying it and giving great increase, so will he multiply their goods and increase them, that there shall be great abundance.

And lest we should think his sayings to be but words, and not truth, we have an example thereof, in the third Book of Kings, which doth confirm and seal it up as a most certain truth. The poor widow that received the banished Prophet of God, Elias, when as she had but an handful of meal, and a vessel and a little oil in a cruse, whereof she

Prov. 28:27

Ibid. 11:24

Ibid. 28:27

2 Cor. 9:10

1 Kings 17:8–16

would make a cake for herself and her son, that after they had eaten that they might die, because in that great famine there was no more food to be gotten; yet, when she gave part thereof unto Elias, and defrauded her own hungry belly, mercifully to relieve him, she was so blessed of God, that neither the meal nor the oil was consumed, all the time while that famine did last, but thereof both the Prophet Elias, she, and her son, were sufficiently nourished, and had enough.

Oh consider this example, ye unbelieving and faithless covetous persons, who discredit God's word, and think his power diminished! This poor woman, in the time of an extreme and long dearth, had but one handful of meal, and a little cruse of oil; her only son was ready to perish before her face, for hunger, and she herself like to pine away: and yet, when the poor Prophet came, and asked part, she was so mindful of mercifulness, that she forgat her own misery; and rather than she would omit the occasion given to give alms, and work a work of righteousness, she was content, presently to hazard her own and her son's life. And you who have great plenty of meats and drinks, great store of motheaten apparel, yea, many of you great heaps of gold and silver (and he that hath least hath more than sufficient, now in this time, when thanks be to God, no great famine doth oppress you, your children being well clothed and well fed, and no danger of death for famine to be feared), will rather cast doubts, and perils of unlikely penury, than you will part with any piece of your superfluities, to help feed and succour the poor, hungry, and naked Christ, that cometh to your doors a begging. This poor and seely widow never cast doubts, in all her misery, what want she herself should have; she never distrusted the promise that God had made to her, by the Prophet; but straightway went about to relieve the hungry Prophet of God, yea, preferring his necessity before her own. But we, like unbelieving wretches, before we will give one mite, we will cast a thousand doubts of danger, whether that will stand us in any stead, that we give to the poor; whether we should not have need of it any other time, and whether here it would not have been more profitably bestowed. So that it is not more hard to wrench a strong nail, as the proverb saith, out of a post, than to wring a farthing out of our fingers. There is neither the fear nor the love of God before our eyes; we will more esteem a mite, than we either desire God's kingdom, or fear the devil's dungeon. Hearken, therefore ye merciless misers, what will be the end of this your unmerciful dealing. As certainly as God nourished this poor widow, in the time of famine, and increased her little store, so that she had enough, and felt no penury when other pined away, so certainly shall God plague you, with poverty in the midst of plenty. Then, when other have abundance, and be fed to the full, you shall utterly waste and consume away yourselves; your store shall be destroyed, your goods plucked from you; all your glory and wealth shall perish; and that which when you had, you might have enjoyed yourself, in peace, and might have bestowed upon other most godly, ye shall seek with sorrow and sighs, and no where shall find it. For your unmercifulness towards other, ye shall find no man that will show mercy towards you. You that had stony hearts towards other, shall find all the creatures of God to youwards as hard as brass and iron.

Alas! what fury and madness doth possess our minds, that in a matter of truth and certainty, we will not give credit to the truth, testifying unto that which is most certain. Christ saith, that if we will first seek the kingdom of God, and do the works of righteousness thereof, we shall not be left destitute; all other things shall be given to us, plenteously. "Nay," say we, "I will first look that I be able to live myself, and be sure that I have enough, for me and mine; and if I have any thing over, I will bestow it to get God's favour, and the poor shall then have part with me." See, I pray you, the perverse judgement of men. We have more care to nourish the carcase, than we have fear to see our soul perish. And as Cyprian saith,

Matt. 6:33

Serm. de Eleemosyna.

> Whilst we stand in doubt, lest our goods fail in being over-liberal, we put it out of doubt, that our life and health faileth, in not being liberal at all. Whilst we are careful for diminishing our stock, we are altogether careless to diminish ourselves. We love mammon, and lose our souls. We fear lest our patrimony should perish from us, but we fear not lest we should perish for it.

Thus do we perversely love that we should hate, and hate that we should love; we be negligent where we should be careful, and careful where we need not.

This vain fear to lack ourselves, if we give to the poor, is much like the fear of children and fools, which when they see the bright glimpsing of a glass, they do imagine straightway, that it is the lightning, and yet the brightness of a glass never was the lightning. Even so, when we imagine that by spending upon the poor, a man may come to poverty, we are cast into a vain fear; for we never heard nor knew, that by that means any man came to misery, and was left destitute, and not considered of God. Nay, we read to the contrary in the Scripture, as I have before showed, and as by infinite testimonies and examples may be proved, that whosoever serveth God faithfully, and unfeignedly, in any vocation, God will not suffer him to decay, much less to perish. The Holy Ghost teacheth us by Salomon, that *the Lord will not suffer the soul of the righteous to perish for hunger.* And therefore David saith unto all them that are merciful, *Oh fear the Lord, ye that be his saints! for they that fear him lack nothing. The lions do lack and suffer hunger; but they which seek the Lord shall want no manner of thing that is good.* When Elias was in the desert, God

Prov. 10:3

Psalm 34:9, 10

1 Kings 17:2–6

fed him by the ministry of a raven, that evening and morning brought him sufficient victuals. When Daniel was shut up in the lions' den, God prepared meat for him, and sent it thither to him. And there was the saying of David fulfilled: *The lions do lack and suffer hunger; but they which seek the Lord shall want no good thing.* For while the lions, which should have been fed with his flesh, roared for hunger and desire of their prey, whereof they had no power, although it were present before them, he in the meantime, was fresh fed from God, that should with his flesh have filled the lions. So mightily doth God work, to preserve and maintain those whom he loveth; so careful is he, to feed them, who in any state or vocation, do unfeignedly serve him. And shall we now think that he will be unmindful of us, if we be obedient to his word, and according to his will, have pity upon the poor? He gives us all wealth, before we do any service for it; and will he see us lack necessaries, when we do him true service? Can a man think, that he that feedeth Christ, can be forsaken of Christ, and left without food? or will Christ deny earthly things, unto them whom he promiseth heavenly things for his true service?

Bel and the
Dragon 30–9

It cannot be, therefore, dear brethren, that by giving of alms, we should at any time want ourselves; or that we, which relieve other men's need, should ourselves be oppressed with penury. It is contrary to God's word; it repugneth with his promise; it is against Christ's property and nature to suffer it; it is the crafty surmise of the devil to persuade us it. Wherefore, stick not to give alms freely, and trust notwithstanding, that God's goodness will minister unto us sufficiency and plenty, so long as we shall live in this transitory life, and after our days here well spent in his service, and the love of our brethren, we shall be crowned with everlasting glory, to reign with Christ our Saviour in heaven. To whom with the Father, and the Holy Ghost, be all honour and glory, for ever. Amen.

AN HOMILY OR SERMON
CONCERNING
THE NATIVITY AND BIRTH
OF OUR SAVIOUR JESUS CHRIST

AMONG ALL THE CREATURES that God made, in the beginning of the world, most excellent and wonderful in their kind, there was none, as Scripture beareth witness, to be compared almost in any point, unto man; who, as well in body and in soul, exceeded all other, no less than the sun, in brightness and light, exceedeth every small and little star in the firmament. He was made according to the image and similitude of God; he was indued with all kind of heavenly gifts; he had no spot of uncleanness in him; he was sound and perfect in all parts, both outwardly and inwardly; his reason was uncorrupt; his understanding was pure and good; his will was obedient and godly; he was made altogether like unto God in righteousness, in holiness, in wisdom, in truth, to be short, in all kind of perfection. When he was thus created and made, Almighty God, in token of his great love towards him, chose out a special place of the earth for him, namely, Paradise; where he lived in all tranquillity and pleasure, having great abundance of worldly goods, and lacking nothing that he might justly require, or desire to have. For, as it is said, *God made him lord and ruler over all the works of his hands, that he should have under his feet all sheep and oxen, all beasts of the field, all fowls of the air, all fishes of the sea*, and use them always at his own pleasure, according as he should have need. Was not this a mirror of perfection? Was not this a full, perfect, and blessed estate? Could any thing else be well added hereunto? or greater felicity desired in this world?

Psalm 8:6–8

But, as the common nature of all men is, in time of prosperity and wealth to forget not only themselves, but also God, even so did this first man Adam: who having but one commandment at God's hand, namely, that he should not eat of the fruit of knowledge of good and ill, did notwithstanding most unmindfully, or rather most wilfully, break it, in forgetting the strait charge of his Maker, and giving ear to the crafty suggestion of that wicked serpent the devil. Whereby it came to pass, that as before he was blessed, so now he was accursed; as before he was loved, so now he was abhorred; as before he was most beautiful and precious, so now he was most vile and wretched, in the sight of his Lord and Maker. Instead of the image of God, he was now become the image of the devil; instead of the citizen of heaven, he was become the bond-slave of hell; having in himself no one part of his former purity and cleanness, but being altogether spotted and defiled; insomuch that now he seemed to be nothing else, but a lump of sin, and therefore, by the just judgement of God, was condemned to everlasting death.

This so great and miserable a plague, if it had only rested on Adam, who first offended, it had been so much the easier, and might the better have been borne. But it fell not only on him, but also on his posterity and children for ever; so that the whole brood of Adam's flesh should sustain the selfsame fall and punishment, which their forefather, by his offence, most justly had deserved. St Paul in the fifth chapter to the Romans saith, *By the offence of only Adam, the fault came upon all men to* Rom. 5:18, 19 *condemnation, and by one man's disobedience, many were made sinners.* By which words we are taught, that as in Adam all men universally sinned, so in Adam all men universally received the reward of sin, that is to say, became mortal, and subject unto death, having in themselves nothing but everlasting damnation, both of body and soul. *They became,* as David Psalm 14:1 saith, *corrupt and abominable; they went all out of the way; there was none that did good, no not one.* Oh what a miserable and woful state was this, that the sin of one man should destroy and condemn all men, that nothing in all the world might be looked for, but only pangs of death and pains of hell! Had it been any marvel if mankind had been utterly driven to desperation, being thus fallen from life to death, from salvation to destruction, from heaven to hell?

But behold the great goodness and tender mercy of God in his behalf. Albeit man's wickedness, and sinful behaviour, was such that it deserved not in any part to be forgiven, yet to the intent he might not be clean destitute of all hope, and comfort in time to come, he ordained a new covenant, and made a sure promise thereof, namely, that he would send a Messias, or Mediator, into the world, which should make inter-cession, and put himself as a stay between both parties, to pacify the wrath and indignation conceived against sin, and to deliver man out of the miserable curse, and cursed misery, whereunto he was fallen head-long, by disobeying the will and commandment of his only Lord and Maker. This covenant and promise was first made unto Adam himself, immediately after his fall, as we read in the third of Genesis, where God

Gen. 3:15

said to the serpent on this wise: *I will put enmity between thee and the woman, between thy seed and her seed: he shall break thine head, and thou shalt bruise his heel.* Afterward, the selfsame covenant was also more amply and plainly renewed, unto Abraham, where God promised him,

Gen. 13:3; 22:18
Gen. 26:4

that *in his seed all nations and families of the earth should be blessed.* Again, it was continued and confirmed unto Isaac, in the same form of words as it was before unto his father. And to the intent that mankind might not despair, but always live in hope, Almighty God never ceased to publish, repeat, confirm, and continue the same, by divers and sundry testimonies of his Prophets; who for the better persuasion of the thing, prophesied the time, the place, the manner, and circumstance of his birth, the afflictions of his life, the kind of his death, the glory of his resurrection, the receiving of his kingdom, the deliverance of his people,

Isai. 8:14
Mic. 5:2

with all other circumstances belonging thereunto. Esay prophesied that he should be born of a virgin, and called Emmanuel. Micheas prophesied that he should be born in Bethleem, a place of Jewry.

Ezek. 34:23, 24
Dan. 8:14
Zech 9:9
Mal. 4:5
Zech. [*sic*] 11:12, 13

Ezechiel prophesied that he should come of the stock and lineage of David. Daniel prophesied *that all nations and languages should serve him.* Zachary prophesied that he should come *in poverty, riding upon an ass.* Malachi prophesied that he should send Elias before him, which was John the Baptist. Jeremy prophesied that he should be sold for thirty pieces of silver, &c. And all this was done, that the promise and covenant of God, made unto Abraham and his posterity, concerning the redemption of the world, might be credited and fully believed.

Gal. 4:4

Now, as the Apostle Paul saith, *when the fullness of time was come,* that is, the perfection and course of years appointed from the beginning, then *God,* according to his former covenant and promise, *sent* a Messias, otherwise called a Mediator, into the world; not such a one as Moyses was, not such a one as Josua, Saul, or David was, but such a one as should deliver mankind from the bitter curse of the law, and make perfect satisfaction, by his death, for the sins of all people; namely, he sent *his* dear and only *Son,* Jesus Christ, *made,* as the Apostle saith, *of a woman, and made under the law, that he might redeem them that were in bondage of the law, and make them the children of God by adoption.* Was not this a wonderful great love, towards us that were his professed and open enemies? towards

Eph. 2:3
1 John 4:9, 10

us that were *by nature the children of wrath,* and firebrands of hell fire? *In this,* saith St John, *appeared the great love of God, that he sent his only begotten Son into the world, to save us,* when we were his extreme enemies. *Herein is love, not that we loved him, but that he loved us, and sent his Son to*

Rom. 5:6, 7, 8

be a reconciliation for our sins. St Paul also saith: *Christ, when we were yet of no strength, died for us, being ungodly. Doubtless a man will scarce die for a righteous man. Peradventure some one durst die for him of whom he hath received good. But God setteth out his love towards us, in that he sent Christ to die for us, when we were yet void of all goodness.* This and such other comparisons doth the Apostle use, to amplify and set forth the tender mercy, and great goodness of God, declared towards mankind, in sending down *a Saviour* from heaven, even *Christ the Lord.* Which one benefit among all other is so great and wonderful, that neither tongue can well express it, neither heart think it, much less give sufficient thanks to God for it.

Luke 2:11

But here is a great controversy between us and the Jews, whether the same Jesus, which was born of the Virgin Mary, be the true Messias and true Saviour of the world, so long promised and prophesied of before. They, as they are, and have always been, proud and *stiffnecked*, would never acknowledge him, until this day, but have looked and gaped for another to come. They have this fond imagination in their heads, that Messias shall come, not as Christ did, like a poor pilgrim and simple soul, riding upon an ass, but like a valiant and mighty king, in great royalty and honour; not as Christ did, with a few fishermen, and men of a small estimation in the world, but with a great army of strong men, with a great train of wise and noble men, as knights, lords, earls, dukes, princes, and so forth. Neither do they think that their Messias shall slanderously suffer death, as Christ did, but that he shall stoutly conquer, and manfully subdue all his enemies, and finally obtain such a kingdom on earth, as never was seen from the beginning. While they feign unto themselves, after this sort, a Messias of their own brain, they deceive themselves, and account Christ as an abject and fool of the world. Therefore *Christ crucified*, as St Paul saith, *is unto the Jews a stumbling-block, and to the Gentiles foolishness*; because they think it an absurd thing, and contrary to all reason, that a Redeemer, and Saviour of the whole world, should be handled after such sort as he was, namely, scorned, reviled, scourged, condemned, and last of all, cruelly hanged. This, I say, seemed in their eyes strange, and most absurd; and therefore neither they would at that time, neither will they as yet, acknowledge Christ to be their Messias, and Saviour. But we, dearly beloved, that hope and look to be saved, must both stedfastly believe, and also boldly confess, that the same Jesus, which was born of the Virgin Mary, was the true Messias, and Mediator between God and man, promised and prophesied of so long before. For as the Apostle writeth, *with the heart man believeth unto righteousness, and with the mouth, confession is made unto salvation.* Again in the same place: *Whosoever believeth in him, shall never be ashamed nor confounded.* Whereto agreeth also the testimony of St John, written in the fourth chapter of his first general Epistle, on this wise: *Whosoever confesseth that Jesus is the Son of God, he dwelleth in God, and God in him.*

Acts 7:51, 52

1 Cor. 1:23

Rom. 10:10, 11

1 John 4:15

There is no doubt but in this point all Christian men are fully and perfectly persuaded. Yet shall it not be a lost labour, to instruct and furnish you with a few places concerning this matter, that ye may be able

Luke 1:11–20, 26–37

to stop the blasphemous mouths of all them that most Jewishly, or rather devilishly, shall at any time go about, to teach or maintain the contrary. First, ye have the witness and testimony of the angel Gabriel, declared as well to Zachary the high priest, as also to the blessed Virgin. Secondly, ye have the witness and testimony of John the Baptist,

John 1:29

pointing unto Christ, and saying, *Behold the Lamb of God, that taketh away the sins of the world.* Thirdly, ye have the witness and testimony of

Matt. 17:5

God the Father, who thundered from heaven, and said, *This is my dearly beloved Son, in whom I am well pleased: hear him.* Fourthly, ye have the

Matt. 3:16

witness and testimony of the Holy Ghost, which came down from heaven, in manner of a white dove, and lighted upon him, in time of his

Matt 2:1–11;
Luke 2:25–38
John 1:40–9;
3:2; 6:69; 11:27

baptism. To these might be added a great number more, namely, the witness and testimony of the wise men that came to Herod, the witness and testimony of Simeon and Anna, the witness and testimony of Andrew and Philip, Nathanael and Peter, Nicodemus and Martha, with divers other: but it were too long to repeat all, and a few places are sufficient in so plain a matter, specially among them that are already persuaded. Therefore, if the privy imps of Antichrist, and crafty instruments of the devil, shall attempt to go about to withdraw you from this true Messias, and persuade you to look for another, that is not yet come, let them not in any case seduce you, but confirm yourselves with these, and such other testimonies of holy Scripture, which are so sure and certain, that all the devils in hell shall never be able to withstand them. For as truly as God liveth, so truly was Jesus Christ the true Messias, and Saviour of the world, even the same Jesus, which as this day, was born of the Virgin Mary, without all help of man, only by the power and operation of the Holy Ghost.

Concerning whose nature and substance, because divers and sundry heresies are risen in these our days, through the motion and suggestion of Satan, therefore it shall be needful, and profitable for your instruction, to speak a word or two also of this part. We are evidently taught in the Scripture, that our Lord and Saviour Christ, consisteth of two several natures; of his manhood, being thereby perfect man; and of his

John 1:14

Godhead, being perfect God. It is written: *The Word,* that is to say the

Rom. 8:3

second person in Trinity, *became flesh. God sending his own Son in the*

Phil. 2:6, 7, 8

similitude of sinful flesh, fulfilled those things which the law could not. Christ, being in form of God, took on him the form of a servant, and was made like

1 Tim. 3:16

unto man, being found in shape as a man. God was showed in flesh, justified in spirit, seen of angels, preached to the Gentiles, believed on in the world, and

1 Tim. 2:5

received up in glory. Also in another place: *There is one God, and one Mediator between God and man, even the man Jesus Christ.* These be plain places, for the proof and declaration of both natures, united and knit together in one Christ.

Let us diligently consider and weigh the works that he did, whiles he lived on earth, and we shall thereby also, perceive the selfsame thing to be most true. In that he did hunger and thirst, eat and drink, sleep and wake; in that he preached his Gospel to the people; in that he wept and sorrowed for Jerusalem; in that he paid tribute for himself and Peter; in that he died and suffered death; what other thing did he else declare but only this, that he was perfect man as we are? For which case he is called in holy Scripture, sometimes *the son of David*, sometimes *the Son of Man*, sometimes *the son of Mary*, sometimes *the son of Joseph*, and so forth. Now in that he forgave sins; in that he wrought miracles; in that he did cast out devils; in that he healed men with his only word; in that he knew the thoughts of men's hearts; in that he had the seas at his command-ment; in that he walked on the water; in that he rose from death to life; in that he ascended into heaven, and so forth; what other thing did he show therein, but only that he was perfect God, coequal with the Father as touching his Deity? Therefore he saith, *The Father and I are all one*: which is to be understood of his Godhead; for, as touching his manhood, he saith, *The Father is greater than I am.* _{Matt. 1:1; 16:13; Mark 6:3; John 6:42}

Matt. 1:1; 16:13;
Mark 6:3;
John 6:42

John 10:30

John 14:28

Where are now those Marcionites, that deny Christ to have been born in flesh, or to have been perfect man? Where are now those Arians, which deny Christ to have been perfect God, of equal substance with the Father? If there be any such, ye may easily reprove them, with these testimonies of God's word, and such other: whereunto I am most sure, they shall never be able to answer. For the necessity of our salvation did require such a Mediator, and Saviour, as under one person should be a partaker of both natures. It was requisite he should be man: it was also requisite he should be God. For as the transgression came by man, so was it meet the satisfaction should be made by man. And because *death*, according to St Paul, *is the* just *stipend* and reward *of sin*, therefore, to appease the wrath of God, and to satisfy his justice, it was expedient that our Mediator should be such a one, as might take upon him the sins of mankind, and sustain the due punishment thereof, namely, death. Moreover, he came in flesh, and in the selfsame flesh ascended into heaven, to declare and testify unto us, that all faithful people, which stedfastly believe in him, shall likewise come unto the same mansion place whereunto he, being our chief captain, is gone before. Last of all, he became man, that we thereby might receive the greater comfort, as well in our prayers as also in our adversity; considering with ourselves, that we have a Mediator, that is true man as we are, *who* also *is touched with our infirmities, and was tempted, even in like sort as we are.* For these and sundry other causes, it was most needful he should come, as he did, in the flesh. But because no creature, in that he is only a creature, hath or may have power to destroy death, and give life, to overcome hell and

Rom. 6:23

Heb. 2:14–17

John 14:2

Heb. 6:19–20

Heb. 4:15

purchase heaven, to remit sins and give righteousness, therefore it was needful, that our Messias, whose proper duty and office that was, should be not only full and perfect man, but also full and perfect God, to the intent he might more fully and perfectly, make satisfaction for mankind.

Matt. 3:17

God saith, *This is my wellbeloved Son, in whom I am well pleased.* By which place we learn, that Christ appeased and quenched the wrath of his Father, not in that he was only the Son of man, but much more in that he was the Son of God.

Thus ye have heard declared out of the Scriptures, that Jesus Christ was the true Messias, and Saviour of the world, that he was by nature and substance, perfect God and perfect man, and for what causes it was expedient he should be so.

Now, that we may be the more mindful, and thankful unto God in this behalf, let us briefly consider, and call to mind, the manifold and great benefits, that we have received by the nativity and birth, of this our Messias, and Saviour. Before Christ's coming into the world, all men

Deut. 32:5
Matt. 7:17;
Mark 4:5, 16;
Heb. 6:8;
Jer. 50:6;
Luke 15:6, 13;
17:10; Matt.
24:48; 25:26
Luke 16:8,
13:27; Matt.
12:34, 23:24;
Luke 1:79;
Rom. 5:12;
1 Cor.15:22
John 1:12

universally were nothing else, but *a wicked and crooked generation*, rotten and *corrupt trees, stony ground, full of brambles and briers, lost sheep, prodigal sons*, naughty and *unprofitable servants, unrighteous stewards, workers of iniquity, the brood of adders, blind guides, sitting in darkness and in the shadow of death*, to be short, nothing else but children of perdition, and inheritors of hell fire. To this doth St Paul bear witness in divers places of his Epistles, and Christ also himself in sundry places of his Gospel. But after he was once come down from heaven, and had taken our frail nature upon him, he made *all them that would receive him* truly, and believe his word, *good trees*, and *good ground, fruitful* and pleasant *branches,*

Matt. 7:17;
13:8, 23; John
15:2; Isai. 60:21;
John 12:36; Phil.
3:20; John 10:16;
Eph. 5:30; James
2:5; John 15:14;
Rom. 8:29;
1 Cor. 5:7
1 Pet. 2:24, 25, 9

children of light, citizens of heaven, sheep of his fold, members of his body, heirs of his kingdom, his true *friends* and *brethren*, sweet and lively bread, the elect and chosen *people of God.* For as St Peter saith, in his first Epistle and second chapter, *he bare our sins in his body upon the cross; he healed us and made us whole by his stripes; and, whereas before, we were sheep going astray, he by his coming brought us home again, to the true Shepherd, and Bishop of our souls*: making us *a chosen generation, a royal priesthood, an holy nation, a peculiar people* of God, in that *he died for our offences, and rose*

Rom. 4:25

again for our justification. St Paul to Timothy, the third chapter: *We were,*

Titus [*sic*] 3:3–7

saith he *in times past unwise, disobedient, deceived, serving divers lusts and pleasures, living in hatred, envy, maliciousness,* and so forth. *But after the loving-kindness of God our Saviour appeared towards mankind, not according to the righteousness that we had done, but according to his great mercy, he saved us, by the fountain of the new birth, and by the renewing of the Holy Ghost; which he poured upon us abundantly, through Jesus Christ our Saviour, that we being once justified by his grace, should be heirs of eternal life, through hope* and faith in his blood. In these and such other places, is set out before our eyes, as it were in a glass, the abundant grace of God, received in Christ Jesu; which is so much the more wonderful, because it came not of any desert of ours, but of his mere and tender mercy, even then when we were his extreme enemies.

But, for the better understanding, and consideration of this thing, let us behold the end of his coming: so shall we perceive, what great commodity and profit his nativity hath brought, unto us miserable and sinful creatures. The end of his coming was, *to save* and deliver *his people,* *to fufil the law* for us, *to bear witness unto the truth,* to teach and *preach the* *words of his Father, to give light unto the world, to call sinners to repentance, to* *refresh them that labour, and be heavy laden, to cast out the prince of this* *world, to reconcile us in the body of his flesh, to dissolve the works of the devil,* last of all, to become *a propitiation for our sins, and not for ours only, but* *also for the sins of the whole world.* These were the chief ends, wherefore Christ became man, not for any profit that should come to himself thereby, but only for our sakes; that we might understand the will of God, be partakers of his heavenly light, be delivered out of the devil's claws, released from the burden of sin, justified through faith in his blood, and finally, received up into everlasting glory, there to reign with him, for ever. Was not this a great and singular love of Christ towards mankind, that *being the express* and lively *image of God,* he would notwithstanding *humble himself, and take upon him the form of a servant,* and that only to save and redeem us? Oh how much are we bound to the goodness of God in this behalf! How many thanks and praises do we owe unto him, for this our salvation, wrought by his dear and only Son Christ! who became a pilgrim in earth, to make us citizens in heaven; who became the Son of man, to make us the sons of God; who became obedient to the law, to *deliver us from the curse of the law*; who *became poor,* *to make us rich*; vile to make us precious; subject to death, to make us live for ever. What greater love could we seely creatures desire, or wish to have at God's hands?

Therefore, dearly beloved, let us not forget this exceeding love of our Lord and Saviour; let us not show ourselves unmindful, or unthankful towards him: but let us love him, fear him, obey him, and serve him. Let us confess him with our mouths, praise him with our tongues, believe on him with our hearts, and glorify him with our good works. Christ is *the* *light*: let us receive the light. Christ is *the truth*: let us believe the truth. Christ is *the way*: let us follow the way. And, because he is our *only* *Master,* our only Teacher, our *only Shepherd* and Chief Captain, therefore let us become his servants, his scholars, his sheep, and his soldiers. As for sin, the flesh, the world, and the devil, whose servants and bondslaves we were, before Christ's coming, let us utterly cast them off, and defy them, as the chief and only enemies of our soul. And seeing

Matt. 1:21, 5:17;
John 18:37;
Luke 4:17–21, 43;
John 8:12; Matt.
9:13, 11:28;
John 12:31;
Col. 1:21, 22;
Heb. 10:10,
1 John 3:8;
Rom. 3:25;
1 John 2:2

Heb. 1:3

Phil. 2:7–8

Gal. 3:13; 4:4–5
2 Cor. 8:9

John 12:46; 14:6

Matt. 23:8, 10
John 6:68; 10:16

we are once delivered from their cruel tyranny, by Christ, let us never fall into their hands again, lest we chance to be in worse case than ever we were before. *Happy are they*, saith the Scripture, *that continue to the end. Be faithful*, saith God, *until death, and I will give thee a crown of life.* Again he saith in another place: *He that putteth his hand unto the plough, and looketh back, is not meet for the kingdom of God.* Therefore let us be strong, *stedfast, and unmoveable, abounding always in the works of the Lord.* Let us receive Christ, not for a time, but for ever; let us believe his word, not for a time, but for ever; let us become his servants, not for a time, but for ever; in consideration that he hath redeemed and saved us, not for a time, but for ever; and will receive us into his heavenly kingdom, there to reign with him, not for a time, but for ever. To him therefore, with the Father, and the Holy Ghost, be all honour, praise, and glory, for ever and ever. Amen.

Dan. 12:12;
Matt. 10:22
Rev. 2:10

Luke 9:62

1 Cor. 15:58

AN HOMILY FOR GOOD FRIDAY CONCERNING THE DEATH AND PASSION OF OUR SAVIOUR JESUS CHRIST

IT SHOULD NOT BECOME US, well beloved in Christ, being that people which be redeemed from the devil, from sin and death, and from everlasting damnation, by Christ, to suffer this time to pass forth without any meditation, and remembrance of that excellent work of our redemption, wrought as about this time, through the great mercy and charity of our Saviour Jesus Christ, for us wretched sinners and his mortal enemies. For if a mortal man's deed, done to the behoof of the commonwealth, be had in remembrance of us, with thanks for the benefit and profit which we receive thereby, how much more readily should we have in memory, this excellent act and benefit, of Christ's death! whereby he hath purchased for us, the undoubted pardon and forgiveness of our sins; whereby he made at one the Father of heaven with us, in such wise that he taketh us now for his loving children, and for the true *inheritors* Rom. 8:17 *with Christ*, his natural Son, of the kingdom of heaven.

And verily, so much more doth Christ's kindness appear unto us, in that it pleased him to deliver himself of all his godly honour, which he Phil. 2:6,7 was equally in with his Father in heaven, and to come down into this vale of misery, to be made mortal man, and to be in the state of a most low servant, serving us for our wealth and profit, us, I say, which were his sworn enemies, and which renounced his holy law and commandments, and followed the lusts and sinful pleasures of our corrupt nature; and yet, I say, did Christ put himself between God's deserved wrath and our sin, and rend that *obligation*, wherein we were in danger to God, and Col. 2:14 paid our debt. Our debt was a great deal too great for us to have paid; and without payment, God the Father could never be at one with us: neither was it possible to be loosed from this debt by our own ability. It pleased him therefore, to be the payer thereof, and to discharge us quite.

Who can now consider the grievous debt of sin, which could none otherwise be paid, but by the death of an innocent, and will not hate sin in his heart? If God hateth sin, so much that he would allow neither man nor angel for the redemption thereof, but only the death of his only and wellbeloved Son, who will not stand in fear thereof? If we, my friends, consider this, that for our sins, this most innocent Lamb was driven to death, we shall have much more cause to bewail ourselves, that we were the cause of his death, than to cry out of the malice and cruelty of the Jews, which pursued him to his death. We did the deeds wherefore he was thus stricken and wounded: they were only the ministers of our wickedness.

It is meet then, we should step low down into our hearts, and bewail our own wretchedness and sinful living. Let us know for a certainty, that if the most dearly beloved Son of God was thus punished, and stricken for the sin which he had not done himself, how much more ought we sore to be stricken, for our daily and manifold sins, which we commit against God, if we earnestly repent us not, and be not sorry for them. No man can love sin, which God hateth so much, and be in his favour. No man can say that he loveth Christ truly, and have his great enemy (sin, I mean, the author of his death), familiar and in friendship with him. So much do we love God and Christ, as we hate sin. We ought therefore to take great heed, that we be not favourers thereof, lest we be found enemies to God, and traitors to Christ. For not only they which nailed Christ upon the cross, are his tormentors and crucifiers, but all they, saith St Paul, *crucify again the Son of God*, as much as is in them, which do commit vice and sin, which brought him to his death.

Heb. 6:6

If *the wages of sin be death*, and death be everlasting, surely it is no small danger to be in service thereof. *If we live after the flesh*, and after the sinful lusts thereof, St Paul threateneth, yea Almighty God in St Paul threateneth, that *we shall* surely *die*. We can none otherwise live to God, but by dying to sin. *If Christ be in us, then is sin dead in us: and if the Spirit of God be in us, which raised Christ from death to life, so shall the same Spirit raise us, to the resurrection of everlasting life*. But if sin rule and reign in us, then is God, which is the fountain of all grace and virtue, departed from us; then hath the devil, and his ungracious spirit, rule and dominion in us. And surely, if in such miserable state we die, we shall not rise to life, but fall down to death and damnation, and that without end.

Rom. 6:23

Rom. 8:13

Rom. 6:11

Rom. 8:10,11

For Christ hath not so redeemed us from sin, that we may safely return thereto again; but he hath redeemed us, that we should forsake the motions thereof, and live to righteousness. Yea, we be therefore washed in our baptism, from the filthiness of sin, that we should live afterward in the pureness of life. In baptism, we promised to renounce the devil and his suggestions, we promised to be, *as obedient children,*

Christ hath not
so redeemed us
Titus 2:14
from sin, that we
should live in sin.

1 Pet. 1:14

always following God's will and pleasure. Then, if he be our Father indeed, let us give him his due honour. If we be his children, let us show him our obedience, like as Christ openly declared his obedience to his Father, which, as St Paul writeth, was *obedient even to the very death, the death of the cross.*

Mal. 1:6

Phil. 2:8

And this he did for us all that believe in him. For himself he was not punished; for he was pure and undefiled of all manner of sin. *He was wounded*, saith Esay, *for our wickedness, and striped for our sins*: he suffered the penalty of them himself, to deliver us from danger. *He bare*, saith Esay, *all our sores and infirmities, upon his own back*: no pain did he refuse to suffer in his own body, that he might deliver us from pain everlasting. His pleasure it was thus to do for us: we deserved it not. Wherefore, the more we see ourselves bound unto him, the more he ought to be thanked for us; yea, and the more hope may we take, that we shall receive all other good things of his hand, in that we have received the gift of his only Son, through his liberality. For *if God*, saith St Paul, *hath not spared his own Son* from pain and punishment, *but delivered him, for us all*, unto the death, *how should he not give us all other things with him*? If we want any thing, either for body or soul, we may lawfully and boldly approach to God, as to our merciful Father, to ask that we desire, and we shall obtain it. For such power is given us, *to be the children of God, so many as believe in Christ's name.* In his name whatsoever we ask, we shall have it granted. For so well pleased is the Father, Almighty God, with Christ his Son, that for his sake he favoureth us, and will deny us nothing. So pleasant was this sacrifice and oblation, of his Son's death, which he so obediently and innocently suffered, that he would take it for the only and full amends, for all the sins of the world. And such favour did he purchase, by his death, of his heavenly Father for us, that for the merit thereof (if we be true Christians indeed, and not in word only), we be now fully in God's grace again, and clearly discharged from our sin.

Isai. 53:4,5

Rom. 8:32

John 1:12

Matt. 21:22,
John 16:23–7

No tongue surely, is able to express the worthiness of this so precious a death. For in this standeth the continual pardon of our daily offences, in this resteth our justification, in this we be allowed, in this is purchased the everlasting health of all our souls; yea, *there is none other thing that can be named under heaven, to save our souls*, but this only work, of Christ's precious offering of his body, upon the altar of the cross. Certes, there can be no work of any mortal man, be he never so holy, that shall be coupled in merits with Christ's most holy act. For no doubt all our thoughts and deeds were of no value, if they were not allowed in the merits of Christ's death. All our righteousness is far unperfect, if it be compared with Christ's righteousness. For in his acts and deeds, there was no spot of sin, or of any unperfectness (and for this cause they were the more able to be the true amends of our unrighteousness); where our

Acts 4:12

Our deeds be
full of
imperfection.
Psalm 115:1

acts and deeds be full of imperfection and infirmities, and therefore nothing worthy of themselves, to stir God to any favour, much less to challenge the glory that is due to Christ's act and merit: for *not to us*, saith David, *not to us, but to thy Name give the glory, O Lord*.

Let us therefore, good friends, with all reverence glorify his Name; let us magnify and praise him for ever. For he hath dealt with us according to his great mercy; by himself hath he purchased our redemption. He thought it not enough to spare himself, and to send his angel to do this

Heb. 1:3

deed; but he would do it himself, that he might do it the better, and make it the more perfect redemption. He was nothing moved with the intolerable pains that he suffered, in the whole course of his long passion, to repent him thus to do good to his enemies; but he opened his heart for us, and bestowed himself wholly, for the ransoming of us. Let us therefore now open our hearts again to him, and study in our lives to be thankful to such a Lord, and evermore to be mindful of so great a benefit.

Yea, let us take up our cross with Christ, and follow him. His passion is not only the ransom, and whole amends for our sin, but it is also a

Acts 17:3,
Luke 24:26,46

most perfect example of all patience and sufferance. For if *it behoved Christ thus to suffer, and to enter into* the *glory* of his Father, how should it not become us, to bear patiently our small crosses of adversity, and the

1 Pet. 2:21

troubles of this world? For surely, as saith St Peter, *Christ therefore*

2 Tim. 2:12

suffered, to leave us an example to follow his steps. And *if we suffer with him,*

Rom. 8:18

we shall be sure also to reign with him, in heaven. *Not that the sufferance of this transitory life, should be worthy of that glory to come*; but gladly should

Matt. 5:10–12,
16

we be content to suffer, to be like Christ in our life, that so by our works we may *glorify our Father, which is in heaven*. And as it is painful and grievous to bear the cross of Christ, in the griefs and displeasures of this

Heb. 12:11

life, so it bringeth forth the joyful fruit of hope, in all them that be

Ibid.:1,2

exercised therewith. Let us not so much behold the pain, as the reward that shall follow that labour.

Nay, let us rather endeavour ourselves, in our sufferance, to endure innocently and guiltless, as our Saviour Christ did. For if we suffer for

James 1:4
1 Pet. 2:19–23

our deservings, then hath not *patience his perfect work* in us; *but if undeservingly we suffer* loss of goods and life, if we suffer to be evil spoken of, for the love of Christ, *this is thankful afore God*; for so did Christ

The patience of
Christ

suffer. *He never did sin, neither was there any guile found in his mouth. Yea, when he was reviled with taunts, he reviled not again; when he was wrongfully dealt with, he threatened not again,* nor revenged his quarrel, *but delivered*

Perfect patience

his cause to him that judgeth rightly. Perfect patience careth not what or how much it suffereth, nor of whom it suffereth, whether of friend or foe; but studieth to suffer innocently and without deserving. Yea, he in whom perfect charity is, careth so little to revenge, that he rather studieth to *do*

good for evil, to bless and say well of them that curse him, to pray for them that Matt. 5:44
pursue him, according to the example of our Saviour Christ, who is the
most perfect example and pattern, of all meekness and sufferance. The meekness of
Christ
Which, hanging upon his cross, in most fervent anguish, bleeding in
every part of his blessed body, being set in the midst of his enemies
and crucifiers, and notwithstanding the intolerable pains which they
saw him in, being of them mocked and scorned despitefully, without
all favour and compassion, had yet towards them such compassion in
heart, that he prayed to his Father of heaven for them, and said, *O
Father, forgive them, for they wote not what they do.* What patience was it Luke 23:34
also which he showed, when one of his own Apostles and servants,
which was put in trust of him, came to betray him unto his enemies
to the death! He said nothing worse to him but, *Friend, wherefore art* Matt. 26:50
thou come?

 Thus, good people, should we call to mind the great examples of
charity, which Christ showed in his passion, if we will fruitfully
remember his passion. Such charity and love should we bear one to
another, if we will be the true servants of Christ. *For if we love but them* Matt. 5:45–8
which love and say well by *us, what great thing is it that we do?* saith Christ:
do not the paynims and *open sinners so?* We must be more perfect in our
charity than thus, *even as our Father in heaven is perfect; which maketh the
light of his sun to rise upon the good and the bad, and sendeth his rain upon
the kind and unkind.* After this manner should we show our charity
indifferently, as well to one as to another, as well to friend as foe, *like* 1 Pet. 1:14
obedient children, after the example of our good Father in heaven. For, if
Christ was *obedient* to his Father, *even to the death,* and that the most Phil. 2:8
shameful death (as the Jews esteemed it), *the death of the cross,* why
should not we be obedient to God, in lower points of charity and
patience?

 Let us forgive then our neighbours their small faults, *as God for* Eph. 4:32
Ecclus. 28:1–5,
Matt. 18:35
Christ's sake hath forgiven us our great. It is not meet, that we should
crave forgiveness of our great offences, at God's hands, and yet will not
forgive the small trespasses of our neighbours against us. We do call for
mercy in vain, if we will not show mercy to our neighbours. For if we will
not put wrath and displeasure forth of our hearts, to our Christian
brother, no more will God forgive the displeasure and wrath, that our
sins have deserved afore him. For under this condition doth God forgive Matt. 6:14, 15
us, if we forgive other. It becometh not Christian men to be hard one to
another, nor yet to think their neighbour unworthy to be forgiven. For
howsoever unworthy he is, yet is Christ worthy to have thee do thus
much for his sake: he hath deserved it of thee, that thou shouldest
forgive thy neighbour. And God is also to be obeyed, which commandeth us to forgive, if we will have any part of the pardon, which our

Saviour Christ purchased once of God the Father, by shedding of his precious blood. Nothing becometh Christ's servants so much, as mercy and compassion.

James 5:16

Let us then be favourable one to another: *and pray we one for another, that we may be healed,* from all frailties of our life, the less to offend one the other; and that we may be *of one mind, and one spirit,* agreeing together in brotherly love and concord, even *like the dear children of God.*

Phil. 1:27, 2:2;
Eph. 5:1, 2

By these means shall we move God to be merciful to our sins. Yea, and we shall be hereby the more ready to receive our Saviour and Maker, in his blessed Sacrament, to our everlasting comfort, and health of soul. Christ delighteth to enter, and to dwell in that soul, where love and charity ruleth, and where peace and concord is seen. For thus writeth St John: *God is charity; he that abideth in charity, abideth in God, and God in*

1 John 4:16

him. And by this, saith he, *we shall know that we be of God, if we love our*

1 John 3:19, 14,
15; 2:11

brothers. Yea, and *by this shall we know that we be shifted from death to life, if we love one another. But he which hateth his brother,* saith the same Apostle, *abideth in death,* even in the danger of everlasting death; and is moreover the child of damnation, and of the devil, cursed of God, and hated (so long as he so remain) of God, and of all his heavenly company. For as peace and charity make us the blessed children of Almighty God, so doth hatred and envy make us the cursed children of the devil.

God give us all grace to follow Christ's example, in peace and charity, in patience and sufferance; that we now may have him our guest, to enter and dwell within us, so as we may be in full surety, having such a pledge of our salvation. If we have him and his favour, we may be sure that we

Rom. 8:34

have the favour of God, by his means. For he sitteth on the right hand of his Father, as our proctor and attorney, pleading and suing for us, in all our needs and necessities. Wherefore, if we want any gift of godly wisdom, we may ask it of God for Christ's sake, and we shall have it.

Let us consider and examine ourselves, in what want we be, concerning this virtue of charity and patience. If we see that our hearts be nothing inclined thereunto, in forgiving them that have offended against us, then let us knowledge our want, and wish of God to have it. But, if we want it, and see in ourselves no desire thereunto, verily, we be in a dangerous case before God, and have need to make much earnest prayer to God, that we may have such an heart changed, to the grafting in of a new. For unless we forgive other, we shall never be forgiven of God. No, not all the prayers and merits of other, can pacify God unto us, unless we be at peace, and at one, with our neighbour: nor all our deeds and good works, can move God to forgive us our debts to him, except we forgive to other. He setteth more by mercy than by sacrifice. Mercy

Hos. 6:6,
Mic. 6:6–8,
Matt. 9:13

moved our Saviour Christ to suffer for his enemies: it becometh us then, to follow his example. For it shall little avail us, to have in meditation the fruits and price of his passion, to magnify them, and to delight or trust to them, except we have in mind his examples in passion, to follow them. If we thus therefore consider Christ's death, and will stick thereto with fast faith, for the merit and deserving thereof, and will also frame ourselves, in such wise to bestow ourselves, and all that we have, by charity, to the behoof of our neighbour, as Christ spent himself wholly for our profit: then do we truly remember Christ's death; and being thus followers of Christ's steps, we shall be sure to follow him, thither where he sitteth now, with the Father, and the Holy Ghost. To whom be all honour, and glory. Amen.

THE SECOND HOMILY CONCERNING
THE DEATH AND PASSION
OF OUR SAVIOUR CHRIST

THAT WE MAY THE BETTER CONCEIVE the great mercy and goodness of our Saviour Christ, in suffering death, universally for all men, it behoveth us to descend into the bottom of our conscience, and deeply to consider the first and principal cause, wherefore he was compelled so to do.

Gen. 3:17–19

When our great-grandfather Adam had broken God's commandment, in eating the apple, forbidden him in Paradise, at the motion and suggestion of his wife, he purchased thereby, not only to himself, but also to his posterity for ever, the just wrath and indignation of God; who according to his former sentence, pronounced at the giving of the commandment, condemned both him and all his to everlasting death, both of body and soul. For it was said unto him: *Thou shalt eat freely of*

Gen. 2:16, 17

every tree in the garden: but as touching the tree of knowledge of good and ill, thou shalt in no wise eat of it; for in what hour soever thou eatest thereof, thou shalt die the death. Now, as the Lord had spoken, so it came to pass. Adam took upon him to eat thereof, and in so doing he died the death; that is to say, he became mortal, he lost the favour of God, he was cast out of Paradise, he was no longer a citizen of heaven, but a firebrand of hell, and a bondslave to the devil. To this doth our Saviour bear witness

Luke 15:4

in the Gospel, calling us *lost sheep*, which have *gone astray*, and wandered

1 Pet. 2:25

from *the* true *Shepherd of our souls.* To this also doth St Paul bear witness,

Rom. 5:12, 18

saying that *by the offence of only Adam, death came upon all men to condemnation.* So that now neither he, nor any of his, had any right, or interest at all, in the kingdom of heaven, but were become plain reprobates and castaways, being perpetually damned, to the everlasting pains of hell fire.

In this so great misery and wretchedness, if mankind could have recovered himself again, and obtained forgiveness at God's hands, then had his case been somewhat tolerable; because he might have attempted some way, how to deliver himself from eternal death. But there was no way left unto him; he could do nothing that might appease God's wrath; he was altogether *unprofitable* in that behalf; *there was none that did good, no not one*. And how then could he work his own salvation? Should he go about to pacify God's heavy displeasure, by offering up burnt sacrifices, according as it was ordained in the old Law? by offering up the blood of oxen, the blood of calves, the blood of goats, the blood of lambs, and so forth? Oh these things were of no force nor strength to take away sins; they could not put away the anger of God; they could not cool the heat of his wrath, nor yet bring mankind into favour again: they were but only figures, and shadows of things to come, and nothing else. Read the Epistle to the Hebrews: there shall you find this matter largely discussed: there shall you learn in most plain words, that the bloody sacrifice of the old Law was unperfect, and not able to deliver man from the state of damnation, by any means: so that mankind in trusting thereunto, should trust to a broken staff, and in the end deceive himself. What should he then do? Should he go about to observe and keep the law of God, divided into two tables, and so purchase to himself eternal life? Indeed, if Adam and his posterity had been able, to satisfy and fulfil the law perfectly, in loving God above all things, and their neighbour as themselves, then should they have easily quenched the Lord's wrath, and escaped the terrible sentence of eternal death, pronounced against them by the mouth of Almighty God. For it is written, *Do this, and thou shalt live*; that is to say, "Fulfil my commandments, keep thyself upright and perfect in them, according to my will; then shalt thou live, and not die." Here is eternal life promised, with this condition: so that they keep and observe the law. But such was the frailty of mankind, after his fall, such was his weakness and imbecility, that he could not walk uprightly in God's commandments, though he would never so fain; but daily and hourly, fell from his bounden duty, offending the Lord his God divers ways, to the great increase of his condemnation; insomuch that the Prophet David crieth out, on this wise: *All have gone astray, all are become unprofitable; there is none that doeth good, no not one*. In this case what profit could he have by the law? None at all. For as St James saith, *he that shall observe the whole law, and yet faileth in one point, is become guilty of all*. And in the book of Deuteronomy it is written, *Cursed be he*, saith God, *which abideth not in all things that are written in the book of the law, to do them*. Behold the law bringeth a curse with it, and maketh us guilty, not because it is of itself naught or unholy (God forbid we should so think), but because the frailty of our sinful flesh is such, that we can never fulfil it, according to the perfection that the Lord requireth. Could Adam then, think you, hope or trust to be saved by the law? No, he could not: but the more he looked on the law, the more he saw his own damnation, set before his eyes, as it were in a most clear glass. So that now of himself

Psalm 53:3,
Rom. 3:12

Heb. 9:9, 12

Heb. 10:1–4, 11

Luke 10:28

Psalm 53:3

James 2:10

Deut. 27:26,
Gal. 3:10

Rom. 4:15

Rom. 7:12–23

he was most wretched and miserable, destitute of all hope, and never able to pacify God's heavy displeasure, nor yet to escape the terrible judgement of God, whereinto he and all his posterity, were fallen, by disobeying the strait commandment of the Lord their God.

Rom. 11:33

But oh the abundant riches of God's great mercy! Oh the unspeakable goodness of his heavenly wisdom! When all hope of righteousness was past on our part; when we had nothing in ourselves, whereby we might quench his burning wrath, and work the salvation of our own souls, and rise out of the miserable estate wherein we lay; then, even then, did Christ, the Son of God, by the appointment of his Father, come down

Isai. 53:12

from heaven, to be wounded for our sakes, to be *reputed with the wicked*, to be condemned unto death, to take upon him the reward of our sins,

Isai. 53:4, 5

and to give his body to be broken on the cross for our offences. *He*, saith the Prophet Esay, meaning Christ, *hath borne our infirmities, and hath carried our sorrows; the chastisement of our peace was upon him, and by his*

2 Cor. 5:21

stripes are we made whole. St Paul likewise saith, *God made him a sacrifice for our sins, which knew not sin, that we should be made the righteousness of God by him*. And St Peter, most agreeably writing in this behalf, saith:

1 Pet. 3:18

Christ hath once died, and suffered for our sins, the just for the unjust, &c. To these might be added an infinite number of other places, to the same effect; but these few shall be sufficient, for this time.

Now then, as it was said at the beginning, let us ponder and weigh the cause of his death, that thereby, we may be the more moved to glorify him, in our whole life. Which if you will have comprehended briefly, in one word, it was nothing else on our part, but only the transgression, and sin of mankind. When the angel came, to warn Joseph that he

Matt. 1:20, 21

should not fear to take Mary to his wife, did he not therefore will the child's name to be called *Jesus*, because he should *save his people from their sins*? When John the Baptist preached Christ, and showed him unto the

John 1:29

people with his finger, did he not plainly say unto them, *Behold the Lamb of God, which taketh away the sins of the world*? When the woman of Canaan besought Christ to help her daughter, which was possessed

Matt. 15:22, 24

with a devil, did he not openly confess, that he was *sent to save the lost sheep of the house of Israel*, by giving his life for their sins? It was sin then, O man, even thy sin, that caused Christ, the only Son of God, to be crucified in the flesh, and to suffer the most vile and slanderous death, of the cross. If thou haddest kept thyself upright, if thou haddest observed

Rom. 5:12–19

the commandments, if thou haddest not presumed to transgress the will of God, in thy first father Adam, then Christ, *being in form of God*,

Phil. 2:6, 7

needed not *to have taken upon him the shape of a servant*; being immortal

John 6:32, 35

in heaven, he needed not to become mortal on earth; being *the true bread*

John 4:10, 7:37
Rev. 21:6

of the soul, he needed not to hunger; being *the* healthful *water of life*, he

John 11:25

needed not to thirst; being *life* itself, he needed not to have suffered death. But to these, and many other such extremities, was he driven by thy sin, which was so manifold and great, that God could be only pleased in him, and no other.

Canst thou think of this, O sinful man, and not tremble within thyself? Canst thou hear it quietly, without remorse of conscience, and sorrow of heart? Did Christ suffer his passion for thee, and wilt thou show no compassion towards him? While Christ was yet hanging on the cross, and yielding up the ghost, the Scripture witnesseth, that *the veil of the Temple did rend in twain*, that *the earth did quake*, that *the stones clave asunder*, that *the graves did open, and the dead bodies rise*; and shall the heart of man be nothing moved, to remember how grievously and cruelly he was handled of the Jews, for our sins? shall man show himself to be more hardhearted than stones? to have less compassion than dead bodies? Call to mind, O sinful creature, and set before thine eyes, Christ crucified; think thou seest his body, stretched out in length upon the cross, his head crowned with sharp thorn, his hands and his feet pierced with nails, his heart opened with a long spear, his flesh rent and torn with whips, his brows sweating water and blood; think thou hearest him now, crying in an intolerable agony to his Father, and saying, *My God, my God, why hast thou forsaken me?* Couldest thou behold this woful sight, or hear this mournful voice without tears, considering that he suffered all this, not for any desert of his own, but only for the grievousness of thy sins? Oh that mankind should put the everlasting Son of God to such pains! Oh that we should be the occasion of his death, and the only cause of his condemnation! May we not justly cry, Woe worth the time that ever we sinned?

O my brethren, let this image of Christ crucified be always printed in our hearts; let it stir us up to the hatred of sin, and provoke our minds to the earnest love of Almighty God. For why, is not sin, think you, a grievous thing in his sight, seeing for the transgressing of God's precept, in eating of one apple, he condemned all the world to perpetual death, and would not be pacified, but only with the blood of his own Son? True, yea, most true is that saying of David: *Thou, O Lord, hatest all them that work iniquity; neither shall the wicked and evil man, dwell with thee.* By the mouth of his Prophet Esay, he crieth mainly out, against sinners, and saith: *Woe be unto you that draw iniquity with cords of vanity, and sins as it were with cart ropes.* Did not God give a plain token, how greatly he hated and abhorred sin, when he drowned all the world, save only eight persons? when he destroyed Sodom and Gomorre with fire and brimstone? when in the three days' space, he killed with pestilence threescore and ten thousand, for David's offence? when he drowned Pharao and all his host, in the Red Sea? when he turned Nabuchodonozor the King, into the form of a brute beast, creeping upon all four? when he suffered

Matt. 27:51, 52

Matt. 27:46,
Psalm 22:1

Psalm 5:4

Isai. 5:18

Gen. 7

Gen. 19:24
2 Sam. 24:13, 15
Exod. 14:28

Dan. 4:33

2 Sam. 17:23;
Acts 1:18,
Matt. 27:5
Achitophel and Judas to hang themselves, upon the remorse of sin, which was so terrible to their eyes? A thousand such examples are to be found in Scripture, if a man would stand to seek them out. But what need we? This one example which we have now in hand, is of more force, and ought more to move us, than all the rest. Christ, being the Son of God, and perfect God himself, who never committed sin, was compelled to come down from heaven, and to give his body to be bruised and broken on the cross, for our sins. Was not this a manifest token of God's great wrath, and displeasure towards sin, that he could be pacified by no other means, but only by the sweet and precious blood of his dear Son? O sin, sin, that ever thou shouldest drive Christ to such extremity! Woe worth the time that ever thou camest into the world! But what booteth it now to bewail? Sin is come, and so come that it cannot be avoided. There is no man living, no, not the justest man on the earth,

Prov. 24:16
but he *falleth seven times a day*, as Salomon saith. And our Saviour Christ, although he hath delivered us from sin, yet not so that we shall be free from committing sin, but so that it shall not be imputed to our

Rom. 8:1
Rom. 6:23
condemnation. He hath taken upon him *the just reward of sin*, which was *death*, and by death, hath overthrown death, that we, believing in him, might live for ever, and not die. Ought not this to engender extreme hatred of sin in us, to consider that it did violently, as it were, pluck God out of heaven, and make him feel the horrors and pains of death? Oh that we would sometimes consider this, in the midst of our pomps and pleasures! It would bridle the outrageousness of the flesh; it would abate and assuage our carnal affections; it would restrain our fleshly appetites, that we should not run at randon, as we commonly do. To commit sin, wilfully and desperately, without fear of God, is nothing else but to crucify Christ anew, as we are expressly taught in the Epistle to the

Heb. 6:6
Hebrews. Which thing if it were deeply printed in all men's hearts, then should not sin reign everywhere so much as it doth, to the great grief and torment of Christ, now sitting in heaven.

Let us therefore remember, and always bear in mind Christ crucified, that thereby we may be inwardly moved, both to abhor sin throughly, and also, with an earnest and zealous heart, to love God. For this is another fruit, which the memorial of Christ's death ought to work in us:

John 3:16
an earnest and unfeigned love towards God. *So God loved the world*, saith St John, *that he gave his only begotten Son, that whosoever believeth in him, should not perish, but have life everlasting*. If God declared so great love towards us, his seely creatures, how can we of right but love him again? Was not this sure pledge of his love, to give us his own Son from heaven? He might have given us an angel if he would, or some other creature, and yet should his love have been far above our deserts. Now he gave us, not an angel, but his Son. And what Son? His only Son, his natural Son,

his wellbeloved Son, even that Son whom he had made Lord and Ruler over all things. Was not this a singular token of great love? But to whom did he give him? He gave him to the whole world, that is to say, to Adam and all that should come after him. O Lord, what had Adam or any other man deserved at God's hands, that he should give us his own Son? We were all miserable persons, sinful persons, damnable persons, justly driven out of paradise, justly excluded from heaven, justly condemned to hell fire: and yet (see a wonderful token of God's love!) he gave us his only begotten Son, us, I say, that were his extreme and deadly enemies; that we, by virtue of his blood, shed upon the cross, might be clean purged from our sins, and made righteous again in his sight. Who can choose but marvel, to hear that God should show such unspeakable love towards us, that were his deadly enemies? Indeed, O mortal man, thou oughtest of right to marvel at it, and to acknowledge therein, God's great goodness and mercy towards mankind; which is so wonderful, that no flesh, be it never so worldly wise, may well conceive it or express it. For as St Paul testifieth, *God* greatly *commendeth* and setteth out *his love*   Rom. 5:8
towards us, in that he sent his Son, Christ, to die for us, when we were yet sinners, and open enemies of his Name. If we had in any manner of wise deserved it at his hands, then had it been no marvel at all; but there was no desert on our part, wherefore he should do it. Therefore, thou sinful creature, when thou hearest that God gave his Son to die, for the sins of the world, think not he did it for any desert or goodness that was in thee, for thou wast then the bondslave of the devil; but fall down upon thy knees, and cry with the Prophet David, *O Lord, what is man, that thou art*   Psalm 8:4
so mindful of him? or the son of man, that thou so regardest him? And, seeing he hath so greatly loved thee, endeavour thyself to love him again *with all*   Luke 10:27;
thy heart, with all thy soul, and with all thy strength, that therein thou   Deut. 6:5
mayest appear not to be unworthy of his love. I report me to thine own conscience, whether thou wouldest not think thy love ill bestowed, upon him that could not find in his heart, to love thee again? If this be true, as it is most true, then think how greatly it belongeth to thy duty, to love God: which hath so greatly loved thee, that he hath not spared his own only Son, from so cruel and shameful a death, for thy sake.

And hitherto concerning the cause of Christ's death and passion, which as it was on our part most horrible and grievous sin, so on the other side, it was the free gift of God, proceeding of his mere and tender love towards mankind, without any merit or desert of our part. The Lord for his mercies' sake grant, that we never forget this great benefit, of our salvation in Christ Jesu, but that we always show ourselves thankful for it, abhorring all kind of wickedness and sin, and applying our minds wholly to the service of God, and the diligent keeping of his commandments.

Now resteth to show unto you, how to apply Christ's death and passion to our comfort, as a medicine to our wounds, so that it may work the same effect in us wherefore it was given, namely, the health and salvation of our souls. For as it profiteth a man nothing to have salve, unless it be well applied to the part affected, so the death of Christ shall stand us in no force, unless we apply it to ourselves, in such sort as God hath appointed. Almighty God commonly worketh by means, and in this thing he hath also ordained a certain mean, whereby we may take fruit and profit, to our souls' health. What mean is that? Forsooth it is faith; not an unconstant or wavering faith, but a sure, stedfast, grounded, and unfeigned faith. *God sent his Son into the world*, saith St John. To what end? *That whosoever believed in him should not perish, but have life everlasting.* Mark these words: *that whosoever believed in him.* Here is the mean whereby we must obtain eternal life; namely, faith. *For,* as St Paul teacheth, in his Epistle to the Romans, *with the heart man believeth, unto righteousness, and with the mouth confession is made, unto salvation.* Paul, being demanded of the keeper of the prison, *what he should do to be saved*, made this answer: *Believe in the Lord Jesus; so shalt thou and thine house be both saved.* After the Evangelist had described, and set forth unto us at large, the life and the death of the Lord Jesus, in the end he concludeth with these words: *These things are written, that we may believe Jesus Christ to be the Son of God, and through faith, obtain eternal life.*

To conclude with the words of St Paul, which are these: *Christ is the end of the law, unto salvation for every one that doth believe.* By this then you may well perceive, that the only mean, and instrument of salvation, required of our parts, is faith: that is to say, a sure trust and confidence in the mercies of God, whereby we persuade ourselves, that God both hath forgiven* and will forgive our sins, that he hath accepted us again into his favour, that he hath released us, from the bonds of damnation, and received us again, into the number of his elect people, not for our merits or deserts, but only and solely, for the merits of Christ's death and passion, who became man for our sakes, and humbled himself to sustain the reproach of the cross, that we thereby might be saved, and made inheritors of the kingdom of heaven. This faith is required at our hands; and this if we keep stedfastly in our hearts, there is no doubt but we shall obtain salvation at God's hands, as did Abraham, Isaac, and Jacob, of whom the Scripture saith, that *they believed, and it was imputed unto them for righteousness.* Was it imputed unto them? and shall it not be imputed unto us? Yes, *if we have* the same *faith* as they had, *it shall be* as truly *imputed unto us* for righteousness, as it was unto them. For it is one faith, that must save both us and them, even a sure and stedfast faith in

Margin references: John 3:16; Rom. 10:10; Acts 16:30, 31; John 20:31; Rom. 10:4; Gen. 15:6, Rom. 4:3, 9, 22, 24

* forgiven *editorial addition*

Christ Jesu; who, as ye have heard, came into the world for this end, *that* John 3:16
whosoever believe in him, should not perish, but have life everlasting.

But here we must take heed that we do not halt with God through an
unconstant and wavering faith, but that it be strong and stedfast to our
lives' end. *He that wavereth*, saith St James, *is like a wave of the sea; neither* James 1:6, 7
let that man think that he shall obtain any thing at God's hands. Peter,
coming to Christ upon the water, because he fainted in faith, was in Matt. 14:28–31
danger of drowning. So we, if we begin to waver or doubt, it is to be
feared lest we shall sink, as Peter did, not into the water, but into the
bottomless pit of hell fire. Therefore I say unto you, that we must
apprehend the merits of Christ's death and passion, by faith; and that
with a strong and stedfast faith: nothing doubting but that Christ, by his Heb. 10:10–18
one oblation, and once offering of himself upon the cross, hath taken
away our sins, and hath restored us again into God's favour, so fully and
perfectly, that no other sacrifice for sin shall hereafter be requisite or
needful, in all the world.

Thus have ye heard in few words, the mean whereby we must apply
the fruits and merits of Christ's death unto us, so that it may work the
salvation of our souls: namely, a sure, stedfast, perfect, and grounded
faith. For, as all they which beheld stedfastly the brasen serpent, were Num. 21:9,
John 3:14, 15
healed and delivered, at the very sight thereof, from their corporal
diseases, and bodily stings, even so, all they which behold Christ
crucified, with a true and lively faith, shall undoubtedly be delivered
from the grievous wounds of the soul, be they never so deadly or many
in number. Therefore, dearly beloved, if we chance at any time, through
frailty of the flesh, to fall into sin, as it cannot be chosen but we must
needs fall often; and if we feel the heavy burden thereof, to press our
souls, tormenting us with the fear of death, hell, and damnation, let us
then use that mean, which God hath appointed, in his word, to wit, the
mean of faith, which is the only instrument of salvation now left unto us.
Let us stedfastly behold Christ crucified, with the eyes of our heart. Let
us only trust to be saved, by his death and passion, and to have our sins
clean washed away, through his most precious blood; that in the end of
the world, when he shall come again to judge both the quick and the
dead, he may receive us into his heavenly kingdom, and place us in the
number of his elect and chosen people, there to be partakers of that
immortal and everlasting life, which he hath purchased unto us, by
virtue of his bloody wounds. To him therefore, with the Father, and the
Holy Ghost, be all honour and glory, world without end. Amen.

AN HOMILY OF THE RESURRECTION OF OUR SAVIOUR JESUS CHRIST

FOR EASTER DAY

IF EVER AT ANY TIME, the greatness or excellency of any matter, spiritual or temporal, hath stirred up your minds, to give diligent ear, good Christian people, and wellbeloved in our Lord and Saviour Jesu Christ, I doubt not, but that I shall have you now, at this present season, most diligent and ready hearers of the matter, which I have at this time to open unto you. For I come to declare that great and most comfortable article of our Christian religion and faith: the resurrection of our Lord Jesus.

So great surely is the matter of this article, and of so great weight and importance, that is was thought worthy, to keep our said Saviour still on earth forty days, after he was risen from death to life, to the confirmation and stablishment thereof, in the hearts of his disciples. So that, as Luke clearly testifieth, in the first chapter of the Acts of the Apostles, he was conversant with his disciples, by the space of forty days continually together, to the intent he would in his person, being now glorified, teach and instruct them, which should be the teachers of other, fully and in most absolute and perfect wise, the truth of this most Christian article, which is the ground and foundation of our whole religion, before he would ascend up to his Father, into the heavens, there to receive the glory of his most triumphant conquest and victory.

Assuredly, so highly comfortable is this article to our consciences, that it is even the very lock and key, of all our Christian religion and faith. *If it were not true*, saith the holy Apostle Paul, *that Christ rose again, then our preaching were in vain, your faith which ye have received were but void, ye were yet in* the danger of *your sins. If Christ be not risen again*, saith the Apostle, *then are they* in very evil case, and utterly *perished, that be entered their sleep in Christ; then are we the most miserable of all men, which have our hope fixed in Christ*, if he be yet under the power of death, and as yet not restored to his bliss again. *But now is he risen again from death*, saith the Apostle Paul, *to be the firstfruits of them that be asleep*, to the

1 Cor. 15:14–22

intent to raise them to everlasting life again. Yea, if it were not true that Christ is risen again, then were it neither true that he is ascended up to heaven; nor that he sent down from heaven unto us the Holy Ghost; nor that he sitteth on the right hand of his heavenly Father, having the rule of heaven and earth, reigning (as the Prophet saith) *from sea to sea*; nor that he should after this world, be the judge as well of the living as of the dead, to give reward to the good, and judgement to the evil.

Psalm 72:8

That these links therefore of our faith, should all hang together, in stedfast establishment and confirmation, it pleased our Saviour, not straightway to withdraw himself, from the bodily presence and sight of his disciples; but he chose out forty days, wherein he would declare unto them, by manifold and most strong arguments and tokens, that he had conquered death, and that he was also truly risen again to life. *He began, saith Luke, at Moses and all the Prophets, and expounded unto them, the prophecies that were written in all the Scriptures of him*, to the intent to confirm the truth of his resurrection, long before spoken of; which he verified indeed, as it is declared very apparently and manifestly, by his oft appearance, to sundry persons at sundry times. First, he sent his angels to the sepulchre, which did show unto certain women the empty grave, saving that the burial linen remained therein; and by these signs were these women fully instructed, that he was risen again, and so did they testify it openly. After this, Jesus himself appeared to Mary Magdalene, and after that to other certain women; and straight afterward he appeared to Peter, then to the two disciples which were going to Emmaus. He appeared to the disciples also, as *they were gathered together, for fear of the Jews, the doors shut*. At another time he was seen at the sea of Tiberias, of Peter and Thomas, and of other disciples, when they were fishing. He was seen of more than five hundred brethren, in the mount of Galilee, where Jesus appointed them to be by his angel, when he said, *Behold, he shall go before you into Galilee; there shall ye see him, as he hath said unto you*. After this he appeared unto James; and last of all he was visibly seen of all the Apostles, at such time as he was taken up, into heaven. Thus at sundry times he showed himself, after he was risen again, to confirm and stablish this article. And in these revelations, sometimes he showed them his hands, his feet, and his side, and bade them touch him, that they should not take him for a ghost or a spirit; sometimes he also did eat with them; but ever was he talking with them, of the everlasting kingdom of God, to assure the truth of his resurrection. For *then he opened their understanding, that they might perceive the Scriptures, and said unto them, "Thus it is written, and thus it behoved Christ to suffer, and to rise from death the third day,"* and that there should be preached openly in his name, penance and remission of sins, to all the nations of the world.

Luke 24:27

Matt. 28:1–8,
Luke 24:1–12

John 20:14–18,
Matt. 28:9–10,
1 Cor. 15:5

Luke 24:13–34

John 20:19

John 21:1–14

1 Cor. 15:6

Mark 16:7,
Matt. 28:7, 10
Acts 1:4–11

Luke 24:39–43,
John 20:27

Luke 24:45–7

Ye see, good Christian people, how necessary this article of our faith is, seeing it was proved of Christ himself, by such evident reasons and tokens, by so long time and space. Now therefore, as our Saviour was diligent, for our comfort and instruction, to declare it, so let us be as ready in our belief, to receive it, to our comfort and instruction. As he

Rom. 4:25

died not for himself, no more did he rise again for himself. *He was dead,* saith St Paul, *for our sins, and rose again for our justification.* Oh most comfortable word, evermore to be borne in remembrance! He died, saith he, to put away sin; he arose again to endow us with righteousness. His death took away sin, and malediction; his death was the ransom of

Heb. 2:14

them both; his death destroyed death, and overcame *the devil, which had the power of death* in his subjection; his death destroyed hell, with all the

1 Cor. 15:54, 57

damnation thereof. Thus *is death swallowed up by Christ's victory*; thus is hell spoiled for ever.

If any man doubt of this victory, let Christ's glorious resurrection declare him the thing. If death could not keep Christ under his dominion and power, but that he arose again, it is manifest that his power was overcome. If death be conquered, then must it follow that

Rom. 6:23

sin, wherefore *death* was appointed as *the wages*, must be also destroyed. If death and sin be vanished away, then is the devil's tyranny vanquished, *which had the power of death*, and was the author and brewer of sin, and the ruler of hell. If Christ had the victory of them all, by the power of his death, and openly proved it, by his most victorious and valiant resurrection, as it was not possible for his great might to be subdued of them; and it is true, that Christ *died for our sins, and rose again for our justification*; why may not we, that be his members by true faith, rejoice, and boldly say with the Prophet Osee, and the Apostle Paul, *Where is thy*

Hos. 13:14,
1 Cor. 15:55, 57

dart, O death? Where is thy victory, O hell? Thanks be unto God, say they, *which hath given us the victory, by our Lord Christ Jesus.*

This mighty conquest of his resurrection, was not only signified

Judges 14: 5–8

before, by divers figures of the Old Testament—as by Samson, when he slew the lion, out of whose mouth came out sweetness and honey, and as

1 Sam. 17:34,
35, 49, 50

David bare his figure, when he delivered the lamb out of the lion's mouth, and when he overcame and slew the great giant Goliath, and as

Jonah 1:17, 2:10

when Jonas was swallowed up of the whale's mouth, and cast up again on land to live—but was also most clearly prophesied, by the Prophets of the Old Testament, and in the New also confirmed by the Apostles.

Col. 2:15

He hath spoiled, saith St Paul, *rule and power*, and all the dominion of our spiritual enemies; *he hath made a show of them openly, and hath triumphed over them, in his own person.*

This is the mighty power of the Lord, whom we believe on. By his death, hath he wrought for us this victory, and by his resurrection, hath he purchased everlasting life and righteousness for us. It had not been

enough, to be delivered by his death from sin, except by his resurrection
we had been endowed with righteousness. And it should not avail us, to
be delivered from death, except he had risen again, to open for us the
gates of heaven, to enter into life everlasting. And therefore St Peter
thanketh *God, the Father of our Lord Jesu Christ, for his abundant mercy,* 1 Pet. 1:3–5
because he hath begotten us, saith he, *unto a lively hope, by the resurrection of
Jesus Christ from death, to enjoy an inheritance immortal, that shall never
perish, which is laid up in heaven, for them that be kept by the power of God,
through faith.* Thus hath his resurrection wrought for us life and
righteousness. He passed through death and hell, to the intent to put us
in good hope, that by his strength we shall do the same. He paid the
ransom of sin, that it should not be laid to our charge. He destroyed the
devil and all his tyranny, and openly triumphed over him, and took away
from him all his captives, and hath raised and set them with himself, Eph. 2:6
amongst the heavenly citizens above. He died to destroy the rule of the
devil in us; and he arose again to send down his Holy Spirit, to rule in
our hearts, to endow us with perfect righteousness. Thus is it true that
David sung: *Veritas de terra orta est, et justitia de coelo prospexit*: the truth of Psalm 85:11
God's promise is in earth to man declared, or *from the earth is the* Eph. 4:8
everlasting *Verity*, God's Son, *risen* to life; and the true *righteousness* of the *Captivam duxit captivitatem.*
Holy Ghost *looking out of heaven*, and is in most liberal largess dealt
upon all the world. Thus is *glory* and praise rebounded upward *to God* Luke 2:14
above, for his mercy and truth; and thus is *peace* come down from
heaven, *to men* of good and faithful hearts. Thus *is mercy and truth*, as Psalm 85:10
David writeth, *together met*; thus *is peace and righteousness* imbracing and *Misericordia et veritas obviaverunt sibi, &c.*
kissing each other.

If thou doubtest of so great wealth and felicity that is wrought for
thee, O man, call to thy mind, that therefore hast thou received into
thine own possession, the everlasting Verity, our Saviour Jesus Christ, to
confirm to thy conscience the truth of all this matter. Thou hast received
him (if in true faith and repentance of heart thou hast received him, if in
purpose of amendment thou hast received him), for an everlasting gage
or pledge, of thy salvation. Thou hast received his body, which was once
broken, and his blood, which was shed, for the remission of thy sin.
Thou hast received his body, to have within thee the Father, the Son,
and the Holy Ghost, for to dwell with thee, to endow thee with grace, to
strength thee against thine enemies, and to comfort thee with their
presence. Thou hast received his body, to endow thee with everlasting
righteousness, to assure thee of everlasting bliss, and life of thy soul. For
with Christ, by true faith art thou quickened again, saith St Paul, from Eph. 2:5–8
death of sin, to life of grace, and in hope translated, from corporal and
everlasting death, to the everlasting life of glory in heaven, where now
thy conversation should be, and thy heart and desire set. Doubt not of

the truth of this matter, how great and high soever these things be. It becometh God to do no little deeds, how impossible soever they seem to thee. Pray to God, that thou mayest have faith, to perceive this great mystery of Christ's resurrection, that by faith, thou mayest certainly believe *nothing* to be *impossible with God.* Only bring thou faith to Christ's holy word and sacrament. Let thy repentance show thy faith; let thy purpose of amendment, and obedience of thy heart to God's law hereafter, declare thy true belief. Endeavour thyself to say with St Paul from henceforth, *Our conversation is in heaven, from whence we look for a Saviour, even the Lord Jesus Christ; which shall change our vile bodies, that they may be fashioned like to his glorious body; which he shall do by the same power* whereby he rose from death, and *whereby he shall be able to subdue all things unto himself.*

Thus, good Christian people, forasmuch as ye have heard these so great and excellent benefits of Christ's mighty and glorious resurrection, as how that he hath ransomed sin, overcome the devil, death, and hell, and hath victoriously gotten the better hand of them all, to make us free and safe from them; and knowing that we be, by this benefit of his resurrection, risen with him by our faith, unto life everlasting; being in full surety of our hope, that we shall have our bodies likewise raised again from death, to have them glorified in immortality, and joined to his glorious body; having in the mean while his Holy Spirit within our hearts, as a seal and pledge of our everlasting inheritance, by whose assistance we be replenished with all righteousness, by whose power we shall be able to subdue all our evil affections, rising against the pleasure of God: these things, I say, well considered, let us now in the rest of our life, declare our faith, that we have in this most fruitful article, by framing ourselves thereunto, in rising daily from sin, to righteousness and holiness of life. *For what shall it avail us,* saith St Peter, *to be escaped and delivered from the filthiness of the world, through the knowledge of the Lord and Saviour, Jesus Christ, if we be entangled again therewith, and be overcome again? Certainly it had been better,* saith he, *never to have known the way of righteousness, than after it is known and received, to turn backward again, from the holy commandment of God given unto us. For so shall the proverb have place in us, where it is said, "The dog is returned to his vomit again, and the sow that was washed, to her wallowing in the mire again."* What a shame were it for us, being thus so clearly and freely washed from our sin, to return to the filthiness thereof again! What a folly were it, thus endowed with righteousness, to lose it again! What madness were it, to lose the inheritance that we be now set in, for the vile and transitory pleasure of sin! And what an unkindness should it be, where our Saviour Christ, of his mercy, is come to us, to dwell within us as our guest, to drive him from us, and to banish him violently out of our souls, and instead of

Luke 1:37, 18:27

Phil. 3:20, 21

2 Pet. 2:20–2

him, in whom is all grace and virtue, to receive the ungracious spirit of the devil, the founder of all naughtiness and mischief! How can we find in our hearts, to show such extreme unkindness to Christ, which hath now so gently called us to mercy, and offered himself unto us, and he now entered within us? Yea, how dare we be so bold to renounce the presence of the Father, the Son, and the Holy Ghost (for, where one is, there is God all whole in Majesty, together with all his power, wisdom, and goodness), and fear not, I say, the danger and peril, of so traitorous a defiance and departure?

Good Christian brethren and sisters, advise yourselves: consider the dignity that ye be now set in. Let not folly lose the thing that grace hath so preciously offered and purchased. Let not wilfulness and blindness put out so great light, that is now showed unto you. Only take good hearts unto you, and *put upon you all the armour of God, that ye may stand against your enemies*, which would again subdue you, and bring you into their thraldom. Remember, *ye be bought from your vain conversation*, and that your freedom is purchased *neither with gold nor silver, but with the price of the precious blood, of that most innocent Lamb Jesus Christ; which was ordained to the same purpose, before the world was made, but he was so declared in the latter time, of grace for your sakes, which by him have your faith in God, who hath raised him from death, and hath given him glory, that you should have your faith and hope toward God.* Therefore, as ye have hitherto followed the vain lusts of your minds, and so displeased God to the danger of your souls, so now, *like obedient children*, thus purified by faith, give yourselves to walk that way which God moveth you to, that ye may receive *the end of your faith, the salvation of your souls*. And *as ye have given your bodies to unrighteousness, to sin after sin, so now give yourselves to righteousness, to be sanctified therein.* Eph. 6:11, 12
1 Pet. 1:18–21

Ibid.:14

Ibid.:9
Rom. 6:19

If ye delight in this article of your faith, that Christ is risen again from death to life, then follow you the example of his resurrection, as St Paul exhorteth us, saying, *As we be buried with Christ, by our baptism into death, so let us* daily *die to sin*, mortifying and killing the evil desires and motions thereof; and *as Christ was raised up from death, by the glory of the Father, so let us rise to a new life, and walk continually therein*; that we may, likewise as natural children, live a conversation to move men to *glorify our Father, which is in heaven. If we then be risen with Christ*, by our faith, to the hope of everlasting life, let us rise also with Christ, after his example, to a new life, and leave our old. We shall then be truly risen, if we *seek for things that be heavenly*, if we *have our affection upon things that be above, and not on things that be on earth.* If ye desire to know what these earthly things be, which ye should put off, and what be the heavenly things above, that ye should seek and ensue, St Paul in the Epistle to the Colossians declareth, when he exhorteth us thus: *Mortify your earthly* Rom. 6:2–4

Matt. 5:16
Col. 3:1, 2

Ibid.::5–10 *members* and old affections of sin, as *fornication, uncleanness, unnatural lust, evil concupiscence, and covetousness, which is worshipping of idols; for which things the wrath of God is wont to fall on the children of unbelief; in which things once ye walked, when ye lived in them. But now, put ye also away from you wrath, fierceness, maliciousness, cursed speaking, filthy speaking out of your mouths. Lie not one to another, that the old man, with his works, be put off, and the new put on.* These be the earthly things, which St Paul moveth you to cast from you, and to pluck your hearts from them. For in following these, ye declare yourselves earthly and worldly. These be the fruits of the earthly Adam. These should ye daily kill, by good diligence in withstanding the desires of them, that ye might rise to righteousness. *Let your affection* from henceforth *be set on heavenly things.* Sue and search for *mercy, kindness, meekness, patience, forbearing one another, and forgiving one another, if any man have any quarrel to another; as Christ forgave you, even so do ye.* If these and such other heavenly virtues ye ensue, in the residue of your life, ye shall show plainly, that *ye be risen with Christ,* and that ye be the heavenly *children of your Father in heaven,* from whom, as from the Giver, cometh these graces and gifts. Ye shall prove by this manner that *your conversation is in heaven,* where your hope is, and not on earth, following the beastly appetites of the flesh.

Ibid.:12, 13

Matt. 5:45

James 1:17

Phil. 3:20

Ye must consider that ye be therefore cleansed and renewed, that ye should from henceforth, *serve God in holiness and righteousness, all the days of your lives,* that ye may reign with him in everlasting life. If ye refuse so great grace, whereto ye be called, what other thing do ye, than heap up your damnation more and more, and so provoke God to cast his displeasure unto you, and to revenge this mockage of his holy Sacraments, in so great abusing of them? Apply yourselves, good friends, to live in Christ, that Christ may still live in you: whose favour and assistance if ye have, then have ye everlasting life already within you, then can nothing hurt you. Whatsoever is hitherto done and committed, Christ, ye see, hath offered you pardon, and clearly received you to his favour again: in full surety whereof, ye have him now inhabiting and dwelling within you. Only show yourselves thankful in your lives: determine with yourselves, to refuse and avoid, all such things in your conversations, as should offend his eyes of mercy. Endeavour yourselves, that way to rise up again, which way ye fell, into the well or pit of sin. If by your tongue ye have offended, now thereby rise again, and glorify God therewith. Accustom it to laud and praise the Name of God, as ye have therewith dishonoured it. And as ye have hurt the name of your neighbour, or otherwise hindered him, so now intend to restore it to him again. For without restitution, God accepteth not your confession, nor yet your repentance. It is not enough to *forsake evil,* except ye set your courage to *do good.* By what occasion soever ye have offended,

Luke 1:74, 75

John 5:24

Col. 3:5, 6

Restitution

Psalm 37:27

turn now the occasion to the honouring of God, and profiting of your neighbour.

Truth it is, that sin is strong, and affections unruly. Hard it is, to subdue and resist our nature, so corrupt, and leavened with the sour bitterness of the poison, which we received by the inheritance of our old father Adam. *But yet take good courage,* saith our Saviour Christ, *for I have overcome the world,* and all other enemies, for you. *Sin shall not have power over you, for ye be now under grace,* saith St Paul. Though your power be weak, yet *Christ is risen again,* to strengthen you in your battle; *his Holy Spirit shall help your infirmities.* In trust of his mercy, take you in hand to *purge this old leaven* of sin, that corrupteth and soureth the sweetness of your life before God; *that ye may be as new* and fresh *dough,* void of all sour *leaven of wickedness:* so shall ye show yourselves to be sweet bread to God, that he may have his delight in you. I say, kill, and offer you up, the worldly and earthly affections of your bodies; *for Christ our Easter lamb is offered up for us,* to slay the power of sin, to deliver us from the danger thereof, and to give us example to die to sin in our life. As the Jews did eat their Easter lamb, and kept their feast, in remembrance of their deliverance out of Egypt, even so, *let us keep our Easter feast,* in the thankful remembrance of Christ's benefits, which he hath plentifully wrought for us, by his resurrection, and passing to his Father; whereby we be delivered, from the captivity and thraldom of all our enemies. Let us in like manner, pass over the affections of our old conversation, that we may be delivered from the bondage thereof, and rise with Christ. The Jews kept their feast, in abstaining from leavened bread, by the space of seven days: *let us* Christian folk *keep our holyday* in spiritual manner, that is, *in abstaining,* not from material leavened bread, but *from the old leaven* of sin, *the leaven of maliciousness and wickedness.* Let us cast from us the leaven of corrupt doctrine, that will infect our souls. *Let us keep our feast,* the whole term of our life, *with eating the bread of pureness* of godly life, *and truth* of Christ's doctrine. Thus shall we declare, that Christ's gifts and graces have their effect in us, and that we have the right belief and knowledge, of his holy resurrection: where truly, if we apply our faith to the virtue thereof, and in our life conform us to the example, and signification meant thereby, we shall be sure to rise hereafter, to everlasting glory, by the goodness and mercy of our Lord, Jesus Christ. To whom with the Father, and the Holy Ghost, be all glory, thanksgiving, and praise, in infinita seculorum secula. Amen.

John 16:33

Rom. 6:14

Rom. 8:11, 26, 34

1 Cor. 5:7, 8

Exod. 12:15–20

Matt. 16:6, 12

AN HOMILY
OF THE WORTHY RECEIVING
AND REVERENT ESTEEMING
OF THE SACRAMENT OF THE BODY
AND BLOOD OF CHRIST

THE GREAT LOVE OF OUR SAVIOUR CHRIST towards mankind, good Christian people, doth not only appear in that dear-bought benefit of our redemption and salvation, by his death and passion, but also in that he so kindly provided, that the same most merciful work might be had in continual remembrance, to take some place in us, and not be frustrate of his end and purpose. For, as tender parents are not content to procure for their children costly possessions and livelihood, but take order that the same may be conserved, and come to their use, so our Lord and Saviour thought it not sufficient, to purchase for us his Father's favour again (which is that deep fountain of all goodness), and eternal life, but also invented the ways most wisely, whereby they might redound to our commodity and profit. Amongst the which means, is the public celebration of the memory of his precious death, at the Lord's table: which although it seem of small virtue to some, yet, being rightly done by the faithful, it doth not only help their weakness, who be by their poisoned nature readier to remember injuries than benefits, but strengtheneth and comforteth their inward man, with peace and gladness, and maketh them thankful to their Redeemer, with diligent care of godly conversation.

Exod. 12:14–27
And as of old time God decreed his wondrous benefits, of the deliverance of his people, to be kept in memory, by the eating of the passover with his rites and ceremonies, so our loving Saviour hath ordained, and Matt. 26:26–8, 1 Cor. 11:23–6 established, the remembrance of his great mercy expressed in his passion, in the institution of his heavenly Supper: where every one of us must be guests, and not gazers, eaters and not lookers, feeding ourselves, and not hiring other to feed for us; that we may live by our own

meat, and not perish for hunger while others devour all. To this his commandment forceth us, saying, *Do ye thus, Drink ye all of this.* To this his promise enticeth us: *This is my body, which is given for you; This is my blood, which is shed for you.*

So then, as of necessity we must be ourselves partakers of this table, and not beholders of other, so we must address ourselves to frequent the same, in reverent and due manner; lest, as physic provided for the body being misused, more hurteth than profiteth, so this comfortable medicine of the soul, undecently received, tendeth to our greater harm and sorrow. As St Paul saith: *He that eateth and drinketh unworthily, eateth and drinketh his own damnation.* Wherefore, that it be not said to us, as it was to the guest of that great supper, *Friend, how camest thou in, not having the marriage garment?* and that we may fruitfully use St Paul's counsel, *Let a man prove himself, and so eat of that bread, and drink of that cup,* we must certainly know that three things be requisite, in him which would seemly—as becometh such high mysteries—resort to the Lord's table, that is: a right and a worthy estimation, and understanding of this mystery; secondly, to come in a sure faith; and thirdly, to have newness or pureness of life, to succeed the receiving of the same.

But before all other things, this we must be sure of specially, that this Supper be in such wise done and ministered, as our Lord and Saviour did, and commanded to be done; as his holy Apostles used it, and the good fathers in the primitive Churches frequented it. For as that worthy man St Ambrose saith, "He is unworthy of the Lord, that otherwise doth celebrate that mystery, than it was delivered by him; neither can he be devout, that otherways doth presume, than it was given by the Author." We must then take heed lest, of the memory, it be made a sacrifice; lest of a communion, it be made a private eating; lest of two parts, we have but one; lest applying it for the dead, we lose the fruit that be alive. Let us rather in these matters, follow the advice of Cyprian in the like cases; that is, cleave fast to the first beginning; hold fast the Lord's tradition; do that in the Lord's commemoration, which he himself did, he himself commanded, and his Apostles confirmed.

This caution or foresight if we use, then may we see to those things that be requisite in the worthy receiver; whereof this was the first, that we have right understanding of the thing itself. As concerning which thing, this we may assuredly persuade ourselves, that the ignorant man can neither worthily esteem, nor effectually use, those marvellous graces and benefits, offered and exhibited in that Supper, but either will lightly regard them, to no small offence, or utterly contemn them, to his utter destruction; so that by his negligence, he deserveth the plagues of God to fall upon him, and by contempt, he deserveth everlasting perdition. To avoid then these harms, use the advice of the Wise Man, who willeth

Margin notes:

Luke 22:19, 20

1 Cor. 11:24, 25,
Matt. 26:27

1 Cor. 11:29

Matt. 22:12

1 Cor. 11:28

Prov. 23:1

thee, *when thou sittest at an earthly king's table*, to *take diligent heed what things are set before thee*. So now much more, at the King of kings' table, thou must search and know, what dainties are provided for thy soul: whither thou art come, not to feed thy senses and belly to corruption, but thy inward man, to immortality and life; not to consider the earthly creatures which thou seest, but the heavenly graces which thy faith beholdeth. "For this table is not," saith Chrysostom, "for chattering jays, but for eagles," who flee *"thither, where the dead body lieth."* And, if this advertisement of man cannot persuade us to resort to the Lord's table, with understanding, see the counsel of God in like matter, who charged his people to teach their posterity, not only the rites and ceremonies of his Passover, but the cause and end thereof: whence we may learn, that both more perfect knowledge is required at this time at our hands, and that the ignorant cannot with fruit and profit, exercise himself in the Lord's Sacraments. But to come nigher to the matter: St Paul, blaming the Corinthians for the profaning of the Lord's Supper, concludeth that ignorance, both of the thing itself, and the signification thereof, was the cause of their abuse; for they came thither unreverently, *not discerning the Lord's body*. Ought not we then, by the monition of the Wise Man, by the wisdom of God, by the fearful example of the Corinthians, to take advised heed, that we thrust not ourselves to this table, with rude and unreverent ignorance? the smart whereof Christ's Church hath rued and lamented these many days and years. For what hath been the cause of the ruin of God's religion, but the ignorance hereof? What hath been the cause of this gross idolatry, but the ignorance hereof? What hath been the cause of this mummish massing, but the ignorance hereof? Yea, what hath been, and what is at this day, the cause of this want of love and charity, but the ignorance hereof? Let us therefore so travail to understand the Lord's Supper, that we be no cause of the decay of God's worship, of no idolatry, of no dumb massing, of no hate and malice: so may we the boldlier have access thither, to our comfort.

Neither need we to think that such exact knowledge is required of every man, that he be able to discuss all high points in the doctrine thereof. But thus much he must be sure to hold, that in the Supper of the Lord there is no vain ceremony, no bare sign, no untrue figure of a thing absent, but as the Scripture saith, *the table of the Lord, the bread and cup of the Lord, the memory of Christ, the annunciation of his death*, yea, *the communion of the body and blood of the Lord*, in a marvellous incorporation; which by the operation of the Holy Ghost, the very bond of our conjunction with Christ, is through faith, wrought in the souls of the faithful, whereby not only their souls live, to eternal life, but they surely trust to win to their bodies a resurrection, to immortality. The true understanding of this fruition and union, which is betwixt the body

Matt. 24:28

Exod. 12:26, 27, 13:8

1 Cor. 11:29

Matt. 26:26, 27; 1 Cor. 10:16, 21; 11:24, 26, 27

Iren. Lib. 4, cap. 34

and the head, betwixt the true believers and Christ, the ancient catholic fathers both perceiving themselves, and commending to their people, were not afraid to call this Supper, some of them, "the salve of immortality, a sovereign preservative against death"; other, "a deifical communion"; other, "the sweet dainties of our Saviour"; "the pledge of eternal health, the defence of faith, the hope of the resurrection"; other, "the food of immortality", "the healthful grace", and "the conservatory to everlasting life". All which sayings—both of the holy Scripture and godly men, truly attributed to this celestial banquet and feast—if we would often call to mind, oh how would they inflame our hearts to desire the participation of these mysteries! and oftentimes to covet after this bread, continually to thirst for this food; not as specially regarding the terrene and earthly creatures which remain, but always holding fast, and cleaving by faith to the *Rock*, whence we may *suck the sweetness of everlasting salvation*. And, to be brief, thus much more the faithful see, and hear, and know, the favourable mercies of God sealed, the satisfaction by Christ towards us confirmed, the remission of sin stablished. Here they may feel wrought, the tranquillity of conscience, the increase of faith, the strengthening of hope, the large spreading abroad of brotherly kindness, with many other sundry graces of God; the taste whereof they cannot attain unto, who be drowned in the deep dirty lake of blindness and ignorance. From the which, O beloved, wash yourselves with the living waters of God's word, whence you may perceive and know, both the spiritual food of this costly Supper, and the happy trustings and effects, that the same doth bring with it.

Now it followeth, to have with this knowledge a sure and constant faith, not only that the death of Christ is available, for the redemption of all the world, for the remission of sins, and reconciliation with God the Father, but also that he hath made upon his cross, a full and sufficient sacrifice for thee, a perfect cleansing of thy sins; so that thou acknowledgest no other Saviour, Redeemer, Mediator, Advocate, Intercessor, but Christ only, and that thou mayest say with the Apostle, that he *loved thee and gave himself for thee*. For this is to stick fast to Christ's promise, made in his institution, to make Christ thine own, and to apply his merits unto thyself. Herein thou needest no other man's help, no other sacrifice or oblation, or sacrificing priest, no mass, no means established by man's invention. That faith is a necessary instrument in all these holy ceremonies, we may thus assure ourselves, for that as St Paul saith, *without faith it is unpossible to please God*. When a great number of the Israelites *were overthrown in the wilderness*, "Moyses, Aaron, and Phinees did eat manna, and pleased God, for that they understood," saith St Augustine, "the visible meat spiritually: spiritually they hungered it; spiritually they tasted it; that they might be spiritually satisfied." And

Marginal notes:

Ignat. *Epist. ad Ephes.*; Dionysius; Origenes; Optatus; Cyprian *de Coen. Dom.*; Athan. *de Pecc. in Spir. Sanct.*

Deut. 32:4, 13, 15; 1 Cor. 10:4

Gal. 2:20

Heb. 11:6

1 Cor. 10:5

in Joan. Hom. 6

truly, as the bodily meat cannot feed the outward man, unless it be let into a stomach to be digested, which is healthsome and sound, no more can the inward man be fed, except his meat be received into his soul and heart, sound and whole in faith. Therefore saith Cyprian, "When we do these things, we need not to whet our teeth, but with sincere faith, we break and divide that holy bread." It is well known, that the meat we seek for in this Supper is spiritual food, the nourishment of our soul, a heavenly refection, and not earthly; an unvisible meat, and not bodily; a ghostly sustenance, and not carnal: so that to think that, without faith, we may enjoy the eating and drinking thereof, or that that is the fruition of it, is but to dream a gross carnal feeding, basely abjecting and binding ourselves to the elements and creatures; whereas, by the advice of the Council of Nicene, we ought to "lift up our minds by faith", and leaving these inferior and earthly things, there seek it, where *the Sun of righteousness* ever shineth. Take then this lesson, O thou that art desirous of this table, of Emissenus, a godly father, that "when thou goest up to the reverend Communion to be satisfied with spiritual meats, thou look up with faith, upon the holy Body and Blood of thy God, thou marvel with reverence, thou touch it with thy mind, thou receive it with the hand of thy heart, and thou take it fully, with thy inward man."

Thus we see, beloved, that resorting to this table, we must pluck up all the roots of infidelity, all distrust in God's promises; we must make ourselves living members of Christ's body. For the unbelievers, and faithless, cannot feed upon that precious Body: whereas the faithful have their life, their abiding, in him; their union, and as it were their incorporation, with him. Wherefore let us prove, and try ourselves unfeignedly, without flattering ourselves, whether we be plants of that fruitful olive, living *branches of the true Vine, members* indeed *of Christ's mystical body*; whether God hath purified our hearts by faith, to the sincere acknowledging of his Gospel, and embracing of his mercies in Christ Jesu: so that at this his table we receive, not only the outward Sacrament, but the spiritual thing also; not the figure, but the truth; not the shadow only, but the body; not to death, but to life; not to destruction, but to salvation. Which God grant us to do, through the merits of our Lord and Saviour: to whom be all honour and glory, for ever. Amen.

de Coen. Dom.

Concilium
Nicen.
Mal. 4:2

Euseb. Emiss.
Serm. de Euchar.

Rom. 11:17, 24
John 15:1–6;
Eph. 5:30, 32

THE SECOND PART OF THE HOMILY OF THE WORTHY RECEIVING AND REVERENT ESTEEMING OF THE SACRAMENT OF THE BODY AND BLOOD OF CHRIST

IN THE HOMILY OF LATE REHEARSED UNTO YOU, ye have heard, good people, why it pleased our Saviour Christ, to institute that heavenly memory of his death and passion; and that every one of us ought to celebrate the same, at his table, in our own persons, and not by other. You have heard also, with what estimation, and knowledge of so high mysteries, we ought to resort thither; you have heard with what constant faith, we should clothe and deck ourselves, that we might be fit and decent partakers of that celestial food. Now followeth the third thing necessary, in him that would not eat of this bread nor drink of this cup unworthily: which is newness of life, and godliness of conversation.

For newness of life, as fruits of faith, are required in the partaker of this table. We may learn, by the eating of the typical lamb, whereunto no man was admitted but he that was a Jew that was circumcised, that was before sanctified. Yea, St Paul testifieth, that although all the people were partakers of the Sacraments under Moses, yet, for that some of them were still worshippers of images, whoremongers, tempters of Christ, murmurers, and coveting after evil things, God overthrew those in the wilderness, and that for our example: that is, that we Christians should take heed we resort unto our Sacraments with holiness of life, not trusting in the outward receiving of them, and infected with corrupt and uncharitable manners. For this sentence of God must always be justified, *I will have mercy, and not sacrifice*. 1 Cor. 10:1–11

Wherefore, [saith Basil], it behoveth him that cometh to the Body and Blood of Christ, *in commemoration of him that died, and rose again*, not only to be pure *from all filthiness, of the flesh and spirit*, lest he eat and drink to his condemnation; but also to show out evidently, a memory of *him that died, and rose again for us*, in this point: that he be *mortified to sin* and *the world*, to *live* now *to God, in Christ Jesu, our Lord*. Hos. 6:1, Matt. 9:13 *de Bapt.* Lib. 1, cap. 3

So then, we must show outward testimony, in following the signification of Christ's death: amongst the which this is not esteemed least: to render thanks to Almighty God, for all his benefits, briefly comprised in the death, passion, and resurrection, of his dearly beloved Son.

The which thing because we ought chiefly at this table to solemnise, the godly fathers named it "Eucharistia", that is, Thanksgiving: as if they should have said, "Now above all other times, ye ought to laud and praise God; now may ye behold the matter, the cause, the beginning, and the end of all thanksgiving; now if ye slack, ye show yourselves most unthankful, and that no other benefit can ever stir you to thank God, who so little regard here so many, so wonderful, and so profitable benefits." Seeing then, that the name and thing itself doth monish us of

Heb. 13:15

thanks, *let us*, as St Paul saith, *offer always to God, the host* or sacrifice *of praise by Christ, that is, the fruit of the lips which confess his Name*. For as

Psalm 50:23

David singeth, *he that offereth to God thanks and praise, honoureth him*. But how few be there of thankful persons in comparison to the unthankful!

Luke 17:12–18

Lo, ten lepers in the Gospel were healed, and but one only returned to give thanks for his health. Yea, happy it were, if among forty communicants, we could see two unfeignedly to give thanks. So unkind we be, so oblivious we be, so proud beggars we be, that partly we care not for our own commodity, partly we know not our duty to God, and chiefly, we will not confess all that we receive. Yea, and if we be forced by God's power to do it, yet we handle it so coldly, so drily, that our lips praise him, but our hearts dispraise him; our tongues bless him, but our life curseth him; our words worship him, but our works dishonour him. Oh let us therefore learn to give God here thanks aright! and so to agnize his exceeding graces poured upon us, that they being shut up in the treasure house of our heart, may in due time and season in our life and conversation appear, to the glorifying of his holy Name.

Furthermore, for newness of life, it is to be noted that St Paul writeth,

1 Cor. 10:17

that *we being many, are one bread, and one body, for all be partakers of one bread*; declaring thereby, not only our communion with Christ, but that unity also, wherein they that eat at this table should be knit together. For by dissension, vainglory, ambition, strife, envying, contempt, hatred, or malice, they should not be dissevered, but so joined by the bond of love, in one mystical body, as the corns of that bread in one loaf. In respect of which strait knot of charity, the true Christians in the tender time of Christ's Church, called this Supper "Love",* as if they would say, none ought to sit down there, that were out of love and charity, who bore grudge and vengeance in his heart, who also did not profess his kind affection, by some charitable relief, for some part of the congregation. And this was their practice. Oh heavenly banquet, then so used! Oh godly guests, who so esteemed this feast! But oh wretched creatures that we be at these days! who be without reconciliation of our brethren, whom we have offended, without satisfying them whom we have caused to fall, without any kind thought or compassion, toward them whom we might easily relieve, without any conscience of slander, disdain, misreport, division, rancour, or inward bitterness; yea, being accombred with the

Gen. 4:5–8;
27:41;
2 Sam. 3:27

cloaked hatred of Cain, with the long covered malice of Esau, with the

* Griffiths notes that the Homilist seems to be confusing the Eucharist with the Love Feast.

dissembled falsehood of Joab, dare yet presume, to come up to these sacred and fearful mysteries. O man, whither rushest thou unadvisedly? It is a table of peace, and thou art ready to fight. It is a table of singleness, and thou art imagining mischief. It is a table of quietness, and thou art given to debate. It is a table of pity, and thou art unmerciful. Dost thou neither fear God, the maker of this feast? nor reverence his Christ, the refection and meat? nor regardest his spouse, his beloved guest? nor weighest thine own conscience, which is sometime thine inward accuser? Wherefore, O man, tender thine own salvation; examine and try thy good will, and love towards the children of God, the members of Christ, the heirs of the heavenly heritage; yea, towards the image of God, the excellent creature thine own soul. If thou have offended, now be reconciled. If thou have caused any to stumble in the way of God, now set them up again. If thou have disquieted thy brother, now pacify him. If thou have wronged him, now relieve him. If thou have defrauded him, now restore to him. If thou have nourished spite, now embrace friendship. If thou have fostered hatred and malice, now openly show thy love and charity; yea, be prest and ready, to procure thy neighbour's health of soul, wealth, commodity, and pleasure, as thine own. Deserve not the heavy and dreadful burden of God's displeasure, for thine evil will towards thy neighbour, so unreverently to approach to this table of the Lord.

Last of all, as there is here "the mystery of peace", and the Sacrament of Christian society, whereby we understand what sincere love ought to be, betwixt the true communicants, so here be the tokens of pureness and innocency of life, whereby we may perceive, that we ought to purge our own soul from all uncleanness, iniquity, and wickedness, "lest, when we receive the mystical bread," as Origen saith, "we eat it in an unclean place, that is, in a soul defiled and polluted with sin." In Moyses' law, the man that did eat of the sacrifice of thanksgiving, with his uncleanness upon him, should be destroyed from his people: and shall we think that the wicked and sinful person shall be excusable, at the table of the Lord? We both read in St Paul, that the Church at Corinth was scourged of the Lord, for misusing the Lord's Supper, and we may plainly see Christ's Church, these many years miserably vexed and oppressed, for the horrible profanation of the same. Wherefore let us all, universal and singular, behold our own manners and lives, to amend them. Yea, now at the least, let us call ourselves to an account, that it may grieve us of our former evil conversation, that we may hate sin, that we may sorrow and mourn for our offences, that we may with tears, pour them out before God, that we may with sure trust, desire and crave the salve of his mercy, bought and purchased with the blood of his dearly beloved Son, Jesus Christ, to heal our deadly wounds withal. For surely, if we do not with earnest repentance, cleanse the filthy stomach of our soul, it must needs

Chrysost. *ad Pop. Ant.* Hom. 60

in Levit. cap. 23, Hom. 14
Num. 5:2, 9:6, 19:15

1 Cor. 11:30

Chrysost. *ad Pop.*
Ant. Hom. 61
come to pass that, "as wholesome meat, received into a raw stomach, corrupteth and marreth all, and is the cause of further sickness," so we shall eat this healthsome bread, and drink this cup, to our eternal destruction. Thus we, and not other, must throughly examine, and not lightly look over, ourselves, not other men; our own conscience, not other men's lives: which we ought to do uprightly, truly, and with just

Ibid. Hom. 60
correction. "Oh," saith St Chrysostom, "let no Judas resort to this table; let no covetous person approach. If any be a disciple, let him be present.

Matt. 26:18
For Christ saith, *With my disciples I make my passover*." Why cried the deacon in the primitive Church, "If any be holy, let him draw near"? Why did they celebrate these mysteries, the choir door being shut? Why were the public penitents, and learners in religion, commanded at this time to avoid? Was it not, because this table receiveth no unholy, unclean, or sinful guests? Wherefore, if servants dare not presume, to an earthly master's table whom they have offended, let us take heed we come not with our sins unexamined, into this presence of our Lord and Judge. If they be worthy blame, who kiss the prince's hand with a filthy and unclean mouth, shalt thou be blameless, which with a filthy stinking soul, full of covetousness, fornication, drunkenness, pride, full of wretched cogitations and thoughts, dost breathe out iniquity and uncleanness, on the bread and cup of the Lord?

Epilogue
Thus have you heard how you should come, reverently and decently, to the table of the Lord, having the knowledge out of his word, of the thing itself, and the fruits thereof; bringing a true and constant faith, the root and wellspring of all newness of life, as well in praising God, and loving our neighbour, as purging our own conscience from filthiness. So that neither the ignorance of the thing shall cause us to contemn it, nor unfaithfulness make us void of fruit, nor sin and iniquity procure us God's plagues; but we* shall by faith in knowledge, and amendment of life in faith, be here so united to Christ, our head in his mysteries, to our comfort, that after, we shall have full fruition of him indeed, to our everlasting joy and eternal life. To the which he bring us, that died for us,

1 John 2:1
and redeemed us, *Jesus Christ the righteous*: to whom, with the Father and the Holy Ghost, one true and eternal God, be all praise, honour, and dominion, for ever. Amen.

---

* we *editorial addition*

AN HOMILY
CONCERNING THE COMING DOWN
OF THE HOLY GHOST
AND
THE MANIFOLD GIFTS OF THE SAME

FOR WHITSUNDAY

BEFORE WE COME to the declaration of the great and manifold gifts of the Holy Ghost, wherewith the Church of God hath been evermore replenished, it shall first be needful, briefly to expound unto you, whereof this feast of Pentecost, or Whitsuntide, had his first beginning. You shall therefore understand, that the feast of Pentecost was always kept, the fiftieth day after Easter, a great and solemn feast among the Jews, wherein they did celebrate the memorial of their deliverance out of Egypt, and also the memorial of the publishing of the Law, which was given unto them in the mount Sinai, upon that day. It was first ordained and commanded to be kept holy, not by any mortal man, but by the mouth of the Lord himself; as we read in Leviticus 23 and Deuteronomy 16. The place appointed for the observation thereof was Jerusalem, where was great recourse of people from all parts of the world; as may well appear in the second chapter of the Acts, wherein mention is made of Parthians, Medes, Elamites, inhabiters of Mesopotamia, inhabiters of Jewry, Cappadocia, Pontus, Asia, Phrygia, Pamphylia, and divers other such places; whereby we may also partly gather, what great and royal solemnity was commonly used in that feast.

Now as this was given in commandment to the Jews, in the Old Law, so did our Saviour Christ, as it were confirm the same, in the time of the Gospel, ordaining after a sort a new Pentecost for his disciples; namely, when he sent down the Holy Ghost visibly, in form of cloven tongues like fire, and gave them power to speak in such sort, that every one might hear them, and also understand them, in his own language. Which miracle, that it might be had in perpetual remembrance, the Church hath thought good to solemnise and keep holy, this day, commonly called Whitsunday. And here is to be noted, that as the Law was given to the Jews, in the mount Sinai, the fiftieth day after Easter, so was the preaching of the Gospel, through the mighty power of the Holy Ghost, given to the Apostles, in the mount Sion, the fiftieth day after Easter. And hereof this feast hath his name, to be called Pentecost, even of the number of the days. For as St Luke writeth, in the Acts of the Apostles, *when fifty days were come to an end,* the disciples being *all together, with one accord, in one place,* the Holy Ghost *came suddenly* among them, *and sat upon each of them, like as it had been cloven tongues of fire.* Which thing was undoubtedly done, to teach the Apostles and all other men, that it is he which giveth eloquence, and utterance in preaching the Gospel; that it is he which openeth the mouth, to declare the mighty works of God; that it is he which engendereth a burning zeal toward God's word, and giveth all men a tongue, yea, a fiery tongue, so that they may boldly and cheerfully profess the truth, in the face of the whole world: as Esay was indued with this Spirit. *The Lord,* saith Esay, *gave me a learned* and skilful *tongue, so that I might know to raise up them that are fallen, with the word.* The Prophet David crieth to have this gift, saying, *Open thou my lips, O Lord, and my mouth shall show forth thy praise.* For our Saviour Christ also in the Gospel, saith to his disciples, *It is not you that speak, but the Spirit of your Father, which is within you.* All which testimonies of holy Scripture, do sufficiently declare, that the mystery of the tongues, betokeneth the preaching of the Gospel, and the open confession of the Christian faith, in all them that are possessed with the Holy Ghost. So that if any man be a dumb Christian, not professing his faith openly, but cloaking and colouring himself, for fear of danger in time to come, he giveth men occasion, justly and with good conscience, to doubt lest he have not the grace of the Holy Ghost within him, because he is tongue tied, and doth not speak.

Thus then have ye heard the first institution of this feast of Pentecost or Whitsuntide, as well in the old Law, among the Jews, as also in the time of the Gospel, among the Christians. Now let us consider what the Holy Ghost is, and how consequently he worketh his miraculous works towards mankind.

The Holy Ghost is a spiritual and divine substance, the third Person in the Deity, distinct from the Father and the Son, and yet proceeding from them both. Which thing to be true, both the Creed of Athanasius beareth witness, and may be also easily proved, by most plain testimonies of God's holy word. When Christ was baptised of John in the river Jordan, we read that the Holy Ghost came down, in the form of a

Margin references:
Acts 2:1, 3

Isai. 50:4

Psalm 51:15
Matt. 10:20

Matt. 3:16, 17

dove, and that the Father thundered *from heaven, saying, This is my dear and well beloved Son, in whom I am well pleased.* Where note, three divers and distinct Persons, the Father, the Son, and the Holy Ghost; which all, notwithstanding, are not three Gods, but one God. Likewise, when Christ did first institute and ordain the Sacrament of Baptism, he sent his disciples into the whole world, willing them to baptise *all nations, in*   Matt. 28:19 *the name of the Father, the Son, and the Holy Ghost.* Also in another place he saith, *I will pray unto my Father, and he shall give you another Comforter.*   John 14:16 Again, *When the Comforter shall come, whom I will send from my Father,* &c.   John 15:26 These, and such other places of the New Testament, do so plainly and evidently confirm the distinction of the Holy Ghost, from the other Persons in the Trinity, that no man can possibly doubt thereof, unless he will blaspheme the everlasting truth of God's word. As for his proper nature and substance, it is altogether one with God the Father, and God the Son, that is to say, spiritual, eternal, uncreated, incomprehensible, almighty; to be short, he is even God and Lord everlasting. Therefore he is called the Spirit of the Father; therefore he is said to proceed from the Father and the Son; and therefore he was equally joined with them, in the commission that the Apostles had, to baptise all nations.

But, that this may appear more sensibly to the eyes of all men, it shall be requisite to come to the other part, namely, to the wonderful and heavenly works of the Holy Ghost, which plainly declare unto the world his mighty and divine power. First, it is evident that he did wonderfully govern and direct the hearts of the Patriarchs and Prophets in old time, illuminating their minds, with the knowledge of the true Messias, and giving them utterance, to prophesy of things that should come to pass, long time after. For, as St Peter witnesseth, *the prophecy came not in old*   2 Pet. 1:21 *time by the will of man, but the holy men of God spake, as they were moved inwardly by the Holy Ghost.* And of Zachary the high priest, it is said in   Luke 1:64, 67 the Gospel that *he, being full of the Holy Ghost, prophesied and praised God.* So did also Simeon, Anna, Mary, and divers other, to the great wonder and admiration of all men.

Moreover, was not the Holy Ghost a mighty worker, in the conception and the nativity of Christ, our Saviour? St Matthew saith that the blessed Virgin *was found with child, of the Holy Ghost, before Joseph and she came*   Matt. 1:18 *together.* And the angel Gabriel did expressly tell her that it should come to pass, saying, *The Holy Ghost shall come upon thee, and the power of the most*   Luke 1:35 *High shall overshadow thee.* A marvellous matter, that a woman should conceive and bear a child, without the knowledge of man! But where the Holy Ghost worketh, there nothing is unpossible: as may further also appear, by the inward regeneration, and sanctification of mankind.

When Christ said to Nicodemus, *Unless a man be born anew, of water*   John 3:3–5 *and the Spirit, he cannot enter into the kingdom of God,* he was greatly amazed in his mind, and began to reason with Christ, demanding *how a man might be born which was old? "Can he enter,"* saith he, *"into his mother's womb again, and so be born anew?"* Behold a lively pattern of a fleshly and carnal man! He had little or no intelligence of the Holy Ghost, and therefore he goeth bluntly to work, and asketh how this thing were possible to be true: whereas otherwise, if he had known the great power of the Holy Ghost in this behalf, that it is he which inwardly worketh the regeneration and new birth of mankind, he would never have marvelled at Christ's words, but would have rather taken occasion thereby, to praise and glorify God. For, as there are three several and sundry Persons in the Deity, so have they three several and sundry offices, proper unto each of them: the Father to create, the Son to redeem, the Holy Ghost to sanctify and regenerate. Whereof the last, the more it is hid from our understanding, the more it ought to move all men to wonder, at the secret and mighty working of God's Holy Spirit, which is within us. For it is the Holy Ghost, and no other thing, that doth quicken the minds of men, stirring up good and godly motions in their hearts, which are agreeable to the will and commandment of God, such as otherwise, of their own crooked and perverse nature, they

John 3:6   should never have. *That which is born of the flesh,* saith Christ, *is flesh, and that which is born of the Spirit, is spirit.* As who should say, Man of his own nature is fleshly and carnal, corrupt and naught, sinful and disobedient to God, without any spark of goodness in him, without any virtuous or godly motion, only given to evil thoughts and wicked deeds: as for the works of the Spirit—the fruits of faith, charitable and godly motions—if he have any at all in him, they proceed only of the Holy Ghost, who is the only worker of our sanctification, and maketh us new men in Christ

1 Sam. 17:33–7   Jesu. Did not God's Holy Spirit miraculously work in the child David, when of a poor shepherd, he became a princelike Prophet? Did not

Matt. 9:9   God's Holy Spirit miraculously work in Matthew, *sitting at the receipt of custom,* when of a proud publican, he became an humble and lowly Evangelist? And who can choose but marvel, to consider that Peter should become, of a simple fisher, a chief and mighty Apostle; Paul, of a cruel and bloody persecutor, a faithful disciple of Christ to teach the Gentiles?

Such is the power of the Holy Ghost to regenerate men, and as it were to bring them forth anew, so that they shall be nothing like the men that they were before. Neither doth he think it sufficient, inwardly to work the spiritual and new birth of man, unless he do also dwell and abide in

1 Cor. 3:16; 6:19   him. *Know ye not,* saith St Paul, *that ye are the temple of God, and that his Spirit dwelleth in you? Know ye not, that your bodies are the temples of the*

Rom. 8:9   *Holy Ghost, which is wthin you?* Again he saith, *You are not in the flesh, but in the spirit; for why, the Spirit of God dwelleth in you.* To this agreeth the doctrine of St John, writing on this wise: *The anointing which ye have received* (he meaneth the Holy Ghost) *dwelleth in you.* And the doctrine of Peter saith the same, who hath these words: *The spirit of glory, and of God, resteth upon you.* Oh what a comfort is this, to the heart of a true Christian, to think that the Holy Ghost dwelleth within him! *If God be with us,* as the Apostle saith, *who can be against us?*

    Oh, but how shall I know that the Holy Ghost is within me? some man perchance will say. Forsooth, as *the tree is known by his fruit,* so is also the Holy Ghost. *The fruits of the Holy Ghost,* according to the mind of St Paul, are these: *love, joy, peace, longsuffering, gentleness, goodness, faithfulness, meekness, temperance,* &c. Contrariwise *the deeds of the flesh are these: adultery, fornication, uncleanness, wantonness, idolatry, witchcraft, hatred, debate, emulation, wrath, contention, sedition, heresy, envy, murder, drunkenness, gluttony, and suchlike.* Here is now that glass, wherein thou must behold thyself, and discern, whether thou have the Holy Ghost within thee, or the spirit of the flesh. If thou see that thy works be virtuous and good, consonant to the prescript rule of God's word, savouring and tasting not of the flesh, but of the Spirit, then assure thyself that thou art endued with the Holy Ghost: otherwise, in thinking well of thyself, thou doest nothing else but deceive thyself.

    The Holy Ghost doth always declare himself, by his fruitful and gracious gifts, namely, by *the word of wisdom,* by *the word of knowledge,* which is the understanding of the Scriptures, by *faith,* in *doing of miracles,* by *healing* them that are diseased, by *prophecy,* which is the declaration of God's mysteries, by *discerning of spirits, diversity of tongues, interpretation of tongues,* and so forth. All which gifts, as they proceed from one Spirit, and are severally given to man, according to the measurable distribution of the Holy Ghost, even so do they bring men, and not without good cause, into a wonderful admiration of God's divine power. Who will not marvel, at that which is written in the Acts of the Apostles, to hear their bold confession, before the council at Jerusalem, and to consider that they went away with joy and gladness, *rejoicing, that they were counted worthy to suffer rebukes* and checks, *for the Name* and faith *of Christ Jesus?* This was the mighty work of the Holy Ghost; who because he giveth patience, and joyfulness of heart, in temptation and affliction, hath therefore worthily obtained this name in holy Scripture: to be called a *Comforter.* Who will not also marvel, to read the learned and heavenly sermons of Peter, and the other disciples, considering that they were never brought up in school of learning, but called even from their nets, to supply rooms of Apostles? This was likewise the mighty work of the Holy Ghost, who because he doth instruct the hearts of the simple, in the true knowledge of God and his holy word, is most justly termed by this name and title, to be *the Spirit of*

1 John 2:27

1 Pet. 4:14

Rom. 8:31

Matt. 12:33

Gal. 5:19–23

1 Cor. 12:7–11

Acts 5:29–32, 41

John 14:16

Ibid.:17

Lib. 10 cap. 3

truth. Eusebius in his *Ecclesiastical History* telleth a strange story, of a certain learned and subtile philosopher, who being an extreme adversary to Christ and his doctrine, could by no kind of learning be converted to the faith, but was able to withstand all the arguments that could be brought against him, with little or no labour. At length there started up a poor simple man, of small wit and less knowledge, one that was reputed among the learned as an idiot; and he on God's Name, would needs take in hand, to dispute with this proud philosopher. The bishops and other learned men standing by, were marvellously abashed at the matter, thinking that by his doings they should be all confounded, and put to open shame. He notwithstanding goeth on, and beginning in the Name of the Lord Jesus, brought the philosopher to such point in the end, contrary to all men's expectation, that he could not choose but acknowledge the power of God in his words, and to give place to the truth. Was not this a miraculous work, that one seely soul, of no learning, should do that which many bishops, of great knowledge and understanding, were never able to bring to pass? So true is that saying of Bede: "Where the Holy Ghost doth instruct and teach, there is no delay at all in learning." Much more might here be spoken, of the manifold gifts and graces of the Holy Ghost, most excellent and wonderful in our eyes: but to make a long discourse through all, the shortness of time will not serve; and, seeing ye have heard the chiefest, ye may easily conceive and judge of the rest.

Hom. 9 *super Lucam*

Now were it expedient, to discuss this question, whether all they which boast and brag that they have the Holy Ghost, do truly challenge this unto themselves, or not? Which doubt, because it is necessary and profitable, shall, God willing, be dissolved in the next part of this Homily. In the mean season, let us, as we are most bound, give hearty thanks to God the Father, and his Son, Jesus Christ, for sending down this Comforter into the world; humbly beseeching him, so to work in our hearts, by the power of this Holy Spirit, that we being regenerate, and newly born again, in all goodness, righteousness, sobriety, and truth, may in the end, be made partakers of everlasting life, in his heavenly kingdom through Jesus Christ, our only Lord and Saviour. Amen.

THE SECOND PART OF THE HOMILY CONCERNING THE HOLY GHOST, DISSOLVING THIS DOUBT, WHETHER ALL MEN DO RIGHTLY CHALLENGE TO THEMSELVES THE HOLY GHOST, OR NO

OUR SAVIOUR CHRIST, *departing out of the world unto his Father*, promised his disciples, to send down *another Comforter, that should continue with them for ever*, and *direct them into all truth*. Which thing to be faithfully and truly performed, the Scriptures do sufficiently bear witness. Neither must we think that this Comforter was either promised or else given, only to the Apostles, but also to the universal Church of Christ, dispersed through the whole world. For, unless the Holy Ghost had been always present, governing and preserving the Church from the beginning, it could never have sustained so many and so great brunts of affliction and persecution, with so little damage and harm as it hath. And the words of Christ are most plain in this behalf, saying that *the Spirit of truth should abide with them for ever*, that *he would be with them always* (he meaneth by grace, virtue, and power) *even to the world's end*. Also, in the prayer that he made to his Father a little before his death, he maketh intercession, not only for himself and his Apostles, but indifferently *for all them that should believe in him through their words*, that is to wit, for his whole Church. Again, St Paul saith, *If any man have not the Spirit of Christ, the same is not his*. Also in the words following, *We have received the spirit of adoption, whereby we cry, "Abba, Father."* Hereby then, it is evident and plain to all men, that the Holy Ghost was given, not only to the Apostles, but also to the whole body of Christ's congregation, although not in like form and majesty as he came down at the feast of Pentecost.

But now herein standeth the controversy, whether all men do justly arrogate to themselves the Holy Ghost, or no. The Bishops of Rome have for a long time made a sore challenge thereunto, reasoning for themselves after this sort. "The Holy Ghost," say they, "was promised to the church, and never forsaketh the Church: but we are the chief heads and the principal part of the Church: therefore we have the Holy Ghost for ever; and whatsoever things we decree, are undoubted verities, and oracles of the Holy Ghost." That ye may perceive the weakness of this argument, it is needful to teach you first, what the true Church of Christ is, and then, to confer the Church of Rome therewith, to discern how well they agree together.

John 13:1

John 14:16, 26 and 15:26, 16:7, 13

John 14:16, 17

Matt. 28:20

John 17:20

Rom. 8:9, 15

The true Church is an universal congregation or fellowship, of God's faithful and elect people, *built upon the foundation of the Apostles and Prophets, Jesus Christ himself being the head corner stone*. And it hath always three notes or marks, whereby it is known: pure and sound doctrine, the Sacraments ministered according to Christ's holy institution, and the right use of ecclesiastical discipline. This description of the Church, is agreeable both to the Scriptures of God, and also to the doctrine of the ancient fathers, so that none may justly find fault therewith.

Now, if ye will compare this with the Church of Rome, not as it was at the beginning, but as it is presently, and hath been for the space of nine hundred years and odd, you shall well perceive the state thereof, to be so far wide from the nature of the true Church, that nothing can be more. For neither are they *built upon the foundation of the Apostles and Prophets*, retaining the pure and sound doctrine of Christ Jesu; neither yet do they order either the Sacraments, or else the ecclesiastical keys, in such sort as he did first institute and ordain them, but have so intermingled their own traditions and inventions, by chopping and changing, by adding and plucking away, that now, they may seem to be converted into a new guise. Christ commended to his Church a Sacrament of his Body and Blood: they have changed it into a sacrifice for the quick and the dead. Christ did minister to his Apostles, and the Apostles to other men, indifferently under both kinds: they have robbed the lay people of the cup, saying that for them one kind is sufficient. Christ ordained no other element to be used in Baptism, but only water, whereunto when the word is joined, it is made, as St Augustine saith, a full and perfect Sacrament: they, being wiser in their own conceit than Christ, think it is not well nor orderly done, unless they use conjuration, unless they hallow the water; unless there be oil, salt, spittle, tapers, and such other dumb ceremonies, serving to no use, contrary to the plain rule of St Paul, who willeth *all things* to be *done* in the Church *unto edification*. Christ ordained the authority of the keys, to excommunicate notorious sinners, and to absolve them which are truly penitent: they abuse this power at their own pleasure, as well in cursing the godly with bell, book, and candle, as also in absolving the reprobate, which are known to be unworthy of any Christian society; whereof he that lust to see examples, let him search their lives. To be short, look what our Saviour Christ pronounced of the Scribes and the Pharisees in the Gospel, the same may we boldly, and with safe conscience, pronounce of the Bishops of Rome: namely, that they have forsaken, and daily do forsake, the commandments of God, to erect and set up their own constitutions. Which thing being true, as all they which have any light of God's word must needs confess, we may well conclude, according to the rule of Augustine, that the Bishops of Rome, and their adherents, are not the

Eph. 2:20

Augustine

1 Cor. 14:26

Matt. 15:3, 6,
Mark 7:9, 13

true Church of Christ, much less then, to be taken as chief heads and rulers of the same. "Whosoever," saith he, "do dissent from the Scriptures concerning the Head, although they be found in all places where the Church is appointed, yet are they not in the Church." A plain place, concluding directly against the Church of Rome.

August. *contra Petil. Donat. Epist.* cap. 4

Where is now the Holy Ghost, which they so stoutly do claim to themselves? Where is now *the Spirit of truth*, that will not suffer them in any wise to err? If it be possible to be there, where the true Church is not, then is it at Rome: otherwise it is but a vain brag, and nothing else. St Paul, as ye have heard before, saith, *If any man have not the Spirit of Christ, the same is not his.* And by turning the words, it may be as truly said, If any man be not of Christ, the same hath not his Spirit. Now, to discern who are truly his, and who not, we have this rule given us, that *his sheep do always hear his voice.* And St John saith, *He that is of God, heareth God's word.* Whereof it followeth, that the popes, in not hearing Christ's voice, as they ought to do, but preferring their own decrees before the express word of God, do plainly argue to the world, that they are not of Christ, nor yet possessed with his Spirit.

John 16:13

Rom. 8:9

John 10:27
John 8:47

But here they will allege for themselves, that there are divers necessary points not expressed in holy Scripture, which were left to the revelation of the Holy Ghost; who being given to the Church, according to Christ's promise, hath taught *many things* from time to time, which the Apostles *could not then bear.* To this we may easily answer, by the plain words of Christ, teaching us that the proper office of the Holy Ghost is, not to institute and bring in new ordinances, contrary to his doctrine before taught, but to expound and declare those things which he had before taught, so that they might be well and truly understood. *When the Holy Ghost,* saith he, *shall come, he shall lead you into all truth.* What truth doth he mean? any other than he himself had before expressed in his word? No. For he saith, *He shall take of mine, and show it unto you.* Again, *He shall bring you in remembrance, of all things that I have told you.* It is not then the duty and part of any Christian, under pretence of the Holy Ghost, to bring in his own dreams and phantasies into the Church; but he must diligently provide, that his doctrine and decrees be agreeable to Christ's holy Testament: otherwise, in making the Holy Ghost the author thereof, he doth blaspheme, and belie the Holy Ghost, to his own condemnation.

John 16:12

Ibid.:13, 14

John 14:26

Now to leave their doctrine, and come to other points. What shall we think or judge of the Pope's intolerable pride? The Scripture saith, that *God resisteth the proud, and showeth grace to the humble.* Also it pronounceth them *blessed, which are poor in spirit,* promising that *they which humble themselves shall be exalted.* And Christ our Saviour willeth all his to *learn of him, because he is humble and meek.* As for pride, St Gregory

James 4:6

Matt. 5:3; 23:12

Matt. 11:29

saith "It is the root of all mischief." And St Augustine's judgement is
this, that it maketh men devils. Can any man then, which either hath or
shall read the popes' lives, justly say that they had the Holy Ghost within
them? First, as touching that they will be termed Universal Bishops, and
Heads of all Christian Churches through the world, we have the
judgement of Gregory expressly against them; who writing to Mauritius
the Emperor, condemneth John Bishop of Constantinople in that
behalf, calling him the prince of pride, Lucifer's successor, and the
forerunner of Antichrist. St Bernard also agreeing thereunto, saith,
"What greater pride can there be, than that one man should prefer his
own judgement, before the whole Congregation, as though he only had
the Spirit of God?" And Chrysostom pronounceth a terrible sentence
against them, affirming plainly, that "Whosoever seeketh to be chief in
earth, shall find confusion in heaven," and that he which striveth for the
supremacy, shall not be reputed among the servants of Christ. Again he
saith, "To desire a good work, it is good; but to covet the chief degree of
honour, it is mere vanity." Do not these places sufficiently convince their
outrageous pride, in usurping to themselves a superiority above all
other, as well ministers and bishops, as kings also and emperors?

But as the lion is known by his claws, so let us learn to know these
men by their deeds. What shall we say of him, that made the noble King
Dandalus to be tied by the neck with a chain, and to lie flat down before
his table, there to gnaw bones like a dog? Shall we think that he had
God's Holy Spirit within him, and not rather the spirit of the devil?
Such a tyrant was Pope Clement the Sixth. What shall we say of him, that
proudly and contemptuously, trod Frederic the Emperor under his feet,
applying that verse of the Psalm unto himself: *Thou shalt go upon the lion
and the adder; the young lion and the dragon thou shalt tread under thy foot?*
Shall we say that he had God's Holy Spirit within him, and not rather
the spirit of the devil? Such a tyrant was Pope Alexander the Third. What
shall we say of him, that armed and animated the son against the father,
causing him to be taken, and to be cruelly famished to death, contrary
to the law both of God and also of nature? Shall we say that he had
God's Holy Spirit within him, and not rather the spirit of the devil?
Such a tyrant was Pope Paschal the Second. What shall we say of him,
that came into his popedom like a fox, that reigned like a lion, and died
like a dog? Shall we say that he had God's Holy Spirit within him, and not
rather the spirit of the devil? Such a tyrant was Pope Boniface the Eighth.
What shall we say of him, that made Henry the Emperor, with his wife
and his young child, to stand at the gates of the city, in the rough winter,
bare-footed and bare-legged, only clothed in linsey woolsey, eating
nothing from morning to night, and that for the space of three days?
Shall we say that he had God's Holy Spirit within him, and not rather

Lib. 4,
Epist. 76, 78

Serm. 3 de
Resur. Dom.

Dialogorum
Lib. iii
Chrysost. *sup*
Matt.

Sabellic. Ennead.
9, Lib. 7

Psalm 91:13

the spirit of the devil? Such a tyrant was Pope Hildebrand, most worthy to be called a firebrand, if we shall term him as he hath best deserved.

Many other examples might here be alleged; as of Pope Jone the harlot, that was delivered of a child in the high street, going solemnly in procession; of Pope Julius the Second, that wilfully cast St Peter's keys into the river Tiberis; of Pope Urban the Sixth, that caused five cardinals to be put in sacks, and cruelly drowned; of Pope Sergius the Third, that persecuted the dead body of Formosus his predecessor, when it had been buried eight years; of Pope John, the Fourteenth of that name, who having his enemy delivered into his hands, caused him first to be stripped stark naked, his beard to be shaven, and to be hanged up a whole day by the hair, then to be set upon an ass, with his face backward towards the tail, to be carried round about the city in despite, to be miserably beaten with rods, last of all to be thrust out of his country, and to be banished for ever. But to conclude and make an end, ye shall briefly take this short lesson: wheresoever ye find the spirit of arrogancy and pride, the spirit of envy, hatred, contention, cruelty, murder, extortion, witchcraft, necromancy, &c, assure yourselves that there is the spirit of the devil, and not of God; albeit they pretend outwardly to the world never so much holiness. For as the Gospel teacheth us, the Spirit of Jesus is a good Spirit, an holy Spirit, a sweet Spirit, a lowly Spirit, a merciful Spirit, full of charity and love, full of forgiveness and pity, *not rendering evil for evil*, extremity for extremity, but *overcoming evil with good*, and *remitting* all offence, even *from the heart*. According to which rule, if any man live uprightly, of him it may be safely pronounced, that he hath the Holy Ghost within him; if not, then it is a plain token, that he doth usurp the name of the Holy Ghost, in vain.

1 Pet. 3:9;
Rom. 12:21
Matt. 18:35

Therefore, dearly beloved, according to the good counsel of St John, *believe not every spirit, but first try them, whether they be of God or no. Many shall come in my name*, saith Christ, and shall *transform themselves into angels of light, deceiving if it be possible, the very elect. They shall come unto you in sheep's clothing, being inwardly cruel and ravening wolves.* They shall have an outward show of great holiness, and innocency of life, so that ye shall hardly, or not at all, discern them. But the rule that ye must follow is this: to *judge them by their fruits.* Which if they be wicked and naught, then it is unpossible, that the tree of whom they proceed, should be good. Such were all the popes and prelates of Rome, for the most part, as doth well appear in the story of their lives; and therefore they are worthily accounted among the number of *false prophets, and false Christs*, which deceived the world a long while.

1 John 4:1;
Matt. 24:5,24,
2 Cor. 11:13–15
Matt. 7:15–20

Luke 6:43–5

Matt. 24:24

The *Lord of heaven and earth* defend us from their tyranny and pride, that they never enter into his vineyard again, to the disturbance of his seely poor flock, but that they may be utterly confounded, and put to

Ibid. 11:25

flight in all parts of the world. And he of his great mercy so work in all men's hearts, by the mighty power of the Holy Ghost, that the comfortable Gospel of his Son, Christ, may be truly preached, truly received, and truly followed in all places, to the beating down of sin, death, the pope, the devil, and all the kingdom of Antichrist; that, the scattered and dispersed sheep being at length gathered into *one fold*, we may in the end rest all together, in the bosom of Abraham, Isaac, and Jacob, there to be partakers of eternal and everlasting life, through the merits and death of Jesus Christ, our Saviour. Amen.

John 10:16

Luke 16:22;
Matt. 8:11

AN HOMILY
FOR THE DAYS OF ROGATION WEEK
THAT ALL GOOD THINGS COMETH
FROM GOD

I AM PURPOSED THIS DAY, good devout Christian people, to declare unto you, the most deserved praise and commendation of Almighty God; not only in consideration of the marvellous creation of this world, or for the conservation and governance thereof, wherein his great power and wisdom might excellently appear, to move us to honour and dread him; but most specially, in consideration of his liberal and large goodness, which he daily bestoweth on us, his reasonable creatures, for whose sake he made this whole universal world, with all the commodities and goods therein: which his singular goodness, well and diligently remembered on our part, should move us, as duty is again, with hearty affection to love him, and with word and deed to praise him, and serve him all the days of our life.

And to this matter, being so worthy to entreat of, and so profitable for you to hear, I trust I shall not need with much circumstance of words, to stir you to give your attendance, to hear what shall be said. Only I would wish your affection inflamed in secret wise within yourself, to raise up some motion of thanksgiving, to the goodness of Almighty God, in every such point as shall be opened by my declaration particularly unto you. For else what shall it avail us, to hear and know the great goodness of God towards us, to know that whatsoever is good, proceedeth from him, as from the principal fountain and the only author, or to know that whatsoever is sent from him, must needs be good and wholesome, if the hearing of such matter moveth us no further, but to know it only? What availed it the wise men of the world, to have a knowledge of *the power and divinity of God*, by the secret inspiration of him, where *they did not* honour and *glorify him* in their knowledges, *as God*? What praise was it to them, by the consideration of the creation of the world, to behold his goodness, Rom. 1:19–22

341

and yet *were not thankful* to him again, for his creatures? What other things deserved this blindness and forgetfulness of them, at God's hands, but utter forsaking of him? And so forsaken of God, they could not but fall into extreme ignorance and error. And although they much esteemed themselves, in their wits and knowledge, and gloried in their wisdom, yet *vanished they away blindly in their thoughts, became fools,* and perished in their folly. There can be none other end of such as draweth nigh to God by knowledge, and yet depart from him in unthankfulness, but utter destruction. This experience saw David in his days. For in his Psalm he saith, *Behold, they which withdraw themselves from thee shall perish; for thou hast destroyed them all that are strayed from thee.* This experience was perceived to be true of that holy Prophet Jeremy. *O Lord,* saith he, *whatsoever they be that forsake thee, shall be confounded; they that depart from thee, shall be written in the earth,* and soon forgotten. It profiteth not, good people, to hear the goodness of God declared unto us, if our hearts be not inflamed thereby, to honour and thank him. It profited not the Jews, which were God's elect people, to hear much of God, seeing that he was not received in their hearts by faith, nor thanked for his benefits bestowed upon them. Their unthankfulness was the cause of their destruction. Let us eschew the manner of these before rehearsed, and follow rather the example of that holy Apostle St Paul, which when in a deep meditation, he did behold the marvellous proceedings of Almighty God, and considered his infinite goodness in the ordering of his creatures, he burst out into this conclusion: *Surely,* saith he, *of him, by him, and in him, be all things.* And, this once pronounced, he stuck not still at this point, but forthwith thereupon joined to these words, *To him be glory, and praise, for ever. Amen.*

Upon the ground of which words of St Paul, good audience, I purpose to build my exhortation of this day unto you. Wherein I shall do my endeavour, first to prove unto you, that all good things *cometh down to us from above, from the Father of light;* secondly, that Jesus Christ, his Son and our Saviour, is the mean, by whom we receive his liberal goodness; thirdly, that in the power and virtue of the Holy Ghost, we be made meet and able to receive his gifts and graces: which things, distinctly and advisedly considered in our minds, must needs compel us, in most low reverence, after our bounden duty, always to render him thanks again, in some testification of our good hearts, for his deserts unto us. And that the intreating of this matter in hand, may be to the glory of Almighty God, let us in one faith and charity, call upon the Father of mercy, from whom *cometh every good gift, and every perfect gift,* by the mediation of his wellbeloved Son, our Saviour, that we may be assisted with the presence of his Holy Spirit, and wholesomely on both our parts to demean ourselves, in speaking and hearing, to the salvation of our souls.

Marginal notes:
Psalm 73:27
Jer. 18:13
Rom. 11:36
James 1:17
Ibid.

In the beginning of my speaking unto you, good Christian people, suppose not that I do take upon me to declare unto you, the excellent power or the incomparable wisdom of Almighty God, as though I would have you believe that it might be expressed unto you by words. Nay, it may not be thought, that that thing may be comprehended by man's words, that is incomprehensible. And too much arrogancy it were, for *dust and ashes* to think that he could worthily declare his Maker. It passeth far the dark understanding and wisdom of a mortal man, to speak sufficiently of that divine Majesty, which the angels cannot understand. We shall therefore lay apart to speak of that profound and unsearchable nature of Almighty God, rather acknowledging our weakness, than rashly to attempt that is above all man's capacity to compass. It shall better suffice us, in low humility to reverence and dread his Majesty, which we cannot comprise, than by overmuch curious searching, to be overcharged with the glory.

Gen. 18:27

We shall rather turn our whole contemplation, to answer a while his goodness towards us; wherein we shall be much more profitably occupied, and more may we be bold to search. To consider this great power he is of, can but make us dread and fear; to consider his high wisdom, might utterly discomfort our frailty, to have any thing to do with him: but in consideration of his inestimable goodness, we take good heart again to trust well unto him; by his goodness, we be assured to take him for our refuge, our hope and comfort, our merciful Father, in all the course of our lives. His power and wisdom compelleth us to take him for God omnipotent, invisible, having rule in heaven and in earth, having all things in his subjection, and will have none in council with him, nor any to ask the reason of his doing: for he may do what liketh him, *and none can resist him*. For *he worketh all things* in his secret judgement, *to his own pleasure, yea even the wicked to damnation*, saith Salomon. By the reason of this nature, he is called in Scripture *consuming fire*, he is called *a terrible* and *fearful God*. Of this behalf therefore, we may have no familiarity, no access unto him: but his goodness again tempereth the rigour of his high power, and maketh us bold, and putteth us in hope that he will be conversant with us, and easy unto us.

Dan. 4:35

Prov. 16:4

Heb. 12:29,
Deut. 4:24, 10:17;
Exod. 15:11

It is his goodness, that moveth him to say in Scripture, *It is my delight to be with the children of men*. It is his goodness, that moveth him to call us unto him, to offer us his friendship and presence. It is his goodness, that patiently suffereth our straying from him, and suffereth us long, to win us to repentance. It is of his goodness, that we be created reasonable creatures, where else he might have made us brute beasts. It was his mercy, to have us born among the number of Christian people, and thereby in a much more nighness to salvation, where we might have been born (if his goodness had not been), among the paynims, clean

Prov. 8:31

void from God and the hope of everlasting life. And what other thing doth his loving and gentle voice, spoken in his word, where he calleth us to his presence and friendship, but declare his goodness only, without regard of our worthiness? And what other thing doth stir him to call us to him, when we be strayed from him, to suffer us patiently, to win us to repentance, but only his singular goodness, no whit of our deserving?

Let them all come together, that be now glorified in heaven, and let us hear what answer they will make, in these points afore rehearsed, whether their first creation was of God's goodness, or of themselves.

Psalm 100:3

Forsooth David would make answer for them all, and say, *Know ye for surety, even the Lord is God; he hath made us, and not we ourselves.* If they were asked again, who should be thanked for their regeneration, for their justification, and for their salvation, whether their deserts, or God's goodness only; although in this point every one confess sufficiently the truth of this matter, in his own person, yet let David answer by the mouth of them all at this time; who cannot but choose but say, *Not to us, O Lord, not to us, but to thy Name give all the thank, for thy loving mercy, and for thy truth's sake.* If we should ask again, from whence came their glorious works and deeds, which they wrought in their lives, wherewith God was so highly pleased and worshipped by them, let some other witness be brought in, to testify in this matter, *that in the mouth of two or three may the truth be known.* Verily that holy Prophet Esay beareth record, and saith, *O Lord, it is thou,* of thy goodness, *that hast wrought all our works in us,* not we of ourselves. And to uphold the truth of this matter, against all justiciaries and hypocrites, which rob Almighty God of this honour, and ascribe it to themselves, St Paul bringeth in his belief. *We be not,* saith he, *sufficient of ourselves, as of ourselves, once to think any thing, but all our ableness is of God's goodness. For he it is, in whom we have all our being, our living, and moving.* If ye will know furthermore, where they had their gifts and sacrifices, which they offered continually in their lives to Almighty God, they cannot but agree with David, where he saith, *Of thy liberal hand, O Lord, we have received that we gave unto thee.*

If this holy company therefore, confesseth so constantly, that all the goods and graces, wherewith they were indued in soul, came of the goodness of God only, what more can be said, to prove that all that is good, cometh from Almighty God? Is it meet to think, that all spiritual goodness cometh from God above only, and that other good things, either of nature or of fortune (as we call them), cometh of any other cause? Doth God of his goodness adorn the soul, with all the powers thereof, as it is, and cometh the gifts of the body, wherewith it is indued, from any other? If he doeth the more, cannot he do the less? To justify a sinner, to new create him, from a wicked person, to a righteous man, is a greater act, saith St Augustine, than to make such a new heaven and

Marginal references:
Psalm 115:1
Matt. 18:16
Isai. 26:12
2 Cor. 3:5; Acts 17:28
1 Chron. 29:14

earth as is already made. We must needs agree, that whatsoever good thing is in us, of grace, of nature, of fortune, is of God only, as the only Author and Worker.

And yet it is not to be thought, that God hath created all this whole universal world, as it is, and thus once made, hath given it up, to be ruled and used after our own wits and device, and so take no more charge therefore: as we see the shipwright, after he hath brought his ship to a perfect end, then delivereth he it to the mariners, and taketh no more care thereof. Nay, God hath not so created the world, that he is careless of it; but he still preserveth it, by his goodness; he still stayeth it in his creation: for else, without his special goodness, it could not stand long in his condition. And therefore St Paul saith, that he preserveth all things, and beareth them up still in his word, lest they should fall, without him, to their nothing again, whereof they were made. If his special goodness were not everywhere present, every creature should be out of order, and no creature should have his property, wherein he was first created. He is therefore invisibly everywhere, and in every creature, and *fulfilleth both heaven and earth* with his presence; in the fire, to give heat; in the water, to give moisture; in the earth, to give fruit; in the heart, to give his strength: yea, in our bread and drink he is, to give us nourishment; where without him, the bread and drink cannot give sustenance, nor the herb health, as the Wise Man plainly confesseth it, saying, *It is not the increase of fruits that feedeth men, but it is thy word, O Lord, which preserveth them that trust in thee.* And Moses agreeth to the same, when he saith, *Man's life resteth not in bread only, but in every word which proceedeth out of God's mouth. It is neither the herb nor the plaster, that giveth health* of themselves, *but thy word, O Lord,* saith the Wise Man, *which healeth all things.* It is not therefore the power of the creatures which worketh their effects, but the goodness of God, which worketh in them. In his word truly, doth all things consist. By that same word, that heaven and earth were made, by the same are they upholden, maintained, and kept in order, saith St Peter, and shall be, till Almighty God shall withdraw his power from them, and speak their dissolution.

If it were not thus, that the goodness of God were effectually in his creatures to rule them, how could it be that the main sea, so raging and labouring to overflow the earth, could be kept within his bonds and banks, as it is? That holy man Job evidently spied the goodness of God in this point, and confessed, that if he had not a special goodness to the preservation of the earth, it could not but shortly be overflowed of the sea. How could it be that the elements, so diverse and contrary as they be among themselves, should yet agree, and abide together in a concord, without destruction one of another, to serve our use, if it came not only of God's goodness, so to temper them? How could the fire not burn, and

Marginal references:
Heb. 1:3, 3:4
Jer. 23:24
Wisd. 16:26
Deut. 8:3
Wisd. 16:12
2 Pet. 3:7
Job 28:11

consume all things, if it were let loose, to go whither it would, and not stayed in his sphere, by the goodness of God, measurably to heat these inferior creatures, to their riping? Consider the huge substance of the earth, so heavy and great as it is: how could it stand stably in the space as

Psalm 104:5

it doth, if God's goodness reserved it not so, for us to travail on? *It is thou, O Lord,* saith David, *which hast founded the earth in his stability*; and during thy word *it shall never reel* or fall down. Consider the great strong beasts and fishes, far passing the strength of man: how fierce soever they be, and strong, yet by the goodness of God, they prevail not against us, but are under our subjection, and serve our use. Of whom came the invention, thus to subdue them, and make them fit for our commodities? Was it by man's brain? Nay, rather this invention came by the goodness of God, which inspired man's understanding, to have his purpose of

Job 38:36
Ibid. 32:8

every creature. *Who was it,* saith Job, *that put will and wisdom in man's head,* but God, only of his goodness? And as the same saith again, *I perceive that every man hath a mind, but it is the inspiration of the Almighty, that giveth understanding.* It could not be, verily, good Christian people, that man, of his own wit unholpen, should invent so many and diverse devices, in all crafts and sciences, except the goodness of Almighty God had been present with men, and had stirred up their wits, and studies, and purpose, to know the natures and disposition of all his creatures, to serve us sufficiently, in our needs and necessities, yea, not only to serve our necessities, but to serve our pleasures and delight, more than necessity requireth. So liberal is God's goodness to us, to provoke us to thank him, if any hearts we have.

The Wise Man, in his contemplation by himself, could not but grant

Wisd. 7:16–21

this thing to be true, that I reason unto you. *In his hands,* saith he, *be we and our words, and all our wisdom, and all our sciences, and works of knowledge. For it is he that gave me the true instruction of his creatures, both to know the disposition of the world, and the virtues of the elements, the beginning and the end of times, the change and diversities of them, the course of the year, the order of the stars, the natures of beasts, and the powers of them, the power of the winds, and thoughts of men, the differences of plants, the virtue of roots; and whatsoever is hid and secret in nature, I learned it. The*

Ibid. 9:16, 14, 17

artificer of all these taught me this wisdom. And further he saith, *Who can search out the things that be in heaven? For it is hard for us, to search such things as be on earth, and in daily sight afore us. For our wits and thoughts,* saith he, *be imperfect, and our policies uncertain. No man can therefore search out the meaning in these things, except thou givest wisdom, and sendest thy Spirit from above.* If the Wise Man thus confesseth all these things to be of God, why should not we acknowledge it, and by the knowledge of it, consider our duty to Godward, to give him thanks for his goodness?

I perceive that I am far here overcharged, with the plenty and copy of matter, that might be brought in, for the proof of this cause. If I should enter to show, how the goodness of Almighty God appeared everywhere, in the creatures of the world, how marvellous they be in their creation, how beautified in their order, how necessary they be to our use, all with one voice must needs grant their author to be none other, but Almighty God; his goodness must they needs extol and magnify everywhere. To whom be all honour and glory, for evermore.

THE SECOND PART OF THE HOMILY FOR ROGATION WEEK

IN THE FORMER PART OF THIS HOMILY, good Christian people, I have declared to your contemplation, the great goodness of Almighty God, in the creation of this world, with all the furniture thereof, for the use and comfort of man; whereby we might the rather be moved to acknowledge our duty again to his Majesty. And I trust it hath wrought not only belief in you, but also it hath moved you to render your thanks, secretly in your hearts, to Almighty God, for his lovingkindness.

But yet peradventure, some will say that they can agree to this: that all that is good pertaining to the soul, or whatsoever is created with us in body, should come from God, as from the Author of all goodness, and from none other; but for such things as be without them both, I mean such good things which we call goods of fortune, as riches, authority, promotion, and honour, some men may think that they should come of our industry and diligence, of our labour and travail, rather than supernaturally.

Now then consider, good people, if any author there be of such things, concurrent with man's labour and endeavour, were it meet to ascribe them to any other, than to God?—as the paynim philosophers and poets did err, which took fortune and made her a goddess, to be honoured for such things. God forbid, good Christian people, that this imagination should earnestly be received of us! that be worshippers of the true God, whose works and proceedings be expressed manifestly in his word. These be the opinions and sayings of infidels, not of true Christians. For they indeed, as Job maketh mention, believe and say, that *God hath his* Job 22:14 *residence* and resting place *in the clouds, and considereth nothing of our matters.* Epicures they be, that imagine that *he walketh about the coasts of the heavens,* and hath no respect to these inferior things; but that all these things should proceed either by chance, and at adventure, or else by disposition of fortune, and God to have no stroke in them. What other thing is this to say, than as *the fool supposeth in his heart, There is no* Psalm 14:1, 53:1

Psalm 50:7, 10–12

God? Whom we shall none otherwise reprove, than with God's own words, by the mouth of David. *Hear, my people,* saith he, *for I am thy God, thy very God. All the beasts of the wood are mine, sheep and oxen, that wandereth on the mountains. I have the knowledge of all the fowls of the air; the beauty of the field is my handywork. Mine is the whole circuit of the world, and all the plenty that is in it.* And again by the Prophet Jeremy: *Thinkest*

Jer. 23:23, 24

thou that I am a God of the place nigh me, saith the Lord, and not a God far off? Can a man hide himself in so secret a corner, that I shall not see him? Do not I fulfil and replenish *both heaven and earth? saith the Lord.* Which of these two should be most believed? fortune, whom they paint to be blind of both eyes, ever unstable and unconstant in her wheel, in whose hands they say these things be? or God, in whose hands and power these things be indeed, who for his truth and constance was never reproved? For his sight looketh thorough heaven and earth, and seeth all things, presently, with his eyes. Nothing is too dark or hidden from his knowledge, not the privy thoughts of men's minds. Truth it is, that of God is all riches, all power, all authority, all health, wealth, and prosperity; of the which we should have no part, without his liberal

Psalm 104:28, 29

distribution, and except it came from him above. David first testifieth it of riches and possessions: *If thou givest good luck, they shall gather; and if thou openest thy hand, they shall be full of* goodness: *but, if thou turnest thy*

Prov. 10:22

face, they shall be troubled. And Salomon saith, *It is the blessing of the Lord*

1 Sam. 2:7–8

that maketh rich men. To this agree that holy woman Anne, where she saith in her song, *It is the Lord that maketh the poor, and maketh the rich: it is he that promoteth and pulleth down: he can raise a needy man from his misery, and from the dunghill he can lift up a poor personage, to sit with princes, and have the seat of glory: for all the coasts of the earth be his.*

James 1:17

Now if any man will ask what shall it avail us, to know that *every good gift,* as of nature and fortune (so called), *and every perfect gift,* as of grace, concerning the soul, is* of God, and that it is his gift only, forsooth for many causes is it convenient for us to know it. For so shall we know, if we confess the truth, who ought justly to be thanked for them. Our pride shall be thereby abated (perceiving naught to come of ourselves but sin and vice), if any goodness be in us, to refer all laud and praise for the same to Almighty God. It shall make us not to advance ourselves before our neighbour, to despise him for that he hath fewer gifts, seeing God giveth his gifts where

Jer. 9:23

he will: it shall make *the wise man not to glory in his wisdom, nor the strong man in his strength, nor the rich to glory in his riches,* but in the living God, which is the Author of all these: lest, if we should do so, we might be rebuked with

1 Cor. 4:7

the words of St Paul, *What hast thou that thou hast not received? and, if thou hast received it, why gloriest thou in thyself, as though thou haddest not received it?*

---

* Griffiths reports that all texts read "to be".

To confess that all good things cometh from Almighty God, is a great point of wisdom, my friends. For so confessing, we know whither to resort, for to have them if we want; as St James biddeth us, saying, *If any man wanteth the gift of wisdom, let him ask it of God, that gives it, and it shall be given him.* As the Wise Man, in the want of such a like gift, made his recourse to God for it, as he testifieth in his book. *After I knew,* saith he, *that otherwise I could not be chaste, except God granted it (and this was,* as he there writeth, *high wisdom, to know whose gift it was), I made haste to the Lord, and earnestly besought him, even from the roots of my heart, to have it.* I would to God, my friends, that in our wants and necessities, we would go to God, as St James bids, and as the Wise Man teacheth us that he did. I would we believed stedfastly, that God only gives them. If we did, we would not seek our want and necessity, of the devil and his ministers, so oft as we do, as daily experience declareth it. For if we stand in necessity of corporal health, whither go the common people, but to charms, witchcrafts, and other delusions of the devil? If we knew that God were the Author of this gift, we would only use his means appointed, and bide his leisure, till he thought it good for us to have it given. If the merchant and worldly occupier, knew that God is the Giver of riches, he would content himself with so much, as by just means, approved of God, he could get to his living, and would be no richer than truth would suffer him; he would never procure his gain, and ask his goods, at the devil's hand. God forbid, ye will say, that any man should take his riches of the devil. Verily, so many as increase themselves by usury, by extortion, by perjury, by stealth, by deceits and craft, they have their goods of the devil's gift. And all they that give themselves to such means, and have renounced the true means that God hath appointed, have forsaken him, and are become worshippers of the devil, to have their lucres and advantages. They be such as kneel down to the devil, at his bidding, and worship him; for he promiseth them for so doing, that he will give them the world, and the goods therein. They cannot other-wise better serve the devil, than to do his pleasure and commandment. And his motion and will it is, to have us forsake the truth, and betake us to falsehood, to lies, and perjuries. They therefore which believe perfectly, in their heart, that God is to be honoured, and requested for the gift of all things necessary, would use no other means, to relieve their necessities, but truth and verity, and would serve God, to have competency of all things necessary. The man in his need would not relieve his want by stealth: the woman would not relieve her necessity and poverty, by giving her body to other in adultery, for gain. If God be the Author indeed of life, health, riches, and welfare, let us make our recourse to him, as to the Author, and we shall have it, saith St James. Yea, *it is high wisdom* by the Wise Man, therefore *to know whose gift it is.*

James 1:5

Wisd. 8:21

For many other skills, it is wisdom to know and believe, that all goods and graces be of God, as the Author. Which thing well considered, must needs make us think, that we shall make account, for that which God giveth us to possess, and therefore shall make us to be more diligent, well to spend them to God's glory, and to the profit of our neighbour; that we may make a good account at the last, and be praised for good stewards; that we may hear these words of our Judge, *Well done, good servant and faithful: thou hast been faithful in little, I will make thee ruler over much: go into thy Master's joy.*

Matt. 25:21

Besides, to believe certainly, God to be the Author of all the gifts that we have, shall make us to be in silence and patience, when they be taken again from us. For, as God of his mercy, doth grant us them to use, so otherwhiles, he doth justly take them again from us, to prove our patience, to exercise our faith, and by the means of the taking away of a few, to bestow the more warily those that remain, to teach us to use them the more to his glory, after he giveth them to us again. Many there be, that with mouth can say that they believe, that God is the Author of every good gift that they have, but in the time of temptation, they go back from this belief. They say it in word, but deny it in deed. Consider me the usage of the world, and see whether it be not true. Behold the rich man, that is indued with substance: if by any adversity, his goods be taken from him, how fumeth and fretteth he! how murmureth he and despaireth! He that hath the gift of good reputation, if his name be any thing touched by the detractor, how unquiet is he! how busy to revenge his despite! If a man hath the gift of wisdom, and fortune to be taken of some evil willer for a fool, and is so reported, how much doth it grieve him to be so esteemed! Think ye that these believe constantly that God is the Author of these gifts? If they believed it verily, why should they not patiently suffer God to take away his gifts again, which he gave them freely, and lent for a time?

But ye will say: "I could be content to resign to God such gifts, if he took them again from me; but now are they taken from me by evil chances and false shrews, by naughty wretches; how should I take this thing patiently?" To this may be answered, that Almighty God is of his nature invisible, and cometh to no man visibly, after the manner of man, to take away his gifts that he lent; but in this point, whatsoever God doeth, he bringeth it about by his instruments ordained thereto. He hath good angels, he hath evil angels; he hath good men, and he hath evil men; he hath hail and rain, he hath wind and thunder, he hath heat and cold; innumerable instruments hath he, and messengers, by whom again he asketh such gifts as he committeth to our trust. As the Wise Man confesseth, the *creature* must needs wait to *serve his Maker*, to be *fierce against unjust men to their punishment*: for as the same author saith, *he armeth the*

Wisd. 16:24
Ibid. 5:17

creature to revenge his enemies. And otherwhiles, to the probation of our faith, stirreth he up such storms. And therefore, by what mean and instrument soever God takes from us his gifts, we must patiently take God's judgement in worth, and acknowledge him to be the Taker and Giver; as Job saith, *The Lord gave, and the Lord took,* when yet his enemies drove his cattle away, and when the devil slew his children, and afflicted his body with a grievous sickness. Such meekness was in that holy King and Prophet David, when he was reviled of Semei in presence of all his host: he took it patiently, and reviled not again; but as confessing God to be the author of his innocency, and good name, and offering it to be at his pleasure, *Let him alone,* saith he to one of his knights, that would have revenged such despite, *for God hath commanded him to curse David, and peradventure God intendeth thereby, to render me some good turn for this curse of him today.* And though the minister otherwhiles doeth evil in his act, proceeding of malice, yet forsomuch as God turneth his evil act, to a proof of our patience, we should rather submit ourself in patience, than to have indignation at God's rod; which peradventure, when he hath corrected us to our nurture, he will cast it into the fire, as it deserveth.

Let us in like manner truly acknowledge, all our gifts and prerogatives, to be so God's gifts, that we shall be ready, to resign them up at his will and pleasure again. Let us throughout our whole lives, confess all good things to come of God, of what name and nature soever they be; not of these corruptible things only, whereof I have now last spoken, but much more of all spiritual graces, behovable for our soul. Without whose goodness no man is called to faith, or stayed therein, as I shall hereafter, in the next part of this Homily, declare to you. In the mean season, forget not what hath already been spoken to you, forget not to be comformable in your judgements, to the truth of this doctrine, and forget not to practise the same, in the whole state of your life; whereby ye shall obtain that blessing, promised by our Saviour Christ, *Blessed be they which hear the word of God, and fulfil it* in life. Which blessing he grant to us all! who reigneth over all, one God in Trinity, the Father, the Son, and the Holy Ghost: to whom be all honour, and glory, for ever. Amen.

Job 1:21

2 Sam. 16:5–12

Luke 11:28

THE THIRD PART OF THE HOMILY FOR ROGATION WEEK

I promised to you, to declare that all spiritual gifts and graces cometh specially from God. Let us consider the truth of this matter, and hear what is testified first of the gift of faith, the first entry into the Christian life, *without which no man can please God.* First, St Paul confesseth it plainly to be God's gift, saying, *Faith is the gift of God.* And again, St

Heb. 11:6

Eph. 2:8

1 Pet. 1:5

Peter saith *it is of God's power that ye be kept, through faith, to salvation.* It is of the goodness of God that we falter not in our hope unto him. It is verily God's work in us, the charity wherewith we love our brethren. If after our fall we repent, it is by him that we repent, which reacheth forth his merciful hand to raise us up. If any will we have to rise, it is he that preventeth our will, and disposeth us thereto. If after contrition we feel our conscience at peace with God, through remission of our sin, and so be reconciled again to his favour, and hope to be his children and inheritors of everlasting life, who worketh these great miracles in us? our deservings and endeavours? our wits and virtue? Nay verily: St Paul will not suffer flesh and clay to presume to such arrogancy, and therefore

2 Cor. 5:18, 19

saith, *All is of God, which hath reconciled us to himself by Jesus Christ; for God was in Christ when he reconciled the world unto himself.* God the Father of all mercy wrought this high benefit unto us, not by his own person, but by a mean, by no less mean than his only beloved Son, whom he spared not from any pain and travail that might do us good. For upon him he put our sins; upon him he made our ransom; him he made the mean betwixt us and himself: whose mediation was so acceptable to God the Father, through his profound and perfect obedience, that he took his act for a full satisfaction of all our disobedience and rebellion; whose righteousness he took to weigh against our sins; whose redemption he would have stand against our damnation.

In this point what have we to muse within ourselves, good friends? I think, no less than that which St Paul said, in the remembrance of this

Rom. 7:25

wonderful goodness of God, *Thanks be to Almighty God, through Christ*

Ephes. 1:3–10

Jesus our Lord. For it is he for whose sake we received this high gift of grace. For as by him, being the everlasting Wisdom, he wrought all the world, and that is contained therein, so by him only and wholly, would he have all things restored again, in heaven and in earth. By this our heavenly Mediator therefore, do we know the favour and mercy of God the Father. By him know we his will and pleasure towards us: for he is

Heb. 1:3

the brightness of his Father's glory, and a very clear *image* and pattern *of his substance.* It is he whom the Father in heaven delighteth to have for his

Matt. 3:17, 18:5

wellbeloved Son, whom he authorised to be our Teacher, whom he charged us to hear, saying, *Hear him.* It is he by whom the Father of

Ephes. 1:3

heaven doth bless us, with all spiritual and heavenly gifts, for whose sake

John 1:16

and favour, writeth St John, *we have received grace* and favour. To this our

Matt. 28:18

Saviour and Mediator, hath God the Father given the power of heaven and earth, and the whole jurisdiction and authority, to distribute his

Ephes. 4:7, 8

goods and gifts committed to him. For so writeth the Apostle: *To every one of us is grace given, according to the measure of Christ's giving.* And thereupon to execute his authority committed, after that he had brought sin and the devil to captivity, to be no more hurtful to his members, he ascended up to his Father again; and from thence sent liberal gifts to his wellbeloved servants; and hath still the power, till the world's end, to distribute his Father's gifts continually in his Church, to the establishment and comfort thereof. And by him, hath Almighty God decreed to dissolve the world, to call all before him, to judge both the quick and the dead. And finally by him, shall he condemn the wicked to eternal fire in hell, and give the good eternal life, and set them assuredly in presence with him in heaven, for evermore. Thus ye see how *all is of God*, by his Son Christ, our Lord and Saviour. Remember, I say once again, your duty of thanks: let them be never to want: still join yourself to continue in thanksgiving: ye can offer to God no better sacrifice; for he saith himself, *It is the sacrifice of praise* and thanks *that shall honour me*. Which thing was well perceived of that holy Prophet David, when he so earnestly spake to himself thus: *O my soul, bless thou the Lord; and all that is within me, bless his holy Name. I say once again, O my soul, bless thou the Lord, and never forget his manifold rewards.* 2 Cor. 5:18 Psalm 50:23 Psalm 103:1–2

God give us grace, good people, to know these things, and to feel them in our hearts! This knowledge and feeling is not in ourself; by ourself it is not possible to come by it; and great pity it were, that we should lose so profitable knowledge. Let us therefore meekly call upon that bountiful Spirit the Holy Ghost, which proceedeth from our Father of mercy, and from our Mediator Christ, that he would assist us, and inspire us with his presence, that in him we may be able to hear the goodness of God declared unto us, to our salvation. For without his lively and secret inspiration, can we not once so much as speak the name of our Mediator, as St Paul plainly testifieth: *No man can once name our Lord Jesus Christ, but in the Holy Ghost.* Much less should we be able to believe and know, these great mysteries that be opened to us by Christ. St Paul saith, that *no man can know what is of God, but the Spirit of God. As for us*, saith he, *we have received, not the spirit of the world, but the Spirit which is of God*, for this purpose, *that* in that holy Spirit, *we might know the things that be given us* by Christ. 1 Cor. 12:3 1 Cor. 2:11, 12

The Wise Man saith, that in the power and virtue of the Holy Ghost, resteth all wisdom, and all ability to know God, and to please him; for he writeth thus: *We know that it is not in man's power to guide his goings: no man can know thy pleasure, except thou givest wisdom, and sendest thy Holy Spirit from above. Send him down*, therefore prayeth he to God, *from thy holy heavens, and from the throne of thy Majesty, that he may be with me, that so I may know what is acceptable before thee.* Let us with so good heart pray as he did, and we shall not fail, but to have his assistance. For *he is soon seen of them that love him; he will be found of them that seek him*: for very liberal and gentle is *the Spirit of wisdom*. Wisd. 9:14–17, 10, Jer. 10:23 Wisd. 6:12; 7:7

In his power shall we have sufficient ability to know our duty to God. In him shall we be comforted, and couraged to walk in our duty. In him shall we be meet vessels to receive the grace of Almighty God. For it is he that purgeth and purifieth the mind, by his secret working, and he

Wisd. 1:7

only is present everywhere, by his invisible power, and *containeth all things* in his dominion. He lighteneth the heart, to conceive worthy thoughts of Almighty God. He sitteth in the tongue of man, to stir him

Ibid.

to speak his honour. No language is hid from him, for *he hath the knowledge of all speech.* He only ministereth spiritual strength to the powers of our soul and body. To hold the way which God hath prepared for us, to walk rightly in our journey, we must acknowledge that it is in

Rom. 8:26

the power of his *Spirit, which helpeth our infirmity.* That we may boldly

Gal. 4:6

come in prayer, and call upon Almighty God as *our Father*, it is by this

Rom. 8:15, 26

Holy Spirit, which *maketh intercession for us, with continual sighs.* If any gift we have, wherewith we may work to the glory of God, and profit of

1 Cor. 12:7–11

our neighbour, all is wrought by *this one and selfsame Spirit, which maketh his distributions peculiarly, to every man as he will.* If any wisdom we have, it is not of our selves; we cannot glory therein, as begun of ourselves; but we ought to glory in God, from whom it came to us, as the Prophet

Jer. 9:24

Jeremy writeth: *Let him that rejoiceth rejoice in this, that he understandeth and knoweth me; for I am the Lord, which show mercy, judgement, and righteousness in the earth; for in these things I delight, saith the Lord.* This wisdom cannot be attained, but by the direction of the Spirit of God, and therefore it is called spiritual wisdom.

And nowhere can we more certainly search for the knowledge of this will of God, by the which we must direct all our works and deeds, but in

John 5:39

the holy Scriptures: for *they be they that testify of* him, saith our Saviour Christ. It may be called knowledge and learning, that is otherwhere

Wisd. 13:1

gotten without the word; but the Wise Man plainly testifieth, that *they all be but vain, which have not in them the wisdom of God.* We see to what vanity the old philosophers came, which were destitute of this science, gotten and searched for in his word. We see what vanity the School doctrine is mixed with, for that in this word they sought not the will of God, but rather the will of reason, the trade of custom, the path of the Fathers, the practice of the Church. Let us therefore read and revolve

Psalm 1:1, 2

the holy Scripture both *day and night*; for *blessed is he that hath his whole*

Psalm 119:105

meditation therein. It is that that giveth *light to our feet*, to walk by. It is that

Psalm 19:7;
John 5:39

which *giveth wisdom to the simple* and ignorant. In it may we find *eternal life*. In the holy Scriptures find we Christ: in Christ find we God; for he

Heb. 1:3,
John 14:9;
Jerome

it is that is *the express image* of the Father; *he that seeth Christ seeth the Father*. And contrariwise, as St Jerome saith, "the ignorance of Scripture is the ignorance of Christ." Not to know Christ is to be in darkness, in the midst of our worldly and carnal light, or reason and philosophy. To be without Christ is to be in foolishness: for he is the only Wisdom of the Father; *in whom it pleased him, that all fullness* and perfection *should dwell.* With whom whosoever is indued *in heart by faith,* and *rooted fast in charity,* hath laid a sure foundation to build on, whereby he *may be able to comprehend with all saints, what is the breadth, and length, and depth, and to know the love of Christ.* This universal and absolute knowledge, is that wisdom which St Paul wished these Ephesians to have, as under heaven the greatest treasure that can be obtained. For of this wisdom the Wise Man writeth thus, of his experience: *All good things came to me together with her, and innumerable riches through her hands.* And addeth moreover in that same place, *She is the mother of all these things. For she is an infinite treasure unto men, which whoso use, become partakers of the love of God.*

I might, with many words, move some of this audience to search for this wisdom, to sequester their reason, to follow God's commandment, to cast from them the wits of their brains, to savour this wisdom, to renounce the wisdom and policy of this fond world, to taste and savour that whereunto the favour and will of God hath called them, and willeth us finally to enjoy by his favour, if we would give ear. But I will haste to the third part of my text; which as it followeth in words more plentifully in the text which I have last cited unto you, wherein is expressed further in Sapience, how God giveth his elect an understanding of the motions of the heavens, of the alterations and circumstances of time, so it must needs follow in them that be indued with this spiritual wisdom. For as they can search where to find this wisdom, and know of whom to ask it, so know they again, that in time it is found, and can therefore attemper themselves to the occasion of the time, to suffer no time to pass away, wherein they may labour for this wisdom. And to increase therein, they know how God, of his infinite mercy and lenity, giveth all men here, time and *place of repentance*; and they see how the wicked, as Job writeth, *abuse the same to their pride*: and therefore do the godly take the better hold of the time, to redeem it, out of such use as it is spoiled in by the wicked. They which have this wisdom of God, can gather, by the diligent and earnest study of the worldlings of this present life, how they wait their times, and apply themselves to every occasion of time, to get riches, to increase their lands and patrimony. They see the time pass away, and therefore take hold on it in such wise, that otherwhiles they will, with the loss of their sleep and ease, with suffering many pains, catch the offer of their time, knowing that that which is once past, cannot be returned again: repentance may follow, but remedy is none. Why should not they then, that be spiritually wise in their generation, wait their time, to increase as fast in their state, to win and gain everlastingly? They reason what a brute forgetfulness it were in man, indued with reason, to be ignorant of their times and tides, when they

Col. 1:19; 2:3, 9

Eph. 3:17–19

Eph. 1:15–19, 3:14–19

Wisd. 7:11, 12, 14

Wisd. 7:17–19

Job 24:23

Jer. 8:7

see the turtledove, the stork, and the swallow to wait their times, as Jeremy saith: *The stork in the air knoweth her appointed times; the turtle and the crane and the swallow observe the time of their coming; but my people knoweth not the judgement of the Lord.*

Eph. 5:16

St Paul willeth us to *redeem the time, because the days are evil.* It is not the counsel of St Paul only, but of all other that ever gave precepts of wisdom. There is no precept more seriously given and commanded, than to know the time. Yea, Christian men, for that they hear how grievously God complaineth, and threateneth in the Scriptures, them which will not know the time of his visitations, are learned thereby the rather, earnestly to apply themselves thereunto. After our Saviour Christ had prophesied, with weeping tears, of the destruction of Jerusalem, at the last he putteth

Luke 19:44

the cause, *For that thou hast not known the time of thy visitation.* O England, which canst not nor wilt not ponder the time of God's merciful visitation, showed thee from day to day, and yet wilt not regard it, neither wilt thou with his punishment be driven to thy duty, nor with his benefits be provoked to thanks; if thou knewest what may fall upon thee, for thine unthankfulness, thou wouldest provide for thy peace.

Brethren, howsoever the world in generality is forgetful of God, let us particularly attend to our time, and win the time with diligence, and apply ourselves to that light and grace that is offered us. Let us, if God's favour and judgements, which he worketh in our time, cannot stir us to call home to ourself, to do that belongeth to our salvation, at the least way let the malice of the devil, the naughtiness of the world, which we see exercised in these perilous and last times, wherein we see our days so dangerously set, provoke us to watch diligently to our vocation, to walk and go forward therein. Let the misery, and short transitory joys, spied in the casualty of our days, move us while we have them in our hands, and seriously stir us, to be wise, and to expend the gracious good will of

Isai. 65:2

God to usward; which *all the day long stretcheth out his hands* (as the Prophet saith) unto us, for the most part his merciful hands, sometime his heavy hands; that we, being learned thereby, may escape the danger

Job 21:13

that must needs fall on the unjust, who *lead their days in felicity* and pleasure, without the knowing of God's will toward them, but *suddenly they go down into hell.*

Let us be found watchers, found in the peace of the Lord; that at the

2 Pet. 3:14

last day we may be *found without spot and blameless.* Yea, let us endeavour ourselves, good Christian people, diligently to keep the presence of his Holy Spirit. Let us renounce all uncleanness; for he is the Spirit of

Wisd. 1:5

purity. Let us avoid all hypocrisy; for this *Holy Spirit will flee from that*

Wisd. 1:4

which is feigned. Cast we off all malice and evil will; for this Spirit *will*

Heb. 12:1

never enter into an evil-willing soul. Let us *cast away all the whole lump of*

Wisd. 1:4

sin, that standeth about us; for he *will never dwell in that body that is subdued to sin.* We cannot be seen thankful to Almighty God, and *work* such Heb. 10:29 *despite to the Spirit of grace,* by whom we be sanctified. If we do our endeavour, we shall not need to fear, we shall be able to overcome all our enemies that fight against us. Only let us apply ourselves, to accept the grace that is offered us. Of Almighty God we have comfort, by his goodness; of our Saviour Christ's mediation we may be sure; and his Holy Spirit will suggest unto us that shall be wholesome, and confirm us in all things. Therefore it cannot be but true, that St Paul affirmeth, *Of* Rom. 11:36 *him, by him, and in him, be all things*: and in him, after this transitory life well passed, shall we have all things. For St Paul saith, *When the Son of* 1 Cor. 15:28 *God shall subdue all things unto him, then shall God be all in all.*

If ye will know how God shall be *all in all,* verily after this sense may ye understand it. In this world ye see that we be fain to borrow many things to our necessity, of many creatures: there is no one thing that sufficeth all our necessities. If we be an hungred, we lust for bread. If we be athirst, we seek to be refreshed with ale or wine. If we be cold, we seek for cloth. If we be sick, we seek to the physician. If we be in heaviness, we seek for comfort of our friends, or of company. So that there is no one creature, by itself, that can content all our wants and desires. But in the world to come, in that everlasting felicity, we shall no more beg and seek our particular comforts and commodities of divers creatures, but we shall possess all that we can ask and desire, in God, and God shall be to us all things. He shall be to us both father and mother; he shall be bread and drink, cloth, physicians, comfort; he shall be all things to us, and that of much more blessed fashion, and more sufficient contentation, than ever these creatures were unto us, with much more delectation than ever man's reason is able to conceive. *The eye of man is not able to behold,* 1 Cor. 2:9 *nor his ear can hear, nor it can be compassed in the heart of man, what joy it is, that God hath prepared for them that love him.*

Let us all conclude then with one voice, with the words of St Paul: *To him which is able to do, abundantly beyond our desires and thoughts,* Ephes. 3:20–1 *according to the power working in us, be glory and praise, in his Church, by Christ Jesus, for ever, world without end.* Amen.

AN EXHORTATION
TO BE SPOKEN TO SUCH PARISHES
WHERE THEY USE THEIR
PERAMBULATIONS IN ROGATION
WEEK FOR THE OVERSIGHT
OF THE BOUNDS AND LIMITS OF
THEIR TOWNS

ALTHOUGH WE BE NOW ASSEMBLED TOGETHER, good Christian people, most principally, to laud and thank Almighty God, for his great benefits, by beholding the fields replenished with all manner fruit, to the maintenance of our corporal necessities, for our food and sustenance; and partly also, to make our humble suits, in prayers to his fatherly providence, to conserve the same fruits, in sending us seasonable weather, whereby we may gather in the said fruits, to that end for which his merciful goodness hath provided them; yet have we occasion, secondarily, given us in our walks on these days, to consider the old ancient bounds and limits, belonging to our own township, and to other our neighbours bordering about us, to the intent that we should be content with our own, and not contentiously strive for others', to the breach of charity, by any encroaching one upon another, or claiming one of the other, further than that in ancient right and custom, our forefathers have peaceably laid out unto us, for our commodity and comfort.

Surely a great oversight it were in us, which be Christian men, and in one profession of faith, daily looking for that heavenly inheritance which is bought for every one of us, by the blood-shedding of our Saviour, Jesus Christ, to strive, and fall to variance, for the earthly bounds of our towns, to the disquiet of our life betwixt ourselves, to the wasting of our goods, by vain expenses, and costs in the law. We ought to remember, that our habitation is but transitory and short, in this mortal life. The more shame it were, to fall out into immortal hatred among ourselves, for so brittle possessions, and so to lose our eternal inheritance, in heaven. It may stand well with charity, for a Christian man quietly to maintain his right and just title; and it is the part of every good townsman to preserve, as much as lieth in him, the liberties, franchises, bounds, and limits, of his town and country. But yet, so to strive for our very rights and duties, with the breach of love and charity, which is the only livery of a Christian man, or with the hurt of godly peace and quiet, by the which we be knit together, in one general fellowship of Christ's family, in one common household of God: that is utterly forbidden, that doth God abhor and detest; which provoketh Almighty God's wrath otherwhiles, to deprive us quite of our commodities and liberties, because we do so abuse them, for matter of strife, discord, and dissension. St Paul blamed the Corinthians for such contentious suing among themselves, to the slander of their profession before the enemies of Christ's religion, saying thus unto them: *Now there is utterly a fault* — 1 Cor. 6:7 *among you, because ye go to law one with another. Why rather suffer ye not wrong? why rather suffer ye not harm?*

If St Paul blameth the Christian men, whereof some of them, for their own right, went contentiously so to law, commending thereby the profession of patience in a Christian man; if Christ, our Saviour, would have us rather to suffer wrong, and to turn our left cheek to him which — Matt. 5:39 hath smitten the right, to suffer one wrong after another, rather than by breach of charity to defend our own; in what state be they before God, who do the wrong? what curses do they fall into, which by false witness defraud either neighbour or township, of his due right and just possession? which will not let to take an oath, by the holy Name of God, the author of all truth, to set out a falsehood, and a wrong? *Know ye not,* — 1 Cor. 6:9 saith St Paul, *that the unrighteous shall not inherit the kingdom of God?* What shall he then win, to increase a little the bounds and possessions of the earth, and lose the possession of the inheritance everlasting? Let us therefore take such heed, in maintaining of our bounds and possessions, that we commit not wrong, by incroaching upon other. Let us beware of sudden verdict, in things of doubt. Let us well advise ourselves, to advouch that certainly, whereof either we have no good knowledge or remembrance, or to claim that we have no just title to.

Thou shalt not, commandeth Almighty God in his Law, *remove thy* — Deut. 19:14 *neighbour's mark, which they of old time have set in thine inheritance. Thou* — Prov. 22:28 *shalt not,* saith Salomon, *remove the ancient bounds, which thy fathers have laid.* And lest we should esteem it to be but a light offence so to do, we shall understand that it is reckoned among the curses of God, pro-

Deut. 27:17

nounced upon sinners. *Accursed be he*, saith Almighty God, by Moses, *who removeth his neighbour's doles and marks: and all the people shall say, answering Amen* thereto, as ratifying that curse, upon whom it doth light. They do much provoke the wrath of God upon themselves, which use to grind up the doles and marks, which of ancient time were laid, for division of meres, and balks in the fields, to bring the owners to their right. They do wickedly, which do turn up the ancient terries of the fields, that old men beforetime, with great pains did tread out; whereby the lord's records (which be the tenant's evidences), be perverted and translated, sometime to the disheriting of the right owner, to the oppression of the poor fatherless, or the poor widow. These covetous men know not what inconveniences they be authors of. Sometimes, by such craft and deceit, be committed great discords and riots, in the challenge of the lands, yea sometime murders and bloodshed; whereof thou art guilty, whosoever thou be, that givest the occasion thereof.

1 Thess. 4:6

This covetous practising therefore, with thy neighbour's lands and good, is hateful to Almighty God. *Let no man subtilly compass or defraud his neighbour*, biddeth St Paul, *in any manner of cause. For God*, saith he, *is a revenger of all such*. God is the God of all equity and righteousness, and therefore forbiddeth all such deceit and subtilty, in his Law, by these

Lev. 19:35, 36

words: *Ye shall not do unjustly in judgement, in line, in weight, or measure: you shall have just balances, true weights, and true measures. False balances*,

Prov. 11:1, 20:23

saith Salomon, *are an abomination unto the Lord*. Remember what St

Rom. 13:4

Paul saith, *God is the revenger* of all wrong and injustice; as we see by daily experience: how ever it thriveth ungraciously, which is gotten by falsehood and craft. We be taught by experience, how Almighty God never suffereth the third heir to enjoy his father's wrong possessions; yea, many a time they are taken from himself, in his own lifetime. God is not bound to defend such possessions, as be gotten by the devil and his counsel. God will defend all such men's goods and possessions, which by him are obtained and possessed, and will defend them against the

Prov. 15:25

violent oppressor. So witnesseth Salomon: *The Lord will destroy the house of the proud man; but he will stablish the borders of the widow. No doubt of it*,

Psalm 37:16

saith David, *better is a little, truly gotten, to the righteous man, than the innumerable riches of the wrongful man*. Let us flee therefore, good people, all wrong practices in getting, maintaining, and defending our possessions, lands, and livelodes, our bounds and liberties, remembering that such possessions be all under God's revengeance.

But what do I speak of house and land? nay, it is said in Scriptures, that God, in his ire, doth root up whole kingdoms, from one nation to another, for unrighteous dealing, for wrongs and riches gotten by

Dan. 4:17

deceit. This is the practice of the Holy One, saith Daniel, *to the intent that living men may know, that the Most High hath power over the kingdoms of men, and giveth them to whomsoever he will.* Furthermore, what is the cause of penury and scarceness, of dearth and famine, any other thing but a token of God's ire, revenging our wrongs and injuries one done to another? *Ye have sown much,* upbraideth God by his Prophet Aggei, *and yet bring in little; ye eat, but ye be not satisfied; ye drink, but ye be not filled; ye clothe yourselves, but ye be not warm; and he that earneth his wages, putteth it in a bottomless purse. Ye look for much increase, but lo! it came to little, and when ye brought it home into your barns, I did blow it away, saith the Lord.* Oh consider therefore the ire of God, against gleaners, gatherers, and encroachers upon other men's lands and possessions! | Hag. 1:6, 9

It is lamentable to see in some places, how greedy men use to plough and grate upon their neighbour's land, that lieth next them; how covetous men nowadays, plough up so nigh the common balks and walks, which good men beforetime made the greater and broader, partly for the commodious walk of his neighbour, partly for the better shack in harvest time, to the more comfort of his poor neighbour's cattle. It is a shame, to behold the insatiableness of some covetous persons, in their doings; that where their ancestors left of their land, a broad and sufficient bierbalk, to carry the corpse to the Christian sepulture, how men pinch at such bierbalks, which by long use and custom, ought to be inviolably kept for that purpose; and now they either quite ear them up, and turn the dead body to be borne further about in the high streets, or else, if they leave any such mere, it is too strait for two to walk on. These strange encroachments, good neighbours, should be looked upon, these should be considered, in these days of our perambulations; and afterward the parties admonished, and charitably reformed, who be the doers of such private gaining, to the slander of the township, and to the hindrance of the poor.

Your highways should be considered in your walks, to understand where to bestow your days' works, according to the good statutes provided for the same. It is a good deed of mercy, to amend the dangerous and noisome ways, whereby thy poor neighbour, sitting on his seely weak beast, foundereth not in the deep thereof, and so the market the worse served, for discouraging of poor victuallers to resort thither, for the same cause.

If now therefore, ye will have your prayers heard, before Almighty God, for the increase of your corn and cattle, and for the defence thereof, from unseasonable mists and blasts, from hail and other such tempests: love equity and righteousness, ensue mercy and charity, which God most requireth at our hands. Which Almighty God respected chiefly, in making his civil laws, for his people the Israelites, in charging the owners not to gather up their corn too nigh, at harvest season, nor the grapes and olives in gathering time, but to leave behind some ears of | Lev. 19:9, 10, Deut. 24:19–21 corn, for the poor gleaners. By this, he meant to induce them to pity the poor, to relieve the needy, to show mercy and kindness. It cannot be lost, which for his sake, is distributed to the poor. For *he which ministereth seed to the sower*, and *bread to the hungry*, which sendeth down *the early and latter rain* upon your fields, so to fill up *the barns with corn*, and *the winepresses with wine and oil*; he, I say, who recompenseth all kind benefits, *in the resurrection of the just*; he will assuredly recompense all merciful deeds, showed to the needy, howsoever unable the poor is, upon whom it is bestowed. *Oh*, saith Salomon, *let not mercy and truth forsake thee. Bind them about thy neck*, saith he, *and write them on the table of thy heart: so shalt thou find favour at God's hand.* Thus *honour thou the Lord with thy riches, and with the firstfruits of thine increase: so shall thy barns be filled with abundance, and thy presses shall burst with new wine.* Nay, God hath promised to *open the windows of heaven*, upon the liberal righteous man, that he shall want nothing. He will repress the devouring caterpillar, which should devour your fruits. He will give you peace and quiet, to gather in your provision, that ye may *sit every man under his own vine*, quietly, without fear of the foreign enemies to invade you. He will give you not only food to feed on, but stomachs and good appetites, to take comfort of your fruits, whereby in all things ye may have sufficiency. Finally, he will bless you with all manner abundance, in this transitory life, and endue you with all manner benediction, in the next world, in the kingdom of heaven, through the merits of our Lord and Saviour. To whom, with the Father, and the Holy Ghost, be all honour, everlastingly. Amen.

2 Cor. 9:10,
Psalm 146:7;
Joel 2:23–4

Luke 14:14

Prov. 3:3, 4, 9, 10

Prov. 11:25,
Mal. 3:10, 11

Mic. 4:4

AN HOMILY
OF THE STATE OF MATRIMONY

THE WORD OF ALMIGHTY GOD doth testify and declare, whence the original beginning of matrimony cometh, and why it is ordained. It is instituted of God, to the intent that man and woman should live lawfully, in a perpetual friendly fellowship, to bring forth fruit, and to avoid fornication: by which means, a good conscience might be preserved on both parties, in bridling the corrupt inclinations of the flesh, within the limits of honesty; for God hath straitly forbidden all whoredom and uncleanness, and hath from time to time taken grievous punishments of this inordinate lust, as all stories and ages hath declared. Furthermore, it is also ordained, that the Church of God and his kingdom, might by this kind of life, be conserved and enlarged, not only in that God giveth children, by his blessing, but also, in that they be brought up by the parents godly, in the knowledge of God's word; that thus the knowledge of God, and true religion, might be delivered by succession, from one to another, that finally, many might enjoy that everlasting immortality.

Wherefore, forasmuch as matrimony serveth as well to avoid sin and offence, as to increase the kingdom of God, you, as all other which enter that state, must acknowledge this benefit of God, with pure and thankful minds, for that he hath so ruled your hearts, that ye follow not the example of the wicked world, who set their delight in filthiness of sin, but both of you stand in the fear of God, and abhor all filthiness. For that is surely the singular gift of God, where the common example of the world declareth, how the devil hath their hearts bound, and entangled in divers snares, so that they in their wifeless state, run into open abominations, without any grudge of their conscience. Which sort of men, that liveth so desperately and filthily, what damnation tarrieth for them, St Paul describeth it to them, saying, *Neither whoremongers, neither adulterers,* 1 Cor. 6:9, 10 *shall inherit the kingdom of God.* This horrible judgement of God ye be escaped, through his mercy, if so be that ye live inseparately, according to God's ordinance.

But yet I would not have you careless, without watching. For the devil will assay to attempt all things, to interrupt and hinder your hearts and godly purpose, if ye will give him any entry. For he will either labour to break this godly knot, once begun betwixt you, or else at the least he will labour, to encumber it with divers griefs and displeasures. And this is his principal craft: to work dissension of hearts of the one from the other; that whereas now there is pleasant and sweet love betwixt you, he will in the stead thereof, bring in most bitter and unpleasant discord. And surely, that same adversary of ours doth, as it were from above, assault man's nature and condition. For this folly is ever from our tender age grown up with us, to have a desire to rule, to think highly of ourself, so that none thinketh it meet to give place to another. That wicked vice, of stubborn will and self love, is more meet to break and to dissever the love of heart, than to preserve concord. Wherefore, married persons must apply their minds in most earnest wise, to concord, and must crave continually of God, the help of his Holy Spirit, so to rule their hearts, and to knit their minds together, that they be not dissevered, by any division of discord.

This necessity of prayer must be oft in the practice and using of married persons, that ofttime the one should pray for the other, lest hate and debate do arise betwixt them. And because few do consider this thing, but more few do perform it (I say, to pray diligently), we see how wonderfully the devil deludeth and scorneth this state, how few matrimonies there be without chidings, brawlings, tauntings, repentings, bitter cursings, and fightings. Which things whosoever doth commit, they do not consider that it is the instigation of the ghostly enemy, who taketh great delight therein: for else they would with all earnest endeavour, strive against these mischiefs, not only with prayer, but also with all possible diligence; yea, they would not give place to the provocation of wrath, which stirreth them either to such rough and sharp words or stripes, which is surely compassed by the devil: whose temptation, if it be followed, must needs begin and weave the web of all miseries and sorrows. For this is most certainly true, that of such beginnings must needs ensue, the breach of true concord in heart, whereby all love must needs shortly be banished. Then cannot it be but a miserable thing to behold, that yet they are of necessity compelled to live together, which yet cannot be in quiet together. And this is most customably everywhere to be seen. But what is the cause thereof? Forsooth, because they will not consider the crafty trains of the devil, and therefore give not themselves to pray to God, that he would vouchsafe to repress his power. Moreover, they do not consider, how they promote the purpose of the devil, in that they follow the wrath of their hearts, while they threat one another, while they in their folly turn all upside down, while they will never give over their right, as they esteem it, yea while many times they will not give over the wrong part indeed. Learn thou therefore, if thou desirest to be void of all these miseries, if thou desirest to live peaceably and comfortably in wedlock, how to make thy earnest prayer to God, that he would govern both your hearts, by his Holy Spirit, to restrain the devil's power, whereby your concord may remain perpetually.

But to this prayer must be joined a singular diligence, whereof St Peter giveth his precept, saying, *You husbands, deal with your wives accord-*   1 Pet. 3:7 *ing to knowledge, giving honour to the wife, as unto the weaker vessel, and as unto them that are heirs also of the grace of life, that your prayers be not hindered.* This precept doth peculiarly pertain to the husband: for he ought to be the leader and author of love, in cherishing and increasing concord; which then shall take place, if he will use measureableness, and not tyranny, and if he yield some things to the woman. For the woman is a weak creature, not endued with like strength and constancy of mind: therefore they be the sooner disquieted, and they be the more prone to all weak affections and dispositions of mind, more than men be; and lighter they be, and more vain in their fantasies and opinions. These things must be considered of the man, that he be not too stiff; so that he ought to wink at some things, and must gently expound all things, and to forbear.

Howbeit, the common sort of men doth judge, that such moderation should not become a man: for they say, that it is a token of a womanish cowardness; and therefore they think that it is a man's part, to fume in anger, to fight with fist and staff. Howbeit, howsoever they imagine, undoubtedly St Peter doth better judge what should be seeming to a man, and what he should most reasonably perform. For he saith, reasoning should be used, and not fighting. Yea, he saith more, that the woman ought to have a certain *honour* attributed to her; that is to say, she must be spared and borne with, the rather for that she is *the weaker vessel,* of a frail heart, inconstant, and with a word soon stirred to wrath. And therefore, considering these her frailties, she is to be the rather spared. By this means thou shalt not only nourish concord, but shalt have her heart in thy power and will; for honest natures will sooner be retained to do their duty, rather by gentle words than by stripes. But he which will do all things with extremity and severity, and doth use always rigour in words and stripes, what will that avail in the conclusion? Verily nothing, but that he thereby setteth forward the devil's work; he banisheth away concord, charity, and sweet amity, and bringeth in dissension, hatred, and irksomeness, the greatest griefs that can be in the mutual love and fellowship of man's life.

Beyond all this, it bringeth another evil therewith; for it is the destruction and interruption of prayer. For in the time that the mind is occupied with dissension and discord, there can be no true prayer used.

For the Lord's Prayer hath not only a respect to particular persons, but to the whole universal; in the which we openly pronounce, that we will forgive them which hath offended against us, even as we ask forgiveness of our sins of God. Which thing how can it be done rightly, when their hearts be at dissension? How can they pray each for other, when they be at hate betwixt themselves? Now, if the aid of prayer be taken away, by what means can they sustain themselves in any comfort? For they cannot otherwise, either resist the devil, or yet have their hearts stayed in stable comfort, in all perils and necessities, but by prayer. Thus all discommodities, as well worldly as ghostly, follow this froward testiness, and cumbrous fierceness in manners; which be more meet for brute beasts, than for reasonable creatures. St Peter doth not allow these things, but the devil desireth them gladly. Wherefore take the more heed! And yet a man may be a man, although he doth not use such extremity, yea, though he should dissemble some things in his wife's manners. And this is the part of a Christian man, which both pleaseth God, and serveth also in good use, to the comfort of their marriage state.

Now as concerning the wife's duty. What shall become her? Shall she abuse the gentleness and humanity of her husband, and at her pleasure turn all things upside down? No surely; for that is far repugnant against

1 Pet. 3:1

God's commandment. For thus doth St Peter preach to them: *Ye wives, be ye in subjection, to obey your own husband.* To obey is another thing than to control or command; which yet they may do to their children, and to their family; but as for their husbands, them must they obey, and cease from commanding, and perform subjection. For this surely doth nourish concord very much, when the wife is ready at hand at her husband's commandment, when she will apply herself to his will, when she endeavoureth herself to seek his contentation, and to do him pleasure, when she will eschew all things that might offend him. For thus will most truly be verified the saying of the poet, "A good wife by obeying her husband, shall bear the rule": so that he shall have a delight and a gladness, the sooner at all times to return home to her. But on the contrary part, when the wives be stubborn, froward, and malapert, their husbands are compelled thereby to abhor and flee from their own houses, even as they should have battle with their enemies.

Howbeit, it can scantly be, but that some offences shall sometime chance betwixt them: for no man doth live without fault; specially for that the woman is the more frail part. Therefore let them beware, that they stand not in their faults and wilfulness; but rather let them acknowledge their follies, and say, "My husband, so it is, that by my anger I was compelled to do this or that: forgive it me, and hereafter I will take better heed." Thus ought women the more readily to do, the more they be ready to offend. And they shall not do this only to avoid strife and debate, but rather in the respect of the commandment of God, as St Paul expresseth it in this form of words: *Let women be subject to their husbands, as to the Lord: for the husband is the head of the woman, as Christ is the Head of the Church.* Here you understand, that God hath commanded, that ye should acknowledge the authority of the husband, and refer to him the honour of obedience. And St Peter saith in that same place before rehearsed, that *holy matrons did sometimes deck themselves,* not with gold and silver, but in *putting their whole hope in God,* and in *obeying their husbands; as Sara obeyed Abraham, calling him lord: whose daughters ye be,* saith he, if ye follow her example. This sentence is very meet for women to print in their remembrance. Truth it is, that they must specially feel the griefs and pains of their matrimony, in that they relinquish the liberty of their own rule, in the pain of their travailing, in the bringing up of their children; in which offices they be in great perils, and be grieved with great afflictions, which they might be without, if they lived out of matrimony. But St Peter saith that this is the chief ornament of *holy matrons,* in that they *set their hope* and trust *in God;* that is to say, in that they refused not from marriage for the business thereof, for the griefs and perils thereof, but committed all such adventures to God, in most sure trust of help, after that they have called upon his aid. O woman, do thou the like, and so shalt thou be most excellently beautified before God, and all his angels and saints. And thou needest not to seek further for doing any better works. For, obey thy husband, take regard of his requests, and give heed unto him, to perceive what he requireth of thee; and so shalt thou honour God, and live peaceably in thy house. And beyond this, God shall follow thee with his benediction, that all things shall well prosper, both to thee and to thy husband, as the Psalm saith. *Blessed is the man which feareth God, and walketh in his ways. Thou shalt have the fruit of thine own hands: happy shalt thou be, and well shall it go with thee. Thy wife shall be as a vine, plentifully spreading about thy house. Thy children shall be as the young springs of the olives about thy table. Lo, thus shall that man be blessed,* saith David, *that feareth the Lord.*

This let the wife have ever in mind, the rather admonished thereto by the apparel of her head, whereby is signified that she is under covert, and obedience of her husband. And as that apparel is of nature so appointed to declare her subjection, so biddeth St Paul, that all other of her raiment should express both *shamefastness and sobriety.* For if it be not lawful for the woman to have her head bare, but to bear thereon the sign of her power, wheresoever she goeth, more is it required that she declare the thing that is meant thereby. And therefore, these ancient women of the old world called their husbands lords, and showed them reverence, in obeying them.

Eph. 5:22, 23

1 Pet. 3:3–6

Psalm 128:1–4

1 Tim. 2:9

1 Cor. 11:10

But peradventure, she will say that those men loved their wives indeed. I know that well enough, and bear it well in mind. But when I do admonish you of your duties, then call not to consideration what their duties be. For when we ourselves do teach our children to obey us, as their parents, or when we reform our servants, and tell them that they should obey their masters, not only at the eye, but as to the Lord; if they should tell us again our duties, we would not think it well done. For, when we be admonished of our duties and faults, we ought not then to seek what other men's duties be. For though a man had a companion in his fault, yet should not he thereby be without his fault. But this must be only looked on: by what means thou mayest make thyself without blame. For Adam did lay the blame upon the woman, and she turned it unto the serpent; but yet neither of them was thus excused. And therefore bring not such excuses to me at this time; but apply all thy diligence to hear thine obedience to thy husband. For when I take in hand to admonish thy husband, to love thee and to cherish thee, yet will I not cease to set out the law that is appointed for the woman, as well as I would require of the man what is written for his law. Go thou therefore about such things as becometh thee only, and show thyself tractable to thy husband. Or rather, if thou wilt obey thy husband for God's precept, then allege such things as be in his duty to do, but perform thou diligently those things which the Lawmaker hath charged thee to do: for thus is it most reasonable to obey God, if thou wilt not suffer thyself to transgress his law. He that loveth his friend, seemeth to do no great thing; but he that honoureth him that is hurtful and hateful to him, this man is worthy much commendation. Even so, think thou, if thou canst suffer an extreme husband, thou shalt have a great reward therefore; but if thou lovest him only because he is gentle and courteous, what reward will God give therefore? Yet I speak not these things, that I would wish the husbands to be sharp towards their wives; but I exhort the women, that they would patiently bear the sharpness of their husbands. For when either parts do their best to perform their duties, the one to the other, then followeth thereon great profit to their neighbours, for their example's sake. For when the woman is ready to suffer a sharp husband, and the man will not extremely entreat his stubborn and troublesome wife, then be all things in quiet, as in a most sure haven.

Even thus was it done in old time, that every one did their own duty and office, and was not busy to require the duty of their neighbours. Consider, I pray thee, that Abraham took to him his brother's son: his wife did not blame him therefore. He commanded her* to go with him a long journey: she did not gainsay it, but obeyed his precept. Again, after all those great miseries, labours, and pains of that journey, when Abraham was made

Eph. 6:5–7

Gen. 3:12–19

Ibid. 12:4, 5

---

* Griffiths reports that all texts read *him*, which is possible (= Lot) but *her* seems more likely.

as lord over all, yet did he give place to Lot of his superiority. Which Gen. 13:8–11
matter Sara took so little to grief, that she never once suffered her tongue
to speak such words, as the common manner of women is wont to do, in
these days: when they see their husbands in such rooms to be made underlings, and to be put under their youngers, then they upbraid them with
cumbrous talk, and call them fools, dastards, and cowards for so doing.
But Sara was so far from speaking any such thing, that it never came into
her mind and thought so to say, but allowed the wisdom and will of her husband. Yea, beside all this, after the said Lot had thus his will, and left to
his uncle the lesser portion of land, he chanced to fall into extreme peril: *Ibid.* 14:12–14
which chance when it came to the knowledge of this said Patriarch, he
incontinently put all his men in harness, and prepared himself with all
his family and friends, against the host of the Persians. In which case
Sara did not counsel him to the contrary, nor did say, as then might have
been said, "My husband, whither goest thou so unadvisedly? Why runnest
thou thus on head? Why dost thou offer thyself to so great perils, and art
thus ready to jeopard thine own life, and to peril the lives of all thine, for
such a man as hath done thee such wrong? At least way, if thou regardest
not thyself, yet have compassion on me, which for thy love have forsaken
my kinred, and my country, and have the want both of my friends and
kinsfolks, and am thus come into so far countries with thee. Have pity
on me, and make me not here a widow, to cast me to such cares and
troubles." Thus might she have said: but Sara neither said nor thought
such words, but she kept herself in silence in all things. Furthermore, all
that time when she was barren, and took no pain, as other women did,
by bringing forth fruit in his house, what did he? He complained not to
his wife, but to Almighty God. And consider how either of them did *Ibid.* 15:2, 3,
16:1, 2
their duties, as became them: for neither did he despise Sara because she
was barren, nor never did cast it in her teeth. Consider again, how
Abraham expelled the handmaid out of his house, when she required it: *Ibid.* 21:9–14
so that by this I may truly prove, that the one was pleased and contented
with the other, in all things. But yet set not your eyes only in this matter,
but look further what was done before this, that Agar used her mistress *Ibid.* 16:4–6
despitefully, and that Abraham himself was somewhat provoked against
her; which must needs be an intolerable matter, and a painful to a
freehearted woman, and a chaste. Let not therefore the woman be too
busy to call for the duty of her husband, where she should be ready to
perform her own; for that is not worthy any great commendation. And
even so again, let not the man only consider what belongeth to the
woman, and to stand too earnestly gazing thereon; for that is not his part
or duty. But, as I have said, let either party be ready and willing to
perform that which belongeth specially to themself. For, if we be bound
to hold out our left cheek to strangers, which will smite us on the right Matt. 5:39

cheek, how much more ought we to suffer an extreme and unkind husband!

But yet I mean not that a man should beat his wife. God forbid that! for that is the greatest shame that can be, not so much to her that is beaten, as to him that doeth the deed. But if by fortune* thou chancest upon such an husband, take it not too heavily; but suppose thou, that thereby is laid up no small reward hereafter, and in this lifetime no small commendation to thee, if thou canst be quiet. But yet to you that be men, thus I speak: let there be none so grievous fault, to compel you to beat your wives. But what say I your wives? No, it is not to be borne with, that an honest man should lay hands on his maidservant, to beat her. Wherefore, if it be a great shame for a man to beat his bond-servant, much more rebuke it is, to lay violent hands upon his free-woman. And this thing may we well understand, by the laws which the paynims hath made, which doth discharge her any longer to dwell with such an husband, as unworthy to have any further company with her, that doth smite her. For it is an extreme point, thus so vilely to entreat her, like a slave, that is fellow to thee of thy life, and so conjoined unto thee beforetime, in the necessary matters of thy living. And therefore a man may well liken such a man, if he may be called a man rather than a wild beast, to a killer of his father or his mother. And whereas we be com-

Gen. 2:24,
Matt. 19:5

manded to forsake our father and mother, for our wife's sake, and yet thereby do work them none injury, but do fulfil the law of God, how can it not appear then, to be a point of extreme madness, to intreat her despitefully, for whose sake God hath commanded thee to leave parents? Yea, who can suffer such despite? Who can worthily express the inconvenience that is, to see what weepings and wailings be made, in the open streets, when neighbours run together to the house of so unruly an husband, as to a Bedlam man, who goeth about to overturn all that he hath at home? Who would not think, that it were better for such a man, to wish the ground to open, and to swallow him in, than once ever after to be seen in the market?

But peradventure thou wilt object, that the woman provoketh thee to this point. But consider thou again, that the woman is a frail vessel, and thou art therefore made the ruler and head over her, to bear the weakness of her, in this her subjection. And therefore, study thou to declare the honest commendation of thine authority; which thou canst no ways better do, than to forbear to urge her, in her weakness and subjection. For, even as the king appeareth so much the more noble, the more excellent and noble he maketh his officers and lieutenants, whom if he should dishonour, and despise the authority of their dignity, he should deprive himself of a great part of his own honour; even so, if thou dost

* All texts read "such fortune".

despise her that is set in the next room beside thee, thou dost much derogate and decay, the excellency and virtue of thine own authority. Recount all these things in thy mind, and be gentle and quiet. Understand that God hath given thee children with her, and art made a father, and by such reason appease thyself. Dost not thou see the husbandmen, what diligence they use, to till that ground which once they have taken to farm, though it be never so full of faults?—as for an example, though it be dry, though it bringeth forth weeds, though the soil cannot bear too much wet, yet he tilleth it, and so winneth fruit thereof. Even in like manner, if thou wouldest use like diligence, to instruct and order the mind of thy spouse, if thou wouldest diligently apply thyself to weed out, by little and little, the noisome weeds of uncomely manners, out of her mind, with wholesome precepts, it could not be, but in time thou shouldest feel the pleasant fruit thereof, to both your comforts. Therefore, that this thing chance not so, perform this thing that I do here counsel thee. Whensoever any displeasant matter riseth at home, if thy wife hath done aught amiss, comfort her, and increase not the heaviness. For, though thou shouldest be grieved with never so many things, yet thou shalt find nothing more grievous than to want the benevolence of thy wife at home; what offence soever thou canst name, yet shalt thou find none more intolerable than to be at debate with thy wife. And for this cause most of all, oughtest thou to have this love in reverence. And if reason moveth thee, to bear any burden at any other men's hands, much more at thy wife's. For if she be poor, upbraid her not; if she be simple, taunt her not, but be the more courteous: for she is thy body, and made *one flesh* with thee.

Gen. 2:24,
Eph. 5:28, 31

But thou peradventure wilt say, that she is a wrathful woman, a drunkard, and beastly, without wit and reason. For this cause bewail her the more. Chafe not in anger, but pray to Almighty God. Let her be admonished, and holpen with good counsel, and do thou thy best endeavour, that she may be delivered of all these affections. But, if thou shouldest beat her, thou shalt increase her evil affections; for frowardness and sharpness is not amended with frowardness, but with softness and gentleness. Furthermore, consider what reward thou shalt have, at God's hand: for where thou mighest beat her, and yet for the respect of the fear of God thou wilt abstain, and bear patiently her great offences— the rather in respect of that law which forbiddeth that a man should cast out his wife, what fault soever she be cumbered with—thou shalt have a very great reward. And before the receipt of that reward, thou shalt feel many commodities; for by this means she shall be made the more obedient, and thou, for her sake, shalt be made the more meek.

It is written in a story of a certain strange philosopher, which had a cursed wife, a froward, and a drunkard, when he was asked for what consideration he did so bear her evil manners, he made answer, "By this means," said he, "I have at home a school-master, and an example how I should behave myself abroad: for I shall," saith he, "be the more quiet with other, being thus daily exercised and taught, in the forbearing of her." Surely it is a shame, that paynims should be wiser than we; we, I say, that be commanded to counterfeit angels, or rather God himself, through meekness. And for the love of virtue, this said philosopher, Socrates, would not expel his wife out of his house; yea, some say that he did therefore marry his wife, to learn this virtue, by that occasion. Wherefore, seeing many men be far behind the wisdom of this man, my counsel is, that first, and before all things, a man do his best endeavour to get him a good wife, indued with all honesty and virtue; but, if it so chance that he is deceived, that he hath chosen such a wife, as is neither good nor tolerable, then let the husband follow this philosopher, and let him instruct his wife in every condition, and never lay these matters to sight. For the merchant man, except he first be at composition with his factor, to use his interaffairs quietly, he will neither stir his ship to sail, nor yet will lay hands upon his merchandise. Even so let us do all things, that we may have the fellowship of our wives, which is the factor of all our doings at home, in great quiet and rest. And by these means all things shall prosper quietly, and so shall we pass through the dangers of the troublous sea of this world. For this state of life will be more honourable and comfortable than our houses, than servants, than money, than lands and possessions, than all things that can be told. As all these, with sedition and discord, can never work us any comfort; so shall all things turn to our commodity and pleasure, if we draw this yoke, in one concord of heart and mind.

Whereupon do your best endeavour, that after this sort ye use your matrimony, and so shall ye be armed on every side. Ye have escaped the snares of the devil, and the unlawful lusts of the flesh; ye have the quietness of conscience, by this institution of matrimony ordained by God: therefore use oft prayer to him, that he would be present by you, that he would continue concord and charity betwixt you. Do the best ye can of your parts, to custom yourselves to softness and meekness, and bear well in worth such oversights as chance; and thus shall your conversation be most pleasant, and comfortable. And although (which can no otherwise be) some adversities shall follow, and otherwhiles now one discommodity, now another shall appear, yet in this common trouble and adversity, lift up both your hands unto heaven; call upon the help and assistance of God, the Author of your marriage; and surely the promise of relief is at hand. For Christ affirmeth in his Gospel, *Where two or three be gathered together, in my Name, and be agreed, what matter soever they pray for, it shall be granted them, of my heavenly Father.* Why therefore

Matt. 18:19, 20

shouldest thou be afeard of the danger, where thou hast so ready a promise, and so nigh an help? Furthermore, you must under-stand, how necessary it is for Christian folk to bear Christ's cross; for else we shall never feel, how comfortable God's help is unto us.

Therefore give thanks to God for his great benefit, in that ye have taken upon you this state of wedlock; and pray you instantly, that Almighty God may luckily defend and maintain you therein, that neither ye be overcome with any temptation, nor with any adversity. But before all things, take good heed that ye give no occasion to the devil, to let and hinder your prayers, by discord and dissension. For there is no stronger defence and stay in all our life, than is prayer: in the which we may call for the help of God, and obtain it; whereby we may win his blessing, his grace, his defence, and protection, so to continue therein, to a better life to come. Which grant us he that died for us all: to whom be all honour and praise, for ever and ever. Amen.

AN HOMILY AGAINST IDLENESS

FORASMUCH AS MAN, being not born to ease and rest, but to labour and travail, is by corruption of nature, through sin, so far degenerated, and grown out of kind, that he taketh idleness to be no evil at all, but rather a commendable thing, seemly for those that be wealthy, and therefore is greedily embraced of most part of men, as agreeable to their sensual affection, and all labour and travail is diligently avoided, as a thing painful, and repugnant to the pleasure of the flesh: it is necessary to be declared unto you, that by the ordinance of God, which he hath set in the nature of man, every one ought in his lawful vocation and calling, to give himself to labour; and that idleness, being repugnant to the same ordinance, is a grievous sin, and also, for the great inconveniences and mischiefs which spring thereof, an intolerable evil; to the intent that, when ye understand the same, ye may diligently flee from it, and on the other part earnestly apply yourselves, every man in his vocation, to honest labour and business; which as it is enjoined unto man, by God's appointment, so it wanteth not his manifold blessings, and sundry benefits.

Almighty God, after that he had created man, put him into Paradise, that he might dress and keep it: but when he had transgressed God's commandment, eating the fruit of the tree which was forbidden him,

Gen. 3:17–24

Almighty God forthwith did cast him out of Paradise, into this woful vale of misery, enjoining him to labour the ground that he was taken out of, and to eat his bread in the sweat of his face, all the days of his life. It is the appointment and will of God, that every man, during the time of this mortal and transitory life, should give himself to some honest and godly exercise and labour, and every one to do his own business, and to

Job 5:7

walk uprightly in his own calling. *Man*, saith Job, *is born to labour*. And

Ecclus. 7:15

we are commanded by Jesus Sirach, *not to hate painful works, neither husbandry*, or other such mysteries of travail, *which the Highest hath*

Prov. 5:15

created. The Wise Man also exhorteth us, to *drink the waters of our own cistern, and of the rivers that run out of the midst of our own well*; meaning thereby, that we should live of our own labours, and not devour the

2 Thess. 3:6–14

labours of other. St Paul, hearing that among the Thessalonians, there

374

were *certain that lived* dissolutely, and *out of order*—that is to say, *which did not work, but were busybodies,* not getting their own living with their own travail, but eating other men's bread of free cost—did command the said Thessalonians, not only *to withdraw themselves,* and abstain from the familiar company of such inordinate persons, but also, that *if there were any such among them, that would not labour, the same should not eat,* nor have any living at other men's hands. Which doctrine of St Paul, no doubt, is grounded upon the general ordinance of God, which is, that every man should labour; and therefore it is to be obeyed, of all men, and no man can justly, exempt himself from the same.

But when it is said, all men should labour, it is not so straitly meant, that all men should use handy labour: but as there be divers sorts of labour, some of the mind, and some of the body, and some of both, so every one (except by reason of age, debility of body, or want of health he be unapt to labour at all), ought, both for the getting of his own living honestly, and for to profit others, in some kind of labour to exercise himself, according as the vocation, whereunto God hath called him, shall require. So that, whosoever doeth good to the common weal and society of men, with his industry and labour—whether it be by governing the common weal publicly, or by bearing public office or ministry, or by doing any common necessary affairs of his country, or by giving counsel, or by teaching and instructing others, or by what other means soever he be occupied, so that a profit and benefit redound thereof unto others— the same person is not to be accounted idle, though he work no bodily labour, nor is to be denied his living (if he attend his vocation), though he work not with his hands. Bodily labour is not required of them, which by reason of their vocation and office, are occupied in the labour of the mind, to the profit and help of others.

St Paul exhorteth Timothy, to eschew and *refuse idle widows, which go about from house to house,* because they are *not only idle, but prattlers also, and busybodies, speaking things which are not comely.* The Prophet Ezechiel, declaring what the sins of the city of Sodom were, reckoneth idleness to be one of the principal. *The sins,* saith he, *of Sodom, were these: pride, fullness of meat, abundance, and idleness: these things had Sodom and her daughters;* meaning the cities subject to her. The horrible and strange kind of destruction of that city, and all the country about the same, which was fire and brimstone raining from heaven, most manifestly declareth, what a grievous sin idleness is, and ought to admonish us to flee from the same, and embrace honest and godly labour. But if we give ourselves to idleness and sloth, to lurking and loitering, to wilful wandering and wasteful spending, never settling ourselves to honest labour, but living like drone bees, by the labours of other men: then do we break the Lord's commandment, we go astray from our vocation,

1 Tim. 5:11, 13

Ezek. 16:49

Gen. 19:24, 25

and incur the danger of God's wrath and heavy displeasure, to our endless destruction, except by repentance we return again unfeignedly unto God.

The inconveniences, and mischiefs, that come of idleness, as well to man's body as to his soul, are more than can in short time be well rehearsed. Some we shall declare and open unto you, that by considering them, ye may the better with yourselves gather the rest. *An idle* hand, saith Salomon, *maketh poor, but a quick labouring hand maketh rich.* Again, *He that tilleth his land, shall have plenteousness of bread; but he that floweth* in idleness is a very fool, and shall have poverty enough.* Again, *A slothful body will not go to plough, for cold of the winter: therefore shall he go a begging in summer, and have nothing.* But what shall we need to stand much about the proving of this, that poverty followeth idleness? We have too much experience thereof (the thing is the more to be lamented!) in this realm. For a great part of the beggary, that is among the poor, can be imputed to nothing so much as to idleness, and to the negligence of parents; which do not bring up their children either in good learning, honest labour, or some commendable occupation or trade; whereby, when they come to age, they might get their living. Daily experience also teacheth, that nothing is more enemy, or pernicious to the health of man's body, than is idleness, too much ease and sleep, and want of exercise.

But these, and suchlike incommodities, albeit they be great and noisome, yet because they concern chiefly the body, and external goods, they are not to be compared, with the mischiefs and inconveniences, which through idleness, happen to the soul: whereof we will recite some. Idleness is never alone, but hath always a long tail of other vices hanging on, which corrupt and infect the whole man, after such sort, that he is made at length, nothing else but a lump of sin. *Idleness,* saith Jesus Sirach, *bringeth much evil and mischief.* St Bernard calleth it "the mother of all evils, and stepdame of all virtues"; adding moreover, that it doth prepare, and as it were tread the way to, hell fire. Where idleness is once received, there the devil is always ready to set in his foot, and to plant all kind of wickedness and sin, to the everlasting destruction of man's soul. Which thing to be most true, we are plainly taught, in the thirteenth of Matthew, where it is said, that *the enemy came while men were asleep, and sowed naughty tares among the good wheat.* In very deed, the best time that the devil can have to work his feat, is when men be asleep, that is to say, idle: then is he most busy in his work; then doth he soonest catch men, in the snare of perdition; then doth he fill them with all iniquity, to bring them, without God's special favour, unto utter destruction.

Hereof we have two notable examples, most lively set before our eyes. The one in King David, who tarrying at home idly, as the Scripture

Prov. 10:4

Prov. 12:11 and 28:19

Prov. 20:4

Ecclus. 33:27

Matt. 13:25

2 Sam. 11

---

* *floweth*: Griffiths suggests *followeth*.

saith, *at such times as* other *kings go forth to battle,* was quickly seduced of Satan, to forsake the Lord his God, and to commit two grievous and abominable sins in his sight, adultery and murder. The plagues that ensued these offences, were horrible and grievous, as it may easily appear to them that will read the story. Another example, of Samson: who, so long as he warred with the Philistines, enemies to the people of God, could never be taken or overcome; but after that he gave himself to ease and idleness, he not only committed fornication, with the strumpet Dalila, but also was taken of his enemies, and had his eyes miserably put out, was put in prison, and compelled to grind in a mill, and at length was made the laughing-stock of his enemies. If these two—who were so excellent men, so well beloved of God, so endued with singular and divine gifts, the one namely of prophecy, and the other of strength, and such men as never could by vexation, labour, or trouble be overcome— were overthrown, and fell into grievous sins, by giving themselves for a short time to ease and idleness, and so consequently incurred miserable plagues at the hands of God, what sin, what mischief, what inconvenience and plague, is not to be feared of them, which all their life long, give themselves wholly to idleness and ease?

2 Sam. 12:10, 11

Judges 16:1–25

Let us not deceive ourselves, thinking little hurt to come of doing nothing. For it is a true saying, "When one doeth nothing, he learneth to do evil." Let us therefore always be doing of some honest work, that the devil may find us occupied. He himself is ever occupied, never idle; but *walketh* continually, *seeking to devour* us. Let us *resist him,* with our diligent watching, in labour and in welldoing. For he that diligently exerciseth himself, in honest business, is not easily catched in the devil's snare. When man, through idleness, or for default of some honest occupation or trade to live upon, is brought to poverty, and want of things necessary, we see how easily such a man is induced, for his gain, to lie, to practise how he may deceive his neighbour, to forswear himself, to bear false witness, and oftentimes to steal and murder, or to use some other ungodly mean to live withal; whereby not only his good name, honest reputation, and a good conscience, yea his life, is utterly lost, but also the great displeasure and wrath of God, with divers and sundry grievous plagues, are procured. Lo here the end of the idle and sluggish bodies, whose hands cannot away with honest labour: loss of name, fame, reputation, and life here in this world, and, without the great mercy of God, the purchasing of everlasting destruction, in the world to come. Have not all men then, good cause to beware, and take heed of idleness, seeing they that imbrace and follow it have commonly, of their pleasant idleness, sharp and sour displeasures?

1 Pet. 5:8, 9

Doubtless, good and godly men, weighing the great and manifold harms, that come by idleness to a commonweal, have from time to time provided with all diligence, that sharp and severe laws might be made, for the correction and amendment of this evil. The Egyptians had a law, that every man should weekly, bring his name to the chief rulers of the province, and therewithal declare what trade of life he occupied, to the intent that idleness might be worthily punished, and diligent labour duly rewarded. The Athenians did chastise sluggish and slothful people, no less than they did heinous and grievous offenders, considering, as the truth is, that idleness causeth much mischief. The Areopagites called every man to a strait account, how he lived; and if they found any loiterers, that did not profit the commonweal by one means or other, they were driven out and banished, as unprofitable members, that did only hurt and corrupt the body. And in this realm of England, good and godly laws have been divers times made, that no idle vagabonds, and loitering runagates, should be suffered to go from town to town, from place to place, without punishment; which neither serve God nor their Prince, but devour the sweet fruits of other men's labour, being common liars, drunkards, swearers, thieves, whoremasters, and murderers, refusing all honest labour, and give themselves to nothing else, but to invent and do mischief, whereof they are more desirous and greedy, than is any lion of his prey.

To remedy this inconvenience, let all parents, and others which have the care and governance of youth, so bring them up, either in good learning, labour, or some honest occupation or trade, that* they may be able in time to come, not only to sustain themselves competently, but also to relieve and supply the necessity and want of others. And St Paul saith, *Let him that hath stolen steal, no more,* and he that hath deceived others, or used unlawful ways to get his living, leave off the same, *and labour rather, working with his hands that thing which is good, that he may have* that which is necessary for himself, and also be able *to give unto others, that stand in need of his help.*

The Prophet David thinketh him happy that liveth upon his labour, saying, *When thou eatest the labours of thine hands, happy art thou, and well is thee.* This happiness or blessing consisteth in these and suchlike points. First, *it is the gift of God,* as Salomon saith, *when one eateth and drinketh, and receiveth good of his labour.* Secondly, when one liveth of his own labour, so it be honest and good, he liveth of it with a good conscience; and an upright conscience is a treasure inestimable. Thirdly, he eateth his bread, not with brawling and chiding, but with peace and quietness, when he quietly laboureth for the same, according to St Paul's admonition. Fourthly, he is no man's bondman for his meat sake, nor needeth not for that, to hang upon the good will of other men; but so liveth of his own, that he is able to give part to others. And to conclude,

Herodotus

Eph. 4:25, 28

Psalm 128:2

Eccles. 3:13

* All texts read *whereby.*

the labouring man and his family, whiles they are busily occupied in their labour, be free from many temptations, and occasions of sin, which they that live in idleness are subject unto.

And here ought artificers and labouring men, who be at wages for their work and labour, to consider their conscience to God, and their duty to their neighbour; lest they abuse their time in idleness, so defrauding them which be at charge, both with great wages and dear commons. They be worse than idle men indeed, for that they seek to have wages for their loitering. It is less danger to God to be idle for no gain, than by idleness to win out of their neighbours' purses, wages for that which is not deserved. It is true, that Almighty God is angry with such as do defraud the hired man out of his wages: the cry of that injury ascendeth up to God's ear for vengeance. And as true it is, that the hired man who useth deceit in his labour, is a thief before God. *Let no man*, saith St Paul to the Thessalonians, *subtilly beguile his brother, let him not defraud him in his business: for the Lord is revenger of such deceits.* Whereupon, he that will have a good conscience to God, that labouring man, I say, which dependeth wholly upon God's benediction, ministering all things sufficient for his living: let him use his time in faithful labour; and when his labour, by sickness or other misfortune, doth cease, yet let him think, for that in his health he served God and his neighbour truly, he shall not want in time of necessity. God, upon respect of his fidelity in health, will recompense his indigence, to move the hearts of good men, to relieve such decayed men in sickness; where otherwise, whatsoever is gotten by idleness, shall have no foison to help, in time of need. Let the labouring man therefore, eschew for his part, this vice of idleness and deceit, remembering that St Paul exhorteth every man, to *lay away* deceit, dissimulation, and *lying*, and to *use truth* and plainness *to his neighbour, because*, saith he, *we be members together* in one body, under one head, Christ our Saviour.

And here might be charged the serving men of this realm, who spend their time in much idleness of life, nothing regarding the opportunity of their time, forgetting how service is no heritage, how age will creep upon them; where wisdom were, they should expend their idle time, in some good business, whereby they might increase in knowledge, and so the more worthy to be ready for every man's service. It is a great rebuke to them, that they study not either to write fair, to keep a book of account, to study the tongues, and so to get wisdom and knowledge, in such books and works as be now plentifully set out in print, of all manner languages. Let young men consider the precious value of their time, and waste it not in idleness, in jollity, in gaming, in banqueting, in ruffians' company. Youth is but vanity, and must be accounted for before God. *How merry and glad soever thou be in thy youth, O young man*, saith the

Deut. 24:15, James 5:4

1 Thess. 4:6

Eph. 4:25; 4, 12, 15

Eccles. 11:9

Preacher, *how glad soever thy heart be in thy young days*, how fast and freely soever thou *follow the ways of thine own heart, and the lust of thine own eyes; yet be thou sure, that God shall bring thee into judgement, for all these things*.

God in his mercy, put it into the hearts and minds, of all them that have the sword of punishment in their hands, or have families under their governance, to labour to redress this great enormity, of all such as live idly and unprofitably in the commonweal, to the great dishonour of God, and the grievous plague of his seely people! To leave sin unpunished, and to neglect the good bringing up of youth, is nothing else but to kindle the Lord's wrath against us, and to heap plagues upon our own heads. As long as the adulterous people were suffered to live licentiously, without reformation, so long did the plague continue and increase in Israel, as ye

Num. 25:1–8   may see in the book of Numbers. But when due correction was done upon them, the Lord's anger was straightway pacified, and the plague ceased. Let all officers therefore look straitly to their charge. Let all masters of households reform this abuse in their families. Let them use the authority that God hath given them. Let them not maintain vaga-bonds and idle persons, but deliver the realm, and their households, from such noisome loiterers; that idleness, the mother of all mischief, being clean taken away, Almighty God may turn his dreadful anger away from us, and confirm the covenant of peace upon us for ever: through the merits of Jesus Christ, our only Lord and Saviour. To whom, with the Father, and the Holy Ghost, be all honour and glory, world without end. Amen.

AN HOMILY OF REPENTANCE
AND OF TRUE RECONCILIATION
UNTO GOD

THERE IS NOTHING that the Holy Ghost doth so much labour, in all the Scriptures, to beat into men's heads, as repentance, amendment of life, and speedy returning unto the Lord God of hosts. And no marvel why: for we do daily and hourly, by our wickedness and stubborn disobedience, horribly fall away from God, thereby purchasing unto ourselves, if he should deal with us according to his justice, eternal damnation. So that no doctrine is so necessary in the Church of God, as the doctrine of repentance and amendment of life. And verily, the true preachers of the Gospel of the kingdom of heaven, and of the glad and joyful tidings of salvation, have always, in their godly sermons and preachings unto the people, joined these two together, I mean repentance and forgiveness of sins; even as our Saviour Jesus Christ did appoint, himself saying, *So it behoved Christ to suffer, and to rise again the third day, and that repentance and forgiveness of sins should be preached in his Name, among all nations.* And therefore the holy Apostle doth in the Acts speak after this manner: *I have witnessed, both to the Jews and to the Gentiles, the repentance towards God, and faith towards our Lord Jesu Christ.* Did not John Baptist, Zachary's son, begin his ministry with the doctrine of repentance, saying, *Repent, for the kingdom of God is at hand?* The like doctrine did our Saviour Jesus Christ preach himself, and commanded his Apostles to preach the same.

I might here allege very many places out of the Prophets, in the which this most wholesome doctrine of repentance, is very earnestly urged, as most needful for all degrees and orders of men; but one shall be sufficient at this present time. These are the words of Joel the Prophet, *Therefore also now the Lord saith, Return unto me with all your heart, with fasting, weeping, and mourning; and rend your hearts, and not your clothes, and return unto the Lord your God: for he is gracious and merciful, slow to anger, and of great compassion, and ready to pardon*

The doctrine of repentance is most necessary.

Luke 24:46, 47

Acts 20:21

Matt. 3:2

Matt. 4:17

Joel 2:12, 13

A perpetual rule
which all must
follow

wickedness. Whereby it is given us to understand, that we have here a perpetual rule appointed unto us, which ought to be observed and kept at all times; and that there is none other way, whereby the wrath of God may be pacified, and his anger assuaged, that the fierceness of his fury, and the plagues or destruction, which by his righteous judgement he had determined to bring upon us, may depart, be removed, and taken away.

Where he saith, *But now therefore saith the Lord, Return unto me,* it is not without great importance that the Prophet speaketh so. For he had afore set forth at large unto them, the horrible vengeance of God, which no man was able to abide; and therefore he doth move them to repentance, to obtain mercy: as if he should say, "I will not have these things to be so taken, as though there were no hope of grace left; for, although ye do by your sins deserve to be utterly destroyed, and God, by his righteous judgements, hath determined to bring no small destruction upon you, *yet, now* that ye are in a manner on the very edge of the sword, if ye will speedily *return unto him,* he will most gently, and most mercifully, receive you into favour again." Whereby we are admonished, that repentance is never too late, so that it be true and earnest. For, sith that God in the Scriptures will be called *our Father,* doubtless he doth follow the nature and property, of gentle and merciful fathers, which seek nothing so much as the returning again, and amendment of their children, as Christ doth abundantly teach, in the parable of the Prodigal Son. Doth not the Lord himself say by the Prophet, *I will not the death of the wicked, but that he turn from his wicked ways, and live?* And in another place: *If we confess our sins, God is faithful and righteous, to forgive us our sins, and to make us clean from all wickedness.* Which most comfortable promises are confirmed, by many examples of the Scriptures. When the Jews did willingly receive and embrace, the wholesome counsel of the Prophet Esay, God by and by did reach his helping hand unto them, and by his angel did in one night, slay the most worthy and valiant soldiers of Sennacherib's camp. Whereunto may King Manasses be added, who after all manner of damnable wickedness, returned unto the Lord, and therefore was heard of him, and restored again into his kingdom. The same grace and favour did the sinful woman, Magdalene, Zaccheus, the poor thief, and many other feel. All which things ought to serve for our comfort, against the tentations of our consciences, whereby the devil goeth about to shake, or rather to overthrow our faith. For every one of us ought to apply the same unto himself, and say, *Yet now return unto the Lord*; neither let the remembrance of thy former life discourage thee; yea, the more wicked that it hath been, the more fervent and earnest let thy repentance or returning be; that forthwith thou shalt feel *the ears of the Lord wide open unto thy prayers.*

Matt. 6:9

Luke 15:11–32
Ezek. 18:23
Isai. 1:18

1 John 1:9

Isai. 37

2 Chron. 33:1–13

Luke 7:48, 8:2,
19:9, 23:43

1 Pet. 3:12

But let us more narrowly look upon the commandment of the Lord, touching this matter. *Turn unto me*, saith he by his Prophet Joel, *with all your hearts, with fasting, with weeping, and mourning; rend your hearts, and not your garments*, &c. In which words, he comprehendeth all manner of things that can be spoken of repentance, which is a turning again of the whole man unto God, from whom we be fallen away by sin. But, that the whole discourse thereof, may the better be borne away, we shall first consider in order, four principal points; that is, from what we must return, to whom we must return, by whom we may be able to convert, and the manner how to turn to God.

First, from when or from what things we must return. Truly, we must return from those things whereby we have been withdrawn, plucked, and led away from God. And these generally are our *sins*, which as the holy Prophet Esay doth testify, *do separate God and us, and hide his face, that he will not hear us*. But under the name of sin, not only those gross words and deeds, which by the common judgement of men are counted to be filthy and unlawful, and so consequently abominable sins, but also the filthy lusts, and inward concupiscences of the flesh, which as St Paul testifieth, do resist the will and Spirit of God, and therefore ought earnestly to be bridled, and kept under. We must repent of the false and erroneous opinions that we have had of God, and the wicked superstition, that doth breed of the same, the unlawful worshipping and service of God, and other like. All these things must they forsake, that will truly turn unto the Lord, and repent aright. For sith that *for such things, the wrath of God cometh upon the children of disobedience*, no end of punishment ought to be looked for, as long as we continue in such things. Therefore they be here condemned, which will seem to be repentant sinners, and yet will not forsake their idolatry and superstition. *(margin: From whence we must return; Isai. 59:2; Gal. 5:17; Eph. 5:6)*

Secondly, we must see unto whom we ought to return. *Revertimini usque ad me*, saith the Lord, that is *Return as far as unto me*. We must then *return unto the Lord*: yea, we must return unto him alone; for he alone is the truth, and the fountain of all goodness. But we must labour, that we do return *as far as unto* him, and that we do never cease and rest, till we have apprehended and taken hold upon him. But this must be done by faith; for, sith that *God is a spirit*, he can by none other mean be apprehended, and taken hold upon. Therefore, first, they do greatly err which do not turn unto God, but unto the creatures, or unto the inventions of men, or unto their own merits; secondly, they that do begin to return unto the Lord, and do faint in the midway, before they come to the mark that is appointed unto them. *(margin: Unto whom we ought to return; John 4:24)*

Thirdly, because we have, of our own selves, nothing to present us to God, and do no less flee from him after our fall, than our first parent *(margin: By whom we must return unto God)*

Gen. 3:8
Adam did, which when he had sinned, did seek to hide himself from the sight of God, we have need of a Mediator, for to bring and reconcile us unto him who, for our sins, is angry with us. The same is Jesus Christ: who being true and natural God, equal and of one substance with the Father, did at the time appointed, take upon him our frail nature, in the blessed Virgin's womb, and that of her undefiled substance; that so he might be a Mediator, betwixt God and us, and pacify his wrath. Of him

Matt. 3:17, 17:5
doth the Father himself speak from heaven, saying, *This is my wellbeloved Son, in whom I am pleased.* And he himself in his Gospel doth cry out and

John 14:6
say, *I am the way, the truth, and the life: no man cometh unto the Father, but*

John 1; 3; 1 Pet. 1
by me. For he alone did, with the sacrifice of his body and blood, make satisfaction unto the justice of God, for our sins. The Apostles do testify

Acts 5:31
that he was *exalted, for to give repentance and remission of sins unto Israel*:

Luke 24:47
both which things, he himself did command to be *preached in his Name.* Therefore they are greatly deceived, that preach repentance without Christ, and teach the simple and ignorant, that it consisteth only in the works of men. They may indeed speak many things of good works, and

John 15:4,5
of amendment of life and manners; but without Christ, they be all vain and unprofitable. They that think that they have done much of themselves towards repentance, are so much more the further from God, because that they do seek those things, in their own works and merits, which ought only to be sought in our Saviour Jesu Christ, and in the merits of his death, passion, and bloodshedding.

The manner of
our returning
Fourthly, this holy Prophet Joel, doth lively express the manner of this our returning, or repentance, comprehending all the inward and outward things that may be observed. First, he will have us to return unto God *with our whole heart*; whereby he doth remove and put away all

Isai. 29:13;
Matt. 15:8
hypocrisy, lest the same might justly be said unto us, *This people draweth near unto me with their mouth, and worshippeth me with their lips, but their heart is far from me.* Secondly, he requireth a sincere and pure love of godliness, and of the true worshipping and service of God; that is to say, that forsaking all manner of things that are repugnant, and contrary unto God's will, we do give our hearts unto him, and all the whole strength of our bodies and souls, according to that which is written in

Deut. 6:5
the Law, *Thou shalt love the Lord thy God, with all thy heart, with all thy soul, and with all thy strength.* Here therefore, nothing is left unto us, that we may give unto the world, and unto the lusts of the flesh. For, sith that the heart is the fountain of all our works, as many as do with their whole heart, turn unto the Lord, do live unto him only. Neither do they yet

Halting on both
sides
repent truly that, halting on both sides, do otherwhiles obey God, but by and by do think, that laying him aside, it is lawful for them to serve the world and the flesh. And because that we are letted, by the natural corruption of our own flesh, and the wicked affections of the same, he

doth bid us also to return *with fasting*; not thereby understanding a superstitious abstinence and choosing of meats, but a true discipline or taming of the flesh, whereby the nourishments of filthy lusts, and of stubborn contumacy and pride, may be withdrawn, and plucked away from it. Whereunto he doth add *weeping and mourning*, which do contain an outward profession of repentance; which is very needful and necessary, that so we may partly set forth the righteousness of God, when by such means we do testify, that we deserved punishment at his hands, and partly stop the offence that was openly given unto the weak. This did David see, who being not content to have bewept and bewailed his sins privately, would publicly, in his Psalms, declare and set forth the righteousness of God, in punishing sin, and also stay them that might have abused his example, to sin the more boldly. Therefore they are furthest from true repentance, that will not confess and acknowledge their sins, nor yet bewail them, but rather do most ungodly, glory and rejoice in them.

Now, lest any man should think, that repentance doth consist in outward weeping and mourning only, he doth rehearse that wherein the chief of the whole matter doth lie, when he saith, *Rend your hearts, and not your garments, and turn unto the Lord your God.* For the people of the East part of the world, were wont to rend their garments, if anything had happened unto them that seemed intolerable. This thing did hypocrites sometime counterfeit and follow, as though the whole repentance did stand in such outward gesture. He teacheth then, that another manner of thing is required: that is, that they must be contrite in their hearts, that they must utterly detest and abhor sins, and being at defiance with them, return unto the Lord their God, from whom they went away before. For God hath no pleasure in the outward ceremony, but requireth *a contrite and humble heart*; which *he will never despise*, as David doth testify. There is therefore, none other use of these outward ceremonies, but as far forth as we are stirred up by them, and [they] do serve to the glory of God, and to the edifying of other.

Now doth he add unto this doctrine or exhortation, certain goodly reasons, which he doth ground upon the nature and property of God, and whereby he doth teach, that true repentance can never be unprofitable, or unfruitful. For as in all other things men's hearts do quail and faint, if they once perceive that they travail in vain, even so, most specially in this matter, must we take heed and beware, that we suffer not ourselves to be persuaded that all that we do is but labour lost; for thereof either sudden desperation doth arise, or a licentious boldness to sin, which at length bringeth unto desperation. Lest any such thing then should happen unto them, he doth certify them of the grace and goodness of God, who is always most ready to receive them into favour

True fast

Psalm 25; 32; 51; 103; 143

Psalm 52: 1–5

Hypocrites do counterfeit all manner of things.

Psalm 51:17

How repentance is not unprofitable

again, that turn speedily unto him. Which thing he doth prove, with the same titles wherewith God doth describe and set forth himself unto

Exod. 34:6

Moses, speaking on this manner: *For he is gracious and merciful, slow to anger, of great kindness, and repenteth him of the evil,* that is, such a one as is sorry for your affliction. First, he calleth him gentle, and *gracious,* as he who of his own nature, is more prompt and ready to do good, than to punish. Whereunto this saying of Esay the Prophet seemeth to pertain,

Isai. 55:7

where he saith, *Let the wicked forsake his way, and the unrighteous his own imaginations, and return unto the Lord, and he will have pity on him, and to our God, for he is very ready to forgive.* Secondly, he doth attribute unto him *mercy,* or rather, according to the Hebrew word, the bowels of mercies, whereby are signified the natural affections of parents towards

Psalm 103:13, 14

their children. Which thing David doth set forth goodly, saying, *As a father hath compassion on his children, so hath the Lord compassion on them that fear him: for he knoweth whereof we be made, and remembereth that we are but dust.* Thirdly, he saith that he is *slow to anger,* that is to say, longsuffering and which is not lightly provoked to wrath. Fourthly, that he is *of much kindness:* for he is that bottomless well of all goodness, who rejoiceth to do good unto us. Therefore did he create and make men, that he might have whom he should do good unto, and make partakers of his heavenly riches. Fifthly, he *repenteth of the evil,* that is to say, he doth call back again, and revoke the punishment which he had threatened, when he seeth men repent, turn, and amend.

Against the Novatians

Whereupon we do not without a just cause, detest and abhor the damnable opinion of them, which do most wickedly go about, to persuade the simple and ignorant people, that if we chance, after we be once come to God, and grafted in his Son, Jesu Christ, to fall into some horrible sin, repentance shall be unprofitable unto us—there is no more hope of reconciliation, or to be received again into the favour and mercy of God. And that they may give the better colour unto their pestilent and pernicious error, they do commonly bring in the sixth and tenth chapters of the Epistle to the Hebrews, and the second chapter of the second Epistle of Peter; not considering, that in those places, the holy Apostles do not speak of the daily falls that we, as long as we carry about this body of sin, are subject unto, but of the final falling away from

Matt. 12:31, Mark 3:29 The sin against the Holy Ghost

Christ and his Gospel: which is a sin against the Holy Ghost, that shall never be forgiven; because that they that do utterly forsake the known truth, do hate Christ and his word, they do crucify and mock him (but to their utter destruction), and therefore fall into desperation, and cannot repent. And that this is the true meaning of the Holy Spirit of God, it appeareth by many other places of the Scriptures, which promiseth unto all true repentant sinners, and to them that with their whole heart do return unto the Lord their God, free pardon and remission of their sins.

For the probation hereof we read this: *O Israel*, saith the holy Prophet Jeremy, *if thou return, return unto me, saith the Lord; and, if thou put away thine abominations out of my sight, then shalt thou not be moved.* Again, these are Esay's words, *Let the wicked forsake his own ways, and the unrighteous his own imaginations, and turn again unto the Lord, and he will have mercy upon him, and to our God, for he is ready to forgive.* And in the Prophet Osee, the godly do exhort one another after this manner: *Come and let us turn again, unto the Lord: for he hath smitten us, and he will heal us; he hath wounded us, and he will bind us up again.* It is most evident and plain, that these things ought to be understood of them that were with the Lord afore, and by their sins and wickedness were gone away from him; for we do not turn again unto him with whom we were never before, but we come unto him.

Now unto all them that will return unfeignedly unto the Lord their God, the favour and mercy of God, unto forgiveness of sins, is liberally offered. Whereby it followeth necessarily, that although we do—after we be once come to God, and grafted in his Son, Jesu Christ—fall into great sins (*for there is no righteous man upon the earth, that sinneth not*, and *if we say we have no sin, we deceive ourselves, and the truth is not in us*), yet if we rise again, by repentance, and with a full purpose of amendment of life, do flee unto the mercy of God, taking sure hold thereupon, through faith in his Son, Jesu Christ, there is an assured and infallible hope of pardon and remission of the same, and that we shall be received again, into the favour of our heavenly Father.

It is written of David, *I have found a man according to mine own heart*; or, *I have found David the son of Jesse, a man according to mine own heart, who will do all things that I will.* This is a godly commendation of David. It is also most certain, that he did stedfastly believe the promise that was made him, touching the Messias, who should come of him touching the flesh, and that by the same faith, he was justified and grafted in our Saviour Jesu Christ to come. And yet afterwards he fell horribly, committing most detestable adultery, and damnable murder: and yet, as soon as he cried *Peccavi, I have sinned unto the Lord*, his sin being forgiven, he was received into favour again.

Now will we come unto Peter, of whom no man can doubt but that he was grafted in our Saviour Jesu Christ, long afore his denial. Which thing may easily be proved, by the answer which he did in his name, and in the name of his fellow Apostles, make unto our Saviour Jesu Christ, when he said unto them, *Will ye also go away? Master*, saith he, *to whom shall we go? thou hast the words of eternal life; and we believe and know, that thou art the Christ, the Son of the living God.* Whereunto may be added the like confession of Peter, where Christ doth give this most infallible testimony: *Thou art blessed, Simon son of Jonas; for neither flesh nor blood*

Marginal references:

Jer. 4:1

Isai. 55:7

Hos. 6:1

Note!

Eccles. 7:20,
1 John 1:8

1 Sam. 13:14,
Psalm 89:20,
Acts 13:22

2 Sam. 7:12–16,
28, 29

2 Sam. 11

Peter

John 6:67–9

Matt. 16:17

hath revealed this unto thee, but my Father, which is in heaven. These words are sufficient, to prove that Peter was already justified, through this his lively faith in the only begotten Son of God, whereof he made so notable and so solemn a confession. But did not he afterwards most cowardly deny his Master, although he had heard of him, *Whosoever denieth me before men, I will deny him before my Father?* Nevertheless, as soon as with weeping eyes, and with a sobbing heart, he did acknowledge his offence, and with earnest repentance did flee unto the mercy of God, taking sure hold thereupon, through faith in him whom he had so shamefully denied, his sin was forgiven him, and for a certificate and assurance thereof, the room of his Apostleship was not denied unto him. But now mark what doth follow. After the same holy Apostle had on Whitsunday, with the rest of the disciples, received the gift of the Holy Ghost most abundantly, he committed no small offence in Antiochia, by bringing the consciences of the faithful into doubt, by his example; so that Paul was fain to rebuke him to his face, because that he *walked not uprightly*, or went not the right way, *in the Gospel.* Shall we now say, that after this grievous offence, he was utterly excluded, and shut out from the grace and mercy of God, and that this his trespass, whereby he was a stumbling-block unto many, was unpardonable? God forfend we should say so!

But, as these examples are not brought in, to the end that we should thereby take a boldness to sin, presuming on the mercy and goodness of God, but to the end that, if through the frailness of our own flesh, and the temptation of the devil, we fall into the like sins, we should in no wise despair of the mercy and goodness of God; even so must we beware, and take heed, that we do in no wise think in our hearts, imagine, or believe, that we are able to repent aright, or to turn effectually unto the Lord, by our own might and strength. For this must be verified in all men, *Without me ye can do nothing.* Again, *Of ourselves we are not able as much as to think a good thought.* And in another place, *It is God that worketh in us, both the will and the deed.* For this cause, although Jeremy had said before, *If thou return, O Israel, return unto me, saith the Lord*, yet afterwards he saith, *Turn thou me, O Lord, and I shall be turned; for thou art the Lord my God.* And therefore that holy writer and ancient father, Ambrose, doth plainly affirm, that the turning of the heart unto God is of God; as the Lord himself doth testify by his Prophet, saying, *And I will give thee an heart to know me, that I am the Lord; and they shall be my people, and I will be their God; for they shall return unto me with their whole heart.*

These things being considered, let us earnestly pray unto the living God, our heavenly Father, that he will vouchsafe by his Holy Spirit, to work a true and unfeigned repentance in us; that after the painful labours and travails of this life, we may live eternally with his Son, Jesus Christ. To whom be all praise and glory, for ever and ever. Amen.

Matt. 26:67–75

Matt. 10:33

Acts 2:1, 4, 14, 37, 38

Gal. 2:11–14

What we must beware of

John 15:5
2 Cor. 3:5
Phil. 2:13

Jer. 4:1
Jer. 31:18

Ambros. *de Vocat. Gent.* Lib. 1, cap. 9
Jer. 24:7

THE SECOND PART
OF THE HOMILY OF REPENTANCE

HITHERTO HAVE YE HEARD, wellbeloved, how needful and necessary the doctrine of repentance is, and how earnestly it is throughout all the Scriptures of God urged, and set forth, both by the ancient Prophets, by our Saviour, Jesu Christ, and his Apostles; and that forasmuch as it is the conversion, or turning again, of the whole man, unto God, from whom we go away by sin, these four points ought to be observed: that is, from whence or from what things we must return, unto whom this our returning must be made, by whose means it ought to be done, that it may be effectual, and last of all, after what sort we ought to behave ourselves in the same, that it may be profitable unto us, and attain unto the thing that we do seek by it. Ye have also learned, that as the opinion of them that deny the benefit of repentance, unto those that after they be come to God, and grafted into our Saviour Jesu Christ, do through the frailness of their flesh, and the temptation of the devil, fall into some grievous and detestable sin, is most pestilent and pernicious; so we must beware, that we do in no wise think that we are able, of our own selves, and of our own strength, to return unto the Lord our God, from whom we are gone away by our wickedness and sin. Now it shall be declared unto you, what be the true parts of repentance, and what things ought to move us to repent, and to return unto the Lord our God with all speed.

Repentance, as it is said before, is a true returning unto God, whereby, men forsaking utterly their idolatry and wickedness, do with a lively faith embrace, love, and worship the true living God only, and give themselves to all manner of good works, which by God's word they know to be acceptable unto him. Now there be four parts of repentance, which being set together, may be likened unto an easy and short ladder, whereby we may climb, from the bottomless pit of perdition, that we cast ourselves into by our daily offences and grievous sins, up into the castle or tower, of eternal and endless salvation. *There be four parts of repentance.*

The first is the contrition of the heart. For we must be earnestly sorry for our sins, and unfeignedly lament and bewail, that we have by them so grievously offended our most bounteous and merciful God; who *so* *John 3:16* tenderly *loved us, that he gave his only begotten Son,* to die a most bitter death, and to shed his dear heart blood, for our redemption and deliverance. And verily, this inward sorrow and grief, being conceived in the heart, for the heinousness of sin, if it be earnest and unfeigned, is as a sacrifice to God: as the holy Prophet David doth testify, saying, *A sacrifice* *Psalm 51:17* *to God is a troubled spirit; a contrite and broken heart, O Lord, thou wilt not despise.* But, that this may take place in us, we must be diligent, to read and hear the Scriptures and word of God, which most lively do paint out, before our eyes, our natural uncleanliness, and the enormity of our sinful life. For, unless we have a thorough feeling of our sins, how can it

2 Sam. 12:1–13

be, that we should earnestly be sorry for them? Afore David did hear the word of the Lord, by the mouth of the Prophet Nathan, what heaviness, I pray you, was in him for the adultery and murder that he had committed? So that it might be said right well, that he slept in his own sin.

Acts 2:37

We read in the Acts of the Apostles, that when the people had heard the sermon of Peter, they were compunct, and *pricked in their hearts.* Which thing would never have been, if they had not heard that wholesome sermon of Peter. They therefore that have no mind at all, neither to read nor yet to hear God's word, there is but small hope of them, that they will as much as once set their feet, or take hold upon the first staff or step of this ladder, but rather will sink deeper and deeper, into the bottomless pit of perdition. For if at any time, through the remorse of their conscience, which accuseth them, they feel any inward grief, sorrow, or heaviness for their sins, forasmuch as they want the salve and comfort of God's word, which they do despise, it will be unto them rather, a mean to bring them to utter desperation, than otherwise.

The second, is an unfeigned confession, and acknowledging of our sins unto God; whom by them we have so grievously offended, that if he should deal with us according to his justice, we do deserve a thousand

Ezek. 18:21, 22

hells, if there could be so many. Yet if we will, with a sorrowful and contrite heart, make an unfeigned confession of them, unto God, he will freely and frankly forgive them, and so put all our wickedness out of remembrance, before the sight of his Majesty, that they shall no more be thought upon. Hereunto doth pertain the golden saying of the holy

Psalm 32:5

Prophet David, where he saith on this manner: *Then I acknowledged my sin unto thee, neither did I hide mine iniquity: I said, "I will confess against myself my wickedness unto the Lord,"* and thou forgavest the ungodliness of

1 John 1:9

my sin. These are also the words of John the Evangelist: *If we confess our sins, God is faithful and righteous, to forgive us our sins, and to make us clean from all our wickedness.* Which ought to be understood of the confession

in Epist. ad Jul. Comit. 30

that is made unto God. For these are St Augustine's words: "That confession which is made unto God, is required by God's law; whereof John the Apostle speaketh, saying, *If we confess our sins, God is faithful and righteous, to forgive us our sins, and to make us clean from all our wickedness*: for without this confession, sin is not forgiven." This is then the chiefest and most principal confession, that in the Scriptures and word of God we are bidden to make, and without the which, we shall never obtain pardon and forgiveness of our sins.

Indeed, besides this there is another kind of confession, which is needful and necesssary. And of the same doth St James speak, after this manner, saying, *Acknowledge your faults one to another, and pray one for* James 5:16 *another, that ye may be saved*: as if he should say, "Open that which grieveth you, that a remedy may be found." And this is commanded, both for him that complaineth, and for him that heareth: that the one should show his grief to the other. The true meaning of it, is that the faithful ought to acknowledge their offences—whereby some hatred, rancour, grudge, or malice have risen or grown among them, one to another— that a brotherly reconciliation may be had; without the which, nothing that we do can be acceptable unto God, as our Saviour, Jesus Christ, doth witness himself, saying, *When thou offerest thine offering at the altar, if* Matt. 5:23–4 *thou rememberest that thy brother hath aught against thee, leave there thine offering, and go, and be reconciled, and when thou art reconciled, come and offer thine offering.* It may also be thus taken, that we ought to confess our weakness and infirmities, one to another, to the end that, knowing each other's frailness, we may the more earnestly pray together, unto Almighty God, our heavenly Father, that he will vouchsafe to pardon us our infirmities, for his Son Jesus Christ's sake, and not to impute them unto us, when *he shall render to every man according to his works.* Matt. 16:27, Rom. 2:6

And whereas the adversaries go about to wrest this place, for to Answer to the adversaries which maintain auricular confession maintain their auricular confession withal, they are greatly deceived themselves, and do shamefully deceive others. For if this text ought to be understood of auricular confession, then the priests are as much bound to confess themselves unto the lay people, as the lay people are bound to confess themselves to them. And if to pray is to absolve, then the laity, by this place, hath as great authority to absolve the priests, as the priests have to absolve the laity. This did Johannes Scotus, otherwise Joh. Scotus, Lib. 4 *Sent.*, Dist. 17, Quaest. 1 called Duns, well perceive, who upon this place writeth on this manner:

> Neither doth it seem unto me, that James did give this command-
> ment, or that he did set it forth, as being received of Christ. For, first
> and foremost, whence had he authority to bind the whole Church,
> sith that he was only Bishop of the Church of Jerusalem? Except
> thou wilt say, that the same Church was at the beginning, the head
> Church, and consequently that he was the head Bishop; which thing
> the see of Rome will never grant.

> The understanding of it then is, as in these words, *Confess your sins
> one to another*, a persuasion to humility, whereby he willeth us to
> confess ourselves generally unto our neighbours, that we are sinners,
> according to this saying, *If we say we have no sin, we deceive ourselves,* 1 John 1:8
> *and the truth is not in us.*

And where that they do allege this saying, of our Saviour, Jesu Christ unto the leper, to prove auricular confession to stand on God's word, *Go* Matt. 8:4 *thy way, and show thyself unto the priest*, do they not see, that the leper was cleansed from his leprosy, afore he was by Christ sent unto the priest, for to show himself unto him? By the same reason, we must be cleansed from our spiritual leprosy, I mean, our sins must be forgiven us, afore that we come to confession. What need we then to tell forth our sins into the ear of the priest, sith that they be already taken away? Therefore holy Ambrose, in his second Sermon upon the hundred and nineteenth Psalm, doth say full well "*Go, show thyself unto the priest*: who is the true Priest, but he which is *the Priest for ever, after the order of Melchisedech?*" Whereby this holy father doth understand, that *both the priesthood and the law being changed*, we ought to acknowledge none other priest, for deliverance from our sins, but our Saviour, Jesus Christ; who, being our sovereign Bishop, doth with the sacrifice of his body and blood, offered once for ever upon the altar of the cross, most effectually cleanse the spiritual leprosy, and wash away the sins, of all those that with true confession of the same, do flee unto him.

It is most evident and plain, that this auricular confession hath not his warrant of God's word; else it had not been lawful for Nectarius, Bishop of Constantinople, upon a just occasion, to have put it down. For when any thing ordained of God, is by the lewdness of men abused, the abuse ought to be taken away, and the thing itself suffered to remain. Moreover, these are St Augustine's words:

> What have I to do with men, that they should hear my confession, as though they were able to heal all my diseases? A curious sort of men, to know another man's life, and slothful to correct or amend their own! Why do they seek to hear of me what I am, which will not hear of thee what they are? And how can they tell, when they hear by me of myself, whether I tell the truth or not? sith that *no mortal man knoweth what is in man, but the spirit of man which is in him.*

Augustine would not have written thus, if auricular confession had been used in his time. Being therefore not led with the conscience thereof, let us, with fear and trembling, and with a true contrite heart, use that kind of confession that God doth command in his word; and then doubtless, as *he is faithful and righteous, he will forgive us our sins, and make us clean from all wickedness.* I do not say but that, if any do find themselves troubled in conscience, they may repair to their learned curate or pastor, or to some other godly learned man, and show the trouble and doubt of their conscience to them, that they may receive at their hand, the comfortable salve of God's word: but it is against the true Christian liberty, that any man should be bound to the numbering of his sins, as it hath been used heretofore, in the time of blindness and ignorance.

The third part of repentance is faith, whereby we do apprehend and take hold upon the promises of God, touching the free pardon and forgiveness of our sins; which promises are sealed up unto us, with the death and bloodshedding of his Son, Jesu Christ. For what should avail

Ambrose

Psalm 110:4,
Heb. 5:6, 6:20
Ibid. 7:12

Nectarius
Sozom. *Eccles.
Hist.* Lib. 7,
cap. 16

Lib. 10 *Conf.*
cap. 3

1 Cor. 2:11

1 John 1:9

and profit us, to be sorry for our sins, to lament and bewail that we have offended our most bounteous and merciful Father, or to confess and acknowledge our offences and trespasses, though it be done never so earnestly, unless we do stedfastly believe, and be fully persuaded, that God, for his Son Jesu Christ's sake, will forgive us all our sins, and put them out of remembrance, and from his sight? Therefore they that teach repentance, without a lively faith in our Saviour, Jesu Christ, do teach none other but Judas' repentance; as all the Schoolmen do, which do only allow these three parts of repentance: the contrition of the heart, the confession of the mouth, and the satisfaction of the work. But all these things we find in Judas' repentance, which in outward appearance, did far exceed and pass the repentance of Peter. For first and foremost, we read in the Gospel, that Judas was so sorrowful and heavy, yea, that he was filled with such anguish and vexation of mind, for that which he had done, that he could not abide to live any longer. Did not he also, afore he hanged himself, make an open confession of his fault, when he said, *I have sinned, betraying the innocent blood?* And verily, this was a very bold confession, which might have brought him to great trouble; for by it he did lay to the high priests' and elders' charge, the shedding of innocent blood, and that they were most abominable murderers. He did also make a certain kind of satisfaction, when he did cast their money unto them again. No such thing do we read of Peter, although he had committed a very heinous sin, and most grievous offence, in denying of his Master. We find that *he went out, and wept bitterly*: whereof Ambrose speaketh on this manner. "Peter was sorry and wept, because he erred as a man. I do not find what he said; I know that he wept. I read of his tears, but not of his satisfaction." But how chance, that the one was received into favour again with God, and the other cast away, but because that the one did, by a lively faith in him whom he had denied, take hold upon the mercy of God, and the other wanted faith, whereby he did despair of the goodness and mercy of God? It is evident and plain then, that although we be never so earnestly sorry for our sins, acknowledge and confess them, yet all these things shall be but means to bring us to utter desperation, except we do stedfastly believe, that God, our heavenly Father, will for his Son Jesu Christ's sake, pardon, and forgive us, our offences and trespasses, and utterly put them out of remembrance in his sight. Therefore, as we said before, they that teach repentance without Christ, and a lively faith in the mercy of God, do only teach Cain's or Judas' repentance.

The fourth is an amendment of life, or a new life, in bringing forth *fruits worthy of repentance*. For they that do truly repent must be clean altered and changed; they must become new creatures; they must be no more the same that they were before. And therefore, thus said John Baptist unto the Pharisees and Sadducees, that came unto his baptism:

The repentance of the Schoolmen

Judas and his repentance

Matt. 27:3–5

Peter and his repentance

Matt. 26:75

de Poenit. Dist. 1, cap. Petrus

Matt. 3:7–8

O generation of vipers, who hath forewarned you, to flee from the anger to come? Bring forth therefore fruits worthy of repentance. Whereby we do learn, that if we will have the wrath of God to be pacified, we must in no wise dissemble, but turn unto him again, with a true and sound repentance, which may be known and declared by good fruits, as by most sure and infallible signs thereof. They that do from the bottom of their hearts, acknowledge their sins, and are unfeignedly sorry for their offences, will cast off all hypocrisy, and put on true humility, and lowliness of heart. They will not only receive the physician of the soul, but also with a most fervent desire, long for him. They will not only abstain from the sins of their former life, and from all other filthy vices, but also flee, eschew, and abhor, all the occasions of them. And as they did before give themselves to uncleanness of life, so will they from henceforwards, with all diligence, give themselves to innocency, pureness of life, and true godliness.

Jonah 3:4–10

We have the Ninivites for an example, which at the preaching of Jonas, did not only proclaim a general fast, and that they should every one put on sackcloth, but they all did *turn from their evil ways, and from the wickedness that was in their hands.* But above all other, the history of Zaccheus is most notable: for being come unto our Saviour, Jesu Christ,

Luke 19:8

he did say, *Behold, Lord, the half of my goods I give to the poor; and if I have defrauded any man, or taken aught away by extortion or fraud, I do restore him fourfold.* Here we see, that after his repentance, he was no more the man that he was before, but was clean changed and altered. It was so far off that he would continue to abide still in his unsatiable covetousness, or take aught away fraudulently from any man, that rather he was most willing and ready, to give away his own, and to make satisfaction, unto all them that he had done injury and wrong unto. Here may we right

Luke 7:37, 38

well add the sinful woman, which when she came to our Saviour, Jesu Christ, did pour down such abundance of tears, out of those wanton eyes of hers, wherewith she had allured many unto folly, that she did with them wash his feet, wiping them with the hairs of her head, which she was wont most gloriously to set out, making of them a net of the devil. Hereby we do learn, what is the satisfaction that God doth

Psalm 34:14,
Isai. 1:16, 17

require of us, which is, that we *cease from evil, and do good,* and if we have done any man wrong, to endeavour ourselves to make him true amends, to the uttermost of our power; following in this the example of Zaccheus, and of this sinful woman, and also that goodly lesson that John Baptist, Zachary's son, did give unto them, that came to ask counsel of him.

John 5:14, 8:11

This was commonly the penance that Christ enjoined sinners: *Go thy way, and sin no more.* Which penance we shall never be able to fulfil,

Ibid. 15:5

without the special grace of him that doth say, *Without me ye can do nothing.* It is therefore our parts, if at least we be desirous, of the health and salvation of our own selves, most earnestly to pray unto our heavenly Father, to assist us with his Holy Spirit, that we may be able to hearken unto the voice of the true Shepherd, and with due obedience, to follow the same. Let us hearken to the voice of Almighty God, when he calleth us to repentance. Let us not harden our hearts, as such infidels do, who do abuse the time given them of God to repent, and turn it to continue their pride and contempt, against God and man; which know not how much they *heap God's wrath upon themselves, for the hardness of their hearts, which cannot repent at the day of vengeance.* Where we have offended the law of God, let us repent us of our straying from so good a Lord. Let us confess our unworthiness before him; but yet let us trust in God's free mercy, for Christ's sake, for the pardon of the same. And from henceforth, let us endeavour ourselves, to walk in a new life, *as newborn babes*, whereby we *may glorify our Father, which is in heaven*, and thereby to bear in our consciences, a good testimony of our faith; so at the last, to obtain the fruition of everlasting life, through the merits of our Saviour. To whom be all praise, and honour, for ever. Amen.

Rom. 2:5

1 Pet. 2:2
Matt. 5:16

THE THIRD PART
OF THE HOMILY OF REPENTANCE

IN THE HOMILY LAST SPOKEN unto you, right well beloved people in our Saviour Christ, ye heard of the true parts and tokens of repentance; that is: hearty contrition and sorrowfulness of our hearts; unfeigned confession in word of mouth, for our unworthy living before God; a stedfast faith to the merits of our Saviour Christ, for pardon; and a purpose of ourselves, by God's grace, to renounce our former wicked life, and a full conversion to God, in a new life, to glorify his Name, and to live orderly and charitably, to the comfort of our neighbour in all righteousness, and live soberly and modestly to ourselves, by using abstinence and temperance, in word and deed, in *mortifying our earthly members here upon earth.* Now for a further persuasion, to move you to those parts of repentance, I will declare unto you some causes, which should the rather move you to repentance.

Col. 3:5

First, the commandment of God, who in so many places of his holy and sacred Scriptures doth bid us return unto him. *O ye children of Israel*, saith he, *turn again from your infidelity, wherein ye drowned yourselves.* Again, *Turn you, turn you, from your evil ways: for why will ye die, O ye house of Israel?* And in another place thus doth he speak, by his holy Prophet Osee: *O Israel, return unto the Lord thy God; for thou hast taken a great fall by thine iniquity. Take unto you these words with you, when ye turn unto the Lord, and say unto him, "Take away all iniquity, and receive us*

The causes that should move us
Isai. 31:6
to repent

Ezek. 33:11

Hos. 14:1, 2

graciously; so will we offer the calves of our lips unto thee. " In all these places, we have an express commandment, given unto us of God, for to return unto him. Therefore we must take good heed unto ourselves lest, whereas we have already, by our manifold sins and transgressions, provoked and kindled the wrath of God against us, we do, by breaking this his commandment, double our offences, and so heap still damnation upon our own heads. By our daily offences and trespasses, whereby we provoke the eyes of his Majesty, we do well deserve, if he should deal with us according to his justice, to be put away for ever from the fruition of his glory. How much more then, are we worthy of the endless torments of hell, if when we be so gently called again after our rebellion, and commanded to return, we will in no wise hearken unto the voice of our heavenly Father, but walk still after the stubbornness of our own hearts!

Secondly, the most comfortable and sweet promise, that the Lord our God, did of his mere mercy and goodness, join unto his commandment.

Jer. 4:1

For he doth not only say, *Return unto me, O Israel*; but also, *If thou wilt return, and put away all thine abominations out of my sight, thou shalt never*

Ezek. 18:21, 22

be moved. These words also have we in the Prophet Ezechiel: *At what time soever, a sinner doth repent him of his sin, from the bottom of his heart, I will put all his wickedness out of my remembrance, saith the Lord, so that they shall no more be thought upon.* Thus are we sufficiently instructed, that God will according to his promise, freely pardon, forgive, and forget all our sins, so that we shall never be cast in the teeth with them, if obeying his commandment, and allured by his sweet promises, we will unfeignedly return unto him.

Thirdly, the filthiness of sin: which is such that, as long as we do abide in it, God cannot but detest and abhor us; neither can there be any hope that we shall enter into the heavenly Jerusalem, except we be first made clean and purged from it. But this will never be, unless, forsaking our former life, we do with our whole heart, return unto the Lord our God, and with a full purpose of amendment of life, flee unto his mercy, taking sure hold thereupon, through faith in the blood of his Son, Jesu Christ.

Similitude

If we should suspect any uncleanness to be in us, wherefore the earthly prince should loath and abhor the sight of us, what pains would we take, to remove and put it away! How much more ought we, with all diligence and speed that may be, to put away that unclean filthiness that doth

Isai. 59:2

separate and make a division *betwixt us and our God*, and that *hideth his face from us, that he will not hear us*! And verily, herein doth appear how filthy a thing sin is, sith that it can by no other means be washed away, but by the blood, of the only begotten Son of God. And shall we not, from the bottom of our hearts, detest and abhor, and with all earnestness flee from it, sith that it did cost the dear heart blood, of the only begotten Son of God, our Saviour and Redeemer, to purge us from it? Plato doth in a certain place write, that if virtue could be seen with bodily eyes, all men would wonderfully be inflamed, and kindled with the love of it. Even so on the contrary, if we might with our bodily eyes, behold the filthiness of sin, and the uncleanness thereof, we could in no wise abide it, but as most present and deadly poison, hate and eschew it. We have a common experience of the same, in them which, when they have committed any heinous offence, of some filthy and abominable sin, if it once come to light, or if they chance to have a thorough feeling of it, they be so ashamed, their own conscience putting before their eyes the filthiness of their act, that they dare look no man in the face, much less that they should be able to stand, in the sight of God.

Fourthly, the uncertainty and brittleness of our own lives: which is such, that we cannot assure ourselves, that we shall live one hour or one half quarter of it. Which by experience we do find daily to be true, in them that being now merry and lusty, and sometimes feasting and banqueting with their friends, do fall suddenly dead in the streets, and otherwhiles under the board, when they are yet at meat. These daily examples, as they are most terrible and dreadful, so ought they to move us, to seek for to be at one, with our heavenly Judge; that we may with a good conscience, appear before him, whensoever it shall please him for to call us, whether it be suddenly or otherwise. For we have no more charter of our life, than they have: but as we are most certain that we shall die, so are we most uncertain when we shall die. For our life doth lie in the hand of God, who will take it away when it pleaseth him. And verily, when the highest somner of all, which is death, shall come, he will not be said nay, but we must forthwith be packing, to be presented before the judgement seat of God, as he doth find us; according as it is written, *Where as the tree falleth, whether it be toward the south, or toward the north, there it shall lie.* Whereunto agreeth the saying of the holy Martyr of God, St Cyprian, saying, "As God doth find thee when he doth call, so doth he judge thee." Let us therefore follow the counsel of the Wise Man, where he saith, *Make no tarrying to turn unto the Lord, and put not off from day to day; for suddenly, shall the wrath of the Lord break forth, and in thy security thou shalt be destroyed, and thou shalt perish in time of vengeance.* Which words I desire you to mark diligently, because they do most lively put before our eyes, the fondness of many men, which abusing the longsuffering and goodness of God, do never think on repentance, or amendment of life. *Follow not,* saith he, *thine own mind and thy strength, to walk in the ways of thy heart; neither say thou, "Who will bring me under, for my works?" For God the revenger, will revenge the wrong done by thee. And say not, "I have sinned, and what evil hath come unto me?" For the Almighty is a patient rewarder, but he will not leave thee unpunished.*

Plato

Death the Lord's somner

Eccles. 11:3

contra Demetrianum

Ecclus. 5:7

Ibid.: 2–6

Because thy sins are forgiven thee, be not without fear to heap sin upon sin. Say not neither, "The mercy of God is great, he will forgive my manifold sins." For mercy and wrath come from him, and his indignation cometh upon unrepentant sinners. As if he should say, "Art thou strong and mighty? art thou lusty and young? hast thou the wealth and riches of the world? or, when thou hast sinned, hast thou received no punishment for it? Let none of all these things make thee to be the slower to repent, and to return with speed unto the Lord; for in the day of punishment, and of his sudden vengeance they shall not be able to help thee." And specially, when thou art either by the preaching of God's word, or by some inward motion of his Holy Spirit, or else by some other means, called unto repentance, neglect not the good occasion that is ministered unto thee; lest, when thou wouldest repent, thou have not the grace, for to do it. For to repent is a good gift of God, which he will never grant unto them, which living in carnal security, do make a mock of his threatenings, or seek to rule his Spirit as they list, as though his working and gifts, were tied unto their will.

Fifthly, the avoiding of the plagues of God, and the utter destruction, that by his righteous judgement, do hang over the heads of them all that

Jer. 24:9–10

will in no wise return unto the Lord. *I will,* saith the Lord, *give them for a terrible plague, to all the kingdoms of the earth, and for a reproach, and for a proverb, and for a curse, in all places where I shall cast them, and will send the sword, the famine, and the pestilence among them, till they be consumed out of the land.* And wherefore is this? Because they hardened their hearts, and

Jonah 3:8, 9

would in no wise *return from their evil ways,* nor yet forsake *the wickedness that was in their own hands,* that the fierceness of the Lord's fury might depart from them. But yet this is nothing, in comparison of the intolerable and endless torments of hell fire, which they shall fain to suffer, who

Rom. 2:5

after their hardness of heart, that cannot repent, do heap unto themselves wrath, against the day of anger, and of the declaration of the just judgement of God. Whereas, if we will repent, and be earnestly sorry for our sins, and with a full purpose of amendment of life, flee unto the mercy of our God, and taking sure hold thereupon, through faith in our Saviour, Jesu

Matt. 3:8

Christ, do *bring forth fruits worthy of repentance,* he will not only pour his manifold blessings upon us, here in this world, but also, at the last, after the painful travails of this life, reward us, with the inheritance of his children: which is the kingdom of heaven, purchased unto us, with the death of his Son, Jesu Christ, our Lord. To whom, with the Father, and the Holy Ghost, be all praise, glory, and honour, world without end. Amen.

AN HOMILY
AGAINST DISOBEDIENCE
AND WILFUL REBELLION

THE FIRST PART

As GOD, THE CREATOR AND LORD of all things, appointed his angels and heavenly creatures, in all obedience to serve and to honour his Majesty, so was it his will that man, his chief creature upon the earth, should live under the obedience of him, his Creator and Lord; and for that cause God, as soon as he had created man, gave unto him a certain precept and law, which he being yet in the state of innocency, and remaining in Paradise, should observe as a pledge and token of his due and bounden obedience; with denunciation of death if he did transgress, and break the said law and commandment. And as God would have man to be his obedient subject, so did he make all earthly creatures subject unto man; who kept their due obedience unto man, so long as man remained in his obedience unto God.

Psalm 97:7, 103:20, 148:2; Song of the Three Holy Children 37, Dan. 7:10; Matt. 26:53; Col. 1:16; Heb. 1:4, 14; Rev. 19:10 Gen. 2:17

Gen. 1:28.

In the which obedience if man had continued still, there had been no poverty, no diseases, no sickness, no death, nor other miseries wherewith mankind is now infinitely, and most miserably, afflicted and oppressed. So here appeareth the original kingdom of God, over angels and man, and universally over all things; and of man over earthly creatures, which God had made subject unto him; and withal the felicity and blessed state, which angels, man, and all creatures had remained in, had they continued in due obedience unto God, their King. For, as long as in this first kingdom, the subjects continued in due obedience to God, their King, so long did God embrace all his subjects with his love, favour, and grace; which to enjoy is perfect felicity. Whereby it is evident, that obedience is the principal virtue of all virtues, and indeed the very root of all virtues, and the cause of all felicity.

But, as all felicity and blessedness should have continued, with the continuance of obedience, so with the breach of obedience, and breaking in of rebellion, all vices and miseries did withal break in, and

Matt. 4:9, 25:41,
John 8:44, 2 Pet.
2:4, Jude 6,
Rev. 12:7
overwhelm the world. The first author of which rebellion (the root of all vices, and mother of all mischiefs), was Lucifer, first God's most excellent creature, and most bounden subject, who by rebelling against the Majesty of God, of the brightest and most glorious angel, is become the blackest and most foulest fiend and devil, and from the height of heaven is fallen, into the pit and bottom of hell. Here you may see the first author and founder of rebellion; and the reward thereof. Here you

Gen. 3:1 &c.,
Wisd. 2:24

Gen. 3:8, 9 &c.,
17, 23, 24
may see the grand captain and father of all rebels: who persuading the following of his rebellion against God, their Creator and Lord, unto our first parents, Adam and Eve, brought them in high displeasure with God; wrought their exile and banishment out of Paradise, a place of all pleasure and goodness, into this wretched earth, and vale of all misery; procured unto them sorrows of their minds, mischiefs, sickness, diseases, death of their bodies; and which is far more horrible than all worldly and bodily mischiefs: he had wrought thereby, their eternal and

Rom. 5:12 &c.,
19 &c.
everlasting death and damnation, had not God, by the obedience of his Son, Jesus Christ, repaired that which man, by disobedience and rebellion, had destroyed, and so of his mercy had pardoned and forgiven him: of which all and singular the premises, the holy Scriptures do bear record, in sundry places. Thus you do see, that neither heaven nor paradise, could suffer any rebellion in them, neither be places for any rebels to remain in. Thus became rebellion, as you see, both the first, and greatest, and the very root of all other sins, and the first and principal cause, both of all worldly and bodily miseries, sorrows, diseases, sicknesses, and deaths, and, which is infinitely worse than all these, as is said, the very cause of death and damnation eternal also.

After this breach of obedience to God, and rebellion against his Majesty, all mischiefs and miseries breaking in therewith, and over-flowing the world; lest all things should come unto confusion and utter

Gen. 3:17
ruin, God forthwith, by laws given unto mankind, repaired again the rule and order of obedience, thus by rebellion overthrown: and, besides

Gen. 3:16;
Eph. 6:1–5
the obedience due unto his Majesty, he not only ordained that in families and households, the wife should be obedient unto her husband, the children unto their parents, the servants unto their masters; but also, when mankind increased, and spread itself more largely over the world, he by his holy word did constitute and ordain, in cities and countries, several and special governors and rulers, unto whom the residue of his

Job 34:30, 36:7,
Eccles. 8:2,
10:16, 17, 20,
Psalm 18:50,
20:6, 21:1,
144:1, Prov. 8:15
people should be obedient. As in reading of the holy Scriptures we shall find, in very many and almost infinite places, as well of the Old Testament as of the New: that kings and princes, as well the evil as the good, do reign by God's ordinance, and that subjects are bounden to obey them; that God doth give princes wisdom, great power, and

authority; that God defendeth them against their enemies, and destroyeth their enemies horribly; that *the anger and displeasure of the prince, is as the roaring of a lion, and the very messenger of death*; and that *the subject that provoketh him to displeasure, sinneth against his own soul*; with many other things, concerning both the authority of princes, and the duty of subjects.

Prov. 19:12, 16:14, 20:2

But here let us rehearse two special places, out of the New Testament, which may stand in stead of all other. The first out of St Paul's Epistle to the Romans, and the thirteenth chapter, where he writeth thus unto all subjects. *Let every soul be subject unto the higher powers. For there is no power but of God, and the powers that be are ordained of God. Whosoever therefore resisteth the power, resisteth the ordinance of God; and they that resist, shall receive to themselves damnation. For princes are not to be feared for good works, but for evil. Wilt thou then be without fear of the power? Do well; so shalt thou have praise of the same; for he is the minister of God, for thy wealth. But if thou do evil, fear: for he beareth not the sword for naught; for he is the minister of God, to take vengeance upon him that doeth evil. Wherefore ye must be subject, not because of wrath only, but also for conscience sake. For for this cause ye pay also tribute; for they are God's ministers, serving for the same purpose. Give to every man therefore his duty; tribute to whom tribute belongeth; custom to whom custom is due; fear to whom fear belongeth; honour to whom ye owe honour.* Thus far are St Paul's words.

Rom. 12:1–7

The second place is in St Peter's first Epistle, and the second chapter, whose words are these. *Submit yourselves unto all manner of ordinance of man, for the Lord's sake: whether it be unto the king, as unto the chief head; either unto rulers, as unto them that are sent of him, for the punishment of evildoers, but for the cherishing of them that do well: for so is the will of God, that with well doing ye may stop the mouths of ignorant and foolish men: as free, and not as having the liberty for a cloak of maliciousness, but even as the servants of God. Honour all men: love brotherly fellowship: fear God: honour the King. Servants, obey your masters with fear; not only if they be good and courteous, but also though they be froward.* Thus far out of St Peter.

1 Pet. 2:13–18

By these two places of the holy Scriptures, it is most evident, that kings, queens, and other princes (for he speaketh of authority and power, be it in men or women), are ordained of God, are to be obeyed, and honoured of their subjects; that such subjects as are disobedient, or rebellious against their princes, disobey God, and procure their own damnation; that the government of princes, is a great blessing of God, given for the commonwealth, specially of the good and godly (for the comfort and cherishing of whom God giveth and setteth up princes), and on the contrary part, to the fear and for the punishment of the evil and wicked; finally, that if servants ought to obey their masters, not only being gentle, but such as be froward, as well, and much more, ought subjects to be obedient, not only to their good and courteous, but also to their sharp and rigorous princes. It cometh therefore neither of chance and fortune (as they term it), nor of the ambition of mortal men and women, climbing up of their own accord to dominion, that there be kings, queens, princes, and other governors over men being their subjects; but all kings, queens, and other governors, are specially appointed by the ordinance of God.

And as God himself, being of an infinite majesty, power, and wisdom, ruleth and governeth all things in heaven and in earth, as the universal Monarch, and only King and Emperor over all, as being only able to take and bear the charge of all; so hath he constituted, ordained, and set earthly princes over particular kingdoms and dominions in earth, both for the avoiding of all confusion (which else would be in the world, if it should be without such governors), and for the great quiet and benefit of earthly men, their subjects, and also that the princes themselves, in authority, power, wisdom, providence, and righteousness in government of people and countries committed to their charge, should resemble his heavenly governance, as the majesty of heavenly things, may by the baseness of earthly things, be shadowed and resembled. And for that similitude that is between the heavenly monarchy, and earthly kingdoms well governed, our Saviour Christ in sundry parables saith, that *the kingdom of heaven is resembled unto a man a king*. And, as the name of *the King* is very often attributed and given unto God, in the holy Scriptures, so doth God himself, in the same Scriptures, sometimes vouchsafe to communicate his name with earthly princes, terming them *gods*; doubtless for that similitude of government which they have, or should have, not unlike unto God their King.

Unto the which similitude of heavenly government, the nearer and nearer that an earthly prince doth come in his regiment, the greater blessing of God's mercy is he, unto that country and people, over whom he reigneth: and the further and further that an earthly prince doth swerve, from the example of the heavenly government, the greater plague he is of God's wrath, and punishment by God's justice, unto that country and people, over whom God, for their sins, hath placed such a prince and governor. For it is indeed evident, both by the Scriptures and by daily experience, that the maintenance of all virtue and godliness, and consequently, of the wealth and prosperity of a kingdom and people, doth stand and rest more, in a wise and good prince, on the one part, than in great multitudes of other men, being subjects; and, on the contrary part, the overthrow of all virtue and godliness, and consequently the decay and utter ruin of a realm and people, doth grow and come more, by an undiscreet and evil governor, than by many

Psalm 10:16,
45:6 &c., 47:2
Ecclus. 17:17

Matt. 18:23,
22:2
Psalm 10:16,
45, 47:2 &c.,
Matt. 22:13,
25:34

Psalm 82:6

thousands of other men, being subjects. Thus say the holy Scriptures. *Well is thee, O thou land*, saith the Preacher, *whose king is come of nobles, and whose princes eat in due season, for necessity and not for lust.* Again, *A wise and righteous king maketh his realm and people wealthy*: and, *A good, merciful, and gracious prince is as a shadow in heat, as a defence in storms, as dew, as sweet showers, as fresh watersprings in great droughts.* Again, the Scriptures, of undiscreet and evil princes, speak thus: *Woe be to thee, O thou land whose king is but a child, and whose princes are early at their banquets.* Again, *When the wicked do reign, then men go to ruin.* And again, *A foolish prince destroyeth the people*: and, *A covetous king undoeth his subjects.* Thus speak the Scriptures, thus experience testifieth, of good and evil princes.

  Eccles. 10:17

  Prov. 16:15, 19:12, 29:4
  Eccles. 10:17,
  Isai. 32:1, 2

  Eccles. 10:16

  Prov. 28:12, 16, 29:4

  What shall subjects do then? Shall they obey valiant, stout, wise, and good princes, and contemn, disobey, and rebel against children being their princes, or against undiscreet and evil governors? God forbid. For first, what a perilous thing were it, to commit unto the subjects the judgement, which prince is wise and godly and his government good, and which is otherwise; as though the foot must judge the head; an enterprise very heinous, and must needs breed rebellion. For who else be they that are most inclined to rebellion, but such haughty spirits? From whom springeth such foul ruin of realms? Is not rebellion the greatest of all mischiefs? And who are most ready to the greatest mischiefs, but the worst men? Rebels therefore, the worst of all subjects, are most ready to rebellion, as being the worst of all vices, and furthest from the duty of a good subject; as on the contrary part, the best subjects are most firm and constant in obedience, as in the special and peculiar virtue of good subjects. What an unworthy matter were it then, to make the naughtiest subjects, and most inclined to rebellion and all evil, judges over their princes, over their government, and over their counsellors! to determine which of them be good or tolerable, and which be evil, and so intolerable that they must needs be removed by rebels; being ever ready, the naughtiest subjects, soonest to rebel against the best princes, specially if they be young in age, women in sex, or gentle and courteous in government; as trusting by their wicked boldness, easily to overthrow their weakness and gentleness, or at the least, so to fear the minds of such princes, that they may have impunity of their mischievous doings. But whereas indeed a rebel is worse than the worst prince, and rebellion worse than the worst government, of the worst prince that hitherto hath been, both are rebels unmeet ministers, and rebellion an unfit and unwholesome medicine, to reform any small lacks in a prince, or to cure any little griefs in government; such lewd remedies being far worse, than any other maladies and disorders that can be, in the body of a commonwealth.

But whatsoever the prince be, or his government, it is evident that for the most part, those princes whom some subjects do think to be very godly, and under whose government they rejoice to live, some other subjects do take the same to be evil and ungodly, and do wish for a change. If therefore, all subjects that mislike of their prince, should rebel, no realm should ever be without rebellion. It were more meet, that rebels should hear the advice of wise men, and give place unto their judgement, and follow the example of obedient subjects; as reason is, that they whose understanding is blinded with so evil an affection, should give place to them that be of sound judgement, and that the worse should give place to the better: and so might realms continue in long obedience, peace, and quietness.

But what if the prince be undiscreet and evil indeed, and it also evident to all men's eyes that he so is? I ask again, what if it be long of the wickedness of the subjects, that the prince is undiscreet or evil? Shall the subjects, both by their wickedness provoke God, for their deserved punishment, to give them an undiscreet or evil prince, and also rebel against him, and withal against God, who for the punishment of their sins, did give them such a prince? Will you hear the Scriptures concerning this point? *God*, say the holy Scriptures, *maketh a wicked man to reign, for the sins of the people.* Again, *God giveth a prince in his anger,* meaning an evil one, *and taketh away a prince in his displeasure,* meaning specially, when he taketh away a good prince, for the sins of the people, as in our memory, he took away our good Josias, King Edward, in his young and good years, for our wickedness. And contrarily the Scriptures do teach, that God giveth wisdom unto princes, and maketh a wise and good king to reign over that people whom he loveth, and who loveth him. Again, *if the people obey God, both they and their king shall prosper, and be safe; else both shall perish,* saith God, by the mouth of Samuel. Here you see that God placeth as well evil princes as good, and for what cause he doth both. If we therefore will have a good prince, either to be given us, or to continue now we have such a one, let us by our obedience to God, and to our prince, move God thereunto. If we will have an evil prince (when God shall send such a one) taken away, and a good in his place, let us take away our wickedness, which provoketh God to place such an one over us, and God will either displace him, or of an evil prince make him a good prince, so that we first will change our evil into good. For will you hear the Scriptures? *The heart of the prince is in God's hand: which way soever it shall please him, he turneth it.* Thus say the Scriptures. Wherefore let us turn from our sins unto the Lord, with all our hearts, and he will turn the heart of the prince, unto our quiet and wealth. Else for subjects to deserve, through their sins, to have an evil prince, and then to rebel against him, were double and treble evil, by provoking God more to

Job 34:30

Hos. 13:11

2 Chron. 2:11, 12, 9:8, 23, Prov. 16:10
1 Sam. 12:14, 15, 25

Prov. 21:1, Ezra 7:27

plague them. Nay, let us either deserve to have a good prince, or let us patiently suffer and obey such as we deserve.

And whether the prince be good or evil, let us, according to the counsel of the holy Scriptures, pray for the prince; for his continuance and increase in goodness, if he be good, and for his amendment, if he be evil.

Will you hear the Scriptures, concerning this most necessary point? *I exhort therefore*, saith St Paul, *that above all things, prayers, supplications, intercessions, and giving of thanks, be had for all men: for kings, and all that are in authority, that we may live a quiet and peaceable life, with all godliness: for that is good, and acceptable in the sight of God, our Saviour,* &c. This is St Paul's counsel. And who, I pray you, was prince over the most part of Christians, when God's Holy Spirit, by St Paul's pen, gave them this lesson? Forsooth, Caligula, Clodius, or Nero; who were not only no Christians, but pagans, and also either foolish rulers, or most cruel tyrants. Will you yet hear the word of God to the Jews, when they were prisoners under Nabuchodonozor, King of Babylon, after he had slain their king, nobles, parents, children, and kinsfolks, burned their country, cities, yea Jerusalem itself, and the holy Temple, and had carried the residue remaining alive, captives with him unto Babylon? will you hear yet, what the Prophet Baruch saith unto God's people, being in this captivity? *Pray you*, saith the prophet, *for the life of Nabuchodonozor, King of Babylon, and for the life of Balthasar his son, that their days may be as the days of heaven upon the earth; that God also may give us strength, and lighten our eyes, that we may live under the defence of Nabuchodonozor, King of Babylon, and under the protection of Balthasar his son, that we may long do them service, and find favour in their sight. Pray for us also, unto the Lord, our God, for we have sinned against the Lord, our God.* Thus far the Prophet Baruch his words; which are spoken by him unto the people of God, of that king who was an heathen, a tyrant, and cruel oppressor of them, and had been a murderer of many thousands of their nation, and a destroyer of their country, with a confession, that their sins had deserved such a prince to reign over them.

And shall the old Christians, by St Paul's exhortation, pray for Caligula, Claudius, or Nero? shall the Jews pray for Nabuchodonozor?— these emperors and kings being strangers unto them, being pagans and infidels, being murderers, tyrants, and cruel oppressors of them, and the destroyers of their country, countrymen, and kinsmen, the burners of their villages, towns, cities, and temples—and shall not we pray for the long, prosperous, and godly reign of our natural Prince, no stranger (which is observed as a great blessing in the Scriptures)?—of our Christian, our most gracious Sovereign, no heathen nor pagan prince? Shall we not pray for the health of our most merciful, most loving Sovereign; the preserver of us and our country in so long peace,

1 Tim. 2:1–3

Bar. 1:11–13

Deut. 17:15

quietness, and security; no cruel person, no tyrant, no spoiler of our goods, no shedder of our bloods, no burner and destroyer of our towns, cities, and country, as were those, for whom yet (as ye have heard), Christians, being their subjects, ought to pray? Let us not commit so great ingratitude, against God and our Sovereign, as not continually to thank God for this government, and for his great and continual benefits and blessings, poured upon us by such government. Let us not commit so great a sin against God, against ourselves, and our country, as not to pray continually unto God, for the long continuance of so gracious a ruler, unto us and our country. Else shall we be unworthy, any longer to enjoy those benefits and blessings of God, which hitherto we have had by her, and shall be most worthy, to fall into all those mischiefs and miseries, which we and our country have, by God's grace, through her government, hitherto escaped.

What shall we say of those subjects (may we call them by the name of subjects?) who neither be thankful, nor make any prayer to God for so gracious a Sovereign; but also themselves take armour wickedly, assemble companies and bands of rebels, to break the public peace so long continued, and to make, not war, but rebellion; to endanger the person of such a gracious Sovereign; to hazard the estate of their country, for whose defence they should be ready to spend their lives; and being Englishmen, to rob, spoil, destroy, and burn, in England, Englishmen; to kill and murder their own neighbours and kinsfolk, their own country-men; to do all evil and mischief, yea, and more too, than foreign enemies would or could do? What shall we say of these men, who use themselves thus rebelliously against their gracious Sovereign; who, if God, for their wickedness, had given them an heathen tyrant to reign over them, were by God's word, bound to obey him, and to pray for him? What may be spoken of them? So far doth their unkindness, unnaturalness, wickedness, mischievousness in their doings, pass and excel, any thing, and all things, that can be expressed, or uttered by words. Only let us wish unto all such, most speedy repentance, and with so grievous sorrow of heart, as such so horrible sins against the Majesty of God do require, who in most extreme unthankfulness do rise, not only against their gracious Prince, against their natural country, but against all their countrymen, women, and children, against themselves, their wives, children, and kinsfolks, and by so wicked an example, against all Christendom, and against whole mankind, of all manner of people throughout the wide world; such repentance, I say, such sorrow of heart, God grant unto all such, whosoever rise, of private and malicious purpose, as is meet for such mischiefs, attempted and wrought by them.

And unto us and all other subjects, God of his mercy, grant that we may be most unlike to all such, and most like to good, natural, loving, and obedient subjects; nay, that we may be such indeed, not only showing all obedience ourselves, but as many of us as be able, to the uttermost of our power, ability, and understanding, to stay and repress all rebels and rebellions, against God, our gracious Prince, and natural country, at every occasion that is offered unto us.

And that which we all are able to do, unless we do it, we shall be most wicked, and most worthy to feel in the end, such extreme plagues, as God hath ever poured upon rebels. Let us all make continual prayers unto Almighty God, even from the bottom of our hearts, that he will give his grace, power, and strength, unto our gracious Queen Elizabeth, to vanquish and subdue all, as well rebels at home, as foreign enemies; that all domestical rebellions being suppressed and pacified, and all outward invasions repulsed and abandoned, we may not only be sure, and long continue, in all obedience unto our gracious Sovereign, and in that peaceable and quiet life, which hitherto we have led under her Majesty, with all security; but also, that both our gracious Queen Elizabeth, and we her subjects, may all together, in all obedience unto God, the King of all kings, and unto his holy laws, lead our lives so in this world, in all virtue and godliness, that in the world to come, we may enjoy his everlasting kingdom. Which I beseech God to grant, as well to our gracious Sovereign, as unto us all, for his Son, our Saviour, Jesus Christ's sake. To whom, with the Father, and the Holy Ghost, one God and King immortal, be all glory, praise, and thanksgiving, world without end. Amen.

Thus have you heard the First Part of this Homily: now, good people, let us pray.

THE PRAYER

O MOST MIGHTY GOD, the Lord of hosts, the Governor of all creatures, the only Giver of all victories, who alone art able to strengthen the weak against the mighty, and to vanquish infinite multitudes of thine enemies, with the countenance of a few of thy servants, calling upon thy Name, and trusting in thee: defend, O Lord, thy servant, and our Governor under thee, our Queen Elizabeth, and all thy people committed to her charge.

O Lord, withstand the cruelty, of all those which be common enemies, as well to the truth of thy eternal word, as to their own natural Prince and country, and manifestly to this crown and realm of England, which thou hast, of thy divine providence, assigned in these our days, to the government of thy servant, our Sovereign and gracious Queen.

O most merciful Father, if it be thy holy will, make soft and tender, the stony hearts of all those, that exalt themselves against thy truth, and seek either to trouble the quiet of this realm of England, or to oppress the crown of the same; and convert them to the knowledge of thy Son, the only Saviour of the world, Jesus Christ; that we and they may jointly glorify thy mercies.

Lighten, we beseech thee, their ignorant hearts, to embrace the truth of thy word; or else so abate their cruelty, O most mighty Lord, that this our Christian realm, with others that confess thy holy Gospel, may obtain, by thine aid and strength, surety from all enemies, without shedding of Christian blood; whereby all they which be oppressed with their tyranny, may be relieved, and they which be in fear of their cruelty, may be comforted; and finally, that all Christian realms, and specially this realm of England, may by thy defence and protection, continue in the truth of the Gospel, and enjoy perfect peace, quietness, and security; and that we for these thy mercies, jointly all together, with one consonant heart and voice, may thankfully render to thee, all laud and praise; that we, knit in one godly concord, and unity amongst ourselves, may continually magnify thy glorious Name; who, with thy Son, our Saviour, Jesus Christ, and the Holy Ghost, art one eternal, almighty, and most merciful God; to whom be all laud and praise, world without end. Amen.

THE SECOND PART OF THE HOMILY AGAINST DISOBEDIENCE AND WILFUL REBELLION

As IN THE FIRST PART of this Treaty, of obedience of subjects to their princes, and against disobedience and rebellion, I have alleged divers sentences out of the holy Scriptures, for proof; so shall it be good, for the better declaration and confirmation, of the said wholesome doctrine, to allege one example or two, out of the same holy Scriptures, of the obedience of subjects, not only unto their good and gracious governors, but also unto their evil and unkind princes.

As King Saul was not of the best, but rather of the worst sort of princes, as being out of God's favour, for his disobedience against God, in sparing, in a wrong pity, the King Agag, whom Almighty God commanded to be slain, according to the justice of God against his sworn enemy; and although Saul, of a devotion, meant to sacrifice such things as he spared of the Amalechites, to the honour and service of God, yet Saul was reproved for his wrong mercy and devotion, and was told that obedience would have more pleased him, than such lenity; which sinful humanity, saith holy Chrysostom, is more cruel before God, than any murder or shedding of blood, when it is commanded of God. But yet, how evil soever Saul the King was, and out of God's favour, yet was he

1 Sam. 15:11, 22, 35

Chrys. Tom. 1, Hom. 1 adversus Judaeos

obeyed of his subject David, the very best of all subjects, and most valiant in the service of his prince and country in the wars, the most obedient and loving in peace, and always most true and faithful to his sovereign and lord, and furthest off from all manner rebellion. For the which his most painful, true, and faithful service, King Saul yet rewarded him not only with great unkindness, but also sought his destruction and death, by all means possible; so that David was fain to save his life, not by rebellion, nor any resistance, but by flight, and hiding himself from the King's sight. Which notwithstanding, when King Saul upon a time came alone, into the cave where David was, so that David might easily have slain him, yet would he neither hurt him himself, neither suffer any of his men to lay hands upon him. Another time also David, entering by night with one Abisai, a valiant and a fierce man, into the tent where King Saul did lie asleep, where also he might yet more easily have slain him; yet would he neither hurt him himself, nor suffer Abisai, who was willing and ready to slay King Saul, once to touch him. Thus did David deal with Saul his Prince, notwithstanding that King Saul continually sought his death and destruction.

It shall not be amiss, unto these deeds of David to add his words, and to show you what he spake, unto such as encouraged him to take his opportunity and advantage, to slay King Saul, as his mortal enemy, when he might. *The Lord keep me,* saith David, *from doing that thing, and from laying hands upon my lord, God's anointed. For who can lay his hand upon the Lord's anointed, and be guiltless? As truly as the Lord liveth, except that the Lord do smite him, or his days shall come to die, or that he go down to war, and be slain in battle, the Lord be merciful unto me, that I lay not my hand upon the Lord's anointed.* These be David's words, spoken at sundry times to divers his servants, provoking him to slay King Saul, when opportunity served him thereunto.

Neither is it to be omitted and left out, how when an Amalechite had slain King Saul, even at Saul's own bidding and commandment (for he would live no longer now, for that he had lost the field against his enemies the Philistines), the said Amalechite making great haste to bring first word and news thereof unto David, as joyous unto him for the death of his mortal enemy, bringing withal the crown that was upon King Saul's head, and the bracelet that was upon his arm, both as a proof of the truth of his news, and also as fit and pleasant presents unto David, being by God appointed to be King Saul his successor in the kingdom; yet was that faithful and godly David, so far from rejoicing at these news, that he rent his clothes, wept, and mourned, and fasted; and so far off from thanksgiving to the messenger, either for his deed in killing the King, though his deadly enemy, or for his message and news, or for his presents that he brought, that he said unto him, *How happened it, that thou wast*

1 Sam. 16:14, 15, 18:10, 12, 19:9, 20; *Ibid.* 17:26 &c., 18:27, 19:5, 8, *Ibid.*:23, 27
Ibid. 16:23, 19:4, 24:9

Ibid. 18:9, 25, 29
Ibid. 19:19, *Ibid.*:21, 22

Ibid. 26:6, 9

Ibid. 24:4

Ibid. 24:6 &c.
Ibid. 26:9, 10 &c.

2 Sam. 1:7, 9

Ibid.:10

Ibid.:12

Ibid.:13–16

not afraid to lay thy hands upon the Lord's anointed, to slay him? whereupon immediately he commanded one of his servants to kill the messenger, and said, *Thy blood be upon thine own head; for thine own mouth hath witnessed against thyself, in confessing, that thou hast slain the Lord's anointed.*

This example, dearly beloved, is notable, and the circumstances thereof are well to be considered, for the better instruction of all subjects, in their bounden duty of obedience, and perpetual fearing of them, from attempting of any rebellion, or hurt against their prince. On the one part, David was not only a good and true subject, but also such a subject as, both in peace and war, had served and saved his prince's honour and life, and delivered his country and countrymen, from great danger of infidels, foreign and most cruel enemies, horribly invading the King and his country: for the which, David was in singular favour with all the people; so that he might have had great numbers of them at his commandment, if he would have attempted any thing. Besides this, David was no common or absolute subject, but heir apparent to the crown and kingdom, by God appointed to reign after Saul; which as it increased the favour of the people that knew it, towards David, so did it make David's cause and case, much differing from the case of common and absolute subjects. And, which is most of all, David was highly and singularly in the favour of God. On the contrary part, King Saul was out of God's favour, for that cause which is before rehearsed, and he as it were God's enemy, and therefore like, in war and peace, to be hurtful and pernicious unto the commonwealth; and that was known to many of his subjects, for that he was openly rebuked of Samuel, for his disobedience unto God; which might make the people the less to esteem him. King Saul was also unto David a mortal and deadly enemy, though without David's deserving; who by his faithful, painful, profitable, yea, most necessary service, had well deserved, as of his country, so of his prince; but King Saul far otherwise; the more was his unkindness, hatred, and cruelty, towards such a good subject, both odious and detestable. Yet would David neither himself slay nor hurt such an enemy, for that he was his prince and lord; nor would suffer any other to kill, hurt, or lay hand upon him, when he might have been slain without any stir, tumult, or danger of any man's life.

Now let David answer, to such demands as men desirous of rebellion do use to make. "Shall not we, specially being so good men as we are, rise and rebel, against a prince hated of God, and God's enemy, and therefore like not to prosper, either in war or peace, but to be hurtful and pernicious to the commonwealth?" "No," saith good and godly David, God's and such a king's faithful subject, and so convicting such subjects as attempt any rebellion against such a king, to be neither good subjects nor good men. "But," say they, "shall we not rise and rebel

Marginal notes:

1 Sam. 18:16, 30

Ibid. 16:12 &c.

Ibid. 18:12

Ibid. 15:11, 18:10, 12

Ibid. 15:19, 22, 26

The demand

The answer

The demand

against so unkind a prince, nothing considering or regarding our true, faithful, and painful service, or the safeguard of our posterity?" "No," saith good David, whom no such unkindness could cause to forsake his due obedience to his sovereign. "Shall we not," say they, "rise and rebel against our known, mortal, and deadly enemy, that seeketh our lives?" "No," saith godly David, who had learned the lesson that our Saviour afterward plainly taught, that we should do no hurt to our fellow subjects, though they hate us, and be our enemies; much less unto our prince, though he were our enemy. "Shall we not assemble an army of such good fellows as we are, and by hazarding of our lives, and the lives of such as shall withstand us (and withal hazarding the whole estate of our country), remove so naughty a prince?" "No," saith godly David; "for I, when I might without assembling force or number of men, without tumult or hazard of any man's life, or shedding of any drop of blood, have delivered myself and my country, of an evil prince, yet would I not do it." "Are not they," say some, "lusty and courageous captains, valiant men of stomach, and good men's bodies, that do venture by force to kill or depose their king, being a naughty prince and their mortal enemy?" "They may be as lusty, as courageous, as they list, yet," saith godly David, "they can be no good nor godly men, that so do: for I not only have rebuked, but also commanded him to be slain, as a wicked man, which slew King Saul mine enemy; though he, being weary of his life, for the loss of the victory against his enemies, desired that man to slay him." What shall we then do, to an evil, to an unkind prince, an enemy to us, hated of God, hurtful to the commonwealth, &c? "Lay no violent hand upon him," saith good David; "but let him live, until God appoint and work his end, either by natural death, or in war, by lawful enemies, not by traitorous subjects." Thus would godly David make answer: and St Paul, as ye heard before, willeth us, to pray also for such a prince.

If King David would make these answers, as by his deeds and words, recorded in the holy Scriptures, indeed he doth make, unto all such demands concerning rebelling against evil princes, unkind princes, cruel princes, princes that be to their good subjects mortal enemies, princes that are out of God's favour, and so hurtful, or like to be hurtful to the commonwealth; what answer, think you, would he make to those that demand whether they (being naughty and unkind subjects), may not—to the great hazard of the life of many thousands, and the utter danger of the state of the commonwealth, and whole realm—assemble a sort of rebels, to put in fear, or to depose or destroy, their natural and loving Princess, enemy to none, good to all, even to them the worst of all other; the maintainer of perpetual peace, quietness, and security, most beneficial to the commonwealth, most necessary for the safeguard of the whole realm? What answer would David make to their demand, whether

Margin notes:
The answer
The demand
The answer
Matt. 5:44
The demand
The answer
The demand
The answer
The demand
The answer
An unnatural and wicked question

they may not attempt, cruelly and unnaturally, to destroy so peaceable and merciful a Princess? What, I say, would David, so reverently speaking of Saul, and so patiently suffering so evil a king, what would he answer and say to such demands? What would he say, nay, what would he do, to such high attempters, who so said and did as you before have heard, unto him that slew the King his master, though a most wicked prince? If he punished with death, as a wicked doer, such a man, with what reproaches of words would he revile such, yea, with what torments of most shameful deaths would he destroy such, hell-hounds rather than evil men, such rebels, I mean, as I last spake of? For if they who do disobey an evil and unkind prince, be most unlike unto David, that good subject, what be they who do rebel against a most natural and loving Prince? And, if David, being so good a subject that he obeyed so evil a king, was worthy, of a subject, to be made a king himself, what be they, who are so evil subjects, that they will rebel against their gracious Prince, worthy of? Surely no mortal man can express with words, nor conceive in mind, the horrible and most dreadful damnation, that such be worthy of, who disdaining to be the quiet and happy subjects of their good Prince, are most worthy to be the miserable captives, and vile slaves, of that infernal tyrant Satan, with him to suffer eternal slavery and torments.

This one example of the good subject David, out of the Old Testament, may suffice, and for the notableness of it, serve for all.

In the New Testament, the excellent example of the blessed Virgin Mary, the mother of our Saviour, Christ, doth at the first offer itself. When proclamation or commandment was sent into Jewry, from Augustus the Emperor of Rome, that the people there should repair unto their own cities and dwelling-places, there to be taxed, neither did the blessed Virgin—though both highly in God's favour, and also being of the royal blood of the ancient natural kings of Jewry—disdain to obey the commandment of an heathen and foreign prince, when God had placed such a one over them; neither did she allege for an excuse, that she was great with child, and most near her time of deliverance; neither grudged she at the length and tediousness of the journey, from Nazareth to Bethlehem, from whence and whither she must go to be taxed; neither repined she at the sharpness of the dead time of winter, being the latter end of December, an unhandsome time to travel in, specially a long journey, for a woman being in her case; but all excuses set apart, she obeyed, and came to the appointed place: where at her coming, she found such great resort and throng of people, that finding no place in any inn, she was fain after her long, painful, and tedious journey, to take up her lodging in a stable, where also she was delivered of her blessed Child; and this also declareth, how near her time she took that journey.

Luke 2:1 &c.

Ibid.:7

This obedience, of this most noble and most virtuous lady, to a foreign and pagan prince, doth well teach us, who in comparison to her are most base and vile, what ready obedience we do owe, to our natural and gracious Sovereign. Howbeit in this case the obedience of the whole Jewish nation (being otherwise a stubborn people), unto the commandment of the same foreign heathen prince, doth prove that such Christians as do not most readily obey their natural gracious sovereign, are far worse than the stubborn Jews, whom yet we account as the worst of all people.

*Ibid.:*3

But no example ought to be of more force with us Christians, than the example of Christ, our Master and Saviour; who, though he were the Son of God, yet did always behave himself most reverently, to such men as were in authority in the world in his time; and he not rebelliously behaved himself, but openly did teach the Jews, to pay tribute unto the Roman Emperor, though a foreign and a pagan prince; yea, himself with his Apostles paid tribute unto him; and finally, being brought before Pontius Pilate, a stranger born and an heathen man (being lord president of Jewry), he acknowledged his authority and power, to be given him from God, and obeyed patiently, the sentence of most painful and shameful death, which the said judge pronounced, and gave most unjustly against him, without any grudge, murmuring, or evil word once giving. There be many other examples of the obedience to princes, even such as be evil, in the New Testament, to the utter confusion of disobedient and rebellious people: but this one may be an eternal example, which the Son of God, and so the Lord of all, Jesus Christ, hath given to us, his Christians and servants; and such as may serve for all, to teach us to obey princes, though strangers, wicked, and wrongful, when God, for our sins, shall place such over us. Whereby it followeth unavoidably, that such as do disobey, or rebel against, their own natural gracious sovereigns, howsoever they call themselves or be named of others, yet are they indeed no true Christians, but worse than Jews, worse than heathens, and such as shall never enjoy the kingdom of heaven; which Christ, by his obedience, purchased for true Christians, being obedient to him, the King of all kings, and to their prince, whom he hath placed over them. The which kingdom, the peculiar place of all such obedient subjects, I beseech God, our heavenly Father, for the same our Saviour Jesus Christ's sake, to grant unto us. To whom, with the Holy Ghost, be all laud, honour, and glory, now and for ever. Amen.

Matt. 17:25 &c.,
Mark 12:17,
Luke 20:25

Matt. 27:2,
Luke 23:1
John 19:11

Matt. 27:26,
Luke 23:24

Thus have you heard the Second Part of this Homily: now, good people, let us pray.

THE PRAYER AS BEFORE

Above, p. 407

THE THIRD PART OF THE HOMILY AGAINST DISOBEDIENCE AND WILFUL REBELLION

As I HAVE in the First Part of this Treatise, showed unto you the doctrine of the holy Scriptures, as concerning the obedience of true subjects to their princes, even as well to such as be evil, as unto the good; and in the Second Part of the same Treaty confirmed the said doctrine, by notable examples, likewise taken out of the holy Scriptures: so remaineth it now, that I partly do declare unto you, in this Third Part, what an abominable sin against God and man, rebellion is; and how dreadfully the wrath of God, is kindled and inflamed against all rebels, and what horrible plagues, punishments, and deaths, and finally eternal damnation, doth hang over their heads; as how on the contrary part, good and obedient subjects are in God's favour, and be partakers of peace, quietness, and security, with other God's manifold blessings in this world, and by his mercies, through our Saviour Christ, of life everlasting also, in the world to come.

How horrible a sin against God and man rebellion is, cannot possibly be expressed according unto the greatness thereof. For he that nameth rebellion, nameth not a singular or one only sin, as is theft, robbery, murder, and suchlike; but he nameth the whole puddle and sink of all sins, against God and man; against his prince, his country, his countrymen, his parents, his children, his kinsfolks, his friends, and against all men universally: all sins, I say, against God and all men heaped together, nameth he that nameth rebellion.

The first table of God's law broken Rom. 13:1–7 by rebellion and the sins of rebels against God

For, concerning the offence of God's Majesty, who seeth not, that rebellion riseth first by contempt of God, and of his holy ordinances and laws, wherein he so straitly commandeth obedience, forbiddeth disobedience and rebellion? And besides the dishonour done by rebels unto God's holy Name, by their breaking of the oath made to their prince—with the attestation of God's Name, and calling of his Majesty to witness—who heareth not the horrible oaths, and blasphemies of God's holy Name, that are used daily amongst rebels, that is either amongst them, or heareth the truth of their behaviour? Who knoweth not, that rebels do not only themselves leave all works necessary to be done upon workdays undone, whiles they accomplish their abominable work of rebellion, and do compel others, that would gladly be well occupied, to do the same; but also how rebels do not only leave the Sabbath day of the Lord unsanctified, the temple and church of the Lord unresorted unto, but also do, by their works of wickedness, most horribly profane and pollute the Sabbath day?—

serving Satan, and by doing of his work, making it the devil's day, instead of the Lord's day; besides that they compel good men, that would gladly serve the Lord, assembling in his temple and church upon his day, as becometh the Lord's servants, to assemble and meet armed in the field, to resist the fury of such rebels. Yea, and many rebels, lest they should leave any part of God's commandments in the first table of his law unbroken, of any sin against God undone, do make rebellion for the maintenance of their images and idols and of their idolatry, committed or to be committed by them; and in despite of God, cut and tear in sunder his holy word, and tread it under their feet; as of late ye know was done.

As concerning the second table of God's law, and all sins that may be committed against man, who seeth not, that they be all contained in rebellion? For first, the rebels do not only dishonour their prince, the parent of their country, but also do dishonour and shame their natural parents, if they have any; do shame their kinred and friends, do disherit and undo for ever their children and heirs. Thefts, robberies, and murders, which of all sins are most loathed of most men, are in no men so much, nor so perniciously and mischievously, as in rebels. For the most arrant thieves, and cruellest murderers that ever were, so long as they refrain from rebellion, as they are not many in number, so spreadeth their wickedness and damnation unto a few; they spoil but a few; they shed the blood but of a few, in comparison. But rebels are the cause of infinite robberies, and murders of great multitudes, and of those also whom they should defend, from the spoil and violence of other; and as rebels are many in number, so doth their wickedness and damnation spread itself unto many. And if whoredom and adultery, amongst such persons as are agreeable to such wickedness, are (as they indeed be) most damnable, what are the forcible oppressions of matrons and men's wives, and the violating and deflowering of virgins and maids, which are most rife with rebels? how horrible and damnable, think you, are they? Now, besides that rebels, by breach of their faith given, and oath made to their prince, be guilty of most damnable perjury, it is wondrous to see what false colours, and feigned causes, by slanderous lies made upon their prince and the counsellors, rebels will devise, to cloak their rebellion withal; which is the worst, and most damnable, of all false witness bearing that may be possible. For what should I speak of coveting or desiring of other men's wives, houses, lands, goods, and servants, in rebels who by their wills would leave unto no man any thing of his own?

Thus you see, that all God's laws are by rebels violated and broken, and that all sins possible to be committed against God or man, be contained in rebellion: which sins if a man list to name, by the accustomed names of the seven capital or deadly sins—as pride, envy,

The fifth commandment

The sixth and the eighth commandment

The seventh commandment

The ninth commandment

The tenth commandment

wrath, covetousness, sloth, gluttony, and lechery—he shall find them all in rebellion, and amongst rebels. For first, as ambition and desire to be aloft, which is the property of pride, stirreth up many men's minds to rebellion, so cometh it of a Luciferian pride and presumption, that a few rebellious subjects should set themselves up, against the majesty of their prince, against the wisdom of the counsellors, against the power and force of all nobility, and the faithful subjects and people of the whole realm. As for envy, wrath, murder and desire of blood, and covetousness of other men's goods, lands, and livings: they are the inseparable accidents of all rebels, and peculiar properties, that do usually stir up wicked men unto rebellion. Now such as by riotousness, gluttony, drunkenness, excess of apparel, and unthrifty games, have wasted their own goods unthriftily, the same are most apt unto, and most desirous of rebellion, whereby they trust to come by other men's goods, unlawfully and violently. And where other gluttons and drunkards, take too much of such meats and drinks, as are served to tables, rebels waste and consume in short space all corn in barns, fields, or elsewhere—whole garners, whole storehouses, whole cellars, devour whole flocks of sheep, whole droves of oxen and kine. And as rebels that are married, leaving their own wives at home, do most ungraciously, so much more do unmarried men, worse than any stallands or horses, being now by rebellion set at liberty from correction of laws, which bridled them before; which abuse by force other men's wives and daughters, and ravish virgins and maidens, most shamefully, abominably, and damnably. Thus all sins, by all names that sins may be named, and by all means that all sins may be committed and wrought, do all wholly, upon heaps, follow rebellion, and are to be found all together amongst rebels.

2 Sam. 24:13   Now whereas pestilence, famine, and war, are by the holy Scriptures declared to be the greatest worldly plagues and miseries, that likely can be, it is evident that all the miseries, which all these plagues have in them, do wholly, all together, follow rebellion; wherein as all their miseries be, so is there much more mischief then* in them all. For it is known, that in the resorting of great companies of men together (which in rebellion happeneth, both upon the part of true subjects and of the rebels), by their close lying together, and corruption of the air and place where they do lie, with ordure and much filth in the hot weather, and by unwholesome lodging, and lying often upon the ground, specially in cold and wet weathers in winter; by their unwholesome diet and feeding at all times, and often by famine, and lack of meat and drink in due time, and again by taking too much at other times: it is well known, I say, that as well plagues and pestilences, as all other kinds of sickness and maladies, by these means grow upon and amongst men, whereby mo men are

* probably in the common sense *than*

consumed at length, than are by dint of sword, suddenly slain in the field. So that not only pestilences, but also all other sickness, diseases, and maladies, do follow rebellion; which are much more horrible than plagues, pestilences, and diseases sent directly from God, as hereafter shall appear more plainly.

And as for hunger and famine, they are the peculiar companions of rebellion. For, whiles rebels do in short time, spoil and consume all corn and necessary provision, which men with their labours, had gotten and appointed upon, for their finding the whole year after; and also do let all other men, husbandmen and others, from their husbandry, and other necessary works, whereby provision should be made for times to come; who seeth not, that extreme famine and hunger, must needs shortly ensue and follow rebellion?

Now whereas the wise King, and godly Prophet David, judged war to be worse than either famine or pestilence, for that these two are often suffered by God, for man's amendment, and be not sins of themselves, but wars have always the sins and mischiefs of men, upon the one side or other, joined with them, and therefore is war the greatest of these worldly mischiefs; but of all wars civil war is the worst; and far more abominable yet is rebellion, than any civil war, being unworthy the name of any war, so far it exceedeth all wars, in all naughtiness, in all mischief, and in all abomination; and therefore our Saviour, Christ, denounceth desolation and destruction to that realm, that by sedition and rebellion is divided in itself: now, as I have showed before that pestilence and famine, so is it yet more evident that all the calamities, miseries, and mischiefs of war, be more grievous, and do more follow rebellion, than any other war, as being far worse than all other wars. For not only those ordinary and usual mischiefs and miseries of other wars, do follow rebellion, as, corn and other things necessary to man's use to be spoiled; houses, villages, towns, cities to be taken, sacked, burned, and destroyed; not only many wealthy men, but whole countries, to be impoverished and utterly beggared; many thousands of men to be slain and murdered; women and maids to be violated and deflowered; which things, when they are done by foreign enemies, we do much mourn (as we have great causes), yet are all these miseries, without any wickedness, wrought by any of our countrymen. But when these mischiefs are wrought in rebellion, by them that should be friends, by countrymen, by kinsmen, by those that should defend their country and countrymen from such miseries, the misery is nothing so great, as is the mischief and wickedness—when the subjects unnaturally do rebel against their prince, whose honour and life they should defend, though it were with loss of their own lives; countrymen to disturb the public peace, and quietness of their country, for defence of whose quietness they should spend their lives; the brother to

Ibid.:14

Matt. 12:25

seek and often to work the death of his brother, the son of the father; the father to seek or procure the death of his sons, being at man's age; and by their faults, to disherit their innocent children, and kinsmen their heirs for ever; for whom they might purchase livings and lands, as natural parents do take care and pains, and be at great costs and charges; and universally, instead of all quietness, joy, and felicity (which do follow blessed peace, and due obedience), to bring in all trouble, sorrow, disquietness of minds and bodies, and all mischief and calamities; to turn all good order upside down; to bring all good laws in contempt, and to tread them under feet; to oppress all virtue and honesty, and all virtuous and honest persons, and to set all vice and wickedness, and all vicious and wicked men, at liberty to work their wicked wills, which were before bridled by wholesome laws; to weaken, to overthrow, and to consume the strength of the realm, their natural country, as well by the spending and wasting of the money and treasure of the prince and realm, as by murdering of the people of the same, and their own

Prov. 14:28

countrymen, who should defend the honour of their prince, and liberty of their country, against the invasion of foreign enemies; and so finally to make their country, thus by their mischief weakened, ready to be a prey and spoil, to all outward enemies that will invade it, to the utter and perpetual captivity, slavery, and destruction of all their countrymen, their children, their friends, their kinsfolks left alive, whom by their wicked rebellion they procure, to be delivered into the hands of foreign enemies, as much as in them doth lie.

In foreign wars, our countrymen in obtaining the victory, win the praise of valiantness; yea, and though they were overcomed and slain, yet win they an honest commendation in this world, and die in a good conscience, for serving God, their prince, and their country, and be children of eternal salvation. But in rebellion, how desperate and strong soever they be, yet win they shame here, in fighting against God, their prince, and country, and therefore justly do fall headlong into hell if they die, and live in shame and fearful conscience, though they escape. But commonly, they be rewarded with shameful deaths, their heads and carcases set upon poles, or hanged in chains, eaten with kites and crows, judged unworthy the honour of burial; and so their souls, if they repent not (as commonly they do not), the devil harrieth them into hell, in the midst of their mischief. For which dreadful execution, St Paul showeth the cause of obedience, not only for fear of death, but also in conscience

Rom. 13:1–5

to Godward, for fear of eternal damnation, in the world to come.

Wherefore good people, let us, as the children of obedience, fear the dreadful execution of God, and live in quiet obedience, to be the children of everlasting salvation. For as heaven is the place of good obedient subjects, and hell the prison and dungeon of rebels against God, and their prince; so is that realm happy, where most obedience of subjects doth appear, being the very figure of heaven; and contrariwise, where most rebellions and rebels be, there is the express similitude of hell, and the rebels themselves are the very figures of fiends and devils, and their captain, the ungracious pattern of Lucifer and Satan, the prince of darkness: of whose rebellion as they be followers, so shall they of his damnation in hell, undoubtedly be partakers; and as undoubtedly, children of peace, the inheritors of heaven, with God the Father, God the Son, and God the Holy Ghost. To whom be all honour and glory, for ever and ever. Amen.

Thus have you heard the Third Part of this Homily: now, good people let us pray.

THE PRAYER AS BEFORE Above, p. 407

THE FOURTH PART OF THE HOMILY AGAINST DISOBEDIENCE AND WILFUL REBELLION

FOR YOUR FURTHER INSTRUCTION, good people, to show unto you how much Almighty God doth abhor disobedience and wilful rebellion—specially when rebels advance themselves so high, that they arm themselves with weapon, and stand in field, to fight against God, their prince, and their country—it shall not be out of the way, to show some examples set out in Scriptures, written for our eternal erudition.

We may soon know, good people, how heinous offence the treachery of rebellion is, if we call to remembrance the heavy wrath, and dreadful indignation, of Almighty God, against such subjects as do only but inwardly grudge, mutter, and murmur against their governors, though their inward treason, so privily hatched in their breasts, come not to open declaration of their doings: as hard it is, whom the devil hath so far enticed against God's word, to keep themselves there; no, he meaneth still to blow the coal, to kindle their rebellious hearts to flame into open deeds, if he be not with grace speedily withstanded. Some of the children of Israel, being murmurers, against their magistrates appointed over them by God, were stricken with foul leprosy: many were burnt up with fire, suddenly sent from the Lord: sometime a great sort of thousands, were consumed with the pestilence: sometime they were stinged to death, with a strange kind of fiery serpents: and, which is most horrible, some of the captains with their band of murmurers, not dying by any

Num. 11:1, 12:10, 16:35, 46–9, 21:5, 6, Psalm 78:31

Num. 16:27–33

usual or natural death of man, but the earth opening, they with their wives, children, and families, were swallowed quick down into hell. Which horrible destructions of such Israelites as were murmurers against Moyses, appointed by God to be their head and chief magistrate, are recorded in the book of Numbers, and other places of the Scriptures, for perpetual memory and warning to all subjects, how highly God is displeased, with the murmuring and evil speaking of subjects against their princes; for that as the Scripture recordeth, their *murmur* was *not against* their prince only, being a mortal creature, *but against God* himself also. Now, if such strange and horrible plagues, did fall upon such subjects as did only murmur, and speak evil against their heads, what shall become of those most wicked imps of the devil, that do conspire, arm themselves, assemble great numbers of armed rebels, and lead them with them against their prince and country, spoiling and robbing, killing and murdering all good subjects that do withstand them, as many as they may prevail against? But those examples are written to stay us, not only from such mischiefs, but also from murmuring, or speaking once an evil word against our prince; which though any should do never so secretly, yet do the holy Scriptures show that *the* very *birds of the air will bewray them*, and these so many examples before noted, out of the same holy Scriptures, do declare that they shall not escape horrible punishment therefore.

Exod. 16:7 &c.

Eccles. 10:20

Now concerning actual rebellion: amongst many examples thereof set forth in the holy Scriptures, the example of Absolon is notable; who entering into conspiracy against King David, his father, both used the advice of very witty men, and assembled a very great and huge company of rebels. The which Absolon, though he were most goodly of person, of great nobility (being the King's son), in great favour of the people, and so dearly beloved of the King himself, so much that he gave commandment that (notwithstanding his rebellion), his life should be saved; when for these considerations most men were afraid to lay their hands upon him, a great tree stretching out his arm, as it were for that purpose, caught him, by the great and long bush of his goodly hair, lapping about it as he fled hastily, bareheaded under the said tree, and so hanged him up, by the hair of his head, in the air, to give an eternal document, that neither comeliness of personage, neither nobility, nor favour of the people, no, nor the favour of the King himself, can save a rebel from due punishment; God, the King of all kings, being so offended with him, that rather than he should lack due execution for his treason, every tree by the way will be a gallows or gibbet unto him, and the hair of his own head, will be unto him instead of an halter, to hang him up with, rather than he should lack one: a fearful example of God's punishment, good people, to consider! Now Achitophel, though otherwise an exceeding wise man, yet

2 Sam. 15:12, 17:1 &c., 11; 18:7,8

Ibid.: 18:5

Ibid.:9

Achitophel

the mischievous counsellor of Absolon in this wicked rebellion, for lack of an hangman (a convenient servitor for such a traitor), went and hanged up himself: a worthy end of all false rebels! who rather than they should lack due execution, will by God's just judgement, become hangmen unto themselves. Thus happened it to the captains of that rebellion, beside forty thousand of rascal rebels, slain in the field and in the chase. Likewise is it to be seen in the holy Scriptures, how that great rebellion, which the traitor Seba moved in Israel, was suddenly appeased, the head of the captain traitor (by the means of a seely woman) being cut off.

2 Sam. 15:12,
16:21, 23, 17:23

Ibid. 18:7, 8
2 Sam. 20

And as the holy Scriptures do show, so doth daily experience prove, that the *counsels*, conspiracies, and attempts of rebels, never took effect, neither came to good, but to most horrible end. For though God do oftentimes prosper just and lawful enemies, which be no subjects, against their foreign enemies, yet did he never long, prosper rebellious subjects against their prince, were they never so great in authority, or so many in number. Five princes or kings (for so the Scripture termeth them), with all their multitudes, could not prevail against Chodorlaomor, unto whom they had promised loyalty and obedience, and had continued in the same certain years, but they were all overthrown, and taken prisoners by him; but Abraham with his family and kinsfolks, an handful of men in respect, owing no subjection unto Chodorlaomor, overthrew him and all his host in battle, and recovered the prisoners, and delivered them. So that, though war be so dreadful and cruel a thing as it is, yet doth God often prosper a few, in lawful wars with foreign enemies, against many thousands; but never yet prospered he subjects being rebels, against their natural sovereign, were they never so great or noble, so many, so stout, so witty and politic; but always they came by the overthrow, and to a shameful end: so much doth God abhor rebellion more than other wars, though otherwise being so dreadful, and so great a destruction to mankind. Though not only great multitudes of the rude and rascal commons, but sometime also men of great wit, nobility, and authority, have moved rebellions, against their lawful princes (whereas true nobility should most abhor such villainous, and true wisdom should most detest such frantic rebellion); though they would pretend sundry causes, as the redress of the commonwealth (which rebellion of all other mischiefs doth most destroy), or reformation of religion (whereas rebellion is most against all true religion); though they have made a great show of holy meaning, by beginning their rebellions with a counterfeit service of God (as did wicked Absolon begin his rebellion, with sacrificing unto God); though they display and bear about, ensigns and banners, which are acceptable unto the rude ignorant common people, great multitudes of whom, by such false pretences and shows, they do deceive and draw unto them: yet, were the multitudes of the rebels never so huge and

Psalm 21:11

Gen. 14

2 Sam. 15:12

great, the captains never so noble, politic, and witty, the pretences feigned to be never so good and holy, yet the speedy overthrow of all rebels, of what number, state, or condition soever they were, or what colour or cause soever they pretended, is and ever hath been such, that God thereby doth show, that he alloweth neither the dignity of any person, nor the multitude of any people, nor the weight of any cause, as sufficient, for the which the subjects may move rebellion against their princes. Turn over and read the histories of all nations; look over the chronicles of our own country; call to mind so many rebellions of old time, and some yet fresh in memory; ye shall not find that God ever prospered any rebellion, against their natural and lawful prince, but contrariwise, that the rebels were overthrown and slain, and such as were taken prisoners, dreadfully executed. Consider the great and noble families, of dukes, marquesses, earls, and other lords, whose names ye shall read in our chronicles, now clean extinguished and gone, and seek out the causes of the decay: you shall find that not lack of issue, and heirs male, hath so much wrought that decay, and waste of noble bloods and houses, as hath rebellion.

And for so much as the redress of the commonwealth, hath of old been the usual feigned pretence of rebels, and religion now of late, beginneth to be a colour of rebellion, let all godly and discreet subjects consider well of both, and first concerning religion. If peaceable King Salomon was judged of God, to be more meet to build his temple (whereby the ordering of religion is meant), than his father King David, though otherwise a most godly king—for that David was a great warrior, and had shed much blood, though it were in his wars against the enemies of God—of this may all godly and reasonable subjects consider, that a peaceable prince, specially our most peaceable and merciful Queen, who hath hitherto shed no blood at all, no, not of her most deadly enemies, is more like, and far meeter, either to set up, or to maintain, true religion, than are bloody rebels, who have not shed the blood of God's enemies, as King David had done, but do seek to shed the blood of God's friends, of their own countrymen, and of their own most dear friends and kinsfolk, yea, the destruction of their most gracious Prince, and natural country, for defence of whom they ought to be ready to shed their blood, if need should so require. What a religion it is, that such men, and by such means would restore, may easily be judged—even as good a religion surely, as rebels be good men, and obedient subjects, and as rebellion is a mean and redress, and reformation, being itself the greatest deformation of all that may possibly be. But as the truth of the Gospel of our Saviour, Christ, being quietly and soberly taught, though it do cost them their lives that do teach it, is able to maintain the true religion; so hath a frantic religion, need of such furious maintenances as is rebellion,

2 Chron. 22:7–10

and of such patrons as are rebels, being ready, not to die for the true religion, but to kill all that shall or dare speak against their false superstition, and wicked idolatry.

Now concerning pretences of any redress of the commonwealth, made by rebels: every man that hath but half an eye, may see how vain they be, rebellion being, as I have before declared, the greatest ruin and destruction of all commonwealths, that may be possible. And whoso looketh on the one part, upon the persons and government of the Queen's most honourable counsellors, by the experiment of so many years proved honourable to her Majesty, and most profitable and beneficial unto our country and countrymen; and on the other part, considereth the persons, state, and conditions of the rebels themselves, the reformers (as they take upon them) of the present government, he shall find that the most rash and harebrained men, the most greatest unthrifts, that have most lewdly wasted their own goods and lands, those that are over the ears in debt, and such as for thefts, robberies, and murders dare not, in any well governed commonwealth, where good laws are in force, show their faces; such as are of most lewd and wicked behaviour and life, and all such as will not or cannot live in peace, are always most ready to move rebellion, or to take part with rebels. And are not these meet men, trow you, to restore the commonwealth decayed, who have so spoiled and consumed all their own wealth and thrift? and very like to mend other men's manners, who have so vile vices, and abominable conditions themselves? Surely that which they falsely call reformation, is indeed not only a defacing or a deformation, but also an utter destruction, of all common wealth; as would well appear, might the rebels have their wills, and doth right well and too well appear, by their doing, in such places of the country where rebels do rout; where though they tarry but a very little while, they make such reformation, that they destroy all places, and undo all men where they come, that the child yet unborn may rue it, and shall many years hereafter curse them.

Let no good and discreet subjects therefore follow the flag or banner displayed to rebellion, and borne by rebels, though it have the image of the plough painted therein, with GOD SPEED THE PLOUGH written under, in great letters—knowing that none hinder the plough more than rebels, who will neither go to the plough themselves, nor suffer other that would go unto it. And though some rebels bear the picture of the five wounds, painted against those who put their only hope of salvation, in the wounds of Christ, not those wounds which are painted in a clout, by some lewd painter, but in those wounds which Christ himself bare, in his precious body; though they, little knowing what the cross of Christ meaneth, which neither carver nor painter can make, do bear the image of the cross painted in a rag, against those that have the cross of Christ printed in their hearts; yea, though they paint withal in their flags, HOC SIGNO VINCES, By this sign thou shalt get the victory (by a most fond imitation of the posy of Constantinus Magnus, that noble Christian Emperor, and great conqueror of God's enemies), a most unmeet ensign for rebels, the enemies of God, their prince, and country, or what other banner soever they shall bear: yet let no good and godly subject, upon any hope of victory or good success, follow such standard-bearers of rebellion. For, as examples of such practices are to be found, as well in the histories of old, as also of later rebellions, in our fathers' and our fresh memory; so, notwithstanding these pretences made, and banners borne, are recorded withal, unto perpetual memory, the great and horrible murders, of infinite multitudes, and thousands of the common people slain in rebellion, the dreadful executions of the authors and captains, the pitiful undoing of their wives and children, and disheriting of the heirs of the rebels for ever, the spoiling, wasting, and destruction of the people and country, where rebellion was first begun, that the child then yet unborn might rue and lament it, with the final overthrow, and shameful deaths of all rebels, set forth as well in the histories of foreign nations, as in the chronicles of our own country; some thereof being yet in fresh memory, which if they were collected together, would make many volumes and books; but on the contrary part all good luck, success, and prosperity, that ever happened unto any rebels, of any age, time, or country, may be contained in a very few lines or words.

Wherefore to conclude: let all good subjects, considering how horrible a sin against God, their prince, their country, and countrymen, against all God's and man's laws, rebellion is—being indeed not one several sin, but all sins against God and man heaped together—considering the mischievous life and deeds, and the shameful ends and deaths, of all rebels hitherto, and the pitiful undoing of their wives, children, and families, and disheriting of their heirs for ever; and above all things, considering the eternal damnation that is prepared, for all impenitent rebels in hell, with Satan, the first founder of rebellion, and grand captain of all rebels; let all good subjects, I say, considering these things, avoid and flee all rebellion, as the greatest of all mischiefs, and embrace due obedience to God, and our Prince, as the greatest of all virtues; that we may both escape all evils and miseries, that do follow rebellion in this world, and eternal damnation in the world to come; and enjoy peace, quietness, and security, with all other God's benefits and blessings, which follow obedience in this life, and finally may enjoy the kingdom of heaven, the peculiar place of all obedient subjects to God and their prince, in the world to come. Which I beseech God, the King of all kings, grant unto us, for the obedience of his Son, our Saviour, Jesus Christ. Unto whom, with the Father, and the Holy Ghost, one

God and King immortal, all honour, service, and obedience of all his creatures, is due for ever and ever. Amen.

Thus have you heard the Fourth Part of this Homily: now, good people let us pray.

THE PRAYER AS BEFORE

Above, p. 407

THE FIFTH PART OF THE HOMILY AGAINST DISOBEDIENCE AND WILFUL REBELLION

WHEREAS, AFTER BOTH DOCTRINE and examples of due obedience of subjects to their princes, I declared lastly unto you, what an abominable sin against God and man rebellion is, and what horrible plagues, punishments, and deaths, with death everlasting finally, doth hang over the heads of all rebels: it shall not be either impertinent of unprofitable, now to declare who they be, whom the devil, the first author and founder of rebellion, doth chiefly use, to the stirring up of subjects to rebel against their lawful princes; that knowing them, you may flee them, and their damnable suggestions; avoid all rebellion; and so escape the horrible plagues, and dreadful deaths, and damnation eternal, finally due to all rebels.

Though many causes of rebellion may be reckoned, and almost as many as there be vices in men and women, as hath been before noted, yet in this place, I will only touch the principal and most usual causes, as specially, ambition and ignorance. By ambition, I mean the unlawful and restless desire in men, to be of higher estate than God hath given or appointed unto them. By ignorance, I mean no unskilfulness in arts or sciences, but the lack of knowledge of God's blessed will, declared in his holy word; which teacheth, both extremely to abhor all rebellion, as the root of all mischief, and specially to delight in obedience, as the beginning and foundation of all goodness; as hath been also before specified. And as these are the two chief causes of rebellion, so are there specially two sorts of men, in whom these vices do reign; by whom the devil, the author of all evil, doth chiefly stir up all disobedience and rebellion. The restless ambitious, having once determined by one means or other, to achieve to their intended purpose, when they cannot, by lawful and peaceable means, climb so high as they do desire, they attempt the same by force and violence; wherein when they cannot prevail, against the ordinary authority and power of lawful princes and governors, themselves alone, they do seek the aid and help of the ignorant multitude, abusing them to their wicked purpose. Wherefore, seeing a few ambitious and malicious are the authors and heads, and multitudes of ignorant men are the ministers and furtherers, of rebellion, the chief point of this Part shall be, as well to notify to the simple and ignorant men, who they be that have been and be the usual authors of rebellion, that they may know them; and also to admonish them to beware, of the subtile suggestions of such restless ambitious persons, and so to flee them; that rebellions, though attempted by a few ambitious, through the lack of maintenance by any multitudes, may speedily and easily, without any great labour, danger, or damage, be repressed, and clearly extinguished.

It is well known, as well by all histories as by daily experience, that none have either more ambitiously aspired, above emperors, kings, and princes, nor have more perniciously moved the ignorant people, to rebellion against their princes, than certain persons which falsely challenge to themselves, to be only counted and called spiritual. I must therefore here, yet once again, briefly put you, good people, in remembrance, out of God's holy word, how our Saviour, Jesus Christ, and his holy Apostles, the heads and chief of all true spiritual and ecclesiastical men, behaved themselves towards the princes and rulers of their time, though not the best governors that ever were; that you be not ignorant, whether they be the true disciples, and followers of Christ, and his Apostles, and so true spiritual men, that either by ambition do so highly aspire, or do most maliciously teach, or most perniciously do execute, rebellion against their lawful princes, being the worst of all carnal works, and mischievous deeds. The holy Scriptures do teach most expressly, that our Saviour Christ himself, and his holy Apostles St Paul, St Peter, with others, were unto the magistrates and higher powers, which ruled at their being upon the earth, both obedient themselves, and did also, diligently and earnestly, exhort all other Christians, to the like obedience unto their princes and governors: whereby it is evident, that men of the clergy, and ecclesiastical ministers, as their successors, ought both themselves specially, and before others, to be obedient unto their princes, and also to exhort all others unto the same. Our Saviour Christ likewise, teaching by his doctrine, that *his kingdom was not of this world*, did by his example, in fleeing from those that would have made him king, confirm the same; expressly also forbidding his Apostles, and by them the whole clergy, all princely dominion over people and nations: and he, and his holy Apostles likewise, namely Peter and Paul, did forbid unto all ecclesiastical ministers, dominion over the Church of Christ. And indeed, whiles that ecclesiastical ministers continued in Christ's Church, in that order that is in Christ's word prescribed unto them, and in Christian kingdoms kept themselves obedient to their own princes, as the holy Scriptures do teach them, both was Christ's Church more clear from

Matt. 17:25,
Mark 12:17,
Luke 20:25,
Matt. 27,
Luke 23,
Rom. 13:1 &c.,
1 Tim. 2:1, 2,
1 Pet. 2:13

John 6:15, 18:36

Matt. 20:25,
Mark 10:42,
Luke 22:25

Matt. 23:8,
Luke 9:46,
2 Cor. 1:24,
1 Pet. 5:3

ambitious emulations and contentions, and the state of Christian kingdoms less subject unto tumults and rebellions.

But after that ambition, and desire of dominion, entered once into ecclesiastical ministers (whose greatness, after the doctrine and example of our Saviour, should chiefly stand in humbling themselves), and that the Bishop of Rome (being by the order of God's word, none other than the bishop of that one see and diocese, and never yet well able to govern the same), did by intolerable ambition challenge, not only to be the head of all the Church, dispersed throughout the world, but also to be lord of all the kingdoms of the world, as is expressly set forth in the book of his own Canon Laws, most contrary to the doctrine and example of our Saviour Christ, whose vicar, and of his holy Apostles, namely Peter, whose successor, he pretendeth to be; after this ambition entered, and this challenge once made by the Bishop of Rome, he became at once the spoiler, and destroyer, both of the Church, which is the kingdom of our Saviour, Christ, and of the Christian Empire, and all Christian kingdoms, as an universal tyrant over all. And whereas before that challenge made, there was great amity and love, amongst the Christians of all countries, hereupon began emulation, and much hatred, between the Bishop of Rome, and his clergy and friends, on the one part, and the Grecian clergy, and Christians of the East, on the other part, for that they refused to acknowledge any such supreme authority of the Bishop of Rome over them; the Bishop of Rome, for this cause amongst others, not only naming them and taking them for schismatics, but also never ceasing to persecute them, and the Emperors who had their see and continuance in Greece, by stirring of the subjects to rebellion, against their sovereign lords, and by raising deadly hatred, and most cruel wars, between them and other Christian princes. And when the Bishops of Rome had translated the title of the Emperor, and (as much as in them did lie) the Empire itself, from their lord the Emperor of Greece, and of Rome also by right, unto the Christian princes of the West, they became in short space, no better unto the West Emperors, than they were before unto the Emperors of Greece. For the usual discharging of subjects from their oaths of fidelity, made unto the Emperors of the West, their sovereign lords, by the Bishops of Rome; the unnatural stirring up of the subjects, unto rebellion against their princes, yea, of the son against the father, by the Bishop of Rome; the most cruel and bloody wars, raised amongst Christian princes of all kingdoms; the horrible murder of infinite thousands of Christian men, being slain by Christians; and, which ensued thereupon, the pitiful losses of so many goodly cities, countries, dominions, and kingdoms, sometime possessed by Christians in Asia, Africa, and Europa; the miserable fall of the Empire and Church of Greece, sometime the most flourishing part of Christendom, into the

Matt. 18:4, 20:28, Luke 9:48, 22:27

Sext. Decre. Lib. 3, Tit. 16, cap. unico, & Lib. 5, Tit. 9, cap. 5, in Glossa hands of Turks; the lamentable diminishing, decay, and ruin of Christian religion; the dreadful encrease of paganism, and power of the infidels and miscreants—and all by the practice and procurement of the Bishop of Rome chiefly—is in the histories and chronicles, written by the Bishop of Rome's own favourers and friends, to be seen, and is well known, unto all such as are acquainted with the said histories.

The ambitious intent, and most subtile drifts, of the Bishops of Rome, in these their practices, appeared evidently, by their bold attempt in spoiling and robbing the Emperors of their towns, cities, dominions, and kingdoms in Italy, Lombardy, and Sicily, of ancient right belonging unto the Empire, and by the joining of them unto their bishopric of Rome; or else giving them unto strangers, to hold them of the Church and Bishops of Rome, as in capite, and as of the chief lords thereof, in which tenure they hold the most part thereof, even at this day. By these ambitious, and indeed traitorous means, and spoiling of their sovereign lords, the Bishops of Rome, of priests, and none other by right than the bishops of one city and diocese, are by false usurpation, become great lords of many dominions, mighty princes, yea, or emperors rather, as claiming to have divers princes and kings to their vassals, liegemen, and subjects; as in the same histories, written by their own familiars and courtiers, is to be seen. And indeed, since the time that the Bishops of Rome, by ambition, treason, and usurpation, achieved and attained to this height and greatness, they behaved themselves more like princes, kings, and emperors, in all things, than remained like priests, bishops, and ecclesiastical or (as they would be called) spiritual persons, in any one thing at all. For after this rate, they have handled other kings and princes, of other realms, throughout Christendom, as well as their sovereign lords the Emperors; usually discharging their subjects of their oath of fidelity, and so stirring them up to rebellion, against their natural princes, whereof some examples shall in the last Part hereof be notified unto you.

Wherefore let all good subjects, knowing these the special instruments and ministers of the devil, to the stirring up of all rebellions, avoid and flee them, and the pestilent suggestions of such foreign usurpers, and their adherents, and embrace all obedience to God, and their natural princes and sovereigns; that they may enjoy God's blessings, and their prince's favour, in all peace, quietness, and security in this world, and finally attain, through Christ our Saviour, life everlasting, in the world to come. Which God the Father, for the same our Saviour, Jesus Christ, his sake, grant unto us all. To whom, with the Holy Ghost, be all honour and glory, world without end. Amen.

Thus have you heard the Fifth Part of this Homily: now, good people, let us pray.

Above, p. 407   THE PRAYER AS BEFORE

THE SIXTH AND LAST PART
OF THE HOMILY AGAINST DISOBEDIENCE
AND WILFUL REBELLION

NOW, WHEREAS THE INJURIES, oppressions, raveny, and tyranny of the Bishops of Rome, usurping as well against their natural lords the Emperors, as against all other Christian kings and kingdoms, and their continual stirring of subjects unto rebellions against their sovereign lords, whereof I have partly admonished you before, were intolerable; and it may seem more than marvel, that any subjects would after such sort, hold with unnatural foreign usurpers, against their own sovereign lords and natural country; it remaineth, that I do declare the mean whereby they compassed these matters, and so to conclude this whole Treaty of due obedience, and against disobedience and wilful rebellion.

You shall understand, that by ignorance of God's word, wherein they kept all men, specially the common people, they wrought and brought to pass all these things, making them believe that all they said was true, all that they did was good and godly, and that to hold with them in all things, against father, mother, prince, country, and all men, was most meritorious. And indeed, what mischief will not blind ignorance lead simple men unto? By ignorance, the Jewish clergy induced the common people to ask the delivery of Barabbas, the seditious murderer, and to sue for the cruel crucifying of our Saviour, Christ, for that he rebuked the ambition, superstition, and other vices, of the high priests and clergy. For, as our Saviour Christ testifieth, that those who crucified him wist not what they did, so doth the holy Apostle St Paul say, *If they had known*, if they had not been ignorant, *they would never have crucified the Lord of glory*: but they knew not what they did. Our Saviour Christ himself also foreshowed, that it should come to pass by ignorance, that those who should persecute and murder his true Apostles and disciples, should think they did God acceptable sacrifice, and good service; as it also is verified even at this day.

And in this ignorance have the Bishops of Rome kept the people of God, specially the common sort, by no means so much, as by the withdrawing of the word of God from them, and by keeping it under the veil of an unknown strange tongue. For as it served the ambitious humour of the Bishops of Rome, to compel all nations to use the natural language of the city of Rome, where they were Bishops, which showed a certain acknowledging of subjection unto them; so yet served it much more their crafty purpose, thereby to keep all people so blind, that they not knowing what they prayed, what they believed, what they were commanded by God, might take all their commandments for God's.

Marginal notes:

Of ignorance of the simple people, the latter part

Matt. 27:20, Luke 23:18

Luke 23:34
1 Cor. 2:8

John 15:21, 16:23

For as they would not suffer the holy Scriptures, or Church Service, to be used or had, in any other language than the Latin, so were very few, even of the most simple people, taught the Lord's Prayer, the Articles of the Faith, and the Ten Commandments, otherwise than in Latin, which they understood not: by which universal ignorance, all men were ready to believe whatsoever they said, and to do whatsoever they commanded.

Si cognovissent.
1 Cor. 2:8

Gregorius II &
IIII Anno Dom.
726, &c.

For, to imitate the Apostle's phrase, *if* the Emperor's subjects *had known*, out of God's word, their duty to their prince, they would not have suffered the Bishop of Rome to persuade them, to forsake their sovereign lord the Emperor, against their oath of fidelity, and to rebel against him, only for that he cast images (unto the which idolatry was committed) out of the churches, which the Bishop of Rome bare them in hand to be heresy. *If they had known* of God's word but as much as the

In the Second Commandment

Ten Commandments, they should have found, that the Bishop of Rome was not only a traitor to the Emperor, his liege lord, but to God also, and an horrible blasphemer of his Majesty, in calling his holy word and commandment heresy; and that which the Bishop of Rome took for a just cause, to rebel against his lawful prince, they might have known to be a doubling, and tripling, of his most heinous wickedness, heaped with horrible impiety and blasphemy. But, lest the poor people should know too much, he would not let them have as much of God's word, as the Ten Commandments wholly and perfectly; withdrawing from them the Second Commandment, that bewrayeth his impiety, by a subtile sacrilege.

Henricus IV

Had the Emperor's subjects likewise *known*, and been of any understanding in God's word, would they at other times have rebelled against their sovereign lord, and by their rebellion, have holpen to depose him,

Gregorius VII
Anno Dom.
1076; Paschalis II
Anno 1099

only for that the Bishop of Rome did bear them in hand, that it was simony, and heresy too, for the Emperor to give any ecclesiastical dignities or promotions, to his learned chaplains, or other of the learned clergy, which all Christian Emperors before him had done without controlment? Would they, I say, for that the Bishop of Rome bare them so in hand, have rebelled, by the space of more than forty years together, against him, with so much shedding of Christian blood, and murder of so many thousands of Christians, and finally have deposed their sovereign lord, *had they known*, and had in God's word any understanding at all? Specially, *had they known*, that they did all this, to pluck from their sovereign lord, and his successors for ever, their ancient right of the Empire, to give it unto the Romish clergy, and to the Bishop of Rome, that he might—for the confirmation of one archbishop, and for a Romish rag, which he calleth a pall, scarce worth twelve pence—receive many thousand crowns of gold, and of other bishops likewise, great sums of money for their bulls, which is simony indeed; would, I say,

Christian men and subjects, by rebellion have spent so much Christian blood, and have deposed their natural, most noble, and most valiant prince, to bring the matter finally to this pass, *had they known* what they did, or had any understanding in God's word at all?

And as these ambitious usurpers, the Bishops of Rome, have overflowed all Italy and Germany, with streams of Christian blood, shed by the rebellions of ignorant subjects, against their natural lords the Emperors, whom they have stirred thereunto by such false pretences, so is there no country in Christendom, which by their like means, and false pretences, hath not been oversprinkled with the blood of subjects, by rebellion against their natural sovereigns, stirred up by the same Bishops of Rome.

And to use one example of our own country. The Bishop of Rome did pick a quarrel to King John of England, about the election of Stephen Langton to the bishopric of Canterbury, wherein the King had ancient right, being used by his progenitors, all Christian kings of England before him; the Bishops of Rome having no right, but had begun then to usurp upon the kings of England, and all other Christian kings, as they had before done against their sovereign lords the Emperors; proceeding even by the same ways and means, and likewise cursing King John, and discharging his subjects of their oath of fidelity, unto their sovereign lord. Now, *had* Englishmen at that time *known* their duty to their Prince, set forth in God's word, would a great many of the nobles and other Englishmen, natural subjects, for this foreign and unnatural usurper his vain curse of the King, and for his feigned discharging of them, of their oath of fidelity to their natural lord, upon so slender or no ground at all, have rebelled against their sovereign lord the King? Would English subjects have taken part, against the King of England, and against Englishmen, with the French King and Frenchmen, being incensed against this realm by the Bishop of Rome? would they have sent for and received the Dolphin of France, with a great army of Frenchmen, into the realm of England? would they have sworn fidelity to the Dolphin of France, breaking their oath of fidelity to their natural lord, the King of England, and have stood under the Dolphin's banner, displayed against the King of England? would they have expelled their sovereign lord, the King of England, out of London, the chief city of England, and out of the greatest part of England upon the South side of Trent, even unto Lincoln, and out of Lincoln itself also, and have delivered the possession thereof unto the Dolphin of France, whereof he kept the possession a great while? would they, being Englishmen, have procured so great shedding of English blood, and other infinite mischiefs and miseries unto England, their natural country, as did follow those cruel wars, and traitorous rebellion, the fruits of the Bishop of Rome's blessings? would

King John

Innocentius III

Philip, French King

Lewes, Dolphin of France

they have driven their natural sovereign lord, the King of England, to such extremity, that he was enforced to submit himself unto that foreign false usurper, the Bishop of Rome, who compelled him to surrender up the crown of England, into the hands of his legate; who in token of possession, kept it in his hands divers days, and then delivered it again to King John, upon that condition, that the King and his successors, kings of England, should hold the crown and kingdom of England, of the Bishop of Rome and his successors, as the vassals of the said Bishops of Rome, for ever; in token whereof the kings of England should also pay an yearly tribute, to the said Bishop of Rome, as his vassals and liegemen? would Englishmen have brought their sovereign lord, and natural country, into this thraldom and subjection, to a false foreign usurper, *had they known*, and had any understanding in God's word at all? Out of the which most lamentable case, and most miserable tyranny, raveny, and spoil of the most greedy Romish wolves, ensuing hereupon, the kings and realm of England could not rid themselves, by the space of many years after; the Bishop of Rome by his ministers, continually not only spoiling the realm and kings of England, of infinite treasure, but also, with the same money, hiring and maintaining foreign enemies, against the realm and kings of England, to keep them in such his subjection, that they should not refuse to pay, whatsoever those unsatiable wolves did greedily gape for, and suffer whatsoever those most cruel tyrants would lay upon them. Would Englishmen have suffered this? would they by rebellion have caused this, trow you, and all for the Bishop of Rome's causeless curse, *had they* in those days *known* and understood, that God doth *curse the blessings*, and bless the cursings, of such wicked ursurping bishops and tyrants, as it appeared afterward in King Henry the Eighth his days, and King Edward the Sixth, and in our gracious Sovereign's days that now is, where neither the Pope's curses, nor God's manifold blessings, are wanting? But in King John's time, the Bishop of Rome understanding the brute blindness, ignorance of God's word, and superstition of Englishmen, and how much they were enclined to worship the babylonical beast of Rome, and to fear all his threatenings and causeless curses, he abused them thus; and by their rebellion, brought this noble realm and kings of England, under his most cruel tyranny, and to be a spoil of his most vile and unsatiable covetousness and raveny, for a long and a great deal too long a time.

And to join unto the reports of histories, matters of later memory: could the Bishop of Rome have raised the late rebellions, in the North and West countries, in the times of King Henry and King Edward, our gracious Sovereign's father and brother, but by abusing of the ignorant people? Or is it not most evident, that the Bishop of Rome hath of late attempted—by his Irish patriarchs and bishops, sent from Rome with

Margin notes:
Pandolphus

See the Acts of Parliament in King Edward the Third his days.

Mal. 2:2

his bull (whereof some were apprehended)—to break down the bars and hedges of the public peace in Ireland, only upon confidence, easily to abuse the ignorance of the wild Irishmen? Or who seeth not, that upon like confidence yet more lately, he hath likewise procured the breach of the public peace in England (with the long and blessed continuance whereof he is sore grieved), by the ministry of his disguised chaplains, creeping in laymen's apparel into the houses, and whispering in the ears of certain Northern borderers, being men most ignorant of their duty to God and their Prince, of all people of the realm; whom therefore, as most meet and ready to execute his intended purpose, he hath by the said ignorant mass priests, as blind guides leading the blind, brought those seely blind subjects, into the deep ditch of horrible rebellion, damnable to themselves, and very dangerous to the state of the realm, had not God of his mercy, miraculously calmed that raging tempest, not only without any shipwrack of the commonwealth, but almost without any shedding of Christian and English blood at all.

And it is yet much more to be lamented that, not only common people, but some other youthful or unskilful princes also, suffer themselves to be abused by the Bishop of Rome his cardinals and bishops, to the oppressing of Christian men their faithful subjects, either themselves, or else by procuring the force and strength of Christian men, to be conveyed out of one country, to oppress true Christians in another country, and by these means open an entry unto Moors and infidels, into the possession of Christian realms and countries; other Christian princes in the mean time, by the Bishop of Rome's procuring also, being so occupied in civil wars, or so troubled with rebellions, that they have neither leisure nor ability, to confer their common forces, to the defence of their fellow Christians, against such invasions of the common enemies of Christendom, the infidels and miscreants. Would to God we might only read and hear, out of histories of the old, and not also see and feel these new and present oppressions of Christians, rebellions of subjects, effusion of Christian blood, destruction of Christian men, decay and ruin of Christendom, increase of paganism, most lamentable and pitiful to behold, being procured in these our days, as well as in times past, by the Bishop of Rome and his ministers, abusing their ignorance of God's word, yet remaining in some Christian princes and people.

By which sour and bitter fruits of ignorance, all men ought to be moved, to give ear and credit to God's word, showing, as most truly, so most plainly, how great a mischief ignorance is, and again, how great and how good a gift of God, knowledge in God's word is. And to begin with the Romish clergy, who though they do brag now, as did sometime [Jer. 18:18] the Jewish clergy, that they cannot lack knowledge, yet doth God by his holy Prophets, both charge them with ignorance, and threaten them [Ezek. 7:26, Hos. 4:6]

Psalm 2:10–12

Prov. 19:2,
Wisd. 13:1

Prov. 17:24,
Eph. 4:17, 18,
John 12:35
Isai. 5:13

Luke 19:44,
23:34
Acts multis locis
John 16:2

Isai. 27:11

Hos. 4:6, Bar.
3:10–12, 28;
Isai. 6:9,
Matt.13:14, 15,
John 12:40

Wisd. 5:6, 7

Matt. 13:19
2 Cor. 4:3, 4

Matt. 7:3

John 3:19

Matt. 11:15,
13:9, 43, Luke
8:8, John 5:39
Psalm 1:1–3,
Matt. 7:7,
Luke 11:9
Luke 16:30, 31,
Gal. 1:8
Deut. 5:32, 33
Deut. 17:14, 15
&c.

also, for that they have repelled the knowledge of God's word and law from themselves, and from his people, that he will repel them, that they shall be no more his priests. God likewise chargeth princes, as well as priests, that they should endeavour themselves, to get understanding and knowledge in his word, threatening his heavy wrath and destruction unto them, if they fail thereof. And the Wise Man saith to all men universally, princes, priests, and people, *Where is no knowledge, there is no good nor health to the soul*; and that *all men be vain, in whom is not the knowledge of God*, and his holy word; that *they who walk in darkness, wot not whither they go*; and that the people that will not learn, shall fall into great mischiefs; as did the people of Israel, who for their ignorance in God's word, were first led into captivity, and when by ignorance afterward, they would not *know the time of their visitation*, but crucified Christ, our Saviour, persecuted his holy Apostles, and were so ignorant and blind that, when they did most wickedly and cruelly, they thought they did God good and acceptable service (as do many by ignorance think even at this day); finally, through their ignorance and blindness, their country, towns, cities, Jerusalem itself, and the holy Temple of God, were all most horribly destroyed, the most chiefest part of their people slain, and the rest led into most miserable captivity: for *he that made them, had no pity upon them, neither would spare them*; and all for their ignorance. And the holy Scriptures do teach, that the people that will not see with their eyes, nor hear with their ears, to learn and to understand with their hearts, cannot be converted and saved. And the wicked themselves, being damned in hell, shall confess ignorance in God's word to have brought them thereunto, saying, *We have erred from the way of the truth, and the light of righteousness hath not shined unto us, and the sun of understanding hath not risen unto us. We have wearied ourselves in the way of wickedness and perdition, and have walked cumbrous and crooked ways: but the way of the Lord have we not known.* And as well our Saviour himself as his Apostle St Paul do teach, that the ignorance of God's word cometh of the devil, is the cause of all error and misjudging (as falleth out with ignorant subjects, who can rather espy a little mote in the eye of the prince or a counsellor, than a great beam in their own), and universally it is the cause of all evil, and finally of eternal damnation; God's judgement being severe towards those who, when the *light* of Christ's Gospel *is come into the world, do delight more in darkness* of ignorance, *than in the light* of knowledge in God's word. For all are commanded to read or hear, to search and study the holy Scriptures, and are promised understanding, to be given them from God if they so do; all are charged not to believe either any dead man, nor if an angel should speak from heaven, much less if the Pope do speak from Rome, against or contrary to the word of God; from the which we may *not decline, neither to the right hand nor to the left.* In God's word, princes must learn how to obey God, and to govern men: in God's word, subjects must learn obedience, both to God and their princes. Old men and young, rich and poor, all men and women, all estates, sexes, and ages, are taught their several duties in the word of God. For *the word of God is bright, giving light unto all men's eyes, the shining lamp, directing all men's paths and steps.*

Let us therefore awake from the sleep and darkness of ignorance, and open our eyes, that we may see the light: let us rise from *the works of darkness*, that we may escape eternal darkness, the due reward thereof: and let us *walk* in the light of God's word, *whiles we have light*, as becometh *the children of light*; so directing the steps of our lives in that way which leadeth to light, and life everlasting, that we may finally obtain and enjoy the same. Which God *the Father of lights, who dwelleth in light* incomprehensible and *inaccessible*, grant unto us, through *the Light of the world*, our Saviour, Jesus Christ. Unto whom, with the Holy Ghost, one most glorious God, be all honour, praise, and thanksgiving, for ever and ever. Amen.

Thus have you heard the Sixth Part of this Homily: now, good people, let us pray.

THE PRAYER AS BEFORE

Rom. 13:1–7,
1 Pet. 2:13–17
Psalm 119:9

Psalm 19:8,
119:105

Eph. 5:14,
1 Thess. 5:4–6,
Rom. 13:11, 12

John 12:35, 36

James 1:17
1 Tim. 6:16
John 3:19, 8:12,
9:5

Above, p. 407

A THANKSGIVING FOR THE SUPPRESSION OF THE LAST REBELLION

O HEAVENLY AND MOST MERCIFUL FATHER, the Defender of those that put their trust in thee, the sure Fortress of all them that flee to thee for succour; who of thy most just judgements, for our disobedience, and rebellion against thy holy word, and for our sinful and wicked living, nothing answering to our holy profession, whereby we have given an occasion that thy holy Name hath been blasphemed amongst the ignorant, hast of late, both sore abashed the whole realm and people of England, with the terror and danger of rebellion, thereby to awake us out of our dead sleep of careless security; and hast yet, by the miseries following the same rebellion, more sharply punished part of our countrymen and Christian brethren, who have more nearly felt the same; and most dreadfully hast scourged some of the seditious persons, with terrible executions, justly inflicted for their disobedience to thee, and to thy servant their Sovereign, to the example of us all, and to the warning, correction, and amendment of thy servants, of thine accustomed goodness turning always the wickedness of evil men, to the profit of them that fear thee; who in thy judgements remembering thy mercy, hast by thy assistance, given the victory to thy servant our Queen, her true nobility, and faithful subjects, with so little, or rather no effusion of Christian blood, as also might justly have ensued; to the exceeding comfort of all sorrowful Christian hearts; and that of thy fatherly pity and merciful goodness only, and even for thine own Name's sake, without any our desert at all: Wherefore we render unto thee most humble and hearty thanks, for these thy great mercies showed unto us, who had deserved sharper punishment; most humbly beseeching thee, to grant unto all us that confess thy holy Name, and profess the true and perfect religion of thy holy Gospel, thy heavenly grace to show ourselves in our living, according to our profession; that we truly knowing thee in thy blessed word, may obediently walk in thy holy commandments; and that we being warned by this thy fatherly correction, do provoke thy just wrath against us no more, but may enjoy the continuance of thy great mercies toward us: thy right hand, as in this, so in all other invasions, rebellions, and dangers, continually saving and defending our Church, our realm, our Queen, and people of England; that all our posterities ensuing, confessing thy holy Name, professing thy holy Gospel, and leading an holy life, may perpetually praise and magnify thee, with thy only Son Jesus Christ, our Saviour, and the Holy Ghost: to whom be all laud, praise, glory, and empire, for ever and ever. Amen.

Select Glossary

numbers refer to pages in this edition

advouch avow
affiance faith
again in return 300
agnize recognise
and [sometimes] if
available availing
avoid remove, empty; [intransitive] leave
balk unplowed strip in arable field
bierbalk path for the bier
bonds bounds 215
comfortable encouraging, strengthening
commodity convenience
comprise comprehend
compunct pricked in the heart
confer put together
consonant sounding together
conversation behaviour
convince convict of 338
copy copiousness 347
covert [noun] protection 367
curiosity carefulness
dared dazzled
daws simpletons, jackdaws
debate quarrel
demean behave 342
discredit disbelieve
dizzard idiot
dole share, boundary-mark
dolphin dauphin
eagerly bitterly
ear [verb] plough
epicures Epicureans
ethnics gentiles, races 188
exitious deadly
farced stuffed 188
finding provision
fond foolish
fortune [verb] chance
foison plenty
fulsomely loathsomely 195
gaud joke 268
halting limping
harness armour

his [sometimes] its, 's
imps scions, shoots
incense-ships incense-vessels 184
inseparately inseparably
instant constant
jetting swaggering
kind nature; *kindly* naturally
knowledge [verb] acknowledge
let [sometimes] [noun] hindrance
let [sometimes] [verb] hesitate, [transitive] prevent
list, lust like[d]
livelode livelihood
long of because of
mainly forcefully
mammets idols
meat food
mere pure
meres boundaries 360
mysteries of travail work skills 374
namely especially
naughty-pack tart
next nearest; *next room* nearest place 371
of [sometimes] from
or [sometimes] ere
only [adjective] alone
ousel blackbird
paramours [adverb] erotically
pass upon regard 250
pie magpie
pillers despoilers 98
polling and pilling plundering and despoiling 93, 204
popinjay parrot, vain person
posy motto
pounces powders (?) 225
presently at once
prest eager, ready (French *prêt*)
prevent go before
quail quell 389
randon a charge
regiment rule [noun]
rest [verb] remain
seely simple, innocent, blessed

shack feeding in stubble 361
shalm shawm (a woodwind instrument) 214
single simple, pure
sith since
skills reasons
somner summoner
sort group, party
stale decoy 228
stallands stallions 416
stares starlings
strait narrow
strange foreign; *stranger* foreigner

tell [sometimes] count; *told* counted
tentations temptations 382
terries trodden path or balk 360
too too very
to-rent torn
town settlement
trade trodden path
typical symbolical 325
utter outer 252, peripheral, 242
witty clever
worth be, become; *in worth* patiently 372
wot know

Some Names

Abacuc Habakkuk
Agge, Aggeus, Haggeus Haggai
Elia, Helias Elijah
Esay Isaiah
Ezechias Hezekiah
Hirene, Eirene Irene
Lia Leah
Nabuchodonozor Nebuchadnezzar

Noe Noah
Ose, Osee Hosea
Paralipomenon Chronicles
Semei Shimei
Toby Tobias
Zachary Zechariah (and so with many names ending in -y, as Ury = Uriah)

The same name frequently appears in different forms, so we sometimes have *Moses* and sometimes *Moyses*. A few with variant initial consonants have been standardised. The Homilies sometimes spell *Jerusalem, Jerome* in the modern way, sometimes as *Hierusalem, Hierome*. Spelling has been standardised in the modern forms. *Jeremiah* sometimes appears as *Jeremy* and sometimes as *Hieremy*; the former has been standardised.